D0872300

Wheel of Fortune

Wheel of Fortune

The Battle for Oil and Power in Russia

Thane Gustafson

WITHDRAWN
UTSA LIBRARIES

The Belknap Press of
Harvard University Press
CAMBRIDGE, MASSACHUSETTS
LONDON, ENGLAND
2012

Copyright © 2012 by Thane Gustafson
All rights reserved
Printed in the United States of America

Book design by Dean Bornstein

Library of Congress Cataloging-in-Publication Data

Gustafson, Thane.
    Wheel of fortune : the battle for oil and power in Russia / Thane Gustafson.
      pages ; cm
    Includes bibliographical references and index.
    ISBN 978-0-674-06647-2 (alkaline paper)
    1. Petroleum industry and trade—Russia (Federation)   2. Petroleum industry
and trade—Political aspects—Russia (Federation)   3. Petroleum industry and
trade—Government policy—Russia (Federation)   I. Title.
    HD9575.R82G87   2012
    338.2'7280947—dc23   2012007731

Library
University of Texas
at San Antonio

This book is dedicated to the memory of

Dr. Vadim Isaakovich Eskin,
Russian Academy of Sciences
(1941–2006)
Mentor, Colleague, Friend

Contents

Wheel of Fortune

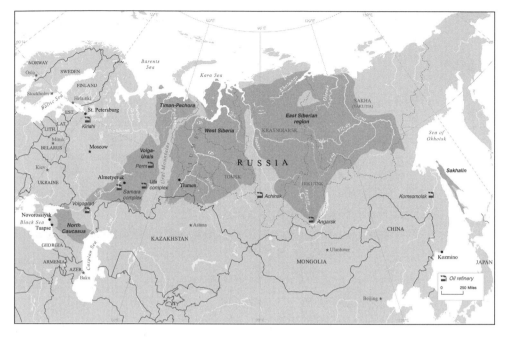

MAP 1 *Russian Federation: Major oil-producing regions and refineries.*

Introduction

This is a book about Russian oil and the making of the new Russia. In December 1991, after seven decades in power, the Soviet Union vanished into history. One of the greatest collapses of modern times was then followed by one of the greatest depressions. The Soviet oil industry, which had been one of the main catalysts of the crash, became one of its chief victims. Soviet oil production, which had led the world in the 1980s, dropped by nearly half through the 1990s, as the oil industry fell apart. One of the most vivid symbols of the Soviet fall was the fabled Samotlor field, the second largest in the world, where output plummeted by nearly 80 percent in less than a decade.

Today, more than two decades after the end of the Soviet Union, those cataclysmic events seem long past. The Russian economy, after a decade of recovery, has nearly regained its Soviet peak, and Russia vies with Saudi Arabia as the world's largest producer and exporter of oil. Oil is again at the center of the story.

No other sector is so vital to Russia's growth and prosperity. Yet in no other sector has the battle for power and wealth been so intense and so bitter. That is because Russia has come to depend on revenue from oil exports far more than it ever did in the Soviet era. This dependence is viewed with growing anxiety by Russia's leaders. But there is no realistic escape. For better and for worse, oil will dominate the future of Russia for years to come.

Oil matters for Russia; it also matters for the world. Russia accounts for nearly 13 percent of the world's oil output, 22 percent of non-OPEC production,[1] and 12 percent of proven oil reserves outside the Middle East.[2] At a time when global oil prices have recently set new records, and instability threatens many oil-producing countries, the performance of the Russian oil sector is a vital part of the world's energy security.[3] The political and economic stability of Russia is equally crucial. Though much diminished compared with Soviet times, Russia remains a great power, and any destabilization of Russia will affect world events all along the periphery of Russia's eleven time zones and beyond.

1

Although I am not an oilman by background, this book is written, in some sense, "from ringside." As a professor and consultant, and a frequent traveler to Russia, I was fortunate to be a witness to many of the events described here, and I know or have met most of the players firsthand. Much of my work over the last thirty years has consisted of studying and writing about the Russian oil and gas industry and its politics. This book is in basic respects a sequel to my earlier history of the Soviet oil and gas industry, *Crisis amid Plenty,* published on the eve of the Soviet demise.[4] *Wheel of Fortune* picks up the oil story and follows its many twists and turns down to the present.

"The Iron Curtain didn't go down," Russians like to say, "it went up." Yet the curtain did not rise on an empty stage. The new Russia has been remade from players and roles carried over from the past, hurriedly adapted to an unpredictable new drama called global capitalism. More than twenty years on, the script is still being rewritten.

The same is true of Russian oil, which together with gas forms the core of the economy and the chief support of the political system. Russia inherited most of the oil industry of the Soviet Union, and despite two decades of tumultuous changes, the pull of the past, of the assets and mind-sets of the Soviet legacy, remains strong. Yet the Russian oil industry is now exposed to a global energy system that is itself in revolution. Consequently, it too is under pressure to change.

This tension between the pull of the past and the forces of change underlies both of the two broad views of Russia that are current in the West today. The first is that Russia is still in "transition" toward political and economic modernity; the second is that Russia has lapsed back into a Soviet-style stagnation where it could remain mired for years to come. Oil is the key to both narratives. The inherited wealth from Soviet oil supports a comfortable system of rents in which it is all too tempting to linger. Yet precisely because oil is a wasting asset, any prolonged stasis is not sustainable. The oil industry must continuously renew itself to avoid decline. Moreover, it is only if the oil industry continues to modernize that Russia will have the revenues to support any sort of transition— and that will happen only if the state and its policies can modernize along with it. The Iron Curtain is still only half-raised. And that is what this book is about.

Collapse and Revival

At the center of the tale is the emergence and evolution of a new oil industry after the breakup of the Soviet Union in 1991, its partial escape from the state in the 1990s, and the reimposition of state power in the 2000s. The book describes the dramatic decline of oil production in the first half of the 1990s and its recovery early in the next decade, the industry's semi-renationalization in the wake of the Yukos Affair, and the impact of the crash and recession of 2008–2009—Russia's third oil-related crisis in twenty-five years.

Any discussion of Russian oil must also include Russian natural gas. In terms of energy content, Russia produces about as much of one as the other—a little over 500 million tons of oil equivalent of each per year (or 10 million barrels per day).[5] But there are two key differences. First, calorie for calorie, gas yields much less value than oil. Second, whereas Russia exports three-quarters of its oil output, it consumes nearly two-thirds of its gas output at home, much of it at prices below "export parity"—that is, at artificially low regulated prices).[6] In terms of money earned, Russia's exports of oil generate over four times the revenue of its exports of gas. Thus, without much exaggeration, one could say there is a division of roles: oil pays the bills abroad, while gas subsidizes the economy at home.[7] But the structure and politics of Russian gas have followed a different path from Russian oil, and that is another book.[8]

Alongside the saga of the Russian oil industry is the parallel story of the collapse and revival of the Russian state. The two are inseparably intertwined. It was the weakness of the Russian state in the 1990s that enabled the oil industry to restructure, privatize, and begin to modernize. The resurgence of strong state power since 2000, supported by rising oil prices, partially reversed those changes and enabled the state to regain control over the oil industry, even as the state itself became increasingly dependent on oil revenues. Throughout both periods, the relationship between the state and the industry has been one of mutual dependence, yet also of constant mistrust and conflict, a ceaseless battle for property, rents, and power.

Even so, by the 2000s the Russian economy had left behind the long depression of the 1990s and returned to strong growth, driven largely by recovering oil production and rising oil prices. A strengthened central state and strong presidential leadership brought a measure of political stability—welcome news to a Russian population tired by a decade of turmoil. The benefits of growth

3

spread throughout Russian society. Real incomes increased by 2.5 times, while unemployment and poverty rates fell by half. Many sectors of the economy made substantial gains in productivity.[9] Although many basic areas continued to decline—most notably the health and education systems and physical infrastructure such as ports and roads—the flood of export revenues supported a decade of strong consumer-led growth, much of it due to oil.[10] For the Russian elites, these were heady times—high oil prices were "here to stay"—and they became cocksure and complacent.

From Dependence to Addiction

But the crash and recession of 2008–2009 and the subsequent slow recovery demonstrated once again Russia's underlying weakness and vulnerability. By the end of the decade it had become apparent that the model on which the growth and prosperity of the 2000s had been based was less and less sustainable. That model is frequently referred to as "state capitalism," but in reality it also reflects a sort of Soviet-style dirigisme. The state takes resource rents from producers and transfers them to the rest of the economy through state-mandated investment programs and state-funded welfare and subsidies.[11] Over time this system's weaknesses have become more and more evident. It is, first of all, highly inefficient and given to waste and corruption. Second, it is engendering an ever-larger dependence, as the population ages, as the inherited Soviet infrastructure deteriorates, and as rent-seeking special interests grow around state programs.

Russian leaders have long been aware of the dangers of oil dependence and the temptations of rentierism. Indeed, some of the sternest warnings have come from President Vladimir Putin himself. In April 2001, then President Vladimir Putin, in his second "State of the Federation" speech to the parliament, warned his countrymen:

> We are still living as we formerly did, in a rent-based, not a production-based economy. Our economic system, at bottom, has hardly changed. Where do we make most of our money? On oil, on gas, on metals, and on other raw materials. Export rents are either spent on consumer goods, or feed capital flight.[12]

But a decade later the dependence on hydrocarbons, especially oil, had only worsened. In 2001, oil accounted for 34 percent of Russian export revenues; by

4

2011, its share had swelled to 52 percent (natural gas exports added another 12 percent). (Of course, oil prices had risen mightily over the years in between.) Oil and gas together, which represented 20 percent of federal tax revenues in 2001, had grown to 49 percent by 2011.[13] Dependence had become addiction.[14]

Sustaining this system requires a steadily growing flow of commodity revenue, chiefly from oil. Yet that is where the biggest problem lies: in coming years the economic surplus from oil is more likely to decline than to increase. The core reason is to be found in the oil industry itself.

The Declining Soviet Oil Legacy

For the past two decades Russia has coasted on an oil legacy inherited from the Soviet Union. Those legacy assets are now wearing down. Russia is not running out of oil, but it is running out of cheap oil. The next generation of oil will be much more difficult and more costly to find and produce. As costs go up, oil margins will decline, unless global oil prices obligingly continue to rise—a risky proposition. In addition, the oil industry will require more of its remaining profits for its own renewal. The combination of Russia's growing dependence on oil, combined with declining surplus value from oil, will force rival claimants to compete for less, leading to greater political conflict, slower economic growth, and possible social destabilization.

But Russia's oil industry and the Russian state are not well prepared to deal with the coming challenge. They have spent the last two decades competing for control of the inherited oil assets and rents, instead of cooperating to better modernize the industry and prepare for the next stage ahead. The state's fiscal and regulatory system, though successful in extracting revenue and controlling the oil sector, constrains investment and stifles innovation. But the state is not the sole problem; the oil industry too is a partner in the rent-distribution system. The result is an industry that, compared with its world peers, lags behind the rapidly moving front of a global oil business that is in the midst of a technological and managerial revolution. As noted by Russia's perennial finance minister, Aleksei Kudrin, the chief architect of Putin's fiscal and budgetary policy until he left the government in 2011, "The oil industry, from being a locomotive for the economy, has become a brake."[15]

Why does Russia find itself in this situation? How did it get to this point? Can it find a way out? These are the central questions of this book.

5

The "Curse of Oil . . . "?

For some, these questions have a simple answer: Russia is what is called a "petro-state." On this reading, Russia's economy exhibits all the classic economic symptoms of "Dutch Disease": a cycle of boom and bust tied to world commodity prices; a built-in tendency toward inflation and currency appreciation, which in turn makes its nonexport sectors uncompetitive, and so forth. Its political system is similarly distorted by its dependence on commodity exports: the state is bloated and corrupt, the private sector is inefficient; and public life is reduced to the politics of rent-seeking.[16] In short, according to this exposition, Russia is yet another victim of the "curse of oil."

But there are a number of problems with this explanation. First, Russia's dependence on oil and the centrality of oil in Russian politics are relatively recent phenomena. The Soviet Union was not a petro-state; on the contrary, it was an advanced (if inefficient) industrial and technological power. If its industry and manufactured exports were uncompetitive, that was not because of dependence on oil or natural resources but because of the communist system and the hot-house conditions in which it functioned, isolated from the world economy and bound to the service of a military-industrial machine.[17] Only in its last decade and a half, as the Soviet system weakened, did its leaders use oil and gas exports as a means of propping up their sagging system while avoiding change.[18] Ironically, this dependence was made possible by an external event, the oil shocks of 1973 and 1979–1980, which caused a massive increase in oil prices—and in Soviet oil revenues. Thus, ironically, a system that had been built around the principle of autarky, in which foreign trade traditionally played the role of residual, came to depend for its stability on a global windfall over which the Soviet central-planning system had no control.

Even so, the Soviet leaders' reliance on oil, even at the end, was not as central as today's. What set the stage for Russia's present massive dependence was the implosion of the Soviet industrial system, which left natural resources, chiefly oil and gas, as the chief remaining sources of value, while Russian manufactured goods became even less competitive in global markets than before. In sum, it was not the "curse of hydrocarbons" that created the setting for Russia's aggravated dependence after the Soviet fall, but the "curse of the collapse" of much of the command economy around it.[19]

The second problem with the "curse of oil" explanation is that it typically applies to countries with much less advanced oil industries and state institutions. The "classic" petro-state is one in which either foreign oil companies or a dominant state-owned oil company and parasitic ruling elites jointly control the hydrocarbon revenues, with little benefit to the local population. Oil acts as a soporific: the leaders and the elites make little effort to escape from their addiction, or if they do, they spend their oil revenues on vast and wasteful projects designed to industrialize their economies overnight, plunging their countries into debt at the next turn in the price cycle. The corrupt and incompetent government bureaucracy exists largely for the purpose of sharing out oil rents among the powerful.[20]

Russia does not fit this picture. Whatever one may say about the Russian political system and bureaucracy, it is a developed state structure, staffed by bureaucrats who are, at least at senior levels, well-educated professionals.[21] The top officials in charge of monetary and fiscal policy are sophisticated people, well aware of the dilemmas of dependence on oil and the policies needed to combat it. The Russian oil industry is home-grown, backed by a large scientific and engineering establishment and highly accomplished technologists. Foreign oil companies, as we shall see, play mostly secondary roles in it. Despite the renationalizations of the mid-2000s, it is still largely privately owned. Most of its equipment and services comes from domestic suppliers, except at the high-tech end of the spectrum. Most of the revenues from hydrocarbons are repatriated to Russia (although a substantial portion may reexit subsequently[22]) and are divided between a bloated welfare system and antiquated state-subsidized industries, both inherited from the Soviet past. In short, despite its weaknesses, Russia is not a third-world petro-state; it remains an industrial power—if an eroded one—with a developed state and a deep-rooted indigenous oil industry. It is the presence of these features, not their absence, that defines the Russian story.

Third, Russia's increased vulnerability to commodity swings is a by- product of its reentry into a global economy that is increasingly unstable and unpredictable. This affects not only the prices of its exports, which have gyrated wildly over the last forty years, but also the price and availability of money, as short-term capital floods across national boundaries in large and unpredictable surges—cheap and abundant one day, dry as a desert the next. Lacking a deep and stable banking and financial infrastructure of its own, Russia has been particularly affected by these fluctuations. Thus it would be equally appropriate to speak of the "curse of globalization."

Lastly, an important part of the Russian story has been the impressive effort by some policy makers to counter the effects of resource dependence and to dampen the impact of global commodity and financial cycles. Led by Russia's longtime finance minister, Aleksey Kudrin, the Russian government after 2000 systematically pursued cautious monetary and budgetary policies—storing up export revenues in two rainy-day funds—that is, sovereign wealth funds—paying off state debt, accumulating foreign currencies, introducing multiyear budgeting, and modernizing the tax system while seeking to capture for the state a larger share of the windfall profits from higher oil prices. This last feature, as we shall see, became one of the main factors in the heightened conflict between the state and the oil industry in the first half of the 2000s and has remained a major source of contention since.

There is no question that money from oil and gas, flooding into Russia after 2000 and seeping into every sector of society and the economy, has fed the appetites of the rich and powerful, aggravating pathologies commonly associated with the "resource curse." Corruption has spread, budgetary discipline has loosened, "good causes" have proliferated, and reforms have been slowed down or frozen. But oil is not the cause of these problems; it has merely amplified them. In this respect, the Russian case confirms the broad conclusion of much of the literature on the "curse of oil," namely, the impact of oil depends on how you got it and what you do with it.

. . . Or the "Curse of the Living Past"?

This book will argue, instead, that the saga of Russian oil and its relationship to the state, including Russia's present dilemma of dependence, is part of a larger and more complex narrative—that of Russia's long and difficult exit from the grip of the Soviet past. It is the Soviet legacy, the shock of the Soviet disintegration, the abruptness of Russia's return to the world economy, the mixed impact of foreign doctrines in the ideological and moral vacuum of post-Soviet Russia, and the continuing issues generated by all of these, not the "curse of oil" or simple rentierism, that explain where Russia is today.

One tends to forget, with the passage of time, just how different the Soviet system was. Isolated behind the Iron Curtain and largely cut off from the outside world, it was in many ways a civilization unto itself, with its own unique institutions and customs. Over three generations it had put its imprint on people, on habits of thought, on language, on institutions, and on the very landscape. The top of the Soviet system blew off in 1991, but most of the underlying foundations did not, and these lived on after the collapse. Despite the sweeping changes of the last two decades, a good deal of the Soviet core remains today.[23]

This is particularly true of the oil industry. The Soviet legacy has been decisive for the oil industry and oil politics on four dimensions—physical, technological, cultural, and political. The first two apply particularly to the oil industry; the second two apply more broadly to Russian society and the political system. All four run throughout the book.

Physical Legacy: Resource Base and Infrastructure. The oil industry that Russia inherited from the Soviet era was highly developed but flawed. Most of its production came from a handful of giant fields in West Siberia, which had been damaged by short-sighted practices caused by political pressure to maximize production.[24] Owing to the financial crisis at the end of the Soviet period and the resulting fall in oil investment, the next generation of oilfields was not yet ready to produce. Output had already begun to decline by the end of 1988. But the final fall of the Soviet Union brought a wholesale disintegration. Russian oil production, which had led the world as late as 1987 with 569.5 million tons (11.4 million barrels per day), dropped steadily over the following eight years, before bottoming out in 1996 at 301.2 million tons (6 million barrels per day), little more than half the Soviet-era peak.[25]

The Soviet oil industry was inefficient in many ways, not the least of which was what the command economy did with the oil it produced. Most of it was passed through basic domestic refineries, which produced a "dark barrel" of products dominated by fuel oil, diesel, and low-octane gasoline, which was then burned in the furnaces and vehicles of one of the world's most wasteful economies. As for exports, a large share went not to the West but to the satellites of the Soviet bloc, as a kind of subsidy to help maintain the empire. In short, much of the value produced by the "upstream" of the oil industry was destroyed by the "downstream." Yet here lay a hidden benefit: as the Soviet economy went down, domestic oil demand went down with it, and the exports to Eastern Europe became cash-only, freeing up oil for badly needed dollar exports. As a result, even though oil-export revenues declined by about 50 percent in the first half of the 1990s compared to the final Soviet years, they were in real money, providing an important buffer for the economy at a time when cash had almost disappeared—but also an added prize to fight over. Therein lay the real beginning of today's increased dependence.

By the end of the decade, once the oil industry had been reorganized and production had turned around, it played an equally central role in fueling the subsequent recovery. But in political and business circles, and even to some extent in the oil industry itself, the renewed growth of oil production encouraged complacency and shortsighted greed. The inherited hydrocarbon wealth—already extensively explored and developed by the Soviet system—came to be taken for granted by the political class, and to some extent by the oil companies themselves, lessening the urgency of investing in new resources or pursuing innovative approaches. The legacy fields still held an abundance of recoverable oil, which could be produced by techniques that were not particularly advanced and could be quickly mastered by local operators. In other words, the Russian oil industry in the 1990s had little immediate need of the next-generation skills required for Arctic offshore projects or unconventional reservoirs, which would necessarily have involved foreign partners or service providers—in contrast, say, to Norway, where the entire petroleum resource was located at sea and the Norwegians faced the problem of dealing with the offshore from scratch, with no prior experience in oil or gas but also no inherited baggage.

Thus, over the longer run, the Soviet legacy assets have acted as an anesthetic, delaying the adaptation of the Russian oil industry to modern management and technology, allowing it to remain relatively isolated and poorly equipped to compete globally. But the next generation of oil and gas will force the oil industry willy-nilly out of its Soviet-era perimeter, toward new oil that will be variously deeper, hotter (or colder), higher in pressure, more sour (i.e., higher in sulfur content), more complex geologically, and more remote, than the present core of the industry—and thus, inevitably, far more costly. This will pose major new challenges, for which the Russian industry is only partly prepared, and in some cases, such as the Arctic offshore, hardly at all.

A further consequence of the nature of the resource in Russia is "giantism." The concentration of oil in a handful of large remote areas favored the creation in Soviet times of large producing entities that controlled their own oilfield services, their own housing and amenities, and their own feeder pipelines to the central pipeline system. This basic structure, thanks to the common efforts of the industry and the state, was then reproduced in the 1990s, except that the new giants now owned their own refineries and gas stations. In this environment it was difficult for smaller independents to function, especially foreign ones, and by the end of the decade most of them were taken over by the larger Russian companies. Thus one potentially important channel of entrepreneurship, learning, and change, which had initially played a significant role in the early to mid-1990s, had practically disappeared by the end of the decade. This will have important consequences as the oil industry addresses the potential of a tight-oil renaissance in its legacy fields, something that will very likely require a parallel renaissance of smaller independents.

The Technological Legacy. The Soviet oil industry was unique in that it had grown up outside the global mainstream. Though founded by local and Western oilmen in Baku, after the 1920s it was virtually isolated from the rest of the world. Drawing on Russia's excellent scientific base and strong industrial and engineering skills, it had developed on its own to become the world's leading producer of oil and gas. It had its own distinctive practices and traditions, coupled with understandable pride in its own achievements.

When the Iron Curtain went up, it was as though two alien civilizations had suddenly come into contact. To the Russian oilmen, the global oil industry was a confusing swirl of unfamiliar players, brash and fast-moving and diverse, and speaking strange tongues (nominally English, but more often Albertan and Texan). The Soviet oilmen were almost exclusively petroleum engineers or geologists, but the global oil business appeared to be run not only by engineers and geoscientists, but also by lawyers, financial analysts, traders, and image makers. The culture shock was extreme, on both sides.

Moreover, the international oil industry was in the midst of a technological upheaval, as innovations in computing, communications, and control transformed the business of finding and producing and selling oil. These forces had been only weakly felt behind the Iron Curtain, and the Russians were shocked to realize that their oil industry had grown stodgy and backward—and worse, was perceived as such by the foreigners, many of whom, as they arrived in Russia, did not bother to hide their views. Much of the oil-equipment sector, never very progressive to begin with, had been lost when the Soviet Union broke up (most of it was located in Azerbaijan and Ukraine), and it had to be rebuilt virtually from zero, mostly on the basis of converted military-industrial plants, a task that took the better part of a decade to yield results and is not completed yet. The Russian oilmen, to their humiliation, found themselves forced to depend on foreign-made equipment and services, which they initially had no money to buy.

In sum, a major theme in the Russian oil story of the last two decades is the uneasy coming together of these two initially alien worlds. For the Russians, it has been a complex combination of acceptance and rejection. Their initial need, as the Soviet system unraveled, was for cash and oiltools to maintain production in the existing fields, and they accepted the presence of foreigners who could provide them. But their welcome was always tinged with reluctance and resentment, and as the new Russian companies evolved, most of them sought to limit the role of the foreign oil companies and above all to prevent them from gaining control of the legacy assets that were the core of Russian production. The foreign companies, for their part, needing to add reserves to their portfolios, looked for "elephants"—large frontier projects where they could deploy their technology and skills. But the Russians were ambivalent about such projects, and indeed about the presence of the large foreign companies themselves, and there was resistance. Although foreign companies led the way in a handful of frontier projects, they have remained marginal players overall. It is only now that early signs have appeared suggesting a new phase in the relationship, in which the international companies may play more substantial roles than before as partners to their Russian peers.

Yet so far the process of transfer of skills and technologies from the global industry to the Russian one has been held back—by the inertia of the Soviet oil legacy, which has impeded innovation and change; by inherited weaknesses in the Russian industrial and research and development (R&D) support systems; by the Russians' own pride and homegrown practices, which resist change coming from outside; and above all, by the Russians' determination not to lose ownership and control of their own industry.

So far I have focused on the aspects of the Soviet legacy that are specific to the oil industry. But the oil industry was embedded in the larger matrix of Soviet culture and political institutions. These too are part of the Soviet legacy shaping the behavior of the oil industry and its relations with the state.

Cultural-Ideological Legacy. The end of the Soviet Union was at once that of an empire, a political system, and an ideology. Over three generations these had been isolated behind the increasingly brittle barrier of the Iron Curtain. Over time they had gradually decayed, and when they collapsed, the flood of capitalism, then at its height of born-again self-confidence and fervor, rushed in. For many Russians, chiefly the young and the enterprising in the major cities, this came as a liberation. But what they perceived was all too often a cartoon version of capitalism that seemed to glorify making money above all else. As the young Mikhail Khodorkovsky and his partner Leonid Nevzlin wrote in a 1992 pamphlet describing their new private bank, Menatep, "What is Menatep? It is the right to get rich." For people such as Khodorkovsky (who as a schoolboy had dreamed of becoming a Soviet factory manager), this anything-goes version of capitalism provided a powerful ideological substitute for the tired slogans of Marxism-Leninism. "Enough of life according to Lenin!" he and his partner wrote, "Our compass is profit."[26]

But for the mass of the population, the sudden influx of foreign ideas and people caused bewilderment and resentment. The formal Soviet ideology might be gone, but a kind of popular socialism, a blend of Soviet Marxism with traditional Russian culture, remained the mental model for most of the population. In the oilfields and the oil towns, in particular, the prevailing culture was in many ways antithetical to the values of the new capitalism. The "oil generals" who ran the Soviet oilfields and refineries were paternalistic figures, responsible not just for their workers' performance but also for their housing, their light and water, and indeed for their entire lives. The kind of relentless cost cutting, downsizing, and outsourcing routinely practiced by Western employers went against the grain of the tight-knit one-company Soviet oil towns, and the private entrepreneur's drive to "optimize" production (a perfectly normal practice in a West that believes that "oil today is worth more than oil tomorrow") only aroused suspicion that the fields would soon be depleted and the livelihood of whole communities destroyed. The immense wealth and power amassed by the Moscow newcomers who quickly penetrated the oil industry were viewed in the oilfields with a deep disapproval tinged with anti-Semitism and xenophobia. In contrast, the handful of Soviet-era bosses who continued to practice the traditional paternalistic system, such as Vladimir Bogdanov, the Siberian driller who still heads Surgutneftegaz today, were revered in the oil towns and still are.

The Soviet system of totalitarian controls and systematic scarcity had led Russians, in self-defense, to form informal networks of collusion and exchange, to trade access, information, protection, and scarce goods. In the absence of legal sanction for private property, in a society in which extreme accumulation of private wealth was by definition criminal, an informal entrepreneur's best protection was to share, lest he be denounced and attacked. In the world "on the left," let alone the underworld, one did not operate alone. Networks of mutual trust were essential for survival, and although the networks themselves have loosened, the norms of exchange and sharing—with neighbors, with partners, with political allies—have carried over to the post-Soviet era, where they fit awkwardly with the arm's-length business relationships prescribed by the market economy. Yet in the absence of secure legal protections and property rights, these informal relations (which we call "corrupt" or "patrimonial") continue to serve the same defensive functions as in Soviet times. As a common Russian business saying goes, "Good friends are worth more than good contracts."

The Political Legacy. The breakup of the Soviet Union took off the top of the political system and greatly weakened the rest of the state, but it did not destroy it. Much of the machinery of government survived, both at the central and especially at the regional and local levels. Large parts of the energy sector remained under state control, even if in the 1990s that control was weak and episodic. The gas industry, in particular, remained state property, as did the electricity sector. The oil industry broke free and became private, but oil resources in the ground still belonged to the state, as did, crucially, the oil-pipeline system. The state still controlled the borders and the customs posts, however porously. It retained the authority, if not always the actual power, to control oil exports, especially crude oil. Thus the oil industry, despite its apparent escape, remained enmeshed in a system of state controls that, although half-comatose in the 1990s, had the potential to be revived at virtually a moment's notice if provided with political energy and resources.

During the 1990s it was commonly said of the Russian state that it had been "privatized," so thoroughly penetrated by the money and power of the new lords of the private sector—who soon came to be known as the "oligarchs"—that it had become their virtual property. The coercive power of the state appeared to have been suspended. But that too proved to be an illusion. The apparatus of coercion—the police, the FSB (the successor to the KGB), and the prosecutors and courts that backed them up—though temporarily stunned and demoralized by the disappearance of the Soviet Union, was still present. When it was deployed by a strong and determined leader, there was no serious contest. In short order, the Kremlin, backed by the coercive elites, succeeded in recapturing the "commanding heights" (as Lenin would have put it) of the economy and the political system, for the state—and for themselves. Crucial to this enterprise was control of the oil industry and its revenues.

In the 1990s the Russian reformers had made impressive efforts to make the new private sector more secure by establishing property rights guaranteed by law. New legal codes legitimized and protected private property and exchange, activities that in the Soviet Union had been criminal. The reformers sought to redefine the mission of the state, from that of all-powerful owner, as it had been in Soviet times, to that of referee and arbitrator. Implicit in this concept was that the state must accept limits on its own power. But those early successes, never more than incomplete, have been partially reversed. State players remain ambivalent about whether they are regulators or owners—with the latter tending to prevail—and they resist legal or constitutional restraints. In short, the chief political legacy of the Soviet Union is weak and uncertain property rights and a state that retains arbitrary power.

Bitter Memories of the 1990s and Resentment of the West. Compounding the lingering hold of the Soviet legacy was the lasting bitterness of the Soviet collapse itself, and Russians' perceptions of the Western responses to it. Many Russians look back on the 1990s as a disaster and a humiliation, a time of invasion by foreign powers, interests, brand names, and values. Some Russians came up winners, as we have noted, but the majority of Russians were losers, including many of those who had had power and prestige under the old system.

Yet even among the winners, negative feelings run strong. Vladimir Putin, in a speech to the parliament following his reelection in 2004, described the end of the Soviet Union as "the greatest geopolitical catastrophe of the 20th Century." Valerii Graifer, the highly respected chairman of the board of LUKoil, Russia's largest private oil company, also calls the fall of the Soviet Union a "catastrophe," although his words reveal an ambivalence that is perhaps more typical of today's business leaders:

15

It was one big oil family throughout all the republics of the Soviet Union. If anyone had told me that this family was about to collapse, I would have laughed. Now, in retrospect, it would be an unfeeling person indeed who would not mourn the Soviet era—but only a fool would want it back. We had a tough time. But I saw that life has gone on.[27]

Many of the former reformers, in particular, are still bitter about what they perceive as the West's betrayal in the desperate days of the early 1990s. Petr Aven, chairman of the powerful Alfa Group, who was minister of foreign trade in the reformist Gaidar government, told an American audience,

> We expected the West to come to our aid. After all, we were the anticommunists, we were the ones who had destroyed communism. A mere billion dollars would have made all the difference. Instead—nothing.[28]

This view remains controversial, both in Russia and in the West, but the point is that many influential Russians believe it to be so.[29]

Such feelings, justified or not, have only deepened with the passage of time. Recent polls show that most Russians today have become, if anything, even more resentful of the West and skeptical of its values—even as they increasingly adopt Western consumer lifestyles.[30] In the wake of the global financial crash of 2008 and the painful aftermath, it is the entire narrative of the superiority of Western-style capitalism and the inevitability of transition that has come into question.[31] The widespread sense of loss and the resentment of the West provide rich material for manipulation by politicians. The past, in Russia as elsewhere, has its uses.

Thus, to sum up the argument so far: if in many respects Russia fits the definition of a rentier state, it is not because of any particular curse of oil, or indeed of any other commodity. Russia is a unique kind of rentier state, one whose dependence is the product of the multiple legacies of the Soviet past. On some levels, this is simply a physical fact—the condition and spacing of wells, the layout of pipelines, the location of refineries and their designs, and so on, are much the same as they were in the Soviet Union. But on the levels of politics and business, the past also exerts its influence through norms and habits of mind and personal ties, which are transposed into new settings but remain strong nonetheless.

I shall return to these themes later in the chapter to put them into the larger context of the evolution and present state of the Russian political system. But first let us sketch the main outlines of the oil story itself—anticipating the more detailed narrative of the chapters ahead—to see the unique role that the politics of oil have played in the emergence of modern Russia.

Conflict Becomes Confrontation

That the legacy of the Soviet era would remain a strong force over the first two post-Soviet decades was only to be expected. It was inevitable, in view of the decline of the Soviet industrial economy, that inherited revenues from oil would be one of Russia's few reliable supports and equally that there would be conflict for control of them. Nor was it surprising that the oil industry did not make massive efforts to move beyond its accustomed "comfort zone," since thanks to the Soviet legacy there was no pressing need to do so. Least surprising of all was that the Russian oil producers, who by their own efforts had been until recently the world's number-one producers, would resist the efforts of outsiders, whether Russian nouveaux riches or foreign companies, to teach them their business or to take control of their industry. Much the same was true in many other commodity-producing sectors of the Russian economy in the 1990s, notably the gas sector.

But in the case of the oil industry the story took a more confrontational turn. The oil industry was exceptional. It was the largest single source of wealth in the country. Alone of any "strategic" sector of the economy, it had succeeded in becoming legally private, yet its privatization had never been fully accepted by more than a fraction of the political elite and the population, and in addition it was incomplete. For these reasons, the oil industry was more politically salient than any other, and its relationship to the state had been fraught from the start. In the early 2000s, as oil production recovered and oil prices rose, the oil industry's autonomy was challenged by a resurgent state. Tension turned into conflict, and then, by 2003–2004, into all-out confrontation. The result was a wholesale recapture of oil rents, and of part of the oil industry itself, by the state.

To understand how that happened, let us begin by turning back the clock to 2002. Russian oil production, after declining in the mid-1990s to half of the Soviet-era peak, had begun growing again in 1999, and by 2002 was increasing at nearly 10 percent per year, with seemingly no end in sight. The recovery was largely the work of the newly privatized oil companies, which controlled over

83 percent of the production of Russian oil in that year. Two new industry leaders, Yukos and Sibneft, were applying production methods and management techniques never seen before in Russia, under the command of two self-made entrepreneurs, newcomers to the oil industry, Mikhail Khodorkovsky and Roman Abramovich. The other private oil companies were following close behind. Their shares were being snapped up on Western stock exchanges. A vigorous new president, Vladimir Putin, spoke of capitalism and economic reform and was initially hailed in the West as a liberal in the European market source. He appeared to have reached a modus vivendi with the private-sector "oligarchs" of the Yeltsin years, based on a principle of mutual noninterference. Foreign oil companies were increasingly active in Russia, and major strategic deals and acquisitions, though not yet public, were being negotiated behind the scenes. The new Russian oil industry was reaching out to the outside world, with ambitious plans for investment in the Caspian Sea, a private pipeline to China, refineries in Europe, and a major new supply line of Russian oil to North America. In the United States, one of the new Russian oil companies, LUKoil, had recently purchased a retail distributor, Getty Oil, and the first U.S. gas stations under the LUKoil brand appeared the following year, including one in Washington, D.C., only blocks from the White House. To many observers at the time, it appeared that the victory of free-market capitalism in Russia was all but complete.

That perception was not altogether an illusion. There were strong forces at work driving the growth of the new private sector and Russia's growing involvement in the world economy—not the least of which was oil. Yet in retrospect, 2002 was a fateful turning point. Behind the apparent dominance of the private sector companies, a newly resurgent state-owned corporation, named Rosneft, was rapidly gaining strength, with the Kremlin's increasingly open support. The Russian government, armed with powerful new tax laws, was already capturing a growing share of the private companies' profits and would go on to capture far more. The ambitions of the foreign oil companies were arousing fear and hostility, which soon led to a political backlash, including a wave of legislation restricting foreign investment in strategic sectors such as oil. Khodorkovsky and Putin were increasingly at odds over a growing range of issues, aggravated by Khodorkovsky's rumored presidential ambitions; the following year Khodorkovsky was arrested and the expropriation of Yukos began. Russian-American relations would soon cool with the beginning of the

18

Iraq war, ending any further talk of energy cooperation. Finally, the double-digit growth in Russian oil production soon subsided, and further gains since then have been slow and irregular. By the end of the decade, in short, the private sector had been curbed, the private entrepreneurs humbled, the private-sector oil boom was over—and the state was back.

Explaining the Turn

How to account for the suddenness and radicalism of this turn? The Soviet legacy alone cannot explain it; that only provided the stage on which the drama played out. Two other factors were also crucial. The first was the boom in world oil prices and the tidal wave of monetary liquidity that began at the very end of the 1990s, and more broadly the impact of global forces on Russia's newly opened economy. The second was the unstable equilibrium that the Russian political and economic system had reached by the end of the first post-Soviet decade. Against this background, accident, circumstance, and personality played crucial roles.

The increase in oil prices that began in 1999 and ran for a decade to mid-2008 sharply raised the stakes in the contest for oil revenues. It turned the new Russian oil companies, which in the post-Soviet depression had been losing money, into highly valuable properties. They had been desirable before; now they were irresistible. Oil became more essential than ever to the economy's survival; but in addition it became the key to power and personal wealth. Note, again, that this is not the same thing as the "curse of oil." A battle for control of the country's oil wealth had been going on for a decade; the oil-price boom simply catalyzed its escalation into all-out war.

At this time, a decade after the Soviet collapse, Russia was in a state of unresolved struggle over its basic political direction. Although some primordial questions had been settled—notably, the creation of the Russian Federation (1991), the commitment to a presidential regime (1993), and the rejection of a return to communism (1996)—others, no less fundamental, remained to be tested. What would be the limits (if any) to executive power, and who or what might impose those limits? What would be the powers of the judiciary, and what protection would it give to property rights? What would be the role of the central state in the economy, that of regulator or, as in Soviet times, that of owner? And last but most important, who would control the state itself, and by what methods—modern institutions or a clique of cronies armed with state power?

Other unresolved issues were specific to the oil industry. There were four main ones. The first was the legitimacy of the oil industry's privatization—a continuing issue, since the privatization was not yet complete, and the question of the existence and roles of a national oil company not yet resolved. The second was the unsettled question of the oil industry's relation to the state, particularly the division of oil rents, but also the extent of the state's regulatory control over the industry's operations. The third was the role of foreign companies and capital. The fourth was control over the movement and sale of oil—exports, export outlets, and pipelines.

All four of these oil questions had been contentious throughout the 1990s, but now the developments of the 2000s made them even more so. The private oil companies, not surprisingly, defended their takeover of the state's assets as legitimate, fought the mounting attempts of the state to increase its take, and trumpeted their right to dispose of their assets and move their oil as they pleased, including through private pipelines and terminals. As oil prices climbed and oil output increased, and as the private oil industry's new owners grew ever richer, their claims grew more confident and assertive. In short, at the beginning of the 2000s, some sort of confrontation seemed inevitable.

Could It Have Been Different?

Many observers, particularly Westerners, look back on the first half of the 2000s as a historic missed opportunity, Russia's road not taken, a battle for the country's soul in which the forces of change were defeated by the forces of reaction. As a former senior executive of Yukos once put it to me, it was a battle between two visions of the future: "Chudo," the Russian word for "miracle"—as in "economic miracle"—a market society based on liberal principles and private-sector entrepreneurship; and "Russian Bear," a scenario of state intervention and authoritarianism—and "Russian Bear" won. Many journalistic and scholarly accounts are similarly apocalyptic. It was "an extraordinary confrontation between the two great forces of modernity, the state and the market," concludes one study. "Two logics of modernity collided."[32]

Yet in reality, the basic outcome was never in doubt. The trumps were on the side of the state. The apparent victory of the private sector and its new owners at the beginning of the 2000s was unstable, unpopular, and incomplete. The Russian state and statist instincts had never vanished; the bureaucracy and the apparatus of coercion had been weakened but not dismantled. Too many potentially powerful groups had been excluded from the initial division of the spoils of the Soviet system in the 1990s, and they were bound to challenge the winners' control at the first opportunity, using the coercive power of the state. The losers' revanche enjoyed wide popular support. Between laissez-faire capitalism, on the one hand, and the seductive myth of a revived Great Russia, on the other, there was never much doubt which would win Russian hearts and minds—and provide the more powerful lever for ambitious politicians.

The motives of the attackers were a complex mixture of sincere policy convictions, offended beliefs, political ambition and thirst for power, and as time went on, cynical greed. The Kremlin leadership, as it sought to reassert control over the oil industry, was able to invoke some fundamental points of policy, which won it elite support or disarmed opposition, both from outside and inside the oil industry. When seen in global context, the claims of the new private Russian oil companies to autonomy from the state were extreme: only in the United States was there a precedent for such a model.[33] In Russia, under the 1993 "Yeltsin" constitution, the state was the sovereign owner of mineral resources in the ground, and as such, it could claim justification in seeking a greater share of the rents from oil, once prices had begun to rise.

Relatedly, the state in its role as owner could argue that it had a legitimate stake in their management; and if the oil establishment perceived the private companies' production practices as harmful or shortsighted, there was at least a case for the state to intervene. In addition, the private sector in the 1990s had demonstrably failed to invest in Russia's future; indeed, the statists could argue that it was incapable of doing so, since it lacked the coherent corporate structures (like the Korean *chaebols*, a favorite model of the statists) or the financial institutions needed to "intermediate," that is, to transfer profits from the export sector to investments in other parts of the economy. Therefore, the statists reasoned, the state would have to do the job instead.

Thus the fight for control of the oil industry and oil revenues was at the same time a deeper contest over the nature of the oil industry's property rights over oil versus those of the state, over the place of oil in the political and economic system, and over the proper roles of the state in a market economy. Not the least interesting role in this contest was played by the Russian "liberals," individuals such as finance minister Aleksey Kudrin and economics minister German Gref, who joined enthusiastically with the new president, Vladimir Putin (himself reputed to be a liberal at the time), to design a new tax code, one of the aims of which was to capture windfall profits from the oil industry. In the early years of the Putin presidency, there was a genuine if fragile consensus between liberal reformers and *silovik*[34] conservatives in the new government in 2000–2001 over the need to raise oil taxes, which helped to set the stage for the confrontation that followed.[35]

Nevertheless, the play of personality and circumstance helped to push what could have been a more consensual renegotiation of rents and power between the private sector and the state toward more radical and violent outcomes. The chief catalyst by 2002–2003 was the role and personality of Mikhail Khodorkovsky, who became a lightning rod for his enemies and provided an opening for their ambitions. In the wake of the "Yukos Affair," the balance of power among elite groups, carefully engineered by Vladimir Putin in his first term, was tipped in favor of the coercive elites. This in turn catalyzed several years of *silovik*-led reaction against private property in oil and against foreign oil companies. The tacit consensus between liberals and statists was broken, complicating relations within the political and business class down to the present. It was not until 2006–2008 that Putin, by manipulating internal rivalries among the *siloviki* and demoting or distancing several of the leading *siloviki,* was able to curb their influence. He then brokered understandings among the elites that led to the election of Dmitri Medvedev as president, and the balance of power among the business and political clans was partially restored.

The leaders of the oil industry, cowed by the attack on Yukos, put their heads down and acquiesced in a systematic tightening of the fiscal and regulatory regime. But the new state of affairs was not without its advantages for them. The state's increasing hostility to foreign oil companies served their short-term interests as well, and so long as oil prices were high and the legacy fields kept on producing, the industry continued to generate enough rents to reward its stakeholders and carry on, despite the state's steadily growing share. In short, the reaction in oil policy that followed in the wake of the Yukos Affair was not entirely the work of the state; the oil industry played its part as well.

The Turning Point of 2008–2010

Toward the end of the 2000s, the Russian political and economic system under Putin seemed to have reached a more stable equilibrium. The central state had been restored; the country was increasingly prosperous; and Putin's popularity was at its height. But then Russia was badly shaken by the crash of 2008 and recession that followed. Yet the shock would have been still worse if Russia had not been partially buffered by large foreign-currency reserves and a rainy-day fund, created by Finance Minister Aleksei Kudrin, in which a portion of Russia's oil revenues was sequestered. By 2010 oil prices were rising again, and as the new decade began it appeared that the "Putin model" had weathered the worst and that the good times would resume.

Yet two fundamental things had changed. First, the optimism of the 2000s had disappeared. Russia's gross domestic product (GDP), which had declined by 7.8 percent during the recession—the steepest drop of any major economy—was slow to resume growing again. The budget had become increasingly difficult to balance: if on the eve of the crash an oil price of $70 per barrel was sufficient to produce a surplus, by 2012 it took nearly $120. Capital flight, which had been chronic through 2005 but had reversed during the peak boom years as Russian capital started to flow home, resumed again after the crash, at a higher rate than ever before. Domestic investment lagged. The political and business elite appeared to be gripped by a malaise over the future of the country, which Putin's return to the presidency in 2012 did not dispel.

Second, since 2004 the growth of Russian oil production had been slowing down, and in 2008 it actually declined for the first time since the first half of the 1990s. Growth resumed again after the crisis had passed, but it was unbalanced, being due solely to the development of a handful of large new fields, while the core of the industry, chiefly West Siberia, appeared to have entered a long-term decline. The costs of finding and producing oil were rising rapidly, while the tax system took over 90 percent of the companies' profits at the margin—the highest tax take in the world. The Russian oil industry, lacking incentive to invest in new fields and new technology, held back. The signs were clear: the Soviet oil legacy, which had sustained the industry for two decades, was running down.

These two developments are linked. On the one hand, the addicted economy and welfare system require larger and larger inputs of oil-derived revenue but respond less and less to each successive dose. On the other, the source of

23

that revenue is threatened, as costs rise and returns diminish. The oil industry requires larger and larger inputs of capital but responds less and less to each successive injection. The result is a gathering crisis of rents from oil, which threatens the basis of the present system.

Rents in the Fabric

Russia under Putin is commonly described as a "rent-based system." But what exactly is "rent," and what does it mean to say that Russia faces a crisis of oil rents? Since the concept is so fundamental to this book, a little detour is in order.

In this book I define rent as any "unearned" profit that accrues to the industry, over and above a "normal return" from oil investment plus any additional return from innovation and efficient management.[36] There are two major sources of oil profits that are clearly "rents" by this definition. The first comes from the legacy assets inherited from the Soviet era. The second is the flow of "windfall" profits resulting from the rise of world oil prices since the end of the 1990s. In both cases the Russian oil industry is the beneficiary of investments made elsewhere or of external forces it does not control. Of these two flows, the "legacy" rents from the Soviet era have clearly been on the decline since the mid-2000s, but this has been more than offset by the decade-long rise of the "global windfall" rents. The key point here is that for the last two decades, the flow of Russia's profits from oil has consisted very largely of rents, which have been maintained at relatively little expense. But both are vulnerable.

A flow of rents inevitably attracts rival claimants. The story of the post-Soviet oil industry is largely that of the battle for rents—in the 1990s for the legacy rents and in the 2000s for the global windfall rents. By the end of the first decade of the 2000s, the state had succeeded in recapturing the lion's share of both. However, the rent stream was so large that it could comfortably accommodate a wide range of other claimants as well, especially since a portion of the rent flow was disguised as inflated costs and unreported side payments. It is in this broader sense that one can say that by the end of the first decade of the 2000s, a large part of the political and economic system had become based on oil rents.

But this situation is now about to change. The decline in the quality and performance of the legacy assets has two consequences. First, as costs go up, the margins from oil decline. Second, the industry's own investment require-ments increase.[37] In other words, the industry will claim (and indeed is already claiming) a higher share of the remaining flow of value from oil. This sets the industry on a collision course with other claimants, and especially the state. Unless the industry is able to recapture some of the state's share for its own needs, it will underinvest, and oil production will eventually decline. If the state responds by forcing the companies to cut dividends to shareholders, the companies' market capitalization—and thus their share prices—will plummet. At the end of that road lies renationalization, but even that would not be more than a stopgap, since the fundamental problem is the shrinking of margins.

The coming decline in the flow of surplus from oil attacks the entire rent-based system and is already raising the level of conflict. Several categories of what in the West would be thought of as costs are actually key parts of the rent-distribution system. Russian oil and gas companies pay taxes to the state, but they also pay informal "taxes," in the form of bribes and "social payments" to localities (known to Russians as *sotsialka*). In addition, production costs are inflated, since much of their equipment and services is purchased through networks of connected companies. The process is subterranean, nontrans-parent, and largely invisible to outsiders, but it is a major channel of rents.[38] Russians, of course, are well aware of its importance. As a veteran Russian oil-man once put it to me with a smile, "You Westerners make money from your profits; we Russians make money from our costs." The implication is that oil and gas rents are ever present, flowing through every artery and vein in the system.

This flow is vital to the maintenance of the economy and the political sys-tem. Rent dependence, in short, is not simply at the heart of the system; it *is* the heart of the system. The obvious implication is that if the flow of petroleum rents were ever to slacken, Russia would be deeply destabilized.

Stasis versus *Zastoi*

Many Russians see growing similarities between today's Russia and the era of Leonid Brezhnev, whose rule spanned much of the late Soviet period from 1964 to 1982. It was a time of political stability, but also of increasing economic stagnation—a period of history known to Russians as *zastoi*. But are the two periods, Brezhnev's and Putin's, in fact similar?

The Soviet system under Brezhnev was indeed in decay. The causes were both external and internal. Decades of military competition with a larger and richer adversary had forced its leaders to concentrate the country's resources on military spending, leaving less and less to support the people's needs and aspirations. Internally, the erosion of the regime's ideological foundations, especially within the ruling Communist Party, had led to widespread corruption.[39] Even so, the regime was reasonably stable down to the mid-1980s, and it might have remained so for another generation, but for the financial crisis catalyzed by the fall of oil prices in the second half of the 1980s, combined with the radical reforms of Mikhail Gorbachev, which disrupted the system and brought on its rapid collapse.

Today's Russia labors under some similar liabilities. The military-industrial system is gone, but much of the obsolete Soviet-era industrial infrastructure remains, as does the Soviet-style social welfare system. These continue to drain the resources of the economy, just as they did in the time of zastoi. The *nomenklatura* as a system is also gone, but its descendants are still very much in place, and they depend on the state and on state-mediated rents, just as they did in the past. In short, there are indeed some key elements of similarity between the Brezhnevian past and Russia's present.

But to say that Russia feels the pull of the past is not to say that it is a prisoner of it. No one who has witnessed the changes that have taken place in Russia over the past twenty years can seriously argue that today's marketized economy, open to the outside world and linked to the Internet, is the same country that Brezhnev knew. Modernization in Russia is a work in progress—but it has come a long way, and it is still in progress.

The oil industry, as this book will attempt to show, is a prime example. An oil industry is by definition modern, in that it rests on a scientific foundation of geology and physics and requires advanced engineering skills and highly disciplined organization. The Soviet oil industry already possessed these traits in abundance, but the end of the Soviet Union, together with the industry's increased exposure to the outside world, have brought about vast changes in the Russian oil industry's structure while increasing its productivity and competitiveness. It still feels the pull of the past, but it is moving forward, and it has no choice but to keep on.

Building new state institutions has been more problematic. The 1990s were a disorderly, if creative, period of transition. The state temporarily lost its grip over the most basic attributes of sovereignty, such as control over its borders and its currency. When he came to power, Putin saw as his prime mission the restoration of stable central power, and in that respect he largely succeeded.

But Putin has been unable to build a stable institutional or ideological mechanism to ensure governability over the longer term. The system is based largely on a rejection of the 1990s, nostalgia for the Soviet empire, and resentment of the West. That is weak glue. What remains is elite self-interest. The result has been a spread of corruption and interclan wars, and, through the selective application of state power, a takeover of the "commanding heights" of the economy by politically favored interests. It is these trends that call to mind the similarities with zastoi.

The oil industry has been one of the sectors most affected. The determination of state players to control the industry and to capture the bulk of its revenues has deprived it of the resources needed to renew itself and weakened its incentive to continue modernizing. In the decade ahead, as the oil industry's inherited assets decline, will it be able to continue supplying the rents that support the political system? The answer of this book is that it will not—unless there is a systematic effort to stimulate the oil industry's continued modernization, which in turn will require improvement of the state system as a whole. To fail to act is to invite destabilization. Thus—to come full circle—the key to the fate of Russia is the fate of Russian oil.

How the Book Is Organized

The book is divided roughly into three parts. Chapters 1–3 and 5 describe the collapse of the Soviet oil industry and its attempted escape from the grip of a weakened state. The result was the rise of five private, vertically integrated oil companies—each with its own distinctive history, leadership, and corporate culture. The central plot in these chapters is the displacement of the old-line Soviet oilmen by a new generation of financial entrepreneurs, of which the most famous example is Mikhail Khodorkovsky and his company, Yukos. The reasons for the spectacular success of Yukos—and its consequent political vulnerability—are analyzed. In the background is the Russian state at its nadir, too weak to prevent the takeover of the industry by the new oligarchs, yet unwilling to release its grip.

Chapters 6–8 describe the rise of Vladimir Putin and the "Pitertsy" (as the Russians call natives of Saint Petersburg), and their role in the revival of the Russian state after 2000. The growth of the power of two groups—the oil oligarchs and Putin's people —led to the massive confrontation of the "Yukos Affair," culminating in the arrest and conviction of Khodorkovsky and the destruction of Yukos. The central argument of these chapters is that the Russian political and business elite rejected Khodorkovsky as a foreign body, because his behavior and policies challenged established norms on a wide front while also competing with the aims and ambitions of the Kremlin leadership. The resulting rise of Rosneft, today Russia's state-owned oil giant, is analyzed and explained.

Chapters 9 and 10 describe the tax and regulatory policies put in place by the state in the wake of the Yukos Affair and their negative consequences for the performance of the oil industry. The argument of this part of the book is that the state went too far in its efforts to tax and control the oil industry and to exclude foreign investment. The shock of the crash of 2008–2009 has prompted a reexamination of these policies, but with only modest results to date.

Woven throughout the book is the theme of mutual learning between Russia and the West following the end of the Soviet Union. Chapters 4 and 11 describe the role of foreign companies and individuals as agents of change and technology transfer, their successes and failures, and their impact in the wake of Russia's reopening to the outside world.

Lastly, Chapter 12 details the case that a crisis is coming as the Soviet oil legacy declines, unless the oil industry and the state undertake strong reforms, and Chapter 13 examines the possible impact of future trends in global oil prices, together with their implications for Russia's stability and growth.

As Vladimir Putin begins his third term as president, there is much talk in Moscow about "modernization," "diversification," and "energy efficiency," which are in fact code words for "escape from oil." The concluding chapter shows why Russia cannot escape from oil. Oil, together with natural gas, remains Russia's chief comparative advantage in the modern world. But Russia can make better use of the opportunities that oil offers as a high-tech sector and as a catalyst for home-grown innovation. Russia still has a window of time to address the oil industry's weaknesses, capitalize on its potential strengths, and put the industry's relationship with the state on a sounder footing. At the same time, success in reforming the oil industry will be unavailing so long as Russia's dependence on oil rents continues to increase.

The title of the book, *Wheel of Fortune,* has many meanings. It describes the cycle of decay, collapse, and restoration through which Russia has passed over the last twenty years; the vast wealth made and unmade; and the rise and fall of political fortunes. It is a metaphor for Russia's dependence on the global economic cycle and resource prices. Above all, it is a symbol of the oil industry itself, the extraordinary business that risks billions on the curve of a well log or the turn of a drill bit. *Wheel of Fortune* is both the journey of the oil industry and that of Russia itself.

But to understand the journey, one must know its beginning. We start the story in a country that no longer exists, run by people who were famous long ago.

chapter 1

The Breakup: The Soviet Oil Industry Disintegrates

Today the veteran "oil generals" who ran the Soviet oil industry look back on their past as though it all happened on a remote planet. Valerii Graifer, now chairman of the board of LUKoil, Russia's largest private oil company, is today a white-haired gentleman in his eighties. His modest and courtly manner gives little hint of the power he once wielded. In the second half of the 1980s, the last years of the Soviet Union, Graifer, as head of the oil ministry's main administration in West Siberia, controlled over 400 million tons per year (8 million barrels per day) of crude oil production, then over 13 percent of the world's total. He held the imposing rank of USSR deputy minister of oil, and technically, that made him the boss of the entire West Siberian oil administration, then known by the jaw-breaking acronym of Glavtiumenneftegaz, or "Glavk" for short.

But in reality Graifer was not the most powerful figure on the scene. There was one man mightier than he, one whose support Graifer badly needed, the head of the Communist Party apparatus in West Siberia's oil capital of Tiumen, Gennadii Bogomiakov. Valerii Graifer recalls:

> I was an unusual combination for the Soviet oil industry—not an engineer but an economist, and even more unusual, a Jew. I had headed the oil industry in Tatarstan and I had a reputation as a manager and troubleshooter. In the mid-1980s, when the West Siberian oil industry ran into trouble, I was sent to Tiumen.
>
> I knew Tiumen well. My grandparents had been exiled there from Saint Petersburg after the revolution of 1905. I had spent summers in Tiumen as a boy. But when I returned as head of Glavtiumenneftegaz I ran into a brick wall. Bogomiakov would not even meet with me. Finally one evening I was invited to a party at his home. I was seated at the bottom end of the table, and everyone ignored me. But as the evening went on Bogomiakov and his

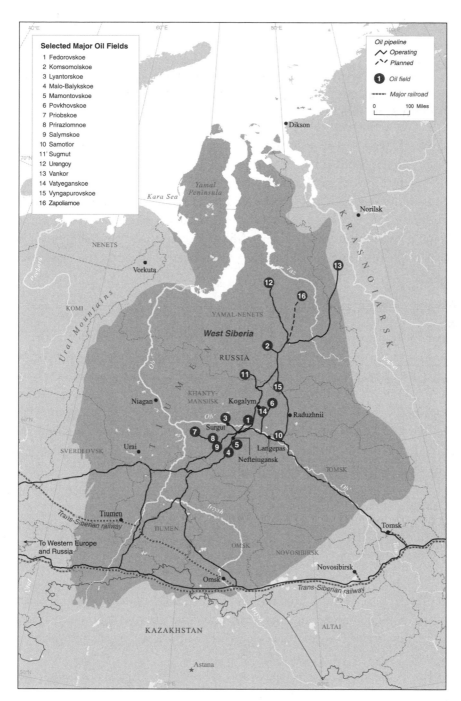

Selected Major Oil Fields

1 Fedorovskoe
2 Komsomolskoe
3 Lyantorskoe
4 Malo-Balykskoe
5 Mamontovskoe
6 Povkhovskoe
7 Priobskoe
8 Prirazlomnoe
9 Salymskoe
10 Samotlor
11 Sugmut
12 Urengoy
13 Vankor
14 Vatyeganskoe
15 Vyngapurovskoe
16 Zapoliamoe

Oil pipeline
— Operating
— Planned
❶ Oil field
···· Major railroad
0   100 Miles

MAP 2 *West Siberian basin: Major oilfields and transportation routes.*

friends began singing Siberian folksongs. To my own surprise—and theirs—I found myself joining in. Those were the songs from my boyhood, buried away in the back of my memory, and I knew them all. We sang all through the night. By morning Bogomiakov and I were fast friends, and I never had any trouble with him after that.[1]

West Siberia by the late 1980s was the powerhouse of the Soviet oil industry, producing two-thirds of all Soviet oil. It was the industry's third generation: from its birthplace in Baku in the early 1900s, it had migrated to the Volga-Urals in the 1940s and 1950s, before reaching its peak as the world's leading producer in the 1970s and 1980s, thanks to the giant oilfields of West Siberia's Tiumen Province. It was in Tiumen, in the Arctic swamps of the middle Ob' River basin, that the final drama of the rise and fall of Soviet oil was played out.

The Stovepipe System

It was a simpler world, in retrospect. There was a vertical chain of command, running from the headquarters of the USSR Ministry of Oil in Moscow, located in a grand prerevolutionary palace facing the Kremlin directly across the Moscow River, down through a hierarchy of divisions and subdivisions to the working level in West Siberia, the "production associations" (in Russian, *proizvodstvennye ob"edineniia*) that controlled the operating units in the field, the so-called NGDUs, later familiar to Western oilmen from Tulsa to Calgary as "engadoos."[2]

But the Ministry of Oil's domain was limited to the production and transportation of crude oil and condensate—in oilspeak, the "upstream." As the crude oil flowed into the pipeline system, the producers turned over title to the pipeline operators, at that time the transportation department of the Ministry of Oil. Title then passed to the next link in the chain, the refineries belonging to the Ministry of Oil Refining and Petrochemicals, which handled all of the "midstream." Refined products moving inside the domestic economy were controlled by yet another monopoly, Transnefteprodukt.[3] A specialized agency of the Ministry of Foreign Trade, Soiuznefteeksport, had a monopoly over oil exports.

Hard-currency proceeds from crude oil sales—the most valuable and politically sensitive part of the oil flow—were kept in special accounts of the

USSR Bank for Foreign Trade (Vneshtorgbank).[4] The key point about this system is that the upstream oil producers, the ones who actually produced the largest single part of the export wealth,[5] saw very little of this hard-currency flow, and none of it directly. The oil ministry bargained, like the others, for its annual share of hard currency, which it then doled out to the upstream producers and the pipeline operators for special projects requiring foreign purchases approved by the planners.

Within these segregated state structures, an upstream crude producer could (and generally did) spend an entire career without ever talking to a refiner, a distributor, or an export trader, except at the very top of the system.[6] Upstream producers had little exposure to the outside world. If they needed equipment from abroad, the Ministry of Foreign Trade bought it for them. For the oil generals, big men though they were in their own home provinces, a trip abroad (where they were herded about in closely watched delegations and given only miserly expense allowances) was just as much of a prized adventure as it was for most other Soviet citizens.

All oil in those days was the property of the state and was managed by the central planning system. The different players in the Soviet system took their cues not from market signals but from the central planners in Moscow, who set production targets and allocated supplies and manpower. Even in the oilfields the Ministry of Oil had little control beyond its own wells and pipelines. All the support systems it needed—power lines and electricity supply, housing and road construction, pipe and drill bits, helicopter transport, and most other key services—were the province of other ministries.[7]

Something was needed to bind these parts together, and for that purpose the Soviets had put in place a separate command structure, the core of which was the regional apparatus of the Communist Party. The true boss of any Soviet region, the all-powerful viceroy of the ruling Politburo, was the first secretary of the party's province committee (known as the *obkom*). His job was to offset the rigidities, the missed cues, the conflicting plans, and the petty jealousies of the local offices of the various ministries, by cajoling, negotiating, knocking heads, and if necessary appealing to Moscow for authority over the closed telephone line, the *vertushka*, that ran straight via a hardwired connection to the Politburo.[8] To bind together the vertical stovepipes of the Soviet command economy, the party apparatus provided the all-important local welding.[9]

33

Gennadii Bogomiakov, whom we have already met at his dinner table, ruled as the party obkom first secretary in Tiumen Province from 1973 to his overthrow in January 1990. He was one of the true veterans of the industry, a geologist by training, formerly head of West Siberia's leading institute for oil geology and exploration. He had worked in Tiumen from the earliest days of the West Siberian oil boom in the 1960s. Bogomiakov had the supremely delicate job of walking the tightrope between Moscow's constant demands for more oil and the local oilmen's equally constant lobbying for lower targets. In those days, the West Siberian oil industry was split between the so-called optimists (who pushed for maximum output growth, under relentless political pressure from the Kremlin) and pessimists (known as *predel'shchiki*), who warned that to push the fields too hard was to invite disaster. Being labeled a *predel'shchik* was likely to cost you your job. Only the celebrated discoverer of Samotlor, Viktor Muravlenko, had the prestige and courage to stand up to the Kremlin and its constant demands for more oil. Muravlenko had a direct line to Prime Minister Aleksey Kosygin and could take his protests straight to the top. But the direct line worked both ways. Muravlenko once told Valerii Graifer that Kosygin called him one day and pleaded, "We're short of bread [*s khlebushkom plokho*]—give us 3 million tons of oil above the plan."[10]

Bogomiakov had the unenviable task of holding the middle between the Kremlin and the oilmen. "He was a serious and intelligent man," recalls Graifer, "and he managed to protect us against the optimists." Others are less forgiving. According to a local historian, Bogomiakov's constant hounding, coupled with that of the ministry in Moscow, broke Muravlenko's health and drove him to an early grave. In 1977 Muravlenko dropped dead of a heart attack in the lobby of the Rossiia Hotel in Moscow, following a particularly stormy exchange with the oil minister, Nikolai Mal'tsev. Following his death, the pressure on the *predel'shchiki* turned into a witch hunt. Muravlenko's successor at Glavtiumenneftegaz, Feliks Arzhanov, was fired in 1980 for trying to hold the 1985 output target at 340 million tons (6.8 million barrels per day) (West Siberia in 1980 had produced 312.7 million) [6.3 million barrels per day], while Bogomiakov demanded an increase to 365 million tons (7.3 million barrels per day).[11] In the early 1980s hundreds of senior managers, including two more heads of the Glavk, were purged from the West Siberian oil industry for failing to meet the higher targets.[12] Whatever Bogomiakov's exact role in these battles, all agree that he was a consummate artist on the tightrope. He survived three political successions and two major shakeouts in the Siberian oil industry all through the 1970s and 1980s, before the death throes of the whole Soviet system finally brought him down.[13]

Markets and economics had no place in this system. The Soviet command economy was not really an economy at all; it was a bureaucratic pump for moving resources according to the priorities set by the political leadership. It was largely indifferent to the fine weighing of value and cost against time and risk that is the essence of free-market economic thinking and business strategy. The skills that the system valued most were those of scientists and engineers—geologists, petroleum engineers, and drillers—who then morphed into political managers as they rose up through the ranks. Whereas a senior executive in a modern international oil company, in addition to technical expertise, is also a specialist in financial strategy and cost management, aiming at optimizing return on capital, Soviet oilmen were engineers who lived in a noneconomic world of administratively set production targets. An international oil company today contracts out much of the actual job of finding and producing oil to service companies. In contrast, an upstream Soviet oil enterprise for all practical purposes was a service company, responsible for every aspect of development and production and directly employing tens of thousands of workers.[14]

Ignoring cost led Soviet leaders and planners to misallocate resources on a grand scale. Throughout the Soviet period, but particularly from the 1960s on, they poured capital and manpower east of the Ural Mountains into the Siberian hinterland, building massive permanent cities in some of the coldest and least hospitable places on earth. In West Siberia, they built large permanent settlements in the middle of Arctic swamp and tundra, one-company towns that later proved hostages to misfortune.[15]

The practical consequence of all this is that the true costs of developing and producing Soviet oil, being largely invisible, were systematically discounted. So long as world oil prices were high and the fields were young—and both conditions prevailed between 1973 and 1980—this could be ignored. But in the first half of the 1980s, world oil prices fell sharply and remained at low levels in the second half of the decade,[16] while at the same time the annual growth in Soviet oil production abruptly slowed, forcing the Soviet government to increase oil investment sharply in order to offset some of the loss in revenues. This reflected, among other things, the fact that the Soviet oil industry was running up against an inexorable fact of nature: the rate of discovery of large new oil fields was slowing down. This had nothing to do with Soviet planning; it simply reflected the log-normal distribution of field sizes characteristic of oil provinces around the world. By the 1980s, the Soviet oilmen were developing ever-smaller and more costly fields.[17]

Thus, from 1980 on, as exploration and production costs increased and oil and gas export revenues declined, the rents from oil plummeted. If it is not quite true, as some studies have concluded, that more money was going down into the wells than was coming up, the drop in oil and gas rents was dramatic enough, from a peak of about $270 billion per year in 1980–1981 to less than $100 billion in 1986 and after.[18] Most of this decline was due to falling world oil prices, but rising production costs were also to blame; between 1983 and 1987, the delivered costs of Soviet oil grew by two-thirds.[19]

The Soviet command economy had always depended on the rents from natural resources—although not so much for export as for internal use.[20] But by the 1980s the Soviet political leadership had grown to rely not only on oil for domestic consumption but also on oil-export revenues, while the oil industry was equally dependent on a high rate of growth of investment. A crisis in the oil industry was bound to translate into a crisis for the entire command economy—and vice versa.[21]

A World of Survivors

The West Siberian oilfields in the 1970s and 1980s were a tough but colorful and boisterous world, a multiethnic melting pot in which, in the early years at least, everyone came from someplace else. Roughnecks and roustabouts, the foot soldiers of any oil industry, were recruited from the older oil provinces, from Ukraine and the Volga Basin and the Caspian Sea, and sent to work in makeshift settlements under incredibly harsh conditions. (Prison labor, however, played no role in the West Siberian oil and gas industries, since they developed even as the Gulag empire was being shut down.[22]) The higher ranks, composed of geologists, engineers, and managers, were an equally varied lot. Farman Salmanov, the most legendary name among the pioneer geologists of the region, recalled that in his Tiumen institute alone, thirty-four different Soviet ethnic groups worked side by side.[23] There was a strong Muslim coloration to the West Siberian workforce (although it was not advisable to make a point of one's cultural or religious origins), and many oilmen from the Muslim republics rose high in the Soviet oil industry.

One of these was Vagit Alekperov, the Baku-born son of an Azerbaijani father and a Russian mother.[24] He had worked on offshore rigs in the Soviet part of the Caspian Sea and had never been up to Russia when he first arrived in West Siberia at the end of the 1970s, at the age of 29. He was assigned to Kogalym, then one of the frontier regions of the West Siberian industry. Owing to his abilities, Alekperov soon attracted the attention of Valerii Graifer, who in 1986 named him to head the Kogalym operation.[25] "It was Valerii Graifer who jump-started my career," Alekperov later said. In 1990, still with Graifer's support, he was promoted over the heads of dozens of more senior men to Moscow, as deputy minister of oil in charge of all Soviet oil production. He had been in that position for less than a year when he teamed up with a group of fellow West Siberian oilmen to create LUKoil, Russia's first private oil company—but here we are getting ahead of the story.

As time went on, West Siberia began to produce its own oilmen. An Industrial Institute was created in the capital city of Tiumen,[26] and an intense rivalry sprang up between the local graduates of "Indus" and the alumni of the prestigious Gubkin Institute of Oil and Gas in Moscow, irreverently known as "Kerosinka" ("Kerosene U"). Many of the leaders of the Siberian oil industry who emerged in the 1980s—including high executives in today's Russian oil majors—graduated from "Indus" within a few years of one another in the early 1970s. They were—and remain—a tight-knit community. The tie often extends to the next generation, father to son. One is apt to hear phrases like, "He's a good guy. His dad and I used to feed the mosquitoes together in the tundra."[27]

In a Soviet-era NGDU, the actual working level of the upstream industry, the drillers were the aristocrats, virtually a separate caste. Vladimir Bogdanov, a 1973 graduate of Indus and today the CEO of Surgutneftegaz, Russia's fourth largest oil company, was typical of the Siberian village boys who went into the oil industry right out of the army, starting at the bottom of the ladder as a *pombur*, a driller's assistant. Almost all of Bogdanov's career was connected with oil drilling in Surgut, where he first arrived in 1976 at the age of twenty-five, after three years at the legendary Samotlor field, the biggest in the Soviet industry. Bogdanov quickly climbed the ranks of the Surgut drillers, becoming head of drilling for all of the Tiumen oil industry in 1983 at the age of thirty-two, when he was transferred back to Surgut to head the production association. Perhaps not surprisingly, Surgutneftegaz today, under the leadership of Vladimir Bodganov, is still known for its devotion to drilling.

Drilling, in Soviet times, was virtually an end in itself. Drilling crews, like everyone else in the command system, were rewarded for meeting targets—though their target was not to produce oil but to drill an assigned number of meters of hole. Drilling crews would arrive on the site of a new field and punch perfectly straight lines of wellbore, a line of injector wells (which injected water into the oilfield, a technique known as "waterflooding") alternating neatly with a line of producer wells, like a sewing machine double-stitching a pair of pants. In the second half of the 1980s, as Moscow became more and more desperate for oil, the drillers drilled more and more frantically, racking up astonishing numbers—over 34 million meters of hole in 1986, over 38 million meters in 1987, finally culminating in a frenzied peak of drilling at over 41 million meters in 1988 before starting the long downhill slide into the 1990s, bottoming out a decade later at one-eighth the peak level of 1988.[28]

That the drillers were able to get such results was itself a miracle. Much of West Siberia is Arctic swamp; in the spring and summer the middle Ob' basin turns into a vast lake. The oilmen had to do most of their work in the Siberian winter, when the ground was frozen hard enough to slide rigs across the ice. They were poorly supplied with inferior-quality drill pipe and bits, which broke frequently and had to be laboriously fished out of the well and replaced. Unable to get hard alloys to make rotary drill bits (the best alloys went to the military-industrial complex), Soviet drillers used less demanding high-speed turbodrills instead, which were hard to control and resulted in wells with strange kinks and curves. (As one Soviet veteran drily recalled, "We drilled horizontal wells by accident.") Drilling muds, cements, and cement pumps were all of poor quality and in unpredictable supply. Drilling teams frequently had to stop operations altogether, as they waited for promised supplies that did not come. People like Bogdanov made their reputations by being resourceful enough, and above all tough enough, to get results despite all the obstacles. It was a game for young men; in the Siberian oil industry you made it young or not at all.

This was obviously an extraordinarily inefficient way to develop oilfields. Although Soviet geological science was highly advanced, reservoir modeling and logging techniques were not, and drilling crews sometimes punched right through productive horizons of oil-bearing rock without even being aware of them. The traditional straight-line pattern of injector and producer wells took no account of the complexities of the reservoirs beneath (which the reservoir engineers of the day were in any case unable to see and model). But above all, the drillers' single-minded focus on drilling hole resulted in thousands of un-produced wells all across the Siberian landscape—drilled and cased but never perforated or produced—as the drillers simply moved on to the next field and the next set of targets.

The rough-and-ready production practices used in West Siberia—responses to the poor Soviet support system and the political pressures placed on the oilmen—were not only inefficient but also damaging. Waterflooding, which was universally used in West Siberia, is a case in point. The idea was to inject water into the fields, creating a massive wall of water that was supposed to push the oil toward the producer wells, but inevitably water broke through fractures in the reservoir rock, bypassing much of the oil and rushing straight to the producer wells. By the 1980s such "swept" fields were producing nine parts of water for each part of oil. The Siberian oilmen had no way to model the problem or even to measure it. The proportion of water in the oil—the so-called water cut—was measured manually by a lowly *laborant* stationed at the exit from the field, who took samples from a valve at the main pipe. As a result, the figure he recorded was an average for the field as a whole, rather than for any one well or group of wells. This crude measure made it impossible to know what was really going on or what to do about it. It was not for another decade and a half that the Russian oil industry began applying modern systems of fluid measurement to each well, together with modeling techniques that made it possible to "see" how the water was actually flowing within the reservoir and to detect zones of bypassed oil.

The Soviet overreliance on drilling and waterflooding, together with a relative neglect of well maintenance and repair and a lack of powerful and reliable down-hole pumps, resulted in damaged and prematurely declining fields. There was also a lasting legacy of falsified data, a particular problem in West Siberia, where the political pressures to produce had been especially intense. A common practice, if a drilling crew drilled a wellbore that missed the targeted pay zone, was for superiors to conceal the mistake by redrawing the maps of the reservoir. The legacy of mislocated wells and falsified data continued to plague Russian reservoir engineers well into the 1990s, and even to the present day.

Such was the unique world of Soviet oil as it was down to the end of the 1980s. The underlying laws of physics were the same as in the rest of the world—oil in Siberia flowed according to Darcy's law just as it did in Texas— yet the Soviet oil industry might as well have been on a separate planet. It had grown up in the unearthly atmosphere of the Soviet command economy and was adapted to the latter's formal rules and—no less important—its informal culture. Its achievements were all the more impressive, won by heroic effort and skill under some of the world's harshest conditions. Although the Soviet Union was the largest oil producer in the world by the second half of the 1980s, some of the very things that had made it great also made it fragile. Many of its practices—adaptations to the constraints of the centrally planned system— aged the fields prematurely. By the end of the 1980s, the Soviet oil industry was struggling.

More than most sectors of the economy—and certainly much more than the gas industry, as we shall see later on—the oil industry was kept together by tight political control. The same political machinery that pressured the Soviet oilmen to overproduce using damaging techniques also kept the system to- gether, forcing the many bureaucracies involved to work more or less together. Once political power weakened, the industry itself was likely to fissure, and that is what happened at the end of the 1980s.

The Soviet oil industry had already stumbled twice, in the late 1970s and, more ominously, in the mid-1980s. It could keep increasing production only by massive increases in inputs—capital, manpower, equipment, and new fields— driven by relentless political pressure. West Siberia, in particular, rested dan- gerously on a handful of first-generation fields, which were now starting to weaken. In the mid-1980s the increasingly anxious oilmen threw their re- sources into developing the next generation of West Siberian fields, but these were smaller and less productive and were not enough to offset the decline of the first generation.[29]

The symbol and centerpiece of the trouble was the fabled Samotlor field, the world's second-largest oilfield, which at its height in 1980 had produced 170 million tons (3.4 million barrels per day), nearly one-quarter of total Soviet output. But it slipped badly in 1984–1985 and again in 1987.[30] Both times the Soviet political leadership responded with additional funds and a vigorous purge of the industry, and output started growing again.[31] The added pressure from Moscow temporarily pushed West Siberian oil output up to its maximum output, never reattained since. In 1988 oil production in West Siberia peaked at 415.1 million tons (8.3 million barrels per day).[32]

Yet this time a third and far more serious oil crisis was at hand. Its source was the reforms of Mikhail Gorbachev.

Oil Crisis Meets *Perestroika*

In far-off Moscow the first winds of a coming hurricane were already starting to blow. In 1985 a new and vigorous leader named Mikhail Gorbachev had come to power as general secretary in the Kremlin, vowing to restart the sputtering Soviet economy. Two years later, frustrated by a lack of results, Gorbachev reached for more radical measures, which he called *perestroika,* or "restructuring." Within three more years, the forces unleashed by perestroika had torn the Soviet oil industry apart and thrown West Siberia into chaos.

Gorbachev's perestroika, in retrospect, was a disastrous blend of good intentions, bad economics, and fatal political naivete. He had come to believe that the main source of stagnation of the Soviet economy was bureaucratic interference by the ministries and the party apparatus. His cure was to curb their power. In 1987 he approved a "Law on the Socialist Enterprise," which was intended to free the enterprise (the basic unit of production in the Soviet system) from the ministries' grip. Enterprise directors were given greater control over their finances and investment budgets, they were allowed to hire freely and offer higher wages, and they were encouraged to maximize profits.

For someone who had come up through the party apparatus, Gorbachev seemed strangely oblivious of the fact that the Soviet command economy rested on wholly artificial administrative prices set by bureaucrats. Unleashing the profit motive, in the absence of a price system that reflected actual supply and demand, invited disaster. In short order these reckless policies disrupted the budget, ignited inflation, and sent output plummeting. By 1990–1991, frightened by the cataclysm he had unleashed, Gorbachev attempted to pull back, but it was too late. Cut loose from its mooring of tight controls bolted by political power, the economy had begun an irreversible drift toward anarchy.[33]

In industry Gorbachev's reforms set off a wage spiral, as enterprise directors competed with one another for scarce labor in a tight market. The West

Siberian oil industry, which relied heavily on workers flown in from other regions, was especially hard-hit. The new law also freed the enterprises from key planning controls, in particularly those governing which products would be produced. For the oil industry this was an ominous move, since it depended on a wide range of equipment from far-away parts of the Soviet Union, particularly from Azerbaijan, where most oil tools were made, and from Ukraine, the source of much of its pipe. The Soviet supply system had never worked well, but from 1988 on it began to disintegrate altogether as key items went out of production or were available only at hefty under-the-table markups.

Thus the costs of labor and supplies both rose sharply, driving up the unit costs of oil. But domestic oil prices were not increased. As a result, from 1988 on the oil producers began to slip into the red. The epidemic of debt and non-payments, which crippled the oil industry for the next decade, began right there.

Most disruptive of all, the 1987 law allowed workers to elect their own directors. Managers, to keep their workers' favor, began granting even larger wage increases and subsidized social programs, adding further to the cost spiral. But the real consequences went deeper. In the Soviet system the most potent lever of power was control over personnel, the power to hire and fire cadres. It was the basis of the nomenklatura system that underpinned the entire Soviet structure of power, not only that of the ministries in Moscow, but also of the Glavk in the field and, even more important, that of the party obkom in Tiumen. Direct election of directors from below threatened anarchy. Little wonder that veterans like Valerii Graifer were horrified.[34] "It created total havoc," he recalled. In later years he pointed to the "Law on the Socialist Enterprise" as the fatal step that marked the beginning of the end of the Soviet system.[35]

Still Gorbachev plunged on. In 1987, he authorized privately owned "cooperatives," in effect opening the door to private enterprise.[36] He broke up the monolithic USSR State Bank, which promptly divided and redivided into a profusion of smaller banks, many of which soon turned themselves into cooperatives, effectively becoming private banks.[37] Soon after, Gorbachev dismantled the state's monopoly control of foreign trade. He granted to the ministries the right to export and import and hold foreign currencies and then extended the same right to individual enterprises. By December 1988, he allowed even the cooperatives to conduct foreign trade on their own.

These measures destroyed the controls of the Soviet command economy. "Coooperatives" became thinly disguised fronts for all sorts of private companies, many of them dodgy devices for enterprise managers to divert company resources into private hands. The new banks, which soon numbered in the hundreds and then in the thousands, borrowed state funds and lent them on to their well-connected friends and relatives. The resulting proliferation of credit caused the money supply to balloon out of control, further feeding inflation. Finally, giving enterprises and cooperatives access to foreign trade and foreign-currency accounts opened up the borders, tearing away the barriers that had isolated the autarkic Soviet Union from the world economy. The new cooperatives and mini-banks—and the well-placed ministry bureaucrats, party officials, and enterprise directors who often stood behind them—rushed to seize the new opportunities. Suddenly everything seemed to be for lease or sale. A spoof want ad in *Izvestiia* captured the gold-rush spirit of the late 1980s: "WANTED: The 'Friends of *Perestroika*' Cooperative wishes to rent three meters of state border." The message was clear: the Iron Curtain itself was on the market.

Gorbachev's other major reform was *glasnost*, meaning "openness." His intention had been to open up the Soviet system, to shed light on the past, to allow citizens to speak their minds, and at the same time to mobilize public opinion against the conservative nomenklatura who opposed his reforms. "Squeeze them from below; we'll squeeze them from above!" became Gorbachev's slogan. It worked all too well. By 1988 a tidal wave of political radicalism swept the country, and by 1989, when Gorbachev called for competitive elections to a reformed legislature, it turned into an all-out attack against anyone identified as a *nomenklaturshchik*. Graifer, who was drafted as a candidate by Bogomiakov and the party obkom, reluctantly hit the campaign trail, where he ran into a wall of popular hostility:

> It was something awful. Besides dealing with production problems, I had to constantly rush about to cities and villages and speak in front of the citizens. My opponent was one of those democrats. His campaign program consisted of pouring mud on me. . . . At these meetings people were all worked up and behaved very aggressively.[38]

Graifer, tagged as a hopeless nomenklaturshchik, went down in humiliating defeat, gaining a mere 17 percent of the popular vote.

Prokruchka: The Wheel of Fortune

For the bold, the well placed, the quick-witted, and the unscrupulous, the doors were now open to instant wealth. From 1988 on, following Gorbachev's loosening of the foreign-trade monopoly, anyone who could get their hands on something exportable stood to make a fortune—if they could reach the border. The basic idea was simple: First create your own cooperative, preferably in the name of a helpful relative. Then found your own bank (typically based on the financial department of your own company). Grant your cooperative an interest-free ruble loan to buy commodities from yourself at fixed low domestic prices. Export them for dollars; repay the initial loan with by-now depreciated rubles; and pocket the remainder. This operation, repeated over and over again on an ever-larger scale, came to be known in Russian as the *prokruchka,* a perpetual-motion machine for the multiplication of wealth, a wheel of fortune for anyone in a position to take advantage of it.

The oil industry was no exception. The differential between the export price of oil and its official domestic price widened steadily as the Soviet system weakened, reaching a peak of 100 to 1 at the time of the Soviet collapse in December 1991.[39] But the upstream producers were initially in a weak position to take advantage of it. They did not own the wells or the oil that came from them; they had no legal status other than state employees; and they had no experience in trading or finance. Title to the oil passed from the production association to the pipeline authority as it entered the system. The oil flowed away into the centralized pipeline system; the great trunk lines were closely monitored, and there was no significant opportunity for physical "leakage."[40] In the vast open spaces of West Siberia, swamp-ridden in summer and frozen in winter, access was difficult and detection almost certain. The West Siberian Pipeline Directorate, an agency of the central ministry's transportation department, maintained a fleet of helicopters that patrolled the main trunk lines constantly, making petty thievery a risky hit-and-run affair. Besides, a tanker truck filled with contraband crude oil would have had to travel hundreds of miles to dispose of its haul, and in any case crude oil without a refinery or an export terminal nearby was worthless.

Instead, the first opportunities for private business in oil opened up at the lower end of the system, at the refineries and storage points, where the oil flow divided into multiple rivulets that were less closely controlled, and refined products such as diesel and gasoline could be moved to the borders by rail or tanker. Those best positioned to take advantage of this, by virtue of their location and their skills, were Moscow-based foreign-trade officials or locally well-connected people close to the refineries, storage points, or export terminals. Thus in 1989 an enterprising foreign-trade official named Andrei Pannikov teamed up with former colleagues in the state oil-export monopoly, a Soviet tanker company called Volgatanker, and the Kirishi refinery on the Gulf of Finland to create Russia's first independent trading company, called "Urals." (Urals later went on to make history as the export trader for Russia's first private oil company, LUKoil.)[41]

Thus as early as 1988–1989 there appeared a theme that would run throughout the 1990s—the complex relationship, part rivalry and part mutual dependence, between those who produced the oil upstream and those who refined it, shipped it, and sold it downstream. They had worked in different regions and ministries; they had different backgrounds, cultures, and political connections. They lacked the long-standing personal ties that kept business going in other sectors as the Soviet system weakened. More divided them than united them. Yet they were inescapably bound together—the refiners and traders could not survive without crude oil, or the oil generals without money.

The initial contacts were hesitant and improvised. As the supply system unraveled, oil producers turned to barter, exchanging crude oil for food and other necessities. This created, for the first time, a pool of independently owned oil. Eager middlemen soon sprang up, improvising chains of barter to reach buyers downstream who could turn oil into cash. Local officials, local gangsters, and many others "left for the market" *(poshli na rynok)*.[42] This "private" oil flowed right along with the "state" oil through the pipeline system; the two were physically indistinguishable, but who was to say who owned what? Thus, even though crude oil did not leak physically from the system, it became part of the prokruchka game just the same.

One important innovation from perestroika was the joint venture. In 1988, to help the oil industry bring new technology and services into the oilfields, the government authorized oil producers to create joint ventures with foreign oil-service companies. Any extra oil their efforts produced could be exported and the proceeds kept in separate hard-currency accounts, to be used for imports of oil tools and other equipment. For the upstream producers, joint ventures suddenly provided, for the first time, a flow of hard currency they could

45

manage themselves, and no less important, they opened up a window on the outside world. Thanks to their foreign partners (or, in some cases, Russian partners who set up companies on foreign soil), an enterprising oil general could travel to the West on a decent expense account or open a personal bank account abroad (still technically quite illegal for Soviet citizens). Not surprisingly, joint ventures spread quickly throughout the upstream. Their share of total Russian oil output and exports was initially insignificant (it grew later, as we shall see in Chapter 4), but they brought the upstream producers into direct contact, for the first time, with people who knew the outside world and the export market.[43]

One such contact would cast a long shadow over the next decade. Iurii Golubev was a senior Soviet foreign-trade official who had spent the 1970s and 1980s in the Soviet foreign-trade office in Canada, eventually rising to chief representative there. One of his tasks was to buy equipment for the oil and gas industry. In 1988 Golubev introduced a company called Canadian Fracmasters to Sergei Muravlenko, then the newly named general director of Yuganskneftegaz. This soon led to the creation of a joint venture, Yuganskfracmaster.[44] The two men became friends and partners. Golubev, thanks to his background in foreign trade and his network of Moscow connections, helped Muravlenko to export oil, and he subsequently played a key role behind the scenes in the creation of Yukos. The two men remained close over the next two decades. When Golubev died in London in January 2007, it was Muravlenko who arranged his funeral in Moscow.

Yet there were few such legal windows. For the most part, upstream producers could not legally appropriate their companies' oil and sell it for personal profit. But by creating a cooperative connected to a joint venture, an oil general could lease "idle wells" to himself as a cooperative and contract with a foreign service company (which might again be himself) to have them "repaired" in exchange for oil.[45] At least some part of the epidemic of idle wells that spread across the Russian upstream in the first half of the 1990s was bogus. The wells were officially listed on the state companies' books as broken, but many of them were producing oil and profits just the same. The first stories of Russian oilmen opening up private accounts in banks in Switzerland and Monaco, using legal investment projects as a cover to launder illegal oil revenues, date from this time.[46] Such personal revenues parked abroad soon amounted to hundreds of millions of dollars (the billions came later), enabling some oil generals, when the time came, to buy stock in their "own" companies from their savings abroad.

Perestroika Drives On

Back in Moscow, perestroika drove on. Banking on the enterprise directors, Gorbachev in 1988 began cutting back the staffs of the ministries, crippling their ability to control developments in the provinces. In June 1989 he chopped the number of ministries in half, consolidating the Ministries of Oil and Gas into a single body and collapsing the seven construction ministries into two. Most of the ministers relevant to the oil industry were fired.[47] Later in the year, Gorbachev made his last fateful move, shutting down the economic departments of the Communist Party apparatus, which had been the principal instrument for coordinating the separate ministries at the regional level.

With the weakening of the central government and the crippling of the party apparatus, there was little to prevent the individual republics of the Soviet Union from going their own way. The years 1989 and 1990 marked the beginning of the "parade of sovereignties," as one republic after another declared autonomy from Moscow. In the Caucasus, this was soon followed by a war between Azerbaijan and Armenia, with disastrous consequences for the supply of equipment to the Russian oil industry from Baku. A supply chain that had become increasingly costly and unreliable since 1987 disappeared altogether in 1990, leaving the Russian oil producers effectively without a home-grown equipment industry and making them reliant on foreign imports.

In the background was a growing financial crisis. The collapse in world oil prices in 1986, and the low oil prices prevailing thereafter, cut deeply into Soviet export revenues. For the first two years, in 1986 and 1987, good weather and good harvests enabled the Soviet leadership to reduce imports of grain and cut back hard-currency expenditures. But in 1988 agricultural output fell back to normal levels, and the government was forced to expend its foreign-currency reserves and borrow massively from abroad, both to pay for grain but also for the increasingly wide range of imported products, including steel pipe and chemicals, on which the Soviet economy had come to depend. By 1989, the Soviet economy was approaching bankruptcy. This was Gorbachev's bad luck, but it was also the result of his failure to take the difficult measures that might have alleviated the crisis. Yegor Gaidar, who as Yeltsin's prime minister subsequently led Russia's market reforms, wrote critically in a memoir of Gorbachev's "lack of understanding of the scale of the problem."[48]

The consequences for the oil industry were disastrous. Capital spending had grown by 47 percent between 1985 and 1989 as the government desperately pumped funds into the oilfields. But after peaking in 1989, investment crashed in 1990,[49] taking oil production down with it.[50] The West Siberian oil producers were especially hard hit: 94 percent of the sudden drop in Soviet oil production in 1990 came in West Siberia.[51] The situation seemed beyond repair. In April 1991 a high-level government commission concluded that restoring oil production to the level of 1989 would require an injection of capital larger than half of the entire USSR state budget—even assuming that the necessary equipment and technology could be found.[52]

These events set the central government and the oil producers against each other in an increasingly tense game of chicken. The oilmen, gasping for oxygen as supplies and funding disappeared, demanded that the government lower its production target and allow them to export a portion of their output independently, in order to buy badly needed foreign equipment.[53] But the government was determined to hold the line—not only because oil exports were its main source of revenue but also because it was afraid that so much oil would head for the borders that the domestic economy would run short. In late 1990, after furious bargaining, the oil producers were able to get the level of state orders for 1991 reduced,[54] thus opening a breach through which they could sell up to 10 percent of their oil independently.[55] Yet the government would allow only a fraction of that amount to be exported—some 10 million tons (200,000 barrels per day) out of 35 million (700,000 barrels per day) authorized for independent sale in 1991.[56] To make sure the oil generals did not miss the message, in late 1990 Prime Minister Valentin Pavlov slapped a 40 percent export tax on the "decentralized" exports, while making export licenses as difficult to obtain as he could. The oil producers reacted by cutting back output. The result was a massive drop in oil exports in the first half of 1991, a major factor in the financial crisis that was engulfing the Soviet Union (see Table 1.1).[57]

The country by this time was in a radical fever. The newly elected Soviet legislature, playing live to a rapt countrywide television audience, spent its time denouncing the nomenklatura and all its works (despite the fact that most of

TABLE 1.1 *Oil exports (crude and products), 1988–1998, in millions of metric tons.*

	1988	1989	1990	1991	1992	1993	1994	1995	1996	1997	1998
Crude oil exports	256.5	263.1	219.9	173.9	149.7	127.6	126.8	122.4	125.6	126.8	137.1
Outside the Former Soviet Union	124.4	102.7	99.3	56.5	66.2	79.8	89.0	91.3	103.0	105.6	111.9
Former Soviet republics	132.1	160.4	120.6	117.4	83.5	47.8	37.8	31.1	22.6	21.3	25.2
Refined product exports	59.3	49.9	50.7	63.6	43.0	44.8	43.4	45.4	56.6	60.6	53.8
Outside the former Soviet Union	42.2	39.2	37.9	41.6	25.3	34.3	38.0	41.4	55.0	58.4	45.6
Within the former Soviet republics	17.1	10.7	12.8	22.0	17.6	10.5	5.4	4.0	1.6	2.2	8.2

SOURCE: *Russian Ministry of Energy.*

the deputies still belonged to the nomenklatura themselves). When the government nominated Gennadii Bogomiakov as the new minister of oil and gas in late 1989, the legislature noisily voted him down as a symbol of the old order.

The mounting crisis pitted the oil producers not only against Moscow but also increasingly against one another. As late as 1989 Glavtiumenneftegaz (or "Glavk"), the main administration for the West Siberian oil industry, still spoke for the oil producers. Thus when the government allowed the West Siberian producers in that year to sell 20 percent of their "above-plan output" for hard currency as so-called decentralized exports, and to use the proceeds to pay for foreign equipment,[58] it was to the Glavk, not to the production associations, that the concession was made. But the Glavk's days were numbered. The reformers viewed it as a symbol of the Soviet past. A new and relatively inexperienced minister of oil and gas, appointed instead of the rejected Bogomiakov, saw it as an inconvenient rival. The oil generals in the production associations clamored for their own individual export quotas and saw the Glavk as an obstacle. Graifer, trying to cope with the crisis, found himself under attack from both sides, without defenders in Moscow or in Tiumen. His letters to Gorbachev went unanswered. The following year, the Glavk was shut down and an embittered Graifer limped back to Moscow.[59]

But at this point an even deeper crisis was at hand. The Gorbachev era was rapidly coming to an end, and with it the Soviet Union.

Revolution Comes to the Oilfields

Boris Yeltsin had been one of Gorbachev's main allies in the Politburo in the early days of perestroika, but Gorbachev, alarmed by Yeltsin's growing radicalism, had sacked him. In the old days, that would have been the end for Yeltsin, or at least for his career. Ironically, it was Gorbachev's reforms that gave Yeltsin a second political life: when Gorbachev, to outflank his opponents in the Communist Party apparatus, opened up the hitherto dormant Soviet legislature to competitive elections in 1989, Yeltsin ran and won.

But that was only the beginning. Like the other members of the nominally "federal" government of the Soviet Union, the Russian republic had long had its own republic-level government. This was little more than a constitutional fiction—until Boris Yeltsin, riding the wave of Gorbachev's electoral reform, was elected deputy to the Russian legislature in the spring of 1990 and subsequently became its chairman. From his expanding power base Yeltsin began building a rival movement, pitting the Russian government against the Soviet one, encouraging the regions of Russia to shift their loyalty to himself, thus systematically undermining Gorbachev. In June 1991, Yeltsin was elected president of Russia.

In Tiumen City the impact of these events was seismic. When Gorbachev abolished the oversight functions of the party apparatus, the power of the party chief in Tiumen, Gennadii Bogomiakov, instantly vanished, and in January 1990 he was forced out. That spring an open election to the *oblast*'[60] legislature produced a body of deputies determined to end the party's rule in Tiumen. The new democratic majority chose as its speaker a young oilman, Iurii Shafranik.[61]

Iurii Shafranik and Vagit Alekperov had been the two prize protégés of Valerii Graifer. In 1986 Graifer had promoted them both to head the two newest and most promising frontier companies, Shafranik in Langepas and Alekperov in Kogalym. (These later became the "L" and the "K" in LUKoil.) But it was Alekperov who then won the glittering prize of promotion to deputy minister in Moscow, while Shafranik, sitting frustrated in Langepas, was drawn toward the new politics instead.[62] Elected a deputy of the Tiumen legislature, he joined the democratic reformers and became a strong Yeltsin supporter.[63]

The two men were at opposite poles of personality. Alekperov was the outsider, the newcomer to West Siberia, reserved and somewhat remote, a leader who inspired respect and even fear but did not invite intimacy. Shafranik was large and expansive, hail-fellow-well-met, with a friendly smile and a huge handshake, the sort of man with whom one could imagine splitting a bottle of vodka after the traditional Russian *banya*.[64] If he had stayed at Langepas, Shafranik might conceivably have become one of LUKoil's founders. But fate soon set the two men on very different and eventually conflicting paths. On August 19, 1991, a cabal of top party, KGB, and military chiefs attempted to overthrow Mikhail Gorbachev and restore the Soviet system. Gorbachev was held hostage at his vacation dacha in Yalta, while Boris Yeltsin holed up in the White House (then the seat of government of the Russian Republic) and defied the plotters. Thanks to Boris Yeltsin's determined resistance—coupled with the plotters' own abysmal lack of organization and resolve—the coup was defeated within three days. But their defeat, and Yeltsin's victory, suddenly thrust the pace of political events into fast forward.[65]

Iurii Shafranik recalls the atmosphere in Tiumen the morning the coup began:

> August 1991. The 19th. I'm getting ready to go to work. On the radio there's nothing but classical music, and I get a feeling something's wrong. I get to work, and I can't get through to anybody on the phone, all the official telephones are dead. So I'm sitting in my office and realizing, "Yes, that's how everything can turn upside down. The farther you are from the center, the less you know about what's going on in Moscow. Either they'll fire everybody tomorrow—or today." But as things turned out, Tiumen was one of the few places where the legislature was summoned immediately. We flew the deputies into Tiumen City, sometimes from two thousand kilometers away. We opened the session. We voted a resolution [opposing the plotters]. Afterward I spoke on television. I don't how I managed it, but people calmed down.[66]

Thanks to Iurii Shafranik, Tiumen was one of the few regions of Russia to back Boris Yeltsin against the plotters. In the fall of 1991, Yeltsin rewarded Shafranik by making him governor of Tiumen Province.

History in Fast Forward

After the failure of the attempted coup of August 1991, the Soviet government crumbled rapidly. Communist Party General Secretary Mikhail Gorbachev was sidelined, an increasingly powerless and pathetic figure. The Russian government—hitherto hardly more than a fig leaf in the fictitious framework of Soviet federalism—now emerged overnight as the dominant power in Moscow and throughout Russia. As the weeks went by, power streamed from the Soviet government to the Russian one. In December, Yeltsin met with the presidents of Belarus and Ukraine and signed an accord dissolving the Soviet Union. By the end of 1991, the Soviet government had ceased to exist and the Russian republic stood alone as its triumphant successor.

Victory, however, did not make the Russian government competent to govern. In the Soviet system, the Russian republic had been charged with second-rate responsibilities, carried out by a third-rate bureaucracy. As Yeltsin became the pole of opposition to Gorbachev, the Russian government attracted a crowd of reformers, dreamers, and careerists but few experienced managers. In the second half of 1991, as the Soviet government weakened, the Russian government began absorbing it. But the Russian government itself was hardly in better shape. Cadres were streaming away from all state agencies, attracted by the rising private sector. Of those who remained, the more dynamic and ruthless were already at work turning state assets to their own profit. The vast mass of the bureaucracy, in shock and denial, drifted aimlessly.

It is hard to imagine a less promising vessel than the Russian ship of state at the end of 1991, as it hauled down the Soviet colors and fought to stay afloat. On the bridge, a crowd of newcomers contended for the wheel, argued over the course, and shouted orders. In the engine room, the remaining officers tried to reverse the engines—or dismantle them for scrap. The rest of the crew milled about in disorder or busied themselves lowering the lifeboats, ignoring all commands.

Over this stormy sea the wind of new ideas blew at hurricane strength, bringing to Russia the West's born-again faith in the doctrines of privatization, marketization, liberalization, and all the other "-izations" then at their height in the West but new and strange to Russians. To those on the bridge of the Russian government at the end of 1991 (although by no means to all of those below), it had become manifest that the Soviet command economy was doomed. But with what to replace it? In October 1991, in a historic speech, Boris Yeltsin announced the abandonment of Soviet socialism and a radical transition to a market economy based on private property.[67] With feverish haste a team of economic advisors, led by a reformist economist named Yegor Gaidar, whom Yeltsin named acting prime minister, devised a program that came to be known in the West as "shock therapy," which went into effect in January 1992.[68] The three centerpieces of the program were an immediate decontrol of prices, massive cuts in state spending, and a rapid privatization of the economy.

For the next few months the Russian government was in the hands of the market radicals, most of whom had never held leadership positions before.[69] Few of them, indeed, had had any significant experience in government at all. They described themselves as "kamikazes" and had little expectation of staying in office long. They were determined to use their brief interval in power—their window in history—to destroy the basis of the Soviet system and prevent it from ever returning. Yet from the first, they were forced to compromise with the remaining Soviet-era stakeholders all around them. One of the most serious compromises, from the standpoint of the oil industry, was that while most prices were decontrolled at the beginning of 1992, energy prices were not.

This policy of half measures—denounced by critics as "shock but no therapy"—only deepened the crisis of the oil industry. Price liberalization, combined with the exclusion of energy prices,[70] put the oil industry between a hammer and an anvil—paying decontrolled prices for its inputs while being paid (and only intermittently at that) at lower state-set prices for its product. Over the next three years, decontrolled prices climbed between 10 and 25 percent per month, with only two brief periods of respite. Oil prices, meanwhile, remained largely fixed.[71] The oil producers began piling up debts. Oil workers and suppliers went unpaid. The only source of relief would have been hard currency from exports. But in an economy that was rapidly becoming demonetized, everyone wanted hard currency, and the oil producers were far back in the queue.

Up to the Soviet Union's final months, as we have seen, the central government's nominal controls over oil exports had remained very tight. But behind the façade of state monopoly, the system was already leaking. Through joint ventures, through various exemptions and special quotas, through upstart "commercial structures" (many quietly sponsored by high-ranking party and other state officials), oil had begun seeping through and around the state monopoly and into the world market. After the failed August coup, the leakage grew to a flood. But it brought little benefit to the upstream producers—not enough, at any rate, for them to keep their companies going and maintain production. Consequently, from this point on, the need to capture export revenues became a life-and-death struggle for the oil generals, driving them downstream in search of allies while pitting them against rival claimants—and against one another.

The West Siberian Industry Breaks Up

As the Soviet regime vanished, the tight hierarchy that had bound the producers together in West Siberia continued to unravel. In 1991 the seven West Siberian production associations prevailed on the ministry in Moscow to replace the abolished Glavk with a voluntary "association of enterprises," each with its own individual state order and its own quota for "decentralized" exports.[72] But the rebellion did not stop there. Uraineftegaz (soon to become the "U" in LUKoil), led by its general director Aleksandr Putilov, broke away from its parent production association, Krasnoleninsk, and obtained its own export quota.[73] Another NGDU, Chernogorneft, rebelled against its parent, Nizhnevartovskneftegaz, and set itself up as an independent oil company. It suddenly dawned on the alarmed oil generals, as even the NGDUs beneath them began struggling to break free, that what they had done could also be done to them. And who would pick up the pieces then—the oil generals, the regions, or somebody else?

Stopping a Locomotive with a Crowbar

Boris Yeltsin, as he campaigned against Gorbachev and the Soviet government, had encouraged the regions to believe that they would be allowed to run their own affairs. Only days before the August coup, Yeltsin had toured the main oil and gas towns of West Siberia—Nadym, Salekhard, Khanty-Mansiisk, Noiabrsk, and Tiumen City itself—repeating as he went the seductive message "Seize as much power as you can swallow!" But Shafranik had not waited for Yeltsin's encouragement to begin drafting plans to recenter the West Siberian oil industry and its wealth around the Tiumen Province government. As early as the summer of 1990 Shafranik had assembled a team of advisors to draw up an economic plan for the province.[74] In December 1990 Shafranik's team drafted a decree for Yeltsin's signature, granting to Tiumen Province authority over oil development and payments for mineral rights.

For a brief time, it seemed he might actually succeed. All through the first half of 1991, Shafranik pressed Yeltsin to sign the decree but in vain—until the August coup. In September, as a reward for his loyalty, Yeltsin finally signed.[75] Armed with this presidential endorsement, Shafranik thought he could keep the West Siberian production associations subordinated to a West Siberian authority with Tiumen City at the hub.

But the radical tide of events quickly outran him. In the Soviet administrative structure there was another level below that of oblast', the so-called okrug, or region. In Tiumen Province there were two of them—Khanty-Mansiisk (where most of the oil industry was located) and Yamal-Nenets (the base of the gas industry in the Far North). In Soviet times the okrugs had been purely administrative conveniences with no power of their own, but in 1990–1991, the okrugs began to break away from the province government, with the support of the oil and gas generals, who wanted nothing to do with Shafranik's ambitions.[76]

The okrugs had only skeleton staffs and no expertise in oil and gas, but they found recruits from an unlikely source, the local geologists. In the Soviet Union the geologists had their own ministry, with ample state funding and an open-ended mission: to find oil. Their *ekspeditsii* (geologists' exploration teams) ranged out ahead of the moving front of oil producers, staking out frontier territories in advance of the main army. The geologists' foreposts were strung out along a line stretching all along the far north of Russia, roughly paralleling the Arctic Circle. There were whole towns populated by geologists and run by geologists. When the Soviet Union collapsed, this northern empire was suddenly stranded, and the geologists, even more than the oilmen to the south of them, were in a desperate fight for survival. Their only asset was their discoveries, and their survival depended on producing and exporting oil from them. But for that the geologists needed to hang on to their claims against the determined opposition of the oil generals, who saw them as rivals for potentially rich prospects. The rise of the okrugs was a blessed lifeline for the geologists, and as the okrugs tooled up and formed local oil and gas committees, these were staffed largely by geologists. This had important consequences later on, as we shall see in the next chapter.

Tiumen City, located far to the south of oil and gas country in the small agricultural part of the province, had no power base or revenues of its own once the Soviet system disappeared. Shafranik had only one trump—Yeltsin's support in Moscow. He appealed again and again for Yeltsin to honor the decree he had signed in the wake of the coup. But Yeltsin, a master of the art of divide and rule, played the okrugs against the oblast'. The oil generals and the okrugs pulled inexorably away, while Shafranik, isolated in the oblast' capital, Tiumen City, was left in command of a rump. Looking back a decade later, Shafranik reflected ruefully, "You can't stop a locomotive with a crowbar."[77]

Churilov's Last Hurrah

In Moscow, meanwhile, the remnants of the USSR oil ministry made a last-ditch effort to keep the oil industry from disintegrating. In October 1991, two months after the coup, the last USSR oil minister, Lev Churilov, floated an idea for a national oil company, to be called Rosneftegaz. It was to be the joint property of its fifty-member enterprises, bringing together, for the first time, the upstream crude producers and the downstream refineries and distributors. In November 1991 he traveled to Tiumen to plead with the directors of the production associations to join. But the oil generals would not hear of it. The head of the Yuganskneftegaz production association, Sergei Muravlenko, returned to his home base at Nefteiugansk and fired off a telex to Moscow: "Our production association will not join the Rosneftegaz Corporation, and does not consider itself a member."[78]

For Sergei Muravlenko, the son of Viktor Muravlenko, to rebel against the parent ministry in Moscow was an act rich in symbolism. His gesture summed up the frustration and resentment that West Siberian oilmen had long felt against the tight rule of the party leadership, the ministry, and the central planners. Now they were declaring independence.

Churilov had no friends either in the new Russian government. Yeltsin had quickly shoved aside his Soviet rival in Moscow after the failure of the August coup, and Yeltsin's people (rightly) suspected Churilov of trying to save the Soviet ministry by resurrecting it in capitalist dress. Churilov appealed to the Russian government to rename his ministry a *kontsern* (an autonomous state-owned corporation), but he was two years and one failed coup too late. The Russian prime minister of the moment, Ivan Silaev, vetoed the idea impatiently.

It would result, he said, in "an oil monster that would try to influence oil poli-cies"[79] Churilov was forced to settle for a structure so weak that it was hardly more than a lobby group, with no power and no money. Instead, Silaev created a new Russian Ministry of Fuel and Power to absorb the Soviet energy minis-tries. This new entity included a Committee on the Oil Industry, which lost no time in luring away people from Rosneftegaz. In the wake of the August coup, as Yeltsin seized control of the levers of government and liquidated or absorbed the last remaining Soviet institutions, Rosneftegaz did not stand a chance.

Yet Churilov never quit trying. In April 1992, four months after the Soviet demise, he submitted a plan to the now-independent Gaidar government to create a national oil company,[80] aimed at regathering the production associa-tions back into a single holding company.[81] But by this time, market reform was in full swing, new ideas were in the air, and Churilov was already a foot-note. In early 1993 Rosneftegaz was officially dissolved, and Churilov was presented with a final humiliation, the post of trade representative to far-off Nigeria.[82] The last remnant of the USSR oil ministry was dead.

But the idea of a state-owned, national oil company never entirely died, as we shall see. Indeed, even as the Gaidar government rejected the idea of a Rosneftegaz, it acted to prevent the breakup of Gazprom, the national gas company.

Gas versus Oil: Why Gazprom Did Not Break Up

Russia entered the 1990s with the largest yet youngest gas industry in the world. It was a unique inheritance: 40 percent of global reserves, three gigan-tic West Siberian fields supplying over 80 percent of Russia's domestic and export needs, and a highway of twenty of the world's largest-diameter pipe-lines to bring the gas to market in western Russia and Europe. Gas already played a key role in the last decade of the Soviet economy, but in the first post-Soviet decade the role of gas grew absolutely critical, as other energy sources faltered. From 43 percent of total primary energy consumption in 1990, the share of natural gas grew to 52 percent by 2000.[83] One of the big stories of the post-Soviet era is that Russia has become in large part a gas-fired economy, and its giant gas company, Gazprom, became Russia's richest and most powerful corporation.[84]

Unlike the oil industry, Gazprom was never broken up. Indeed, over the following decade and a half its reach expanded even further, as it took control of downstream distribution and gas exports, expanded into electrical power and coal, and acquired a large portfolio of gas-related assets, both in Russia and in Europe. It remained majority state-owned throughout the 1990s, and in the Putin era it has come once again under the firm hand of the Kremlin. In its core business—the production and transportation of natural gas—it is largely unchanged from the Soviet era.

Gas Is Different

Why did gas follow such a dramatically different path from oil? There are two reasons. The first, the underlying one, is that gas is different from oil. Unlike oil, gas is comparatively easy to produce but difficult and expensive to transport, and it is worthless unless there is a distribution system in place to bring it to consumers. Until the last three decades, when technologies to turn gas into liquids began to change the industry, the dependence of gas on pipelines was total, and even now the economics and politics of gas are still essentially those of transportation and distribution.

Thus gas is inherently a more centralized business than oil. The Soviet gas industry was especially centralized. The huge trunk lines built in the 1970s and 1980s did not divide and subdivide, as in the West, into myriad low-pressure pipes that feed individual homes and small businesses, but ran instead straight to large factories and power plants, which were assigned annual quotas of gas to meet their assigned production plans. Gas exports, like all foreign trade under the Soviet system, were handled by foreign-trade professionals in the USSR Ministry of Foreign Trade. They sold gas through long-term "take-or-pay" contracts with the major European gas transporters, who did the actual marketing.

These basic facts about gas go a long way toward explaining why it diverged from oil in the growing chaos of 1989–1991. The upstream gas producers were even more isolated than their counterparts in the oil industry and utterly hostage to the monopoly's control of the pipeline system. Even if they had managed somehow to move gas to the Soviet borders, they would have found no one to sell it to, since no spot market for gas would exist in Europe for another decade. At the same time, their young fields and pipelines required little investment. Thus from the beginning, the disintegrative forces of need and greed, which accelerated the breakup of the Soviet oil industry, were contained in the case of gas.

But that alone would not necessarily have kept the gas industry whole in the charged atmosphere of 1991–1992, when the Soviet Union was breaking up and its assets were going up for grabs. The second reason is the role of a handful of key players during the brief critical months when the old system had melted down and a new one had not yet gelled. In fact, the answer to the question "Why didn't Gazprom break up?" ultimately comes down to two people, Viktor Chernomyrdin, the ex–minister of gas who was the first head of Gazprom, and Yegor Gaidar, the acting prime minister who led Russia's radical turn to the market. I discuss the first reason below, postponing the second until the next chapter.

A Familiar World Crumbles

All over Russia, a familiar world was disappearing. Ever since the end of the 1920s, everything had depended on a centrally planned economy run by a one-party dictatorship at the head of an all-powerful state. Money, supplies, food, heat, water—all the essentials of life—had flowed by bureaucratic fiat. Russians now watched in fearful amazement in the fall of 1991 and the winter of 1992 as this system fell apart. Suddenly they were in limbo, their familiar world shattered, their future unknowable. That frightening winter, it seemed to Russians, especially outside Moscow, that with the spinal cord gone, the body would collapse in a heap.

Yet it did not. The state regressed, but it did not disintegrate; the economy slowed but did not stop; the fabric of society frayed but did not rend. Whole institutions vanished—the party apparatus, the machinery of state planning, the secret-police controls—but the administrative base, though weakened and disoriented, survived. For the next decade, the Russian state could only weakly control its borders, manage its budget or its money supply, administer justice, or protect its citizens.[85] Yet remarkably, in most of the country, the lights stayed on and heat still arrived. Buses and trains still ran, however raggedly. Factories remained open, most people still went to work, and their employers continued to provide them with housing and basic welfare, if on a reduced basis and with little or no pay. Apart from localized shortages, there was no famine. Civilian rule never broke down and there were no warlords, except in the North Caucasus (although gang leaders, in some places like Yeltsin's home city of Ekaterinburg, came close). The Soviet-era nomenklatura, if with altered labels and vocabulary and some turnover of people, remained mostly in charge.

What made this possible was the continuing flow of essentially free value from the Soviet legacy of natural resources, especially from oil and gas, which continued to support the economy at subsidized prices and to bring in export income. The result was a "virtual economy" in which Soviet-era industry and the Soviet-era welfare state continued to function at a reduced rate, providing a meager but vital buffer against the shock of political and economic collapse and enabling the Soviet-era elites to adapt and carry on.[86] In retrospect, this was the true "shock therapy"—that is, revenues from oil and gas cushioning the shock of the Soviet collapse.

But in the oilfields, too, the familiar Soviet world was crumbling. By 1991 the entire Soviet-era support system for the oil industry was gone. Oil tools no longer arrived from Azerbaijan, nor did pipe from Ukraine. Workers stopped flying in from Tatarstan and Ukraine—the oil generals could no longer pay them, and in any case Aeroflot was canceling flights because it had no fuel. The Russian oil industry was especially vulnerable to these disruptions, because it had a large stock of older wells to maintain, and it had to drill new wells constantly to offset the decline of older ones. Yet drilling, which had set a record in 1988 and held steady in 1989, began to slide in 1990, as central funding for the oil industry disappeared. The following year brought headlong decline. In 1991 drilling dropped by one-quarter compared with 1988, and by 1992 it had fallen by nearly half (see Figure 1.1).[87]

Yet the oil industry, like the rest of Russia, never stopped completely. This was partly because of the way it had been built—low-tech but rugged, adapted to the dysfunctions of the Soviet system. Thus to make sure that manpower would always be at hand, the oil industry in West Siberia had built large permanent cities near the oilfields. Now these oilworkers and their families had nowhere to go, and they kept working, although often without pay. Similarly, to deal with unreliable oilfield equipment from Azerbaijan, the West Siberian oil producers had long maintained large local repair facilities, which now enabled the industry to limp along. Thanks to bartered oil and IOUs, the oil generals kept food and electricity and equipment arriving, though more irregu-

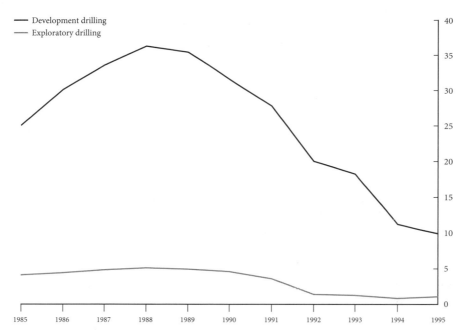

FIGURE 1.1 *Russian exploratory and development drilling, 1985–1995, in millions of metric meters. (Sources: TEK Rossii and Russian Statistical Service.)*

larly and in smaller amounts. For a time, in short, the industry could keep on producing, if at a diminished rate.

Yet this situation was not tenable for long. The different parts of the Soviet oil industry had been held together by the apparatus of the command economy and the party, and now those were gone. But what would replace them? Market reformers might dream of a purely economic value chain, linking privately owned and independent producers to refiners and consumers via market forces. But the elements needed for such a free-enterprise structure did not exist in the early 1990s (indeed, they do not yet fully exist even today). There was no market; buyers did not know where to find sellers; prices ceased to have meaning as the economy teetered on the edge of hyperinflation; and the system of payments stopped working. In principle, the various pieces of the industry, being incapable of surviving alone, were driven toward one another by a common and urgent need. But how would they come together? Who would dominate? Who would take the lion's share of the rents? An all-out war for control of oil rents and property was looming, as a result of which oil production might collapse altogether.

In this situation, it was practically a given that the various players, having lived their whole lives under the Soviet Union, would look instinctively to the state in Moscow for solutions. But, weak and divided as it was, what role would the Russian state play? The central government was like a zombie—decapitated yet still half alive, incoherent yet still capable of obstruction. The outlook for effective state action, in the wake of the Soviet collapse, looked hopeless. Yet few Russian oilmen in the early 1990s seriously believed there could be any alternative to the state.

Thus in the oil industry the era of Soviet Man was passing, but no one could yet know what would replace it. As the upstream oil generals began mobilizing to defend their remote empires against the spreading disorder, they could not know that it would be a decade before an uneasy stability would return. They could not know that the industry would reemerge in a new guise, from the horizontally compartmentalized structure of Soviet ministries to a new generation of mostly private vertically integrated companies, and that these new companies, employing a mixture of new technology and improved management, would ultimately bring about a recovery of the Russian oil industry. They could not know that the global oil industry, from which they had been isolated for half a century, would soon bid for a major role in Russia. And there was one more thing they could not know: that in the struggle that had already begun, most of them would end up as losers.

chapter 2

Riding Chaos: The Battle for Ownership, Money, and Power

Money. You don't know where it's been,
but you put it where your mouth is.
And it talks.

—Dana Gioia, *The Gods of Winter* (1991)

Old buildings have their own stories to tell. In the bleak winter of 1991–1992 the newly created Russian Ministry of Fuel and Power moved into the drafty head-quarters of the former Soviet Ministry of Electrification at Number 7 Kitai-gorodskii Proezd, near Red Square. For a time the old building had no security at all. Visitors entered as they pleased through the creaky swinging doors, brushed past the pensioners posted to check documents that no one bothered to present, then walked up the dusty and chipped marble steps and down dimly lighted hallways, the walls still festooned with fading posters proclaiming the achievements of the Soviet power industry. The offices were dingy, many were empty; everything smelled musty and disused. Only the vast offices of the minister and his deputies retained some vestiges of decayed grandeur.

The Neophyte Minister

Vladimir Lopukhin, who presided there as energy minister from November 1991 through May 1992, was typical of the reformers who headed the Russian government under acting prime minister Yegor Gaidar. They were almost all novices. Lopukhin himself had no prior experience in the energy sector, nor had he ever managed anything larger than an institute laboratory.[1] On oil and gas matters there were few people in his ministry to help him, since it had previously been solely in charge of electricity. A handful of officials had migrated over from the dying Soviet Ministry of Oil and Gas and formed the small Committee on the Oil Industry, headed by a veteran oil official named Viktor

63

Ott, which spent much of its time dealing with emergencies over winter fuel supplies. Lopukhin, like most of the other self-styled kamikazes in the Gaidar government, was not an adept administrator. He worked hard, as they all did, holding meetings in the middle of the night when he ran out of daylight hours, and in fairness his ministry was disintegrating beneath him as officials left in droves for the private sector.

Matters were not helped by the extreme inefficiency of the remaining ministry staff and what was perceived in the oil industry as Lopukhin's non-urgent attitude. For the oil generals, the most pressing strategic question was how to preserve their control over the oilfields. They besieged Lopukhin's office with plans for new rules and structures, but the minister was always too busy. As the plans piled up on his desk and nothing happened, Lopukhin seemed remarkably philosophical. As he commented to an interviewer, "It's like coming out of prison: you don't want to go to work immediately, you want to lie on the grass for a while."[2] The atmosphere was chaotic, as these young academics, suddenly thrust into positions of power, wrestled with dismantling the old system and jury-rigging a new one. For older Soviet-era officials raised on the mythology of the 1917 Revolution, it seemed like history repeating itself as farce. Valerii Cherniaev, the crusty veteran chief of the oil pipeline system Transneft, recalls being summoned to Kitaigorodskii Proezd for one of those 3:00 a.m. meetings:

> The secretaries in the outer office were the same ones who had worked for Neporozhnii, the Soviet minister of electricity. As I came in, I asked, "What's going on in there?" They laughed, "It's like the Smolnyi [the headquarters of the Bolsheviks under Lenin in 1917] all over again." Inside, the office was thick with cigarette smoke; there were butts and coffee bottoms littering the minister's meeting table. Lopukhin sat with one of his deputies, Eduard Grushevenko; they called each other "Lopukh" and "Grush." I've never seen such appalling amateurs.[3]

The oil generals felt much the same way. They did not trust Lopukhin; he was not one of them; he did not speak their language. The new Russian government appeared hostile to them; several of the initial decrees of the Russian government omitted all mention of the production associations (ob"edineniia) and appeared to treat the NGDUs as the key players. Lopukhin appeared helpless to help them or unwilling—they could not tell which.

Crisis Spreads in the Oilfields

Over the winter of 1991–1992, the decline in oil production, which had begun in 1989, threatened to turn into a rout. The revolt against the center was spreading beyond the production associations to the NGDUs.[4] Local politicians were lining up behind the ambitions of these second-tier "mini-generals." As spring came to West Siberia and the other oil provinces of Russia, the oilworkers had gone without pay for months and the oil towns seethed on the verge of open revolt. One of the largest NGDUs, Var'eganneftegaz, broke away from its parent body and declared itself an independent state enterprise; but the parent then retaliated by encouraging Var'eganneftegaz's own subsidiaries to secede.[5] It seemed as though the unraveling of the industry would never stop. There were rumors of impending strikes in the oilfields—although, more often than not, it was the managers of the NGDUs who headed the strike committees and were using the threat of strikes as a bargaining tool against the oil generals.[6] Every day more of the state companies' assets leaked to the private structures that were springing up all over oil country—banks, cooperatives, brokerages, exchanges, fly-by-night producers, joint ventures—as the Soviet-era stakeholders, not knowing what the future held, prepared makeshift lifeboats and began lowering away.[7]

The Rise of Organized Crime

The most urgent challenge to the oil generals came from their own backyard. In West Siberia, as in the rest of Russia, a crime wave broke out as the state weakened. Criminal gangs soon penetrated the oil towns of Tiumen Province—Surgut, Nizhnevartovsk, and Tiumen City itself. These were at first the traditional thieves, the "made men" (in Russian, *vory v zakone*) of the Soviet-era underworld, who emerged from Soviet prisons in the late 1980s and found the atmosphere of Gorbachev's perestroika very much to their liking, especially the opportunity to create "cooperatives." These were fearsome characters, with their tattooed hands and faces and their nicknames acquired over long jail terms—"Shama," and "Arap" ("the Arab") and "Rais from Tobol'sk"—and their thieves' code of silence and revenge. In Surgut a group of recently released ex-convicts set up a cooperative called "Kolkhida," which presented itself as a purveyor of pastries and sweets, but its real business was fronting stolen goods.

65

In Tiumen City they operated practically in the open, with headquarters in the Tourist Hotel.[8]

Before long, the criminals had shouldered aside or co-opted the handful of local entrepreneurs who had started legitimate cooperatives in 1988–1989 with the support of the local Komsomol and party administration, such as the "Soiuz" group, which like Menatep in Moscow had started out importing computers. By 1990–1991 the *vory* controlled large chunks of the economies of the oil towns—the markets, the airports, the train stations, the hotels, the river fishing industry (both licit and illicit), and much else besides. No one was safe from attack. A former deputy director of the Omsk refinery, for example, recalled in an interview being stopped at gunpoint on the road leading to his plant.

The ultimate prize was the oil and gas industry itself, but this remained beyond the grasp of the local thieves, who at this stage were still barely more than petty gangsters. The oil generals managed to protect their oilfields and the actual oil production. But the gangsters' takeover of the oil cities was a threat to them just the same, because the oil cities were where their workers and they themselves lived. The oil companies were not just companies; they owned and operated most of the housing, the power and water systems, the public transportation, lighting, and much of everything else, not to mention the local governments. But now there was no money. The oil generals resorted to barter, paying with crude oil from their "above the state contract" allowances.

Viktor Palii, then general director of Nizhnevartovskneftegaz, reflected on the reasons for the criminalization of the oil trade:

> It's true that the oil industry is being penetrated by crime, but it's not through the fault of the oilmen.... Today the oil producers are getting real money for only about 30% of the oil they produce. The remaining 70% is being bartered, and that's where the criminal part comes in.... I pay my taxes in oil, part to the city and part to the regional governments, and even to the federal government, to say nothing of my electricity and construction bills. But these people, having received oil in place of money, have no way to sell it, no experience in trading. As a result, around my one company, "Nizhnevartovskneftegaz," there have sprung up dozens of sellers. They're all kinds of people and outfits, including some that are criminal.[9]

Consequently, whether they liked it or not, the oil generals had to come to terms with the criminals. One oil general, who asked not to be named, told me:

> We all faced death threats; but at the same time, we had to deal with the gangs. Remember that we were responsible for the oil towns and everything in them. So we had to "organize our relations" [*organizovat' otnosheniia*] with the criminals. We got absolutely no help from the local police or the procuracy—they were bought [*prodazhnye*]—and the local FSB acted as "neutrals" [*statisty*]. We were also under attack from organized criminals from outside, from Sverdlovsk especially; they had more firepower than the local police.

Thus the criminals, like other local businessmen, were getting their hands on oil (or at least oil contracts), but what were they to do with it? Crude oil was virtually impossible to turn into money locally. So the criminals, too, had to "organize their relations," building chains of barter with other gangs that had access downstream to refineries and to refined products. But as these ties developed, they brought danger. The local *vory* soon had competition from other gangs downstream, better organized and financed, that moved upstream along with the flow of refined products, seeking crude oil. Bloody gang wars roiled the oil towns.

The oil generals became increasingly frightened at what they themselves had helped to unleash. It was one thing to declare independence from Moscow, but it was quite another to find themselves isolated and under attack, by the NGDUs, by local politicians, by traders, and by organized crime. But one of the greatest threats came from the radicalized geologists.

Geologists on the March

As we saw in the last chapter, in the power vacuum of the early 1990s the geologists had emerged as significant players. In West Siberia, as the okrugs gained power at the expense of the province government, the geologists found welcome employment in the okrugs' expanding bureaucracy. But by a fluke combination of events, the geologists had created a stronghold in Moscow as well. In the wake of the failed August coup, the remains of the Soviet geology ministry had been taken over by a crowd of environmental activists. The geologists, led by Viktor Orlov, an energetic former geology minister, left and formed a new body of their own under the Russian government, the Committee for Geology and Natural Resources (Roskomnedra). In the early 1990s, this body played a key role, sponsoring legislation favorable to the geologists' interests. For a brief time, the geologists rode high. By late 1992 independent companies descended from the geological ekspeditsii were producing 2 million tons of oil per year (40,000 barrels per day) and exporting 75 percent of their output. Orlov declared triumphantly that within five years there would be ten new integrated oil companies based on geological units, including mini-refineries and export trading.[10]

In February 1992 Viktor Orlov and his committee even stole a march on Lopukhin's energy ministry by pushing through the parliament a framework law on mineral resources that gave the geologists the lead role in licensing oil exploration and development, while granting the regional governments, where the geologists were strongly represented, equal power with the center.[11] President Yeltsin, anxious to retain the support of the regions, signed the bill into law.

The Mineral Resources Law had two far-reaching consequences. It reaffirmed the principle of state ownership of oil resources in the ground and created a legal framework within which oilfields were licensed to explorers and producers under the state's supervision. The state, in other words, remained sovereign, and its relationship to license holders was treated as a matter of administrative law between a principal and its agent, not as a contract between equal parties. But what the sovereign could grant, the sovereign could also take away; and although in the early 1990s the state was too weak to do so, the Mineral Resources Law created the legal basis for the state's subsequent reassertion of wide-ranging regulatory powers over the oil producers.[12]

The second consequence of the Mineral Resources Law was the sharing of power with the regions, in what came to be known as the "two-key principle." This provision became both symbol and cause of the steady weakening of the central state in the 1990s. In West Siberia, the two-key rule proved to be a potent weapon in the hands of the okrugs in their battle against the province government. It was only in the next decade that the power of the okrugs was curbed, when President Vladimir Putin abolished the two-key principle and dramatically cut the power of the regions over the regulation of the oil industry.

For the oil generals, the Mineral Resources Law was deeply alarming. First, though the licensing system represented an important first step toward providing a new legal basis for exploration and production, the law did not specify who would hold the licenses—the oil generals or their various competitors, the NGDUs, the geologists, or others. Therefore, from the standpoint of the oil generals, the law would only further catalyze the breakup of the industry. Second, the law put the licensing process under the control of Roskomnedra, which raised the prospect that geologists would dictate to oilmen how much oil they could produce and how. Thus, the passage of the Mineral Resources Law underscored for the oil generals the ineffectiveness of the market radicals in Moscow and their lack of concern for the generals' interests.

The Radicals Turn Pragmatic: How Gazprom Was Saved

The experience of governing was quickly changing the thinking of the reformers. Lopukhin, like Gaidar and the other market reformers, had initially come into office believing that the oil and gas industries, as arch-symbols of the hated Soviet past, should simply be broken up and privatized in pieces. But in the face of the growing disorder, and pressed by the increasingly panicked oil generals, the reformers began to alter their views.[13] As Lopukhin later told an interviewer, they came to accept that "it was impossible to build an economy of small pieces."[14] They parted company with the more radical reformers and turned instead to a group of more conservative but pragmatic-minded industry technocrats, of whom the most significant was Viktor Chernomyrdin, the head of the gas monopoly Gazprom.

Viktor Chernomyrdin had come up from modest beginnings in remote Orenburg Oblast', next to the border of Kazakhstan. The key moment in his career, both for Chernomyrdin personally and for the gas industry, came in 1978, when he was transferred to the headquarters of the Central Committee of the Communist Party in Moscow, as an *instruktor* in the department responsible for gas.[15] If Brezhnev as general secretary was the one who launched broad policies—such as the high-priority program to develop the country's gas resources in the late 1970s—it was officials like Chernomyrdin who carried them out. As deputy gas minister from 1982 to 1985, based in Tiumen, he led the development of the West Siberian gas system. In 1985, the same year that Gorbachev became general secretary, Chernomyrdin was promoted to minister of gas, where he remained to the end of the Soviet Union.

69

With his stocky frame and square jaw and thick eyebrows that could have rivaled Brezhnev's, Viktor Chernomyrdin looked the classic Soviet bureaucrat, the type invariably described in Western news stories as "stolid," but which Russians commonly call a *muzhik*. His manner was deceptively low-key and deliberate, and he was a poor public speaker—indeed, his habit of speaking in often-hilarious malapropisms later turned him into a media favorite. He will go down in history for one famous phrase, which for Russians sums up the 1990s and has practically entered the language: "We wanted for the best, but it came out like always."[16]

All this tended to cause people to underestimate him, but Chernomyrdin was a shrewd and patient player and a master of bureaucratic maneuver. His moves in the last days of the Soviet Union were not only defensive but offensive as well, revealing his wider strategic ambitions for Gazprom. In the fall of 1991, Chernomyrdin captured a key prize, the gas-export arm of the Soviet Ministry of Foreign Trade, Soiuzgazeksport. From December 1991 on, under the new name of Gazeksport, gas exports became an integral part of Gazprom.[17] This proved to be a master stroke, since gas exports would be the principal source of income for Gazprom throughout the 1990s and indeed down to the present day.

The Pragmatic Radical

Yet Chernomyrdin's efforts to preserve Gazprom might not have prevailed once the reformers gained power in early 1992. The more radical reformers were pushing a plan to break up the company. It would have turned the individual producers into quasi-autonomous joint-stock corporations under a weak state-owned holding company subordinated to the Ministry of Fuel and Power. The pipeline system—the key to Gazprom's power—would have become a common carrier. Transparent gas auctions would have ensured open competition.[18] For Chernomyrdin, the barbarians were at the gate.

But at that point a key player intervened to keep the company whole. That man, ironically, was the architect of shock therapy, the head kamikaze himself—acting prime minister Yegor Gaidar.

Yegor Gaidar was different from the other market radicals. Though he had never actually held office in Soviet times, he was familiar with the corridors of power. As economics editor of *Kommunist,* the official monthly journal of the Central Committee of the Communist Party, he had been an insider and he

was sophisticated about politics. He realized that carrying out the market reforms required staying in power—if only for a few critical months—and that
meant making compromises. From the beginning, as we have seen, he had
agreed as a tactical concession (a temporary one, he hoped) to leave a short list
of strategic commodities out of the price decontrol; at the head of that list was
energy.

The way Gaidar chose to deal with Gazprom was similarly pragmatic. In
May and June 1992, Gaidar overruled the market radicals in his government
and intervened decisively in Gazprom's defense.[19] Gaidar in later years never
disavowed his decision to keep Gazprom whole, nor did he portray it as a
retreat. Even after he had left office, and even after the disadvantages of keeping Gazprom a monopoly had become obvious, Gaidar remained adamant
that breaking up Gazprom would have been a mistake. "The gas industry is a
natural monopoly," he insisted in an interview in late 1995, three years after he
had stepped down as prime minister. "It is not in our interest to break up
Gazprom."[20] By implication, oil did not have the same importance, or at least
not to the same critical extent. Oil kept the budget balanced, but gas kept the
lights on and the homes heated. In the end Gaidar proved himself more of a
pragmatist than an ideologue.

But what about oil?

From Horizontal to Vertical

The reformers, as we have seen, had rejected a Gazprom for oil, and in any case
by this time the disintegration of the oil industry was too far gone for the Soviet ministry to be resurrected. By this time privatization was spreading like
an epidemic, "wildly and spontaneously," as Yeltsin had described it in his
landmark October 1991 speech, as the Soviet-era nomenklatura helped itself
to state property all over the country.[21] The challenge for the reformers was to
create a framework for privatization, so as to bring the process under some
measure of legal control and give it legitimacy. In the fall of 1991, the Russian
government created the State Property Committee. To lead it Yeltsin turned to
one of the earliest reformers, a young economist who had pioneered privatization in the city of Saint Petersburg, named Anatolii Chubais. Chubais and his
small team quickly drafted a framework law on privatization and a program,
which Yeltsin approved by decree at the end of 1991.[22]

But there was widespread resistance to privatizing the oil industry. What the reformers needed was a plan that would reorganize the industry and stave off further disintegration, while temporarily postponing the privatization issue. They found it in Vagit Alekperov and his concept for a vertically integrated company. He called it LUKoil.

Enter Vagit Alekperov and LUKoil

Vagit Alekperov, today the CEO of Russia's largest private oil company, will go down in history as the man who pioneered the concept of the privately owned oil company in Russia and then turned it into reality. As Alekperov, then newly promoted to deputy minister of oil for upstream production, arrived in Moscow in January 1990, he was on the front line as the oil industry disintegrated. "As early as 1990," he told an interviewer two years later, "we saw that the growing disarray of the oil sector could not be reversed by using traditional administrative methods."[23] Later that year, he began talking to his former colleagues in West Siberia about creating an integrated *kontsern,* a term then popular with the Gorbachev reformers to describe a state-owned company that would operate as a quasi-autonomous and voluntary association of enterprises while technically remaining subordinate to a ministry. The idea was not altogether new. Viktor Chernomyrdin had already established Gazprom as a kontsern in the summer of 1989. Gazprom was initially the model for Alekperov. In fact, his initial proposal was to turn the entire Soviet oil ministry into a single integrated Gazprom-like kontsern (unlike Chernomyrdin, who had made an earlier proposal for the oil industry based on several different companies). Here Alekperov describes his proposal:

> In 1990 I prepared and sent to Filimonov (who was then minister) a proposal to create a corporation on the basis of the ministry. He approved it in principle. I had already visited several Western companies (Agip, BP, Chevron) and was convinced that vertical integration was the way to go. In principle it was the same idea as that of Chernomyrdin, who had created the "Gazprom" concern shortly before. But the bureaucrats of the various ministries were unable to come to an agreement and so the state corporation never happened.[24]

Only as a second-best, then, Alekperov fell back on breaking out a piece of the oil ministry and operating it independently, although still under state ownership. There is no sign that at this early date Alekperov was yet thinking seriously of a fully private company. Yet by the spring of 1990 Alekperov's thinking was already far advanced and his main cast of characters already in place, when he made a trip to London. Traveling with Alekperov were three West Siberian oilmen, who were making their first official trips to the West: Ravil' Maganov, formerly Alekperov's chief engineer at Kogalym and recently named head of the Langepas Production Association; Aleksandr Putilov, head of Urai; and Ralif Safin, Maganov's successor as chief engineer of Kogalym.[25] I was part of one group that hosted them, and I recall that we were puzzled why Alekperov had brought with him this particular collection of men, who were fairly low ranking from a protocol standpoint. It was not until a few months later that we realized that their company names formed the L, U, and K of LUKoil and that we had just been introduced to the top command of the future corporation. Legend has it that the name LUKoil was coined by Maganov (today LUKoil's first vice president for exploration and production), who received a bonus of 1,000 rubles (then worth about $500) for his ingenuity.[26]

On his return to Moscow, during the summer and fall of 1990, Alekperov drew up a draft decree for the USSR Council of Ministers, creating an association of upstream producers and downstream refiners. To prepare the way, in December 1990 Alekperov had the potential members sign a cooperation agreement. At this point, it was still a fairly modest proposal: the proposed association was to be voluntary and nonprofit.[27]

Even so, Alekperov ran into a blank wall. "I came under heavy criticism in various quarters at that time." Alekperov recalled, "for 'destroying the oil sector.'" The Soviet oil minister and the hierarchy of the ministry opposed his plan, as did the Council of Ministers of the Soviet government. Alekperov got nowhere—until the failure of the August coup suddenly removed all obstacles.[28] By this time, in the fall of 1991, power was quickly passing into the hands of the victorious Russian government, and as Alekperov recalled, he gained the signature of Gennadii Burbulis, then the Russian deputy prime minister and a close confidant of Yeltsin. Equally crucial, however, was an export license. According to Andrei Pannikov, head of LUKoil's oil-trader "Urals," he and Alekperov sought out the relevant foreign-trade official in the Russian government and quickly secured the all-important document. A special connection took them to the right man. "We knew whom to visit," said Pannikov. "He and I lived in the same apartment building and we used to walk our dogs together."[29]

Nurturing the Pearls in the Oyster

Lopukhin and his team, after initial hesitation, embraced the LUKoil model and decided to extend it to the rest of the oil industry. The basic idea was to create more integrated holding companies like LUKoil. "We will nurture the new companies like pearls in an oyster," he told me in an interview in early 1992. "First LUKoil, then Surgut, and then Yugansk, one after the other." But the oil generals were divided. Some, like Viktor Palii of Nizhnevartovskneftegaz, wanted to go their own way. Others, like Vladimir Bogdanov of Surgutneftegaz, wanted to turn their companies over to their workers, at least nominally. They were wary of the idea of holding companies, and many wanted these to be mere voluntary associations. The one thing that they all agreed on, however, was the need to preserve their own power, by making their ob"edineniia the holder of whatever property rights were created.

There followed several weeks of negotiations as Lopukhin and Ott worked on a draft presidential decree. The drafting required lengthy coordination with the State Committee on Privatization, principally Anatolii Chubais's two deputies, Dmitri Vasil'ev and Petr Mostovoi. Mostovoi was opposed to the plan to create holding companies and tried hard to head it off. The oil generals hovered over the process like a cloud of mosquitoes. The atmosphere, as always, was hectic. Petr Mostovoi recalls,

> The pressure from the oil generals was extremely powerful. When I was completely exhausted from the struggle, Vasil'ev would kick in and would carry on pounding on the lobbyists, to get rid of their more outrageous proposals. Vasil'ev and I had our offices at opposite ends of a long hallway, and we kept them running up and down the fourth floor between us.[30]

By May 1992 the draft decree on restructuring the oil industry was finally ready for President Yeltsin's signature, but time was running out for Lopukhin. In mid-May I attended a stormy summit of the oil industry in Samara, an oil center on the banks of the Volga River in south Russia, where the minister and his deputies faced the wrath of the oil generals. It was a scene straight out of an Eisenstein movie. Outside the apple trees were in blossom, but inside the meeting hall it was more like 1917. The beleaguered minister and his deputies sat lined up on a dais, looking on helplessly while the angry oil generals shouted and waved their fists. Vladimir Bogdanov, the head of the Surgutneftegaz production association, looked ready to charge the dais. He faced a strike of the power workers at Surgut's gas-fired power plant complex, which would have paralyzed his wells and pipelines, and he was getting no help from Lopukhin, whose ministry was nominally in charge of the power sector.[31] The oil generals suspected Lopukhin of double-dealing, of favoring integration in public while quietly encouraging the NGDUs to seize their freedom from the oil generals. As Anatolii Sivak, the head of the Var'eganneftegaz production association, wrote somewhat clinically in early 1992, "An uncontrolled process of disintegration of the oil-producing associations has begun."[32]

But though emotions ran high, there was no unanimity among the oilmen. The one thing they agreed on was that they wanted the government to take action, and they wanted Lopukhin out. Two weeks later, at the end of May, it was President Yeltsin's turn to face the oil generals back in Moscow. By the time they left the capital, Yeltsin had given them two presents—the draft privatization decree and Lopukhin's head.[33] As Yeltsin wrote later,

> If some middle-aged industrialist comes to me and says, "Boris Nikolaevich, I have worked for forty years in the petroleum industry. What is your Lopukhin doing? Such-and-such is happening. It's a nightmare; everything's going to hell in a handbasket," of course I lose my patience. I feel I have to make some changes.[34]

The Old Pro Takes Over

To replace the unfortunate energy minister and stop the disintegration, Yeltsin turned to Chernomyrdin and offered him the energy ministry. Chernomyrdin held out cautiously, demanding greater authority than that of a minister, so Yeltsin made him deputy prime minister for energy, leaving the post of energy minister temporarily vacant.[35] Thus began what turned out to be the most significant political partnership of the 1990s. First as deputy prime minister and subsequently (from December 1992) as prime minister, Chernomyrdin for the next six years became Yeltsin's alter ego and the most significant player in Russian economic policy.

Chernomyrdin was no academic kamikaze. Within days of his appointment he went to West Siberia, accompanied by the top brass of the government's energy establishment. This time the conversation was quite different. The oil generals welcomed Chernomyrdin as one of their own, and Chernomyrdin had not come empty-handed. He promised the oil generals credits for wages and working capital. He faced down the rebellious electricity workers. But most important, he rallied the oil generals' support for the plan to form integrated companies under their leadership.[36]

Chernomyrdin did not attempt to corral the oil generals back into a single centralized structure, a state-owned equivalent of Gazprom for oil. He recognized that the greater threat was disintegration from below and that the one dike that would hold was the oil generals' production associations, duly amalgamated into integrated corporations, with the largest upstream oil generals in overall charge.

In November 1992, President Yeltsin signed a historic decree officially designating the first three integrated holding companies: LUKoil, Yukos, and Surgutneftegaz. With that signature he, in effect, created three new Russian "oil majors." The ob"edineniia comprising them would be turned into joint-stock corporations, which would then turn over to the parent holding company a controlling block of their shares. The state, in turn, would continue to hold a 45 percent share in the holding companies for three years, at which time a decision would be made concerning their privatization.[37] Thus the vision of "nurturing pearls in an oyster" was on its way to being realized.

But the November 1992 decree left out more than it put in. Left undecided was the fate of the other production associations whose generals had not wanted to join a holding company or had not had time to form one. These were gathered together under a temporary state company called Rosneft. As they were turned into joint-stock companies, they too would turn over controlling shares in themselves in trust to Rosneft, likewise for three years, at which point their fate would be decided. Thus a national oil company was retained for the time being, but essentially as a temporary parking lot.

The November decree also did not resolve the fundamental ambiguity surrounding the rights and powers of the oil generals who controlled the ob"edineniia. As the new licensing system went into effect, the licenses to most producing fields were simply transferred to the ob"edineniia, which likewise held title to the oil produced. This put substantial trumps in the hands of the oil generals. Yet the drafters of the November decree seemed to assume that by simply creating shares in the ob"edineniia and handing majority blocs in them to the new majors, the oil generals would be easily brought to heel. But what if the ob"edineniia refused to play their new role and submit meekly to the authority of the new majors? The legal mechanisms by which shareholder power could be enforced through the courts did not yet exist, and the state's regulatory powers were ambiguous and weak. As subsequent events proved, shareholder rights on paper meant little and often had to be enforced through direct action, to the point of pitched battles for physical entry to shareholders' meetings or access to the director's office and his safe and official seal.

Thus the November decree amounted to a starting gun in a race for which the rules had not yet been written or tested. For the new majors, the challenge was to gain effective control of their own subsidiaries before the three years were up and to position themselves to take over the state's majority stake when the time came to privatize.

Rosneft posed a different problem. For the companies that had been temporarily herded into Rosneft, the state company's three-year lease on life gave them an incentive to try to escape—and for rivals to gain control of them. Meanwhile, Aleksandr Putilov, who had left the LUKoil team to become the president of Rosneft, had different ideas about the future of the company. He saw it as a chance to make Rosneft a national oil company or at the least an integrated company in its own right, whereas for his rival oil generals as well as other would-be players, such an obviously temporary structure as Rosneft only invited attack. (We return to the story of Rosneft in Chapter 8.)

The November 1992 decree, in short, only set up the next round of battles for control of oil assets, which lasted through the next three years. Yet in retrospect the decree was a key turning point. It marked the victory of the pragmatic "gradualists" under Viktor Chernomyrdin, a coalition of Soviet technocrats and pragmatic reformers who rejected both the "shock therapy" of the radical reformers and the reactionary views of the "restorationists"—the Soviet-era diehards—and promoted instead what they hoped would be a controlled quasi-privatization under the leadership of the upstream oil generals.[38] It marked the rejection of both extremes—both the all-powerful state company that the restorationists had wanted and the wholesale decentralization that the reformers (and the smaller players in the oilfields) had initially hoped for.

For all that, the legal restructuring of the oil industry, through the February 1992 Mineral Resources Law and the November 1992 presidential decree, was hardly more than the blessing of a weak and divided central government. The reality on the ground fell far short of the powers created on paper. The oil generals—even LUKoil, Yukos, and Surgutneftegaz—had no real control over the refineries, distribution networks, and export outlets that nominally made up their new empires. They had little control over their oil flows or cash flows. A new framework had been created. But would it stick?

"No One Listened to Russian Ministers"

Boris Yeltsin, it seemed, never met a presidential decree he didn't like. In the early 1990s he issued thousands of them, and much of Kremlin politics consisted of the jockeying of powerful palace clans, competing to get the old man to sign their pet document. Most of these remained dead letters. Even once he had put pen to paper, the president's signature brought neither consensus nor compliance, even among his ministers, who in those early years were not only disunited but also largely powerless. This was especially true at the outset, in late 1991 and 1992. As Anatolii Chubais recalled in a memoir, "No one listened to Russian ministers."[39]

How different might things have been if Boris Yeltsin had been a stronger or a more attentive and consistent chief executive? "Boris Yeltsin is a dictator," the former party boss of Tyumen, Gennadii Bogomiakov, told me once in an interview in 1992. But he was quite wrong, or rather, he was no longer right. Yeltsin had been Bogomiakov's opposite number as party leader in the neighboring oblast' of Sverdlovsk up to the mid-1980s, and Bogomiakov recalled that Yeltsin had ruled his industrial fief with a tough hand. But Yeltsin's subsequent rise and fall at Gorbachev's hands, his two years of political exile, and his subsequent resurrection as the elected president of a democratic Russia had transformed him.[40] As president, Yeltsin's approach to governing was hands off and indeed often surprisingly offhand. He knew little of economics, and though he leaned toward private property (mainly because he rightly saw it as the chief obstacle to a return of communism), he was not interested in the details of marketization or privatization.

Yet in reality, Yeltsin had little choice. As province chief, Yeltsin had been a cog in a totalitarian dictatorship. But as president he stood over a weak and divided state. His thousands of dead-letter decrees were a monument to the state's weakness. Indeed, the entire government was seized with a frenzy of decree writing, each more impotent than the last. A massive retrospective review of the privatization campaign, conducted in 2004 by the government's financial watchdog, the Audits Chamber *(Schetnaia Palata)*, observed that there were over 3,000 laws, statutes, and other normative documents pertaining to privatization, many of them conflicting and few of them observed.[41]

The central themes of powerlessness and conflict are essential to any understanding of Russia's rocky path from communism to the market in the 1990s. From 1993 to 1998 Russia jolted from crisis to crisis. At first Russia appeared headed for civil war, as Yeltsin and the Supreme Soviet (the parliament inherited from the defunct Soviet Union) battled for supremacy, until their dispute was settled in tank fire in October 1993. Each year brought fresh disaster—after the siege of the Moscow White House in 1993, there was the debacle of the First Chechen War in late 1994 and 1995, the narrow victory of Boris Yeltsin over the communists in 1996, the "Asian flu" financial crisis of 1997, the collapse of world oil prices and the financial and economic crash of 1998, and many lesser crises in between. These were the years of Boris Yeltsin's physical decline, the fading of the democrats and the market radicals, and the humiliation of Russian patriots. The central state steadily lost what little power remained to it, as government cash flows—customs duties, tax payments, tariffs—leaked to the regional governments and the private sector. All across a wide range of exportable commodities sectors, state property was dissolving and vast wealth was passing into private hands—aluminum, nickel, steel, diamonds, and timber, as well as oil.

Yet one has to be clear on just what the nature of this weakness was. The country had not been defeated in war; its infrastructure had not been destroyed; its ruling class had not been executed on the guillotine. Despite the efforts of the radical reformers to dismantle the apparatus of state power, they were only partly successful. Many of the state's levers of power remained intact. They simply lay inactive, while the new rulers—most of them former members of the Soviet nomenklatura—debated, maneuvered, and fought over what use to make of them, under what rules, and for whose benefit. Would it be the emerging oligarchs, who were already penetrating the state and tapping its resources for their private profit? Or would it be some new combination of state players? And who would end up controlling the oil industry?

In the case of oil, the single most important lever of power was the pipeline system. As John D. Rockefeller had taught the world in the 1870s, at the dawn of the era of oil, whoever controlled the pipelines would control the flow of oil, and therefore the rents, and thus ultimately the industry. This was especially the case in Russia, with its heavy concentration in West Siberia, which recalled the equally heavy concentration of U.S. oil production around Pennsylvania in Rockefeller's day.[42] In the Soviet system, the master of the pipelines had been the state. Who would it be now?

Selling "on the Left"

The pipeline empire of Transneft was one of the engineering marvels of the Soviet era, a vast system of steel arteries over 50,000 kilometers long. In Soviet times, Transneft (then called Glavtransneft) had been the transportation department of the Ministry of Oil. As the Soviet system broke up, Transneft continued to measure and monitor the flow of oil through its system. The Russian government knew to a fair approximation how much oil was entering and leaving its trunk lines. It is a myth that vast quantities of phantom oil were produced but never counted.[43]

But the real questions were: Who actually owned the oil in the pipeline, and what became of it once it reached the end of the Transneft system, at the refineries, the export terminals, and the borders? Here the Russian state's controls practically dissolved. If in principle it still loosely controlled the customs service and could therefore monitor the flow of crude to the Russian borders, it had no control over what happened beyond them. The newly independent western republics of the former Soviet Union—Ukraine, Belarus, and the three Baltic republics—became gaping breaches. Russia continued in those years to ship crude oil to them at below-market prices, to feed the local refineries and support the local economies, but it was quickly apparent that a large portion of the crude was being exported on, while vast arbitrage profits went into private pockets.

Well-placed insiders received export licenses in exchange for favors rendered, such as the Moscow-based "Century" group, which received a license to export 1 million tons (7.3 million barrels) of oil, reportedly in exchange for financial assistance to the Yeltsin camp during the abortive August 1991 coup. A trading company called "Tiumen," which belonged to former members of the Central Committee of the Communist Party and included shareholders on both sides of the political divide during the August 1991 coup and after, served its owners impartially with ample export licenses obtained by special decrees of the USSR Council of Ministers obtained on the eve of the Soviet breakup.[44]

According to Yegor Gaidar, in 1991 150 million tons (3 million barrels per day) of crude, or nearly half of the oil production of West Siberia, was sold "on the left" (i.e., under the table), bypassing the government foreign-trade organization that was still nominally in charge of oil exports. Of 194 shipments of oil exported in 1991, reported the Russian daily *Komsomol'skaia pravda,* only twenty-two reached their nominal destination, while the remainder were diverted to points officially unknown. In November of that year, Yegor Gaidar, then deputy prime minister for economic policy, appeared on Russian television to sound the alarm:

An endless number of [export] licenses has been issued without quotas. . . . If we don't stop this process, then we will have absolutely nothing to burn this winter. The whole national economy will come to a halt.[45]

Yeltsin suspended all existing export licenses and ordered no new ones issued until the end of the year.[46] A commission was hurriedly formed to review the structure of licenses and recommend to the president which ones to renew.[47] The Russian energy minister, Vladimir Lopukhin, subsequently said that the government discovered that it had issued more export licenses for crude oil in December alone than the country's entire annual production.[48] But the hemorrhage did not stop.

If the state's control over crude exports was disorderly, the scene at the refineries bordered on anarchy. Once oil was refined into products such as fuel oil, diesel, and gasoline, it mostly moved on by rail and river tanker and truck instead of pipe.[49] The lots were smaller, and they were much more difficult for the state to monitor and control. From the refineries and storage depots, oil in the form of products could be moved quickly to smaller ports and terminals and turned into cash. Distributors and consumers played the arbitrage game by overreporting what they were consuming at home and quietly exporting the difference or selling it on to someone who could. If you could somehow acquire, say, fifty tank cars of diesel fuel at a refinery in northwest Russia and move it by rail to Kaliningrad or Riga, you were well on your way to becoming very rich—if you survived. Many did not. Criminal gangs soon penetrated the refineries and the local distribution systems, while competing with one another in increasingly bloody pitched battles.

Yet in principle both exporters and refiners were hostage to the pipelines to keep them supplied with crude. Why was the state unable to use its ownership of the pipeline system to retain leverage over the allocation of export quotas and permits for crude oil and to control refining and domestic distribution? Or alternatively, why did Transneft itself not use its strategic position to turn itself into a corporate powerhouse? Where was the Russian Rockefeller who might have used his control over the pipelines to build an oil monopoly, on either the state's behalf or that of the oil generals—or his own?

The Reluctant Rockefeller

There was in fact a Russian Rockefeller, indeed two of them, father and son. Since 1980 Transneft had been headed by a longtime pipeline specialist, Valerii Cherniaev. Cherniaev was one of the most famous names in the history of the Soviet oil industry. His father, Davyd, had begun working at the age of 11, on the eve of the Russian Revolution, in the North Caspian oilfields then owned by the Nobel Oil Company, and rose through the Soviet industry as it expanded from the Caspian to the Volga-Urals basin and then to West Siberia. Starting in the 1940s Davyd Cherniaev built and ran the pipeline system that supported the "Second Baku," as Soviet propagandists liked to call the Volga-Urals, and then led the first big pipeline projects into West Siberia in the 1960s. When he retired in 1970, Valerii took over his post, and ten years later, at age 43, Valerii took over the entire crude-oil transportation system, which he ran until his removal in 1998. Thus the two generations of Cherniaevs, father and son, spanned the entire Soviet period and the key years of the post-Soviet transition and symbolized, perhaps more than any other, the history of the Soviet oil industry, its rise, triumph, and decline.[50]

By 1991, when the Soviet Union broke up, Valerii Cherniaev was deputy USSR minister of oil, responsible not only for all transportation but also for all wholesale sales of crude oil. He was then 54 years old, and after a lifetime spent in the pipeline system, much of it in the regions, Cherniaev was one of the few people in the Soviet oil industry to be acquainted with the main players at every point in the value chain.

This was potentially, on the face of it, a position of great power. Why, then, did Valerii Cherniaev not become an oligarch? In the anything-goes atmosphere of "Wild East" Russia, a time of unlimited opportunity for the bold and the resolute, could he not have become the Russian Rockefeller and the founder and owner of an all-powerful Standard Oil of Russia?

I asked Cherniaev himself that question, although not until a decade and a half later. Many people had thought of using the pipeline system as a lever for power, Cherniaev answered. The man with the biggest ambitions, and the nerve to match, was the burly, tough-talking boss of the West Siberian branch of the pipeline system, Nikolai Leshchiov. Leshchiov was all for creating his own pipeline empire, and in 1991 he led a rebellion of the regional pipeline managers and threatened to take his part of the pipeline system out of Transneft. "Kolya," Cherniaev recalls warning him (using the Russian familiar form of Nikolai), "the oil generals will never let you dictate to them." Cherniaev narrowly managed to contain the rebellion of the regional managers and defeat Leshchiov, who refused to submit to a demotion and defiantly left Transneft for the private sector.

Transneft at the end of the 1980s operated on a "merchant" basis, meaning that it took title to the crude oil from the producers and sold it at the other end of the system, at the refineries and the export terminals. This was what Leshchiov had been banking on as a lever for power. In reality, however, Transneft's "ownership" of the oil was a source of vulnerability so long as domestic prices were controlled by the state. Oil producers sold their crude into the system at a regulated price based on their costs plus a markup. As their costs went up—as they did sharply in the late 1980s—the purchase price Transneft had to pay went up correspondingly. Meanwhile, the prices at which Transneft sold its oil at the other end of the system increased much more slowly. Transneft began piling up debts, and Cherniaev was soon in the same unhappy position as the upstream oil generals, with no operating funds to pay his workers and no working capital for maintenance and repairs. Cherniaev, like everyone else, owed money to other ministries—notably to the electrical utilities, who provided power to keep the pipelines going and who threatened to cut him off if he did not pay up.

Two could play the threat game, and Cherniaev himself on one or two occasions briefly stopped the pipeline system to pressure the government into conceding higher prices. The resulting backups of crude oil quickly caused all the available storage space upstream to fill up, threatening a wholesale shutdown in production. On the surface, the picture was reminiscent of Pennsylvania in the 1870s, when Standard Oil under John D. Rockefeller used its monopoly power over transportation to compel the producers to cut back output, forcing them to dump oil into nearby rivers because they had no place to store it.

But in reality the two situations were quite different. In Pennsylvania the problem was chaotic overproduction, whereas in Russia it was chaotic underproduction. During the critical years 1989–1993, when the fate of the pipeline system was playing out, crude production was declining and the pipeline system was increasingly operating below capacity. From a peak of 125 million tons (2.5 million barrels per day) in 1988, oil exported through Transneft plummeted to barely one-third of that amount, 48 million tons (956,000 barrels per day) in 1991, as Russian crude production declined and the Soviet export system disintegrated. Consequently, far from having leverage over producers, Cherniaev was forced to look for barrels to ship wherever he could find them, just to keep his system going. Moreover, the larger Russian producers were few enough in number (unlike the disorganized crowd of small Pennsylvania oilmen) to join forces and cut production as a group. In other words, Cherniaev had leverage only with the producers, not against them.

It was at this point, in about 1990, that Cherniaev made the crucial decision to take himself out of the vulnerable middle, by giving up title to the oil. He hired Western consultants to help him design a Western-style tariff system, based on a standard fee for service that would not be tied to oil prices.[51] Above all, it would guarantee Transneft a steady source of revenue.

The next step was getting the approval of the Russian government, and in the atmosphere of Moscow after the August 1991 coup, this was not easy. Cherniaev recalls wandering through Moscow, like a voyager through the underworld, in search of someone with the time and the semblance of authority to approve the new tariff. No one cared about something so arcane as a pipeline tariff. Didn't Cherniaev know there was a revolution going on? "People kept telling me, 'Are you crazy?'" But Cherniaev persisted and eventually got official approval. On January 1, 1992, the new tariff system went into effect.

The transportation tariff proved to be a decisive move for Transneft and for the oil generals as well. From January 1992 on the legal owners of the oil in the Transneft system were the producers, who were now in a position—at least theoretically—to find their own buyers. This was the crucial first step toward putting ownership rights in the hands of the producers.

Still, the question remains: Why did Cherniaev give up so easily? Why did he not fight to control the oil flow himself? To Cherniaev's colleagues, the main answer was personality: Cherniaev was widely perceived as a bureaucrat, not an entrepreneur. One of the leading oil generals, speaking to me anonymously, said of Cherniaev, "He had a ministry mentality [*ministerskaia mental'nost'*]. He genuinely did not understand the idea of privatization, until much later, when it was already too late." In short, Cherniaev remained what he had always been and what his father had been before him—an engineer's engineer, dedicated to his pipelines. Cherniaev's greatest source of pride, in retrospect, was that he had kept the Russian pipeline system whole through the turbulent 1990s and indeed, he claimed, in better condition than it had been in Soviet times. Thanks to the steady stream of hard currency from the new tariff system, Transneft by 1997 was repairing seven times as much pipeline as in 1992, and by 1998 nearly all of its repair work used advanced diagnostics.[52] As Cherniaev told this story, a decade and a half later, it was clear that this was what he wanted to be remembered for.

Transneft's shift to a tariff system, little noticed amid the great events of the early 1990s, proved momentous in another way. Since it no longer held title to oil, Transneft did not loom as a target for the oligarchs; it did not generate enough revenue to be worth seizing. Instead, as the various powerful players of the day—the oil generals, the traders, the government officials—fought for control of oil revenues, they were content if Transneft simply did its job of accepting oil from all comers and moving it smoothly to where it could be turned into money. This Cherniaev was careful to do. Although Cherniaev claims that he accepted oil only from "producers," it was a byword at the time, and confirmed by interviews since, that Cherniaev prudently accepted oil from anyone who showed up with an export license or any reasonable semblance of an official paper.

Cherniaev's decision not to fight to privatize Transneft, and his judicious neutrality in granting access to the pipeline system, had two far-reaching consequences. First, it enabled the government to maintain legal authority over the pipeline system, something that gave it little real leverage at first but later turned out to be crucial in establishing a more stable regime for oil exports, as we shall see shortly. Second, the immediate consequence of Cherniaev's neutrality was that it shifted the battleground for ownership and control of oil and oil revenues downstream, to the refineries and terminals, and to the government offices where export quotas were assigned. That was where the battle for control of exports was fought between 1992 and 1995.

The Battle for Access to Exports

To a spectator watching from the sidelines, and even to most of the players, the battle over exports in the first half of the 1990s was like the Red Queen's croquet party in *Alice in Wonderland*. Yet since control over exports was the ultimate prize, it is important to follow the main elements of the tangled plot.

The profits from arbitrage between domestic prices and export prices created an irresistible incentive to rush oil to the border. But with the breakup of the Soviet Union, Russia had lost direct access to most of its export outlets, and consequently there was a shortage of space in Russia's remaining export pipelines and terminals. (This affected exports of crude oil more than refined products because the latter could also be moved by rail and waterways.) Each year the shortage grew worse as domestic consumption plummeted faster than oil production, due to the worsening economic depression, and this created a growing surplus of exportable oil. As a result, allocation of the space in the export-pipeline system became the main prize, and the fact that the pipelines remained state owned gave crucial leverage to whatever state players (and their friends) could control the allocation. But who would that be?

The Widening Circle of Players

As early as 1988, Gorbachev's breakup of the Soviet foreign-trade monopoly had brought in new players interested in exporting oil. Oil exports had traditionally been the preserve of a foreign-trade organization (FTO) called Soiuznefteeksport, part of the USSR Ministry of Foreign Trade. When that ministry was broken up, the first ones to seize the new opportunities were other FTOs, which branched out into oil trading, expanding their roles at the expense of Soiuznefteeksport.[53] (As Yegor Gaidar put it in a memorably acid phrase about the state traders, "As shrewd and mercenary gravediggers they aimed to profit from their own death."[54]) The new FTOs dealt mainly in refined products; indeed, some of them had previously played a modest role in certain specialized oil-product exports.

Meanwhile, the refineries, which had long chafed under the monopoly of Soiuznefteeksport, took advantage of these openings to get into the export game on their own. One of the most significant, in light of later developments, was the Kirishi refinery. Favored by its location on the Baltic Sea, it was one of the first to create its own export subsidiary, Kirishineftekhimeksport, whose Soviet-era name was soon shortened to Kineks.[55] (One of the four founding partners of Kineks was Gennadii Timchenko, today one of the world's most influential oil traders, reputedly a member of Putin's inner circle, and an increasingly visible investor in the Russian energy sector.[56]) To offset their lack of experience in foreign trade, refiners formed joint ventures with professional foreign traders as partners, some of them actually Russian companies already rebased abroad. I have already mentioned Urals, the early joint venture formed by Andrei Pannikov and Kineks.[57] Refineries located inland were not far behind. The Novokuybyshev refinery, located near Samara on the Volga River, was exporting refined products and petrochemicals as early as 1991 through a Belgium-based joint venture called Petroplast, which subsequently played a key role in the origins of Yukos (see Chapter 3).[58] They found ready export outlets through oil-loading terminals, which had been among the first to form "cooperatives" under Gorbachev's reforms. Thus as early as 1989, a cooperative had leased the oil terminal of the port of Leningrad (soon to be renamed Saint Petersburg) and launched into business on its own, exporting over 2 million tons per year of refined products.[59]

At first the erosion of Soiuznefteeksport's monopoly affected mainly refined products, but by mid-1991 it had spread to crude oil as well. In October, two months after the failed coup, Soiuznefteeksport renamed itself Nafta-Moskva. As late as 1992 Nafta-Moskva still handled some two-thirds of Russian crude exports,[60] but its share dwindled rapidly after that. The Russian oil-export business was rapidly becoming wide open.

As the circle of players widened, a new breed of entrepreneurs began to appear, people who were initially strangers to the Soviet-era foreign-trade elite but quickly developed ties to it. Thus the powerful Alfa Group began as a small coooperative under perestroika, led by a young start-up entrepreneur named Mikhail Fridman, but by the beginning of the 1990s Alfa was importing sugar, carpets, and tea from South and Southeast Asia in payment for India's Soviet-era debts. As its business grew, it branched out into finance, buying Russian foreign debt at deep discounts and redeeming it at par from the Russian treasury, and it subsequently moved into oil trading. Clearly these specialized operations required good connections in the Ministry of Foreign Economic Relations, which then deepened as former state officials migrated into the private sector.[61] As Soiuznefteeksport's monopoly of oil trade weakened, such groups were well positioned to move into exports of crude oil.

The only players missing were the upstream oil producers themselves. At this stage, the oil producers were not yet allowed to negotiate their own oil exports directly. For them to be able to monetize oil, a new system and new rules had to be invented. This process, which took place in a constant swirl of politics and intrigue, took about three years, from 1992 to 1995.

Upstream and Downstream: Different Games, Different Players

Crude oil and refined products were two separate battlefields, each with different players and rules. The battle for crude-oil exports centered in Moscow, in the offices and antechambers of politicians in the central government. The prize was access to the state-owned pipelines and customs posts that channeled the export flow and controlled the hard-currency revenues from crude exports.

The struggle over the domestic products market, in contrast, was fought at the regional and local levels. As the command system dissolved, traditional consumers like factories and farms had no money to pay for fuels. Bureaucrats tried to force producers and refiners to deliver fuel to these bankrupt consumers by fiat, while the producers fought to limit their deliveries, diverting as much as possible to exports, where the money was. The few actual sources of cash in the domestic market—real cash rubles from gasoline sales at the pump, for example, or dollars gained from surreptitious exports by rail or barge—were quickly targeted by organized crime. This was the rough end of the business, where life was fast paced and short. If the battle for crude-oil export licenses was mostly a white-collar affair fought in the suites, control over the "cashable" refined products was a dangerous street business, fought over at the refineries and depots, the railroad loading points, and the docks. There was constant warfare among rival gangs, and Russians joked grimly that profitability was best measured by the trail of corpses.

There was on the whole little direct contact between these two worlds. Only a handful of those who survived at the refined products end acquired the skills and the patronage to migrate "upstream" to the crude-export game, where the big money was, although this small group includes some of the famous names at the top of the Russian oil business today. One of these was Roman Abramovich, subsequently the owner of Sibneft. He started from nothing at the beginning of the 1990s, parlaying hometown connections from Ukhta into a modest products-trading operation. By 1992, through his trading company AVK, the 25-year-old Abramovich was moving tank cars of products, chiefly diesel, from the Ukhta refinery to export points on the Baltic. Within a year, however, he had formed close ties with a leading upstream producer, Noiabrskneftegaz, and had become one of the top traders of crude oil out of West Siberia.[62]

"Pragmatists" versus "Restorationists": The Battle for the Russian White House

The struggle over export controls on crude oil was much affected by the stormy politics of 1992–1995. Conservative opposition to the reformers' radical pro-market policies mounted steadily from the spring of 1992 through the summer of 1993. The contest over policies soon turned into a battle for power between Yeltsin and the Supreme Soviet, the legislature inherited from the Soviet regime that was now located, ironically, in the same White House from which Yeltsin had faced down the coup plotters only two years before. The two sides dueled for supremacy, the president threatening to dissolve the legislature and the legislature threatening to impeach the president. Finally, tiring of the game, Yeltsin in September surrounded the legislature and laid siege to it. The stand-off ended only when the military (which had reluctantly contributed a column of tanks in response to Yeltsin's pleas) lobbed two rounds into the White House and the deputies surrendered.

The reformers thought that Yeltsin's victory would put them back in power, but instead they were resoundingly beaten in the legislative elections that followed in December 1993, and only a handful of reformers stayed on in the government. For the next three years, control over economic policy swung back and forth between the two remaining groups—the "pragmatists," led by Prime Minister Viktor Chernomyrdin, and the conservative "restorationists," whose leading figure at the time was First Deputy Prime Minister Oleg Soskovets.

89

The restorationists initially had the upper hand. The ever-moody Yeltsin, sinking into depression as he typically did between crises, retreated from public view and spent most of his time with a private circle of Kremlin cronies and drinking partners, including his chief bodyguard, Aleksandr Korzhakov, and his tennis coach, Shamil' Tarpishchev, plus a handful of favored government officials, notably Mikhail Barsukov, the head of the FSB, and Soskovets, who oversaw industry and energy.

Soskovets was a longtime Soviet-era manager from the metals industry, who strongly opposed the privatization of industries he regarded as strategic, especially the oil industry. His relations with Prime Minister Chernomyrdin were notoriously tense. The prime minister, who regarded Soskovets as a thorn, appealed repeatedly to Yeltsin to get rid of him and in the meantime tried to isolate Soskovets from the flow of business. But Soskovets was a drinking partner of Yeltsin's and thus enjoyed direct connections—in the Kremlin they called them *riumochnye otnosheniia* ("vodka-glass relations")—that Chernomyrdin, whose personal relations with Yeltsin were more formal, did not have.[63] To Chernomyrdin's frustration, Soskovets used his influence to push for tighter state controls over oil exports.[64]

The disorder in the export-control system, however, was not solely due to political conflicts, but reflected the fact that the system itself was still halfway between Soviet-style controls and an evolving privatization. Even as late as 1994 the oil producers were barred from selling more than 20 percent of their oil on the open market; 80 percent still had to go to the state at low fixed prices. The state, having no tax system worthy of the name, relied heavily on oil-export revenues to finance its budget through the so-called state's needs programs, under which favored traders (called special exporters, or "spetsy" for short) bought oil cheaply from producers, then sold it on at world prices, pocketing commissions for themselves and their friends in the government. It was, in effect, a kind of tax farming system.[65] A special exporter was a kind of accredited arbitrageur, working the gap between domestic and export prices on behalf of the state.[66] They helped the government raise money for a wide range of good causes. Thus a trader called Rosnefteimpeks handled oil exports to finance the modernization of the Baikonur space center, while Nafta-Moskva did the same for a military radar station. Yet another, called MES, which was backed by the Russian Orthodox Church, sold oil to finance the regilding of the Kremlin churches.[67] By 1994, at the high point of this arrangement, the spetsy handled 93 percent of Russia's total exports of crude oil, or 83 million tons (1.7 million barrels per day) out of Russia's total of 91 million tons (1.8 million barrels per day) that year.[68]

The system of spetsy quickly acquired an unsavory reputation. To the reformers and to foreign advisors such as the International Monetary Fund (IMF) and the World Bank, the system appeared both corrupt and inefficient, since it amounted to imposing a favored middleman between the producer and the buyer. Yet the system had its defenders, and a kind of pragmatic consensus kept it going. The spetsy, obviously, enjoyed their privileged status. "If the government cancels quotas and licenses," warned one spets trader, access would go "to the guys with the most machine guns."[69]

The only losers were the oil producers. Yet in the background, other forces were in motion that were gradually swinging the balance of power in their direction. During the years 1993–1995, the grip of the traders on oil exports was gradually loosened in favor of a new system under which space in the export pipelines was allocated by a committee of state officials. As we shall see, this development was hailed at the time as a "liberalization," although in truth it turned out to be more of a brokered compromise between the traders and the oil producers.

The Last Kamikaze: The Role of Anatolii Chubais

The pivotal player in the liberalization of the export system that finally took place in 1994–1995 was Anatolii Chubais, one of the last survivors of the original market radicals of the 1980s. As head of the State Property Committee, Chubais had overseen the massive "voucher privatization" of 1993–1994, in which thousands of nonstrategic businesses were auctioned off all over Russia.[70] A skilled politician, Chubais stayed on in the government after most of the reformers had left; indeed, as time went on his standing rose. In 1994 he became minister of economics and then, in November 1994, first deputy prime minister responsible for economic affairs alongside Soskovets; in addition, Chubais led the Commission on Operational Affairs, a senior group that managed day-to-day crises (of which there was no lack, then or later). His influence reached its height in January 1996 when he took over Yeltsin's reelection campaign and masterminded Yeltsin's stunning come-from-behind victory in that year's presidential contest. Chubais waged a steady battle against the restorationists,

91

and in 1996 he succeeded in dislodging Soskovets and the cronies surrounding Yeltsin.

Chubais had a key ally—the IMF. The influence of the IMF was at its height in 1994–1995, because of its power to give or withhold credits, which at this time made the difference between surplus and deficit in the Russian federal budget. It used its leverage to press for eliminating the whole jury-rigged structure of export quotas and licenses, preferential tariffs, customs duties exemptions, and, above all, special exporters. The IMF's threat to withhold credits brought around the pragmatic middle, whose concern was to balance the budget and avoid a financial crisis—the Ministry of Finance, Prime Minister Chernomyrdin, and President Yeltsin himself.

Even so, the pendulum of policy swung crazily back and forth throughout 1994, as the contending sides backed competing draft decrees, which lay unsigned for months on the president's desk. Finally, at the end of 1994 Chernomyrdin signed an order on oil exports, which appeared to give the pragmatists, the oil generals, and the IMF everything they had been campaigning for.[71] It eliminated all reference to export licenses and export quotas and abolished the spetsy. Authority over oil exports was transferred to an interagency committee under the authority of the Ministry of Fuel and Power. Chubais, by now first deputy prime minister, claimed victory:

> The press asserted with one voice that we'd never be able to do anything about oil, that the government kept losing because too powerful interests stood behind it. As you see, their forecast didn't work out.[72]

And the Russian government got its IMF credits.

Why Fight 'Em When You Can Join 'Em?

The outcome was also hailed as a victory for the oil generals, and indeed that was how it initially appeared. Even before the 1994 decree the emerging Russian majors had been figuring out how to work the system to get their oil out, by forming their own trading divisions or making alliances with existing ones. LUKoil and Rosneft had actually joined the list of spetsy, and LUKoil in 1994 was the largest single crude exporter on the list of authorized exporters.[73] Yukos exported crude through a closely affiliated spets trader, Coneks, and

Rosneft did the same through a trader called Rosnefteimpeks.[74] Thus in 1994 the oil generals, directly or indirectly, handled between one-third and one-half of all crude exports and were gradually becoming the dominant players. In contrast, the traders appeared to be losing ground. Some left the oil-export business and turned to other forms of trade. The Ministry of Foreign Economic Relations continued to register spetsy,[75] but they were increasingly being restricted to the state's-needs exports and state contracts.

But the appearance of a clear victory of the producers over the traders was deceiving. In reality, the two sides were moving toward each other, and the result was a series of fusions. In some cases the oil company was the dominant partner. LUKoil, as the first and most powerful of the emerging oil companies, had moved quickly to control its own export operations without an intermediary. Coneks, which had been the export arm of Yukos, sold a controlling interest to Yukos and ultimately merged with it.[76] Rosnefteimpeks, by government order, was turned over to Rosneft. Nafta-Moskva became the principal trader for Surgutneftegaz.[77]

But more often it was the trader that turned out to be dominant, and in those cases the fusion proved to be the prelude to takeover. Thus Runicom had become the dominant partner in the relationship with Noiabrskneftegaz and the Omsk refinery and soon took them over. MES took a stake in Komineft. Where the trader was backed by a large bank or a financial-industrial conglomerate, the relationship was even more lopsided. Thus Alfa and its oil-trading arm, Alfa-Eko, shortly took over the Tiumen Oil Company, or TNK,[78] while Alfa and Oneksimbank jointly became dominant over Sidanco. Less visibly, the traders reemerged as export agents for the smaller independents, the geologicals, and even some of the subsidiaries of the weaker majors.[79]

In other words, the absorption of the weaker oil companies by financial groups began well before the "loans-for-shares" pseudo-auctions of 1995–1996. In these cases, the financial groups, via their oil-trading arms, were already well entrenched inside the oil companies. They had cash, and they had Moscow connections; whereas the weaker oil companies had only their debts. Thus as early as 1994 we see the beginning of the process that led in 1995–1996 to the takeover of much of the weaker side of the oil sector by the emerging oligarchs and their dominance over the next decade.

The outcome of the battle over crude exports was the beginning of the end for the joint ventures and for the geologists. The joint ventures had been a useful loophole for the oil generals so long as they could not export crude themselves. But after January 1995 they had become competitors to the oil companies for space in the pipeline. The new decree mandated that joint ventures would still have 100 percent export access, but in practice they found themselves shunted to exports within the former Soviet Union.[80] (We return to their story in Chapter 4.)

The geologists fared almost as badly. Ironically, thanks to the tax-free export licenses granted to the geological ekspeditsii,[81] they were attractive targets for takeover by the emerging oil majors and the traders, and they were being rapidly gobbled up. A few (such as Arkhangel'skgeoldobycha, or AGD) joined Rosneft, hoping that under the state umbrella they could maintain something of their independent existence. But by early 1995, 35 percent of the geological enterprises previously subject to Roskomnedra had been privatized and the rest were due to follow, laying them open to absorption by the emerging majors.[82]

The Oil Industry Bottoms Out

By the middle of the 1990s, thanks to the gradual liberalization of oil prices, the end of export quotas, the monetization of oil, and the beginnings of reconsolidation of the industry, oil production began to stabilize. As money resumed flowing into the oilfields, the oil generals started repairing broken wells and returning idle wells to production. Annual production declines, which had been in the double digits in 1991–1993, slowed in 1994, and by 1995–1996 were only between 2 and 3 percent. By the end of 1996, the decline in crude output had bottomed out. Russia in 1996 produced only half as much oil as in 1987, its peak year in the Soviet Union, and oil investment stood at less than one-third, but there was now hope that the worst had passed and that the sector was poised for recovery.[83]

That said, the companies' progress was uneven. Some of the oil generals had turned out to be good managers and some poor; some paid their bills and their taxes, while others did not or could not. Some concentrated instead on building fortunes offshore. There were wide variations from one company to another. Where they had made the least headway as a group was in bringing the refineries and distributors to heel. The domestic oil market remained a

94

complex thicket of problems that mostly defied the oil generals' efforts to manage it, as we shall see in the next chapter.

The two companies that had been first off the mark in redesigning themselves as vertically integrated corporations and beginning the process of privatization—LUKoil and Surgutneftegaz—and had been from the beginning the most resolute in establishing financial controls over their subsidiaries, were also the most successful in limiting debt and avoiding penetration. The others, which had been less quick, less decisive, or less lucky, soon became vulnerable to takeover.

At this point, in mid-1995, the state still held majority stakes in all the oil companies. But with the end of the three-year "incubator" created by the November 1992 decree, the time was ripe for the final step, a full and formal privatization. But by this time, the playing field was changing. The oil industry, now partly restabilized on its new foundations, was a juicy target for the financial-industrial giants that had emerged since the end of the 1980s—such as Menatep, Oneksimbank, and Alfa—and their leaders, who were just becoming known as the "oligarchs." As we have seen, their penetration of the oil industry had begun earlier, but the stage was now set for the last act, the formal takeover of much of the oil industry by the oligarchs.

The Great Quasi-Escape

The central story of this chapter has been the evolution of ownership and control over oil and oil revenues and the movement away from the state-controlled system of ministries to a new generation of vertically integrated companies, descended from a fusion of the upstream oil generals with the export traders, as both evolved away from their Soviet antecedents. In the process, the threat of a wholesale collapse of the Russian oil industry was successfully averted.

Two features of this evolution stand out. The first is that it was presided over by state players or, more precisely, by a coalition of reformers and pragmatists, operating from state positions, who sought to halt the unraveling of the oil industry. They did not attempt to preserve a state monopoly over the oil industry—by 1992 it was already too late for that. But they did retain control (however imperfectly in practice at the time) of the "commanding heights" of the industry—the customs offices and the pipelines. They built a hybrid system of licenses and quotas that, however loosely it was enforced at the time, meant that the oil industry never really broke free of state control. This turned out to be critical at the end of the decade, when the power of the central state revived. An important part of the explanation for the rapid recovery of control of the oil industry under Putin a decade later lies here.

The second broad feature of the evolution of the integrated oil companies was the fusion of the upstream oil generals with the export traders in all but two of the Russian majors. The pragmatists had not expected this development, nor was it noticed by most outside observers at the time. Thus the ironic outcome of the long battle for control of oil exports, which appeared at the beginning to have been won by the oil generals, was in fact the backdoor penetration of the upstream by the traders. In only two cases—LUKoil and Surgutneftegaz—was the outcome a victory for the oil generals; in all others the traders became the dominant partners. This puts the subsequent "shares-for-loans" takeovers of 1995–1996 in a different light from the customary telling; they were more like the last act, a final state blessing as it were, to a process that had begun two years before.

The early 1990s left a legacy in the oil industry that is key to understanding the recovery by the state a decade later. Despite the weakening of state control in the first half of the 1990s and the appearance of near-total privatization that followed, the state never fully exited from ownership and control of the oil industry. It retained legal rights over every part of the system: from ownership of oil in the ground to ownership of the pipeline systems; from licensing of exploration and development to regulation of reserves and field development plans; from control over the allocation of export quotas and access to export capacity, to control (by municipal governments) over much of domestic distribution and sales. In legal terms, all that the emerging private sector actually owned was the oil that had been extracted, together with the revenues from it, and even that was subject to major restrictions. There was never a clear delimitation of private property rights and state regulatory powers.

What was built in the first half of the 1990s, in other words, was a system of quasi-private property that restricted the ownership rights of the companies to junior roles vis-à-vis the state. This was not apparent at the time. Indeed, so weak and disorganized was the state at all levels—especially the center—that it appeared to contemporary observers, even to the major players themselves, as though the oil industry had genuinely escaped from state control. But it had not. All that had happened was that the system of state controls had gone dormant. It retained large power over the industry in theory, but in practice that power became largely latent, present mainly as an invitation to evasion. Its symbols were the empty government offices, the telephones that were never answered, the forms that went unsigned, and of course the nearly universal bribes (though still small by today's standards). In short, private ownership was established in the breach, in the spaces temporarily left unoccupied by a corrupt and penetrated state with weak enforcement powers.

There were two consequences—one immediate and the other long-term. The first was the takeover by financial capital in the second half of the 1990s. The second was the subsequent reassertion of state power and its de facto recapture of the oil industry, a decade later.

chapter 3

The Birth of the Russian Majors:
LUKoil, Surgutneftegaz, and Yukos

Getting gas for your car in Russia used to be a test of character. Gas stations were few and far between, generally located on the outskirts of town. Drivers who managed to find one were rewarded with low-octane gasoline and Soviet-style service. But suddenly, around the mid-1990s, Russians began to notice amazing changes. Shiny, brightly lit, brand-new service stations started popping up like mushrooms at local intersections, offering not only high-octane gasoline of dependable quality but an unheard-of innovation—an *avtomoika*, an automatic car wash. The new stations even featured convenience stores with all the benefits of civilization, such as ice cream (much loved by Russians even in winter; in the Far North, gas station operators sold more ice cream than gas), the inevitable Snickers bars, and soft porn. Practically overnight, the larger Russian cities were decked with brightly lit new corporate logos——names like LUKoil, Yukos, Surgutneftegaz, and a gaggle of others—which would soon be as familiar to Russian motorists as the hammer and sickle had recently been. Russians might take a dim view of the privatization of the oil industry, but they hailed the new stations. Say what you like about capitalism and big oil—you can say it better on a full tank of gas.

The New Majors

The mid-1990s, roughly from 1993 to 1998, were the critical years when the Russian "majors"—large integrated oil companies—emerged out of the Soviet ruins. By 1998, an industry that in Soviet times had been layered into horizontal ministries had been turned into vertically consolidated corporations, each one controlling a single integrated business from the well to the gas pump. But the real revolution lay in the ownership. In 1992 the Russian oil industry was still state owned; by the end of 1998 it had become largely private.

Yet the owners of the new companies—with two significant exceptions— were not the Soviet-era oil generals. Instead, by 1998 most of the original *neftianiki,* the Soviet producers and refiners, had been pushed aside, co-opted, or (in a few cases) killed off. The new owners were outsiders, newcomers to the oil industry—regional governors, city mayors, but above all the well-connected, newly rich, and increasingly powerful financial barons who were coming to be known as the "oligarchs." The latter started out knowing nothing about oil— except how to turn it into money, as they quickly seized the opportunities offered by the new economy. Yet this was the critical skill that the oil generals lacked, and for most of them this shortcoming was crippling. Of the famous names of the Soviet-era oil industry at the end of the 1980s—Fomin, Filimonov, Gorodilov, Kuz'min, Muravlenko, Palii, Putilov, Sivak, Vershinin, and many others—none remained at the head of a major company by the end of the 1990s, except, in one or two cases, in honorific positions. Only two of the original Soviet-era *neftianik* generals, Vagit Alekperov of LUKoil and Vladimir Bogdanov of Surgutneftegaz, successfully managed the transition and emerged as leaders of two of the largest majors.

Why did only these two succeed and all the other oil generals fail? Why Alekperov and Bogdanov, and not Sergei Muravlenko, the founder of Yukos? We have seen how the federal government in Moscow opted in the summer and fall of 1992 to create three integrated companies under the general directors of the largest producing ob"edineniia, or production associations, while grouping the others in a temporary holding company, called Rosneft. Over the following three years the government broadly tried to adhere to the game plan laid out in Yeltsin's November 1992 decree. Remarkably, the core of the plan— the creation of the first integrated companies—was actually achieved. But no prepared script could survive intact in the Russian melodrama of the 1990s, and least of all in the oil industry. The state was too weak and divided, the prize too glittering. New and hungry players quickly crowded in, and they wrote their own script as they went along.

The oil industry was privatized in two phases, spread over six years. In the first, from 1993 to 1995, centrifugal forces prevailed, and by the end of 1995, the dispersion of the industry had reached an extreme degree. Thirteen private, quasi-private, and nominally state-owned companies (some federal and some regional), as well as innumerable smaller ones, had filled the void left by the vanished Soviet ministries. In addition to the three "majors" (LUKoil, Yukos, and Surgutneftegaz) and the state residual, Rosneft, there were six new "mini-majors" (Sidanco, Eastern Oil Company, Slavneft, Onako, Sibneft, and TNK), three companies owned by republics (Tatneft, Bashneft, and Komitek), and a handful of companies owned or sponsored by regional governments, some of them descended from the geologicals. With the exception of a handful of truncated companies (Norsi-Oil, for example, consisted solely of a refinery, while Vostsibneftegaz and Sakhaneftegaz had only upstream assets), most claimed some degree of vertical integration, whether at the national or the local level. Yet of the three integrated companies mandated by the Yeltsin decree, only LUKoil and Surgutneftegaz had achieved by the end of 1995 something approaching genuine vertical consolidation, that is, a marriage of upstream and downstream into a single corporate structure. "The others," said one Soviet oil general, "still have a lot of work to do."[1]

Starting in late 1995, the trend shifted to reconsolidation. By 1998 the oil industry had reconcentrated around the six largest private companies, which in that year produced nearly two-thirds of Russian oil. Yet only LUKoil and Surgutneftegaz remained under their original oil-general leaders; the others had been taken over by the emerging financial oligarchs, self-made men who ten years before had had no connection whatsoever to the oil industry. At Yukos, the third "major" scripted in the November 1992 decree, Muravlenko had been relegated to an honorific but powerless status, while the real owners were a group of trader-bankers led by a rising young financial entrepreneur named Mikhail Khodorkovsky. The three other leading companies, TNK, Sidanco, and Sibneft, all carved out of the hapless Rosneft, were likewise owned by the new oligarchs. The new winners began busily mopping up the smaller regional producers and independents; only the local fuel distribution and retail companies continued, for a time, to evade their grasp. The surviving state-owned sector, meanwhile, had shrunk to barely one-quarter of total production. Rosneft was reduced to a remnant, made up of disparate bits and pieces that the larger players either did not want or had been too busy to absorb. Tatneft and Bashneft, meanwhile, became the de facto property of the presidents of Tatarstan and Bashkortostan and their families, beneficiaries of Yeltsin's permissive policy toward the regions.

The reconsolidation of the oil industry in the hands of the oligarchs continued through the end of the decade and into the early 2000s. It reached its peak in

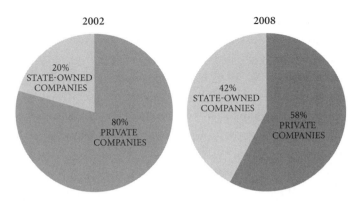

FIGURE 3.1 *Oil production by private and state-owned Russian companies. (Source: Russian Ministry of Energy.)*

2002, when they absorbed two of the last remaining state-owned companies (Onako and Slavneft). By the end of that year, the oligarch-owned companies, then at their height, controlled half of the private production of Russian oil. Then the pendulum began to swing back toward state ownership (see Figure 3.1).[2]

This was not, to put it mildly, the outcome that anyone in the oil industry or the government had intended or foreseen at the beginning of the 1990s. Indeed, the budding oligarchs themselves would have been the most surprised of all to be told that they would become by the end of the decade the dominant stakeholders in the Russian oil industry. How did it happen?

Kidnapped Brides or Arranged Marriages?

Western accounts of the 1990s point to the "loans-for-shares" affair of 1995 as the critical moment of takeover by the oligarchs. Through a series of rigged auctions, in that year a group of the richest and most powerful new financial barons acquired the state's controlling stakes in several of the largest oil companies as security for loans to the state. The following year, when the state (as expected) failed to repay the loans, the shares became the barons' property. In Western tellings this is the defining event of the Russian 1990s, the point where the market reforms went irretrievably wrong. "A Faustian bargain," wrote Chrystia Freeland in her book *The Sale of the Century,* "Russian capitalism's original sin," in which "the young reformers created the oligarchs." For David

Hoffman, author of another major study, *The Oligarchs,* it was "a privatization deal that would change Russian capitalism and politics forever." In this telling there are no heroes.[3]

The loans-for-shares episode was indeed an important event. It transferred a large share of Russian production of oil and other commodities to the new financial empires. It cemented the coalition of oligarchs that financed the re-election campaign of Boris Yeltsin the following year. It gave the oligarchs the richest turn of all on the wheel of fortune, within a few years turning their multimillion-dollar fortunes into billions. And it is also true that it discredited the privatization program and damaged the reputations of the remaining reformers, particularly that of Anatolii Chubais. Largely as a result of the loans-for-shares affair, privatization became the unburied corpse haunting Russian politics. A decade and a half later, Russian officialdom and most ordinary Russians remain convinced that the privatization of large industry, and especially that of the oil sector, was fraudulent.[4] This perception handed Vladimir Putin and the central state, when it reemerged after 2000, a potentially powerful lever against the oligarchs.

But on closer examination a more complex story emerges. "Loans for shares" is actually a shorthand for the whole series of takeovers and attempted takeovers that took place between 1995 and 1998, culminating in the triple failure to privatize Rosneft. The only oil companies that actually went to the new financial oligarchs via the shares-for-loans auctions in 1995–1996 were Yukos, Sibneft, and Sidanco. TNK was privatized later on, via a money tender. Most of the remaining oil companies did not find any buyers until early in the following decade, when they were absorbed by the oligarchs. Rosneft, as we shall see in Chapter 8, was the sole exception, in that it was not privatized at all.[5]

In reality, the takeover of the oil industry by the new moneyed interests was already far advanced well before the rigged auctions of 1995, and the real story is how few of the Soviet-era oil generals managed to survive the process. The companies that were taken over were the ones that had failed to consolidate themselves financially and politically over the previous four years—all of them, in other words, except for LUKoil and Surgutneftegaz. The oil generals who headed them had already lost control of their oil flows and cash flows and had fallen deeply into debt. Yukos, the best-known case, was already closely tied to Mikhail Khodorkovsky and his banking group, Menatep, well before he took over the state's shares at the end of 1995.

Shares for loans, in short, was only an episode in a saga that ran for a decade, in which the oil generals as a group—again except for LUKoil and Surgutneftegaz—lost out against the onslaught of well-connected new money. Some, like Viktor Palii of Nizhnevartovskneftegaz and Aleksandr Putilov of Rosneft, went down fighting (and indeed Putilov managed to hang on to some second-tier assets). Others, like Muravlenko of Yukos, yielded gracefully and were rewarded with a symbolic seat at the new table. One or two were murdered. But collectively they went down to defeat, in a war of multiple fronts extending over a period of years, for control of cash, debt, oil flows, and shares.

The Age of Acquirius

The outcome set the stage for the "age of the oligarchs." In short order the new private owners overturned the management of their companies and revolutionized their corporate cultures. The private oil companies focused on the bottom line. They courted global investors and financial analysts. They revalued their reserves, brought in new technologies, cut costs, and began boosting production as fast as they could. Realizing that their reputations influenced their share prices, they hired Western teams of financial advisors and public-relations experts and switched to Western standards of accounting and corporate governance, to gain acceptance on global financial markets.

But the most important change was their dramatically altered stance vis-à-vis the state. The oligarch-owned companies asserted autonomy from the state, and the state was initially too weak to resist the claim. For the next several years, they ran their part of the Russian oil industry as their own private property—hiring and firing as they pleased, operating their fields and reckoning their reserves as they saw fit, setting their own exploration and investment priorities, asserting the right to build and own their own pipelines and export terminals, and taking every advantage of every loophole and gray zone in the tax laws to "optimize" their payments to the state.

In all of these respects, Yukos under Mikhail Khodorkovsky was the most ambitious, the most entrepreneurial and innovative, and the most daring in its claim to independence from the state. Sibneft and TNK followed close behind. In contrast, LUKoil and Surgutneftegaz hung back more cautiously, aligned themselves with government policies, and avoided overt challenges. Thus the stage was set for the collision of 2003–2005, when a resurgent central state under

Vladimir Putin unleashed its police, its prosecutors, and its tax collectors, destroyed Yukos and bought back Sibneft, and forced the remaining oil companies back under its control, if not its ownership.

But in 1994–1995 all that lay in the mists of an unimaginable future. This chapter focuses on the emergence of the three leading majors, LUKoil, Surgutneftegaz, and Yukos, and shows why, in the contest for privatization and consolidation, Vagit Alekperov of LUKoil and Vladimir Bogdanov of Surgutneftegaz, alone of all the oil generals, steered clear of takeover by the oligarchs and remained in charge of their companies, while Sergei Muravlenko of Yukos, at first sight well positioned to succeed as well, lost control to Mikhail Khodorkovsky and Menatep.

The first part of the answer is timing. The most important advantage enjoyed by LUKoil and Surgutneftegaz was that they were the first ones out of the gate. The more time went by, the more outside players came into the game, making it more and more difficult for the traditional "oil generals" to gain control. As in chess, the game that Russians love and understand so well, the important thing was not to lose tempo. What was possible in 1993 was difficult by 1994, impossible by 1995.

There were three hurdles to clear. The first was to manage the privatization itself. The second was to achieve legal unification. The third, and by far the most difficult, was to establish actual control over oil flows and cash flows. The key word in all three was *control*—legal, financial, and physical. Of all the oil generals and oil companies, only Vagit Alekperov and LUKoil fully succeeded in clearing all three hurdles while preserving independence. Even Vladimir Bogdanov of Surgutneftegaz fell short of achieving full control of his downstream, and although he remained in overall charge of his company, he needed the help of powerful allies who subsequently became major, if quasi-hidden, partners in his company. As for Sergei Muravlenko and Yukos, they failed on all three counts and became the oligarchs' most famous and fateful prize.

But first we return to the beginnings of the privatization story, and to its most famous "father," Anatolii Chubais.

How the Oil Industry Was Privatized

Anatolii Chubais stands out as the one truly talented political leader and manager of the 1990s. In his strategic vision of a liberal and capitalist Russia, in his political skills as an organizer and campaigner, and above all in his relentless tactics, Chubais towered above both his friends and his enemies, both of whom were many. Chubais's role in overseeing the liberalization of the oil market was critical, and he brought to it his signature modus operandi: identify and co-opt the stakeholder—of whatever persuasion—and then neutralize the opposition by any available political means.

In the winter of 1992 Anatolii Chubais and his team of liberal economists in the State Property Committee (Goskomimushchestvo, or GKI) had found quarters in the vast abandoned offices of the Central Committee of the Communist Party of the Soviet Union on Old Square. This had been the seat of power in the old Soviet system, and ghosts of the past regularly came back to haunt Chubais's team in unexpected ways:

> In [Dmitri] Vasilev's office [wrote his colleague Petr Mostovoi] there was a computer, but you couldn't just get into it, because it was linked to some internal network of the CPSU Central Committee, and all the passwords had been lost beyond retrieval. So we had to break into it by brute force and work with programs that were partly disabled. Working on the privatization program, from time to time we would run into documents on the computer from "that time." And for scratch paper we used the reverse side of Central Committee forms.[6]

Polls showed that most Russians opposed privatizing the country's large strategic industries. The oil sector was especially sensitive, and as a consequence it was one of the last to be addressed by the government's privatization program. Even after the Soviet collapse and the beginning of radical market reforms, the reformers' privatization plan focused mainly on small businesses, and the large strategic industries such as the oil and gas sectors were at first explicitly excluded. The ministries opposed it; the oil generals feared it; and public opinion was hostile. Dmitri Vasil'ev, who was then Chubais's deputy at the State Property Committee, wrote in a memoir, "Where the privatization of large enterprises was concerned, the number of those opposed was always larger than those in favor." Indeed, as time went by, public disapproval only deepened.[7] Even the radical reformers on Chubais's team conceded that the oil industry required special handling, and in the privatization program adopted in early 1992 the oil industry was placed in a group of sectors requiring government permission before they could privatize.[8]

The Gorbachev reforms, in seeking to decentralize industry by empowering the enterprise managers and weakening the ministries, had left an awkward legal legacy. They had stripped the power structure down to the individual "state enterprise" *(gosudarstvennoe predpriiatie),* giving it operational autonomy and legal control over its assets. The ob"edinenie, the parent unit that stood over the enterprise, was abolished. But this caused a problem in the oil industry, where the ob"edinenie was the traditional decision-making unit of the industry, not to mention the power base of the oil generals.[9] Thus the late Gorbachev reforms left them in a legal void. In concrete terms, for example, this meant that the giant Nizhnevartovskneftegaz ob"edinenie (which included the Samotlor field) had no legal standing, while its nine producing NGDUs became legally independent. It took two special presidential decrees in mid-1992, following a desperate appeal from the oil generals, to restore the status of the parent ob"edineniia and to spell out their seniority over their divisions.[10] In the end the oil generals in most cases were able to prevent outright secession by the NGDUs. Yet the ambiguity introduced by the late Gorbachev reforms continued into the post-Soviet era, as the Yeltsin government moved on to corporatization and privatization. The NGDUs' legal rights as juridical persons carried over when they were turned from state enterprises into joint-stock corporations, and having tasted legal and financial autonomy, they fought to keep it.[11]

The practical consequence of these legal tangles was that when privatization finally went forward in 1993–1994, it did so simultaneously on two parallel levels—on that of the ob"edineniia and that of the NGDUs and other subsidiaries beneath them. If this were not already complicated enough, creating the new vertically integrated companies—the new "majors"—required creating a new layer of holding companies and corralling the ob"edineniia into them. But both the ob"edineniia and the NGDUs claimed legal rights derived from the previous reforms, which they resisted handing over to the holding companies. Thus legal privatization was delayed by multiple battles for control being waged simultaneously—those of the heads of the ob"edineniia versus their NGDUs and those of the new majors versus the ob"edineniia—to which must be added the remnants of the Soviet ministries in Moscow, with painted-over signs on their front doors but much the same control-minded ideas inside. The federal government in Moscow, distracted by the increasingly bitter constitutional confrontation between the president and the legislature that raged through late 1993, remained divided over the course to follow. The privatization campaign appeared about to stall before it had even begun.

Looking for a way to disarm opposition and get the privatization program moving, Chubais's team hit upon the idea (which they copied from a similar program used in Czechoslovakia) of distributing free vouchers, which could be traded at auction for shares in the companies being privatized. The idea was to hand out to every Russian citizen a certificate with a nominal value of 10,000 rubles, elegantly printed to look like a banknote, which people could then exchange for shares in major companies. Their key innovation was to make the vouchers tradable. A skeptic could sell his voucher for cash or a bottle of vodka; an optimist could buy up as many vouchers as he could afford. Within weeks of their first issue in October 1992, a thriving secondary market in vouchers sprang up all over Russia. In open-air stalls, on street corners, at factory gates, and soon on improvised exchanges, Russians were buying and selling vouchers.[12] The Russian Commodity Exchange (Rossiiskaia Tovarno-Syr'evaia Birzha, or RTSB), housed in the old Moscow Post Office building on Miasnitskaia Street, quickly turned into a nationwide trading floor for vouchers.[13]

But there was strong resistance to using vouchers to privatize the oil industry. The oil generals as a group strongly opposed voucher privatization. Voucher auctions were by definition a giveaway of shares, and they brought no capital to the investment-starved oil companies. Dmitri Vasil'ev, then chairman of the State Property Committee that oversaw the voucher auctions, recalls, "Even though the share packets [reserved for voucher auctions] were small (8 to 14% of the total), the oil generals trembled over every share."[14] Some oil regions, such as Tatarstan and Kalmykiia, refused to conduct voucher auctions at all. Others, such as the northwest Russian republic of Komi, demanded greater local control.[15] The ministries, predictably enough, favored creating large conglomerates managed by themselves. By January 1994 they had succeeded in exempting two-thirds of the enterprises in the energy sector from voucher privatization, and the whole program looked about to stall.[16] Chubais had to appeal to Yeltsin to issue a direct order, listing specific companies and schedules for voucher auctions. The ministries and the oil generals reluctantly complied, and voucher auctions in the oil industry finally got under way in the winter and spring of 1994.

Fortunes in Burlap Bags

The beginning of voucher auctions for oil companies touched off a frenzy of speculation. By this time, enterprising foreigners had joined the chase. One of them, then a young investment banker fresh from New York, recalls the feverish atmosphere:

> It was a crazy time. Just the process for buying the vouchers was crazy. Each voucher, then worth about $20, carried a 13-digit serial number. You had to pay cash for them, and the largest Russian banknote in circulation at that time was worth about $20. Can you imagine how many pieces of paper we had to assemble to make $1 million? That was 50,000 pieces of paper—and we were handling $5 million a day like that. We would go down to the Post Office on Miasnitskaia with duffelbags of banknotes, and turn them in for vouchers. We had to record each 13-digit serial number in triplicate, by hand. We did that every day and every night. It was nuts.[17]

The young brokers were soon inundated with orders from Western investors eager to buy into Russian oil companies:

> The phone would ring from New York. A customer would say, "I'll take $5 million worth of Russian oil-company stock." Sight unseen. We had no research, no information. But clients were willing to spend millions on a pure punt.[18]

Russian speculators quickly set about doing the same, although initially they had nowhere near as much money behind them. But to get voucher privatization off to a fast start, the government had licensed voucher investment funds, which were intended to act like mutual funds. Ordinary Russians, instead of selling their vouchers for cash, could turn them over to a fund, which then exchanged them for shares on their behalf. Several of these turned out to be little more than scams, and many ordinary Russians lost their vouchers. But the voucher funds enabled quick-footed Russian speculators to amass large blocks of vouchers at next to no outlay. As the larger Russian companies began holding voucher auctions, both the Russian voucher funds and the Western brokerages hastened to the company sites with their satchels of vouchers, jostling one another for the shares on offer.

For the oil generals, the voucher auctions presented a mixture of threat and opportunity. The threat was loss of control. This affected the three emerging majors particularly. Under the November 1992 decree, they had been given controlling stakes in the ob"edineniia, which now became their subsidiaries.[19] But because the latter were still legally autonomous entities in their own right, they conducted privatization auctions in parallel with those of the parent holding companies. If the subsidiary's local managers and allies—or some group of outsiders—could acquire as little as a 25 percent stake plus one share at the subsidiary's auction, they could gain troublesome veto power over the parent.

At the same time, voucher privatization offered the oil generals a golden opportunity. By buying vouchers on the secondary market, oil-industry managers could convert the "parallel" cash flows and capital they had acquired over the previous five years through leasing, cooperatives, joint ventures, and so forth, into shares. For anyone who had cash, vouchers were cheap. In effect, the generals could now launder their offshore "gray-zone" revenues by creating their own voucher funds and buying shares on the cheap in their own companies.[20] As a consequence, the oil generals, after initial reluctance, ultimately became strong supporters of voucher privatization.

But voucher privatization was just one aspect of a whole new world of issues related to money and finance. These were new subjects for Soviet-era managers; they had never really had to think about money before. Yet almost overnight, issues of money became matters of life and death for the oil companies. Some of the most critical decisions the Russian oilmen had to make in the early 1990s had to do with the choice of a bank and financial advisors, as well as the construction of their own financial teams. Make the wrong choices, and they would end up losing control of cash flow and drowning in their own debt or, conversely, being taken over by a predatory financial "advisor." The failure to manage money proved to be a far more critical source of weakness than the failure to manage oil.

The only company to get it right from the start was LUKoil. From the earliest days Vagit Alekperov and his team developed a financial strategy that managed risk while exploiting opportunities and maximizing control. They realized very early that their main source of wealth and their best defensive weapon was the value of their stock. Alekperov did not seek to keep the bulk of the shares for himself. Instead, he spread them around among key associates and political allies, building a broad network of support. In a strategy reminiscent of that of John D. Rockefeller and Standard Oil, Alekperov encouraged his closest team members and other well-placed allies to build up their stakes and grow wealthy. And from the beginning LUKoil cultivated a clean image and sought to draw in foreign companies as shareholders and partners. While other oil generals adopted parts of this strategy, Alekperov and his team at LUKoil were the only ones to combine them into a whole that enabled the company to consolidate, to grow, and, later on, to survive.

Alekperov Builds a Financial Team

For someone who had come up from the ranks of Soviet oilmen, Vagit Alekperov proved remarkably adept at grasping the importance of finance. From the earliest beginnings of LUKoil, he saw the challenge of forming an integrated company as essentially financial. We have seen how he traveled to the West as early as 1990 to learn from banks and oil companies how to organize an integrated oil company and mobilize capital for it. He was a great seeker of advice. By 1992 he had hired the Moscow office of KPMG, one of the large global auditing companies then known as the "Big Seven," and had brought in the French bank Paribas, the management consultant McKinsey, and the U.S. law firm Akin Gump.[21]

Yet Western advisors could not be the whole answer. They were expensive (at least for a fledgling Russian company in those days); their interests did not necessarily coincide with LUKoil's; and above all, they were foreigners. Alekperov needed his own team, smart people he could trust. But Russians with money skills were scarce. The initial top command of LUKoil consisted of West Siberian oilmen and a handful of former oil ministry bureaucrats. The handful among them who had economic skills had been trained in Soviet times.[22] The first generation of Russian financial experts who emerged in those years were mostly self-taught and gravitated toward the new oil companies by accidental paths. The two who helped Alekperov make Lukoil were military officers.

Financial Wizards from the Military

At 32, Colonel Leonid Fedun's career looked to be at a dead end. An officer's son, Fedun had graduated from the Higher Military Command College of the

Strategic Rocket Forces and was commissioned as a political officer. By the 1980s he was an instructor in political economy and political science at the Dzerzhinskii Military Academy, the prestigious higher officers' school for the Strategic Rocket Forces. Yet the subjects he taught were hardly more than indoctrination, and so far as he could tell the next quarter century would bring only more of the same.[23]

But by 1988 Gorbachev's perestroika was in full swing, and Fedun began looking around for a new line of work. He became intrigued by the international economics and politics of oil. His first research project, on the impact of the 1973 oil crisis on the economies of the countries comprising the North Atlantic Treaty Organization (NATO), led to him advising the Russian oil producers on oil export markets. One of them was the young general director of Kogalymneftegaz, Vagit Alekperov.[24] The two men hit it off. By 1992, the year he left the Strategic Rocket Forces Academy, Fedun was already Alekperov's indispensable right-hand man on securities and privatization, new subjects in which Fedun schooled himself on the run. Since 1994 Fedun has been vice president of LUKoil in charge of investor strategy, the perennial face of LUKoil to the world's investors and analysts. When in 2002 LUKoil published a list of its principal shareholders, Fedun was the third largest.[25] As Fedun once told an interviewer, in a classic understatement, "I was in the right place at the right time."[26]

But Fedun was hardly alone. In Soviet times the military and the KGB had attracted the best and the brightest, and when it collapsed, over 300,000 younger officers like Fedun left the service for the private sector, many of them turning their mathematical and technical skills into the new financial wizardry of shares and investments.[27] Alekperov, who personally supervised hiring at LUKoil in those days, was said to favor former military officers over oilmen. "The oil we can teach them," he used to say.[28]

The second key recruit to Alekperov's financial team was a former air force colonel named Nikolai Tsvetkov, also in his early thirties. Tsvetkov had taken the plunge into the new private sector even earlier than Fedun, resigning his commission in 1990 to join one of the new start-up oil exchanges. By 1992, the year he met Alekperov, he was running a small two-man brokerage called BrokInvest. In 1993, Tsvetkov founded an investment fund called Nikoil, which became LUKoil's main agent in voucher auctions and financial markets. (According to legend, to finance the launch of Nikoil, Nikolai and his wife Galina pledged their small house in the Moscow countryside, inherited from Galina's family.)[29] By the early 2000s, Alekperov and Tsvetkov had contributed substantially to one another's fortunes. In 2002, Tsvetkov was listed as LUKoil's second-largest shareholder,[30] while in 2004 Alekperov was listed as a major shareholder in Nikoil. Today Nikoil (now renamed Uralsib), with Tsvetkov as chairman, is one of Russia's largest private banks.

Fedun and Tsvetkov had notoriously tense relations. Westerners who worked with them in the mid-1990s perceived Fedun as the insider fending off Tsvetkov the outsider. Yet between 1992 and 1998 they worked in uneasy tandem, until Tsvetkov finally left LUKoil in 1998. Yet harmonious or not, the financial team formed by people like Fedun and Tsvetkov was seen throughout the oil industry as the most skilled in the business, putting LUKoil well ahead of the other oil companies.[31]

This small team of close confidants, seconded by international advisors, enabled Alekperov and LUKoil to control all the key steps in the privatization and consolidation of the company over the critical five years 1991–1995.

On Tap but Not on Top: Finding the Right Bank

The first problem was finding the right bank. In those days Russian banks were as likely to be a threat as a help. When Gorbachev broke up the monopoly of the USSR State Bank, it disintegrated into over 2,000 new banks all across the Russian landscape. They were a mixed lot. Some of them were "pocket banks," born out of the accounting departments of Soviet-era enterprises, which served mainly as conduits for channeling state credits into the oilmen's private pockets, a useful function but not a source of sophisticated advice. Some were nomenklatura banks based in Moscow, descendants of specialist banks that had been part of the USSR State Bank. They were useful for foreign trade and politically well connected, but they were not particularly attuned to the challenges facing the oil industry. Lastly, there were the new start-ups, the brash go-go banks set up by the emerging entrepreneurs to finance their arbitrage operations, such as Mikhail Fridman's Alfa-Bank and Mikhail Khodorkovsky's Menatep.[32]

In those days none of the banks actually financed any oil projects or lent money for working capital; at most they lent modest amounts of money to finance oil exports. Even the biggest of them were miniscule by international standards. They were more interested in speculating on the ruble or securing lucrative state accounts than in betting on reviving the bankrupt oil industry. Revenues from oil exports, on the other hand, aroused their intense interest. From the oil generals' standpoint, it would have been hard to say which was the greater danger, the pocket banks' generally low level of competence or the predatory opportunism of the newer banks, which soon included speculation in vouchers. It was a tricky choice.

LUKoil chose carefully and was fortunate. From late 1993 it concentrated its accounts in a new Moscow bank called Imperial. The bank was large enough to provide modern services, it specialized in oil and gas clients, and it quickly gained a good reputation for professionalism. But to make sure Imperial would do his bidding rather than the other way around, Alekperov bought a 12 percent stake in the bank and kept it under close watch. This was typical of LUKoil's approach. As a leading Russian expert has observed,

> LUKoil stands out because of the active part played by the leadership of the oil company from the very beginning of the relationship. Banks and investment institutions served to consolidate the oil company, but it was the company itself that decided which institutions and which services it wanted to avail itself of, and what it wanted to use them for.[33]

The other oil companies were less successful in finding the right blend of competence and control. Yukos initially chose as an advisor a medium-sized bank with little international experience, Promradtekhbank. Westerners who worked with Yukos in those early days had a poor opinion of Promradtekhbank, and Yukos soon relegated it to a minor role. But Yukos's main problem was its rebellious subsidiary, Yuganskneftegaz, which defiantly ran its own exports and planned its own parallel privatization—and cofounded its own bank, called Tokobank. Yukos's chairman, Sergei Muravlenko, turned instead to one of the new Moscow banks, Menatep, headed by a young man with ambitious ideas, named Mikhail Khodorkovsky. Muravlenko and Yukos quickly began to depend on Menatep and on Khodorkovsky for advice and financing.

The next problem for the oil generals was developing a strategy for managing privatization. Again, LUKoil was the first to get it right.

Privatization: Keeping Out the Outsiders

The basic approach used to privatize the oil companies, when it finally got under way in 1993, reflected an uneasy compromise by the Yeltsin government, the parliament, and the regions, between those who wanted to turn the companies over to the workers, those who wanted to sell them off for cash, and those who wanted to keep control for themselves.[34] Under the GKI's basic plan (so-called Option 1), employees got 25 percent of oil company shares in the form of nonvoting ("preferred") shares and a further 10 percent of voting ("ordinary") shares in a closed distribution at a deep discount. Company managers had the right to buy 5 percent for cash. Some 22 percent of shares were to be offered in public auctions, in exchange for vouchers.[35] This left a controlling block of voting shares in the hands of the state, for later cash sales. Most of the oil companies were privatized under Option 1.

The oil generals were determined not to lose control of their companies, and they devised a variety of tactics to make sure they stayed in charge. They repurchased their employees' shares or held them "in trust." They allied themselves with regional authorities to prevent the NGDUs beneath them from privatizing separately. They limited the number of shares to be traded for vouchers, and they restricted outsiders' access to the voucher auctions through a variety of subterfuges or where necessary by violence.[36] They formed front companies to buy up vouchers and exchange them for shares. In some places, such as Nizhnevartovsk, the oil generals conspired with the regional property committees to block voucher auctions altogether.[37]

The three emerging majors—LUKoil, Yukos, and Surgutneftegaz—faced the additional challenge of establishing control over their designated subsidiaries. Under the November 1992 decree, they had been given a narrow majority stake in these, but their voting control could easily be diluted if the subsidiaries decided to resist.[38] This was a real possibility, since under the GKI's privatization plan both the majors and their subsidiaries privatized in parallel, and indeed, the subsidiaries' voucher auctions were scheduled to take place first, ahead of those of the parent companies.[39] If outsiders or rivals gained a foothold through the voucher auctions, they could promote rebellion.

The strategy developed by LUKoil was to use an external company to manage all financial aspects of LUKoil's privatization. For this purpose Alekperov turned to Nikoil, the investment fund created by Nikolai Tsvetkov. Nikoil held

LUKoil's shareholder registry and voted the employees' proxies. It created two voucher investment funds, called "Roil-Fund" and "LUKoil-Fund," to acquire shares and vouchers from LUKoil employees and on the secondary market.[40] Through Nikoil, LUKoil's management team acquired not only its own shares at voucher auctions and those of its subsidiaries but also those of potential acquisition targets.[41] Last but not least, Nikoil served as LUKoil's investment bank, managing its relations with prospective foreign lenders and investors, whom LUKoil actively tried to draw into the privatization process as partners and allies.

LUKoil was well served by its close connections to the government, notably to Energy Minister Iurii Shafranik and to GKI. To prevent its subsidiaries from privatizing separately, Alekperov persuaded GKI to allow LUKoil to conduct "integrated" auctions, at which shares of both the parent company and its subsidiaries would be offered simultaneously, under LUKoil and Nikoil's close watch. Any local subsidiaries that attempted to break ranks and privatize on their own were firmly brought back into line.[42] And to make sure the subsidiaries kept to the game plan, LUKoil's managers transferred the blocks of their shares on offer at the auction to Nikoil for safekeeping.

Despite the risk of losing tempo, Alekperov took his time, leaving nothing to chance. It was not until March and April 1994 that LUKoil held its first voucher auctions, conducted simultaneously in seventy-six regions nationwide.[43] "LUKoil-Fund" had amassed a war chest of 2 million vouchers, and it was joined by its allies, including Imperial Bank and its French advisor Paribas, who had also purchased vouchers to offer for shares.[44] Broadly, the auction went according to plan, although Alekperov and his team were startled when a pair of young Western traders representing Credit Suisse First Boston (CSFB) showed up at LUKoil's voucher auction in Moscow and made off with a 2.8 percent stake in LUKoil and a 5 percent stake in LUKoil-Kogalymneftegaz.[45] Alekperov was at first under the impression that CSFB intended to become a strategic partner of LUKoil, not realizing that CSFB was acting as an intermediary, buying shares on behalf of portfolio investors in the West.[46] Yet this did not pose a threat, since no one of these offshore shareholders held more than a small stake. Overall, LUKoil's game plan was successful in keeping control during the initial stages of privatization. Thus by mid-1994 Alekperov and his team were well positioned to move quickly to the next stage of privatization: the sale of the remaining state-owned stake for money.

Controlling Oil and Cash: FK-LUKoil

Thanks to its early partnership with Andrei Pannikov and his "Urals" trading company, LUKoil controlled its own exports from an early date, but the more difficult challenge was cutting back the hemorrhage of oil into the domestic market. In 1993 and 1994, the oil companies were still subject to compulsory state orders *(goszakazy)* to deliver oil to domestic consumers. But consumers had largely ceased to pay. Debts piled up quickly. By January 1994 LUKoil was owed 400 billion rubles by nonpaying consumers; by mid-March, 600 billion. As cash ran short, the company was having to use its export revenues to pay wages instead of repairing wells.[47] All the upstream producers faced the same problem; if anything, LUKoil was slightly better off because of its better control over exports. But something had to be done.

In 1993 Alekperov set up a special subsidiary called the LUKoil Financial Company *(Finansovaia Kompaniia LUKoil,* or FK-LUKoil). FK-LUKoil, as it came to be called, was essentially a collection agency, a means of centralizing cash flow in the hands of the corporation. It took title to the crude oil from LUKoil's upstream producers and had it refined on a fee basis ("tolling") at LUKoil's refineries, then moved the refined products to the wholesale distributors. It retained title all the way, signing separate contracts with each participant in the chain and collecting cash at every step.[48] To accelerate payments (and keep track of the cash flows), all the players were required to open accounts in the Imperial Bank. LUKoil required prepayment from the distributors, in exchange for which it offered discounts.[49] To run FK-LUKoil, Alekperov turned to a tough trader named Mukharbek Aushev. Aushev came from the North Caucasus and took no nonsense, hiring enforcers where he found them.[50]

FK-LUKoil was an early step on the way to monitoring and centralizing cash flows, although it was not yet transfer pricing, more like a profit-sharing cooperative.[51] Yet it put LUKoil well ahead of Yukos, which only "proposed to establish a center for financial settlements within the organization," which in the end (as we shall see) it proved unable to implement.[52] LUKoil was also well ahead of Surgutneftegaz, whose relations with the Kirishi refinery and the Saint Petersburg distributors were tense, and consequently Bogdanov was unable to push through a similar arrangement. In contrast, Alekperov's tighter control over his downstream enabled him to move quickly to build a network of wholly owned gasoline stations under the LUKoil brand (by 1995 there were between 900 and 1,000), while selling diesel and fuel oil directly through wholesalers, bypassing the inefficient local distribution companies.[53]

By the spring of 1995, LUKoil was ready to proceed with the next step in consolidating control: a share swap with its subsidiaries, which enabled LUKoil to convert all the company's shareholdings into a single stock. Alekperov offered generous terms, and the share swaps proceeded rapidly and with no apparent opposition from the subsidiaries.[54] Here too LUKoil was ahead of the pack. Vladimir Bogdanov had a tougher time swapping shares with the Kirishi refinery,[55] and he ultimately failed to achieve a share swap with his distributor subsidiaries in Saint Petersburg (indeed, as we shall see, he faced a wholesale rebellion); while Muravlenko of Yukos kept postponing a share unification until finally it was too late and he had lost control of the company.

Having achieved full control over the entire structure of LUKoil, Alekperov was able to proceed to the final step, turning the subsidiaries into corporate divisions of a single centralized corporation. Once this was done, FK-LUKoil had outlived its usefulness and was abolished in early 1996. LUKoil had come of age.[56]

But Alekperov had not waited to launch the strategy that became his trademark. Practically from the first moment he began planning LUKoil, he looked outside Russia, for partners and opportunities. His foreign strategy became an integral part of his success in consolidating and financing his company.

LUKoil Looks Abroad

In July 1994, just three months after its successful voucher auctions, LUKoil announced that it would sell a 15 percent share to foreign investors, in the form of convertible bonds.[57] A LUKoil delegation led by Leonid Fedun traveled to the United States, where they met with banks and with William Donaldson, chair of the New York Stock Exchange. It was a meeting rich in symbols: for the Russians, they were venturing into the very den of capitalism; for Donaldson, it was his first encounter with a Russian oil company. On their return they reported strong interest by U.S. investors in this new phenomenon—a private Russian oil company, and one willing to share ownership with foreigners.[58]

Until now only speculators had bought Russian oil stocks, but LUKoil's financial team now prepared for the sale by the book. This time Alekperov needed the top Western brand names on the masthead. KPMG was named official auditor and began a Western-style audit of the company.[59] (As Fedun commented, "This will put an end to insinuations about the company's financial standing."[60]) Akin Gump was hired to provide legal advice, and Miller and Lents, a Houston-based oil and gas consultant, reevaluated LUKoil's reserves on Western standards. LUKoil's careful homework paid off: foreign strategic investors showed interest. In September 1995, ARCO, at that time the United States' seventh largest oil company, bid $250 million in a tender for LUKoil's convertible bonds and thus became the first major foreign shareholder in a Russian oil company.[61]

Altogether, Alekperov was the first of the Russian oilmen to develop a long-range vision for his company. Unlike the traders and bankers who flooded into the Russian oil business in those early days, for whom a three-month export-credit deal was long-term planning, Alekperov always thought in terms of decades. Alone of all the Russian oilmen in the early 1990s, Alekperov had a vision for LUKoil as a major international player. His initial focus was the Caspian Sea, where he had started as a young man.

Alekperov Returns to Baku

If Alekperov's Baku family had been better connected, he might have stayed in Azerbaijan and become a member of the local political elite or risen to a high position in Azneft', the onshore oil industry, which reported to a local minister in Baku and was staffed largely by Azeris. But Alekperov's father was a modest rank-and-file oil worker and did not belong to either of the two powerful clans that dominated (and still dominate) Azerbaijan under the Alievs, the so-called Yeraz clan of Azeris from Erevan and the Nakhichevanis from southwestern Azerbaijan. Instead, Alekperov went to work for the offshore company Kaspmorneftegaz, which reported directly to Moscow. He rose modestly through the ranks, until he decided, at the age of 29, to seek his fortune in West Siberia.

Over the following decade and a half, Alekperov's Caspian roots grew distant. But in 1993, when Azerbaijan's longtime party boss, Heydar Aliev, returned to power as president, Alekperov came back to Baku leading his new company, intent on gaining for LUKoil a stake in the emerging bonanza of the south Caspian offshore. In that year he took a 10 percent share in the Azerbaijan International Oil Consortium (AIOC), a group of companies led by BP and Amoco, to develop the giant Apsheron Trend, the "string of pearls" (as oilmen called it) stretching under the Caspian between Azerbaijan and Turkmenistan.[62]

Alekperov at that time saw the Caspian as the future of LUKoil. He knew that his West Siberian base faced eventual decline, and he took the established view of the Soviet oil industry that the Caspian was the coming "fourth generation" (after the first three "generations"—Baku, the Volga-Urals, and West Siberia). Azerbaijan's independence appeared to open a unique opportunity for the Baku native son. Yet Alekperov must have been too astute to believe that the republic's initially enthusiastic welcome would last and that he would be given the keys to the kingdom. His fledgling company was by far the weakest partner in the AIOC consortium (except for the Turkish TPAO): he had no cash or international experience, and LUKoil lacked offshore expertise. President Aliev, himself a former member of the Soviet Politburo and no stranger to Moscow, from the first perceived Alekperov less as an Azerbaijani than as a Russian, and his company as a potential spearhead for the Russian state. Thus although he welcomed Alekperov to Baku and eased his way into the AIOC consortium, the crafty president was willing to grant LUKoil only a limited role in Azerbaijan's offshore oil. Aliev was determined to take advantage of Russia's weakness, which he saw as temporary, to attract international support for Azerbaijan's independence. Oil was his only trump. In Aliev's diversification strategy, LUKoil had its place, but only as one of the widest possible range of partners.

Alekperov's vision was not limited to Azerbaijan, however, or even to the Caspian. He was soon pursuing opportunities in the other Muslim republics of the former Soviet Union and throughout the Middle East. As early as January 1994, LUKoil and Eni/Agip announced plans to explore and develop oilfields jointly in North Africa and West Siberia.[63] By October 1994 the two companies were discussing a refinery in southern Russia,[64] and by the following June they had created a joint venture called LUKAgip.[65] Suddenly LUKoil seemed to be everywhere. In the fall of 1995, LUKoil together with ARCO bought a 5 percent stake in Kazakhstan's Tengiz field.[66] In June 1996 the two companies, through their joint venture LUKArco, acquired a stake in the Caspian Pipeline Consortium (CPC), created to connect the Tengiz field to a new export terminal on the Black Sea. LUKoil was also active elsewhere in Kazakhstan (supplying equipment to the Kumkol field), in Uzbekistan (exploring for gas), and even in

Iraq (with an option to explore and develop the South Kurna field after the expected removal of the international embargo).

So active was LUKoil in areas of Russian interest that Alekperov was often portrayed in the Western media as the "soft arm" of Russian diplomacy. It is clear that Alekperov was strongly supported in the south by the Yeltsin government, and especially by Prime Minister Viktor Chernomyrdin and Energy Minister Iurii Shafranik, who together with Alekperov appeared in the mid-1990s to form a kind of troika for the advancement of Russian interests in the southern tier of the former Soviet Union. LUKoil owed its participation in the Tengiz consortium and the Caspian pipeline venture to Chernomyrdin's direct intervention. In Kazakhstan and Uzbekistan Alekperov acted as Russia's unofficial ambassador—he once presented Kazakhstan's president Nursultan Nazarbaev with a personal helicopter—while inside CPC, LUKoil's man, Vladimir Stanev, energetically defended Russian state interests.[67]

Probably the most accurate formulation is to say that in Alekperov's mind, LUKoil's commercial aims and Russia's diplomatic objectives blended smoothly, especially at first, when the Russian government was weak and East-West rivalries were temporarily muted. In Azerbaijan he wanted LUKoil to be accepted as a private company, but he also actively solicited the support of Russian leaders. Thus in early 1997, commenting on the active bidding then going on for a prospect called Inam, Alekperov told an interviewer in Baku, "We receive recommendations from the highest officials of Russia, addressed not only to Aliev but also to Nazarbaev. This is normal."[68] When the powers on the shoreline of the Caspian Sea debated over how the resources of the seabed should be divided, Alekperov endorsed the Russian position, that the Caspian should be treated as a lake and that all the countries bordering on it should have equal access to its natural resources. "Development in the Caspian Sea is a political issue," he said in mid-1994, criticizing what he called the unilateral actions of Azerbaijan, Turkmenistan, and Kazakhstan, "and Russia's Foreign Ministry should play first violin in settling it."[69]

Later on, as Russian-Western rivalries sharpened in the South Caspian, the ever-cautious Alekperov hewed more carefully than ever to Russian state policy, even when LUKoil's commercial interests pointed the other way. Thus when invited to participate in the Baku-Tbilisi-Ceyhan oil pipeline to Turkey, Alekperov refused. Subsequently, as official Russian irritation mounted over the redirection of Azerbaijan's oil flow away from Russia, Alekperov in 2002 sold his equity stake in AIOC and concentrated his attention on the Russian offshore sector in the North Caspian. Yet by this time his 10 percent stake had increased immensely in value, and thus he was cashing out of a very successful investment. Even more to the point, the geology of the South Caspian had failed to confirm the early expectations of large oil reserves, and LUKoil had suffered a string of dry holes. Once again, Alekperov's approach balanced commercial realities and political constraints.

It remains that Alekperov, as a former Soviet minister, never lost sight of the state, even when it was at its weakest.[70] "We do not want to lose our tie to the state," he told an interviewer in 1996, and this summed up his attitude throughout the 1990s. He never forgot who was ultimately the sovereign owner of Russia's oil and gas resources and pipelines, as well as the source of its foreign policy, in which energy has never ceased to play a major part. Whether one calls it statist conviction or risk aversion, this middle road has been the hallmark of Alekperov's behavior down to the present day.

There is no such ambiguity in the case of Vladimir Bogdanov, the head of Surgutneftegaz. Bogdanov was from the outset the most "Soviet" of the oil generals and the one who has remained closest to the state.

Vladimir Bogdanov, the Hermit Oilman

The only thing that Vladimir Bogdanov, founder of Surgutneftegaz, and Vagit Alekperov have in common is that they both rose through the school of hard knocks of the Soviet oil industry in the swamps of West Siberia. In every other respect Bogdanov is the polar opposite of Alekperov, in origins, personal style, and business strategy. Born in 1951 in the tiny West Siberian village of Suerka south of Tiumen City, Bogdanov graduated from "Indus" as a drilling engineer and, like many of his classmates of the early 1970s, started work at Samotlor field, which at that time was nearing its height as the second largest oilfield in the world. In 1976 he moved to Surgutneftegaz, and from that time forward, apart from short stints elsewhere in West Siberia, his entire career is connected to the company that he still heads today. Bogdanov's deep roots in the Tiumen countryside and his three decades in the same company go far to explain his unique style. Bogdanov never moved to Moscow. He and his company remain based in Surgut, where Bogdanov lives modestly, travels little outside Siberia, and resides close to his office. "I'm happy," he says, "that I can walk to work."[71]

Bogdanov is a fiercely authoritarian manager, aloof and secretive.[72] He never lost his grip over Surgutneftegaz in the Gorbachev years or following the Soviet breakup, and from the first he put his own unique stamp on the company. He had no truck with criminals.[73] Alone of all the oil generals, Bogdanov refused any collaboration with foreign companies or foreign investors, except as contractors. He formed no joint ventures; indeed he fiercely opposed them, claiming that they were little more than fronts for illegal exports (which in fact they frequently were). He minimized the use of foreign service providers, preferring to rely on his company's own resources, and he accepted no foreign credits.[74] The populist language, the fierce rejection of outside help, the belligerent tone, all are characteristic of the fiery Bogdanov, who is often described by outsiders as "the hermit oilman."

Bogdanov is unique in one more respect as well: from the first he cultivated a reputation as a good corporate citizen. In an era in which tax evasion was practically the national sport, Bogdanov paid his taxes, or at least as much as he was able.[75] In his rare public interviews he spoke with contempt of oil companies that used offshore tax havens, transfer pricing, or creative tax "optimization" schemes to enrich themselves. He claimed he did not hide export revenues, and the meager data available do not contradict him. In the mid- to late 1990s Surgutneftegaz's declared profits from exports were the highest of any oil company; and it paid eight times more taxes per ton than Sibneft and three times more than TNK.[76] Surgutneftegaz has always emerged unscathed from the many tax investigations that the federal government regularly conducts on the oil industry.[77]

Thus Bogdanov, in his own way, has always minded his political fences, no less than Alekperov, and like him has enjoyed strong political support in return, both from the center and from his home region of Khanty-Mansiisk. Throughout the 1990s Surgutneftegaz was the mainstay of the Khanty-Mansiisk regional government; in the early 2000s, according to a government report, it accounted for over half of the okrug's tax receipts.[78] Bogdanov made a point of spending generously on housing and services for the local towns, especially Surgutneftegaz's home base of Surgut, where the quality of housing and living standards are noticeably higher than in the other oil towns of West Siberia.[79] In 2004 Vladimir Putin, on a trip to the Far North, paid tribute to Bogdanov's role as a good citizen, drawing an unfavorable contrast between Surgut and Yukos's capital city of Nefteiugansk.[80]

In short, Vladimir Bogdanov is perceived by Russians as a rare embodiment of the ideal of the "red manager." But how was he able to keep such remarkable control over his company?

"They Thought They Could Control Him"

Bogdanov was determined to prevent outsiders from using privatization to gain a foothold in his company. He fought in every possible way to concentrate company shares in his own hands. It was only after an extended fight with Chubais's team in Moscow that he was allowed to limit the voucher auctions for Surgutneftegaz shares to two isolated West Siberian locations, from which outsiders could be barred. Frustrated reporters who tried to reach Surgut to find out what was going on were told that the phone lines were "broken."[81] Altogether, Bogdanov succeeded in controlling the privatization of his upstream producer, although as we shall see, he had more trouble with his downstream.[82]

Bogdanov's task was made easier by the fact that Surgutneftegaz in Soviet times had been the most centralized of all the West Siberian ob"edineniia. Unlike Nizhnevartovskneftegaz, whose nine NGDUs were all "juridical entities" and thus had a legal claim to privatize independently, Surgutneftegaz consisted of only one producing entity—of which Bogdanov also happened to be the general director.[83] Downstream, Surgutneftegaz was assigned only one refinery, the strategically placed Kirishi refinery near Saint Petersburg, with its easy access to the Baltic Sea and the export market. His only major potential problem was his distribution territory in Saint Petersburg, which as we shall see ultimately eluded his grasp.

How to Sell an Oil Company to Yourself

Bogdanov's approach to privatization was that of the bear in his den. Not for him the foreign banks and legal advisors. Share issues and registry were handled by the company's head office in Surgut, not by Moscow-based investment banks.[84] Bogdanov's financial team was discreet, obscure, and local. In contrast to LUKoil's Fedun and Nikoil's Tsvetkov, who became major stockholders and public personalities in their own right, Bogdanov's principal aide in managing his privatization strategy and investor relations was a modest accountant from inside the company, named Natal'ia Ol'shanova.[85] Her chief qualities were organization, discipline, and a fierce attention to detail. Every document that passed through her hands was in perfect legal form, with nothing left to chance, and Bogdanov's enemies were never able to trip him up on technicalities. At the end of the 1990s, Ol'shanova retired, her key role largely unknown except to insiders, as obscure as when she began.

Bogdanov mostly used local banks to handle his cash flow, concentrating all the accounts of the mother company and its sixty-nine subsidiaries into a single account that he could control.[86] But to handle his export revenues and finance capital investment, Bogdanov needed something larger and preferably Moscow-based. Bogdanov settled on Oneksimbank, a bank created by a group of foreign-trade companies and headed by a young scion of the Soviet-era foreign-trade aristocracy, Vladimir Potanin.[87] There followed a complex relationship. Surgutneftegaz was receiving little or no payment from its assigned internal market in Saint Petersburg and the Russian Northwest, and despite his best efforts to stay solvent, Surgutneftegaz was falling into debt. In stepped Oneksimbank and its well-connected founder, Vladimir Potanin, who volunteered credit to provide working capital and loans to build a new terminal to help Surgutneftegaz increase its exports of refined products (thus monetizing his output abroad instead of supplying it locally for no return).[88] But with credits came leverage and the threat of takeover, and Bogdanov tried to keep Oneksimbank at arm's length. In early 1995 Surgutneftegaz bought a 16 percent share in Oneksimbank, partly as an investment in a good partner and partly as a defensive move to keep an eye on Oneksimbank's intentions.[89]

Thus it was that when the oligarchs in Moscow dreamed up the shares-for-loans operation, Bogdanov was able to see off the attackers by closing the city of Surgut to air traffic and conducting his own one-man auction. He had timely help from Potanin and Oneksimbank, who obtained from the government a "poison pill" provision that the winning bidder would be required to pay off any of the company's overdue taxes and debts.[90] Thus Bogdanov as president of Surgutneftegaz smoothly handed over the state's controlling stake to Bogdanov as head of Surgutneftegaz's employee pension fund, which he created overnight for the purpose. Rosneft, which had intended to put in a bid, was excluded on a technicality and was not even allowed into Surgut.[91]

Why were Oneksimbank and Potanin so generous with their help? According to the same insider, who was a close witness to the various players' moves:

The reason Bogdanov was allowed to conduct his shares-for-loans auction ahead of the others, and in Surgut, was that Potanin and the others thought they could control him later—but he turned out to be too tough.[92]

Potanin and Oneksimbank, who had viewed Bogdanov as a rough-cut provincial, discovered that they had been outsmarted. Once he had acquired the state's remaining 40.1 percent stake in Surgutneftegaz, Bogdanov turned away from Oneksimbank and soon found other well-placed allies.

Bogdanov was also successful in consolidating control over his key downstream asset, the Kirishi refinery, one of the most modern in Russia at the time and strategically located on the Bay of Finland near Saint Petersburg. Although the refinery had been officially assigned to Surgutneftegaz in 1993, it was far from a foregone conclusion that Bogdanov would manage to hang on to it. Yukos and LUKoil (to which Kirishi had originally been assigned in 1991–1992) were actively bidding for it. Yet the refinery and its export subsidiary, Kineks, were essential to Surgutneftegaz's position in the Russian northwest and even more to its access to exports, thanks to its outlet to the Baltic Sea. Kirishi had been exporting crude and refined products on its own since the late 1980s and was accustomed to having its independence.[93] But in the spring of 1994, through a combination of pressure and negotiation, Bogdanov was able to install his own man, Vadim Somov, as general director at Kirishi.[94] By 1996, Somov had helped Bogdanov engineer a share swap on terms favorable to Surgutneftegaz.

In Russia in those days, such victories were not won peacefully without concessions in return. The identities of several of the most senior shareholders of Surgutneftegaz have never been revealed, but there have been persistent rumors that they include some of the then leading figures in Kirishi and Kineks as well as the city government of Saint Petersburg. If that were so, it would help to explain Bogdanov's successful consolidation of control then and his apparent strong political support today.

Bogdanov and the "Night Governor"

Yet there was one battle that Bogdanov did not win. In 1993 all of the new majors had been assigned their own domestic marketing regions for oil products. Surgutneftegaz had been assigned Saint Petersburg, the surrounding Leningrad

Province, and the Russian Northwest. Like all the other local markets in the 1990s, it was a treacherous swamp of red ink, red tape, and blood. So long as domestic fuel prices remained controlled (as they did through 1995), local distributors of heating oil and diesel regularly resold their stocks to black-market exporters, while the managers of retail service stations sold gasoline to private motorists for hidden cash markups. The supplier—in this case Surgutneftegaz and its refinery at Kirishi—rarely saw the proceeds. In other words, the local fuels business was a rich source of off-the-books cash, and therefore it was quickly penetrated by organized crime, typically with the behind-the-scenes backing of city officials and local law-enforcement agencies. It was a violent scene, as competing gangs battled one another for control, sometimes with the discreet backing of rival political and business coalitions. Even before Bogdanov inherited it, much of the Saint Petersburg fuels system had already been under attack from the much-feared *Tambov* group. Their technique for muscling in to a distributor or a depot or a service station was much the same as everywhere else in Russia at the time: first they offered "protection" to local operators, then they took a share in the profits, and before long they were shareholders and were on their way to becoming de facto owners.[95]

But Bogdanov was not one to take a challenge lying down. In the spring of 1994, having gained control of the Kirishi refinery, he now attempted to do the same in Saint Petersburg. He demanded prepayment in cash and threatened to cut off anyone who did not pay. He convened meetings of the shareholders of his local distributors and tried to impose the same share swaps as at Kirishi. But Bogdanov's tough tactics backfired. The mayor of Saint Petersburg, Anatolii Sobchak (or quite likely his de facto first deputy, Vladimir Putin, acting with Sobchak's blessing),[96] denounced the "dictatorship" of Surgutneftegaz, and in the fall of 1994 he sponsored the creation of a competitor, called the Petersburg Fuel Company (*Petersburgskaia Toplivnaia Kompaniia*, or PTK), which began buying fuels from other refineries, such as Omsk, Yaroslavl, and Nizhnii-Novgorod.[97] The local distributors defected to the new company, turning over local storage tanks and gasoline stations to PTK by the familiar device of "leasing" them. Bogdanov's own handpicked deputy for the northwest region, German Makarov, went over to the enemy.[98] Bogdanov was taken off guard by the scale of the rebellion. "Everything was normal in Petersburg," he told an interviewer, "until we began to restore order in the activity of our subsidiaries, and after that the situation immediately exploded."[99] The result, in December 1994, was a massive fuels famine, as Bogdanov cut off supplies to the city, and PTK and the municipal authorities cast about for more fuel from alternative sources. In January 1995, Sobchak responded by naming PTK the official fuels supplier to the city.[100]

For Surgutneftegaz this was a critical turning point. Over the following two years, Surgutneftegaz's market share in Saint Petersburg and the surrounding province collapsed. Its sales plummeted from 1.3 million tons in 1994 to just over 0.4 million in 1995, as the city and PTK continued diversifying their suppliers.[101] In September 1995 Mayor Sobchak invited the Finnish company Neste to open service stations in Saint Petersburg, and in April 1996 he made the same invitation to LUKoil.[102]

But Bogdanov, and for that matter the city government, was even less prepared for what happened next. In early 1996 a dangerous gang leader, Vladimir Kumarin, a founder of the *Tambov* gang, returned from Germany, where he had spent the previous year and a half recovering from serious wounds suffered when rivals had tried to kill him. During his stay in Germany Kumarin had continued to direct the activities of the *Tambovtsy* from afar, but he had also moved into a circle of influential Russian and German businessmen and had begun to evolve from a mere street gangster to a more outwardly respectable businessman with a more strategic view and connections to the political and security elite of Saint Petersburg. When he returned home, he set about turning gang control into legal ownership, through boardroom coups and courtroom battles, accompanied by violence only where necessary. The local media took to calling Kumarin the "night governor." Bogdanov found himself outmaneuvered at every turn. Through the summer of 1996 he had managed to retain nominal control of "Nefto-Kombi," which owned 111 of Saint Petersburg's 125 gas stations, but in August 1996 Surgutneftegaz was forced off the board of Nefto-Kombi, and over the following months the new management (essentially Kumarin and his partners) diluted Surgutneftegaz down to a 10 percent share through new share issues. Then they subleased Nefto-Kombi's filling stations to an outside group (again themselves), leaving Nefto-Kombi as an empty shell of debts.[103] The threat of violence was everywhere. Shareholders' meetings took place under heavy security. In the summer of 1997, Vice Governor Mikhail Manevich, who headed the city's property fund, and Valerii Mandrykin, vice president of Neste Saint-Petersburg, were murdered by contract killers.[104] As a Surgutneftegaz source put it, in a marvelous understatement, they were dealing with structures "whose activity does not always accord with the law."[105]

By late 1997 Bogdanov was left with the dregs of the market, the rustbelt industries and farms of Leningrad Province, the part that never paid its bills. The retail gasoline market in Saint Petersburg itself had become wide open, at least in nominal terms, with no one controlling more than a 5–10 percent share,[106] but according to police reports Kumarin and his colleagues, backed by the muscle of the Tambovtsy as well as discreet support from the local security organs, actually controlled 80 percent of it.[107] In 1998, after four years of struggle, Bogdanov finally threw in the towel and sold off Surgutneftegaz's last distribution and retail assets in Saint Petersburg, which by this time had been hollowed out to virtually nothing.[108] Vladimir Kumarin, who had engineered much of the offensive, remained in control of the field. Through the Petersburg City Bank, which he and his associates controlled, he held a 75.9 percent share of PTK, enough to override any minority shareholder.[109] The wars for control of the Saint Petersburg fuels market continued into the next decade, but by then Surgutneftegaz was no longer a significant part of them. Bogdanov and Surgutneftegaz never did regain control of the Saint Petersburg fuels market.

For Bogdanov, however, defeat may have been a blessing in disguise. Shut out of the domestic market in Saint Petersburg, he concentrated on exports out of Kirishi, which were profitable, if no longer so overwhelmingly so as in the first half of the 1990s. Defeat undoubtedly helped his cash flow. More than that, he was left with a simplified corporate structure, consisting essentially of one West Siberian producer and one strategically located refinery, together with the powerful exporters grouped in Kineks.[110] He was free to concentrate on restoring production in Surgut.

In actual fact, Bogdanov had never ceased investing in his upstream. Alone of all the oil generals, he managed to find the cash to repair old wells and keep drilling new ones, and even to develop some new fields. Surgutneftegaz was the first important oil company to halt the decline in oil production and the first to generate an increase. His approach remained essentially that of the Soviet era, just as his company remained the most Soviet of all the oil companies, but it was not ineffective, as we shall see in the following chapters.

Thus, each in his own way and style, Alekperov of LUKoil and Bogdanov of Surgutneftegaz succeeded in consolidating their companies (or at least, in the case of Bogdanov, the core of it) while remaining in command themselves. The third case, that of Yukos, is in total contrast. The failure of Sergey Muravlenko, its first CEO, to deal with the same challenges not only led to his personal defeat and the takeover of his company by Mikhail Khodorkovsky, but set the stage for the next act in the drama of Russian oil, the apogee of the oligarchs.

The Pioneer's Son

The first president of Yukos, Sergei Muravlenko, had the most famous last name in West Siberia. He was the son of Viktor Muravlenko, the celebrated discoverer of the oil riches of the Ob' River basin and the first head of the Tiumen oil industry. In the clannish world of the Soviet technocracy, that kind of name ushered you right in to any office in Russia, including the Kremlin. A graduate of "Indus," the Tiumen Industrial Institute, Muravlenko had gone to work at Samotlor and had moved quickly up the ladder of the West Siberian oil industry. In 1987, at the age of 37, he was posted to Yugviskneftegaz as chief engineer. Yuganskneftegaz in the 1980s had the reputation of being the best managed of the West Siberian oil companies, but like the others, it had suffered from the pressures placed on it by Moscow as oil production faltered after 1985. One manager after another had come and gone, and the company had begun to drift.[111] In 1988, senior management positions having been made elective, Muravlenko was elected general director of Yuganskneftegaz, thanks in no small part to his genial personality and his famous name.[112]

Unlike Bogdanov and Alekperov, Muravlenko had not had to rise with his fists and his wits. People who dealt with Muravlenko in later years described him as a courtly gentleman, a perfect hunting companion, but not an incisive leader or brilliant decision maker. He was liked but not feared. And although he was a West Siberian by upbringing, as a recent arrival in Yugansk he did not command the deep loyalty and obedience that Bogdanov did in Surgutneft-egaz. Finally, despite his name, he lacked high-level connections in the new post-Soviet politics of the capital, except for a network of his father's former colleagues in the oil establishment. These features made Muravlenko a much weaker leader than either Bogdanov or Alekperov.

In addition, Muravlenko had a tougher hand to play, as a result of the way Yukos was put together. Ironically, this was partly a consequence of Muravlenko's own earlier actions. Between 1988 and 1991, he had been one of the most secession-minded of all the West Siberian oil generals, but he had soon faced rebellion from the NGDUs beneath him. (One of them, Yugraneft, made off with the southern portion of a giant prospect called Priobskoe, Yuganskneftegaz's crown jewel.[113]) The alarmed Muravlenko saw salvation in Alekperov's model of an integrated oil company, and following Alekperov's example, in 1991 Muravlenko set about creating his own counterpart to LUKoil.

In Soviet times, Yugansk had sent its crude for refining to Samara Province, in the Volga Basin of central Russia,[114] and that is where Muravlenko turned in his search for a downstream partner. He began talks with the local head of the Samara refining sector, Vladimir Zenkin, and soon reached agreement on a voluntary partnership. (The name Yukos is an acronym, derived from a combination of Yuganskneftegaz and Kuibyshevnefteorgsintez, the Soviet-era name of the Samara refinery group.) On the face of it, it seemed a good match, and on paper it gave Yukos a reasonably good balance of upstream production and downstream refining capacity.[115] What Muravlenko could not know was that Zenkin had already lost control. As we shall see, the Samara refineries proved to be an unruly partner and a constant source of headaches for Muravlenko.

But Muravlenko's creation had other liabilities as well, mostly self-inflicted. First, he lacked a strong financial team with a clear strategy for managing the privatization of Yukos and consolidating power around a strong corporate center. Instead of LUKoil's military team of Fedun and Tsvetkov, or the relentlessly disciplined Ol'shanova of Surgutneftegaz, Muravlenko oscillated among several different financial counselors, none of them, as it turned out, of adequate caliber. There was no single voice and no single policy.

As a result, unlike LUKoil and Surgutneftegaz, Yukos never developed a coherent policy for consolidating the company's oil and cash flows or centralizing ownership via share swaps. Yukos never developed a counterpart to FK-LUKoil and systematically failed to collect revenues from its refineries and downstream distributors, and it was unable to gain control over its upstream revenues either.

One defeat led to another, in a chain of reverses. Still hoping to gain control over his subsidiaries, Muravlenko kept postponing the decision to issue shares in the parent major. This had two results. Unlike LUKoil, with its convertible bonds, Yukos did not develop a coherent policy for selling Yukos shares to foreign investors, which would have brought in badly needed investment capital.

But more serious, by the second half of 1995, when the Russian oligarchs and the government developed the shares-for-loans scheme, 78 percent of Yukos shares were still in state hands and were thus sitting ducks for the shares-for-loans handover. Like a chess player with a losing position, as Muravlenko's control over his company weakened, he was increasingly left with no good moves, save that of surrender.

Problems Upstream

Muravlenko's problems began with his own upstream property, Yuganskneft-egaz. From one of the leading ob"edineniia in Soviet times, Yuganskneftegaz went into one of the worst declines in the industry.[116] In the general epidemic of idle wells that gripped the Russian oilfields, Yuganskneftegaz was practically a terminal case: Whereas for the industry as a whole roughly one-fifth of all wells were out of service—broken or simply shut in— at Yuganskneftegaz the share of idle wells ballooned to one-third by 1994 and peaked at 46 percent in January 1996, the highest of any company.[117] Instead, the local management of Yuganskneftegaz sought to keep its labor force employed in the traditional way, by maintaining high levels of infill drilling and new-well development, even though that activity produced little additional oil.[118] Muravlenko and Yukos's corporate headquarters struggled without success to gain control.[119] Vladimir Guliaev, who had been elected to succeed Muravlenko as general director, set his own course and disregarded orders. It was only at the end of 1995, when it was already apparent that Yukos was changing hands, that Muravlenko was able to fire Guliaev and replace Yuganskneftegaz's management.[120] But by then it was too late: Muravlenko's chapter as head of Yukos was about to end.

A key part of the problem was that most of the company's export and cash flows were bypassing Muravlenko and Yukos. Yuganskneftegaz had its own bank and handled its own exports, particularly the lucrative revenues from its principal joint venture, Yuganskfracmaster.[121] In 1992–1995 more than half of the crude produced by Yuganskneftegaz was being sold outside Yukos, to various traders who in turn marketed the crude to refiners and exporters outside the Yukos network. As a result, the company's downstream units were starved for crude and had no incentive to cooperate with the upstream.[122] Meanwhile, two-thirds of Yuganskneftegaz's crude output was not being paid for, and the company's losses for 1995 alone ran into the hundreds of millions of dollars.[123] The company, in turn, was not paying its suppliers, its workers, or the government. By the second half of 1995, Yuganskneftegaz was the second largest tax debtor in Russia.[124]

Rebellious Samara

Nominally, Yukos owned majority stakes in the three refineries that had been assigned to it, but here Muravlenko faced his greatest problem, because the refineries were in open rebellion against him.

The downstream part of Yukos consisted of three refineries in Samara Province, located along the Volga River in central Russia. The largest and oldest of the three, the Novokuibyshev refinery, had begun exporting diesel and heavy fuel oil on its own in the final Gorbachev years. In 1991 the refinery director, Vladimir Zenkin, formed a joint venture with a group of Russian traders based in Belgium, who called themselves "Petroplast." It was a maneuver typical of the times, Russians partnering with Russians masquerading as Westerners in a joint venture. But at the beginning of 1992, a Moscow-based gangster, Vladimir Misiurin, muscled into Petroplast, backed by toughs from his home town of Novokuznetsk, where Misiurin had once been a taxi driver.[125] In April 1992 Petroplast was merged into a larger entity called Nefsam, in which Zenkin was a shareholder but which was actually controlled by Misiurin and a group of fellow gangsters.

Misiurin's arrival set off a long and bloody battle for control of the Samara refineries' export revenues, which ran from 1992 to 1997 and claimed over fifty lives.[126] Zenkin, facing acute danger, was only too glad when Sergei Muravlenko approached him in 1992 to join Yukos. By this time Zenkin was nominally in charge of all three Samara refineries, and he agreed to merge them into the newly created major; in exchange Muravlenko made him a vice president of Yukos. By early 1993 the two men were collaborating to consolidate the refinery's cash flows within the new organization. But this put Zenkin in direct conflict with Misiurin, and Yukos was unable to protect him. In October 1993 Zenkin was knifed to death in front of his house in Samara.[127]

Zenkin's successor as director of the Novokuibyshev refinery was a two-fisted individual named Viktor Tarkhov. The good news, from Muravlenko's perspective, was that Tarkhov had survival skills. Where both of his predecessors had been murdered,[128] Tarkhov somehow managed to live through all the wars that followed (subsequently, in another life, he became mayor of the city of Samara).[129] But he was a prickly customer, determined to preserve his independence. When he learned that under the terms of Yeltsin's November 1992 decree he was expected to surrender a controlling share of his company to the new major headed by an upstream oil general, Tarkhov balked.[130] In the fall of 1993, shortly after the presidential decree creating Yukos, he led his refinery workers in voting against joining the new holding company. Only after the Supreme Court had invalidated their vote was Novokuibyshev finally corralled into Yukos.

But once inside the company Tarkhov was just as unruly. Whereas Yukos's integration plan called for the Samara refineries to take the company's crude and turn it over to Yukos's distributors, Tarkhov refused, on the not unreasonable grounds that the distributors did not pay their bills. Instead he accepted crude from anyone who would pay a fee up front (this arrangement was called a "tolling contract").[131] Since the deeply indebted upstream producers often could not pay the tolling fees, that meant that much of the oil that Tarkhov refined came from "commercial structures" that acquired it by "informal" channels upstream—part of the parallel cash flow described in the last chapter. Much of the cash flow, in other words, was bypassing Yukos.

When Zenkin was murdered in the fall of 1993, Tarkhov took his place as Yukos vice president, and by 1996 he had moved to Moscow as senior vice president for all of Yukos's refining and marketing (a move to which he may have owed his survival).[132] Evidently by this time he had made some sort of peace with Muravlenko, but despite this Yukos was no closer to controlling the cash flows from the Samara refineries. Take exports, which were the lifeblood of the oil companies in those years: in those years a large proportion of Yukos's total export revenues came from refined products. But practically none of the refined-product revenues went into Yukos's corporate coffers; instead, they flowed to the Samara refineries and their local shareholders, to the province government of Samara, and to Misiurin the gangster and his pals.

Misiurin, meanwhile, had grown into one of the first of the new Russian cash-only multimillionaires, trading oil and metals out of Odessa and dabbling in oil in Venezuela and multiple businesses all over the world. He moved to Belgium and tried to run Nefsam by remote control. But he soon fell out with his partners back in Russia, and there followed a fresh round of warfare.[133] Finally, in December 1994, Misiurin's time ran out; in front of his mansion in the posh Brussels suburb of Uccle, he was gunned down by "unknown assailants," who left only the customary calling card of Russian professional *killery*, the murder weapon, carefully placed on the dead body.[134]

The saga of Nefsam finally ended in 1997, when Misiurin's former partner, Igor Legotskii, who had been strongly suspected of arranging Misiurin's murder and had taken over the business after his death, was himself killed on a Moscow street.

The Necessary Foreign Evil

Oilmen are optimists by nature—they have to be, to play dice with geology—and Muravlenko, despite Yukos's mounting troubles, always believed something would turn up to save the company. That something was a prospect called Priobskoe. Priobskoe was a very large field, with estimated reserves of over 700 million tons (5 billion barrels), but it was a tricky play. Its name, "the field by the Ob' River," sounded deceptively bucolic; in actuality it lay right beneath the riverbed, which turned into a pileup of icebergs in the spring and a swampy lake in the summer and fall. The reservoir itself lay deeper than the conventional sands of West Siberia, in irregular landslides that geologists call "turbidites," unpredictable gravelly structures that Soviet oilmen had shied away from in the 1970s and 1980s. Yet for Muravlenko Priobskoe was the future of the company. He expected it would ultimately increase production at Yugansneftegaz by 40 percent, and the revenues from it would drive the growth of Yukos's entire upstream.[135]

The scale and complexity of Priobskoe surpassed the means and capabilities of Russian oilmen in the early 1990s. An experienced foreign partner seemed essential. Yet Muravlenko was ambivalent in his view of foreign companies. "To me," he said, "working with foreign firms is a necessary evil":

> While they are essential partners, they are potential competitors at the same time. . . . I think it can be dangerous to allow foreign firms to take large positions in the newly emerging Russian oil companies. . . . My preference is to undertake joint projects together, but not to sell large blocks of shares to foreign companies.[136]

This approach suited Amoco, which unlike ARCO in the case of LUKoil had no intention of taking a stake in Yukos, so the two companies concentrated on negotiating a deal for Priobskoe. The project was huge, requiring over $28 billion dollars in capital investment. Such a large venture seemed too risky under the ever-changing Russian tax laws, and Amoco was willing to go forward only on the basis of a production-sharing agreement (PSA). PSAs were widely used in the international oil business, mainly in countries lacking a modern tax system (which was certainly the case in Russia in the 1990s). But PSAs never caught on in Russia, as we shall see in Chapters 4 and 11. In the end, only three PSAs ever came into being. Many other projects, caught in the endless queue, died waiting. The long wait proved fatal to Amoco's plans for Priobskoe as well, and for Muravlenko's hopes. By the time Amoco and Yukos finalized their partnership, Muravlenko had lost control of Yukos.

In retrospect, the Priobskoe project symbolized everything that was wrong with Muravlenko's approach to managing Yukos. It was a very long-term project—it was estimated that it would reach its planned peak output of 20 million tons per year only sixteen years after development began. In contrast to LUKoil, whose sale of convertible bonds to foreign investors gave it ready cash right away, Priobskoe for the first several years would only recover its costs; "profit oil" would come afterward. But in the meantime, Muravlenko and Yukos were bleeding money, and the government and the company's creditors were losing patience. Muravlenko's focus on Priobskoe was like sitting on the bridge of the *Titanic* designing the next-generation ice-proof hull even as the seawater poured in below.

The Last Act

By 1994 Muravlenko was having so much difficulty gaining even nominal control over his subsidiaries that he turned to the federal government for help. (At that point the federal government still owned 93 percent of the shares of Yukos.) Petr Mostovoi, by then head of the Federal Bankruptcy Administration, issued a directive to the state's representative on the Yukos board demanding that the parent company hold its subsidiaries to stricter account and make them pay their back debts. The directive issued by the state's representatives transferred authority for trading crude and products directly to the holding company and authorized the holding company to dismiss the directors of subsidiaries that did not comply. It also banned the sale of crude and products without prepayment.[137]

But this protocol was bound to be a dead letter, since it was recognized by all that the state's representatives were hardly more, in the words of an official of the State Antimonopoly Committee, than "wedding generals" (*svadebnye generaly*—the picturesque Russian expression for "figurehead"). By the beginning of 1995 Yukos's weakness in enforcing payments from its subsidiaries and traders had become a byword. In January 1995 the World Bank canceled a planned loan to Yukos to finance the development of Priobskoe.

By the spring of 1995 Muravlenko was so weakened that he even faced demands from the province government of Samara and its assertive governor, Konstantin Titov, to transfer the headquarters of the entire company to the Volga town.[138] As a last-ditch compromise, he resigned himself to a sort of second-best, an integrated subcompany within Yukos, based on Samara alone, to be called "Yukos-Samara." It would include as its components a local crude producer, Samaraneftegaz, and the three Samara refineries. Once that company was set up, Muravlenko hoped he could proceed with a share swap between the Yukos holding and the Samara entity.

But time was running out.[139] Throughout the summer and fall of 1995, Mikhail Khodorkovsky and his partners at Menatep were maneuvering to prepare the way for a takeover of Yukos. Potential rival bidders, including foreign ones, were warned off. The only significant threat was a last-minute challenge from a troika of Russian banks, which attempted to derail the Yukos auction by claiming in the media that it was "ill-prepared and questionably organized" and that Menatep was being unfairly favored by the Kremlin. Both charges were undoubtedly true, as the troika was well aware, since the challengers included some of those who had planned the loans-for-shares operation in the first place. But Chubais was determined to push the auction through on schedule, and he had decided long before who the winner was going to be; according to Mikhail Fridman, whose Alfa Bank was one of the challengers, tax inspectors began circling around his bank in the days before the auction, a clear message from the Kremlin not to interfere. On the day of the auction, December 8, 1995, the challengers were excluded. Khodorkovsky, acting through a front company called "Laguna," acquired the state's stake of 78 percent of Yukos for a total of $303.125 million.[140] Although the Yukos shares did not officially become Menatep's property until the following year, by the end of 1995 Khodorkovsky effectively owned the company. But would he be able to run it any better than Muravlenko had?

Khodorkovsky Takes Over

Mikhail Khodorkovsky knew practically nothing about oil when he took over Yukos in late 1995. The oil establishment took one look at the young man with the raffish moustache and aviator glasses, with his signature leather jacket, turtleneck sweater, and blue jeans, and dismissed him as a brash go-go Moscow kid whom they could easily manipulate. The ever-sardonic Russian press contrasted Khodorkovsky unfavorably with LUKoil's Vagit Alekperov and gave him very low odds of penetrating the closed world of the Russian neftianka (or as U.S. oilmen call their own world, "the oilpatch"). As one Russian reporter wrote:

> The oilworkers accord respect only to their own oil generals, men who rose from the oilwell. Outsiders [chuzhaki] who come into the company are viewed with suspicion and mistrust. One has only to recall the fate of the former energy minister Vladimir Lopukhin, who was rejected by the "generals" and lasted in his job only five months.[141]

But Khodorkovsky knew about money—and about survival.[142] As a student at the Mendeleev Institute of Chemistry in Moscow, he had shown an unusual talent for working the system but above all for finding its loopholes, particularly by attracting influential patrons. As president of the Komsomol youth organization at Mendeleev—the junior version of the Communist Party—Khodorkovsky parlayed his Komsomol connections into a thriving kooperativ, offering "consulting services" to factories and research laboratories.[143] Just what those services consisted of remains obscure, but they initially revolved around trading computers and turning the non-cash state accounts of his customers into usable cash. His business thrived, and with a small group of friends—notably a young computer programmer named Leonid Nevzlin, who became his principal partner and ally—he founded Menatep Bank in the late 1980s. Together they grew rich and then much richer, multiplying their stake with each turn of the wheel of fortune, speculating on the meltdown of the ruble and the near hyperinflation of the early 1990s. As Menatep grew and matured, it began attracting government accounts, acting as an "authorized bank" for state tax and customs revenues. By the mid-1990s, on the eve of their takeover of Yukos, Khodorkovsky and Menatep were the largest holders of Russian government funds, including those of the Ministry of Finance.

It was all highly profitable—and highly dangerous. As the Russian bankers' fortunes grew, so did their death rate, as organized crime tried to muscle into the banking business. In the spring of 1993, when I first visited Khodorkovsky, Menatep was quartered in a converted apartment building in southwest Moscow. Security was tight, but it still had an amateurish air. Guards dressed in scruffy-looking military camouflage suits and seated at worn desks checked visitors' documents in the entryway but glanced only perfunctorily at briefcases and bags—nothing compared with the elaborate high-tech security apparatus at the entrance to Yukos's corporate headquarters a decade later. But it worked: unlike smaller and less fortunate banks, Menatep did not lose a single senior executive in the early 1990s.

Yet as Menatep grew, Khodorkovsky needed more elaborate security, less for self-defense than to take control of Menatep's expanding empire of industrial assets. In early 1993 Leonid Nevzlin hired a senior officer of Moscow's Administration for Combat against Economic Crime (better known to cops and robbers alike as UBEP: *Upravlenie po bor'be s ekonomicheskimi prestupleniiami*), Colonel Mikhail Shestopalov.[144] Shestopalov, reporting to Nevzlin, supplied the muscle behind what soon turned into a grim battle to take over the company's oil and cash flows.[145]

The new management's first task was to understand what was going on. In April 1996 Khodorkovsky named himself first vice president of Yukos and brought in eight new vice presidents from Menatep to report to him on the company's refining and fuel distribution operations, chemicals and petrochemicals, investment, finance, and exports—in short, the most vital oil and cash flows.[146] To pore over Yukos's books he ordered over a hundred senior bankers from Menatep to transfer over, accompanied by their staffs. His approach was typically blunt:

> Two and a half thousand people work at Menatep. When I needed people for Yukos . . . I just called my division heads together and I said, "OK, privatization's over now, I'm probably going to lay you off. But you have a last chance—you can go work at Yukos." I'll shake the tree at the bank another couple of times and the financial team at Yukos will be complete.[147]

At first he concentrated on the company's downstream cash flow, perhaps because that was where the hemorrhage was most severe and also because it was more familiar to him than the upstream.[148] Within weeks he had begun sizing up the massive scale of the losses:

> For Yukos as a whole unknown losses of refined products amount to about 20%. Just where they are going I can't say today, but for certain I soon will. We have the appropriate services working. . . . By theft I don't just mean theft directly inside the company, such as when someone is selling off refined products "on the left." Those are small losses. The biggest theft is from receivables, when fuel is delivered but not paid for.[149]

To track the leakage Khodorkovsky, with Nevzlin's help, set up a centralized security apparatus that reached down into every office of the company. Up to that time security had been the responsibility of each business unit, and the result was a chaotic structure in which the various services got in each other's way.[150] Under the new structure, in each of the fuel distribution divisions, which Khodorkovsky considered to be the major sources of leakage, five-man teams, drawn from former KGB and MVD officers (the Soviet-era secret and uniformed police, respectively), watched over the oil flow.[151] They reported to Nezvlin at Rosprom, not to Yukos. This understandably did not go down well with the old-time oil managers, who complained that Yukos had been taken over by a dictatorship staffed by *gebeshniki*—KGB officers.[152] But Khodorkovsky and Nevzlin were determined to break the local networks of influence, through which oil leaked not only to "commercial structures" but also to local politicians who demanded free fuel for their districts. One senior Yukos executive criticized these "remnants of socialist consciousness," which caused managers to transfer fuel without payment "at the first whistle of the local authorities."[153] As an illustration he related how the governor of Ul'ianovsk Province, a largely agricultural province in Yukos's assigned market area, had refused to make any down payment for Yukos's fuel deliveries to the local farms (a government regulation of the time mandated a 10 percent prepayment) and had threatened to send OMON shock police units to liberate fuel from the company's storage tanks, calling Yukos the "bloodsuckers of the working peasantry."[154]

Samara was a special problem, because all three of Yukos's refineries were clustered there, as well as its second largest crude producer, Samaraneftegaz.[155]

Samara's powerful governor, Konstantin Titov, was alarmed by Menatep's takeover of Yukos. He feared—rightly, as it proved—that Khodorkovsky meant to recentralize the company's revenues around the corporate headquarters in Moscow and that Samara would lose its single most important source of tax revenue. In March 1996 Muravlenko and Khodorkovsky traveled to Samara for negotiations with Titov. They promised him that Yukos would remain a good friend to the province, and they agreed to continue to use a local bank, Solidarnost', as the vehicle for Yukos's tax payments.[156] Yet upon returning to Moscow, Khodorkovsky lost no time in shutting down Samara-Yukos as a quasi-independent subsidiary.[157] As for Samara's Solidarnost' bank, Khodorkovsky hired its president, Leonid Simanovskii, and made him a vice president of Yukos in charge of managing the finances of Yukos's regional subsidiaries, thus turning his inside knowledge and connections into assets for Yukos instead of Titov.[158] This smooth co-optation of regional influentials became a trademark maneuver in Khodorkovsky's dealings with regional leaders over the following years.

Thus within less than a year of Menatep's initial acquisition of Yukos in the shares-for-loan operation, Mikhail Khodorkovsky and his partners had gone a long way toward taking control of Yukos's downstream refining, distribution, and exports, although they admitted that there was still much that escaped them.

The upstream proved tougher to master. Khodorkovsky did not make his first visit to Yuganskneftegaz until a year later, in the spring of 1997. He was greeted with skepticism and suspicion by the oilworkers. Even the general director of Yuganskneftegaz, Vladimir Parasiuk, conceded that "99% of the workers think it's all for show. Only a few believe he actually wants to go deeply into our problems and find out how everything works."[159] In fact, Khodorkovsky's first concern, as usual, was the leakage of money. According to press reports at the time, he discovered that crude oil from Yuganskneftegaz was being sold by over twenty different traders, several of which were connected to gangs in Moscow.[160] But an even more pressing concern to Khodorkovsky was Yuganskneftegaz's "social" payments to the local community, which had cost the company 3.5 trillion rubles (or about $970 million[161]) over the previous four years. Khodorkovsky, who had brought a team of consultants from Arthur Andersen, set about transferring responsibility for local housing, day-care centers, and the like to the local city government. But the city, lacking a tax base, had no money to pay for these services and consequently was totally dependent on handouts from Yukos. The stage was set for a bitter conflict, which exploded the following year.

Nevertheless, by mid-1996 Khodorkovsky's control was sufficient to enable him to proceed with formal unification of the company, exchanging shares in the subsidiaries for shares in Yukos—a final step that Muravlenko had been unable to achieve, owing to the determined resistance of the shareholders of Yukos's subsidiaries, backed by regional authorities and the various "commercial structures" that controlled much of the company's oil. In short, within six months Khodorkovsky and his team achieved what Muravlenko had hardly begun to do after three years.

One of the casualties of the takeover of Yukos by Menatep was the partnership with Amoco at Priobskoe. By early 1996, when the Russian government finally passed a framework law authorizing production-sharing agreements, Amoco and Yukos had created a special operating company, owned 50–50 by the two companies, to which they planned to transfer the license to the field.[162] As late as April 1996 the two companies were exploring transportation routes for exporting oil from Priobskoe and were even talking about jointly producing and marketing refined products.[163]

But at that point Khodorkovsky arrived on the scene. Relations were rocky from the start, and they rapidly grew worse. As one participant recalled, "Misunderstanding turned into mistrust and finally alienation." Khodorkovsky would not agree to Amoco's terms; indeed, from Amoco's perspective, he seemed unwilling to talk seriously at all. "He was working in one cosmos," recalled Amoco's lead manager, "and I was in a totally different one. We just could never get him to come to the bargaining table."[164] Back at Amoco Eurasia's Houston headquarters, the reaction was frustration and rage but also bafflement. As T. Don Stacy, the CEO of Amoco Eurasia, told me in a conversation at the time, "That man Khodorkovsky—his idea of a long-term oil project is three months." In the end, the two companies patched up an agreement, but by then Amoco itself was in the process of being taken over by BP and the joint venture was never implemented.

And what of Muravlenko himself? How did the son of the most famous oil general in West Siberia react to the systematic takeover of his company by the junior bankers from Moscow? At first, Muravlenko appeared to believe that he would remain on top. "Nobody is swallowing anybody, there is a mutual penetration," he told an interviewer in the spring of 1996, even as Menatep's troops were taking charge.[165] He still appeared to see production as central and finances as secondary. "As far as production is concerned," he told an interviewer in June 1996, "that's my prerogative and that of my [Yukos] colleagues. As for financial questions, we of course consult with the leadership of Menatep."

Khodorkovsky and Nevzlin took care to spare Muravlenko's ego. They named him first vice president and chairman of the board of Rosprom, Menatep's holding company for the bank's industrial assets—perhaps to take his mind off oil.[166] But as always in Russia, informal relations are central, and here it was Iurii Golubev, Muravlenko's longtime strategic advisor and friend, who came up with the breakthrough idea. As a senior Yukos executive told the story:

> Relations between Khodorkovsky and Muravlenko were awkward at first—until Golubev organized a hunting trip. Khodorkovsky, who had never been hunting, was totally captivated. In subsequent years, he became a passionate hunter, and from that day on, Khodorkovsky and Muravlenko became fast friends, joined by their common passion for hunting. Over the following decade they went on many hunting trips together, including Asia and Africa.

Khodorkovsky spoke of Muravlenko, at least in public, with outward respect, though tinged with condescension. "We took half a year to wear in, but now I know exactly what to expect from Muravlenko, and Muravlenko knows exactly what to expect from me. We are objectively essential to one another," he told one interviewer, "and that is why the team has worked."[167] Coming from a young man who less than a decade before had been an ordinary student while Muravlenko was one of the famous names of the Soviet oil industry, this statement must have sounded to the ears of veteran oilmen like breathtaking hubris, but it left little doubt who was the dominant partner.

The following year, in early 1997, when Menatep took official ownership of the shares of Yukos it had previously held in trust, Khodorkovsky further tightened his grip over Yukos, edging Muravlenko into an honorific but clearly secondary role.

Thus Yukos passed into the hands of Menatep, a group that had no roots in the culture of the Soviet-era oil industry and who would shortly revolutionize the company. Muravlenko's fellow generals were contemptuous and traced it all to Muravlenko's personal weakness. Years later, Valerii Graifer, who knew the generals well, having personally made the career of most of them, had this comment:

> Why did Sergei Muravlenko lose control to Menatep and Khodorkovsky? He fell into bad company, of people who were psychologically [*nravstvenno*] stronger than he, a wolf pack, people who would stop at nothing. His father, Viktor Ivanovich, would not have lost control of the company. Why, do you know we used to call Viktor Ivanovich "Bat'ka" ["Little Father"]—that's how much authority he had with us. He was the father figure. Seryozha was at opposite poles from his father.[168]

Revealingly, Graifer called Muravlenko by his nickname, "Seryozha"—little Sergei—while referring to his father by his full formal patronymic. In that detail there was a world of difference.

Conclusion

The creation of the new vertically integrated Russian oil companies took the better part of the 1990s and the early 2000s. During that tumultuous period, most of the Soviet-era oil generals—the *neftianiki*—lost out to the new financial oligarchs. The sole exceptions were LUKoil and Surgutneftegaz, which remained under the control of their Soviet-era "red directors."[169] Both Alekperov of LUKoil and Bogdanov of Surgutneftegaz turned out to be strong and resourceful leaders; above all, they were quick to make the transition from producing oil to managing money. They used their leverage over crude oil to gain control of export revenues; fought to collect debts owed to them by refineries and distributors; and deployed their cash to buy vouchers and shares and thus to control the privatization of their own companies and subsidiaries. Failure to control oil and cash flows meant loss of independence and ownership—and this was the ultimate fate of most of the oil generals.

They were joined in defeat by most of the Soviet-era refiners. The refineries were surrounded by forces and players over which they had no control—local politicians, influential consumers, and organized crime—who commandeered their production but did not pay for it. But their greatest weakness was their inability to control the supply of crude oil, on which their operations ultimately depended. In the end, their best hope lay in joining the emerging oil majors. One by one, the refineries were absorbed, and their managers either moved to Moscow to join the new corporate headquarters or left the oil business to become local politicians and businessmen.

There was another group of losers as well—the handful of foreign oilmen who came to Russia at the beginning of the 1990s and formed joint ventures. Yet their fate is an important part of our story. In the next chapter we turn to the experience of the first foreign players.

chapter 4

Worlds in Collision: The Foreigners Arrive in Russia

Early on a winter morning in Calgary in 1995, I joined a planeload of Canadian drillers on their way to north Russia. Our chartered Boeing 737 had never been built to fly so far—its main virtue was that it was cheap—and it made five refueling stops as it lumbered its way across the Canadian north and over Iceland, landing in Murmansk on the Russian Kola Peninsula. There we cleared passport control and customs before flying the last leg to our destination, Usinsk, an isolated oil town in the Russian northwest, where we finally disembarked, twenty-four hours after takeoff. This is the daily life of the itinerant roughnecks and roustabouts, the foot soldiers of the oil business, who like migrating birds fly across half the globe to work their shifts, typically one month on and one month off, in remote places with even remoter languages and customs.

The oil industry in Alberta was still recovering from the oil-price collapse of 1986, and there were plenty of underemployed oilworkers and companies looking for new opportunities. Even before the Iron Curtain came down they had discovered Russia. As early as 1988, as Gorbachev's reforms pried open the closed Soviet world, Western oilmen began arriving, attracted by the prospect of forming joint ventures, which Gorbachev had first authorized in 1987 as a means of attracting foreign technology.[1] To the Albertans northern Russia looked like familiar territory: instead of muskeg the locals called it tundra, but it was the same swampy stuff, the temperature oppressively hot in summer and properly frigid in winter. The Russians played a decent game of ice hockey, held their liquor pretty well by Alberta standards, and the mosquitoes were Canadian size. The Russian oilmen were also, as the Albertans came to recognize, men who knew their oil.

But beneath the apparent similarities lay worlds of difference, and finding common ground would turn out to be far more difficult than either side imagined. This chapter, the first of two on the foreign oil companies in Russia, tells the story of their initial arrival and difficult relations during the years of the

Russian oil industry's decline and gradual stabilization, up to the 1997–1998 crash. What did the foreign oilmen contribute during those years of crisis, and what roles did they play in the rise of the new Russian oil industry?

When they entered Russia, the Western companies embodied, so to speak, modern capitalism in action. They brought with them far more efficient management and advanced technology and radically higher standards of execution, job safety, and environmental protection than anything seen in the Soviet Union. Along with the large international oil companies arrived a phalanx of service companies and equipment suppliers and smaller operators, not to mention law firms, financial advisors, management consultants, and other modern missionaries, who promptly set up shop in Moscow, to the fascinated amazement of the Russians, for whom all of this was wholly new.

Given the importance of oil to the prostrate economy of Russia of the early 1990s and the deep crisis in the Russian oil industry itself, one might have expected the foreign oil companies to carve out major roles, both as partners and as models, in the post-Soviet adaptation and recovery of the oil sector. But except for a handful of exceptions they have not. The same broad observation holds also for the foreign oil companies' larger impact on Russian oil policy and legislation: they have had only minor roles in the key issues that have shaped the Russian oil industry over the last twenty years. For the most part, foreign companies have been bystanders, hardly more than bit players—typically in the roles of pretexts or prizes—in a Russian passion play they could only partly follow and over which they have had hardly any influence. The broad drivers that have shaped the post-Soviet evolution of the oil industry—the cycle of state collapse and recovery, the battle for control of the oil sector and oil rents, and the evolving relationship between the state and the industry—have hardly involved foreign players at all (see Figure 4.1).

On the face of it, this is surprising. After three generations of near complete isolation from the West, Russia had reopened itself to the outside world. Russia's overthrow of the communist system and the end of the Iron Curtain made Russia initially quite receptive to new ideas. Rejoining the global mainstream had a powerful appeal: one of the phrases heard most often from Russians in the 1990s was that Russia would at last become "civilized" *(tsivilizovanno),* a "normal country," by which they meant, among other things, a two-way relationship of exchange and learning.

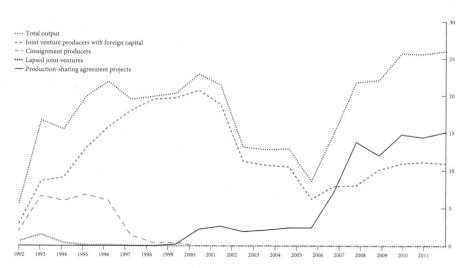

FIGURE 4.1 *Oil production by foreign-owned companies in Russia, 1992–2011, crude oil and condensate production, in millions of metric tons; includes all oil-producing enterprises with large foreign ownership. (Sources: TEK Rossii and Russian Ministry of Energy.)*

This enthusiasm over Russia's new openness implied, at least in principle, that foreign investment and foreign players would be welcome, and indeed this point of view was strongly represented, if not consistently dominant, in the Russian government throughout the 1990s and into the 2000s. If a sector needed capital and technology, the case could be made for a foreign presence. The oil industry clearly qualified, and so long as the market reformers were in positions of influence (that is, intermittently through mid-1998), they favored a strong role for the foreign companies, including operating control and even ownership.

But receptiveness in principle among a handful of reformers was one thing; actual integration into the industry was another. The Russian industry's past as the world's leading oil producer, its homegrown science and technology, its cadre of proud Soviet-era oil generals and hard-bitten oilworkers, made it prickly and defensive, quick to resent any suggestion that it was in any way deficient or backward. Combine that with the oil generals' determination not to lose control, the long history of isolation and the lack of ready precedents for foreign involvement, plus a suspicion of foreigners throughout the oil industry and in the population at large—and it is clear that the very factors that made Russia unique were also bound to make it a uniquely difficult place for the foreign companies to do business.

Two Worlds of Petroleum

For over half a century, the Soviet oil industry had developed in near total isolation from the rest of the world. Western oilmen, who had played the lead roles in the Baku oil industry at the turn of the twentieth century, had left Russia during the Revolution and the Civil War, and few were tempted back by the Soviet government's offers of oil concessions during Lenin's new economic policy in the 1920s.[2] With the beginning of the Soviet Five-Year Plans at the end of the 1920s, the Soviet Union essentially withdrew from the world economy. The Soviet oil industry, as it moved from Baku to the Volga-Urals basin in the 1940s and then to West Siberia in the 1960s, did so largely on the basis of homegrown geology and engineering. Yet the Soviet regime, building on foundations laid in tsarist times, developed a strong scientific and engineering base, and by the late 1970s the Soviets had become the world's largest oil producers, essentially by their own bootstraps. Russia's own resource endowment was so large that the Russians never had to go abroad to look for oil. It was proud of its achievements and, at least until the 1980s, quite content to go its own way.

Yet Soviet oilmen, when they had the opportunity, peered over the Iron Curtain with curiosity. As the Cold War thawed in the 1960s and 1970s, some limited contacts began. There were technical conferences in Moscow. At one point, a consortium of U.S. companies discussed joining cooperative projects with the Soviet government. Most of the contacts, however, consisted of brief and elaborately choreographed visits by high-ranking official delegations. Oil Minister Valentin Shashin, for example, made four trips to the United States and Canada between 1957 and 1974, as well as others to Japan and Western Europe.[3] These were part tourism and part shopping expeditions, sometimes with wives and sometimes not, but always with the inevitable Soviet security in discreet tow. (A favorite parlor game among the Western oilmen was to try to spot the KGB man in the group.) A 1970 photograph shows Shashin and his delegation visiting the Cameron Iron Works in Houston, smiling broadly in Texas-style ten-gallon hats, and later on watching a baseball game at the Houston Astrodome, with puzzled expressions on their faces.

148

The Soviets wanted to see the latest Western developments, such as Prud-hoe Bay in Alaska and the UK Continental Shelf, but they were also interested in specific kinds of equipment that Soviet industry did not produce for itself—for example, blowout preventers, offshore drilling rigs, or Arctic all-terrain vehicles. Occasionally they made large purchases. In the 1970s, major U.S. companies such as Cameron, Dresser, and Baker-Hughes made sales worth tens of millions of dollars, as did some of the large European and Japanese companies.[4] When the Soviets bought something, it was usually for some specific high-priority purpose, and then money was no object. Where the oil industry's domestic suppliers could not provide the necessary quality, a whole plant might be purchased from abroad. One U.S. tool-company executive recalls touring a state-of-the-art Japanese-made factory in Russia, devoted solely to making tool joints, the critical threaded piece that connects sections of drill pipe, without which no deep well is possible.

But these tended to be exceptions, and on the whole the Western companies found the Soviet visitors disappointingly frugal spenders. Yet by the late 1970s and early 1980s there was increasingly frank recognition inside the Soviet Union that the oil industry lacked good-quality and up-to-date equipment.[5] As the law of diminishing returns set in in the Soviet oilfields, and as the Soviets' dependence on oil revenues grew, one might have expected them to buy more from Western equipment makers and service companies. But their purchases remained modest.[6] The same pattern continued into the 1980s, despite the fact that Soviet oil production by then had begun to falter. Most Soviet imports of oilfield equipment until the late 1980s came from inside the Soviet bloc, chiefly Romania, which supplied well over half of the total, mostly basic, low-technology oil tools that did not require spending hard currency.[7] And even though upstream oil investment increased sharply during the second half of the 1980s, as the industry struggled against the oncoming crisis, imports of Western equipment and services remained minuscule.[8] On the eve of the Soviet collapse, the Russian oil industry was more autarkic than ever.

There were many reasons. The abrupt end of détente at the end of the 1970s (following the Soviet invasion of Afghanistan) played a major role. Even during the thaw of the 1970s, Western export controls had limited the kinds of technology the Soviets were allowed to import. Some sensitive items had been permitted, such as the sale of three Cyber supercomputer systems for seismic data processing in the mid-1970s, which apparently came as a godsend to Soviet geologists, who were starved for computer power: one of them was installed in Tiumen, the oil capital of West Siberia, and reportedly played a major role in improving the success rate of Soviet oil and gas exploration.[9] But for the most part, U.S. export controls managed to filter out most of the high-tech types of equipment that could have had military applications, and after the Soviet invasion of Afghanistan in 1979, the U.S. government banned exports of oilfield equipment to the Soviet Union altogether.

There were also domestic obstacles to imports, and in the end these were probably more important than the external controls. The domestic machinery industry vigorously opposed competition from outside. There was also a strong habit of pride within the oil industry itself. But aside from that, the main obstacle was that the oil industry did not control the decision making. The allocation of "hard currency" was a high-stakes game that took place at the level of the USSR Council of Ministers.[10] The oil industry was not at the top of the government's import priorities; the leadership was more concerned to use its export revenues to placate public opinion by importing food and clothing.[11] Until the mid-1980s the politicians were slow to wake up to the urgency of the oil industry's problems. Thus ironically, the oil industry, which generated the bulk of the Soviet Union's hard-currency earnings in the 1970s and 1980s, stood far back in the queue of claimants for the use of them. By the second half of the 1980s, as world oil prices collapsed and Soviet oil revenues along with them, there was little money left to spend on imported oil equipment or services, even though the oil industry was by then in serious trouble.[12] Thus isolation was sustained from both sides, from the West and from inside the Soviet Union, right down to the end of the Soviet era.

The Walls Go Down

Few of the foreigners who started arriving in the early 1990s knew anything at all of the Soviet Union, and they were astonished by what they perceived as the industry's backwardness. In 1992 the U.S. government commissioned a survey of the state of Russian oilfield equipment and services. The consultants, respected specialists in this field, traveled to Russia and interviewed dozens of Russian and foreign oilmen on the ground. Their extensive report provides a comprehensive picture of an industry in disarray.[13]

Throughout virtually the entire spectrum of oil industry operations, the consultants found, the productivity of the Russian industry ran between 10 and 30 percent of Western levels. The gap was sometimes as great as a half century. Western industry veterans sometimes had the impression they had returned to their youth, as they discovered old field-processing vessels originally donated to Russia under the Lend-Lease Agreement of World War II that were still in service. Russian cement trucks were copies of a U.S. design from the mid-1950s. Soviet wire-line services still used analog equipment, whereas their Western counterparts had moved to digital equipment two decades earlier.[14] It was, the report said, like wandering through a historical museum.

There were, to be sure, exceptions. In 1991 the Western operators at the Anglo-Suisse Var'egannefiegaz joint venture pitted one of their best American-made rigs against a Russian contractor with equipment from the leading Russian rig manufacturer, Uralmash. The drill-off lasted nine months and the Russians beat the Americans cold, drilling three wells to the Americans' one:

> The Russian rigs, developed for work in West Siberian swamps, were mounted on rails. They could drill a whole row of wells without being disassembled, punching them out like an assembly line. The American rigs, adapted to work in West Texas, had to be broken down and lifted by crane to drill the next hole. Thanks to the low exchange rate of the ruble and high Russian inflation in the early 1990s, the Russian rig and crew could drill a well for $250,000, as against $1 million for the Western rig.[15]

But such cases were few. The greatest gap was in exploration. The Russian scientific tradition in geology was very strong, but Soviet seismic technology and data processing capability were poor, a direct consequence of the Soviet lag in computer power.[16] As a result, the success rate of Soviet exploration teams, measured as barrels of oil discovered per kilometer of seismic survey, was only about one-fifth of the worldwide average.[17]

More surprisingly, the Soviet lag was also great in the area of well drilling and completion. Drill bits were a case in point:

> In 1991, Hughes Tool Co. compared their top of the line ATM bit against Russian bits in Western Siberia. To drill the 2,000–3,000 meter interval in Siberian wells, 10–11 Russian bits were needed; only one Hughes ATM was

needed. The extra 9–10 trips to swap out bits will double or quadruple the time needed to drill the 1,000 meter interval.[18]

There were similar quality gaps, if not quite so glaring, in most other types of equipment for well completions—muds, cements and cement pumps, downhole pumps, and tubular goods. In addition, everything was in short supply, since most of the Soviet oil tools had come from Azerbaijan, and that source was now disrupted, following the collapse of the USSR.

It wasn't just a question of hardware. The Western oilmen perceived throughout the Russian oil industry a culture of neglect and inefficiency. A striking example was the area of field processing, that is, the stage at which crude oil is gathered and treated to remove natural gas and impurities such as sediments and water before it is put in a pipeline. Field processing involves no high technology but fairly simple assemblies of separation vessels, heaters, and so forth. Yet Soviet operators lost as much as a quarter of the crude oil they produced; vast quantities of water and oil were routinely spilled on the ground; and most of the associated gas was "flared," that is, burned off. Western specialists estimated that the Russians could increase net production by 10–15 percent through simple improvements.[19]

As time went by, thoughtful Westerners observed that the level of scientific and engineering talent among the Russian oilmen was actually very high. For example, well logs were copied by hand with colored pencils, because the Russian operators did not yet have up-to-date color reprographics, but the geoscientists who used them were extremely proficient. But a more common reaction among the newcomers was to dismiss Russia's oil expertise, not understanding that there were specific reasons for the weaknesses they saw. Many foreigners treated Russia as a defeated country, wide open and for sale, virtually a tabula rasa. This attitude, although not universal, was widespread and was understandably galling to the Russians.

The Russians would not have disagreed with the foreigners' criticism of their industry; the Soviet literature had long said many of the same things. But they also understood that much of the gap was a matter of circumstances and incentives. The giant fields of West Siberia lay close to the surface in relatively simple geological formations. The Soviet geologists found nearly all of them with the techniques they possessed at the time (revealingly, only one new giant has been discovered in West Siberia since the end of the 1980s).[20] The Russians had not needed anything more advanced and consequently had gone to no great trouble to develop it.

Much of the inefficiency and waste of the Russian industry was likewise due to the environment it worked in. Leaving one-quarter of oil production on the ground (although losses were not typically that large) was no different from losing one-half of the potato crop to spoilage on the way to market. Yet no one, from ministers to field workers, had any incentive to stem the waste. But if the incentives changed, behavior would surely change as well.

If the Westerners misperceived the Russians, the Russians also misperceived the Westerners. Apart from a handful of senior industry officials, as described earlier, few or none of the local operators had ever been outside the Soviet Union. They had no scorecard by which to judge the foreign players, no way to tell the fly-by-nighters from the genuine article. They imagined that a capitalist businessman, being a capitalist, had the power to make investment decisions on the spot and on his own signature—and indeed some readily fit the Russians' stereotypes of a Western oilman: brash, swashbuckling wildcatters of the old school, prepared to close a deal on a hunch and a prayer after a vodka-sodden fishing trip. But those were exceptions. The Russian oilmen were astonished to discover that the smaller Western companies were cautious in the extreme about incurring costs, and the larger ones were in some ways as bureaucratic as the Russians themselves were. I remember meeting with a frustrated Russian oil official in early 1992, who opened a filing cabinet stuffed with business cards from Western companies. "Look," he exclaimed in exasperation, "hundreds of cards and not a single deal."

As a result, it was difficult for Western and Russian oilmen to find a common language—literally, of course, since both sides relied on interpreters—and although they could converse more or less comfortably about wells and reservoirs, when the talk turned to deals they might as well have come from different planets. Russian oilmen were utterly unaccustomed to thinking of oil in terms of finance and profit. As T. Don Stacy, the head of Amoco Eurasia in the mid-1990s, put it,

The financial piece of the pie was like talking to them in Greek. All they saw was the technical and the bureaucratic. Their rationale was, "We are as good technically as you are, and it's our bureaucracy. All we need is money. Give us the money." And we would say no.[21]

153

Yet as the Soviet Union neared its end and oil production began to falter, the Russian oilmen grew desperate. Consequently, they were prepared to welcome any foreigner who could plausibly promise to increase production, particularly if they brought their own tools and money. They swallowed their pride and accepted what they had to, but they didn't have to like it, and most did not, particularly those who had been at the top of the Soviet industry—the oil generals and the oil establishment in the ministries and the institutes.[22] Thus, from the beginning their feelings about the foreigners' presence were ambivalent, colored by the fact that the foreigners' arrival coincided with national collapse and humiliation. The Russians were caught between conflicting emotions—admiration, suspicion, apprehension—and the higher their rank, the more conflict they felt.

In the Russian government at large, feelings were similarly divided. Only a handful—essentially the small group of market reformers—were committed to foreign investment as a matter of principle, as part of a general opening up of the Russian economy. But the acceptance of foreign investors and players elsewhere in the government was uneven at best, particularly where a strategic resource such as oil was concerned. Russians did not mind if foreigners took over the beer or candy industries, but oil was a different matter. Thus the foreign oilmen coming into Russia were entering an emotional and political minefield.

Yet for a brief time, the Russians' acute need for rapid help outweighed everything else. The result was the joint ventures.

The Brief Flowering of Joint Ventures

Joint ventures, as we saw earlier, had been one of Mikhail Gorbachev's experiments to restart the faltering Soviet economy, by allowing Russian enterprises to partner with foreign companies to attract capital and technology from abroad. They proved an immediate hit. When the Soviet government first authorized joint ventures with foreign companies in the spring of 1987, there was a rush to sign up. By mid-1989 there were already nearly 700 registered. But the oil and gas sector was still off limits at the time, and most of the industrial joint ventures were in chemicals and petrochemicals—sectors that had a long history of relying on imported Western equipment. Initially only two joint ventures were in the oil industry, both of them involving small West German partners.[23]

But by the end of the Soviet Union in December 1991, over 100 joint ventures were being negotiated in the area of oil, of which some seventy were eventually registered, and about forty actually became active. It was a broad effort all across the Russian upstream: the joint ventures represented over sixty foreign companies from seventeen countries (although U.S. and Canadian companies were the most numerous), located at fifty fields with total reserves of around 960 million tons (7 billion barrels).[24] In 1996, their peak year, the joint ventures produced nearly 22 million tons (440,000 barrels per day) of oil, or 7 percent of total Russian production, while their exports peaked two years later, in 1998, at 12.6 million tons (252,000 barrels per day), or 11 percent of total Russian oil exports that year.[25] From that point on, however, their output and exports stagnated. By 2000–2001 the joint ventures were being systematically absorbed by the newly powerful Russian companies, and within a few more years they had nearly all disappeared.

Why did the joint ventures vanish? There is no single answer. To the emerging Russian oil companies, they became competitors for access to the export system. To the Russian oilmen in the field, they were an unpleasant reminder of their own failures—all the more since the Western expatriates often took little trouble to hide their feelings of superiority. The Russian government saw them as noisy claimants for special treatment. But perhaps more than anything else, their time simply passed. They helped to stabilize production at the depths of the post-Soviet depression, but as the Russian economy recovered and the new structure of the Russian oil industry emerged, the joint ventures came to seem an inconvenient anachronism.

But in the early 1990s the joint ventures were the only legal vehicle available for a foreign company wanting to work in Russia. Thus they had a significance that went far beyond their modest size and output. For the Westerners, joint ventures were their first experience on the ground of actual collaboration with the Russian oilmen. Even the international majors, as we shall see, experimented with joint ventures, as one means of learning the territory. For the Russians, joint ventures were their first real exposure to Western ways of producing oil and conducting business, and thus they were the first major vehicles of technology transfer into the Russian oil industry. For the Russian oil generals, in particular, the joint ventures were the first real outlet to the outside world and, not least important, the first conduit by which they were able, more or less legally, to move and store money offshore.

All Shapes and Sizes

There were three kinds of joint ventures in Russia.[26] The earliest, the so-called consignment joint ventures, were essentially service companies, hired mainly to rehabilitate idle or underproducing wells. They applied mostly standard low-technology techniques: repairing or replacing pumps, fishing out abandoned tools or other objects blocking the wellbore, redrilling and recompleting wells. Hydraulic fracturing (universally called "fraccing" in the oil world), which was introduced to Russia by Canadian Fracmasters, produced spectacular results and spread quickly.[27] Fracmasters, in addition to its initial joint venture at Yuganskneftegas, created in 1989, had by 1991 formed three other joint ventures in West Siberia, which specialized in fraccing but also performed a wide range of rehabilitation services.[28] (We return to the fraccing story in the next chapter.)

These service joint ventures invested little except the very basic equipment they employed; their essential contribution was know-how in applying standard techniques familiar to any Alberta or West Texas oilman. But they were very effective in reviving idle wells and increasing well flows quickly. They were paid out of the incremental oil they produced, which they were initially allowed to export freely.

The second kind of joint ventures worked entire fields, which they leased, performing a mixture of rehabilitations and new drilling, sometimes extending to new development at the edges of existing fields. These operations, known as "joint ventures with foreign capital," were likewise credited for the incremental oil they produced, and they were allowed to export it, initially on preferential terms. They tended to be larger than the service joint ventures, they invested more money and equipment, and they typically held the licenses to their fields.

Lastly, about fifteen joint ventures consisted of large projects to develop completely new fields. These were the riskiest joint ventures, since starting from scratch required a major commitment of money and time, only partly offset by the fact that they usually held the licenses to their fields. The most important of these was Polar Lights, a joint venture partnership of Conoco and Komineft in northwestern Russia, which became by far the largest joint venture in terms of capital invested.

Thus joint ventures came in all shapes and sizes, and each one was a pioneer with its own colorful history. Geoilbent, for example, was born of an improbable alliance between a geophysicist from California and a Siberian geologist. Alexander Benton, the Californian, had a classic American story. His parents had fled Russia in World War II and landed in Gilroy, California, the self-proclaimed "garlic capital of the world." Benton worked in a local garlic-processing plant to put himself through college, where he majored in geophysics. Recruited by Amoco, he became one of the early pioneers of "bright spot analysis," a revolutionary technique for detecting oil and gas based on three-dimensional seismic analysis.[29] Striking out on his own, he became the first independent to employ the new technique, which he used to locate untapped oil and gas in depleted fields. In 1988 he formed Benton Oil, and within a short time he gained a reputation as a technically savvy entrepreneur and a man who was not afraid to take risks.[30]

Meanwhile, in the far north of West Siberia, a group of Russian geologists called Purneftegazgeologiia were looking for a Western partner.[31] Their story was typical of the Russian geologists of the late 1980s, who faced disaster as their funding from the state disappeared. They had discovered two promising fields, but they had no money or expertise to develop them, and they were separated from the nearest pipeline by 59 kilometers of virgin tundra. In 1990 Iosif Levinzon, the chief of the geologists, heard about Benton Oil and invited Alexander Benton to come for a visit. Benton, who had never been to Russia but spoke Russian as his mother tongue, traveled 2,000 miles north of Moscow in January 1991, in sixty-degrees-below-zero weather, to meet Levinzon, and the two men struck a deal. Benton would build a pipeline and supply know-how and capital; Purneftegazgeologiia would provide labor and equipment and secure the license to the fields. Geoilbent, then, was a joint venture of the third category, one of the fifteen developing new fields.

It proved to be one of the more successful ones. The local ob"edinenie, Purneftegaz, had little interest in two remote prospects in the far north of its domain and willingly turned over its licenses to the joint venture, while retaining a 33 percent interest. Purneftegazgeologiia held another 33 percent, and Benton 34 percent—an ideal arrangement for him, since no single partner could dictate to the others, and the two Russian players, divided as geologists and oilmen typically were, were unlikely to unite against him. Levinzon was the boss and ran operations, while Benton's people ran the finances. It was an unusually smooth arrangement, and it became smoother still after 1996 when Levinzon left Purneftegazgeologiia to become the deputy governor of the Yamal-Nenetsk okrug but continued to support his brainchild.[32] With $18 million in seed money from Benton, Geoilbent quickly built a connecting pipeline to the nearest trunk line, and by mid-1994 it was shipping large volumes of crude for export.

But Geoilbent was hard-hit by the political currents that soon buffeted all the joint ventures. In 1996, it was slapped with a heavy excise tax and lost its guaranteed export access, and the company began losing money. Then came the 1997 "Asian flu" and the worldwide crash in oil prices the following year. Geoilbent was saved by a timely loan from the European Bank for Reconstruction and Development (EBRD), but help came too late for Alexander Benton, who was ruined by the collapse of oil prices in 1998 and went bankrupt in 1999, resigning as chairman of Benton Oil. In 2005 Geoilbent finally ended its fourteen-year existence as an independent entity when it was sold to LUKoil—ironically, in the same year that it reached its maximum output, finally topping 1 million tons. By the standards of most joint ventures, it had a very good run.

Muskeg Meets Tundra: Komiarcticoil

Another joint venture, a "joint venture with foreign capital," was Komiarcticoil—the one I had flown from Canada to visit. It was a joint venture of Gulf Canada and British Gas with the Russian ob"edinenie Komineft'. It was located at the northern edge of Komineft's domain, near the Pechora River, at a point where it makes a sharp bend on its way to the Arctic Ocean. The Upper Vozei field, where the joint venture worked, had already been developed in Soviet times, but the oil was heavy with paraffin and well flow rates were poor. (Farther north, near the river's estuary, the Soviets had experimented with nuclear explosives to try to crack open the tight rock formations. They succeeded only in fusing the sandstone into glass instead.)

The joint venture began operation in 1991, drilling new wells and refurbishing old ones. Within four years, from late 1991 to 1995, it doubled the average daily well flow (from 60 tons [around 440 barrels] to 130–150 tons [about

950–1,100 barrels]) and delivered a hefty increment of production, nearly all of which was credited to the joint venture as its own "incremental" oil and was therefore eligible for unrestricted export. Thanks to Komineft's close relations with its parent, the government of the Komi Republic, the joint venture enjoyed good political protection and was initially able to realize its export quotas without much difficulty. In short, Komiarcticoil, like Geoilbent, was a relative success story.

Relations between the Canadians and their Russian counterparts in the field were good. The veteran Canadian drilling foreman who took me around the field site and put up good-naturedly with my elementary questions, grumbled about the Russian drillers' seeming inability to drill a straight line but acknowledged that it was largely a result of the Russians' use of the turbodrill, which was fast but wholly unpredictable.[33] The Canadians found they could lessen the damage it did by slowing it down. Through such rough-and-ready adjustments, the Canadians learned to respect the Russian equipment for its ruggedness, while the Russians came to appreciate (if grudgingly) the Albertans' exacting drilling and well-completion standards.

To be sure, there were some sources of friction between the Russians and the Canadians, at Komiarcticoil and other sites, where the Canadians were initially present in large numbers. The Canadians were vastly better paid than the Russians, and as itinerant workers they were housed and fed on a standard that left the Russians gasping. One of the first things Komiarcticoil did was to create a modern base for its offices and sleeping quarters, which though normal by Alberta standards struck Russians as the ultimate in self-indulgent luxury. (Another joint venture, White Nights, was famous for its Portuguese catering service, which flew in hot meals for the foreign oilworkers.) Inevitably, the joint ventures became the target of petty extortions by local authorities, who used their control over local fire and health regulations to extract favors. Yet Komiarcticoil was strongly supported by the government of Komi Republic and on the whole enjoyed good relations with the local community.

The Welcome Mat Frays

Komiarcticoil and Geoilbent were more fortunate than most. Within one or two years of their creation, most of the joint ventures found the welcome mat growing frayed. There were two basic reasons: the joint ventures failed to live up to the Russians' expectations as a source of investment and technology, and the emerging Russian oil companies, which had initially found them useful, began to see them as annoying competitors for access to the increasingly crowded export pipeline system (as explained below). By the second half of the 1990s, most of their initial privileges had eroded away. Once that happened, they were living on borrowed time, their initial reason for existence having disappeared.

To attract foreign investors into the joint ventures, the Soviet government initially offered them a low tax rate and the right to export 100 percent of their production.[34] This appealed to the foreign players but even more to their Russian partners, who at this time (1991–1992) were not yet allowed to export their own production or keep the proceeds. Inevitably, there was a temptation for the Russian companies to abuse what amounted to a loophole, and practically from the first there were accusations that the joint ventures were cheating.

In 1992–1993 I became a frequent visitor to the office of Tamara Trunilina, who kept watch over the joint ventures' exports at the Ministry of Energy. Trunilina was the very image of cultured Russian femininity, courteous to every visitor to her cramped office, where one could always count on a good cup of tea. But when she suspected the joint ventures were engaged in funny business—which she happened to believe was nearly always—the courtly lady became a terror. Along with my cup of tea came a regular earful on the misdeeds of the joint ventures.

For Russian officials like Trunilina, what clinched the case was that the joint ventures' exports were larger than their reported production.[35] The Russian government, not unreasonably, took the view that the joint ventures should be entitled to export privileges only for that portion of extra oil that was directly due to their efforts. But it was tricky business to determine just what the joint ventures could honestly claim as "theirs," especially since the rules of the game varied from one joint venture to another. For example, the previously mentioned White Nights, a joint venture between Anglo-Suisse and Phibro with the Russian company Nizhnevartovskneftegaz, had an agreement that defined its "own" oil on the basis of a projected "natural" decline rate, a highly subjective yardstick and certainly open to "interpretation."[36] In other cases, the joint venture's original agreement entitled it to claim all of its production, and thus the issue was sanctity of contract. Some joint ventures did not actually produce oil at all but only provided services such as well diagnostics,

160

for which they were paid in kind. Did that qualify? Officials like Tamara Trunilina were suspicious.[37]

Yet behind these ambiguities the basic game was clear enough: many Russian partners were using the joint ventures as a convenient means of getting as much oil out of the country as they could, and the Russian bureaucracy, though ultimately helpless to stop them, was determined to make their life as difficult as possible. The result was constant disputes and changes in rules and tax increases, accompanied by steady harassment, which ate into the joint ventures' profits and poisoned the atmosphere on all sides.[38]

The Russians had hoped that joint ventures would attract big players for big projects, thus bringing a badly needed injection of foreign capital, and when they failed to do so the Russians were disappointed. But the larger foreign companies considered the joint ventures too fragile a foundation for large multibillion-dollar projects. As a result, most of them remained small affairs. Only one joint venture moved into virgin territory to develop an entirely new field, the so-called Polar Lights project, in which Conoco invested over $400 million between 1992 and 1995, the largest foreign investment in the Russian oil sector at that time.[39] But Polar Lights was the exception. Phibro invested about $120 million in its project at Nizhnevartovsk, while another small independent, Anderman Smith, put some $86 million into a West Siberian field called Chernogorskoe. The average investment in a joint venture by the Western partner was only about $35 million, and much of that was reinvested profits, which as far as the Russians were concerned did not count.[40] Wherever possible the foreign partners in joint ventures tried to "bootstrap" their operations, that is, to make the joint ventures generate their own investment capital from their profits, thus limiting the Western companies' risk to the original seed capital and credits they had brought in. The cumulative total of foreign direct investment in Russia's oil sector (including credits) stood at only about $1.6 billion by the end of 1995, of which the joint ventures accounted for just under a $1 billion—a disappointing score compared with the needs of the industry.[41] Moreover, after 1995 the flow of new foreign investment and credits declined sharply. That left only the reinvested profits, which to the Russians did not represent net new "outside" capital.

International financial institutions, notably the World Bank and the European Bank for Reconstruction and Development (EBRD), initially played a valuable role in the first half of the 1990s in supplying credits to the Russian oil industry, which helped to finance the joint ventures. In 1993 and 1994 the World Bank approved two major "oil rehabilitation projects," for $610 million and $600 million, respectively, which were intended to help stabilize production from existing fields while providing technical assistance "to transfer international technical, environmental and managerial practice to the operation of oil fields in Western Siberia."[42] The loans encountered problems, however, notably because of the government's insistence that equipment purchased under them was subject to taxation. In addition, the Russian companies were often reluctant to take on debt under the World Bank's strict conditions. As a result, by mid-1996 only a fraction had been disbursed.[43] By that time the bank's initial enthusiasm for oil lending had faded. The Russian government resisted the bank's attempts to use its lending as leverage to promote reforms; and the constant policy changes to which the joint ventures were subjected made further loans seem risky. The last straw was the shares-for-loans auctions of 1996 and the takeover of several of the oil companies by the new oligarchs. A planned third major loan of $500 million, to support Amoco's joint venture with Yukos for the development of the Priobskoe field, was dropped in 1996 when Menatep took over and the joint venture was aborted. From that point on, the World Bank shifted its energy lending to other fuels, particularly coal. The falloff in oil lending by the World Bank in the mid-1990s coincided with a similar decline by other institutional financial institutions and private investors, as Western frustration mounted over Russia's unpredictable tax and export policies.[44]

These two problems fed on each other: the more conflict there was over tax exemptions and export rules, the more the foreign investors held back; and the more they held back, the more frustrated the Russians became. Rightly or wrongly, the joint ventures became objects of suspicion and disappointment, even derision, among Russians, particularly in the Moscow media, the parliament, and the ministries. But what ultimately did them in was something else: their very success in producing more oil. As the joint ventures' production grew, the more they found themselves in competition with the emerging Russian majors—in other words, their own co-owners—for space, that is, for access to scarce export outlets. As we saw in Chapter 2, the loss of the Soviet Union's main export outlets had set up a fierce battle for Russia's remaining pipeline capacity. In the ensuing melee, the joint ventures were the weakest combatants and soon began to be squeezed out.

From 1995 on, the Russian government tightened the terms available to the joint ventures. Whereas initially they had been promised tax breaks and unrestricted exports, after 1995 those privileges were gradually taken away. In 1996 the energy minister of the day, Iurii Shafranik, changed the rules to make the joint ventures' exports count against the exports of the Russian parent company, unless they held their own production licenses. The Russian parents promptly shut off the joint ventures' access to exports, leaving them only with the lower priced and cash-starved domestic market as an outlet for their production. This spelled the end for the service joint ventures, which promptly went out of business. The principal victim was Fracmasters, which was so heavily invested in Russia that the failure of its joint ventures there drove the entire company into bankruptcy back in Alberta.

Most of the other Alberta-based players, such as Gulf Canada, also left Russia at this time. Yet as late as 1998–1999, forty-five joint ventures were still active, producing 20 million tons per year (400,000 barrels per day), about 6.5 percent of total Russian production.[45] They did not last much longer. Over the following five years, most of the remaining joint ventures were absorbed by the Russian majors.

What the Joint Ventures Achieved

A decade later, the joint ventures have been largely forgotten. There have been no retrospectives; no scholar, Western or Russian, has written their history. Old comrades-in-arms stay in touch—the veterans of Komiarcticoil, for example, maintain a website, and others doubtless do so as well. But both Westerners and Russians have tended to write off the joint ventures almost as a quaint historical experiment, part of the naive fizz of the early days of marketization.

Yet the joint ventures were the first real point of contact between the two previously isolated worlds of oil, the first vehicles of mutual discovery and transfer of techniques and know-how.[46] Yet what exactly was transferred? What was the contribution of the joint ventures to the "great reknitting" of the Russian oil industry with the outside world?

It was not state-of-the-art technology. Few if any of the joint ventures in Russia used what would be called "high-tech," in the sense of big innovative techniques at the leading edge of the industry. The advanced technology and engineering deployed by large international exploration and production companies—whether floating drilling platforms or 3-D reservoir models with space-age visuals or high-precision "long reach" horizontal wells—required big projects with big capital budgets, but these did not get under way until the end of the 1990s. Almost all of the joint ventures, as we have seen, were low-budget affairs involving small companies.

Most of the techniques they used were standard in the West.[47] Their most important import—hydraulic fracturing—was new to Russia but not to North America, where it had long been used, especially in the gas industry. But fraccing was the exception. For the most part, the joint ventures used standard equipment and approaches wherever possible, together with Russian tools and crews.[48] The same anxious concern for their bottom line caused the joint ventures to limit their purchases of foreign high-tech services, such as those offered by Schlumberger, Halliburton, and other leading Western providers, whose sales in Russia remained small until late in the decade, when the rise of the new Russian giants and the expanding activity of the Western majors expanded the market for their services.

For this reason, the joint ventures were considered by many Russians to have been a failure, because they did not accomplish the two objectives the Soviet government and the oil industry had originally set for them—to bring in capital and high technology. The joint ventures' stubborn insistence on "bootstrapping" their operations (i.e., funding their growth from their profits instead of new capital) and employing only technologies that were "fit for purpose" was perceived by the Russians as an insult. They accused the Western companies of fobbing off obsolete, second-rate equipment on them—unconscious of the irony that much of that equipment was Russian. But in reality the joint ventures' behavior was the result of the high-risk environment that the Russians themselves had created. The joint ventures failed to invest money and technology because the fiscal regime and the export rules made it impossible for them to do so.

Yet the joint ventures brought something else, which in its way was even more far-reaching. It was a simple but radical change of mindset—that the purpose of producing oil was not to meet a plan target but to make money. That elementary precept drove the Westerners' entire approach to their business, in ways that ran counter to long-established Soviet practices. Whereas it was routine for Soviet drilling crews to spend weeks drilling a well—much of that time spent sitting and waiting for supplies—the Westerners aimed to complete a well in a matter of days. Higher standards of execution meant better yields and lower costs; hence the Westerners' insistence on close tolerances in drilling and completions. Good communications were essential to efficiency, so the Westerners bypassed the traditional Soviet reliance on hardwired phone systems by using satellite-based telephony and data transfer. The same principle governed their choices of field technology. The golden rule was "fit for purpose": the point was not how technologically advanced a tool or technique might be but whether it got the job done profitably. And lastly, the Westerners' entire approach to profit and loss demanded a close tracking of the joint ventures' cash flow, using up-to-date computer-based accounting software, together with incentive systems that rewarded transparency and controlled internal theft and fraud—endemic problems in the early 1990s.

The Russians at first found all this deeply unsettling. The traditional Soviet work culture was all about hierarchy, bargaining, concealment, and the apportionment of blame. Satellite telephony disrupted the traditional command structure in which the *vertushka* on the general director's desk was a symbol of his power. Making profit the sole criterion of performance amounted to shining a raw spotlight on a world of extralegal but long-accepted practices, the whole point of which was to prevent higher-ups from finding out what was going on. The fact that it was foreigners who, with the brashness and self-assurance of conquerors, challenged this familiar world, only made the experience all the more irritating.

Yet in the new post-Soviet world, in which money was once again king, it did not take the Russians long to catch on. They were struck by the sharp differences in work ethic and motivation between the Western oilworkers and their Russian counterparts. "We see how every American specialist is personally incentivized and uses his time valuably," commented the chief engineer of a Russian company that had partnered with Texaco in a joint venture at the Sutormin field in West Siberia, and his comment was typical. "There's a very high degree of performance in all technical operations, and he avoids mistakes as much as possible." The point was also not lost on the emerging new owners of the Russian companies, and once they had consolidated control over their companies, they began applying similar methods.

From their early experience with the joint ventures the Russians also made one more crucial discovery: the Western oilmen were not magicians—or rather, their magic could be learned or hired. "We haven't seen much that was unknown to us," commented the same chief engineer. "We would like to have the same type of equipment, the same chemical agents, then we would be able to compete with our colleagues from the United States."[49] Very quickly, the Russians began using the new techniques and approaches themselves. The Russians also discovered that just about anything they did not have themselves, they could contract out. What they did not need to do was surrender ownership or control.

Thus the joint ventures prepared the way for the next phase of the evolution of the Russian oil industry: the emergence of the privately owned, entrepreneurial oil company, focused on the bottom line and prepared to innovate to make a profit. The joint ventures, in other words, were an important way station to Yukos and Sibneft and the Russian "oil miracle," the topics of the next chapter.

The joint ventures were significant in one last respect. They showed that small companies could make a major contribution to the efficient management of Russia's huge stock of "legacy" fields. In the "Lower 48" of the United States, independent companies account for roughly half of the oil produced, and the methods they use to coax oil out of depleted or secondary fields represent one of the most important areas of application of high technology. The absorption of the joint ventures by the new Russian giants at the beginning of the 2000s marked at the same time the rejection of the Lower 48 model of development of the Russian brownfields. The joint ventures, in retrospect, were the road not taken. A decade later, as the tight-oil boom swept across the United States (discussed in Chapter 12), the Russian bet on big companies and the absorption of the smaller ones came to loom large.

Meanwhile, what of the large international oil companies—the "majors"? While the joint ventures mostly involved smaller Western players, the large companies had not been inactive. But as we shall see, their initial efforts were much less successful. It was only at the beginning of the following decade that the Western majors began to make headway. We now look at the reasons why.

The Majors Move to Center Stage

The international oil companies (IOCs) had begun looking around Russia as early as 1987.[50] Within two or three years, most of the leading companies had formed "Russia teams," opened offices in Moscow, and were actively scouting for projects. But whereas smaller players had focused mainly on local opportunities in established producing areas, the larger companies were after bigger game. Their aim was to locate whole new plays, large strategic prospects that they could add to their portfolio of reserves, diversifying their production and ensuring their future as major players. But to achieve this ambitious goal, the international companies had to learn the unfamiliar Russian terrain. This took time. Even when successful, large-scale projects involving foreign companies in Russia have taken between five and ten years to negotiate, before work on the ground even begins. As a result, while the smaller players were producing oil within a year or two after their arrival, none of the large international companies did so on any meaningful scale until the following decade—except in a handful of cases where they formed a joint venture themselves, usually as a pilot project.[51]

Cautious Survivors

Who were the Western majors? The large IOCs that entered Russia in 1989–1990 were no longer the all-powerful "Seven Sisters" that decades of Soviet propaganda had taught the Russians to expect. The days of the monopoly power of the big U.S.-based companies were long gone. The turbulent 1970s and 1980s had transformed the ways oil was produced and sold in the world economy, with far-reaching consequences for the companies themselves. In the 1970s, the IOCs had been expelled from many of the developing countries that had provided their growth since the end of World War II. By the end of the 1970s over eighteen countries had nationalized their oil production. New oil reserves were becoming expensive and difficult to acquire. Throughout the 1980s the oil companies had faced declining oil prices and margins, which left them with little capital to invest in new exploration and development. Credit was chronically tight, aggravated by the fact that the oil sector was out of favor with investors. Several of the weaker oil companies had gone under, victims of hostile takeovers, and many of the rest were in shaky financial condition. Size seemed the best protection. Some oil companies diversified into other industries or were themselves acquired by non-energy conglomerates, while others grew by taking over smaller rivals.[52] Mobil bought Montgomery Ward. Conoco became part of DuPont. BP went into telecommunications and food. As it turned out, none of these maneuvers were particularly successful, and some were disastrous.

Thus the majors that came to Russia in 1989–1991 were, in a sense, survivors in varying states of health. Over the previous decade they had had to adapt and evolve, and their personnel and culture had changed. A whole generation of experienced workers and technical teams left the industry and never returned, while young people avoided a sector that had come to be viewed as backward—a sunset industry, they thought, doomed to decline. In the boardrooms company executives tailored their strategies to the available means. Instead of investing in new projects, they looked for acquisitions and ways to cut costs. Rather than maintain large permanent staffs, they "downsized" and "out-sourced." The times favored the promotion of financial experts and lawyers instead of explorers or production engineers. Some companies abandoned the time-honored model of the integrated oil company and increasingly acquired crude by trading on commodity exchanges. The joke in the industry, in the early 1990s, was that the international oil company of the future would consist of just one financial guy, sitting alone in a large office with a computer.

The international companies were also becoming a more varied lot. Five out of the Seven Sisters had been U.S. companies (the exceptions being BP and Royal Dutch Shell), but by the late 1980s two new groups had appeared on the international stage. U.S. "near-majors," such as Conoco and Unocal, which had traditionally operated primarily in the Lower 48, sought to offset their shrinking reserve base at home by expanding abroad, where finding costs were half what they were in the United States. They were joined by a handful of state companies, notably Statoil, Eni, Petrobras, and Petronas, the vanguard of an emerging "new wave" of national oil companies that were becoming increasingly entrepreneurial, on their way to becoming private or quasi-private companies in the 1990s. They too were seeking to break out of traditional markets and become more international, but in comparison with the established majors they were still relative beginners.

The other change was technology. The powerful advances in computing, information sciences, imaging, guidance, modeling, and communications that were transforming the world economy in the 1970s and 1980s were also penetrating and revolutionizing the oil industry. But by and large these creative forces originated outside the oil industry, and the majors, in particular, were more the recipients than the originators. There was, in other words, a far-reaching process of technology transfer taking place, in which advances developed outside the oil industry were absorbed and adapted inside. The early career of John Browne, subsequently CEO of BP, illustrates the point. Browne first attracted notice in the early 1970s, when as a young petroleum engineer in Alaska, he took the initiative of applying programming skills he had learned at Cambridge to develop the first computer algorithms and visualization techniques that enabled BP to do computer-based mapping of its oil reservoirs in Alaska. But BP did not yet have computers; Browne had learned programming on his own, almost as a hobby; and his initiative was viewed as exotic in a company that in those days was still highly conservative in its approach to technology.[53]

As time went on, the main vehicle of innovation—and the principal agent of technology transfer—was not the majors themselves but the service industry. The majors, under pressure to cut costs, slashed their own spending on research and development and closed their research centers, and as they downsized, they outsourced (to use the industry's terms). In other words, they increasingly relied on service companies and external consultants for new technology.[54] As a risk-management strategy, this made sense. New technology could pay spectacular dividends, such as the explosion of production in the Overthrust Belt in the western United States in the 1980s, made possible by advances in computer-assisted interpretation of seismic data, in which Amoco's Research Center in Tulsa played a major role. But it could also lead to expensive failures, such as Amoco's unsuccessful investment in injecting carbon dioxide into the older fields of Texas's Permian Basin.[55] By the beginning of the 1990s, in short, the large international companies were no longer the technological leading edge of the oil industry. Instead, they viewed their forte as management, the ability to run large projects efficiently, combining and adapting new technologies in the most cost-effective ways.

The oil-service sector too had gone through wrenching changes. The large oil-tool and engineering companies had been savaged by the price collapse of 1986. Houston in the late 1980s was a place of devastation. As Houstonians grimly joked, "What's the difference between a pigeon and a Texas oilman?" The answer: "The pigeon can still make a deposit on a Mercedes." Many famous names had gone under, absorbed by the handful of survivors. But in the background a new technological revolution was gathering pace, led by smaller high-tech start-ups that were busy translating advances in computer technology, control, imaging, and communications, into new dark digital arts like "3-D seismic" and "measurement while drilling" that enabled operators to visualize an entire field and to locate potential pockets of oil, and then to guide a drill bit unerringly to the target through miles of rock, with the precision of a silk thread running through the eye of a needle. Innovations such as these were rapidly transforming the art of finding and producing oil.

Even more revolutionary changes lay ahead. As the world's remaining conventional reserves became increasingly closed to the majors, the international companies ventured beyond their traditional perimeter into deeper waters, colder climates, and more complex geologies. All this implied higher costs and bigger risks, but the competition for new reserves was relentless.

Against this backdrop, the opening up of Russia looked like a godsend. Suddenly one of the world's largest remaining onshore provinces, one of the last treasure troves of conventional oil, a place that had already been extensively explored and developed, looked to be available for business. For the international companies, eager to add reserves, the appeal was irresistible.

First Contact

Of these changes in the global industry the Russians were only distantly aware. In the early 1990s the first meetings between IOCs and Russian oilmen had something of the feel of two alien races making initial contact. The Russians still thought vaguely of the international oil majors as giants of entrepreneurial capitalism and innovation with unlimited means and power and ambition. They were quick to perceive, however, that there were major differences from one company to another, and particularly in their leaders and culture. Some companies landed in Moscow with armies of accountants and lawyers who spoke an unfamiliar jargon with phrases like "shareholder return," "net present value," "cost stop," and above all, "country risk." To the Russians all this was new.

For the Western IOCs, Russia represented extreme opportunity coupled with extreme risk. The combination was particularly delicate for the weaker second-tier companies. For Amoco, whose reserves had dwindled as the result of a series of unsuccessful exploration ventures, the lure of Russia was powerful, yet the risks seemed overwhelming. "If Amoco could capture only 1 percent of the industry upstream opportunities in Russia by 2000," commented a senior Amoco executive at the time, "we could add new oil reserves equivalent to the company's 1991 total reserves."[56] Yet Amoco's management in Chicago was apprehensive, and Amoco moved more slowly into Russia than did the other IOCs, limiting its outlay (it did not open an office in Moscow until 1992) and constantly searching for strategies to mitigate risk. It had more to lose: one big unsuccessful bet in Russia, and the company's future could be at stake.[57]

Other companies were more venturesome in style, reflecting the charismatic personalities of their leaders. Ken Derr, then CEO of Chevron, had opened the way to the giant Tengiz field by negotiating directly with Gorbachev and then went on make a wager on Tengiz that practically bet the company. Dino Nicandros, CEO of Conoco, and his successor Archie Dunham, were the first Western oilmen to venture a large stake in a greenfield project in Northwest Russia, the Polar Lights project at the Ardalin field. Mark Moody-Stuart, chairman of Shell, saw the former Soviet Union as the all-important "next wedge" of production for the company after Nigeria and began the negotiations that led to Shell's participation in an offshore project on Sakhalin Island. Mike Bowlin of ARCO made the first Western purchase of a large equity stake in one of the new Russian oil companies, LUKoil, when he bought $250 million of LUKoil stock—a daring move at the time. As for Exxon, its leadership was more entrepreneurial than its somewhat conservative reputation, as it proved when it too joined a consortium to explore the Sakhalin offshore.[58]

But Where Is the Money?

As the majors arrived, there was a great flurry of activity as their corporate jets flew in and out and their executives met with government officials and oil generals, signing memoranda of understanding accompanied by press conferences and fanfare. It sounded as though a vast flood of capital was about to roll into Russia. Yet the Russians soon realized that the majors were cautious about spending real money, and they were surprised and disappointed. Since they had only recently been the world's largest producers of oil, the Russians imagined that the majors would rush in and spend freely on exploring and developing large projects. They had viewed themselves as the belles of the ball. So where was the big money?

The explanation was straightforward. As one former Shell executive put it,

The international companies would put 5 or 6 chips on different parts of the table, betting that one might win. But when it came time to commit money, their boards would ask, "How much exposure do we really want in any one country?" They diversified risk globally, putting a cap on the share of their capital employed in any one country. This the Russians did not quite understand or accept.[59]

Yet corporate boards and senior management, and even the most entrepreneurial CEOs, would not sanction multibillion-dollar projects without a clear business plan and a strategy for managing risk. But developing and testing strategies in such a fluid and unfamiliar place took the majors the better part of the first decade. They had three broad decisions to make: what kinds of plays to look for; which partners to work with; and how to manage risk. And once they had arrived at the answers—or at least what they thought were the answers (for Russia was always full of surprises)—they faced the challenge of sitting down and negotiating a viable deal.

Where to Play?

The first major choice in the former Soviet Union was whether to focus on Russia or the newly independent states bordering the basin of the Caspian Sea. At first the Caspian seemed the more uncertain of the two. The onshore plays (such as Tengiz and Karachaganak in Kazakhstan) had been reasonably well explored by Soviet geologists, but they were technically and economically challenging—the oil was deep and sour, the gas far from market. The Caspian offshore was still mostly a question mark. By the late 1980s, Soviet geologists had mapped the basin and identified many promising structures, but most of them remained to be proven. The one well-identified prospect in the South Caspian was the so-called Apsheron Trend, located east of Baku in Azerbaijani waters. BP and Amoco were soon locked in battle for the right to explore and develop it. When the first test wells revealed an abundance of oil in the three main fields in the trend, a perfect string of pearls virtually within sight of Baku, it touched off an oil fever. Dozens of companies from all over the world rushed to the South Caspian to lock up licenses and begin exploring.

Russia was a different story. The principal onshore regions, at least in the western half of the country, had already been well explored. The geology of

West Siberia and the Volga-Urals was well understood (although the potential of deeper formations had not yet been much investigated). In the northwest several major prospects had been identified. The main remaining blank spot on the map was East Siberia, which was still largely unknown, especially the Arctic estuaries of the great East Siberian rivers, the Yenisei and the Lena.

The Russian offshore had not yet been actively investigated, except for the Barents Sea in the northwest and Sakhalin Island north of Japan, where because of their strategic military location Soviet geologists had done some basic mapping. Since they lacked offshore technology of their own, the Soviets had worked with foreign companies—one of the few exceptions to the general pattern of isolation. At Sakhalin, the Soviets had collaborated since 1975 with a Japanese consortium called Sodeco. But it was still the Soviet era, and the collaboration was strictly limited: although the Soviets allowed the use of foreign equipment, they insisted that only Soviet personnel could work on site.[60]

Thus, in contrast to the Caspian, where the prize lay offshore and the main risks were geological, in Russia most of the apparent opportunities were onshore and the risks were primarily political, stemming from the highly unsettled state of the country after the Soviet collapse. The two types of risk called for different approaches: reducing geological risk could only be done by spending money, whereas managing political risk required negotiation and relationship building, which was initially cheaper but took longer. As a result, the lion's share of the foreign oil capital actually invested in the 1990s went to the Caspian, not to Russia.

The next strategic question, assuming one went for Russia, was whether to aim for the established core of the industry, West Siberia and the Volga-Urals, or to focus on the periphery, the as-yet undeveloped provinces of the Russian Far East (including Sakhalin Island), East Siberia, and the Russian northwest, known as the Timan-Pechora. All the larger companies—with the significant exception of BP, as we shall see—ended up placing their bets mainly on the periphery. These were virgin opportunities, tough Arctic frontier plays where the foreign companies could best use their experience from Alaska or the North Sea. They also seemed the easiest for foreigners to penetrate. There were fewer established players (most of the powerful Russian oil generals were concentrated in West Siberia), and local governments in the outlying regions, which had been devastated by the post-Soviet depression and virtually abandoned by the central government in Moscow,[61] appeared to welcome the prospect of foreign investors.

Above all, the periphery appeared to provide the easiest export outlets. Russia had a network of pipelines already in place, but it came with a risk: delivering one's oil into the nearest pipeline automatically meant being hostage to its owner, whether the central government (as in the case of Transneft) or a local Russian oil company (as in the Komi Republic and in much of West Siberia). A foreign company in this situation faced the unpleasant choice of competing with Russian producers for scarce space in the export system or getting trapped in the domestic market. The joint ventures had discovered this the hard way. The larger companies, pondering the lessons, looked for spots on or close to the sea, where they could build their own export terminals served by their own pipelines. This made Sakhalin Island, despite its severe Arctic climate, especially attractive. In West Siberia, there were few prospects with such direct outlets, but the foreign companies focused on those.[62] In the northwest, the foreign companies were drawn to promising prospects in the Nenets okrug bordering on the Barents Sea. In contrast, East Siberia was to be avoided, because, on top of its uncertain geology, it had no pipelines at all or indeed infrastructure of any kind.

Finally, one last strategic choice was whether to focus on oil or gas. This was partly a matter of corporate culture and skills. Shell, the leading global gas specialist at the time, quickly homed in on the potential of liquefied natural gas at Sakhalin. It also saw the promise of linking the gas fields of northern Siberia to its gas business in Europe. Consequently, Shell based much of its Russia strategy on gas, as did the Italian Eni, which was interested in expanding Russian gas exports to the Mediterranean. Most of the other companies concentrated on oil—although the choice of oil versus gas was sometimes more a matter of chance than choice. Exxon, for example, initially saw the Sakhalin offshore as a gas play; it was only as it explored further that it realized that its license area was actually richer in oil.

"In Russia, Good Friends Are Better Than Good Contracts"

An even greater challenge was the choice of a partner. As experienced international players, the foreign majors understood that they could not operate in Russia without friends. But whom to deal with, in a country with no settled authority and an oil industry in upheaval? And whom could one count on, when the Russians themselves had no idea what they owned or what the rules were? In the war of each against all that raged in Russia in the 1990s, the danger was to bet on the wrong side, or even to be seen to be taking sides at all. As the Russian saying goes, "He who interferes in a fight between brothers will be beaten by both, and rightly."

As they looked for political support, the foreign companies faced a difficult choice between Moscow and the regions. Given the weakness of the central state at the time, it was tempting to look to local governments instead. A strong regional governor could be the foreign companies' best friend. Iurii Spiridonov, who had been the top Communist Party official in Komi Republic and moved over smoothly to become governor in 1991, provided essential political backing for Conoco's Polar Lights project throughout the early 1990s. On Sakhalin Island, a reformist governor from Moscow, Valentin Fedorov, provided the initial entrée for the foreign companies, but it was his successor, Igor Farkhutdinov, a charismatic figure who soon dominated the island's politics, who became the chief ally of ExxonMobil at Sakhalin-1 and the Shell-led consortium at Sakhalin-2, until his death in a helicopter accident in 2003. In contrast, where local politics were unsettled or the governor was unsupportive, the lack of political cover at the regional level could cause a project to stall. In Irkutsk Province in East Siberia, for example, BP located a promising gas field that could potentially supply gas to China but found little support from the local elites. The province's economy was dominated at the time by coal and power interests that were suspicious of foreign investors generally and favored a quite unrealistic plan to export coal-generated electricity to China by high-voltage lines.

The central government, riven by rival personalities, interests, and ideologies, was of little help and indeed was more often a problem than a solution. The foreign companies' most likely allies in Moscow were the market reformers, but after mid-1992 the reformers were only occasionally in positions of power, and in any case they were no more than a handful, of whom Anatolii Chubais was the most consistent and effective supporter. Only on a few occasions was the direct intervention of the president or the prime minister decisive. Mikhail Gorbachev had personally opened the way for Chevron at Tengiz, but that was in Soviet times and that project was now in Kazakhstan. President Yeltsin was generally supportive of foreign investment but rarely became personally involved. Prime Minister Viktor Chernomyrdin, who was more directly responsible for relations with the foreign companies, was occasionally helpful, particularly in the framework of his biannual meetings with Vice President Al Gore. One of the few instances in which Chernomyrdin's intervention led directly to a major outcome was in overcoming opposition to the Caspian Pipeline Consortium, a pipeline connecting the Tengiz field in Kazakhstan to the Russian Black Sea export terminal at Novorossiisk. But the edicts of the top leaders were frequently reversed or evaded at lower levels. And in the Duma, nationalist opposition to the foreign companies mounted as the 1990s went on.

The choice of an industry partner was equally fraught. In the early 1990s one could not identify the new players flooding into the oil industry: there was no scorecard, no track record, no credit ratings, no better business bureau. How could one know whom one was dealing with? But one essential rule about doing business in Russia is that it is all about relationships. As the saying goes, "In Russia, good friends are better than good contracts," and the Western companies that did best were those whose top leaders invested the time and interest to travel to Russia and form personal ties with their counterparts. The senior Russian oilmen in the early 1990s were hard-bitten engineers who had come up from the field, and they tended to get on best with people of similar backgrounds. But whether the spark crossed was above all a matter of personality and chemistry. Dino Nicandros, the CEO of Conoco who led his company into Russia, was not a petroleum engineer but an economist who had risen through the planning department and had never worked in an oilfield in his life. Yet he was a charismatic figure and got on well with the Russian oilmen. His successor, Archie Dunham, was similarly successful. Conversely, sometimes the chemistry failed to work. John Browne of BP and Vagit Alekperov of LUKoil famously did not hit it off, despite (or perhaps because of) the technical and managerial brilliance of both men and their common background as petroleum engineers who had risen from the field. It was partly a matter of language. Browne was a master of diplomatic subtlety, which sometimes baffled the Russians. Browne's interpreter struggled valiantly to render Browne's ornate phrases into plainer Russian, but Alekperov sat unmoved. The two men simply did not get along, and BP and LUKoil never did conclude a partnership in Russia.

Yet having a Russian partner was indispensable. Only a Russian partner could fly political cover for the foreign company; only a Russian partner could navigate the uncharted shoals of Russian business culture; and only a Russian partner could handle the bureaucrats, the police, the endless "consultants" offering services that could not be refused, and the mafia. Only one significant Western group chose to go it alone in a major project in Russia—Shell and its Japanese partners Mitsui and Mitsubishi at Sakhalin-2. Perhaps considering that the powerful governor Farkhutdinov was partner enough, the Shell-led consortium went forward alone, while in contrast, ExxonMobil in its Sakhalin-1 project teamed up with Sakhalinmorneftegaz, the local offshore company, which soon became a subsidiary of Rosneft.[63] These early choices proved fateful: a decade later, ExxonMobil has established a far-reaching strategic alliance with Rosneft, while the role of senior shareholder at Sakhalin-2, after a long battle, ended up being taken over by Gazprom.

In retrospect, Shell had no other option, because at the time Sakhalin-2 was formed, there was no plausible partner other than the regional government. In the 1990s Gazprom virtually ignored the eastern half of Russia and the Pacific Basin, and it was only in the following decade that it began reaching out to the east. Yet far from ignoring Gazprom, Shell engaged in lengthy negotiations with the Russian gas giant over the better part of a decade to create a strategic alliance covering a broad range of projects and markets, both east and west. Shell had built a powerful gas market in Europe and was one of the early leaders in the new technology of liquefying natural gas and transporting it by ship. Thus on paper Gazprom looked like an ideal partner, and Gazprom was keenly interested. But in the end the alliance failed to close, partly due to unlucky timing and partly to competing priorities on both sides, but mainly because the two sides tried to do too much at once.[64] The lesson of Shell's experience, broadly matched by that of the other foreign companies, is that successful partnerships in Russia require—as a necessary condition although not necessarily as a sufficient one—concrete projects that build trust and knowledge through actual teamwork, solving problems project by project and achieving real results on the ground. Yet that was precisely the dilemma: putting actual chips on the table meant running the risk of losing them.

Managing "Russia Risk"

In Russia in the 1990s, risk seemed to be everywhere. An epidemic of violent crime swept over Russian cities, as rival gangs fought for control of the assets pried loose from the moribund Soviet state system. Russian businessmen were fair game for extortion and murder, and the police stood by, unable or unwilling to protect them. A contract killer could be hired for $500 or less, and it became a byword that the surest sign of a profitable business was a trail of dead bodies. Yet, paradoxically, in this war foreigners were neutrals, and for them personally Russia was one of the safest places on earth. Unlike in Caracas or Rio de Janeiro, a foreign businessman could walk the streets of any major Russian city without fear of being murdered or kidnapped or even mugged.[65]

But business risk was another matter. Russian courts, boardrooms, and government offices were as much of a no-man's-land as the streets outside, and there foreigners were fair game. Soviet law was clearly inadequate, and Russian law was being invented on the run, especially tax law, which changed every day. Property rights were still an exotic notion—after all, until just the day before, the state had been the only property owner. Foreigners, with their talk of "contract sanctity" and "transparency" seemed naive. It was not that the Russians didn't play by rules; rather, the only rules that had survived the Soviet breakup, more or less, were informal ones of friendship and loyalty among former Soviet-era colleagues, and those did not apply to foreigners.

Searching for the Holy Grail: Production-Sharing Agreements

It was clear that no foreign investment in major projects would go forward (Conoco's Polar Lights was the one exception that proved the rule, and it too had its share of challenges) unless there was a safer legal and fiscal framework than the flimsy structure underpinning the joint ventures. As early as 1991 the foreign companies began urging the Russian government to adopt production-sharing agreements (PSAs) as the basis for large projects.

PSAs are direct contracts between an investor and a host government to share the proceeds of a project, and they are used by the oil industry worldwide (including Russian companies outside Russia). PSAs have three big advantages for the investor: first, they lie outside the host country's regular tax laws and licensing regulations; second, they are tailored individually to each project; and third, they allow the investor to recover costs up front. Once oil begins to flow, the initial production is "cost oil" and goes to the investor; but once costs have been recovered, all remaining production is "profit oil" and is split between the investor and the host. In other words, a PSA creates a customized "ring fence" around a project, which insulates it (at least in principle) from the vagaries of politics and tax policies in the host country. It is thus ideally suited to places with unstable investment regimes and unpredictable or weakly developed tax systems, as in many third-world countries.

But it was precisely the link to "third-world countries" that created a problem in Russia. To Russian ears, PSAs sounded like a scam designed for primitives. "We are not Papua New Guinea" ("My ne Papuasy") was the common indignant reaction, especially among the more nationalist deputies in the Duma. There was widespread suspicion that PSAs were a giveaway to the foreign companies. To the "red-brown" deputies of the left and the far right, who made up the majority in the Duma after 1993, PSAs looked like a humiliating sellout. Vladimir Zhirinovskii, the leader of the quasi-fascist Liberal Democratic Party, drew a sarcastic parallel between the oil industry and the plight of the army: "We don't have money for the army," he quipped. "So let's give the army to NATO, NATO will be able to maintain it."[66]

In reality, a PSA can favor either the host or investor, depending on how much of the costs the investor is allowed to recover and over what period ("cost stop") and what share of the profit oil goes to each ("profit split"). A PSA can specify how much of the oil must be reserved for the host's internal market and what share of labor and equipment must be sourced domestically. In short, whether a PSA favors the host or the foreigner is a matter of the bargaining position and the negotiating skill of each side. But that too was part of the problem. To the Russians' suspicious minds, always prompt to see a plot by the foreigners or corruption among their own, the foreign companies, with their armies of negotiators and lawyers, were bound to have the edge.

It was only with the greatest difficulty, after three years of debate and compromise, that liberals in the government were able to push a PSA law through the Duma, which Yeltsin signed at the end of December 1995. But in Russia a law is only a framework, and the real battle is over the enabling legislation that comes after. Over the following four years, every attempt to pass the enabling legislation either died in committee or was voted down on the floor.

The battle over production sharing turned into the longest running saga in Russian legislative politics in the 1990s. The market liberals broadly supported it, but they were never more than briefly in command, either in the executive branch or in the legislature. Rival ministries jockeyed for control; the parties in the Duma were divided and ambivalent; some regions were in favor, others

179

opposed; and the Russian oil companies blew hot and cold by turns. When all was said and done, production sharing simply lacked a robust base of support. "Bursts of legislative activity in 1995 and 1998 were separated by long periods of inactivity and stalemate," writes a Western authority on Russian legislative politics. "There was never a consistently dominant pro-PSA majority in Russian politics."[67]

The two PSAs on Sakhalin Island—the Exxon-Rosneft alliance at Sakhalin-1 and the Shell-led consortium at Sakhalin-2—plus another small one in Northwest Russia, involving the French company Total—were the exceptions that underscored the general rule. Because they were approved before the framework law on PSA was signed, they have been known ever since as the "grandfathered PSAs." Lucky timing plus strong local support—and no doubt Sakhalin's remoteness from Moscow—enabled the grandfathers to slip through. After a decade and a half of politicking and debate, they are still the only PSAs to have become reality.

In retrospect, one might argue that the IOCs held out too long for PSAs as their chief answer to the problem of managing risk, costing themselves time and position as a result. The IOCs' insistence on PSA was understandable. It would have taken a brave investor indeed to venture billions on the totally unpredictable Russian tax regime such as it was in the 1990s. Yet the failure to find an acceptable basis for large risky investments was the single most direct reason for the IOCs' lack of success in Russia in the 1990s. It was not until 2003 that BP finally broke ranks with the other IOCs and formed a strategic alliance with TNK, not on the basis of a PSA but a joint venture. Others soon followed—ConocoPhillips at South Khylchuiu with LUKoil and Shell at Salym. It was not that the tax regime had improved by then, as we shall see in later chapters, but simply that oil prices had risen far above their levels of the late 1990s, making the potential upside more commensurate with the risk.

But the deeper question really is, why were the Russians unwilling to accept a regime that would have secured technology and capital for large-scale oil projects? In the end, the answer is that there was a fundamental misalignment between what the two sides needed and offered. The Russians needed capital and revenue, but they wanted it fast, and without surrendering either control or pride. The IOCs were prepared to offer capital and ultimately revenue, but unlike the joint ventures they could not deliver results quickly, and they insisted on control. In this respect the contrast between Russia and the

Caspian countries in the 1990s was instructive. The needs of the Caspian countries were greater, while their own capabilities were weaker. Consequently they were prepared to grant the IOCs greater control—and a greater share of the upside. It was not until the following decade that the Caspian countries took steps to change the balance.

The Chess Game for Novyi Port

Cynics say it is no accident that chess is Russia's national sport. Chess, after all, is a zero-sum game—if one side wins, the other must lose. You can be sure there is a plot, and you know the other guy is always out to get you. Whatever the case, chess performs a unique male-bonding function in Russian culture. If two Russian males discover that they are a match for one another over the chessboard, they develop mutual respect and trust, which then carries over to their other dealings. It is a ritual, however, that seldom applies to foreigners.

In the winter of 1992, two men were sitting in a steaming banya in a remote north Siberian settlement. Valerii Remizov, then head of Nadymgazprom and a rising star in the Gazprom hierarchy, was hosting a Western visitor, a young vice president of Amoco. The two had spent long hours negotiating over a promising field called Novyi Port, and now they were taking a break. As they sat together Remizov pulled out a chessboard and said, "You want the right to the Noyvi Port project? I'll play you for it." For Remizov it was no contest: the one thing all Russians know about Americans is that they can't play chess. But unbeknownst to him his visitor was a ranked player in the United States—merely decent by Russian standards, but no patsy. To Remizov's shocked amazement the American beat him.

It was all in fun, of course, but one can imagine that Remizov began to sweat a little more profusely, and not just from the steam. Who would believe, back at Gazprom hadquarters, that Remizov had actually lost to an American? Surely he must have thrown the game. Fortunately, there were no witnesses. Remizov tightened his towel, challenged his guest to a rematch, and over the next two games blew the American off the board. Russian honor, and Novyi Port, were saved.

There were many such stories. For the hundreds of foreign oilmen who roamed all over Russia in the early 1990s, it was a time of discovery and high adventure. Most of them had worked around the world, in Alaska, the North

Sea, Indonesia, the Middle East. But they all agreed that Russia was something altogether different. They were intrigued by the world revealed by the fall of the Iron Curtain, impressed by the skill and resourcefulness of the Russian geologists and petroleum engineers, baffled by the politics and the bizarre business culture, and charmed by the warm hospitality of ordinary people. They were used to exotic places, but they discovered that Russia, like love or malaria, gets into your blood and never quite leaves you. Indeed, many learned Russian, found Russian spouses and founded families, and have never left. Mutual learning ultimately takes place through people working together. During the 1990s, starting from virtually nothing, the number of Westerners with experience in Russia, and Russians with experience with foreign companies, gradually built up.

Yet the interface—the zone of contact between Russians and Westerners—was still limited. The main setting in which Russians and foreigners actually worked together side by side was the joint ventures, and the technologies and know-how that passed between them focused mainly on the rehabilitation of existing wells in legacy fields—as yet small-bore stuff, limited in scale and reach, representing only a small part of the rapidly growing arsenal of experience and knowledge possessed by the global oil industry. Only large projects, mobilizing the full management and technological resources of large companies and teams, would provide the setting in which wholesale integration and learning could take place.

1996–1997: On the Verge of a Breakthrough?

By 1997, the majors had been in Russia for a half-dozen years, and despite variations from company to company, they had all made the same discovery—that there were no magic keys to the kingdom. They had all identified prospective locations and seemingly promising partners, yet none had found the answers to the fundamental problems of Russian risk. The Russian oil generals were unpredictable; oil properties changed hands as the Russian companies warred with each other and with outsiders; and regional governments competed for rights and rents with the center and with their own often rebellious subregions. Joint ventures proved vulnerable; tax legislation changed practically daily; and PSA became an endless quest for the Holy Grail. No strategy was foolproof. The one seeming exception was Sakhalin, where the two "grandfathered" PSAs were proceeding; yet even there progress was difficult. As one rueful company executive summed up the companies' early experiences, "Russia turned out to be more of a minefield than an oilfield."

Yet 1996–1997 brought three events that looked to open up new opportunities for the IOCs. Boris Yeltsin miraculously won the presidential election of 1996 and the market liberals returned to power, while the specter of a communist revanche abruptly disappeared. The shares-for-loans auctions of 1996–1997, though the immediate effect had been unfortunate for Amoco, created a new situation in the oil industry by putting several major oil companies in the hands of new people without traditional ties to the Soviet oil industry. The government announced a new round of privatization auctions for 1998, and this time it promised that foreign investors would be allowed to compete.[68] Lastly, the long decline in oil production bottomed out. By 1997 oil output, having stabilized at roughly half the Soviet peak, began timidly growing again, as the Russian companies overcame the worst effects of the Soviet collapse.[69] By the summer of 1997, a decade after Mikhail Gorbachev had launched Russia down the fateful path of reform and unwittingly started a revolution, Russia looked as though it might be settling down and the oil sector opening up.

But the stabilization proved fleeting. At the end of the year, the world—and Russia—caught the flu.

The "Asian Flu" and the Crash of 1998

The financial crash that began in East Asia in July 1997 with the collapse of the Thai baht and the flight of "hot money" from East Asia spread over the global economy over the next year and a half. It came to be known as the "Asian flu." As it traveled westward it claimed victims worldwide. Foreign capital fled from the so-called emerging markets. Oil prices plummeted. Russia, as a leading oil exporter, was hit especially hard. By the middle of June 1998, Urals crude was trading below $9.00 per barrel—on June 15 it briefly hit a low of $8.23—and over the rest of the year it meandered between $9.00 and $14.00, for an annual average of about $12.00 per barrel.[70] Oil export revenues melted away, from $23.5 billion in 1996 (the high point of the 1990s) to $14.6 billion in 1998.[71] On August 17, 1998, the Russian government, no longer able to finance its massive budget deficits through short-term borrowing, defaulted on its debts and devalued the ruble, and the economy went into a tailspin. The Russian oil companies survived, as other companies did, by stopping all payments—taxes, wages, or payables of any kind—while they hunkered down to wait out the storm.

The crash of 1998 changed the Russian political and economic landscape, in ways that were not apparent at the time. The Russian *kollaps* (as Russians took to calling it, borrowing the English word) and its aftermath, like a bad morning-after hangover, brought a rueful sobering up to the political and business class, a kind of collective staring into the shaving mirror, accompanied by a resolve that things had to change. Ironically, the very fact that the nascent Russian market economy had survived such a bruising finally convinced many Russians that private property and the market had come to stay—something that had been in doubt as recently as the presidential election of 1996, when the communists had seemed about to win. But liberals and conservatives drew different lessons from the experience. For liberals, the state had failed, and the solution was to strengthen the market, to make private property secure, and to increase the attractiveness of the Russian private companies to global investors. For conservatives, the state had indeed failed—but the solution was to make it stronger and more centralized. Thus both of the competing agendas of the next decade stemmed directly from the wreckage of 1998, and so did the inevitability of conflict between them.

But for the moment that conflict still lay far ahead. The immediate consequence of the crash of 1998 was a massive devaluation of the ruble, which restored the profitability of Russian exports. When in the following year the "devaluation dividend" was combined with a turnaround in world oil prices, the result was a massive boost to the Russian oil industry. This set the stage for a sharp recovery of oil production, in what came to be known over the next five years as the Russian "oil miracle."

chapter 5

The Russian "Oil Miracle": 1999–2004

An oilwell is a scientific experiment.

—Joe Mach

"Russia is down the tubes," concluded one guest gloomily, and no one disagreed. It was a despondent group that gazed into their dinner plates on the seventh floor of the State Department, as Secretary of State Madeleine Albright hosted a group of specialists to discuss the state of Russia. The revival of relations with Russia had been one of the major foreign policy projects of the Clinton administration, and now it looked all for nought. On August 17, 1998, the Russian government had defaulted on $40 billion of foreign debt and devalued the ruble fourfold. Overnight the country had been thrown back to the darkest days of the early 1990s. Unemployment and inflation were up sharply. Russia's nascent private sector and middle class looked to have been all but wiped out, and a crowd of Soviet-era officials had returned to power. The country's credit rating was nil as its international reserves of currency and good will hit bottom. The Washington group's dark mood mirrored that of governments and the media around the world. Russia looked headed back into depression and chaos.

Yet remarkably, by year's end the Russian economy had turned around. GDP started growing again in early 1999. By mid-2000, Russia had largely recovered from the post-1998 recession,[1] and soon the recovery accelerated. By the end of 2005, real GDP had grown 58 percent from the trough of 1998. The country's finances, in ruins seven years before, were unrecognizable. The Russian Central Bank held $144 billion in foreign-exchange reserves, the world's fifth largest total, plus a $25 billion "stabilization fund," and the Finance Ministry was busily paying off its foreign debt. Wages and investment were growing strongly. In the space of seven years, Russia had gone from one of the weakest economies in the world to one of the strongest.[2]

What the world's governments and pundits had missed was oil. Yet it is oil, then as now, that makes the weather in the Russian economy.[3] It was declining

185

oil prices, aggravated by the "Asian flu" of 1997, that had catalyzed the Russian financial crash in 1998, and it was rising oil prices that put it afloat again starting in early 1999. Between the low point of 1998 and 2005, the average price of Russia's Urals export blend increased over four times, from about $12 per barrel in 1998 to nearly $51 in 2005. At the same time, the Russian oil companies' own costs, mostly denominated in rubles, were abruptly slashed by three-quarters by the devaluation that followed the crash, which continued to pay dividends, like a fading echo, over the next several years.

The Surprise Turnaround

Overnight the Russian oil industry, thanks to higher oil prices and lower ruble costs, became profitable again, for the first time since the mid-1980s.[4] How would the new owners react? One might have expected them simply to skim the profits—but they did not. Badly frightened by the near meltdown of 1998 but comforted that capitalist Russia had somehow survived it, the new private owners began putting money into their oil companies. It was high time: investment in oil production by 1998 had sunk to only 30 percent of the level of 1990, to about $3 billion. But over the next six years, capital investment tripled, returning to roughly the 1990 level.[5] This was an extremely significant turning point. With real money going into the oilfields for the first time since the late 1980s, oil production turned around nearly instantly, reversing a decade of catastrophic decline.

Over the next six years Russian oil output rose strongly. By the end of 2004, when the explosion of growth slowed, Russia was producing half again as much oil as in 1998 (see Figure 5.1). This was important not just for Russia but also for the world energy economy. Between 1998 and 2004 Russia accounted for nearly half of the world's net growth of oil production.[6] The impact of the Russian oil growth on the world economy was all the greater since Russian domestic oil consumption remained low, and therefore most of the increase was exported. Russian oil exports rose even faster than production, from 163 million tons (3.3 million barrels per day) in 1998 to 300 million tons (6.0 million barrels per day) in 2005.[7] If it had not been for the recovery of Russian production and exports in 1999–2004, world oil prices would have risen much faster and higher—as indeed they did in 2005 and after, when the growth in Russian oil production tapered off.

186

Russia
West Siberia

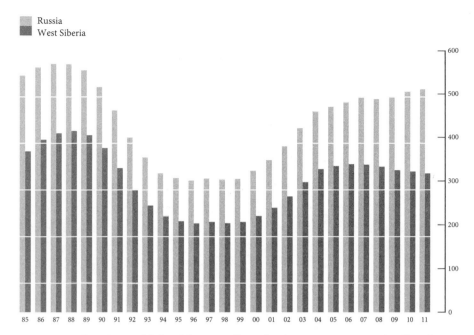

FIGURE 5.1 *Russian and West Siberian oil production, 1985–2011, crude oil and condensate production, in millions of metric tons. (Sources: Russian Statistical Committee and Russian Ministry of Energy.)*

The political consequences of the Russian oil boom were equally far reaching. The Russian oil recovery set the stage for a massive confrontation between the private oil industry and the state. Without the increase in oil revenues that began in 1999, the political stakes would arguably not have been so high, the ambitions of the private sector so great, and the response of the state so determined. It was the oil boom of 1999–2004 that turned the budding oligarchs from mere multimillionaires into multibillionaires and transformed one failed banker, Mikhail Khodorkovsky, into a man so wealthy and powerful that he imagined he could control the state itself. At the same time, it was the oil boom that put a weak and bankrupt central state back afloat and gave Vladimir Putin (who became prime minister in 1999, the year the oil-price recovery began) the resources to rebuild the central state's apparatus of coercion and control.

Two striking numbers give the whole picture: in 1998 total Russian export revenues were only $74.4 billion, of which oil and gas accounted for only $28

187

billion (or 38 percent). By 2005, total exports had swelled to $243.6 billion, of which oil and gas were $143.4 billion (or 59 percent).[8] By this time, oil and gas represented 37 percent of the central government's tax receipts.[9] Without the lever of expanded funds, arguably, Vladimir Putin would not have been able to challenge the power of the regional governors and secure the loyalty of the police and the military as quickly and effectively as he did.[10]

"Scores of Fields Producing More and Hundreds Losing Less"

The abrupt recovery in Russian oil production was due not to new discoveries but to the revival and development of assets inherited from the Soviet era, stimulated by higher oil prices. These were of two main sorts: new fields discovered in Soviet times but never developed, and so-called brownfields, older fields that had already been producing in the Soviet era but had been declining since the end of the 1980s. At the end of the 1990s, the Russian oil companies, by now largely private, began developing the handful of the most promising new fields while massively rehabilitating the old ones. As one leading Western expert put it, "The recovery in Russian production came from scores of fields producing more and hundreds losing less."[11]

The Russian companies concentrated most of their effort on West Siberia, the same region that had powered the growth of Soviet oil production in the 1970s and 1980s. The Russian oil renaissance, therefore, did not require going off to new provinces at the periphery of Russia. The companies mined the Soviet legacy, which lay right at hand, in the middle of the existing infrastructure of West Siberian roads, power lines, and pipelines, in fields already licensed.

In the oil world outside Russia, the margin of known but undeveloped fields has become razor thin. In 1980, over 360 billion barrels of discovered oil lay undeveloped worldwide, two-thirds of it not even covered by a development plan. Now, in the new century, nearly 90 percent of all discovered oil resources are under development, and much of what remains undeveloped consists of difficult or inferior prospects.[12] In other words, the world oil industry depends on constant exploration to replenish the stock of new-field opportunities, but new discoveries are not keeping up with production. Good prospects, once discovered, are developed immediately. The world oil industry is increasingly operating on a "just in time" basis.

Not so in Russia, at least not at the end of the 1990s, when the oil renaissance began. From the Soviet era the Russian oil industry had inherited a vast stock of explored but undeveloped prospects, the legacy of a system in which geologists were paid by the state to discover as much as they could.[13] The development of new fields had virtually stopped in Russia in the 1990s. But at the end of the decade, thanks to the devaluation of 1998 and the rise of oil prices, Russian oil companies finally had the cash and the incentive to turn to their undeveloped stock. They went after the biggest ones first, just as they had in Soviet times (and just as Western oilmen would have done). Just four large fields accounted for over one-quarter of the net growth in Russian crude production in 1999–2004 (or 42.7 million tons [854,000 barrels per day] out of 153.2 million tons [3.1 million barrels per day]). All four were located in West Siberia, and all but the smallest had been discovered in Soviet times.[14]

Several hundred smaller new fields, many of them satellites and "step-outs" located near established fields, added another quarter of the net growth in Russian oil production over the period.[15] Thus, in all, about half of the growth in 1999–2004 came from new fields and satellites, all but a handful in West Siberia.

The Real Miracle: The Revival of the Brownfields

The real achievement was the other half—the growth that came from the revival of older fields.

Much of the operating stock held by the Russian oil industry in the late 1990s consisted of fields that had been badly damaged by Soviet-era practices and had then been allowed to run down in the first half of the 1990s. The symbol of the mismanagement of the West Siberian oilfields in Soviet times, and of the disarray that followed, was the giant Samotlor field. At its peak in the early 1980s, Samotlor was the largest field in Russia and the second largest on the globe. It peaked at 171.8 million tons (3.4 million barrels per day) in 1980,[16] and then collapsed, the victim of badly managed waterflooding and poor well maintenance. By the end of the 1990s Samotlor hit bottom at just over 20 million tons per year (or 400,000 barrels per day).[17]

But Samotlor was only the most spectacular example of the wholesale degradation of the West Siberian brownfield legacy.[18] In the first half of the 1990s, annual decline rates in the older wells of West Siberia ran at more than 20

189

percent per year. Although the worst of the decline was arrested in the mid-1990s, notably by restarting nonoperating wells, between 1995 and 1998 decline rates in the inherited well stock still averaged over 10 percent per year. It would have strained the imagination, at the time of the financial crash of mid-summer 1998, to believe that this sorry collection of tapped-out giants was fated for anything but continued decline.

Yet the brownfield decline was not merely arrested; for a time it was even reversed. Half of the 51 percent net growth in Russian oil production from 1999 to 2004 came from the brownfields. Again the symbol is Samotlor. After bottoming out at 20 million tons (400,000 barrels per day) in 1999, by 2005 production at Samotlor had increased by more than 50 percent.[19] Dozens of older West Siberian fields turned around in the same way.

An oil field is what economists call a "wasting asset." As oil is drawn out of the reservoir rock that holds it, it is not renewed. The natural pressure that drives it up the well soon declines. In a sense, as soon as an oil field is tapped, it loses energy and begins to die, though (because additional wells are drilled) it may take a decade to reach its peak before actually declining. But once it has begun to fall, everything that oilmen do to it amounts to a rearguard action, a steady retreat in the face of inexorable decline.

But the decline can be fast or slow, and for brief periods of time it can even be reversed. Much of the art of the U.S. onshore oil industry in the Lower 48, in places like Texas and Oklahoma and California, consists of coaxing along old wells and old fields, slowing their decline with an ingenious and ever-evolving bag of tricks. In exceptional cases, a technological breakthrough can even bring old fields a second life, as in today's tight-oil boom in the United States. But in the end it is only a reprieve.

Producing the brownfields, in the United States and in much of the rest of the world, is the domain of the service companies and small independents, not the large multinational majors. Collectively the independents account for more than half of U.S. production, and all the U.S. companies, large and small, draw on the innovations of the service sector.

The Soviet oil industry had made little use of these techniques, however, and for good reason. From the late 1960s to the 1980s, Soviet geologists and oil engineers applied all of their energies to opening up the newly discovered bonanza of West Siberia. They were "elephant hunters"—they went after the largest fields first, and after they had bagged those, they moved on to the next largest, prodded by the constant demands of the Communist Party leadership for higher and higher production. They ignored fields that were too hard to produce and formations that were too subtle to identify clearly with the rough-and-ready technology at their disposal. Their field techniques were equally basic. To augment the natural flow of the oil wells, Soviet engineers drilled rows of injection wells and pumped massive amounts of water into the reservoirs to drive the oil forward. By the end of the 1980s, for every ten barrels of liquid that came up from the wells, nearly nine barrels were water. The Soviet oil industry became the largest water company in the world.

This massive mistreatment of the West Siberian oil fields had led Western analysts in the late 1970s to predict an early collapse of Soviet oil production. Those predictions would have come true on schedule, if it had not been for the equally massive injections of capital that the Soviet leadership put into the oil industry during their final decade in power. But the money went to pay for the same methods as before, and the wholesale destruction of the West Siberian oilfields continued, right down to the end of the 1980s, when the Soviet machine could no longer pay the bill. The legacy was an industry that appeared permanently ruined.

But in reality it was a situation tailor-made for the salvaging techniques that had been developed over the decades in West Texas, Oklahoma, and Alberta. In the early 1990s, as we saw in the last chapter, the first Western independents and service companies began arriving in Russia. Some had already taken the plunge even earlier. In the late 1980s an Alberta oilman, Ron Bullen, bet a skeptical Soviet oil ministry official that he could hydrofracture a handful of West Siberian oil wells and multiply production severalfold. His company, Canadian Fracmasters, hit hard by the collapse of world oil prices in 1986, faced bankruptcy. Bullen offered to do the job for free, to show what his equipment could do. The results so impressed the Soviet oilmen that it led to one of the first joint ventures of the Gorbachev era. Over the following years, Canadian Fracmasters fractured hundreds of wells in Yuganskneftegaz, rescuing Bullen and his company from ruin—at least until Iurii Shafranik, by then the Russian energy minister, changed the tax rules in 1996.[20]

Russians maintain that "hydraulic fracturing" was actually pioneered in the Soviet Union, although Kansans will tell you differently.[21] The basic idea is to shoot water-based fluids at high pressure into the oil-bearing rock around a well, cracking the rock and creating long channels through which the oil will flow faster toward the wellbore. These long fractures, which can extend for hundreds of feet into the surrounding reservoir, are kept open by small ceramic beads, called "proppants," that are injected together with the water. As the water is pumped back up out of the well, the beads remain, propping open the fractures.

The first Russian experiments with hydraulic fracturing were conducted in the 1950s. But as so frequently happened in that system, a good idea went undeveloped. The Soviet military had first call on all materials and equipment, and the oil industry was never able to obtain pumps powerful enough to crack the reservoir rock. "When I went to the Soviet Union," recalled Ron Bullen, "They were using 300-horsepower pumpers just like in Kansas in the 1940s, river sand, and water, to fracture their wells."[22] The results weren't very impressive, and the ministry was skeptical. But the Russian oilmen didn't really care. They had their hands full with the new supergiants in West Siberia, and apart from a few experiments in Azerbaijan, hydraulic fracturing was left on the shelf—until it was reintroduced by Western contractors. By the mid-1990s, there were a dozen joint ventures specializing in hydraulic fracturing, producing over 6 million tons of oil (120,000 barrels per day) per year.[23]

But that was only the beginning. By the end of the 1990s the Russians had learned how to do fracs for themselves. Within a short time most of the frac crews and large parts of their kit were Russian.[24] The reintroduction of hydraulic fracturing into Russia is a classic story of "technology transfer," the transfer of new technology and know-how from one country or company to another.

The Subtle Art of Technology Transfer

During the Cold War, the issue of technology transfer was much on Western strategists' minds. The Soviets operated a huge worldwide espionage network to capture and import Western technology, most of it for military applications.[25] But the lesson both sides learned—and this is the universal lesson of technology transfer everywhere—is that acquiring technology is one thing; putting it to work is quite another. An imported technology must take root in the local soil; and if the soil is inhospitable, the foreign technique will fail. The classic story from the Cold War is the fate of the German rocket scientists from Peenemünde who ended up in Soviet *sharagi* (the KGB's prison labs) after World War II: their sophisticated German instruments immediately burned out when connected to the unpredictable Soviet power system.

Broadly, the transfer of a new technology works smoothly if three conditions are met: the receiving side must be motivated to adopt it; the agents of transfer must be live human beings working on location, not inanimate samples or stolen blueprints; and last but not least, a new technology must be adapted to the environment and culture of the receiving side. The result is invariably a hybrid, arrived at through trial and error, a process that can extend over a decade or more but can also be surprisingly rapid if the three conditions are met. If they are not, a new technology, no matter how promising, will be rejected or subverted, or if implemented simply fail. Conversely, once successfully adopted, it may well be taken over and quickly developed further, while its foreign originators are pushed out or bypassed or absorbed. The whole process is typically marked by controversy and conflict, as those who have a stake in the old ways resist the new, until they are won over or swept aside.[26]

This is precisely what happened in the Russian oil industry in the 1990s. When the first Western oilmen rushed into Russia, they expected a bonanza. They confidently expected that Western oilfield technologies would quickly prove their superiority and that the innovations they brought would be welcomed enthusiastically by Russian oilmen, opening up vast vistas of profit and ownership in a previously closed territory.

But as we saw in the last chapter, it all turned out to be much more complex than they had imagined. The experience of a joint venture called White Nights was typical. The Western expatriates arrived with advanced technologies and expensive support systems. They brought with them a new technique called horizontal drilling. When applied to West Siberian sandstones it initially produced phenomenal flows of oil, but within a few days the flow rates mysteriously collapsed, and the chastened Westerners were forced to fall back on humbler but tried-and-true well rehabilitations, using much the same techniques as their Russian counterparts. Horizontal drilling subsequently became one of the leading techniques of oil production in West Siberia, but like hydraulic fracturing it had to be adapted to local conditions. In the meantime, many of those early Westerners came to seem to the Russians like high-cost braggarts. The Westerners have not entirely overcome that early reputation even today.

The Russian oilmen—who until the Soviet collapse had, after all, led the world in oil production and could be forgiven for thinking they knew a thing or two—began to push back. Subversion began at the local level, as Russian field managers began laying traps for their Western colleagues, such as deliberately steering them to areas where waterfloods had saturated the reservoirs with water.[27] Such "swept fields" yielded no oil, even to the most advanced techniques. In parallel, Russian oilmen began copying the Western methods and applying them themselves, except more cheaply and effectively. As early as the mid-1990s, fraccing was rapidly being taken over by Russians. The emerging Russian majors, as they gained strength, began absorbing the joint ventures and packing the expats off home. By the time of the 1998 crash, as we saw in the last chapter, the joint ventures and related forms of in-kind service contracts were on their way out.

One might conclude from this that the first generation of technology transfer largely failed. But in reality it was the indispensable first phase. The Russians observed the mixed successes of the Westerners and began adopting their techniques, blending them with local equipment and know-how. The Westerners who survived in Russia, as well as those who returned later on, also learned to adapt their skills and equipment, along with their attitudes and lifestyles, to Russian conditions. Above all, they learned to form mixed teams and work together with their hosts.

Mining the Soviet legacy, in other words, called for a subtle blend of technological and cultural change, a synthesis of new and old, of homegrown and foreign. The receiving soil was crucial. Just as every oilfield was different, so also every Russian oil town and company had its own history and character, the subtle variations among them initially invisible to the Westerners. This explains why the Russian oil renaissance, when it came at the end of the 1990s, took different forms from company to company, with sharply different results.

The Russian Rainbow: Why Some Companies Did Better Than Others

Nearly all the Russian companies grew strongly in the period 1999–2004. As a group, the ten integrated companies increased their crude oil production by 56 percent. But the differences among them were more significant than the similarities. Two companies, Yukos and Sibneft, led the pack, nearly doubling their output between 1999 and 2004. Surgutneftegaz came close behind, with an increase of over two-thirds. The rest pedaled along in loose formation behind the leaders (see Table 5.1).

TABLE 5.1 Oil production by company, 1995–2011, in millions of metric tons; shading indicates state-owned companies.

	1995	1996	1997	1998	1999	2000	2001	2002	2003	2004	2005	2006	2007	2008	2009	2010	2011
Russian Federation, total	307	301	306	303	305	323	348	380	421	459	470	481	491	488	494	505	511
Rosneft	12	13	13	13	12	13	14	15	19	22	74	82	110	114	106	112	114
LUKoil	58	54	57	57	59	62	72	74	72	84	88	86	91	88	92	90	85
TNK-BP[a]	n.a.	n.a.	n.a.	n.a.	n.a.	n.a.	n.a.	n.a.	n.a.	70	75	84	80	79	80	81	82
Surgutneftegaz	33	33	34	35	36	41	44	49	54	60	64	66	64	62	60	60	61
Gazprom Neft[b]	20	19	18	17	16	17	21	26	31	34	33	44	43	41	39	39	39
Tatneft	25	25	25	24	24	24	25	25	25	25	25	25	26	26	26	26	26
Slavneft	13	13	13	12	12	12	14	15	18	22	24	n.a.	n.a.	n.a.	n.a.	n.a.	n.a.
Bashneft	18	16	15	13	12	12	12	12	12	12	12	12	12	12	12	14	15
Gazprom	9	9	9	9	10	10	10	11	11	12	13	13	13	13	11	14	15
Russneft	n.a.	n.a.	n.a.	n.a.	n.a.	n.a.	n.a.	n.a.	2	7	12	15	14	14	13	13	14
TNK	28	25	24	22	23	29	34	38	43	n.a.	n.a.	n.a.	n.a.	n.a.	n.a.	n.a.	n.a.
Sidanko	18	15	15	16	16	16	16	16	19	n.a.	n.a.	n.a.	n.a.	n.a.	n.a.	n.a.	n.a.
Onako	8	8	8	8	8	8	n.a.	n.a.	n.a.	n.a.	n.a.	n.a.	n.a.	n.a.	n.a.	n.a.	n.a.
Yukos	47	46	47	45	44	50	58	70	81	86	25	22	n.a.	n.a.	n.a.	n.a.	n.a.

SOURCE: Russian Ministry of Energy.

NOTES: Companies are designated as private from the first year when private-sector control of a majority stake in a holding company can be identified for a full year.

n.a.: Not applicable (company not in existence or acquired by other company or companies).

a. Includes production of one-half of Slavneft from 2006.

b. Includes production of Sibneft before 2006 and one-half of Slavneft from 2006.

What accounted for these differences? Except for the two companies in the declining Volga-Urals province (Tatneft and Bashneft), which had been producing for over two generations, the differences in resource base among the companies were not crucial. Sibneft had several good prospects (Sugmut and Sporyshev). Yukos had one attractive new field (Priobskoe) and one giant (Mamontovo) that was in comparatively good shape. LUKoil, Surgutneftegaz, and Slavneft were less favored, but their subsequent performance suggests that these differences were not crucial.

The form of ownership was clearly more important. The privately owned companies as a group increased production by nearly two-thirds (66.9 percent), while the state-owned companies grew by only one-quarter (25.5 percent). But the private companies themselves performed very differently from one another. As we have seen, two sorts of private oil companies emerged from the 1990s: the companies that had been taken over by the post-Soviet financiers in the mid-1990s (Yukos, Sibneft, and TNK); and the companies that were still controlled by Soviet-era oil generals (LUKoil and Surgutneftegaz). (For convenience, I shall call the first group the *finansist* companies and the second group the *neftianik* companies.) As a group, the finansist companies did best, increasing their output of crude oil by over three-quarters between 1999 and 2004, while the neftianik companies grew by barely more than half.

Thus the fact of private ownership, plus the culture and style of the owners, appears to account for most of the differences in performance from company to company. But what did the privately owned companies actually do that made them more successful? For answers we turn first to the two leaders, Yukos and Sibneft.

1998–1999: Yukos Turns the Corner

On the eve of the financial crash of August 1998, despite Khodorkovsky's efforts, Yukos was still in financial trouble. Oil export prices had been dropping steadily since the previous year. By the summer of 1998 they had sunk to between $8 and $10 per barrel, two-thirds of the levels of early 1997.[28] Yukos's own production, which had briefly increased in 1997 after an eight-year decline, sagged again in 1998. And while each barrel fetched less, it cost more. At the beginning of 1998, Yukos's lifting costs were $9.30 per barrel,[29] and although the company was able to cut costs throughout the first half of the year, they were still $7.20 per barrel on the eve of the August 1998 crash.[30]

Khodorkovsky fought back hard. Some of his responses were what any chief executive anywhere in the world would have done: He canceled dividends.[31] He slashed investment by half.[32] He cut back sharply on drilling and new-well completions.[33] He also used "Russian methods": He stopped tax payments.[34] He stiff-armed suppliers. He held off creditors. By paying his subsidiaries ultra-low prices (so-called transfer prices), he concentrated his resources in the holding company where he had better control.

In the midst of all this, the crash of August 17, 1998, came like the crack of doom. It crippled Menatep Bank, Khodorkovsky's main bank asset and the initial source of his fortune,[35] forcing him to fall back on his main oil asset, Yukos. From that point on, willy-nilly, Khodorkovsky was no longer a banker but an oilman. Yet his oil company too was on the verge of bankruptcy. By the fall of 1998, the situation looked desperate.

In retrospect, it was the low point, but no one could have known that at the time. The August crash and the massive devaluation of the ruble that followed abruptly cut the oil companies' ruble costs.[36] By the end of 1998, Yukos's lifting costs had dropped below $5 per barrel,[37] and they kept on falling from there. Export prices did not begin rising again until mid-1999, but the ruble continued to depreciate slowly in real terms for another six months after the crash (and in nominal terms for another three years), generating a continuous "depreciation dividend," since most of the oil companies' costs—labor, local supplies, power, and transportation—were denominated in rubles, while export revenues accrued in dollars.[38] As the gap widened between rising export prices and falling lifting costs, the flow of profits swelled and brought blessed relief. Cautiously, not quite daring to believe that oil export prices would continue to recover, the oil companies began investing to boost production.[39] By the fourth quarter of 1999, Yukos's flow of crude began rising. The "oil miracle" had begun.

But first Khodorkovsky had to survive 1998. Already that spring, he had announced he was cutting the company's wage bill by 30 percent, through a combination of pay cuts, layoffs, and reorganization.[40] His plan was to spin off Yukos's service divisions into separate companies, which would then compete for service contracts with the company's operating divisions. Implicit in the concept was that the new service companies, to cut costs and be competitive, would lay off excess workers—but since they would be technically separate entities, Yukos itself would not be blamed for the layoffs, which were bound to be unpopular in the oil towns. The goal was ambitious: Khodorkovsky aimed to cut employment at Yukos's three main operating divisions (Yugansk, Samara, and Tomsk) from 70,000 to 40,000 by the end of 1998 and ultimately to 25,000.[41]

Laying off oil workers was bound to cause trouble. In the Soviet era the oil industry (defying official policy) had settled hundreds of thousands of oil workers in company towns in the far north of West Siberia, which soon became permanent one-industry cities.[42] In the early 1990s these workers were stranded. In a country with no housing market, with no jobs outside their region and their savings wiped out by the near hyperinflation of 1991–1993, the oilworkers had nowhere to go and no choice but to keep laboring in the oil-fields. They would put up with lower wages—they had little choice—but to fire them was to break the implicit contract that bound them to their towns and their livelihoods.

In late May 1998, well before the August crash, tensions had already reached a peak. Thousands of angry oilworkers and citizens converged on the town center of Nefteiugansk and blockaded a group of Yukos executives, including the chairman of the board, Sergei Muravlenko, who had been attending a Yuganskneftegaz shareholder meeting. For twelve hours the company officers were trapped inside their building, while outside the mayor of Nefteiugansk, Vladimir Petukhov, led a raucous town meeting to protest against Yukos's pay cuts and backlogs in payments to city employees. "The town square was packed," said a Moscow broker who was present at the scene. "They were making very angry speeches against Yukos, protesting a 30 percent salary cut. Neither Surgutneftegaz and LUKoil cut salaries, and these people know that."[43]

Mayor Petukhov had been from the beginning an outspoken opponent of the takeover of Yuganskneftegaz by Menatep. He too was a graduate of "Indus" from the early 1970s and had several of the future oil generals as his classmates, but instead of going into the oilfields he chose to work in one of the local institutes. In 1990 he had started a small private service company, which provided oilfield services to Yuganskneftegaz. He had earlier opposed the absorption of Yuganskneftegaz by the Yukos holding company, calling it "robbery," and when the Menatep group took over Yukos in the "shares-for-loans" deal, Petukhov as early as May 1996 began organizing protest meetings in Nefteiugansk against the policies of the new owners. In October of that year he ran for mayor, winning by a large majority.[44]

From his mayor's office Petukhov continued to attack Yukos as Khodorkovsky and his team tightened their control over the company. In the spring of 1998, as Khodorkovsky fought to cut costs, the conflict sharpened. Petukhov denounced the parent company's resort to transfer pricing, charging that the company had broken a promise to the governor of the Khanty-Mansiisk okrug that it would not do so. He demanded that Yukos restore cuts in tax payments to the city. City employees, he said (including schoolteachers, doctors and nurses, and other key categories), had not been paid since February. This was the background to the June 1998 blockade. Muravlenko and the company executives at the shareholder meeting, in effect being held prisoner by the crowd outside, finally met with the mayor and agreed to transfer 30 million rubles (then about $5 million) to the city government to pay February wages to city employees. That round went to Petukhov, but the outlook was for more escalation. "We will continue until they stop their senseless decision-making and mismanagement," vowed the embattled mayor, and one of his assistants spoke darkly of blocking a key bridge in the region.[45] In mid-June 1998 Petukhov went on a hunger strike and made a series of demands that, if met, effectively would have forced Yukos to abandon its entire financial strategy for its subsidiary.[46]

Later that month Petukhov was gunned down by unknown assailants. From the beginning, there were rumors in the town that the conflict with Yukos had cost the mayor his life. The company issued vigorous denials, but a cloud of suspicion continued to hang over the circumstances of Petukhov's death.[47] The scandal mobilized the local governments and unions—normally passive allies of management—and Yukos was forced to abandon its plans for massive layoffs.

After the crash of August 17, the threat of violence hung everywhere over the West Siberian oilfields. On September 18, organized by a militant new labor union, oil workers went out on strike at Sibneft's Kholmogor field, shutting down fifteen of the field's highest-producing wells. Ominously, the local police supported the strikers against the company's security force, and strikebreakers sent to restart the wells were roughed up. Clearly, local mayors and police in the oil towns were on the workers' side, just as Petukhov had been. The strike lasted only one day, and Yukos was not directly affected. But oilworkers at Yukos's "capital city," Nefteiugansk, signed a contract with the new labor union, and the danger of a strike was extreme. The union demanded indexation of the workers' wages and an end to layoffs. In October, the oil workers sent delegations to Moscow to picket the White House, waving red banners with angry slogans: "A hungry oilworker is Russia's shame!" and "We want to live and work with dignity!" Remarkably, actual strikes proved rare. But would that last?

Casting about for any way to cut his costs and his debts, Khodorkovsky came up with an unlikely plan to spin off unprofitable wells into separate companies, which would obtain special tax breaks from local governments in order to be able to break even, thus preserving the jobs of the workers.[48] It was, in effect, a thinly disguised plan to cut local taxes (which, according to Yukos sources, accounted for between 20 and 60 percent of the oil companies' total tax bill), and the local governments were understandably opposed.[49] Talks dragged on into the winter without result. But the practical result was the same: Yukos simply stopped paying local taxes.

Yet by the late months of 1998, Khodorkovsky's back was to the wall. Coworkers recall that cash was so short that even a cable breaking in a remote well caused a crisis at the head office, sending Khodorkovsky himself racing around trying to find money to pay for a new cable.[50] A senior foreign executive later recalled:

> In late 1998 Khodorkovsky was paying his creditors on a monthly basis. Each month they were opening up every single drawer. The staff were under orders to print on both sides of each sheet of paper. When I went off on holiday at the end of December 1998, I asked Khodorkovsky if I should even plan to return. Khodorkovsky said, "If we make it to April, we'll turn the corner."[51]

Yet as fall turned into winter, Yukos's cash flow continued to dwindle. Khodorkovsky could not pay his oil workers. As he grew more anxious, his expedients grew more exotic. Don Wolcott, a crack waterflood expert from Schlumberger who arrived at Yukos in early 1999, recalls, "In those days Khodorkovsky was paying his workers in TV sets. They had a TV in every room, including the bathroom.... He measured payroll by how many months he was behind."[52] Yet Yukos's West Siberian oil workers were relatively lucky:

not wanting to risk another explosion, Khodorkovsky channeled what cash he had into payrolls at Nefteiugansk, while largely cutting off his other subsidiaries altogether.[53] He was not alone. An epidemic of wage arrears spread throughout the oil industry.

Holding off the tax collector called for equal creativity. Throughout the 1990s a culture of tax evasion had developed throughout the country, in response to the state's constantly changing tax laws and its weak enforcement of them.[54] The oil companies, faced with tax bills that—in theory—would have exceeded their gross revenues, became ingenious in finding loopholes. They paid their taxes in kind or offset them against the state's purchases of oil (even though after 1997 such offsets were officially forbidden). They mostly paid the regions ahead of the federal government, since the regions were more apt to grant concessions. The origins of the "tax optimization schemes" that later became the chief pretext for Yukos's destruction can be found in these early survival practices, which accustomed the oil companies to treating both the tax laws and the tax man lightly. In this respect, Yukos was no exception—it was only more aggressive.

Yet what Khodorkovsky needed most was more oil, and he needed it quickly and cheaply. In October 1998 he signed a five-year strategic agreement with a leading international oil-service company, Schlumberger. Schlumberger agreed to provide not only services for Yukos's ailing wells but also—in an arrangement unique in the oil industry—financial management and personnel throughout the company. A senior Schlumberger executive was named Yukos's chief financial officer, and another took over human resources. But the key development was the arrival in Moscow in early 1999 of a veteran Schlumberger well specialist, Joe Mach. His mission: to design a plan to turn around Yukos's declining fields and put the company on the path to growth—and above all to do it fast.

Enter Joe Mach

Joe Mach enjoyed playing the part of the tough, rough-spoken Tulsa petroleum engineer, complete with cowboy boots and cigar. His language was so colorful it was said he spelled "oil" as a four-letter word. But Mach was one of Schlumberger's leading production specialists and managers and an outstanding oil-well expert. Fifty years old when he came to Yukos, he had been a vice president of Schlumberger's Dowell division and then its Wireline and Testing division, with two decades of experience in North America and overseas.[55] He was no stranger to Russia; he had made his first trip to the Soviet Union in 1977 and had returned several times since.[56]

Back in the United States, Mach had been one of the leaders in developing a revolutionary new concept of oilfield service, which Dowell had pioneered in the 1970s and 1980s. In the North American oil business, the oil companies are traditionally the dominant players, while the service contractors wait at their beck and call. Faced with a problem, oil companies call in the contractors for specific tasks, but the oil companies remain very much in charge, specifying what needs to be done and where. But since the 1980s, the leading service companies have sought to convince the operators that this traditional job-by-job contracting leaves profits in the ground. Instead, they offer a "full service" approach, in which the oil companies and the service contractor work together as a team to get the most out of the company's entire well stock. This is obviously a self-interested proposition, but it reflects a basic trend, that the service companies are increasingly the main channels of technology transfer in today's oil industry.

The Schlumberger approach consisted of two parts. First, in the second half of the 1970s, Joe Mach and his colleagues had begun applying computers and systems analysis to determine how oil and water flow during production.[57] By monitoring pressure losses and fluid rates at every stage as oil moved from the reservoir to the interface with the wellbore, then up to the surface and on to the gathering system, analysts could identify the discrete locations, called nodes, where bottlenecks occurred and compare the actual performance of a well against a theoretical ideal. The difference between the two—the "performance gap"—enabled the analyst to select the best candidates for well treatment. The model could then predict the effects of various enhancements, such as reperforation, well stimulations, or changing pump and tubing sizes.[58] The end result was to put the analysis of oilwells on a more systematic and scientific basis than the traditional ad hoc approach. Joe Mach always insisted on this scientific aspect; as he liked to say, "An oilwell is a scientific experiment."

But the implications for company strategy were far-reaching and dramatic. In traditional practice, companies called in the service companies to work on their worst wells. Nodal analysis proved that was wrong: the most impressive reductions in performance gap came from focusing on the best wells instead.

By the early 1990s, Schlumberger had introduced computerized prediction of well performance, based on nodal analysis, and developed a program to identify the best wells for remedial treatment.

Yet the idea of systematically selecting the best candidates for treatment had one major implication, and this is where the second part of the Schlumberger doctrine came in. Under the traditional "beck-and-call" relationship between a service company and an operator, service companies tended to be highly specialized; they would be called in to perform just one specific task on one specific well. Nodal analysis, on the contrary, required evaluating the total well stock and proposing a full menu of well treatments. In response, Schlumberger developed the concept of placing a full-service team, so-called DESC engineers, inside the client company.[59] The mission of this "Production Enhancement Group," as it was called, was to work with the client company to evaluate the entire well stock, select candidates, and recommend the appropriate mix of treatment in a total profit-maximizing strategy.

The DESC approach could not have been more different from the traditional arm's-length relationship between clients and contractors. It amounted to embedding a foreign team inside an operating company's most intimate decision-making structure. It implied a great deal of trust on the part of the client and a willingness to change long-established procedures.[60] Such a far-reaching change in company culture necessarily required leadership from the top.

Schlumberger had begun experimenting with putting its engineers "in residence" in company offices as far back as the 1960s. The growing technical complexity of the systems that radioed log data from rigs in the Gulf of Mexico to the mainland required dedicated specialists to run them.[61] By the early 1980s, the technologies had evolved further, and they required even more skilled specialists, working in residence inside the operating company to interpret logs generated by the VAX computers of the day. But the relationship between contractor and operator remained much as it had been before. What changed everything was the development of the personal computer. By the mid-1990s, engineers equipped with PCs could analyze the performance of wells in the field and report back the results to a central network. The evaluation of candidate wells, which previously took several days, was reduced to a few hours.

These were the core ideas that Schlumberger and Joe Mach brought to Yukos in early 1999. They could hardly have found more fertile ground, beginning in the office of the CEO himself. Mikhail Khodorkovsky, then not yet 40 years old, was a chemical engineer by first training, a graduate of Moscow's Mendeleev Institute. He was not a petroleum engineer and knew nothing of wells and reservoirs, but he had a brilliant, eager mind and possessed the thorough mathematical grounding typical of Soviet engineering education. He was intensely interested in the science underlying the technology, and the logic of nodal analysis appealed to him immediately. It was more than a passing interest. Throughout the next five years, Khodorkovsky remained intimately involved in the technical aspects of production. Every Monday morning, he convened a "chalk session" on technical issues in his office; each week a different expert was assigned a topic for discussion, and Khodorkovsky was always engaged.

"I explained to him my know-how in detail," Mach recalled. "That was in 1999." What Khodorkovsky liked most, of course, was Mach's proposition that he could deliver a fast turnaround in production at low cost, focusing on Yukos's existing well stock, and with relatively little capital investment. With Khodorkovsky's blessing, Mach spent 1999 reproducing inside Yukos what amounted to the DESC model of embedded service teams, dedicated to performing nodal analysis, identifying performance gaps, and selecting candidate wells for treatment. He bought large numbers of laptop computers and trained over a thousand young Yukos engineers in nodal analysis. "In 1999, I put members of my team in each production unit of the company," Mach said. "These people had one job—to look at each well, calculate its performance gap and sort them in descending order. The well with the biggest gap went on top and we worked on that well."

For Joe Mach, West Siberia was an oilman's dream. "Siberia is the simplest environment in the world. . . . It's one big beach front," he would tell visitors:

> The Ob' River is flowing today right over where it was 130 million years ago. It's the same place. You can see it on seismic, you can see it on the logs. The West Siberian landscape has not changed in 130 million years.

The result was a uniquely uniform and prolific environment for oil:

> You can go a thousand kilometers—it's the same goddamned sand. All across, it's 18 percent porosity. The water saturation is very consistent. The other no-brainer is, the reservoir pressure is 4,500 pounds, and the bubble

point's 1,800. In other words, it is pure oil. Man, it doesn't get any simpler than that.[62]

Far from being played out, Mach concluded, West Siberia was still full of opportunity:

The Soviets did all the beaches; they just went in and high-graded those beaches—which is fine, that just left the rest of it for us. They were easy to see on the logs and produce like hell.

In other words, there remained plenty of untapped formations.

But the main immediate opportunity lay in the existing well stock. "The Russian wells," said Mach, "were systematically underproduced in Soviet times." As he surveyed the situation in the legacy fields, Mach saw that several things could be quickly fixed. First, the flow rates from the wells could be increased, by installing bigger down-hole pumps. Second, the hydraulic fracturing technology used by previous teams had never been properly adapted to the looser sands of West Siberia and could be improved. Third, the waterflooding patterns developed in Soviet times were bypassing a lot of oil. "Pumps, fracs, and floods"—these became Mach's mantra over the next five years.

But he might as well have said, "Shibboleths, bad practice, and screw-ups," because making changes in these three basic techniques ran straight up against established ways, beliefs, and rules. From the moment Mach arrived at Yukos, the fight was on, both inside the company and out, in Moscow and in the field.

Pumps and Shibboleths

As he started out in 1999, Mach did not have the time to do elaborate field models—those came later—so he looked for the most obvious "nodes" to attack quickly to get immediate results. At the top of the list was pumps. In the 1970s and 1980s, as Russian wells produced more and more water, the Soviet oil industry had installed tens of thousands of electrically driven pumps, known in the business as "electrical submersible pumps," or ESPs. Unlike the familiar "nodding donkey" rod pumps that dot the landscape of Texas and Oklahoma—practically a symbol of the oil industry in most people's minds—ESPs are powered by an electric motor at the bottom of the well, which drives propellers that move the mixture of oil and water up the wellbore.[63] In the first half of the

1980s, as the "water cut" from Siberian wells grew inexorably, ESPs spread all over Western Siberia; between 1981 and 1985, the share of wells equipped with ESPs jumped from 18 to 45 percent.[64] By the end of the Soviet era, over 60 percent of all Soviet oil came from wells equipped with ESPs, mostly built in Soviet factories. The Soviet Union at that time had more installed ESPs than the rest of the world combined.[65]

But Soviet-made submersibles had serious problems, which were compounded when the Soviet system broke up in 1991. The early Soviet ESPs broke down after only about 100 days of operation.[66] Even after the operators set up their own network of repair shops to fix defects and provide maintenance, by the late 1980s the mean time before failure of Soviet ESPs had increased to only about 350 days,[67] compared with the several years of operation considered normal in the West.

One early point of conflict between Mach and the Russian operators, which underscores the constant battle of Western versus Russian practice inside Yukos, arose over Mach's insistence that the ESPs be placed lower down in the well. The Soviet pumps could not work above a certain temperature, which meant they couldn't be set below a certain depth in the hole. So, the Russian operators set them higher up, where the wellbore was cooler, but the pumps operated less efficiently. An amused Khodorkovsky related to an interviewer what happened next:

> When Joe first arrived, our guys said, "We know everything better than anybody." But Joe said, "Set the pump lower!" And they said, "Go fuck yourself! [*Da poshel ty!*]" Because we knew that if you set the pump low in the well, it'd burn out. Joe insisted. So we lowered it—and it burned out. Another one—and it burned out too. Six pumps burned out. . . . But Joe kept saying, "Lower, lower, goddammit! One out of three will burn out, but the other two will work so well that you won't miss the third one."[68]

But the more fundamental problem, from the standpoint of Mach and other Western specialists, was that the Russian ESPs were seriously underpowered—and here lay a major opportunity for quick gains. Replace the Soviet-era pump with a more powerful one, and you could grow production overnight. In 1999–2000 much of the initial increase in Russian oil output was driven by the simple installation of higher-capacity ESPs.[69] As Mach put it, "The wells had been producing ten tons per day. You could have pissed in the well and put the right pump in it and made fifty tons per day."[70]

But could Russian pump manufacturers respond? The crash of 1998 and the devaluation of the ruble had suddenly opened up a wide window of opportunity for Russian equipment suppliers. A standard ESP of Western manufacture cost $80,000 and up, whereas a Russian model, priced in now-cheap rubles, cost only $10,000. But capacity and reliability remained serious issues, and the Russian manufacturers, after a decade of virtual inactivity, lacked the capital to retool on their own. At this point the Russian oil companies stepped in and began investing in the domestic equipment manufacturers to upgrade their production. The Russian pump companies used part of the capital to buy up the Soviet-era repair stations, which had languished during the 1990s. These moves were successful: between 2000 and 2003, Russian ESP manufacturers sold the oil companies over 50,000 pumps, effectively replacing the entire Soviet-era stock.[71]

But Khodorkovsky went one step further, using the Russian pump manufacturers to shake up Yukos's own internal service departments. In 2000, Khodorkovsky signed a full-service contract with the largest Russian pump manufacturer, ALNAS, giving it access to some of its oil fields and pitting it against Yukos's own service departments. ALNAS won the contest hands-down, showing up the in-house department's inefficiency.[72] Predictably, this provoked resentment and resistance in the field. Local Russian operators, even more than their Western counterparts, were accustomed to keeping the service companies and manufacturers at arm's length and did not take kindly to having outsiders criticize their performance.

But there was a deeper reason why the move to higher-capacity pumps proved controversial. A more powerful pump increases the flow of liquids through the wellbore, but this lowers the pressure drop between the reservoir and the well. To understand what happens next, remember that crude oil contains a substantial amount of dissolved gas, so-called associated gas, which is normally separated from the oil fraction only after the crude reaches the surface. If the pressure drop at the bottom of the well is too great, then the dissolved gas in the liquid comes bubbling out of solution, like soda in a bottle that has been shaken and then abruptly opened. This bubbling cuts the well's production sharply. Traditional Soviet rules commanded operators to keep pressures well above the "bubble point," and official field development plans (FDPs) were written accordingly. In contrast, reservoir managers in the West had learned how to increase production by hovering near or even below bubble-point pressures, and consequently they were unbothered by the higher flow rates produced by more powerful pumps. But traditional Russian well operators were horrified—and frightened of reprisals by state regulators. The issue of "producing below bubble point" became one of the early charges leveled against Joe Mach, both outside Yukos and inside.

"Fracs" and Friction

We have seen how fraccing returned to Russia at the end of the 1980s, but by the late 1990s the pioneering Yugansk-Fracmasters joint venture had folded. When Mach arrived at Yukos, no wells were being fracced, and the Fracmasters equipment lay parked in a Yukos yard. Mach lay down a new rule: "Frac every well." This became Mach's hallmark at Yukos and also his most controversial innovation. As Mach's deputy commented, "We got more criticized for our doctrine on fraccing than for any other issues such as producing below bubble point."[73]

Why was Mach's use of fracs so controversial? The Russians had no problem with the small fracs used by the Canadians, which essentially did little more than break through the accumulations of hard minerals that sometimes form around the wellbore and prevent the oil from flowing into the well. Oilmen call these "skin," and these early fracs were called "skin fracs." Mach began using more powerful fracturing equipment, which produced longer fractures and used more tons of proppant. "When I came here they were fraccing 4 to 10 tons," Mach told me. "We immediately upped it to 50 to 100 tons." No one had done such large frac jobs in Russia before.

But Mach was just getting started. Within a year, working with Russian contractors, he was shooting fracs with 200 tons of proppant and planning 400- and 500-ton jobs, huge explosions that fractured the reservoir rock for hundreds of yards. Soon he was way beyond the limits of conventional technology. To prop open the wide fractures he was making, he commissioned specially made large ceramic spheres, which soon became known in West Siberia as "Joe's balls." It was a brute-force approach, unlike anything that had been tried in West Siberia before. One competitor likened it to "blasting a superhighway through the geology." Others called it "carpet-bombing."

As we shall see in the next chapter, Mach's fracs became one of the charges leveled against Yukos, as the Russian oil establishment mounted its attack on what it had come to regard as a rogue company.

"Floods" and Thief Wells

When oil comes out of the ground, the pressure in the reservoir drops. The oilfield is losing energy. To replace it, oilmen inject water into the reservoir, by drilling injector wells at some distance from the producer wells. This not only restores the reservoir's pressure, but it also creates an advancing wall of water that pushes oil toward the wellbores. Waterflooding has been a basic technique practically since the dawn of the oil industry in post-Civil War Pennsylvania. But waterflooding is a tricky technique. If water breaks through the wall of oil and runs directly to the well, the operator gets nothing but water. Because of this and other problems, waterflooding was viewed with suspicion in nineteenth-century Pennsylvania, and it was actually illegal in the United States until 1921. It was not widely accepted there until the late 1930s and did not spread much outside Pennsylvania until the late 1940s.[74]

Waterflooding was first used in Russia in the early 1960s, at the giant Romashkino Field in the Volga-Urals, which was then starting its long decline.[75] By the late 1960s, when the Soviet oil industry began moving to West Siberia, waterflooding had become such a standard part of the Russian toolkit that it was used from the start of production. Since not much was known in those days about the structure of the West Siberian reservoirs, the Russian drillers used a very simple technique, drilling parallel rows of injector and producer wells, closed off by an occasional crosscutting line of wells. The result looked like a box, and indeed was known (at least to Westerners) as the "Siberian box." In effect, you corralled the oil and forced it toward a common center. By world standards, this box pattern was unusual, but it had the advantage of being simple and fast—a classic example of the "making do" approach of the Soviet oil industry—and it didn't require a lot of technology or knowledge of the formation. Later on, as they tackled more complex horizons, Russian drillers developed a pattern of interlocking hexagons, in which one producer was surrounded by six injectors. The hexagons were rather reminiscent of screw heads, so the Russians called them *gaiki* (screws). As you look at a field map of Samotlor, the center of the field shows the early Siberian boxes, then the next outer perimeter shows the hexagon pattern.

The pattern was elementary in the extreme, ready-made for the convenience of Soviet-era drillers with plan targets to meet. But geology is subtle. Water soon broke through to the wells, leaving large amounts of stranded oil behind. Bad waterflooding had been the prime suspect in an analysis of signs of premature aging at Samotlor in the mid-1970s by the Central Intelligence Agency, and when Western specialists arrived in West Siberia they confirmed the story. "Russian wells in Soviet times were producing at less than 8 percent of their potential," said Mach of what he found at Yuganskneftegaz. "The main reason was they screwed up their waterfloods."

Mach hired some of the world's leading waterflood specialists to map the flood patterns at Yukos's main fields, employing three-dimensional seismic imaging to model the flows in the reservoirs. They could see where water had broken through and where pockets of oil lay isolated. They could also see on their models that some oil wells were "thief wells"—that is, they drew the water flow to themselves, leaving other parts of the reservoir isolated. They changed the flood patterns by selectively closing off some injector wells and drilling new ones and by shutting down thief wells, even when, in some cases, the thief wells were large producers—much to the horror of the traditional Russian operators.

Mach Goes to War

Armed with innovative approaches to these three basic techniques—pumps, fracs, and floods—Mach set about revolutionizing the way Yukos produced oil. Yet the most revolutionary part of his program—the part that caused the most controversy both inside Yukos and out—had little to do with technology. The techniques themselves, in fact, were hardly more than the standard West Texas toolkit that any independent oilman from the Lower 48 would have deployed. Rather, what was revolutionary was the systematic selection of candidates for treatment. This required developing a file of accurate information about every well at Yukos, centralizing real-time information at company headquarters in Moscow, and making daily decisions on which wells would get priority attention. It was the simple yet systematic application of priorities. Mach's doctrine, taken straight from nodal analysis, was, "Fix the best wells first." His "Top Twenty" program focused on Yukos's top producer wells, to nudge them closer to their theoretical limit. "A lot of oil companies say, 'No, fix the broken stuff first,'" Mach would say. "I don't care if they never fix the broken well. If it doesn't pop up on the priority list, it doesn't get fixed."[76]

Instead, Mach ordered a massive shutdown of Yukos's poorest producers. From 14,000 active wells when Mach arrived in early 1999, Yukos's producing well stock dropped to 7,000 by the beginning of 2004. Mach regarded this wholesale triage as one of his proudest achievements.[77]

Yet there was one small problem with shutting down wells in this way: it was illegal. In Russia every field must have a development plan, which must be approved by the state authorities. It specifies the number of wells and their placement. The total plan aims at maximum ultimate recovery of the oil in place. In traditional Russian oilfield doctrine, the poorer wells are part of the total pattern. Shutting them down selectively to focus on the best wells is not just bad practice; it is a violation of the field development plan, and as such against the law.[78]

In this and other ways, the Yukos approach consisted less of introducing new technologies than of applying standard know-how and changing long-established Russian practices. But this put Yukos in direct conflict not only with the authorities but first and foremost with many people inside Yukos itself, as Khodorkovsky's team challenged some of the most deep-seated traits of Soviet-era organizational culture.

Soviet organizational culture was all about survival, which meant evading the system, concealing facts and knowledge, and avoiding blame. Doctoring payrolls, rigging tenders, overstating payments, concealing production—all these were the classic arts of the Soviet manager. But as Russia moved into the post-Soviet era, the techniques developed for self-protection blended into skimming for private profit. Workers and managers in the field frequently falsified logs and well records, overstating successes (but not too much) and hiding failures. Oil would disappear or, to be more precise, would never officially appear, thanks to inaccuracies in measurement at the various nodes between the well and the Transneft pipeline system. Whereas "technical losses" in a Western system might be a few tenths of a percentage point per year, in the Russian system they were routinely 3 to 5 percent. Decision makers at the top could not cut through the fog to tell reality from illusion.

Planners in Moscow had struggled with this problem throughout the Soviet era, trying one scheme after another to combat disinformation from below, without ever licking it. In the 1970s they thought computers and computerized management systems would be the answer. But local managers were unfazed; they fed the central planners in Moscow false information—impeccably computerized—until the State Planning Committee (Gosplan) and the Politburo finally gave up and reverted to the traditional "planning by negotiation."[79] When the Soviet Union finally collapsed and the planners disappeared, instead of underreporting results to avoid higher targets, local managers switched to underreporting them to dodge taxes—but the basic game was the same. And when the oil industry was privatized and the integrated companies emerged, local managers thought it would be no different. As a timeless Siberian saying goes, "Moscow is far away."

Except that by the 1990s two things had changed. The advent of the personal computer and modern telecommunications made it genuinely possible to gather, analyze, and transmit information quickly and accurately from the field to corporate headquarters. Today's oil wells are wired up. Senior managers sitting at a central command post control a digital information empire at their fingertips, in real time, through a technology called SCADA (Supervisory Control and Data Acquisition).[80] It has become increasingly difficult for local field operators, however remote, to conceal from senior management back at corporate headquarters what is going on.

And corporate headquarters was no longer a Soviet-style state ministry. At the top of Yukos was a determined private-sector entrepreneur who had total power over the organization. Khodorkovsky's top priority was control—control over crude flow and cash flow, top to bottom throughout the company. In a country in which insider crime was endemic, Khodorkovsky made it clear that fraud and theft would not be tolerated, and to prevent leakage he set up the tightest security system in the industry. We saw in the last chapter how Khodorkovsky, when he took over Yukos, set up a formidable security apparatus. He summarily fired hundreds of Yukos employees until the message sank in. Controlling leakage of information was just as important to him as leakage of oil or money. Visitors to Yukos had to surrender their laptop computers to armed guards on the way in and recovered them only on the way out. (These arrangements have since become standard, but Yukos was first.)

To maximize central power over field operations, Khodorkovsky built a chain of command so short it was unique for a major oil company. The line of authority consisted of just three people: Mikhail Khodorkovsky; his first vice chairman for exploration and production, Iurii Beilin; and Joe Mach.

In effect, Khodorkovsky managed production at Yukos like a small independent, putting his technologists at the top of the organization. "In any other large oil company," Mach said,

> there would have been twelve layers of financial guys down from the CEO before you got to the first field specialist. Yukos was an absolutely unique case. By some definitions, this was the largest oil company in the world at the time, yet between me and Khodorkovsky there was only one man, Beilin, and he was totally on our side. I had total power over every field and every well. Nowhere else in the world could you find a setup like that.[81]

In reality, there was a second chain of command, reporting to Beilin, which handled relations with state regulators and local politicians, mollifying opposition with discreet lubrication. And there was a third chain, dealing with external security, under Khodorkovsky's partner, Leonid Nevzlin. But these parts of the structure, which consisted solely of Russians, were seldom visible to the Westerners at Yukos.

Mach relished his unique freedom to focus solely on the business of producing oil. "The senior levels of the majors today consist of people who are managing financial portfolios and doing deals," he said, "but Khodorkovsky made a deal with me. He said, 'You just make those wells produce and recover the oil. I'll handle all the other stuff.'" From his desk computer in Moscow, Mach oversaw every one of Yukos's wells in real time. He reproduced inside Yukos the DESC concept of analysts embedded in the client field structure. But in Mach's hands it became an instrument of power and cultural change, designed to break through the "shale layer" of local resistance and concealment.

Automation alone was not enough. Without a network of loyal cadres at the local level, the information coming in would have been suspect and the orders going out would have been ignored. In 1999 Mach handpicked a team of twenty-seven young engineers, one for each NGDU in Yukos, and trained them in candidate recognition. They bypassed completely the traditional management system. He gave them tight incentives, and they were paid directly from Moscow. The aim was to use them to uncover the true state of production, the actual production from each well. This was enormously subversive; the traditional field managers did everything in their power to prevent this kind of information from being communicated to Moscow.

Five years later the enforcement team had evolved into a small elite army, who came to be known informally as "Yukos's Black Belts." Inside each NGDU was a special department for production enhancement and waterfloods. Working from their laptops, the analysts monitored the local well stock, calculated performance gaps, and recommended candidate wells for treatment, reporting directly to Mach's computer at Yukos headquarters in Moscow. They were all young production engineers, recruited by Mach and trained by visiting international experts whom Yukos flew in from all over the world. The headquarters of the network was Yukos's Field Development Center in Moscow, opened in late 2001 and conceived both as a training facility and as a "home away from home," where the young nodalists could come in from the field for a refresher course, a pep talk, and a pizza.[82] They were brash and assertive, self-confident to the point of arrogance, and totally empowered. In a culture in which twenty-somethings are traditionally supposed to keep their mouths shut, their mission was to barge in on grizzled Siberian field chiefs twenty years their seniors, pry loose their most closely held information, and force them to change their ways—and increase production.

For all its surface resemblance to the American-derived DESC model, this management structure would have been instantly familiar to a Communist Party *aparatchik* back in Soviet times. Khodorkovsky and his top command were the Politburo. Mach and his Moscow staff were the Central Committee Secretariat at Old Square, and the local departments of production enhancement were the *partkomy* in the field. The Field Development Center was the Higher Party School. Like the Bolsheviks during the Russian Civil War, Yukos management installed a hierarchy of loyal *politruk* commissars that paralleled the established officer corps at every rank. All that was missing—just barely—was the Bolshevik commissars' standing orders to use their sidearms if they detected treason.

The atmosphere too was occasionally reminiscent of Bolshevik times. A staple management tool in Russia is instilling terror in subordinates. A Russian manager must be able to put on a suitably terrifying alpha-male display of rage to dress down a subordinate. This ceremony is known as a *raznos*. Khodorkovsky himself was an exception. He never raised his voice. But other Russians at Yukos favored the old-fashioned way. Here Mach fit right in. He was famous for his authoritarian style. He did not discriminate between Russians and Westerners—he was brusque with everybody. He wove four-letter Anglo-Saxon into a unique language, which his interpreters struggled to render into Russian equivalents—no small achievement in Russia, the homeland of *mat,* the elaborate obscenity that is an art form among Russian males. As an admiring Khodorkovsky told an interviewer in 2002: "Joe Mach. He's a typical cowboy in leather boots. He swears like a Russian." The unbelieving interviewer then asks: "In Russian?" To which Khodorkovsky answers proudly, "In English, but the interpreter translates into Russian."[83]

Yet Mach also enjoyed great respect among the Russians for his extraordinary technical expertise. Even his enemies described him as one of the most talented well experts of his generation. Mach constantly emphasized the basic physics of oil wells. "Not our experience, and not your experience," he used to say. "Use Darcy's law and Bernoulli's law, use the fundamental physics to derive a calculated standard that is suited to the situation." To his young Russian engineers, with their deep training in mathematics and basic science, this had tremendous appeal.

But the older Russians at Yukos headquarters, and especially the line managers in the field, despised the Khodorkovsky-Beilin *vertikal'*, and they positively hated Mach. Mach had authority to hire and fire, and he did not hesitate to use it, although when the victim was Russian, Khodorkovsky would sometimes discreetly hire him back. Mach's Black Belts reminded them less of the Bolshevik commissars than of the *oprichniki,* the black riders of death of sixteenth-century tsar Ivan the Terrible, who dispatched them to terrorize the *boyars,* the nobles who resisted his power. "They had power without responsibility," one senior Russian executive at Yukos told me. "They were totally unaccountable." Behind the older Russians' attitude was undoubtedly a measure of Russian resentment of the Western intruders, but there was also uneasiness. They knew how deeply Mach's methods conflicted with established ways and rules. The government regulators' offices might be half empty and rules unenforced, but how long would that remain the case? The Russian executive went on:

The Black Belt guys would terrorize local operators into departing completely from the official field development plans. For Mach these legal documents did not exist. You're allowed a 5–10% margin of error above the production levels specified in the FDPs, but not 100% or 200%. Mach was a barbarian. This is Russia, after all.[84]

There was indeed tremendous resistance in the field, and for more than just legal reasons. In Western thinking, oil today is worth more than oil tomorrow. Therefore, accelerating production, if it can be done without lessening total recovery, is in itself a good thing. Yukos under Khodorkovsky adopted this doctrine wholesale. But it ran directly counter to the culture and the interests of the Siberian oilworkers. From their point of view, Yukos management's insistence on boosting production was simply a replay in capitalist drag of the Soviet Politburo's constant demands for higher production targets. They did not buy the view that Western methods could boost production and increase total recovery at the same time. They called Yukos's methods "rape and pillage" (khishchnichestvo) and believed they would damage the fields, just as Soviet methods had done. Accelerating production hastened the day when the fields would be exhausted and the oilworkers' jobs would be gone. And what would become of them then, in a Russia in which there were no jobs and no housing outside the oil towns? Mach, who enjoyed being provocative, would say to visitors, "Do we ruin oilfields? Sure we do—that's our goal. We're trying to empty the oilfields by getting all the oil out." Yet that only deepened the oilworkers' worst fears.

But enforcement and fear were only half the story. The other half was an elaborate structure of positive incentives. The top tier of Moscow executives, both Russian and Western, received high salaries in dollars and, after 2001, stock and stock options as well.[85] Senior managers in the field, the heads of ob"edineniia and NGDUs, were also paid in dollars, much of it in the form of performance bonuses tied to the company's aggressive production targets.

One of the chief aims of the incentive system was to encourage accurate reporting of the facts. "From hiding facts to constructive evaluation of reality" was the slogan of the Schlumberger secondees, who helped to design the incentive system.[86] Khodorkovsky looked for young talent, preferably people from outside the conventional oil system who would be free from the old ways. Like Alekperov of LUKoil, he liked to hire physicists and mathematicians, even graduates of military schools, rather than alumni of the conventional "oil academies" like the Gubkin Institute, whom he found conservative and unimaginative. Instead, he hired the best and the brightest, then taught them the oil business on the job, through innovative training programs that set a new standard for the Russian industry. His showcase was Tomsk Polytechnic University, where Yukos set up a joint program with Heriot-Watt, a Scottish university, to create a curriculum in advanced reservoir engineering. Khodorkovsky promoted his recruits quickly and rotated them throughout the company.

Yet Khodorkovsky drew a sharp line between the indispensable and the replaceable. Teams that exceeded their targets and reported their results accurately were rewarded generously, but the average wage for Yukos oilworkers in the field was actually lower than in other companies. In 1998–1999 there was a surplus of oilworkers in nearly every category, and in Khodorkovsky's mind this meant he could afford to keep pay low. Only later on, as competition tightened and workers started to be bid away by Surgutneftegaz and others, was Khodorkovsky forced to raise wages.

Far more controversial was Khodorkovsky's policy of curbing spending on the oil cities. Unlike Vladimir Bogdanov of Surgutneftegaz, who followed the Soviet tradition of the paternalistic enterprise director who supports the whole community, Khodorkovsky refused to finance "social" projects, such as housing, hospitals, and schools. This caused deep resentment, not least among the local oil generals, whose power rested on their role as providers. This was precisely the kind of local structure that Khodorkovsky was determined to break up, but in the process he acquired a reputation as a bad corporate citizen, one of the many things held against him later on.

Yet Khodorkovsky's system was tremendously effective. Within a year and a half after the crash of 1998, Yukos had moved to the head of the industry. Its output grew faster, more efficiently, and more profitably than any other Russian oil producer. The average flow rate from Yukos's wells more than doubled between 1997 and 2002, while for the industry as a whole it increased by only 14 percent.[87] The increase in flow rates for new wells was even more spectacular. For Yuganskneftegaz alone, new well flow rates soared from a low of 13.8 tons (100.7 barrels) per day in 1993 to 125.7 tons (917.6 barrels) in 2003,[88] while in the industry new well flow rates doubled from 11.0 tons per day (80.3 barrels) to 40.3 tons (294.2 barrels) per day over the same period.[89] At the same time, Yukos produced more cheaply than any other Russian company. In 2002 its lifting costs were $1.47 per barrel, while its closest competitor, LUKoil, was at $2.50 per barrel.[90] Yukos was also more efficient at finding and developing new

oil: its finding and development costs in 2002 stood at $1.07 per barrel, com-
pared with $1.21 for Sibneft and $1.48 for LUKoil.[91]

Labor productivity was an especially revealing—and politically sensitive—
indicator. In Russia in the 1990s, where oil was one of the few sectors actually
functioning, the industry became an employer of last resort. As the economy
declined, upstream employment went up. It was not until the economy turned
around in the new decade that most of the oil companies dared to shed workers. As a result, labor productivity in the industry went down.

Yukos under Khodorkovsky did precisely the opposite. Whereas others
added employees to their balance sheets, Khodorkovsky moved them off, spin-
ning them into independent service companies or transferring them to the
budgets of city governments, mainly Nefteiugansk. Thus whereas Yukos had
lagged far behind the rest of the industry in labor productivity from 1993 to
1996, after 1998 Yukos's production per upstream worker increased by five,
leaving the rest of the industry far behind.

Greenfield versus Brownfield

What Mach liked most to tell visitors about was his rehabilitation of the Soviet-
era brownfields. "We've gotten our results by drilling less, not more," he told
me in early 2002:

> We've focused instead on remodeling the fields, correcting the water flows,
> recompleting wells, watching for bottlenecks, and automating well opera-
> tions. We don't use state-of-the-art technology, but plain old know-how
> and equipment. Our motto is not "best in class" but "fit for purpose."

The aim was to maximize output while controlling costs. "The other companies
haven't gotten the point yet," Mach said. "They keep trying to drill more wells."

But in reality Yukos owed much of its production growth to one major new
field, Priobskoe. After negotiating with several Western companies in turn,
Khodorkovsky decided to begin developing Priobskoe himself, and he turned
Priobskoe over to Joe Mach and his team. Joe Mach attacked it with his entire
arsenal: large-diameter well casings with powerful pumps, "step-out" wells that
branched out from the main wellbore and provided, in effect, several wells at
once, and more powerful fracs than the Russian industry had ever seen before.

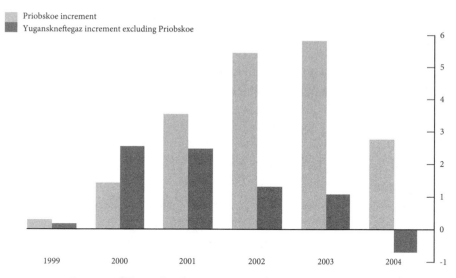

Priobskoe increment
Yuganskneftegaz increment excluding Priobskoe

FIGURE 5.2 *Sources of Yuganskneftegaz net growth, 1999–2004, in millions of metric tons of growth per year. (Sources: Russian Statistical Committee and Russian Ministry of Energy.)*

Priobskoe soon dominated Yukos's upstream effort. Production from the giant field began building rapidly in 2000, and already by 2001 the share of Priobskoe in Yugansk's total growth was greater than that of the older fields. Thereafter, with each passing year the share of growth from Priobskoe grew, while that of the older fields declined. In 2003 and 2004, the story was all Priobskoe (see Figure 5.2).

Meanwhile, production growth at Yukos's Soviet-era brownfields was clearly slowing. By 2004, the last year in which Yugansk operated as a unit of Yukos before it was taken away from the company, the older fields began to decline again. In sum, the spectacular spurt in brownfield production that had begun in 2000, one year after Mach arrived at Yukos, lasted for barely three years.

Had the "cream" been skimmed? Had the "Soviet dividend" been harvested? If Yukos had remained under Khodorkovsky and the troika of Khodorkovsky-Beilin-Mach had stayed in charge, would the decline of the Yukos brownfields have been slowed or even reversed once more? Might

Yukos have gone on to pioneer more advanced technologies, moving on to the techniques that have generated the tight-oil boom in the United States today?

This is a near impossible question to judge, even for oilfield professionals. In the many conversations I have had, including with the key players themselves, I have heard a wide range of opinions. But I think many would agree with the following. The initial burst of double-digit production growth observed at Yukos—a pattern that was later seen at TNK-BP and LUKoil as well—came from applying basic improvements to the wells, mainly by installing more powerful pumps, repairing and recompleting wells, and using hydraulic fracturing. Once this initial phase was over, a second frontier lay beyond, which required moving from rehabilitating wells to optimizing whole reservoirs, particularly by rationalizing waterflooding. This second phase was more difficult, more costly, and longer range. Above all, it required more time—to train the people, to study the fields, to draw up the plans, to convince the regulators, and to put it into action.

By mid-2003 Joe Mach's reservoir optimization program was just moving into high gear. His cadre of young reservoir engineers was trained and deployed; his team had divided up Yukos's fields into cells and was modeling the patterns in which water and oil flowed inside each cell. He had hired (and was in the process of buying) a consultancy company in Texas, which provided some of the most advanced modeling techniques in the world. Given time, insiders say, Yukos would have continued to generate strong growth, through a combination of stabilization in the brownfields and production from new fields (chiefly from Priobskoe). The experience of TNK-BP, in some ways the closest analog to Yukos in its approach to the brownfields, suggests as much. But in the case of Yukos, we shall never know, because the experiment was abruptly terminated by the destruction of the company.

Khodorkovsky, Beilin, and Mach were revolutionaries. They built a system of centralized power unique to a major oil company, one that put a team of technologists in sole charge of production, backed up by the direct daily authority of the chief executive. Through this system they brought in new methods of management, new technologies, and new systems of reporting and communication, borrowed from Western practice, and imposed them by fiat, overcoming resistance in the field through a mixture of incentives and sanctions. The core of the revolution lay not so much in advanced technologies—

there were actually few of those—but in the systematic application of priorities and a customized approach to each well and reservoir. Mach himself summed it up as "not technology, but leadership and know-how."

Their contribution lay in demonstrating the huge potential of the "Soviet legacy" and showing how it could be exploited quickly to yield dramatically higher well flows. By arresting the decline of the legacy fields and developing quickly a difficult but major new field that conventional wisdom in the industry had assumed could be developed only by an international major, Khodorkovsky, Beilin, and Mach doubled Yukos's oil production and multiplied the market value of the company many fold.[92] They showed it could be done and how.

Yet their very success, and the methods by which they achieved it, became one of the causes of the destruction of the company. Their increased production and their fabulous profits excited envy and greed. Equally important, their identity and their methods aroused controversy, resentment, and bitter resistance, both inside the company and out.[93] A group of upstart financiers (perceived by many Russians to be Jewish), using foreigners and a cadre of brash youngsters, threatened the established networks of power and interest in the Russian oilfields, challenged regional leaders, went against too many entrenched traditions, bent too many established rules, and offended too many people. The subsequent attack on Khodorkovsky and Yukos, though driven at the top by politics, was also fed at the bottom by the widespread fear and dislike the Russian oil establishment felt for the company.

Meanwhile, what of the other industry leader, Sibneft?

Sibneft: The Quiet Revolutionary

The other outstanding success story of the Russian "oil miracle" was Sibneft. Yukos and Sibneft had both been taken over by financiers in the "Deal of the Century" in 1995–1996. Both companies' oil output came from aging upstream properties that had declined steadily through much of the 1990s.[94] Both companies nearly doubled their production between 1999 and 2004. And both companies ended up being partly or totally renationalized in 2005—Yukos through takeover by Rosneft, Sibneft through purchase by Gazprom.

Yet the similarities end there. The creation of Sibneft in 1995 is associated with the names of Boris Berezovsky and Roman Abramovich, who persuaded

President Yeltsin to approve the creation of a new oil company, formed out of the Noiabrskneftegaz production association and the Omsk refinery, then Russia's newest.[95] But Berezovsky never played an active role in the management of the company; neither did Abramovich once he took control. Instead, Abramovich turned Sibneft over to a professional manager and tax expert, Evgenii Shvidler. Shvidler never sought the limelight, while Abramovich positively shunned it. Sibneft, unlike Yukos, was never used as a platform for its owners' political ambitions or social causes. Neither did Shvidler attempt to turn Sibneft into a showcase for capitalism, importing Western executives wholesale and turning over to them the financial management and public relations of the company. Shvidler himself was only 34 years old when he was named president of Sibneft, and most of the senior people he hired, a mixture of oilfield veterans and financial experts, were barely older than he.[96] Although several of them had Western training and international exposure,[97] the Sibneft team was almost entirely Russian. Unlike the hybrid management developed by Khodorkovsky at Yukos, Sibneft remained very much a Russian operation.

Yet in its field operations Sibneft was at least as revolutionary as Yukos, and in some respects even more so. At Sibneft as at Yukos, Schlumberger played the key role of catalyst. Schlumberger had opened up an office in Noiabrsk, Sibneft's main base town in West Siberia, in 1997. In August 1998 (the same month as the financial crash), Schlumberger's Dowell division began the first of 150 fracs at four of Sibneft's older subsidiaries, under a $20 million one-year contract.[98] In October 1999, the initial experiment having been a success, Schlumberger and Sibneft went on to sign a strategic alliance, aimed at developing Sibneft's two main new fields, Sugmut and Sporyshev.[99]

The main technical problem to beat at Sugmut and Sporyshev was that the oil was concentrated in extremely thin strata, shaped rather like lenses, only 2 to 4.5 meters thick, and lying on top of water. This called for a very different approach from Priobskoe. Hydraulic fracturing had to be used with caution, because of the danger that water would penetrate the oil zones from below, and in any case it would not have been as effective, because of the thinness of the oil zones.

The solution chosen by Sibneft and Schlumberger was horizontal drilling. Using advanced steering technology, drillers were able to guide drill bits to even the thinnest targets, hitting sweet spots 3,000 meters deep and 1,000 meters horizontally. But the technique had never been tried in Russia before, and the initial results were discouraging. The man whom Schlumberger had sent to lead the effort was a young petroleum engineer named Iskander Diyashev. Diyashev recalls:

> Our first well, in 2000 at the Yerainer field, failed. I was blamed for the failure and sent back to Texas. But then they made such a mess of the second well that my boss Matevosov called me back. The next well, at Romanov field, turned out pretty well. But the fourth well, at Sugmut, was a big success—so much so that we changed the entire development strategy for the field. That was in 2001.[100]

That fourth well was a game changer for Sibneft. Eventually the best wells at Sugmut came in at over 1,200 tons (9,000 barrels) per day,[101] more than forty times the average rates for new wells in West Siberia up to that time. Soon Diyashev had moved over to Sibneft and was promoted to chief engineer.

On the surface, there were significant parallels between Diyashev and Mach. Both had initially worked for Schlumberger, leading its strategic alliances with Yukos and Sibneft, respectively. Both were resident inside the client company, having both left Schlumberger to work for their clients. In short, both represented variations on the Schlumberger approach to client service (i.e., nodal analysis of the total well stock, candidate selection, resident DESC engineer), and when they went over to their Russian clients they both embodied essentially the same mechanism of technology transfer into a Russian organizational setting.

But there the similarities ended. Diyashev was a graduate of Texas A&M, but though he proudly wore an Aggie class ring and a trademark pair of cowboy boots in his office in West Siberia, he was a Russian citizen and a Tatar to boot. He was also a graduate of one of Russia's leading scientific universities, the famous "Fiz-Tekh," Moscow's elite Physics and Engineering Institute, and was the son of a prominent Russian geophysicist, Rasim Diyashev, formerly the deputy chief geologist of Tatneft. Diyashev himself had begun his career at Tatneft before going on to Texas A&M for his doctorate, after which he joined Schlumberger's Holditch Reservoir Technologies in the United States. In other words, Diyashev was one of the best and the brightest of the Russian system and through his family he was a scion of the Soviet-era oil technocracy.

When he returned to Russia in 1997, to head Schlumberger's field office in Noiabrsk, Diyashev was 29 years old, a generation younger than Joe Mach.

When he moved over to Sibneft in 2001, to the newly created position of chief engineer, Diyashev was four rungs below the owner of Sibneft, and unlike Mach, he did not have line authority over production decisions.[102] In short, the short chain of command that gave Mach absolute power at Yukos, with the direct daily backing of an actively engaged owner, did not exist at Sibneft.

This may help to explain why Sibneft's relationship with Schlumberger also evolved in a different way. Mach was soon at loggerheads with his former employer; and by 2003 the strategic alliance had been severed. For his innovations in fraccing, Mach contracted directly with suppliers and became, in effect, his own service company. Sibneft retained the close tie with Schlumberger; indeed, it turned over several of its service divisions—and sometimes whole projects—to Schlumberger. By 2002, there were over 800 Schlumberger employees working for Sibneft, many of them former Sibneft service workers. Although there was some effort to diversify (in 2002 Sibneft formed a strategic alliance with Schlumberger's principal Western rival in Russia, Halliburton), Sibneft maintained a policy of treating its service contractors as partners, whereas at Yukos, Mach's policy (ironically, for someone who had pioneered the DESC approach) was to keep contractors at a distance. This fit with Khodorkovsky's own evolving priorities: by 2002–2003 he had terminated Schlumberger's role in the company's overall management and moved on to other foreign advisors.

Sibneft's challenge to Russian established ways and conventional wisdom was less extreme and abrasive than that of Yukos. This was partly because of differences in the two companies' culture and leadership, but it also reflected differences in the two companies' strategies. Yukos began by putting top priority on its old fields and only gradually shifted its emphasis to its main new field, Priobskoe. But at Sibneft it was the opposite: most of the new technology was directed to its new fields, chiefly Sugmut and Sporyshev, and it was only later, as production at those two fields peaked, that Sibneft shifted its attention back to its brownfields. Because he attacked the brownfields first, Mach necessarily had to confront established Russian practice head-on. Yukos was all about confrontation; Sibneft was more about adaptation.

The hallmark technologies used by the two companies—wide-fracture fraccing in the case of Yukos and horizontal drilling in that of Sibneft—were viewed differently by the Russian oil establishment and consequently had a different political resonance. Wide-fracture fraccing, as we have seen, was controversial from the first and remains so today. Mach's aggressive use of it was bound to put him and Yukos in the line of fire. In contrast, horizontal drilling has never been controversial in Russia. The biggest users of horizontal drilling in Russia are LUKoil and Surgutneftegaz, which have never been criticized for it.

Surgutneftegaz: Success Soviet-Style

This brings us to Surgutneftegaz. Surgutneftegaz was nearly as successful as Yukos and Sibneft in harvesting the remaining "Soviet dividend" between 1999 and 2004, but it represents a different model altogether. Despite its reputation for technological conservatism, Surgutneftegaz has been in fact one of the more innovative Russian companies and has made abundant use of technologies transferred from the West. But unlike Yukos and Sibneft, the mechanism of transfer has made only limited use of foreign companies or personnel. Indeed, Surgutneftegaz in its basic management is little changed from Soviet times. Thus it stands out as the antithesis of Yukos and Sibneft. What accounted for its success?

With Surgutneftegaz, as with Yukos and Sibneft, leadership was the main key. Vladimir Bogdanov ran his company in the same Soviet style as he had founded it. He dug in at Surgutneftegaz's stronghold in the middle Ob' River basin, seeking neither acquisitions nor expansion outside his home grounds. He rejected all foreign suitors, advisors, and consultants. He steered clear of newfangled strategies and focused instead on the one skill he had used all his life: drilling.

Bogdanov's approach was the absolute opposite of Yukos's. Instead of shutting down wells, he added new ones. Instead of installing new high-powered down-hole pumps, he stuck with the underpowered Soviet-era models, thus avoiding the "bubble point" issue. He opposed big fracs. So conservative was Bogdanov in his approach to production that one leading Western analyst called him a *staroverets,* an "Old Believer," a reference to the seventeenth-century Russian schismatics who retreated to the deep woods, made the sign of the cross with two fingers instead of three, and rejected all Western-style innovations as the work of the Antichrist.

By 2000–2001, the contrast between Surgutneftegaz and its high-flying competitors, Yukos and Sibneft, was so extreme that Bogdanov had become an object of ridicule among sophisticated Moscow analysts. He even paid his bills and his taxes on time and in cash, which was considered positively exotic. Yet Bogdanov was getting results that were nearly as good as those of the industry leaders, at least in terms of total production. Surgutneftegaz did not get the same spectacular new-well flow rates as Yukos and Sibneft, but it made up for it with more efficient drilling, and more of it, as Surgutneftegaz tackled more new fields than any other Russian company.

All that tended to confirm the industry's judgment that Bogdanov was a one-trick Soviet pony, but after a while people began to notice some other things. When it came to controlling his bottom line, Bogdanov did not hesitate to buy the best and the newest, even if it was not Russian. In the mid-1990s he was the first to implement an advanced "enterprise resource management" software from SAP, the leading German provider, to monitor and control costs. His approach to new technology was cautious, but when he had made up his mind he sent his best people abroad by the hundreds to be trained. By 2002, for example, Surgutneftegaz was drilling more horizontal wells than any other Russian company. Drilling a horizontal well involves guiding a drill bit horizontally through the length of a pay zone, with the same surgeon's delicacy as threading a catheter through an artery. It requires extreme precision, using state-of-the-art telemetry, but Surgutneftegaz quickly mastered it, even if its results were not quite as eye-popping as those of Sibneft. By 2004, Surgutneftegaz was rapidly catching up in other advanced techniques as well, such as modeling waterflood patterns. By this time, Surgutneftegaz was increasing production at over 10 percent per year. Bogdanov's only problem was that he was beginning to run out of new acreage in Surgutneftegaz's license area, and after 2004 the company's growth fell back.[103]

To many Russian observers, and particularly those in the Kremlin, Bogdanov's record meant that a private oil company could be run along traditional lines and still be successful, a lesson that became politically significant later on.

LUKoil: A Late Me-Too Conversion

Finally, what of LUKoil, the first Russian oil company to privatize and the pioneer of the concept of vertical integration? LUKoil had become accustomed since the mid-1990s to being the favorite of the Russian stock market, and Alekperov and his partners watched with growing irritation as Yukos, by

2000–2001, became the company with the fizz. LUKoil, by contrast, looked distinctly flat. Between October 2000 and April 2002, in a booming Russian stock market, LUKoil shares doubled, but Yukos shares rose fivefold,[104] and by the spring of 2002 Yukos was worth more than LUKoil. But there was worse news. In early April 2002 Alekperov told journalists that LUKoil's profits would be down for both 2001 and 2002.[105] To offset the impact on its stock price, the company doubled its dividend for 2001,[106] but that did not help. Something else was needed to put the company back in front.

In late April LUKoil unveiled a sweeping plan for change. Significantly, it was Leonid Fedun who took the microphone: this was a message intended for investors. LUKoil, he said, was being forced by its "competitive environment" (read Yukos and Sibneft) to change its whole approach to production and management. Over the next few years it would shut down 5,000 wells, or nearly a quarter of its well stock. It would lay off 20,000 of its 140,000 workers. It would sell off a big part of its service sector, beginning with its drilling subsidiary, LUKoil-Burenie. Conceding that it lagged far behind its competitors in well flow rates and lifting costs, LUKoil vowed to catch up, with a vast brownfield program focused on its core assets in West Siberia.[107]

In effect LUKoil was trading in its old business model for a souped-up one analogous to Yukos. For a decade Alekperov had insisted that LUKoil's West Siberian fields were doomed to irreversible decline and that the company's future lay outside, in the Caspian and in Northwest Russia. The company had invested its resources accordingly, buying properties in Russia's northwest and drilling offshore in the Caspian. But in the spring of 2002 Alekperov vowed to stabilize the company's production in Khanty-Mansiisk at the 2001 level. "We will maintain that level of production in Khanty-Mansiisk Autonomous District for the next five to seven years," he said.[108]

Unlike its competitors, LUKoil had no new elephants in West Siberia. Only one new field, Tevlinsko-Russkinskoe, had reserves of more than 100 million tons (730 million barrels); its other explored prospects had much more modest reserves. That meant that stabilizing production required working the older fields, using Mach-like techniques like fraccing and bigger pumps. Even as he announced LUKoil's new program, Fedun showed some apprehension. LUKoil was resorting to the "accelerated development method," he conceded. "This decision was more difficult for us *neftianiki* than it was for the *finansisty* running the other oil companies."[109] As we shall see in the next chapter, LUKoil soon retreated from its new course after Yukos ran into trouble and conse-quently did not enjoy as large a spurt of organic growth as the other private companies did, although the modest increase that did take place suggests that if LUKoil had persevered, it might have gotten essentially the same results.[110]

Nevertheless, LUKoil's change of rhetoric symbolized the fact that by mid-2002 the Yukos-Sibneft model was at its height of acceptance. Even the Russian government, keen to get the best price as it sold off its remaining oil assets, ap-peared to go along.[111] Yet this moment of triumph was destined to last less than a year. The clouds were already gathering around Yukos.

Lessons of the Russian "Oil Miracle"

The immediate stimulus for the turnaround in Russian oil production was the devaluation that followed the crash of 1998 and the recovery of world oil prices in early 1999. This was no mere reprise of the two earlier crash recoveries of West Siberian production in the 1980s. Those had been based on a fresh tier of new oilfields, hastily hustled into production by a desperate and self-destructive Soviet government.[112] In the intervening decade, the Russian oil industry had gone through a revolution, which recast the industry into privately owned, vertically integrated companies. The difference in behavior was that the new companies responded to economic signals, not political ones.

Yet getting to that point had taken a decade of gestation. Throughout the 1990s Western technology and management had gradually seeped into Russia, blending with the experience and skills of the Russian oil industry. It took nearly ten years of difficult trial and error for Russian and Western oilmen, overcoming a half century of isolation, to find a common language, based on hybrid technologies and know-how adapted to the Russian environment. By the end of the 1990s the synthesis was still far from smooth or complete, but the leading private companies in the Russian industry were ready to attack the brownfields of West Siberia with a new set of tools. They showed that they could produce oil abundantly and efficiently from what had been some of the most catastrophically damaged assets of the Soviet era. All of the private com-panies, despite their diverse origins, management styles, and approaches, achieved convincing growth. None of the state-owned companies did. If one was looking for proof of the superiority of private entrepreneurship, at least in generating near-term responses to short-term economic signals, this was it.

228

What role did foreigners play in the revival of the Russian industry? The "oil miracle" was not due to the international majors, which played practically no part in it. Much of the initial example came from the joint ventures; but by the end of the 1990s the latter were already on the decline. Rather, Western technology penetrated the Russian oil industry through multiple channels—through service companies and equipment suppliers, through financial advisors and management consultants, and through the Russians' own increasingly direct exposure through travel abroad. Above all, innovation came through motivated individuals working with other motivated individuals, cooperating in concrete situations, learning from one another, and together overcoming inertia and opposition. In these respects, the recovery of 1999–2004 was a classic illustration of effective technology transfer in action.

By early 2003 the growth of the private Russian oil companies seemed unstoppable. Their output of crude was growing at annual rates of over 10 percent. Their worth on the stock markets of the world was breaking records almost daily. Their founders were at the height of their wealth and prestige. In February 2003 *Forbes* magazine listed seventeen Russian billionaires, twelve of them in the oil sector alone. Mikhail Khodorkovsky, whose fortune *Forbes* put at $8 billion, was Russia's richest man.

Yet the oil miracle would shortly come to an end. Behind its spectacular success were liabilities that made it fragile, vulnerable, and temporary.

First, it was narrowly based. The revival of production in 1999–2004 was based almost entirely on the Soviet legacy, essentially the inherited brownfields plus a handful of new fields that had already been discovered in Soviet times. But the industry gave little attention to exploration and there were few new discoveries. As for the "legacy" fields, the application of standard well rehabilitation and stimulation techniques produced in each company that adopted them a brief two-year burst of spectacular growth, after which growth rates rapidly fell back. By the end of 2004, the Russian industry had reached the end of the "miracle." From that point on, holding back the decline of the legacy fields would require much more capital and more advanced technology.

The second broad liability of the private oil miracle could perhaps best be called cultural. It was in the oilfields that the core doctrines and practices of capitalism collided with the deeply rooted Soviet legacy of populist socialism, with its blend of egalitarianism, communitarianism, dissimulation, anti-Semitism, and xenophobia. All of the standard practices of a capitalist company were viewed as suspect in the oil towns, the geological and petro-engineering institutes, and the government offices. Acceleration of production based on unfamiliar new techniques was widely perceived as destructive and shortsighted. Downsizing and outsourcing and transferring social costs to local budgets were seen as rapacious and irresponsible. Tight financial and production controls were repressive—and got in the way of traditional local arrangements. Profit maximization was predatory. Tax optimization was criminal. And all this, many Russians muttered to themselves, was the work of foreigners and non-Russians. It was a potent brew of resentments, well suited, as it frothed up, to nourishing political agendas and ambitions.

But here is where the differences among the private oil companies were critical. The neftianik companies, LUKoil and especially Surgutneftegaz, were more cautious and conservative, always mindful of the potential political dangers of defying the traditional norms of the Soviet era. Vagit Alekperov and Vladimir Bogdanov, as former Soviet officials, never doubted that the weakness of the state was temporary. Thus they limited their liabilities.

But the finansist companies plunged ahead, changing their own internal cultures and asserting their autonomy from the state. Yet even among the finansist companies there were differences. Sibneft remained largely Russian, and though highly innovative it hewed to Russian norms. TNK was only moderately innovative, until its Russian owners merged it into a joint venture with BP in 2003, a topic discussed in Chapter 11. Yukos, by contrast, was a full-scale rebel practically from the moment Khodorkovsky took it over in late 1995. In a culture of exchange in which rents are shared among wide networks of notables and influentials, Khodorkovsky shared only on his own terms. In a statist culture in which companies and individuals look first to the government for direction (if perhaps to evade it later), Khodorkovsky proclaimed total independence. In the way he ran his company, in the way he produced oil, in the way he enriched himself and his colleagues, Khodorkovsky set many in the oil establishment and the political sphere against him. The consequences would soon follow.

chapter 6

The Brothers from Saint Petersburg:
The Origins of Putin's State Capitalism

Moscow and Saint Petersburg have always been rivals. Ever since Tsar Peter the Great founded his northern capital in the spring of 1703, cutting a cross in the barren peat of the Neva River delta, Muscovites have derided it as an upstart, an administrative city with imperial pretensions. Saint Petersburgers, for their part, have long dismissed Moscow as a crass merchant town. The two cities compete for the soul of the country, each rising and falling in a struggle that has lasted 300 years. But in the 2000s, as the rivalry entered its fourth century, the elites of Saint Petersburg developed a novel strategy—under Vladimir Putin, they invaded Moscow.

Thousands of *Pitertsy* (as Russians call the inhabitants of Saint Petersburg) have migrated to Moscow and taken up many of the most powerful positions in the government and big business. While the communists ruled the Soviet Union from Moscow, Saint Petersburg became a shabby backwater. But under Putin federal funding and state-sponsored investment have flowed like a mighty river to the northwest, and Saint Petersburg has regained its wealth and its pride. Moscow remains the political center and by far the largest and richest city in the country, but in the 2000s the *Pitertsy* took over many of the capital's power structures. Though far outnumbered by the many officials from other places who work in the Kremlin and the White House, the influence of the Pitertsy outweighed all other groups. During Vladimir Putin's first two terms they were the core of his formula of power and rule. It was only toward the end of the decade, as Putin and Dmitri Medvedev began to draw cadres from more diverse sources, that their numbers and influence faded.

A first wave from Saint Petersburg had already arrived long before Putin, between the late 1980s and the mid-1990s. They were the young pro-market economists from academic institutes who came to the capital to help launch the radical market reforms.[1] Anatolii Chubais was the best known and most successful of these. But by the end of the 1990s, only a handful of them remained in the government (Chubais himself had moved on in 1998 to head the Russian electricity monopoly). One of the last of this initial wave, however, was Aleksei Kudrin—a man as important to the 2000s as Chubais was to the 1990s—who came to the capital in 1996 as a protégé of Chubais and subsequently became Putin's perennial minister of finance and the chief architect of his fiscal and budgetary policy, until his sudden dismissal in September 2011. It was also Kudrin, as we shall see, who introduced another Saint Petersburg migrant to Moscow: Vladimir Putin himself.

The second wave of Pitertsy—Putin's people—was much larger and more diverse. They came from the security, administrative, and scientific elite of Saint Petersburg. Many were former KGB officers, like Putin himself, but they also included academics and jurists, entrepreneurs and businessmen, and many of Putin's former colleagues and protégés from his days as deputy mayor of Saint Petersburg. They began migrating to Moscow in the late 1990s, as Putin moved up the Kremlin hierarchy.

By the second half of the 2000s, a third group of Pitertsy began to emerge into public view, consisting of private businessmen whose chief asset was their early association with the Saint Petersburg mayoralty and Putin's activities there. They were neither "liberals" nor *siloviki*; they had not held major posts in Saint Petersburg and did not hold any in Moscow; for the most part they did not even migrate there. They took no public part in policy issues; thus, they were not a political "clan," in the same sense as the other two groups. The initial rise of this new class of oligarchs was unheralded, marked mainly by their quiet acquisition of one major state asset after another, through a process that suggested powerful connections. By the end of the 2000s, however, this third group—the "deep Pitertsy," one might call them—had become so visible that they drew growing publicity and public disapproval. Unlike the first two groups, which had been an essential political asset for Putin as he built his power, the third group increasingly became a political liability, symbolizing what many Russians perceived as the decay of the system and the spread of patrimonial rule.[2]

This chapter tells the story of Putin's Pitertsy and especially Putin himself. For over a decade, the men from Saint Petersburg have been Putin's chief instrument in consolidating his power, recapturing rents, and rebuilding a strong centralized state. They have been amply rewarded, to put it mildly, for their service, and they have grown rich and powerful. At the same time, the often bitter battles among them for profit, precedence, and property have repeatedly disrupted the facade of stability that Putin has so carefully crafted, forcing him to engage in constant rebalancing. The rivalries and tensions among the various Pitertsy and their complex relations with Putin himself have been a major driver in the politics of oil and gas, the two most important prizes in the system.

Liberals and Siloviki

Putin's Pitertsy are like any large family. Their complex divisions and rivalries have deep roots in the politics of Soviet-era Leningrad and the Saint Petersburg of the early 1990s under reformist mayor Anatolii Sobchak. There is no simple unity of views and motives among them, and one would look in vain for a "Saint Petersburg" view that would explain the politics and policies of the Putin era. As Putin himself put it in an interview in 1999, "We feel a little like fellow-countrymen . . . but there is a wide spread in our views."[3]

For the sake of simplicity, it helps to think of the Pitertsy as comprising two broad streams, which subsequently, as they moved to Moscow, became rival clans with competing institutional strongholds. The first consisted mainly of economists and lawyers, who viewed Russia's marketization as an overall success and accepted the new private sector, although many felt it needed a stronger and more competent state to regulate it. The second consisted of security people, mostly former officers, policemen, and prosecutors.[4] They disliked Russia's chaotic marketization, denounced the scandalous "shares-for-loans" privatizations of the 1990s, and despised the oligarchs who had inherited the commanding heights of Soviet industry (although that did not prevent them from doing business with the oligarchs). The first group came to be called the "liberals" and the second group the siloviki, that is, those who came from the security sector, although in practice the boundary between them was shifting and fluid, and the differences between the two were based as much on opportunism and group interest as on principle.[5]

The term *silovik,* though it became widely known in the West only under Putin, has long been used by Russians to designate those who work in the *silovye struktury,* the "power structures." In traditional Russian parlance the

233

term applies to the police and the secret police, the prosecutors and the judges, but also the military and more broadly any state officials who wear uniforms and wield coercive power. But under Putin the term came to apply as well to anyone with a prior career as a silovik, and more specifically to the ex-siloviki among the Pitertsy who migrated to Moscow in the Putin years and held top positions in the FSB and the General Procuracy, as well as the handful of agencies that had been spun off from the KGB in the early 1990s.

The views of both the liberals and siloviki were naturally colored by how they had fared personally in the 1990s. Within each group there were some who had done well, but most had missed out on the first post-Soviet division of the assets in the 1990s and were determined not to miss a second one. As with any group arriving in power, their behavior was shaped by past careers, group loyalties, self-interest, and one thing more: a sense of urgency, since they could not know how long their time in the sun would last.

When they arrived in the capital, the two groups tended to gravitate to different jobs. The liberals predominated in the financial and economic positions; the siloviki moved into the coercive apparatus. The result was an unspoken division of labor: the liberals fashioned a new fiscal and budgetary machinery,[6] while the siloviki built a new structure of central political control.[7] Both sides shared a common interest in strengthening the central state, and for much of Putin's first term, they were able to work reasonably smoothly together. (Indeed, the strengthened financial and coercive controls were simply two faces of the same reconstruction of central power.) Yet from the beginning there was a built-in tension between the goals of political control and economic liberalism. The tension mounted as resource prices climbed, the flow of rents increased, and the competition for power sharpened within the ruling elites, eventually erupting into the open over the Yukos Affair and the subsequent battle for Rosneft, described in the next two chapters.

Thus, insofar as one can speak of a "Saint Petersburg style," it may lie precisely in the split collective personality of the Pitertsy. It is perhaps no accident that Saint Petersburg over the last generation has produced both some of the most radical liberals and the most dyed-in-the-wool reactionaries in the Russian political spectrum. The combination of Saint Petersburg's location at the edge of the West, together with the heavy concentration of military industry there, may provide a clue. In Soviet times, it was Saint Petersburg that was viewed by the Kremlin as potentially the most vulnerable to dangerous ideas from the West, and it was all the more tightly controlled on that account. This pair of opposite influences can be felt in the city even now.

But what of the man himself? Who was Putin?

"Steadfast in the Military Manner"

It was the summer of 1996, and Vladimir Putin was out of a job. His liberal patron, Anatolii Sobchak, had lost the recent mayoral election in Saint Petersburg. Putin, who had risen under Sobchak to become first deputy mayor and Sobchak's right-hand man, was suddenly at loose ends. But his friend and former mayoralty colleague, Aleksei Kudrin, had just landed a top job as head of the Kremlin's Inspection Administration *(Kontrol'noe Upravlenie)*. Kudrin invited Putin to come to Moscow; Kudrin would introduce him around. But Putin was offered only a disappointingly minor post, which he turned down, and Kudrin was driving him to the airport to catch a plane back to Saint Petersburg. As the car neared the airport, Kudrin made a last-minute call to another high Kremlin official, which unexpectedly yielded a better offer. Kudrin turned the car around. Putin was hired. His life and that of Russia were about to change.[8]

Over the next three years Putin rose rapidly in the Kremlin hierarchy. He was hard-working, self-effacing, disciplined, and loyal—qualities that soon attracted the attention of President Boris Yeltsin. In his last autobiography, *Presidential Marathon,* Yeltsin wrote that he had been on the lookout for someone "steadfast in the military manner."[9] In July 1998, at Yeltsin's order, Putin was promoted over hundreds of more senior eligibles to head the Federal Security Service (FSB), the successor to the KGB. Another promotion soon followed,[10] and in August 1999 Yeltsin named Putin prime minister, explicitly designating Putin as his intended heir.

At the time, this did not look to be the epoch-making event that it does now. Yeltsin's latest choice seemed like only the latest episode in the aging patriarch's erratic search for a successor. He had designated "heirs" before. Putin was Yeltsin's fourth prime minister in sixteen months, and the Kremlin, in that late summer of 1999, seemed at sea, without a strategy or a candidate.[11] Yet in fewer than 100 days, in what must surely rank as one of the supreme feats of political engineering, the new prime minister morphed from a near total unknown into a presidential front-runner. In the election of March 2000 Putin swept to a first-round victory as president of Russia.[12]

When he took the oath of office in May, Putin had none of the obvious power assets of a career politician. He had behind him no party, no coterie of allies and trusted protégés, no favor bank built up over a lifetime in office, no policy record, and no mass following. On inauguration day, as he walked down an endless red carpet through the vast halls of the Kremlin to take the oath of office, he looked nervous and alone. Few imagined he could be a strong ruler.[13] But within a fortnight of his inauguration Putin had begun to build a framework of power that would restore the primacy of the central state and make him the undisputed leader of Russia.[14]

An essential part of the story was Putin's reassertion of state control over the oil and gas industry, then as now the most essential resource for power and wealth in Russia. In 2000, the oil sector appeared to have escaped irretrievably from the grasp of the state, and the gas sector looked to be slipping away as well.[15] Yet only four years later, by the end of Putin's first term, the Kremlin was back in charge of both. Their revenues, now buoyed up by rising global commodity prices, were recaptured for the Kremlin's uses. What appeared in 2000 to be the invincible power of the oligarchs quickly began to crumble against the reasserted power of the Kremlin and the state, and by 2004–2005 Putin's victory appeared complete. In the process, however, the initial alliance between the liberals and the siloviki was torn apart, to the advantage of a hardline group within the latter.

The Putin Formula: "Left" and "Right"

How did Putin do it? The broad answer is that state power easily trumped the power of private money, once the former was revived and deployed by a determined leader. The machinery of state control over the energy sector had never been abolished but had merely gone dormant. The police, the Procuracy, and the courts were still there. When new political life was breathed into them, the effect was almost instantaneous.

But why was money not able simply to subvert force, buying policemen and judges, just as it had done throughout the 1990s (and indeed has never ceased doing)? What enabled Putin to regain control over the apparatus of coercion and to use it so effectively against the oligarchs' money? And what enabled him, from a weak starting position in 1999–2000, to achieve that control in so short a time?

The answer was a political formula that blended the ideological appeal of Russian patriotism and renewed state strength with the motive of self-interest, wrapped in the language of market liberalism. During Putin's first term, this formula drew the support of both liberals and conservatives, particularly among Putin's previous associates and acquaintances from Saint Petersburg.[16] The core of that consensus, the point on which both liberals and statists agreed, was that the state had lost control over oil and gas rents—the single most important source of wealth in the country—and had to regain it. This "coalition of discontent" was key to Putin's early bid for control over the energy sector.[17] Putin revealed himself to be a skillful and determined tactician, engaging the powerful motives of patriotism and self-interest against the oil and gas oligarchs, through the classic devices of divide-and-conquer, intimidation, and co-optation. But the main key to his success is that there was a broad consensus, both among the Pitertsy and in much of the political and business elite generally, that the weakening of the state needed to be reversed. During his first term, the "left-right" Putin embodied that consensus.

The formula had originated in Saint Petersburg in the late 1980s and early 1990s. Russian sociologist Ol'ga Kryshtanovskaia, describing the Soviet officers and officials who left state service for the private sector in the early 1990s, sums up their evolution:

> These young retirees with their communist views went to work for the nouveaux riches, whom they initially hated. However, material incentives did their work, and the longer these people worked in business and the more they came to depend on the oligarchs and the new Russians, the more liberal their views became. . . . Their views evolved: the communist pathos weakened, the Soviet mythology lost its former power over their minds. The Marxist-Leninist phraseology was replaced by patriotism and slavophilism, while their economic views became more and more market-oriented.[18]

Vladimir Putin, Kryshtanovskaia believes, was the ultimate illustration of this evolution:

> Raised as a communist, he found himself in the alien world of the democrats. The metamorphosis of his views was typical of all the former officers in the reform years: [he developed] an ambivalent consciousness, which accepted both the new market economy and the old ideas of great-power

Russia and socialist equality. Putin, like many other officers, became simultaneously left and right.[19]

In Putin's case the culture shock was particularly great because he had spent the second half of the 1980s—virtually the entire Gorbachev period—in East Germany. There he had witnessed at first hand the disintegration of the Soviet empire, but he had missed the entire experience of Gorbachev's reforms, the ferment and euphoria of *perestroika* and *glasnost* that affected all Russia in those years.[20]

Precisely because he was "simultaneously left and right," Putin was uniquely placed to attract the loyalty and support of both the liberals and the conservatives. His appeal lay precisely in his ambiguity. Both sides saw him as one of them. He had credibility with both, and he could draw recruits from both. But more fundamentally, his views were also a blend of both. In Putin's own mind, "left" and "right" fit smoothly together. His views on foreign investment are a good illustration. A strong state is a stable state, one in which foreign investors will feel they can "plow their money into Russian soil." In a revealing television interview in February 2000, on the eve of his election, Putin drew the lessons of his experience in Saint Petersburg in the first half of the decade:

> You know, I worked in Saint Petersburg on a great many different projects. I simply know these negotiations from the inside. A potential investor comes along. Let's say, an investment of a hundred million. First he's got to plow this money into our soil, right? Then a certain period of time has to pass while he recoups his investment, and a further period before he earns a profit, otherwise there's no sense in his getting into this business.
>
> But if we're going from one putsch to another, and no one knows when the next putsch is coming and how it will end, then who will invest? There will be no large-scale investment until we have a steady political system, stability, and a strong state that protects market institutions and creates favorable investment conditions.[21]

In Putin's mind, market and state meshed smoothly. But it was a vision that assumed, as a matter of course, that the state would be the dominant partner.

But by what steps did this ideology evolve, and how did its application to energy policy develop? To answer that, one must go back to Saint Petersburg, at the beginning of the 1990s.

Northern Origins

The Soviet era had been a disaster for Saint Petersburg. The proud capital of Russia under the tsars, the symbol of Russia's Silver Age, was relegated by the Bolsheviks to the status of a distant second city. Peter the Great's window on the West was shuttered behind the Iron Curtain. For three-quarters of a century, Saint Petersburg—denied even its name after the Communists dubbed it Leningrad in 1924—lived in the shadow of Moscow.[22]

Yet this early center of industry under the tsars found a new vocation under the Soviets, as the country's military workshop. By the 1980s, some three-quarters of all military orders from the nine military-industrial ministries (known in Russian as the *oboronka*) went to plants in the Leningrad region.[23] But when Yeltsin's market reformers came to power in 1991–1992, they canceled nearly all military contracts. Thus, when the second Russian revolution undid the first, Saint Petersburg regained little more than its name. Unlike Moscow, which soon exploded in a roar of private-sector activity, Saint Petersburg in the wake of communism's collapse lay prostrate.

This was the impoverished and demoralized city to which KGB Lieutenant-Colonel Vladimir Putin returned in 1990, after five years on assignment in East Germany. He went to work for the reformist mayor of Saint Petersburg, Anatolii Sobchak, initially as an advisor, and from late 1991 as deputy mayor for foreign economic relations. From 1992 on, Putin's influence grew steadily, until in March 1994 Sobchak named him first deputy mayor, thus making official a role that Putin had already played informally for the previous two years.[24] By this time, Putin was in charge of an increasingly broad range of the city's affairs, including, notably, relations with all the city's "power structures": the KGB, the police, and the judiciary. It was said of Sobchak that he "presided rather than governed," leaving wide latitude to his subordinates, and as a result Putin and his fellow deputy mayors effectively ran the city. There was an informal division of labor: Putin's fellow first deputy Vladimir Yakovlev ran the "old" economy of the city, while Putin oversaw the "new" economy—the joint ventures, the privatized businesses, and foreign investments. Putin served in the Sobchak government for five years, until Sobchak was defeated in the election of 1996 and Putin resigned from the city government.[25]

As Saint Petersburg struggled against the deep depression that gripped all of Russia—but especially its northwest—its one asset was its strategic location on the Bay of Finland, which opened onto the Baltic Sea. Saint Petersburg had regained its window on the world, and in the new wide-open Russian economy, the city had the potential to develop into an international trade hub. But, as Putin was to describe in a doctoral thesis he defended the year after leaving the mayoralty, the breakup of the Soviet Union left Saint Petersburg poorly equipped to seize the opportunity. The major Soviet commercial ports on the Baltic were now in foreign countries: Tallinn (now in independent Estonia) handled grain; Riga (in Latvia) specialized in container traffic; Klaipeda and Ventspils (in Lithuania and Latvia, respectively) were the oil ports. Russian exports also went out via Finland's oil refinery and terminal at Porvoo. These did very well in this transitional period, as they continued to handle Russia's exports of raw materials and bulk commodities.

In contrast, Saint Petersburg and its surrounding ports had been mainly naval bases, and the city lacked modern commercial facilities. What little did exist was old and dilapidated. An antiquated oil terminal exported a small volume of oil products but could be reached only by barge, which limited its use to the summer months. The city urgently needed an up-to-date "multifunctional port complex" (as Putin noted in his dissertation) that could stimulate the city's economy.

Saint Petersburg would have to wait another decade for its new port, by which time its one-time deputy mayor had become president of Russia. But the region's depressed economy did not prevent private enterprise from springing up just the same, in a local version of the mass privatization taking place throughout the country. "Going to the market," state officials exited their offices and launched private businesses with state connections and newly privatized state assets.[26] At the Smolny Palace (now the seat of the Saint Petersburg mayoralty), a Committee for Foreign Economic Relations (known as KVS) was responsible for registering companies involving foreign partners. Starting in the spring of 1991 and running over the next five years, KVS registered over 9,000 new companies.[27] Its chairman was Deputy Mayor Putin.

In some of these, KVS itself was a cofounder and minority shareholder. Thus on July 4, 1991 (one week after Putin's start on the job), KVS took a 5 percent interest in a "Saint Petersburg Center for World Trade," alongside another 5 percent investor, the newly created "Bank Rossiya," several of whose senior shareholders have since remained close to Putin.[28] KVS under Putin helped launch several other businesses as well, such as Petromed, created to buy medical equipment for Saint Petersburg's hospitals.[29] For a municipal office to take a stake as a shareholder in a private company was an innovation; and according to one well-informed report, the young legal scholar who first figured out how this could be done within the rules was Dmitri Medvedev, who served as KVS's legal consultant and subsequently became Putin's protégé and Russia's president from 2008 to 2012, and current prime minister.[30]

The Brothers from Saint Petersburg

Putin was a visible figure in the Saint Petersburg of the early 1990s. Hundreds of Western businessmen visited his office, seeking the mayoralty's support for ventures of all kinds: real estate, timber, metals, food-for-fuel barter deals, and much else. They remember Putin as a helpful and efficient official, who helped them cut through the city's endless red tape and who did not take bribes.[31] The office of the deputy mayor for external relations became known as a place to get things done. Putin's near native command of German was particularly welcome to European visitors. (He did not speak English at the time, although as president he took lessons and became reasonably proficient.) With Putin's assistance many German companies opened representative offices in Saint Petersburg, including notably Dresdner Bank, whose president in Saint Petersburg, Matthias Warnig, had been a friend of Putin's during the latter's service in Dresden;[32] and the German engineering company Siemens, whose Saint Petersburg representative was Nikolai Shamalov. Both men subsequently became prominent figures in the business circles associated with the Putin era.

If one could travel in time back to that corner of the Smolny Building where KVS had its offices, one would see a remarkable number of familiar faces—two decades younger, a little slimmer perhaps and less well turned out, but recognizably the same. Igor Sechin, Putin's perennial aide, and Mariia Ental'tseva, his secretary, busily manage the office's flow of visitors and papers— just as they would in later years in the Kremlin. (We shall meet Sechin again at several points throughout this book.) Putin's deputies Oleg Markov (a law school classmate of Putin's, subsequently a presidential aide) and Oleg Safonov (today deputy head of the Federal Antinarcotics Service) are hard at work nearby. In a neighboring office sits Aleksei Miller (today the CEO of Gazprom), in those days a shy and hesitant figure with a thin moustache. Sometimes a surviving news clip shows them in action. In one scene from 1991, Putin's deputy Viktor Zubkov (future prime minister and today chairman of the board of Gazprom), a gruff veteran of the Leningrad party apparatus, leads a news conference next to his visibly uncertain chief. It is clear from the body language that Zubkov is the mentor, Putin the student. As Putin rises to first deputy mayor, his responsibilities broaden, and other deputies begin to report to him. Through his office pass other colleagues with famous names today: Aleksei Kudrin (then responsible for the city's budget and finances, later Putin's minister of finance and deputy prime minister), Kudrin's deputy Sergei Naryshkin (subsequently head of the Presidential Administration under Dmitri Medvedev and today speaker of the Duma), Dmitri Kozak (then head of Sobchak's legal affairs committee, today deputy prime minister), Viktor Ivanov (a retired KGB colonel who then headed the mayoralty's personnel department and later held the same job in the Kremlin under Putin, now head of the Federal Antinarcotics Service). Viktor Zolotov (today the head of Putin's personal security service) discreetly provides security and other services through his private company, Baltik-Escort. There are occasional visitors from the Saint Petersburg legislature and the local offices of the Tax Police and the FSB, all prominent figures in Moscow today.[33]

The record of the owners of the businesses registered by KVS in the first half of the 1990s would become practically a roll call of several hundred of the most influential business leaders in Russia, many of whom followed Putin and Medvedev to Moscow in the second half of the 1990s. The media have sensationalized this group's KGB connections, but what is in fact more striking is the diversity of their origins and their overlapping career paths, especially after 1991. Former KGB officers account for perhaps a third of the founding shareholders of the companies on the list. The rest are drawn from a wide range of backgrounds in the political, managerial, and scientific elite of Saint Petersburg.[34]

One name that recurs frequently in the accounts of the time and illustrates the complex networks among the Pitertsy is that of Vladimir Yakunin, today the head of the Russian railways, a man who has been close to Putin since the mayoralty days and was later prominently mentioned in 2006–2007 as a possible successor to Putin as president. In the early to mid-1980s, while head of the international department of the prestigious Yoffe Institute of Physics, Yakunin joined with other institute staff members Yuri Koval'chuk, Viktor Miachin, and Andrei Fursenko—all prominent names in Putin's inner business circle today—to create several private consulting companies, which generated foreign currency for the institute. Assigned to the Permanent Mission of the USSR at the United Nations in New York, Yakunin continued developing his business activities in Russia in the late 1980s. By 1990, Yakunin was a board member and (through four of his companies) one of the major shareholders of the influential "Bank Rossiya", which brings together many of the key figures in Putin's inner circle, including Yakunin's former partners from the Yoffe Institute.[35] According to some accounts, Yakunin, a former KGB officer who combines business acumen with international experience and connections, was the principal innovator and the chief motive force in several of the numerous businesses that KVS registered in Putin's time.

Just how much Putin may have benefited personally from KVS's participation in such businesses has never been established, and Russians in a position to know are understandably discreet. If Putin himself did well at the time, he was remarkably unostentatious about it. People who knew him in those days remember how modestly, even shabbily, he dressed, in a drab suit and mousy overcoat.[36] His wife, Liudmila, recalls that the couple built their first dacha with bricks she had bought herself (although by other accounts the dacha was far from plain).[37] A fire at the dacha in the summer of 1996 consumed the couple's savings, which like most Russians at the time they kept in cash in their home, since banks were not to be trusted. In subsequent years, though, Putin's standard of living clearly improved, even before he became president. One documented business connection between Putin and what is sometimes called the "Yoffe" group or the "Bank Rossiya" group was their common membership in a luxurious gated community of summer homes, the "Ozero" complex, built in the later 1990s.[38] Yet for all the rumors that swirl about Putin's private business ties in the early 1990s, there is little definite to point to.[39]

Among the companies with ties to KVS was the Petersburg Fuel Company (PTK), previously discussed in Chapter 3. KVS was not itself a cofounder of PTK (the actual shareholder of record was the city's Property Committee[40]), but Putin took an active part in the creation of PTK in the fall of 1994,[41] and he oversaw it until the summer of 1996, when he left the city government. Even after Putin's departure for Moscow, his former colleagues and associates continued to hold key positions in PTK as well as Surgutneftegaz's local fuel distribution subsidiary.[42] Putin took no direct part in the battles between Surgutneftegaz and PTK, but once he had become prime minister he may have brokered (or at least supported) an accommodation among the warring factions in the Saint Petersburg fuels market, enabling Surgutneftegaz to return to the city as a fuels supplier by the end of the decade.[43]

Terminal Politics

The local fuels market was small-time compared with the much bigger rewards Saint Petersburg stood to gain from oil exports, if only it could break free of its dependence on Ventspils, Tallinn, and Klaipeda, which charged high transit tariffs and export taxes to handle Russian crude and products, taking $10–$12 per ton away from the Russian export revenues. The Russians agreed they needed their own oil terminal. But there were several rival concepts in play, with competing backers. In January 1992 Putin's KVS committee teamed up with the operators of the small existing Saint Petersburg oil terminal to form a company called "Golden Gates," which leased the terminal and launched a plan to expand it.[44] According to a subsequent account in the *Financial Times* (FT), Kineks and its cofounder, Gennadii Timchenko, whom we met earlier, were also shareholders in the deal. According to the FT, the project soon clashed with a rival group backed by a criminal gang, and "the dispute escalated to the point at which Mr. Putin was personally threatened and had to send his daughters to Germany for safety."[45]

The reality seems to have been less dramatic. The Golden Gates project was a modest one, and it was soon overtaken by more ambitious ventures with bigger backers. In 1993 the Russian government issued a directive approving three major terminal projects—Primorsk (for crude oil), Ust'-Luga (for container traffic), and Batareinaia (for refined oil products).[46] Golden Gates was not on the list.[47] This was not to the city government's liking, since the three approved projects benefited the surrounding oblast' (and its government) but did little directly for the city itself. Between 1993 and 1995 the mayoralty strenuously opposed the three big projects, arguing in favor of a reconstruction of the port of Saint Petersburg instead, on the grounds that a reconstruction would be faster and cheaper than a grandiose new project. To keep the peace, Moscow had to dispatch the transportation minister, Vitalii Efimov, to try to reconcile the various positions.[48]

Putin was actively involved in this dispute. In his capacity as first deputy mayor, he chaired an Administrative Council of the Ports, which directly oversaw the various local plans to reconstruct the port of Saint Petersburg, contracting for feasibility studies and looking for investors.[49] The mayoralty held out for two other local projects in addition to Golden Gates—a sugar terminal and a complex for refrigerated goods—but found few allies. The Golden Gates project, in particular, was overshadowed by the Batareinaia project, to be connected to the Kirishi refinery by a new pipeline.[50] But the problem shared by all these projects was a lack of money. The Batareinaia terminal was no exception; after fifteen years of promises and press releases, it has never been built.[51]

These local battles over terminals and pipelines in the early 1990s, and Putin's active involvement in them at the time, are ancient history now, yet they are significant in retrospect for two reasons. First, almost as soon as he became prime minister Putin returned to the Baltic oil-export issue; clearly in his mind it was an important component of Russian energy policy. Revealingly, however, when he did so, it was on the opposite side. As deputy mayor of Saint Petersburg he had supported local solutions, which led him to oppose a large crude pipeline to the Baltic that would bypass the city, but as prime minister and president he became the crude pipeline's most fervent backer, because it promised a major Russian outlet for Russian oil and thus was of national significance.

Second, in these early battles, key alliances and personal relationships were formed that have endured to the present day. For example, Gennadii Timchenko, the one-time Kirishi official and cofounder of Kineks who was briefly Putin's early partner in the Golden Gates project, remains a social friend who shares Putin's interest in martial arts.[52] Both men deny that there were any business connections between them or that there are any now. Timchenko (who is so secretive that until recently there were only two known photographs of him) has long since left Russia to live in Switzerland, where he cofounded what soon became one of the world's largest oil-trading companies, Gunvor.[53] Gunvor is the leading trader of Russia's oil exports, notably through Surgutneftegaz, which owns the Kirishi refinery.[54] In recent years Timchenko has reemerged as a major investor in Russia, notably in several strategic energy companies and projects of interest to the Kremlin, such as an LNG (liquefied natural gas) project on the Yamal Peninsula in the far north of Tiumen Oblast'.[55]

In Russia such things do not happen by accident. The possible ties between the two men have become the object of intense scrutiny by the Russian media and opposition politicians,[56] as has the entire range of Putin's early associations.[57] But where Timchenko is concerned, the precise origins of the friendship, and its nature today, remain obscure.

What is quite clear, however, is that Putin was deeply involved in the emerging world of private business in the Saint Petersburg of the early 1990s—as regulator, facilitator, arbitrator, and conceivably as stakeholder—and was well acquainted with its principal players, many of whom subsequently followed him to Moscow. It is in this sense that one can speak of Putin as being "both left and right," that is, both "private" and "state," in the skills and relationships he brought with him to Moscow.

Putin Moves to Moscow

By the fall of 1996 Putin had left the city government of Saint Petersburg and moved to Moscow. His first post in the Kremlin was as deputy head of the Kremlin's Administration of Affairs *(Upravlenie delami)*. This innocuously named body administers the Kremlin's far-flung network of real-estate properties, resorts, hunting lodges, luxury sanatoria, and so forth, much of it taken over from the Communist Party and other defunct Soviet institutions in the wake of the Soviet collapse.[58] Putin's boss in his first assignment was the colorful Pavel Pavlovich Borodin (known to all by his first name and patronymic as "Pal Palych"). Pal Palych was the powerful master of Kremlin patronage and favors, who judiciously measured out largesse to a wide range of good causes, from credit cards for the Yeltsin family's foreign shopping trips to the multiple regildings of the Kremlin palaces and churches, not to mention the odd election campaign. It was a good place to learn the inner workings of the Kremlin, and Putin soon established a reputation as a hard-working, loyal, and discreet aide.

It was during this first year in Moscow that Putin defended a doctoral dissertation at the Saint Petersburg Mining Institute, on the subject of planning the mineral-resource base of the Saint Petersburg region.[59] This very Russian custom of bylining a scholarly tome in midcareer is a virtually obligatory rite of passage, a sign of rising rank, for state officials and politicians (and more recently, business executives).[60] Putin appears to have begun the project in 1995, when he was still first deputy mayor of Saint Petersburg, and completed it in 1997, by which time he was already in the Kremlin.

The text of Putin's thesis has recently become available, but analysts who hoped to find in it a key to Putin's thinking about economic policy, and energy affairs in particular, have been disappointed to discover a workmanlike but entirely conventional three-part essay dealing with development issues in the region of Saint Petersburg—and not in the least with energy. The first part analyzes the local market in the area around Saint Petersburg for construction materials (mainly granite and other kinds of stone); the third part discusses the prospects for developing the transportation network and port system of Saint Petersburg; and linking the two parts is a middle section on decision-making strategy, drawn from an American textbook. The dissertation does not cover energy at all, with the curious exception of a single paragraph, seemingly dropped into the text as an afterthought, opposing any extension of the proposed Baltic pipeline to Finland.

In short, the Putin thesis suggests that as late as 1997 Putin was paying no particular attention to energy policy. This in itself would not be so surprising. He was a rising Kremlin official but not yet a national policy leader. The following year, when he was named chairman of the FSB, he was quickly immersed in security matters.[61] The Putin thesis, then, could be interpreted as just what it so commonly is in Russia—a ticket to support a career that, at the time he started it, appeared to be on hold.

Yet this may understate the extent to which Putin and an early circle of associates were already thinking about the role of energy in Russian policy. From the middle of the decade, a small group of officials, most of them previously connected with Putin at the Saint Petersburg mayoralty, had formed an informal discussion group on natural-resource policy under the aegis of a well-known senior scientist, Vladimir Litvinenko, rector of the Saint Petersburg Mining Institute. Their discussions resulted in a number of published works between 1997 and 1999, of which Putin's dissertation was only the first. Taken together they form a detailed agenda for natural-resource and energy policy. Among them was a doctoral dissertation by Viktor Zubkov on tax policy in the natural-resource sector, which prefigures several major themes of Putin's subsequent approach to taxation.[62] But by far the most significant product of the "Litvinenko circle" was another dissertation, defended in 1998, by Putin's long-time aide and confidant, Igor Sechin.

The Alter Ego: Igor Sechin

The significance of Igor Sechin in the politics of the Putin era is hard to overstate. Starting out as Putin's personal assistant in 1991, Sechin accompanied

Putin in nearly every subsequent assignment on the way to the top.[63] Over the years Sechin evolved from assistant to key inside player, an unofficial leader of the silovik wing of the Kremlin elite, and one of the central figures behind the scenes in the rise of Rosneft and the destruction of Yukos. Yet so long as Putin was president, Sechin remained out of public view, a self-effacing éminence grise, the shadow at Putin's side, the ultimate Kremlin insider. It was only after 2008, when Putin became prime minister and Dmitri Medvedev took his place as president, that Sechin took on a public persona, as Putin's deputy prime minister in charge of energy affairs, and now as president and chairman of Rosneft, as well as executive secretary of Putin's newly created Energy Commision. The bond between the two men, established over nearly two decades, though sometimes tested, appears indestructible.

The central topic of Sechin's dissertation is oil. Sechin had no background in economics or energy affairs, having majored in Romance languages at Leningrad State University, with a specialty in Portuguese.[64] Yet the dissertation is a sophisticated economic exercise, containing a lengthy analysis of the condition of the Russian oil industry and the outlook for the global oil market.

Putin and Sechin: A Doctrine Evolves

Thanks to the two men's theses we have some clues to the genesis and evolution of the thinking of Vladimir Putin, Igor Sechin, and their associates in Saint Petersburg on the eve of their move to a national stage. They are initially a small-town crowd, focused on local issues, working second-tier deals, with little inkling that they will soon be running the affairs of the country. Neither work really departs from the native setting of Saint Petersburg.

Yet some of the major themes of the Putin approach to economic policy, and to energy in particular, can already be seen in both works, as well as Putin and Sechin's early involvement in the oil politics of the Baltic region in the early to mid-1990s. Both men perceive that the market has not worked. For the Russian Baltic region, and for Saint Petersburg in particular, it has brought only depression, decline, and disorder, while the newly independent Baltic states have prospered at Russia's expense.

Yet it is not private enterprise itself that is to blame; it is the lack of state leadership. The solution is a pragmatic state-private partnership, in which the state plays a leading role in defining strategy, and the lines between private and public entrepreneurship are blurred. There is no condemnation of capitalism per se, but there is a strongly held view that capitalism is incapable of restoring growth and prosperity on its own. It needs state guidance. But more than that, it needs direct state intervention in the most strategic sectors, such as oil exports. The two theses are, in short, an early call for precisely the kind of state capitalism that the two men subsequently implemented at the top, and to which they remain faithful today.

In neither thesis, incidentally, is there any condemnation of the Soviet past. The record of the centrally planned economy is viewed rather favorably. Its crowning achievement is the creation of a high-tech military industry. The real disaster is the breakup of the Soviet Union and particularly the loss of territory and the rise of commercial rivals on Russia's doorstep. Putin and Sechin accept that Russia now functions in a global economy, but the goal of Russian policy should be to regain control of the country's trade outlets and to displace foreign competitors. Their outlook, from the first, is resolutely mercantilist, nationalist, and patriotic.

The Move to a National Stage, 1999–2000

By early 1999 Putin is no longer a local politician focused on the narrow issues of Saint Petersburg. He has been exposed to new ideas and influences, and the views that appear under his name evolve as well. His broad outlook remains recognizably the same, but as he begins applying it to actual policies, he increasingly stresses the importance of state power and control. State power is the precondition for stability and economic growth, and control of natural resources is the precondition for state power.

Tracing this evolution is rather like digging up fossils—a lot of work for a few bones. The prize fossil in this case is an article signed by Putin in the scientific journal of the Saint Petersburg Mining Institute (where Putin defended his thesis in 1997) published in early 1999. It links the "local" Putin of the earlier 1990s and the emerging "national" one and is the first major statement of his doctrine as applied to natural resources and energy.[65] The journal is obscure, its circulation a few hundred at most; and few beyond Saint Petersburg are likely to have seen the lead article in the first issue early that year, with its unsmiling Soviet-style photograph of the author, whose position as chairman of the FSB is not identified. When it first came to the attention of foreign journalists and scholars in later years, they logically assumed that the article must have been based on Putin's PhD thesis. But as we have seen, his thesis had nothing to do with energy at all. The 1999 article is a new work, Putin's first major statement of his policy views, written at a time when no one, least of all Vladimir Putin himself, imagined that within less than a year he would be president.

A Blueprint of Putin's Energy Policy?

What did the 1999 article imply for energy policy? Several of the major themes of his later policies are already there: Putin's stress on the resource sector as the basis for future growth, his aim of recapturing rents from the resource sector to support social programs and rebuild the rest of the economy, his encouragement of large financial-industrial groups with mixed public-private ownership, his emphasis on moving up the value chain from raw materials to processed goods, his call for tax reform and budgetary discipline. The 1999 article contained no specifics on energy policy, but oil transportation and oil taxes would have been predictable targets, as, above all, would gas. Gazprom, Putin's first major energy initiative, is virtually the embodiment of the program described in the 1999 article in action: building the national energy champion that invests widely throughout the economy; turning gas into processed tradables like petrochemicals, fertilizers, and steel; helping to upgrade the power sector; and competing with the Western multinationals on the global stage. In these respects the 1999 article has elements of prophecy.

Yet as Putin's actual policies evolved over the decade, they went well beyond the 1999 model. Reading the article as a blueprint, one would not have predicted the extensive renationalization of the oil sector that took place after 2004 or the large-scale use of coercion by which it happened. One might have expected more of an attempt to restructure the gas monopoly, rather than its systematic recapture and preservation as a rent machine for the Kremlin and various Saint Petersburg-based private interests. Much of the lateral transfer of oil rents under Putin has been achieved not through private-sector *chaebols,* as the 1999 article proposes, but through direct state action, via taxation and direct state subsidy or via state-owned banks and state-owned corporations. The 1999 article also did not advertise the coming "second *peredel,*" the wholesale redistribution of property to influential players with high state positions and

250

close connections to the Kremlin. In short, the path taken has turned out to be less reform-oriented and more statist, more coercive, more authoritarian, and more partial to favored interests than one might have expected from the blueprint.

Perhaps this was inevitable. Any program calling for the restoration of state power was bound to provoke strong and vocal opposition from the oligarchs. Putin, it soon became clear, was not a leader to tolerate defiance. Moreover, any reinforcement of the state was bound to benefit its best-placed servants. But in 1998–1999 none of this seemed foreordained. Putin's actual energy policies, as they evolved, were much shaped by events as they came along, and particularly by the Yukos Affair, as we shall see in the next chapter.

In particular, there is no evidence of any advance plan, concocted at FSB headquarters in the Lubyanka in 1998 or in the Security Council in 1999, when Putin briefly headed both organizations, to expropriate the oil oligarchs or purge the leadership of Gazprom, much less to renationalize the oil and gas industry around state-owned energy champions.[66] Putin had no inkling until the last moment that he would shortly be named prime minister, and his reported duties as FSB chairman and secretary of the Security Council were narrowly focused on military and security issues.[67] There are no signs of an "energy staff" or an "economic staff" surrounding Putin in the spring and summer of 1999. On the eve of his accession to the prime ministership in August, he had a broad doctrine in which energy played the key role, but he did not yet have a detailed energy program.

The same impression comes from a document published under Putin's signature in late 1999, called "Russia on the Threshold," in which Putin, by now the odds-on favorite for the succession, laid out his ideas for his presidency. It is an ambitious essay, which prefigures many of the themes later associated with Dmitri Medvedev's modernization campaign a decade later.[68]

The "Russia on the Threshold" essay starts with Russia's dire condition but puts the blame, far more than the 1999 article did, on the evils of the Soviet system. Totalitarianism, repression, a smothering official ideology—Putin does not blink from using the harshest terms. On the economy, he condemns the Soviet system's "excessive emphasis on the development of the commodities sector and defense industry," the lack of competition, the suppression of entrepreneurship and initiative, and the insufficient attention given to the key sectors of a modern economy, such as information technology, communications, and electronics. "However bitter it is to admit it,' the document concluded, "for nearly seven decades we were going down a dead-end street." This was a much more radical condemnation of the past than that of Putin's dissertation or Sechin's.

Yet the "Threshold" essay is mainly a Russian hymn to the strong state as the core of the essential Russia idea:

> Russia will not soon become, if ever, a second edition of the USA or England. . . . In our country the state, its institutions and structures have always played an exceptionally important role in the country's life and people. For the Russian people a strong state is not an anomaly, not something to be struggled against, but on the contrary a guarantor of order, the initiator and chief moving force of all changes.[69]

Even more than the earlier 1999 article, the "Threshold" essay condemns the market radicalism of the 1990s as a revolutionary doctrine drawn from abstract models in foreign textbooks. "We must find our own Russian road," Putin writes, through national unity and a reassertion of timeless Russian values, all under the guidance of a strengthened, reformed state.

Yet Putin's specific views on energy issues remained a mystery. As the 2000 election approached, the oil and gas generals knew little about the man who had suddenly emerged as the likely next president. Was he, as some believed, a tool of the "Family" around Yeltsin? Was he a silovik, given his KGB background? A liberal, from his days under Sobchak? Putin seemed in no hurry to enlighten them. By early 2000, as Putin became the anointed successor-in-waiting, his presidential campaign was chiefly remarkable for his studied vagueness about what he would do when elected. He traveled about the country, speaking often but saying little.

By early March, on the eve of the election, the oil and gas generals were clamoring for Putin, by now the favorite, to state his positions on key energy issues. At their urging Putin flew to the frozen West Siberian oil town of Surgutneftegaz and delivered his first detailed policy statement on energy.

First Inklings: Putin Speaks to the Oil Generals

The weather was in the low twenties below zero, but everyone who was anyone in the Russian energy world was present in Surgutneftegaz that day. With his opening words, Putin acknowledged that the energy generals had challenged him to lay out his plans. What followed contained something for everyone, an artful blend of carrots and sticks, but remarkable for its command of detail and technical issues. For the assembled generals, it was their first look at a side of Putin that subsequently became familiar—the policy "wonk," the confident master of his brief, surprisingly knowledgable on details, a man attracted to technical issues. (In that respect, as many subsequently observed, he was not unlike Mikhail Khodorkovsky.)

Three themes must have struck the audience. First, the state's needs were paramount, and the mission of the energy sector was to serve the state's goals. Now that energy prices were climbing again and energy profits were growing, the oil and gas sector would be expected to play a constructive role in the rebuilding of Russia. Putin lashed out at the oil companies for exporting capital out of Russia: "What is the share of the energy complex in the $1.5 billion that leave the country each month?" he asked rhetorically. Why are the energy companies investing outside, when there is an "investment famine" inside? And Putin concluded with the significant reminder, "In the end, the mineral resources belong to the state." This would be a recurring theme over the following decade and down to the present.

Yet Putin also brought the generals reassurance. He did not criticize private ownership of the oil industry and made no hint of renationalizing it (despite calls from some conservatives, including his former deputy at the FSB, Sergei Ivanov). At the same time he did not endorse the liberals' calls to break up state monopolies like Gazprom, at least not "without a detailed understanding of the consequences of such steps for the state." Instead, they would be more closely regulated and held to account. In short, Putin appeared to support the status quo.

Lastly, Putin turned to the critical subject of taxes. He first offered a headline that must have sounded like music to the oil generals—an apparent promise of lower taxes:

> Tax policy needs adjusting. . . . I won't go into details now, but of course, the basis of all our policy will be directed at reducing the tax burden, not only on the economy as a whole, but on the fuels and power sector as well.

But Putin's tax message also contained a hint of a tougher approach to come. "Profits from higher prices are being unjustly appropriated," he said.

"It's not a secret for anyone that the oil companies are using tax havens, both foreign and home-grown ones."[70] In retrospect, this was a clear warning, fore-shadowing the government's offensive against tax loopholes and nonpayments that began just a few months later.

Yet the generals could be forgiven if they did not hear the tougher parts of the message clearly. By early 2000 the overall tone of Putin's rhetoric had suddenly shifted in a noticeably liberal direction. Indeed, the shift went well beyond rhetoric. Putin named a group of liberals as his principal economic advisors, and the liberal wing of the Pitertsy took over all the leading positions in his economic team.[71] This caused a great buzz at the time, particularly in the foreign media, which hailed Putin as a "market liberal." But was he really?

Putin the Liberal?

During a trip to the Far East in October 1999, Putin had called for the creation of an economic think tank to advise him. By the turn of the year, the Center for Strategic Projects was actively churning out policy papers, with abundant funding from the Presidential Administration. Led by a reform-minded economist, German Gref, a Chubais protégé who had served in the Saint Petersburg mayoralty in Putin's time there, the Center was staffed mainly by liberals from Saint Petersburg. Once Putin was elected, the Center became an unofficial transition team, whose members subsequently became the core of the government's liberal economic wing during Putin's first term.

An intense man, who at the time sported a black goatee that gave him something of the appearance of an early Russian revolutionary, Gref spoke with the nervous air of someone who had come from the provinces to the big city and was still not quite sure he belonged there. He had grown up on a farm in Kazakhstan in an ethnic German family that had been exiled from wartime Leningrad, earning a law degree from Omsk in Siberia before continuing law school in Saint Petersburg.[72] He was on the liberal reform side from the beginning, getting his start, as so many reformers did in the 1990s, in the privatization committee in Saint Petersburg, working for Anatolii Chubais. But instead of following Chubais to Moscow in 1991, Gref rose in the city administration of Saint Petersburg, becoming deputy to Putin's close friend and ally Mikhail Manevich in the city's Property Committee, in charge of the highly sensitive real estate sector. By 1997, following Manevich's murder by organized crime,

Gref was named head of the committee and deputy mayor. The following year, with Chubais's sponsorship, Gref took a big jump in rank, landing in Moscow as first deputy head of the Ministry of State Property.[73]

In the winter of 2000, with Putin now acting president and increasingly a certainty to be elected, German Gref and his institute were suddenly in the spotlight.[74] For a time he appeared everywhere, the magnet of foreign hopes for a renewal of market reforms under the new leadership taking shape in the Kremlin. Tax reform, legal reform, restructuring state monopolies—everything appeared to be in the works, under study in Gref's policy laboratory. Its influence was particularly noticeable during Putin's first year or two in the presidency. In 2000 German Gref became Putin's minister of economic reform.

It was a heady and hopeful time for liberals. In March Gref's team presented Putin with a "manifesto," which Gref described grandly as a "new Social Contract"—like Rousseau's, he said. But as Gref acknowledged with disarming candor, "We have a patron, and we are just trying to figure out what this patron actually wants."[75] One skeptical Russian observer summed up a widespread view: Gref's program was "nice but irrationally unspecific."[76] Nevertheless, during these early days Gref appeared to have his boss's strong support.

The idea that the new president was a "market liberal" gained a further boost when in April 2000 Putin unexpectedly picked one of the most radical of the market reformers of the early 1990s, Andrei Illarionov, to be his economic advisor. Trained as an economist at Leningrad State University, Illarionov had been one of the original Saint Petersburg marketeers and, as an advisor to Yegor Gaidar, had participated in the feverish planning of the "shock therapy" of 1992. But he had gradually distanced himself from the government after Chernomyrdin became prime minister, and he remained an outsider throughout the rest of the 1990s—keeping up a steady drumbeat of iconoclastic criticism, mainly aimed at what he viewed as the disastrous fiscal and monetary policies of the Chernomyrdin government. He was one of the few to have predicted the disastrous crash of 1998. But he had the reputation of an unpredictable gadfly, and few in Moscow thought he would last long as Putin's advisor. Surprisingly he stayed in the Kremlin for nearly six years, and during the initial ones—until the Yukos Affair—he had access to Putin and apparently some influence over his thinking.

The high point of Putin's early "liberal phase" came that summer, when, as the constitution required, Putin delivered his first State of the Federation address (known in Russian as the *Poslanie*[77]) to a joint session of the two houses of parliament. Putin has never adopted a teleprompter—he still prefers to read his speeches from a paper script. As he read his maiden *Poslanie* to the assembled deputies, he exuded a nervous determination, periodically glancing down to take a fresh breath of text.[78]

He sounded the same basic themes as his signed article of the previous year: Russia's vulnerability and decline and the mission of restoring the country's place in the world. But the speech must also have startled the deputies with its unexpectedly liberal language. "The state intervenes too much where it should not, and not enough where it should," Putin declared. "It is too much present in the areas of property, entrepreneurship, and consumption, but not enough in the protection of property rights and enforcement of the laws." At times Putin managed to sound almost like a Russian version of Adam Smith: "The key economic role of the state, without a doubt, is the protection of economic freedom—freedom to produce, to trade, to invest." The government should not conduct private business. It should not choose champions but protect private initiative. It should support transparency, governance, and property rights.[79]

Yet the speech was liberal only in parts. Most of it, in fact, was devoted to Putin's familiar theme of the need to strengthen the state, and its real message was that a true market economy could function only in a single national space, without regional restrictions and obstacles to the flow of capital and trade. In short, it was Putin's trademark message, that true capitalism could function only under a strong state.

The first *Poslanie,* in other words, summed up Putin's consistent approach since his 1997 thesis and his 1999 article: a market-oriented economic policy combined with a radical political recentralization. Putin's earlier "Threshold" essay had already stated its essence in a single phrase: "We must be guided by the principle, 'As much state as is essential; as much freedom as is necessary.'"[80] Even as they listened, the deputies were well aware that Putin was already moving fast to recentralize political power. Within days of his inauguration, he had created a new layer of government to control the regions, and he had taken the first steps to weaken the legislature. Putin himself evidently saw no contradiction between the liberal and the statist sides of his message. He was simply being, as always, "left and right."

But to strengthen the role of the state, Putin needed money, and the obvious place to get it was the oil industry, which by 2000–2001, thanks to rising oil prices and recovering production, was finally becoming profitable. In the fall of 2000, over the liberals' protests, Putin backed the plan of his finance minister, Aleksei Kudrin, to raise taxes on the oil companies.

Aleksei Kudrin and the Tax Reform of 2000–2002

If there was anyone in Putin's entourage who wove together the multiple strands of the president's thinking, it was Aleksei Kudrin. One of the original Saint Petersburg market reformers and an early associate of Anatolii Chubais,[81] Kudrin had a unique relation to Putin. The two men had worked together in the Saint Petersburg mayoralty, where Kudrin was in charge of the city's finances. Subsequently, as we have seen, Kudrin played a key role in Putin's move to the Kremlin. Kudrin served as Putin's finance minister throughout his two terms as president, and he was the chief architect of the government's fiscal and budgetary policy throughout the 2000s, until his abrupt departure from the government in the fall of 2011. No one, with the possible exception of Igor Sechin, enjoyed as close and long-standing a tie to Putin as Aleksei Kudrin, with decisive consequences for the politics of oil.

Kudrin was invariably described in the Western media as a "liberal," but in reality his liberalism was no more (and no less) than the strictest fiscal and monetary orthodoxy. The path to a well-functioning market economy, Kudrin believed, lay through financial order—balanced budgets, transparent taxes, low debts and low inflation, and sound treasury controls—which only a well-ordered state could provide. His one overriding concern throughout his long tenure was the solvency and stability of the state.[82] Kudrin, every bit as much as Putin but in his own way, was determined that Russia should never again endure the traumas of the 1990s and the crash of 1998.

But so long as the state remained weak, financial order did not stand a chance. For this reason, an economic liberal such as Kudrin could only welcome the prospect of a stronger and more disciplined state, and Putin, Kudrin's old colleague, seemed to embody that promise. Between 2000 and 2004, Kudrin could reconcile, with no discomfort whatever, his liberal economics, his financial orthodoxy, and Putin's statism. As rising world prices drove up the oil companies' oil-export profits in the 2000s, Kudrin as finance minister was one of the principal leaders in the drive to capture the resulting windfall for the state, and he viewed the oil companies' efforts to "optimize" their taxes as little better than criminal. In these respects, Kudrin was at one with Putin, and Putin, in return, backed his finance minister to the full. It was only in the second half of the 2000s, as the corruption and inefficiency of the model of "state capitalism" became glaring, that Kudrin's disquiet grew and he found himself increasingly at odds not only with Putin and his business entourage but also with the Medvedev camp of modernizers and their doctrine of state-led investment and deficit spending. By the time he left office in 2011, Kudrin had become an unwelcome Cassandra, isolated and increasingly powerless.

After August 1999, owing to his previous ties to Putin, Kudrin quickly emerged as the leader of the tax reform effort. Now deputy minister of finance, he drew to his side a team of reformers, including a close friend and ally, Sergei Shatalov. Shatalov played such an important role in the tax reform that he is often called "the father of the Russian tax code." When Kudrin became minister of finance in 2000, he took Shatalov with him as his principal deputy. Between the two of them, they ran Russia's fiscal policy for a decade, creating Russia's first modern tax system.

"The Devil Would Break His Leg"

The Soviet Union, strictly speaking, did not have a tax system. There was little need for one, in a regime in which the state owned virtually everything. The state levied most of its revenue through the simple device of manipulating prices. The producer received a low price; the consumer paid a higher price; and the state pocketed a percentage of the difference (typically around 80 percent in the case of the oil industry). It was direct, efficient, and, because the prices were set administratively, totally arbitrary.

But in a market economy, the game changes: the state is removing the property of private property owners. Clear rules and predictability are (or ideally should be) the conditions for consent and compliance, and the removal of property occurs only as sanctioned by law.[83] Yet in the growing financial chaos of the late Gorbachev period and the initial post-Soviet years, the state was completely unprepared for such a radical change, which required not only a transformation in mind-set but also a competent bureaucracy to apply it. The first attempts to develop a new tax system began only in 1990, and in 1991–1992 the new Russian government essentially improvised on the run. By 1993, Russian taxes had become a thicket of hundreds of federal and regional taxes, applied (as Shatalov told an audience in 2005) through "instructions, cables, and clarifications distributed by newly set-up tax authorities" and plagued by a "plethora of problems and abuses originating from tax concessions."[84]

By the late 1990s the thicket of tax laws had grown into a jungle. It was so complicated that, as the Russian saying goes, "the devil would break his leg" trying to understand it. It was both punitive yet easily evaded, because it was so tangled, inconsistent, and poorly enforced. It encouraged an entire nation to become experts in tax avoidance, not least the oil companies, which developed sophisticated methods of concealing profits, from parking export revenues abroad to manipulating prices and profits at home. Although the regional governments had some success in collecting taxes in kind, the federal government's efforts to gather revenue steadily lost ground, and by the eve of the crash of August 1998 the federal government was effectively bankrupt.[85]

At the center of the fiscal problem was the constant game of hide-and-seek between the government and the oil industry, the largest single source of export revenues in the cash-starved Russian economy. The government made up for its failure to tax the broad economy by selectively targeting the largest companies and especially the oil companies. On the eve of the 1998 crash, just nineteen corporations supplied over two-thirds of federal revenues; and the oil industry alone accounted for one-quarter.[86] But this was actually a very low number; the fact is that the government was failing to capture much of the rent from oil. The oil companies quickly became skilled at sidestepping the tax collectors, and the government was able to capture only between one-quarter and one-third of their revenues. Moreover, the system was arbitrary, unpredictable, and ridden by conflict. The government's methods ranged from negotiation and threats to raids, arrests, freezing of bank accounts, and denials of export licenses and quotas, accompanied by a constant drumbeat of denunciations in the media. The companies responded with more dissimulation, misreporting, and ever more ingenious forms of evasion. It was a kind of rough-edged game of fiscal theater, in which both sides played familiar parts—the tax raids, complete with ski-masked OMON troops, became known in Russian as *maski-show*—and the final tax bill, as so much else in Russia, was a negotiated compromise. A witty Russian journalist reconstructed the tax collector's language to the oilmen:

> Of course we know that in theory you could pay us nothing at all, but in that case watch out: there will be tax inspections, and raids, and rumors of renationalization, which will mess up your stock price. So think hard how much of your profit you're going to show us.[87]

By 1999, as the smoke cleared from the crash and default of the previous year, everyone agreed that the system was broken. But could a new one be devised that would be more efficient and consensual?

Capturing the Oil Rents

From the moment he was inaugurated, Putin put tax reform at the top of his economic agenda. He gave Kudrin wide authority, not only as finance minister, but simultaneously as deputy prime minister for all fiscal and budgetary matters. Kudrin chaired a key coordinating body, the Interdepartmental Commission on Protective Measures in Foreign Trade, Customs, and Tariff Policy, which gave him the lead role in tax reform. At the same time, the power of the Ministry of Fuel and Power, hitherto the main lobbyist for the oil industry inside the government, was weakened. Thus the "liberals" were securely in control, and they had the president's total support.

From the first, the oil companies were the prime target. To gather intelligence on their financial operations, Kudrin created a special investigative body within the Finance Ministry, called the Committee on Financial Monitoring (Rosfinmonitoring). Its primary mission was to track money laundering by Russian entities. Money laundering had become epidemic in the 1990s, causing Russia to be blacklisted by the international watchdog, the Financial Action Task Force.[88] To head the committee, Putin and Kudrin turned to the veteran Viktor Zubkov, Putin's onetime mentor at the mayoralty, who had subsequently spent much of the 1990s as Saint Petersburg's chief tax collector. Wily and experienced, Zubkov acted as Kudrin's chief sleuth all through the coming battles with the oil companies, seconded after 2004 by Zubkov's protégé and son-in-law, Anatolii Serdiukov, who became head of the Federal Tax Service in that year.[89] Thus, in the run-up to the Yukos Affair, the government had an increasingly detailed picture of the previously occult flows of oil money.

The reformers had three aims: to simplify the tax system and make it more transparent and equitable, to strengthen the central government by drawing revenues away from the regions, and to toughen enforcement while making it more predictable. In this way, they believed, they could provide dependable revenues to the state while lowering the overall tax burden on the population. In addition, there was a fourth goal: to lessen the overall tax burden on the economy.

Such changes almost certainly implied that the oil companies would end up paying more. A simpler and more transparent system would leave fewer loopholes and hiding places for concealing revenues, while tougher enforcement would raise the penalties for being found out. The center would be less accommodating than the regions and more likely to demand payment in real money. Moreover, what was implicit in the liberals' program was explicit in the writings of the president: the whole point of the reform, as far as he was concerned, was to capture oil rents and put them to work to rebuild the economy.

The oil companies do not seem at first to have recognized the full extent of the threat. To be sure, they could feel growing tax pressure from the government, but they dealt with it in the usual way, by negotiation and concession, followed by "creative optimization," in what they considered essentially a game among equals. Indeed, the familiar jousting over taxes had resumed right after the crash. In January 1999, Prime Minister Evgenii Primakov reinstated the oil-export tax, which had been abandoned in 1997 at the urging of the IMF. The oil companies retaliated by threatening to go to the president and have his finance minister, Mikhail Zadornov, fired, and through this and similar hardball tactics they succeeded in negotiating a lower rate. Primakov countered by tightening loopholes, lifting profit-tax exemptions, and levying a special transportation tariff on the oil companies to pay for new pipelines. The oil companies replied with a lawsuit to stop the special tariff. In August 1999, two prime ministers and one finance minister later, Vladimir Putin led off the next round by raising the export-tax rate again. The oil companies responded with their usual protests, and the game began all over again. Nevertheless, as a result of this jousting, the government did succeed in both forcing the oil companies to pay their back taxes and increasing the government's overall take.[90] But even though they were conceding ground, it must have seemed to the oil companies pretty much business as usual.

By the turn of the year 1999–2000, rumors of the reformers' plans for tax reform increasingly worried the oil companies, but they took hope from Putin's apparent promise in his Surgut speech in March to lower taxes on the energy sector, which he repeated before the Duma in May. Putin's benevolence seemed confirmed when the oil generals learned of the promotion of Aleksei Kudrin to finance minister that same month.

At this point the oil generals still considered Kudrin to be a friendly figure. In Saint Petersburg in the mid-1990s, as head of the city's finance committee, he had been known as an advocate of lower taxes. At first the oil companies were reassured when, in his first public appearances as finance minister, Kudrin continued to call for lower taxes.[91] At the same moment, Putin was pressing the Duma to pass the long-delayed Part II of the Tax Code, which likewise provided for cutting the tax burden.[92] Thus, to the oil generals, the new president appeared to be offering more secure property rights and lower taxes, in exchange for greater transparency and compliance, which the oil companies were confident they could continue to manage to their advantage.[93]

The oil generals were unprepared, therefore, for the storm that broke over their heads in the summer of 2000. It began with a joint report by the Tax Ministry and the Tax Police on the methods used by the oil companies to avoid taxes. Topping the list was the technique known as "transfer pricing," by which the oil companies "optimized" their taxes by paying a very low internal price to their producing divisions, thus lowering all local taxes based on that price. The report denounced this and similar techniques as tax evasion. In July the government launched a series of tax raids on the major oil companies, notably LUKoil, which hitherto had been considered one of the better fiscal citizens.[94] Later that same month, in a tense meeting with Putin, the oil generals challenged the findings of the tax report, arguing that their methods were legal. But Putin was adamant. At one point he turned on Vagit Alekperov of LUKoil, criticizing him for being "Number 1 in oil production but Number 7 in tax payments." Alekperov, taken aback, answered confusedly that the reports Putin was receiving from the tax people were mistaken.[95]

Charging the atmosphere—and greatly raising the political stakes—was the unexpectedly strong growth of world oil prices. In 1999 they were still relatively low, and few expected them to keep rising for long. As late as June 2000, when Kudrin announced his preliminary budget for 2001, he based it on the pessimistic assumption that oil prices would decline to $18–$19 per barrel. The government was initially more concerned with putting a floor under its revenues than in expanding its share. Its first increases in the export tax were thus essentially defensive, as Putin sought to secure funding to pay pensions during the winter of 1999–2000. But as the months went by and oil prices kept rising, the government saw that its share of the revenues was going down, and it resolved to push back. By the end of the year, Kudrin announced another sharp increase in the export tax. The oil companies were indignant. "The government is violating its own rules of the game," exclaimed Vagit Alekperov. "It's substituting itself for Vladimir Putin, who at the Surgut meeting promised the oilmen fiscal stability." Mikhail Khodorkovsky of Yukos warned that the government's proposed tax increases would cause oil production to drop sharply, wiping out the production gains achieved since 1998.[96] But Kudrin was adamant, and Putin backed him. The tax increases went through.

The oil companies tried to argue that as oil rents increased, the government's first priority, once it had balanced its budget, should be to leave them enough to invest in new exploration and production. After all, they were the government's chief source of future revenues. But Kudrin did not see it that way. As he explained to a journalist a few months later, "Favorable prices have given the oil companies extra earnings that have nothing to do with their activity. Simply, global rents have poured down on them."[97]

The flood of oil revenues was causing the ruble to appreciate, Kudrin went on, stimulating imports and damaging the competitive position of other sectors. Should the oil sector, which had done nothing special to earn a windfall, be allowed to ruin the rest of the economy?

> So the question looks very simple: What do we want, to remain a commodity producer and export only hydrocarbons, or do we want to support the export of other kinds of production, including high technology? I don't know about the oil magnates, but for me the answer is clear. . . . We have got to take away the extra foreign currency from the oil companies, not just a little, as they want, but a lot.

With these words the battle was joined. The reformers' determination to wrest the growing windfall from the oil companies made them increasingly impatient with the oil companies' optimization schemes, and the rhetoric quickly became bitter. Announcing the government's increase in export-tax rates in December 2000, Kudrin criticized the oil companies for "avoiding taxes on a scale that even the Ministry of Finance had not suspected."[98] This led Kudrin and his team to change their entire approach. Sergei Shatalov had initially drawn on the accepted Western view, which held that the most efficient approach, both for the industry and for the government, was to tax profits, not gross revenue. But by the second half of 2000 Kudrin and Shatalov had concluded that the government had neither the power to compel the oil companies to reveal their true profits nor the expertise to ferret them out. "Profits," in any case, were subject to manipulation, in these officials' view. (This was one of the reasons they created the Committee on Financial Monitoring the following year.) They therefore decided to cut through the problem by a radical simplification. The two key taxes applying to oil—the export tax and a new consolidated production tax (usually referred to by its Russian initials as NDPI[99])—were simply tied to the export price, thus bypassing at one stroke the entire issue of transfer prices.

The new system was a blunt instrument—its creators acknowledged as much—because it was based on gross revenues regardless of field quality or performance. But because of its extreme simplicity it was easily collectible, and as oil prices continued to mount, it proved remarkably effective in capturing the lion's share of the windfall. Over the following six years, between 1999 and 2005, the share of oil-company profits collected by the government grew from 45.1 percent to 83.8 percent,[100] and by 2008, as oil prices reached their peak, the state's take at the margin swelled to well over 90 percent. In dollar terms, the state's oil-tax revenues exploded from $5.6 billion in 1999 to $83.2 billion in 2005.[101]

Ironically (especially in light of later events), the original source of the draft law incorporating these changes was not Kudrin or Shatalov but Yukos, which had seen in the simplified system a means of gaining a competitive advantage over its rivals. Yukos had strong support among the deputies—the Moscow grapevine whispered that Khodorkovsky had a substantial part of the Duma on his payroll (Muscovites called this "material lobbying")—and it was confident that it could control the setting of the actual tax rates. Kudrin and Shatalov, looking for a way to defeat the companies' concealment tactics, suddenly found in the Yukos draft the solution to their problem, and it became the basis of the government's proposals.[102]

What followed was a wholesale defeat for the oil companies. By May 2001, despite vigorous lobbying, the generals were unable to prevent the government from submitting, and the Duma from passing, the new natural-resources chapter of the Tax Code, which included the new "one size fits all" formula for the export tax and the production tax.[103] If the companies had calculated that the Duma would be left to decide the actual rates of the new production and export taxes, they were disappointed. The most they were able to win was an amendment allowing the Duma to specify a general range that varied with world oil prices,[104] but the actual tax was determined by Kudrin's commission, which was chaired by himself and dominated by his allies. Beginning in the summer of 2001, the commission started adjusting the tax rate "by hand" (as Gref put it) four to six times per year, as oil prices fluctuated.[105]

The oil companies found themselves with few friends. As oil prices increased, so did public resentment over their profits, as well as the government's determination to capture them. From that time on, finding the front door to the parliament closed, the companies increasingly resorted to the back door, thus setting the stage for the confrontations with the Kremlin, and particularly with Yukos, that followed in 2002 and 2003.

What is striking about the tax reform is how quickly it happened. The alliance between Putin and the economic liberals (who as we have seen were "liberal" in the sense that they were committed to a market economy but orthodox on fiscal and monetary matters, and some of whom, such as Zubkov and Serdiukov, were hardly liberal at all) took shape in the fall of 1999, helped by personal ties that had been formed in Saint Petersburg in the first half of the 1990s. By the spring of 2000, Putin had placed the liberals in all the key economic decision-making spots in his government. By the summer and fall of 2000, rising oil prices and the growing oil windfall had catalyzed the "coalition of discontent" that led to the radical simplification of the oil chapter of the Tax Code, while weakening the oil industry's power to resist it. But the basis for the coalition had been laid much earlier, in the broad search for new fiscal policies in the mid- to late 1990s and the emerging consensus view that capturing revenues from the natural-resource sector, and oil in particular, was the indispensable means to prevent "Dutch disease" and to finance, via state action, the recovery of the country.

The oil companies' stubborn resistance only played further into the reformers' hands. The companies' stance was understandable: For the first time in a decade they were making big money, and in defending it they were simply continuing what they had done successfully in the 1990s. But that was then, and the oil companies as a group failed to see that times had suddenly changed. (The one significant exception, typically, was Vladimir Bogdanov of Surgut-neftegaz, who ignored all newfangled talk of "fiscal optimization" and paid his taxes.)

But the companies' uncompromising stance turned the politics of oil taxation into a bitter zero-sum game, which prefigured the showdown to come in 2004–2005. The more lasting consequence, however, was an oil-tax regime that had been deliberately designed as a bludgeon, the consequences of which both the oil industry and the state are still struggling with today.

Taking Control: The Beginnings of Putin's Energy Policy

Even as he moved to increase the state's tax take from the oil companies, Putin reached out to regain control of the gas industry and the oil-pipeline system. These were the first concrete indications of what Putin's energy policies would look like in practice. The ruthless way in which they were carried out was soon unsettling to the liberals in his administration, as they were to the foreign media. Yet Putin was careful not to disrupt the political balance; he kept most of the senior figures of the Yeltsin team (the so-called Family) in place in the Kremlin and in the government; and he continued to endorse key liberal ideas, notably in fiscal and judicial reform. Thus the "coalition of discontent" between liberals and siloviki continued to hold.

Putin's first target was Gazprom. During the 1990s the gas industry, though never officially privatized, had gradually drifted out of the state's control. Gazprom prospered. It expanded into sectors it had never occupied before—first into gas distribution and then into gas-consuming industries, such as metals and petrochemicals, both inside Russia and outside. By the end of the 1990s, Gazprom had become one of the largest companies in Russia and one of the richest.[106]

But although Gazprom remained nominally under state ownership, actual control of the company had increasingly passed into the hands of its senior managers, beginning with Rem Viakhirev, a protege of former prime minister Chernomyrdin, and his friends and relations. His son Iurii headed Gazeksport, Gazprom's export arm; his daughter Tat'iana was a major shareholder in

Stroitransgaz, Gazprom's pipeline builder, as were Chernomyrdin's two sons; and cousin Viktor was in charge of Burgaz, Gazprom's main drilling contractor. But that was not all. Over time, a steady stream of assets and licenses migrated to friendly companies, which were either independent or soon became so, as Gazprom's stakes in them were diluted. Gazprom's monopoly control over the gas sector was rapidly eroding, seemingly with the Viakhirev management's full acquiescence. But Viakhirev remained—until Putin became president.

From the start Putin made it clear he meant to be the boss and that Viakhirev's continuation in office depended on his active cooperation, beginning with Putin's campaign against the media oligarchs Vladimir Gusinsky and Boris Berezovsky. But when the Kremlin arrested Vladimir Gusinsky, Viakhirev made the mistake of joining seventeen other business leaders in a collective letter of protest. From that time on, his fate was sealed. On May 30, 2001, when his contract as general director expired, Viakhirev was summoned to the Kremlin and dismissed.

Putin replaced Viakhirev with a 39-year-old Piterets, Aleksei Miller, who had been a minor staffer in Putin's Committee on International Relations (KVS) in the Saint Petersburg mayoralty in the early 1990s. When Putin moved to Moscow in 1996, Miller had stayed on in Saint Petersburg, managing two local projects, the port of Saint Petersburg and the Baltic Pipeline consortium, both, as it turned out, of interest to the future president. Miller, who had originally started out in Anatolii Chubais's circle of liberal reformers before joining the mayoralty, was viewed by his former colleagues as a competent and loyal administrator but not a leader. But this was precisely the mix of qualities Putin was looking for, in addition to one other: Miller had never worked in the gas industry, and thus he had no connection whatsoever to the Viakhirev management.

Over the following two years, Miller conducted a systematic purge of the senior ranks of Gazprom. Although he left the technical leadership of the company largely untouched, he removed Viakhirev's people from all the key positions connected to Gazprom's revenues, contracting and procurement, and control of property and assets. To replace them, he brought in trusted subordinates from his previous two jobs. In parallel, he successfully regained control of most of the assets that had drifted away from Gazprom under the previous management. By the end of 2003, he had largely carried out the mission that

Putin had entrusted to him, that of restoring Gazprom's control over the gas industry and bringing Gazprom back under the control of the Kremlin.

The liberals in the administration, beginning with German Gref, imagined that with Gazprom once more under the government's control, they could now proceed to modernize it along Western lines, much as the market reformers had recommended at the beginning of the 1990s. The company would be broken up; the upstream would be privatized and different producers would compete against one another; and the pipeline system would be turned into a regulated public utility. What they could not foresee was that none of this would happen. Putin had different plans for Gazprom. He kept Gazprom's monopoly intact, while encouraging the company to resume its expansion, this time as Russia's national energy champion.[107] But none of this was yet visible in the early years of the decade, and the liberals, still believing they had the president's support, continued laying their plans.[108] (I remember attending a Christmas Eve meeting in German Gref's office in 2004 at which he vowed, "Next year we will break up Gazprom." It didn't happen, either that year or since.)

Back to the Baltic: The Baltic Pipeline System

Oil transportation was next. When Putin was deputy mayor of Saint Petersburg, as we have seen, he looked for ways to restore the city's role as a window on the Baltic. But he had opposed the plan to build a pipeline to the nearby terminal of Primorsk, on the grounds that it did little for Saint Petersburg itself. He need not have worried: over the following years, as Putin worked his way up the Kremlin hierarchy, the Baltic Pipeline System (or BPS, as it was commonly called), remained stalled.

But by this time Putin had rethought his earlier opposition to BPS. Russia was losing a fortune in tariffs and fees to Latvia and Estonia, but more important, Russia was increasingly dependent on foreign countries for export of a key strategic commodity. Within two months of his appointment, the new prime minister made it clear he now supported BPS and expected the government to press ahead with it.[109] Even as Russia went back to war in Chechnya and succession politics in the Kremlin reached a peak of intensity, Putin—by now acting president—pushed the Baltic project hard, scolding and prodding the companies and the ministries. He hectored them like schoolboys: "Since 1997 nothing has been done . . . and the cup keeps getting passed back and forth."[110] By February 2000 money had been found and the state machinery had begun to move; and by the beginning of April, on the eve of Putin's election as president, construction was finally under way. The first phase was completed ahead of schedule, and in late December 2001, Putin flew to Saint Petersburg to attend the opening ceremony.[111]

In retrospect, Putin's campaign for the Baltic pipeline is the first concrete example of his long-standing views being translated into energy policy. It is also a telling indicator of Putin's rising power. Month by month, as his political star rose, opposition melted away and officials gravitated to his side. A key event—and a fateful one for the future course of Putin's energy policy—was the arrival in September 1999 of a strong personality, Semyon Vainshtok, at the head of Transneft, the state's oil pipeline monopoly. Vainshtok had come up through the LUKoil organization to become one of Vagit Alekperov's top lieutenants; as head of LUKoil-West Siberia, he was responsible for the bulk of LUKoil's production of crude oil.[112] When he took over Transneft it was widely perceived as a sign of LUKoil's growing influence over government policy, a view that was reinforced by the simultaneous presence of another former LUKoil vice president, Vladimir Stanev, as deputy minister of energy. But matters turned out very differently: Vainshtok became Putin's man instead. Long known for his toughness, strict punctuality, long memory, and resolute manner, Vainshtok lost little time in establishing his power inside Transneft and in staking out a strong statist position. As soon as Putin announced his support for the BPS in October 1999, Vainshtok aligned himself with it,[113] and the oil companies hurriedly began scrambling for an equity stake in the corporation he created to manage the project.[114] Thus Putin found in Vainshtok the ideal instrument, both for the BPS project initially and then, more broadly, for reinforcing the Kremlin's control over the oil pipeline system and thus over the oil industry. Over the following years Vainshtok would champion the principle of state ownership of all oil-export pipelines—a position that soon placed him in the front line of battle against Mikhail Khodorkovsky.

But that was later. The significant thing about the BPS initiative in 1999–2000 is that Putin left open the key question of ownership. The oil companies were allowed to believe that it might be privately owned or at least could be managed as a state-private corporation in which the private oil companies would be shareholders. It was not until 2003 that the Kremlin finally ruled that the state, through Transneft, would remain the monopoly owner of all oil-export pipelines. For the time being, Putin did not reveal his preference—perhaps he was still genuinely undecided—but in this early episode his statist bias was already plain.

Conclusion

Two key themes run through this chapter. The first is the continuing importance of the friendships and loyalties—as well as the rivalries and enmities—formed during the present elite's early years in Saint Petersburg in the late 1980s and the first half of the 1990s. The "brothers from Saint Petersburg" are the latest embodiment of a long-standing theme in Russian politics, namely, the enduring personal essence of Russian political power. This is the part that scholars, groping for formulas, variously call the "patrimonial," the "pre-modern," the "non-institutionalized," or the "administrative" side of the Russian state and that Russian commentators, with their usual love of hyperbole, simply call, "the mafia." This shifting network of personal relationships, with all its various factions and subfactions, forms the inner core of Putin's "vertical of power." But the key point is that there is not one such group but several, and no single one is dominant. Putin's unceasing efforts to keep the balance among them, to maintain their loyalty, to exploit their self-interest, and ultimately to control them take up much of his time and attention and have been a central feature of the politics of the Putin era. As we shall see, this interplay of clans has also been a major force affecting the oil industry throughout the Putin era, as it continues to be today.

The second key point is the overall continuity and consistency in the thinking of Putin and his circle on the leading role of the state and its relationship to the private sector, as the all-important key to Russia's wealth and power as well as their own. The state is the dominant partner, and its chief instrument is control of strategic resources. The economy needs to be organized on market principles, but the market alone cannot work without state leadership. In the most strategic sectors, direct state intervention is required; and energy is one of those sectors. On the level of general principles but also that of concrete projects (notably, pipelines), there is a straight line between the deputy mayor of the mid-1990s and the president of the 2000s.

Putin's public words early in his first term had a strong liberal tinge—hence the widespread view that he was a liberal reformer. But his actions in energy policy—on oil taxation, on natural gas, on oil transportation—were resolutely statist and conformed to his general doctrine.

The ambiguities in Putin's initial energy policies suggest that he was genuinely divided between "left" and "right," that on many issues he had not yet made up his mind. He left the door open at first for a restructuring of Gazprom; he did not initially rule out the oil companies' plans for privately owned oil pipelines; he genuinely favored broadening the tax base and supported a broadly liberal tax reform; lastly, he did not rush to commit himself to a national oil company. This ambiguity, whether deliberate or not, had the consequence of keeping the liberals and the conservatives among the Pitertsy united around the president and his policies.

But it is with policy, as it is with human character, that it is in action that ambiguity is resolved, when actual choices are made, options exercised, and alternatives closed. And what Putin's actual policies showed, as they began to unfold in the energy sector as in other domains, was a consistent bias toward control, a preference for state ownership, an instinct for domination, and an intolerance of opposition. As time went by and Putin consolidated his power, these traits would lead inexorably toward conflict with the new oligarchs of the oil industry, and particularly with the most outspoken among them, Mikhail Khodorkovsky of Yukos.

chapter 7

"Chudo" Meets "Russian Bear": The Yukos Affair

Но те, которым в дружной встрече
Я строфы первые читал . . .
Иных уж нет, а те далече,
Как Сади некогда сказал.

But of those to whom, in a circle of friends,
These lines I first read,
Some are gone, and some far away,
As Sa'adi once said.

—Pushkin, *Evgenii Onegin*

The season's first big snow swirled across Siberia. Shortly before dawn, a white Tupolev 134 with no markings cut through the dark frigid morning and touched down at Tolmachevo Airport in Novosibirsk to refuel. The plane's sole passenger was the CEO of Yukos, Mikhail Khodorkovsky. At first, all seemed normal. But as the plane taxied to a stop, Khodorkovsky looked out the cabin window and saw a party of armed troops. In seconds the plane was surrounded. The soldiers, a unit of the FSB's elite Alfa antiterrorist brigade, stormed aboard. Khodorkovsky was led away, in handcuffs and with a hood over his head, to the airport's militia post, where he was informed that he was wanted in Moscow as a "witness." Two hours later, still hooded and handcuffed, he was marched to a transport plane bound for the capital. It was October 25, 2003. He has been in prison ever since.[1]

The arrest of Mikhail Khodorkovsky led over the next four years to the breakup of Yukos, then Russia's largest and most successful oil company, and the prosecution of dozens of its executives. There followed a partial renationalization of the oil industry, a heightened tax take by the state, a hardening of the Kremlin's relations with the West, and a wave of legislation tightening oil regulation and restricting foreign investment. The Yukos Affair alone was not the cause of these developments—they had all begun earlier—but it acted as a powerful amplifier of them. The repercussions of the Yukos Affair continued to echo through the Russian oil world for the next several years. It affected the balance of power in Russian oil politics; it altered the course of oil policy; and it changed the structure and behavior of the oil industry. Today it stands as the single most important event in the story of the Russian oil industry in the post-Soviet era.

Moreover, the Yukos Affair is not yet over. Like slowly cooling lava, it has formed a crust, over which ordinary life has moved on. On most days the Affair seems remote, almost forgotten. Yet underneath, the ground is still shifting. The policy issues involved in the Affair have been only partly resolved—some of them not at all—and they continue to rumble. In courtrooms and law offices around the world, litigation over the remains of Yukos simmers on. Vladimir Putin, to his annoyance, still regularly faces questions about the Affair at press conferences. And last but not least, Mikhail Khodorkovsky himself appears no closer to freedom: in December 2010, he was sentenced to a second prison term of eight years. Yet so long as Khodorkovsky remains behind bars, the Yukos Affair is not closed.

The subject of this chapter, however, is not Khodorkovsky's fate or his guilt or innocence.[2] Rather, my concern here is to analyze the significance of the Yukos Affair for the relationship of the Russian oil industry to the state. I will focus on the way Khodorkovsky was perceived by the Russian political class and the oil establishment, since these perceptions shaped their subsequent actions against him. Indeed, those perceptions are the essence of the story. My argument comes down to this: Khodorkovsky and Yukos were attacked because they were seen by a wide range of Russian elite opinion as a foreign body and a threat. What could be absorbed was absorbed; the rest was destroyed.

Origins of the Yukos Affair

We begin by turning back the clock to the crash of 1998. In the aftermath of that cataclysm, three key events occurred. The first was the appointment of Vladimir Putin as prime minister, with his longtime aide, Igor Sechin, at his side. The second was the beginning of Mikhail Khodorkovsky's restructuring of Yukos, in a strategic alliance with the Franco-American oil-service company

Schlumberger. The third was Sergei Bogdanchikov's consolidation of control over Rosneft. By the late summer of 1999, the main actors in the coming drama were assembled on the stage.

At this point these men were not thinking about confrontation. All were in new and unfamiliar situations. Khodorkovsky had narrowly survived bankruptcy and had just begun turning around a company that, only months before, had been on the verge of failure, in an industry about which he still had much to learn. Bogdanchikov had been unexpectedly brought to Moscow from a provincial career on remote Sakhalin Island, to head Rosneft, a residual entity that no one appeared to want, except in pieces. Putin was a political unknown, the fourth in a line of failed prime ministers since April 1998, with only months, if not weeks, to prove himself as the Kremlin's last-ditch presidential candidate in the upcoming 2000 election. Sechin was an anonymous assistant, a gray figure at the entrance to Putin's office. For all four, failure seemed more likely than success. Yet within three years they would be among the most powerful men in Russia, and they would be headed for battle at the highest of stakes.

What made all the difference was the quiet beginnings of a sustained and ultimately massive rise in global oil prices. Oil prices had been mostly depressed for over a decade. When the turnaround came in early 1999, the beleaguered Russian oilmen—and the Russian treasury—did not dare believe it. Yet within twelve months Russia's demonetized "virtual economy" was reaping tens of billions of dollars, and soon hundreds of billions, in windfall profits.

The surge in oil rents, as it multiplied the wealth of the oilmen and the other new owners of the privatized industries of Russia, fed their power and ambitions. In the mid-1990s, Boris Berezovsky famously described "half of Russia" as owned by a handful of "oligarchs," but their means and dreams in those days were still modest compared with just a few years later. Multimillionaires soon became billionaires. They saw themselves as the new seat of power and believed that their money ruled all.

But the oligarchs were not the only ones who gained from the increase in oil revenues; the Kremlin too was strengthened. In 1998 the central government's tax take had sunk to a low of 9.2 percent of GDP, but beginning in 1999 the trend turned. By the end of 2002 the center's share of revenues had doubled to 18.8 percent.[3] And as the center's means grew, so did its strength. Within days of his accession as president, Putin began reeling back the powers that

Yeltsin had ceded, partly by design but mostly by default, to the regional and local governments. By 2002, Putin had largely succeeded. In the process he gave new authority and confidence to the policemen, the prosecutors, and above all the FSB—the men who came to be called the siloviki. They saw Putin as their man, and after some initial hesitation (he had left the service, after all, as an obscure lieutenant-colonel) they gave him their support. But his plan to recentralize the state could hardly have been as successful as it turned out to be if it had not been backed by ample oil funds.[4]

"The Injustice of Life"

Thus two broad groups evolved in parallel, each gaining strength as the oil revenues increased. On one side were the oligarchs; on the other, the siloviki. Those, at least, are the labels commonly given them. In reality, the makeup of the two groups and the boundaries between them were hazy. What defined them was less their past or present jobs than two opposed sets of perceptions, experiences, and resources. The oligarchs were the "winners of the 1990s," who now looked set to be the even bigger winners of the 2000s. To them had gone the leading roles and the biggest prizes. For them the first post-Soviet decade, whatever its blemishes, had been a brilliant success story. Russia had been freed from totalitarianism and the market had returned. Privatization had brought rich dividends—at least to them—and the best was yet to come. The arbitrary power of the central state and its organs of coercion had been curbed. A new legal foundation had been laid to protect the property rights of the new "haves." Russia had reentered the world and was open for business, led by its new rich.

On the other side were the relative "losers of the 1990s," those who had played the lesser roles and won the smaller pieces or none at all. They had watched with mounting resentment as others, seemingly no better than themselves, grew rich beyond imagination. Many of them had stayed in their state jobs, resisting the urge (or finding no opportunity) to join the migration to the private sector. Others, particularly the siloviki among the Pitertsy who arrived with Putin, had been confined for a decade to the relative minor leagues outside Moscow. For them the 1990s had been a period of frustration and humiliation, for themselves and for the country. The state had lost its leading role. Its most loyal servants had been dishonored, their perquisites and status

275

destroyed. Foreigners were taking over the strategic assets. Corruption and crime ruled the country. Russia was betrayed and adrift.

In late 2003, the liberal Moscow weekly *Novaia gazeta* ran what it claimed to be an interview with an unnamed senior officer of the FSB, a member of the investigative unit assigned to the Yukos case. There is, of course, no way of knowing whether the source is genuine. But genuine or not, his words have an eerily plausible ring as a summation of the second group's pent-up resentment and their sense that their time had come:

> There's a lot of bitterness among our guys—both against Khodorkovsky and against the injustice of life. . . . Under Yeltsin a lot of things started to be perceived as dogma. Private property was sacred! But it's not sacred at all. You guys started to believe that all those liberal values were here forever, right? Don't delude yourselves! All the rules can still be revised—and they will be.[5]

For a decade Russia had been poised between these two groups and their diametrically opposite readings of the 1990s. The fact that their narratives were both self-serving myths only reinforced their hold on each side. But the trends of the early 2000s made the contrast between them even more compelling. For the oligarchs, the accelerating "oil miracle" and the rising tide of oil profits, by multiplying their wealth and their apparent power, cemented their conviction that Russia's future lay with the booming private sector—or, in other words, with themselves. Didn't the phenomenal growth in oil output itself prove that a private oil company, applying modern technology and management, was the best instrument to bring prosperity to the country? Didn't the soaring market valuations of their companies signify the endorsement of the global financial community, the ultimate sign that they were among the elect?

For the siloviki, on the contrary, the new oil bounty only deepened their determination to capture it for the central state and to use it to rebuild the state's power, redistributing the oil wealth through the state to the rest of the economy—including themselves. It was not so much the alleged illegitimacy of the privatization of state property that bothered them as the fact that it had ended up in the wrong hands and was being used for the wrong ends. As for the source of the "oil miracle," the statists were readily persuaded (or pretended to be) by the chorus of condemnation from the Soviet-era oil establishment, to the effect that the private companies were committing rape and pillage in the oilfields. Besides, it was all Western technology anyway, and applying it took no talent. As our unnamed FSB officer put it scornfully, in words that reflected a long-established attitude of many state officials toward the oil industry, "What kind of brains do you need to pump oil? Just build yourself some rigs. All the technologies they buy from the West. You don't need any brains at all."[6] Thus, what was a matter of pride for the leading oil companies and (in their own eyes, at least) the clearest point in their favor was at the same time, for their enemies, the surest proof of the companies' fraudulent claims—and a convenient point of attack.

The Power of Money versus the Power of Coercion

The emerging confrontation was not simply between two sorts of people but between two sorts of power. For the oligarchs, the chief lesson of the 1990s was that private money trumped state coercion. They had become accustomed to a situation in which the traditional power of the state—its power to coerce—had become paralyzed. If one had money, what did one have to fear? Or to quote our FSB general:

> [In the 1990s] everything was predictable: if we went after an oligarch, he would give money to the media, who would start blaring in his defense. He'd give money—and buy his way out. If he wasn't let go right away, that meant he hadn't paid enough. But now no oligarch can reckon the odds in advance. Everything is in motion, and the rules of the game are changing. Now they're afraid of us, because they don't know what to expect from us.

What the oligarchs had missed was that the state's coercive power had not been broken in the 1990s, only suspended. There were several reasons for that. The ideological shock of the end of the Soviet Union had caused a lasting demoralization among the siloviki. The collapse of the central state's power and funding had led those who remained in state service to transfer their loyalties to the richer regional governments, which had the resources to pay them. Above all, they lacked a leader and a cause. Vladimir Putin provided both. Thus the economic recovery and the beginnings of the oil boom, coinciding with the election of the new president, brought together the two essential elements for a revival of the coercive power of the central state—an expanding budget and the will to use it.

Thus during the years of Putin's first term the setting for the Yukos Affair gradually begins to form. While commodity prices continue to climb, inflating the wealth and self-confidence of the oligarchs, the power of the statists grows inexorably in parallel. As the two sides move toward confrontation, the issues between them deepen and multiply. The ultimate issue is straightforward: Who shall rule Russia?

Within days of his inauguration in May 2000, Putin began tightening central control over the coercive elites (chiefly the uniformed police) and weakening the regional governors.[7] Shortly after that he turned to deal with the oligarchs. In retrospect, it is clear that Putin never really observed the "equal distance" doctrine he had enunciated to the oligarchs at the beginning of his presidency, and he was prepared to be as tough as required to get his way. What guided his actions was not only whether one or another oligarch "played by the rules" but also the strategic importance of the target—"strategic" meaning not only its importance for national policy but also its importance as a source of rents. To those who observed the pattern, the implication must have been clear: it would only be a matter of time before it was the turn of the oil industry. It was at about this time that Igor Sechin, happening to meet Iurii Golubev of Yukos, said to him, "Wait and see. Within two more years you will not recognize the situation."[8]

Over the following two years, as Putin rebuilt the power of the central government, the areas of conflict between the Kremlin and the private oil companies multiplied and intensified. The passage of the new Tax Code in 2001, with its "one size fits all" chapter on mineral resources, and the steady ratcheting up of tax rates as oil prices rose, brought the state into constant collision with the companies over oil revenues. Putin's preference for a continued state monopoly in oil transportation ran up against the oil companies' ambition to build and own pipelines themselves. His purge of Gazprom's leadership and his appointment of a loyal new CEO from Saint Petersburg, and the systematic regathering of gas assets that followed, was another signal of Putin's intentions. The Kremlin's increasing favor toward Rosneft as an emerging national oil company created a new rival to the private companies for the privatization of the remaining state-owned oil assets and for control of oil licenses in East Siberia and the Far East. Putin's determination to exploit the potential of oil and gas as instruments of foreign policy clashed with the oil companies' insistence that profitability alone should determine the choice of production levels and export markets. And behind all of these points of conflict there was the same fundamental issue: Who, in the end, would be sovereign over oil?

Why Yukos?

Despite these growing tensions between the state and the oil industry, it was not obvious, even as late as 2002, that Mikhail Khodorkovsky and Yukos would be the ones singled out for attack. In kind, Yukos's behavior was not different from that of the other oil companies. Thus if Yukos aggressively practiced "tax optimization" through the use of transfer pricing and dubious offshore tax havens, so did all the others. Although it sparred with Transneft over its plan for a privately owned pipeline to China, so did LUKoil, which was promoting a consortium of private oil companies to build and operate an export pipeline to Murmansk. Yukos tangled with Rosneft over the licensing of key prospects and the absorption of smaller companies, but LUKoil did so even more, and Surgut was not far behind. Yukos was attacked for its "oil now" approach to production, but so were Sibneft and LUKoil. (Indeed, in April 2002, LUKoil announced a "restructuring" of its operations that was modeled on those of its two leading rivals,[9] and even Surgutneftegaz quietly began adopting "foreign" production methods.[10]) Yukos was criticized for underinvesting in exploration while squirreling away licenses and doing nothing with them, but so were the other oil companies.[11] Yukos used strong-arm tactics in dealing with minority shareholders, but what Russian company did not? TNK could hardly complain of its treatment at the hands of Yukos in the battle for control of the Eastern Oil Company in 2002, since TNK's own methods in earlier conflicts had been little different. If Yukos pursued what amounted to its own foreign policy toward China and the United States, it was closely followed by LUKoil. When the Russian government attempted to impose export limits in support of OPEC, all the oil companies cheerfully disregarded them. And last but not least, if as early as 2002 Yukos was already negotiating with Chevron the possible sale of an equity stake in the company, so was LUKoil (which in addition was already negotiating a strategic agreement with ConocoPhillips), while TNK was talking both to BP and Texaco with the same object.

279

Thus Yukos resembled the other oil companies in kind—but it stood out in degree. Finance Minister Aleksei Kudrin spoke for many in the government when he said, a few months after Khodorkovsky's arrest,

> What Yukos managers were doing until recently was right before everybody's eyes. [Others] did not create such obvious schemes of tax evasion. I have been holding dialogues with Yukos for four years and I know the situation from the inside. They were coming to me and saying, "We won't let this law pass the Duma; it does not matter how much it costs." And they didn't just act in the Duma, where their former vice-president [Vladimir Dubov] was a member of the tax subcommittee. Lobbyists of other companies were not so aggressive.[12]

On every point of contention, in short, Yukos was more strident, more aggressive, and more radical than the other oil companies. And what made it appear so was its CEO, Mikhail Khodorkovsky himself.

The Man Outside the System

Only the unique environment of the Russian 1980s and 1990s could have produced a phenomenon like Mikhail Khodorkovsky. His beginnings were conventional enough. He was a classic product of a Moscow working-class family and the Soviet educational system—highly educated in the sciences and engineering but untutored, for obvious reasons, in subjects like modern economics and business, let alone business ethics. Like most of his generation, he dismissed as cant the required official teachings in "scientific communism" and "historical materialism" (despite his active role in the Lenin Youth League, the Komsomol, in his student days), but he had nothing to put in their place. He knew little about the outside world. He was in his mid-twenties before he visited the West, and his knowledge of it thereafter was gained on the run, in the middle of business trips. He struck the foreigners who met him in the early 1990s as a brilliant but unformed mind, essentially an autodidact. He absorbed full strength the extreme version of laissez-faire capitalism that blew into Russia at the end of the 1980s and turned it into a personal creed that gave the entrepreneur absolute license and made greed not only good but the supreme good. The Russians have an expression for such people: "he was drunk on the sweet air of freedom."

As the 1990s went on, Khodorkovsky's worldview expanded rapidly. His mind was hyperactive, his curiosity insatiable, and he was constantly constructing theories, trying to understand the world about him, frequently reinventing the wheel as he went along. Much of his theorizing was based on an idealized picture of the United States. (It is not for nothing that the Russian expression for "reinventing the wheel" is "discovering America.") His picture of the oil industry, in particular, seemed to be based on a caricature of the era of the Seven Sisters, a time when U.S. private oil companies ruled the world as they pleased, or so it seemed to Khodorkovsky, who derived from it that to be successful an oil company should be autonomous from the state, both in domestic and in foreign policy.

To fellow Russians, Khodorkovsky came across as a blend of Soviet and post-Soviet, a mixture of the go-go entrepreneur and the cynical Komsomol operator. Ever since the shares-for-loans privatizations of 1996–1997, Khodorkovsky had been identified in the political and business elite, and particularly in the oil world, as the archetype of the brash finansisty who had taken over the core strategic sectors. His reputation was hardly improved when, in the wake of the crash of 1998, Khodorkovsky and his associates walked away from Menatep Bank, carting off its assets and leaving it an empty shell.[13]

"Rape and Pillage"

The methods used by Yukos and Sibneft were controversial from the start, as we saw in Chapter 5, and their very success made them even more so. Everything about the sudden boom in oil production was offensive to the Russian oil establishment, and old-time Soviet-era geologists and oilmen reacted with indignation bordering on rage. They had many reasons to be affronted. Yukos and Sibneft were the companies that had been taken over in the "shares-for-loans" scandal of just a few years before. The veteran oilmen who ran them— friends and associates of long decades' standing—had been summarily purged by brash young financiers who admitted they knew nothing about oil. The new men staffed their companies with Western expatriates who treated their Russian counterparts, hard-bitten men with decades of experience and power in the Soviet oil industry, with incomprehension and barely disguised contempt. They were now applying methods that were viewed by the oil establishment as risky and destructive and in any case unapproved—and therefore illegal. They largely ignored, or at best treated lightly, the rigorous reporting and approvals mandated by Soviet-era rules, which remained on the books even if dormant. And worst of all, the companies' very success was offensive to the professional pride of the veteran Russian oilmen, because it was hailed as a result of the reversal of the harmful and incompetent practices of the Soviet era.

To the veterans, it must have seemed like déjà vu all over again. Many of them had spent the 1970s and 1980s warning against the harm done by Moscow's unremitting pressure for higher production, driven by the state planners and the hierarchs of the Communist Party. Yet here were their capitalist successors, pushing for what seemed to the Soviet-era veterans exactly the same thing. To the geologists and engineers, the Western doctrine of acceleration ("oil today is worth more than oil tomorrow"), which to Western ears is as obvious as ABC, sounded no different from the "maximizers" of the 1980s, with their constant ratcheting up of output targets and their slogans.

It would be a mistake, therefore, to view the Russian oil establishment simply as dinosaurs, Soviet-era obscurantists. What they really are is geological and engineering fundamentalists, whose concept of sound practice is to maximize total recovery: to produce as much as possible of the geological potential of the oil in the ground over the lifetime of the field, regardless of cost or time. No matter how much time has passed or how much the oil companies have evolved, something of the former attitude remains, especially among the veterans. Even as innovative an oilman as Valerii Graifer, now chairman of the board of LUKoil, once told me, nearly twenty years after the fall of the Soviet Union, "I object to an approach that turns everything into profit and loss. One has to respect the resource. Yukos's approach was a desecration [*profanatsiia*]."[14] The hearts of men such as Graifer belong with the rocks.

Khodorkovsky's abrupt conversion the following year to the virtues of corporate transparency and accountability struck many Russian observers as hypocrisy, yet another shady maneuver. The description of Yukos in the last two chapters showed clearly that Khodorkovsky's restructuring of Yukos along international lines after 1998 was genuine and deep. Yet informed Russians were aware, as most Westerners were not, of the parallel command structure he had built inside Yukos, in which Westerners managed technology policy, finance, and investor relations, but Russians handled security, media management, and relations with officialdom, in much the same heavy-handed way as before. Many were also aware of the tough battles that had taken place for control of

282

the company. Even inside Yukos, many were skeptical about the "new" post-crash Khodorkovsky. As one former senior Yukos executive, who worked closely with Khodorkovsky, put it to me,

> You have to understand that Khodorkovsky did not change. He was at the end as he was at the beginning—cynical and calculating. The key change in [Khodorkovsky's] strategic thinking came when he realized that raising the company's market capitalization was far more profitable than increasing the cash flow. That turned him from a short-term tactician to a long-term strategist. . . . But he was no different from before.

Yet paradoxically, Khodorkovsky's cynical ruthlessness was combined with a streak of what can only be called naivete, both about the West and about his own country. Khodorkovsky came of age just as the Gorbachev era began. Unlike the Soviet-era oil generals, who were on average a decade older than he, Khodorkovsky had grown up without personal experience of working in the Soviet system. From his student days as a Komsomol activist he had grown used to dealing with a state that was malleable, in which officials could be co-opted, intimidated, or bought. He had never learned to fear it; he had never grown the carapace of dissimulation that protected every Soviet citizen. As Khodorkovsky himself put it, "I was too young!" His Russia was one in which all inherited truths appeared to have been thrown to the ground, in which state coercion had disappeared, and in which foreign governments, corporations, and banks were alternative sources of power and protection. For Khodorkovsky, the new doctrines from the West were the new reality, and however cynically he might play on them, at the same time he believed them wholly. Moreover, he believed they would justify him and protect him.

By 2002 Khodorkovsky had become a one-man conversion society for the values of the global, transparent, efficient, and of course privately owned corporation. These, Khodorkovsky asserted, accounted for Yukos's success and justified his own wealth. In the summer of 2002, in an interview with the Moscow tabloid *Moskovskii komsomolets*, Khodorkovsky laid out his formula:

> Today the company is worth $20 billion. But that doesn't mean that I sold Russia's oil and grabbed the $20 billion for myself. No—that $20 billion is the value of the brains by which the company produces and refines oil *efficiently*. That means that if Khodorkovsky leaves Yukos tomorrow, the company will

be worth a lot less. For example, as much as Tatneft is worth. And the share that goes to Khodorkovsky today will be worth not $3 billion but $400 million. And if the state nationalizes the company tomorrow, that share will be worth zero—absolutely nothing. State companies, as we know, are absolutely not valued on the world market—until they're sold off.[15]

Words like these were bound to set on edge the teeth of many an influential Russian, both inside and outside the oil world. Clearly, in Khodorkovsky's mind the real secret of Yukos's success was himself. He was the indispensable man, the capitalist hero fighting against the bureaucratic enemy, doing battle against value-destroying state ownership. The key words were brains and reputation:

> If you have resources, but no reputation—that's worth zero. Take Yukos for example. In 1999 the company's profit was $1.5 billion, and it was worth $300 million. By 2001 our profit was one-and-a-half to two times bigger. But the company's worth reached $20 billion—70 times more! That was because our reputation had improved.

But the reputation that Khodorkovsky had in mind was his reputation with the global financial community—the key to world-class wealth—not with the Russian elites or the oil establishment. Inside Russia, Khodorkovsky's reputation was increasingly that of a man who had forgotten what country he lived in, who had failed to form the defensive relationships that provide protection, and who seemed to delight in flouting the rules both written and unwritten. He surrounded himself with foreigners, while he treated fellow Russians with contempt. He made enemies and seemed glad of it. One former Yukos executive concluded that Khodorkovsky "had defined himself as a man outside the system."

In these respects, Khodorkovsky was not untypical of other "new Russians" of his generation. Indeed, he was far less flamboyant than they in his personal lifestyle. But what set him apart from the other oil barons and business oligarchs was his fervor as a prophet for the new values, his very public contempt for the old, and his energy in translating his views into radical action, both in oil and in politics. By the end of 2002 these were already turning him into a marked man.

284

The Richest Oligarch—and the Most Visible

As time went on, Khodorkovsky became steadily more visible as a public figure. If one compares the growing frequency of references to Khodorkovsky in the central Russian press with those of the other leading oil oligarchs, in 1999 Khodorkovsky is well behind LUKoil's Vagit Alekperov and Sibneft's Roman Abramovich, but with each passing year Khodorkovsky is more and more in the public eye. By late 2002 he is far and away the most frequently mentioned oligarch in the Russian print media.[16]

By this time Khodorkovsky was also fixed in the public mind as Russia's richest man. In June the core shareholders of Menatep Group, which owned 61 percent of Yukos, revealed their holdings in Yukos, a step required by the U.S. Securities and Exchanges Commission before Yukos could launch so-called Level 3 ADRs on the U.S. market.[17] At Yukos's share price at the time, their holdings in Yukos alone made six of them dollar billionaires.[18] LUKoil, competing hard with Yukos to keep its position as market leader, followed suit two months later.

At the time, the disclosure was hailed—at least in financial circles—as yet another step forward in corporate transparency. Analysts at one major Moscow brokerage wrote enthusiastically, "We believe that this openness is a sign of improving political stability in Russia, with Yukos again acting as corporate governance role model."[19] In retrospect, one wonders if a little less transparency might not have been wiser. The effect of the disclosure was to focus media attention on everything Khodorkovsky said and did. He was not only Russia's richest man; a few months prior to this disclosure, Yukos had become the country's leading oil producer, having taken over first place from LUKoil in January 2002. By the spring of 2003, Yukos's market worth had passed that of LUKoil, and it had become the largest oil company in Russia.

But then came a bombshell: a merger with Sibneft. An earlier attempt, when Sibneft was still owned by Boris Berezovsky, had produced the stillborn "Yuksi," which was quickly buried amid mutual accusations of bad faith. But by early 2003 Sibneft had passed into the hands of Berezovsky's onetime protégé Roman Abramovich, who appeared keen to cash out of active involvement in the oil business and concentrate on his overseas investments, including his British soccer club, Chelsea. The merger, had it been fully consummated, would have created a supergiant, far and away the largest oil company in Russia, and by some measures the largest in the world. In early September 2003, a month and a half before Khodorkovsky's arrest, the market valued Yukos at $31.2 billion and Sibneft at $13.3 billion. With reserves of nearly 160 billion tons (22 billion barrels), YukosSibneft (as the company was provisionally called) would have towered above all the world's private companies, including BP, ExxonMobil, and Shell.

All this undoubtedly attracted the thoughtful gaze of powerful figures, for whom such sudden and immense wealth, especially accruing to someone they regarded as an interloper and a parvenu, was practically a provocation. Indeed, Khodorkovsky's public behavior seemed calculated to provoke. By late 2002, his tone in media interviews had become increasingly sarcastic, contemptuous, and dismissive of the Russian bureaucracy and policy makers. He openly described state officials as fools and incompetents and called for them to be disciplined or dismissed. Khodorkovsky's general opinion seemed to be that anyone who had remained a Russian state official through the 1990s was either incompetent or venal, and he didn't seem to care who knew it. Thus his view of the technical experts in the Central Commision on Oilfield Developement (TsKR), the powerful body that reviewed the companies' field development plans, managed to be both patronizing and disparaging in the same sentence:

> There are some highly qualified experts in the TsKR, although some of them have been hired by the oil companies, because the "battle for brains" has been no less intense in the oil sector than in others. . . . It would not be a bad thing if they were retrained in their technological skills, acquired up-to-date software, and some of their personnel were changed.[20]

In Khodorkovsky's eyes, it was a constant battle between the companies' innovativeness and the regulators' benighted conservatism. "A whole year may be spent convincing bureaucrats that the methods of operating licensed parts of oil fields, proposed by companies, are correct," he said in the spring of 2002.[21] This was true, but it was hardly politic to say so in public.

In sum, by the beginning of 2003 Khodorkovsky stood out from the other oligarchs as the most determined and outspoken defender of positions and practices that were increasingly in conflict with the state's own growing ambitions and those of its preferred agents, Transneft and Rosneft. But more than that, his attitude and his language were increasingly incautious, verging on the reckless.

Two key examples make the point in more detail: Khodorkovsky's approach to "tax optimization" and his attempts to build an export pipeline to China.

Onshore Offshores: Haven Is Where You Find It

The landlocked republic of Ingushetiia, just next door to Chechnya in the mountainous North Caucasus, is not exactly known for its palm trees and sandy beaches. But in the 1990s it became one of Russia's most thriving off-shore tax havens, a favorite location for nameplate companies, mostly trading subsidiaries of Moscow-based Russian corporations. Together with other remote regions of the Russian Federation, mostly non-Russian enclaves such as Chukotka, Mordoviia, and Kalmykiia, "inland offshores" like Ingushetiia in the late 1990s were costing the federal treasury billions of dollars in tax receipts every year. But that was just the tip of the iceberg. In the 1990s hundreds of tax-privileged locations, typically individual towns or technology parks, sprang up throughout Russia, all offering exemptions to their corporate guests on regional and local taxes, and frequently on federal taxes as well.[22]

The irony of these tax havens was that they had been created by the Russian federal government in the first place. Until 2000, when Russian laws began to be tightened, the favorite tax havens of Russian corporations were the so-called ZATOs (*Zakrytye Administrativno-Territorial'nye Obrazovaniia*, or Closed Administrative-Territorial Entities). Most of these were former military-industrial "closed cities and territories," such as the notorious "post-office box" cities like Cheliabinsk-70 and Arzamas-16. In Soviet times, such closed cities and territories occupied 20 percent of the land area of the Soviet Union. To this day the full list of these locations is not known, but currently 2 million Russian citizens live and work in forty-one ZATOs, twenty-six of which belong to the Ministry of Defense and ten to the Atomic Industry Agency.[23]

In the 2001 version of the Tax Code, regions were allowed to grant exemptions from the regional and local portions of the corporate income tax (i.e., up to 16.5 percent out of 24 percent) to companies that signed agreements to invest in local economic growth. Oil companies rushed to take advantage of the loophole. Instead of the statutory 24 percent, they paid rates as low as 9 percent or less.[24] The way to use these "domestic offshores" was to open a trading subsidiary in one of the special economic zones and to channel exports through that entity. Corporate headquarters would then instruct their oil-producing divisions to sell their oil to the trading subsidiary at a low, so-called transfer price, thus displacing the company's profits to the domestic offshore, where they would be lightly taxed. Yukos had been one of the earliest and most aggressive users of such tax optimization.

The dispute over domestic tax havens and transfer prices is emblematic of the deep divide between the private companies' interpretations of the law and those of the Russian state in the early 2000s. For the oil companies, the law was perfectly clear—and using the domestic offshores for "tax optimization" was legal.[25] But for the Russian government, the policy's intent was being flouted. But was "tax optimization" a criminal act? On this point officials were divided. Mikhail Kasyanov, still prime minister at the time, said in 2003: "If legal tax optimization is declared illegal retroactively, I think that's unjust. If optimization is allowed by the law, we should follow the letter of the law, and not some idea of 'justice,' as some are doing today."[26] The Russian courts broadly agreed with him. The civil-law tradition tends to encourage a close adherence to the letter of the law, and Russian judges up to that point had resisted the government's attempts to prosecute private companies for taking advantage of loopholes.

The view of Deputy Finance Minister Sergei Shatalov is of special interest, because he had spent the years between the 1998 crash and Putin's election as head of the tax department of the Moscow office of one of the major Western auditing companies. "I consider tax minimization within the framework of the law to be entirely admissible," Shatalov told an interviewer in the fall of 2003:

> But from an ethical perspective it looks different, everyone knows that. . . . I've run into consultants who warn their clients, "In theory, this scheme is acceptable, you won't be prosecuted for it, but it smells bad." . . . But we have to admit that in the tax laws there are rather a lot of holes, which enable people to use tax minimization schemes perfectly legally, even though they smell bad.[27]

His boss, however, showed no such ambivalence. Finance Minister Kudrin argued that the intent of Russian legislation had been quite clear. If the government's tax officials could prove in court that a company was using domestic offshores to minimize its taxes, the court would be perfectly justified in declaring the arrangement null and void. As an example he cited a case in which LUKoil had been found guilty of setting up a shell company to exploit the tax breaks given by the Russian government to support the Baikonur space center. LUKoil had not contested the verdict and had paid up. As for Yukos, which had not, Kudrin said darkly, "We have only just begun pressing our claims."[28]

Kudrin remained one of the hard-liners on Yukos down to the end. One year later, on the day Khodorkovsky was sentenced to nine years in prison, Kudrin repeated his view that tax optimization was a violation of the law: "The attitude today is: if you avoid taxes 'honestly,' using loopholes in the law, then this is a proper way. But 'honest' avoidance is impossible."[29] The companies called it "tax optimization," but the Ministry of Finance called it "tax minimization."

The Ministry of Finance began closing down the "offshores." As it did so, Mikhail Khodorkovsky was scathing in his criticism, belittling the intelligence of the tax officials and calling for them to be punished:

> Do you know how many times over the last ten years there have been changes in tax policy toward the oil sector? Around fifty, on average five times a year. . . . I have already told the estimable leadership of our government that officials should be punished for their irresponsible chatter on this subject. . . . Some officials have constantly wagging tongues [*iazyki bez kostei*].[30]

Warming to the theme of irresponsible bureaucrats, Khodorkovsky added darkly, "In Stalin's time this was called sabotage—premeditated, malevolent sabotage on the part of some state officials." Such language, whether he consciously meant it or not, naturally implied to his listeners that the only appropriate remedy was arrest and prosecution. Just which officials Khodorkovsky had in mind he did not say, but they would surely have been understood to include Aleksei Kudrin, the finance minister, who for the previous three years had led the battle against the oil companies to raise the state's take from oil.

We return in Chapter 10 to a more detailed look at the politics of oil taxes, but the key point here is that Khodorkovsky did not simply oppose the government's attempts to tighten the tax system; he publicly impugned the tax officials' motives and intelligence, which only served to mobilize his enemies against him.

The same can be seen in Khodorkovsky's handling of the debate over oil policy toward China and the related issue of who would own pipelines and control oil-export policy.

"Beating a Dragon with a Stick"

Yukos had been working for the previous three years on a project to build a pipeline to China, and it had become central to Yukos's strategic plans.[31] The all-important anchor for the project was Tomsk Province, the southeastern-most corner of the West Siberian basin, where Yukos was already building up production and where its experts (Joe Mach, in particular) believed that much more oil would be found. Khodorkovsky set himself the goal of gaining sole control of Tomskneft, the local producer. A Western banker I spoke to recalled being struck by Khodorkovsky's single-minded determination:

> I had teamed up with [two Russian bankers] in 1997 to acquire Tomskneft (then known as Eastern Oil). We were trumped by Khodorkovsky, who bid three or four times above our top bid. We asked him, "Why are you bidding such an insane price for this property?" He answered, "I'm building an empire, and this is a key part of it."

In the summer of 2002, Yukos was reported to be talking to Sinopec and the China National Petroleum Corporation (CNPC) about taking a stake in the Talakan field in Sakha, which Yukos was seeking to control. The Talakan field would have been the centerpiece of the third stage of the pipeline. Thus in Khodorkovsky's mind the Chinese were an integral part of his grand strategy for the development of East Siberia.

But by late 2002 Khodorkovsky was beginning to realize that the Kremlin had turned against the Yukos pipeline and indeed against his attempts to build a strategic relationship with China. In November 2002 Putin chaired a meeting of the Security Council at which he expressed support for a route to the Pacific at the port of Nakhodka, bypassing China.[32] In contrast, less than a month later, during his state visit to Beijing, Putin omitted any mention of Yukos's China pipeline. Sensing that the project was escaping from his grasp, Khodorkovsky escalated. In early February, he warned that if the government chose the Pacific route, Yukos would refuse to use it to export oil.[33] At about the same time, in an interview with the weekly *Ekspert*, he vented his frustration:

> They tell me, "At Nakhodka you'll have access to the world market." I say, "Really? Just think: I drag my oil an extra three thousand kilometers, find a buyer, instead of getting my money at the Chinese border, under a twenty-

year guarantee from the Chinese government, at world prices. What am I—crazy?"[34]

In the same interview, Khodorkovsky charged that the Russian government had gone back on a commitment, and in the process had caused the Chinese government to lose face. In actual fact, the Russian government had never made a formal promise; a "tripartite agreement" of September 2001, under which CNPC had agreed to help finance the Yukos pipeline, was signed by Transneft, not the Russian state. But the Chinese government had included the pipeline in its five-year plan and had lobbied hard for it in Moscow. Prime Minister Mikhail Kasyanov had supported it; both he and the deputy prime minister for energy, Viktor Khristenko, had traveled to Beijing in August to discuss the details.[35] Khodorkovsky warned that by turning away from the China pipeline, the Kremlin was insulting a rising great power:

> The Chinese told me once that you can beat a dragon with a stick so long as it's asleep. But that dragon now has a GDP three or four times larger than ours, its growth rates are two to three times greater, and its population is ten times ours. But we're running up with a club and beating that dragon on the tail. For the moment the dragon is taking no notice—but I wouldn't want it to change its mind.[36]

Khodorkovsky's public comments on a matter of foreign policy could hardly have been welcomed in the Kremlin. Putin, like Yeltsin before him, regarded foreign policy and defense as his own preserve. Khodorkovsky's intrusion into an area of presidential prerogative only reinforced rumors that he had wider political ambitions, and Khodorkovsky himself did nothing to dispel them.

All this came to a head in February 2003, during a fateful personal exchange between Khodorkovsky and Putin.

"I'm Returning the Hockey Puck to You"

It has become one of the iconic scenes of the Putin era. In February 2003, Putin met with the members of the Russian Union of Industrialists and Entrepreneurs (RSPP) in the ornate Catherine Hall of the Kremlin. Since his election in 2000, Putin had met annually with this group, which included all of the leading private industrialists, essentially the oligarchs' lobby.

It was before a similar group, in July 2000, that Putin had enunciated the principle of "equal distance," according to which no private businessman would be allowed to have privileged access to the corridors of power. "No clan, no oligarch should come close to regional or federal authorities," Putin had said. "They should be kept equally distanced from politics."[37] The meetings with the RSPP, at which the assembled oligarchs sat facing the president like obedient schoolchildren, symbolized their "equal distance."

Subsequent sessions had been uneventful discussions of routine matters, but the topic this time was the sensitive issue of corruption. Khodorkovsky came armed with an elaborate slide presentation, titled "Corruption in Russia: A Brake on Economic Growth." It was soon apparent, as he spoke, that his target was the state.

State corruption was everywhere, declared Khodorkovsky, especially among the tax collectors. For every vacancy in the Tax Academy there were four to five applicants waiting in line—proof that it was viewed as a road to riches. The Ministry of Energy had been the "most corrupt ministry in the country," until its power to set oil-tax rates had been taken away. Then turning to face Sergei Bogdanichikov, the chairman of Rosneft, Khodorkovsky charged that Rosneft had resorted to corruption to gain control of Northern Oil, a small company in Russia's Timan-Pechora region. It was tantamount to a direct accusation that Bogdanchikov himself was corrupt.

For Putin, this was quite enough. At this point he came to Bogdanchikov's defense, pointing out that Rosneft needed new reserves. As everyone in the room knew, the private oil companies had repeatedly raided Rosneft throughout the 1990s, carrying off its best properties; and only at the last minute had LUKoil been prevented from taking over Purneftegaz, Rosneft's last jewel. But now Putin counterattacked. "Some companies, including Yukos, have excessive reserves," he said. "How did it obtain them?" Observing that Yukos had had tax problems and had worked with the government to resolve them, he asked, "But how did they arise in the first place?" Putin added slyly, "Maybe that's why there are five applications for every vacancy at the Tax Academy?" "In other words," Putin concluded with a slight smile, "I'm returning the hockey puck to you." The hall of assembled oligarchs echoed with derisive laughter.[38]

But that was not the end of the exchange. According to one eyewitness, Viktor Gerashchenko, former chairman of the Russian Central Bank and subsequently chairman of Yukos, Khodorkovsky pressed on with a plea to Putin to approve Yukos's pipeline to China. Putin refused point-blank, saying that he supported Transneft's plan to build a pipeline to the Pacific. Khodorkovsky insisted, and Putin again refused, whereupon Khodorkovsky, according to Gerashchenko, exclaimed, "Vladimir Vladimirovich, you do not understand the importance of developing relations with China."[39] We don't know Putin's reaction, but we can be sure he did not appreciate being lectured on grand strategy.

In retrospect, several of the major themes of the coming Yukos Affair were already present in this exchange: Putin's irritation over Yukos's tax practices and hoarding of licenses, his annoyance at Khodorkovsky's independent foreign policy, his growing opposition to private pipelines in general and to Yukos's China pipeline in particular, and his concern to defend the interests of the state-owned Rosneft. But above all it was Khodorkovsky's extraordinary bravado that turned the exchange into an open conflict. It was one thing to criticize unnamed state officials, quite another to accuse the president of incompetence—and worse—to his face in front of assembled witnesses. It was a fatal blunder. In one flash Khodorkovsky's incaution, his underestimation of the forces against him, and his contempt for the president himself were on display for all to see. In addition, Bogdanchikov's public humiliation by Khodorkovsky turned normal corporate competition into a personal vendetta. On that day in February 2003, Khodorkovsky's position began to crumble. He had just eight months of freedom left.

The issue over which Khodorkovsky had publicly assailed Bogdanchikov was the purchase of Northern Oil by Rosneft. From that moment on, Bogdanchikov became an implacable enemy. Khodorkovsky's public personal attack on Bogdanchikov was all the more puzzling because it was gratuitous. Neither Khodorkovsky nor his partners in Menatep, so far as is known, were directly affected by the sale. Why then did he venture to step on a political third rail—and before such an audience—over a matter in which he had no personal stake? The conventional interpretation is that Khodorkovsky's growing power and wealth had produced in him a megalomaniacal "master of the universe" state of mind in which he recognized no limits. But that is likely only half the explanation. Khodorkovsky's attitude, even before the hockey-puck exchange, suggested growing frustration, anger, and the beginnings of fear.

Well before the Yukos Affair began, Khodorkovsky must have sensed that the tide was turning. By the end of 2002 he was facing increasingly intractable opposition, from the Kremlin, from the tax authorities, from Transneft, and above all from Rosneft, which appeared to be winning the Kremlin's favor. He was losing ground over key issues, and to people he regarded as wrong-headed if not outright fools. His opponents' actions not only offended economic common sense and went against Russia's national interests, he felt; they threatened his carefully laid strategic plans for Yukos. By early 2003 Khodorkovsky was behaving like an increasingly angry and frustrated man.

Under the circumstances, one might have expected Khodorkovsky to take a lower profile, as the other oil generals did. Instead, as winter passed into spring, he took even more provocative public positions. The best example is Yukos's lobbying activity in the Duma and its open resistance to the government's efforts to pass new legislation on taxation and foreign investment. This ratcheted up even further Khodorkovsky's conflict with the state.

No Lobbying, Please—We're Russian

It was a byword in the 1990s that the Russian parliament, especially its lower house, the Duma, was thoroughly penetrated by private interests. Most deputies were more or less openly on the payroll of one oligarch or another. Yet a kind of Victorian *pudeur* prevailed on the subject: everyone did it, but one didn't mention it in polite society. Lobbying was not viewed as legitimate; the very word, *lobbirovanie,* was one of those words imported from the West to signify something distasteful. Indeed, perhaps precisely because lobbying had not been institutionalized as a recognized part of legislative life, influence buying took extreme and exotic forms. Rather than support registered lobbyists and contribute to campaigns through political action committees, Russian businessmen ran for parliament and represented themselves or installed their straw men. Party lists were openly for sale. Key committees became corporate outposts. In the Russia of the 1990s, K Street ran right through the center aisle of the Duma.

Yukos played the game as others did, but true to form, it was far more open and brazen than anyone else. Vladimir Dubov, chairman of the tax subcommittee of the Duma's budget committee between 1999 and 2003, was one of Mikhail Khodorkovsky's earliest partners. He had been a research chemist at the prestigious Institute of High Temperatures of the USSR Academy of Sciences, whose director, academician Aleksandr Sheindlin, had given Khodor-kovsky and his fledgling cooperative their first big fee—the then glittering sum of 160,000 rubles.[40] In 1989, when Khodorkovsky turned his cooperative into a bank called Menatep, Vladimir Dubov, then 31 years old, joined him as a member of the executive board.

Throughout the 1990s Dubov remained largely invisible to the public. But in 1999 Dubov was elected deputy in the federal parliament and became chairman of the tax subcommittee of the Duma budget committee. In this position he became known as the "man from Yukos." As the Putin administration fought to raise taxes on oil production, Dubov coordinated the oil companies' rearguard defenses. For three years the battle raged. The higher oil prices climbed, the more frustrated the government became over the oil companies' constant resistance. In parallel, Yukos was fighting a legislative battle of its own against the government's efforts to pass new legislation on production sharing agreements (PSAs). Dubov was the central figure in both of those actions.

In the spring and summer of 2003, the conflict over Yukos's lobbying came to a head.[41] Khodorkovsky had taken a strong stance against production sharing and was lobbying hard in the parliament to block the government's legislation on the subject. Yukos's people scarcely bothered to conceal their hand. In May, as Dubov guided the markup of the government's draft PSA bill in committee, members of the Yukos legal department sat next to him, providing advice on proposed amendments as they came up. Later in the month, as the PSA bill came to the floor of the Duma for debate, Sergei Shtogrin, who though a member of the Communist Party faction was loyal to Yukos, stood at the speakers' rostrum, presenting a series of amendments. Vladimir Dubov stepped up to him and handed him a mobile telephone. Shtogrin interrupted his speech and listened intently as the Yukos legal department, at the other end of the line, coached Shtogrin on the language to use. For the speaker, Gennadii Seleznev, this was too much. Addressing Shtogrin, he exploded: "Sergei Ivanovich, have you no fear of God? This is an outrage! It's Dubov who is making you do this! Put away your telephone—what disrespect for the Duma!"[42]

A few weeks later, at a press conference at the Kremlin for Russian and foreign media in late June, Putin, who had been briefed about the incident, spoke out angrily against what he described as Yukos's interference with the government's priorities:

The large oil companies are actively opposing the tax on mineral resources, arguing that the government is putting too heavy a burden on them. . . . We must not allow certain business interests to influence the political life of the country in their narrow group interests.

Putin then added menacingly, "But as for those who do not agree with this position, well, as they used to say, 'Some are gone, and some are far away.'"[43] The quotation, from Russia's national poet, Pushkin,[44] was instantly familiar to every Russian. The clear implication was that if Khodorkovsky did not stop interfering in what Putin regarded as the preserve of the state, he would either be arrested or exiled.

It was at about this time, in June 2003, that an incendiary report appeared, with the title "The State and the Oligarchs." Claiming that Russia was on the verge of an "oligarchic coup," it argued that the substance of power was passing to a group of powerful men, led by Mikhail Khodorkovsky and Mikhail Fridman and a handful of others, who aimed to turn Russia into a parliamentary regime and weaken the powers of the presidency. The paper denounced the weakness of the "capitulationist state" and argued that the recentralization of power that had taken place under Putin had in fact only opened the way for rule by the oligarchs. By implication, the report, though without naming him, was calling Putin weak.[45]

The report was written by an obscure group called the Council for National Strategy, but it is believed that the principal author was a publicist and political strategist named Stanislav Belkovskii, who served as an occasional political advisor to the Kremlin. According to persistent rumors and *kompromat* material circulating in Moscow at the time, Belkovskii had been commissioned to write the report by Sergei Bogdanchikov, the CEO of Rosneft, who was still seething with anger over Khodorkovsky's personal attack against him in the "hockey puck" episode.[46] Behind Bogdanchikov there were said to be still more powerful figures; some accounts pointed to Igor Sechin himself as the report's ultimate sponsor. There is no way to judge the truth of these rumors, but the report was well timed, to say the least. Putin was apparently swayed by it, at least to judge from the fact that at the end of June he himself spoke out against the idea of turning Russia into a parliamentary system.

Khodorkovsky's own actions at this time provided food for the Kremlin's suspicions. Through his financial support for opposition parties and nongovernmental organizations, his lobbying activity in the Duma, and his public positions on foreign policy, he did indeed appear to be positioning himself as a challenger. His own public musings about his political future only strengthened the impression. In an interview in the German weekly *Der Spiegel* in April 2003, for example, Khodorkovsky said he intended to step down from his position as chairman of the board of Yukos when he turned 45. "I may well go into politics," he said. As it happened, his forty-fifth birthday would fall in 2008—at the end of Putin's second presidential term.[47]

Thus the growing conflict between Khodorkovsky and the Kremlin was over not a single issue but a multitude. But there was one more, which for some was decisive. Khodorkovsky seemed to be about to sell his company to the foreigners.

Houdini's Last Escape: The Near Sale of Yukos

In the final months before his arrest, Khodorkovsky attempted the most spectacular and controversial deal of his career: to merge Yukos with an international oil company. It was an extraordinary gamble, a double-or-nothing bet that would have created the largest oil giant in the world, providing protection—or so Khodorkovsky hoped—against arrest and expropriation at home. Yet the move symbolized the strategic flaw in Khodorkovsky's thinking: his exaggerated view of the power of external actors to influence events inside Russia and his misperception of the way his foreign ties would play at home. There is no way of knowing whether, as some claim, the near merger was the last straw for Putin. But added to the other issues we have seen, Khodorkovsky's last gamble, one may be sure, only strengthened the mistrust and antipathy with which he was viewed in the Kremlin.

Khodorkovsky's gamble was not a last-minute improvisation; its origins go back to mid-2002. Up to that time he had been well known among foreign oil companies for his resistance to any sort of equity sale. But by mid-2002 he had evidently decided that Yukos's valuation had reached the point where selling a stake made sense. In July 2002, he approached Chevron. The U.S. company formed a team and talks began. The initial proposal was for a 25 percent stake, with an option to increase to 50 percent. In the fall of 2002, Khodorkovsky began parallel talks with ExxonMobil, and from that point on the two conversations continued simultaneously. Yukos took elaborate precautions to preserve secrecy, maintaining separate data rooms on separate floors as the talks mounted in intensity over the summer, ushering the two companies' teams in and out by separate doors. But the bustle of foreign guests was such that everyone in Yukos was aware of it. Characteristically, according to one Yukos executive, "Chevron brought in platoons of experts, Exxon brought in whole armies."

But in the spring of 2003, as the Kremlin's pressure on Yukos intensified, Khodorkovsky decided to up the ante with Chevron. Chevron was willing: a new senior vice president had recently taken over at Chevron with the mission of expanding the company's activity abroad. By late September a summer of intense talks had produced a letter of agreement between Chevron and Yukos. The deal had expanded dramatically. Instead of Chevron simply taking a stake in Yukos, the leaders of the two companies had decided to attempt something unprecedented in the Russian oil industry: an outright merger. In terms of production and reserves (although not quite in market capital) the combined company would have been a giant, the largest oil company in the world. If the deal had gone through, Khodorkovsky would have become vice chairman and an executive member of the board of the combined company. As one senior Yukos executive, who was close to the talks, commented, "Khodorkovsky was not selling out of the oil business. He was buying a window on to the world."

All that remained was to agree on Yukos's share in the new joint company. But for that the two CEOs needed sit down together and actually close the deal. The U.S.-Russian Energy Summit in Saint Petersburg gave them the opportunity. During a break, four men—Chevron's CEO Dave O'Reilly, Khodorkovsky, and two top aides—looked about for a discreet place to meet. But the ever alert editor of the *Financial Times,* Chrystia Freeland, was standing nearby, perhaps sensing something was afoot. According to an eyewitness:

> Yukos's head of public affairs was assigned to divert Chrystia Freeland's attention to another part of the conference hall, while the four men ducked into a side room. There was only one issue left on the table: the percentage of the combined company that YukosSibneft would get. But the two sides failed to close. O'Reilly offered 37.6 percent; Khodorkovsky held out for 43.5 percent; and neither side would budge. It turned out to be the last time they met.

The deal would have been fabulous for Khodorkovsky. Chevron's offer looked generous, amounting to a 15 percent premium above Yukos's current valuation, reflecting its anticipated rapid future growth and Yukos's expanding reserves. But Khodorkovsky insisted on a 30 percent premium and would not yield. If Yukos's position had prevailed, Khodorkovsky, who owned 36 percent of Yukos, or 25 percent of the anticipated YukosSibneft combined company, would have ended up with 10 percent of YukosSibneftChevTex. But more than that, in Khodorkovsky's eyes, the merger represented life insurance. The Kremlin might not hesitate to go after a Russian oligarch, but surely it would think twice about expropriating the world's largest oil company.

The near deal with Chevron sheds some interesting light on Khodorkovsky's own vision of himself and his future. As we saw in Chapter 5, Khodorkovsky took an eager part in the most technical details of oil production. Those who had daily working contact with him observed that he clearly enjoyed the oil business and was fascinated by it. If the merger had come off, Khodorkovsky would have been one of the giants of the global oil business, at a time of revolutionary change in the industry. The near merger between Chevron and Yukos stands as one of the most tantalizing might-have-beens in the recent history of the oil industry.

In reality, even if O'Reilly and Khodorkovsky had shaken hands on a number, they were still a long way from closing. O'Reilly would have had to gain the assent of Chevron's board. Several members were thought to be reluctant. "After all," said one high-placed Chevron executive, "we were betting the company, nothing less." In the end, O'Reilly might well have prevailed, but it would have taken time.

And time was running out. In parallel with speculation over the possible mergers, the prosecutors' attacks on Yukos mounted in intensity. In the final weeks before Khodorkovsky's arrest a kind of schizophrenia gripped Moscow. Yukos's stock, along with the rest of the Russian stock market, climbed daily from peak to peak, as acquisition rumors continued to fly. Less than a week after the U.S.-Russian summit, Putin visited New York, accompanied by LUKoil CEO Vagit Alekperov. There he met privately with Lee Raymond, the CEO of ExxonMobil, who briefed Putin on Yukos's talks with ExxonMobil. The following week, on October 2, Lee Raymond arrived in Moscow, officially for the World Economic Forum but reportedly for meetings with Khodorkovsky, and acquisition fever mounted another notch,[48] driving the Russian stock market even higher. On the same day, Yukos and Sibneft announced the completion of their merger.[49] On October 3, Raymond met with Prime Minister

Kasyanov and informed him officially of the ongoing talks between Yukos and ExxonMobil.

Yet even as Raymond departed Moscow, the prosecutors struck again. On October 3, agents of the General Procuracy raided a school supported by Yukos outside Moscow, on the grounds of which Khodorkovsky's parents also happened to live, as well as the Yukos business center in the suburban village of Zhukovka.[50] Tensions were mounting by the day. It was increasingly difficult to see how negotiations over a sale could continue in such an atmosphere.

It has been suggested that it was the prospect of a sale of Yukos to a foreign company that was the tipping point that caused Putin to order Khodorkovsky's arrest. According to this view, Putin was unaware of the scale of the proposed deal, or that ExxonMobil was involved as a contender, until his meeting with Lee Raymond in New York. "Are you from Chevron?" Putin is said to have exclaimed in surprise, when Lee Raymond informed him of his talks with Khodorkovsky. Putin then supposedly returned to Moscow seething with anger, determined to head off the deal before it was final. This account seems unlikely. It is not plausible to suppose that Putin was unaware of the talks with Exxon. Both companies had been talking with Yukos for over a year. Consequently, if the Kremlin's intelligence system was at all competent, Putin was presumably aware of Exxon's presence. If nothing else, there was a steady stream of leaks to the international media, which fed the mounting excitement among investors in Moscow. All this was impossible for the Kremlin to ignore. Moreover, Putin had direct knowledge of the talks with ExxonMobil, because various public figures had spoken to him or his staff directly on the company's behalf. It is unlikely, in other words, that the proposed mergers were the trigger that caused Putin to act. But what did?

So What "Caused" Khodorkovsky's Arrest?

By the summer of 2003 there was a long list of contentious issues between Yukos and the Kremlin: Yukos's lobbying over tax issues, its proposed export pipeline to China, Khodorkovsky's rumored political ambitions, and the negotiations to sell Yukos to foreign investors. But one could extend the list almost at will, to include Yukos's support for opposition parties, Khodorkovsky's pro-American stance (at a time when the onset of the Iraq War had cast a cloud over Russian-American relations), his funding of nongovernmental organizations, not to mention the way he ran his oil company and disposed of its profits. Which of these ultimately caused Khodorkovsky's arrest, or was it something else? Was there a single episode that finally caused Putin's anger to run over?

By October, Putin's anger was palpable. In a lengthy interview with the *New York Times,* he lashed out at the unnamed billionaires who had attempted to "create a system of oligarchic rule":

> We have a category of people who have become billionaires, as we say, overnight. The state appointed them as billionaires. It simply gave out a huge amount of property, practically for free. . . . Then as the play developed, they got the impression that the gods themselves slept on their heads, that everything is permitted to them.[51]

For his part, Khodorkovsky seemed practically to be inviting arrest. At a news conference on October 4, commenting on the government's tactics, Khodorkovsky exclaimed, "If they want me to go into exile, I'm not going to. If they want to put me in prison, then . . . be my guest, go ahead."[52] What set Khodorkovsky apart from the other oligarchs Putin had fought and defeated—Gusinskii, Berezovsky, and especially Viakhirev—was that Khodorkovsky refused to back down or leave Russia. Was that, in the end, what caused Putin to move against him?

According to one account, two days before Khodorkovsky's arrest the general prosecutor, Vladimir Ustinov, presented Putin a report on Khodorkovsky's supposed crimes. After reading it, Putin finally said, "Let the law take its course,"[53] and the trap closed.

We will probably never know. But the larger answer is that what ultimately caused Khodorkovsky's downfall was the totality of his actions and, above all, the way the Russian political and business elite reacted to them. Khodorkovsky's wealth and visibility, his control of the single most successful oil company in Russia, his open contempt for the state's officials, his challenge to established conventions on oil production, and his positions on a dozen sensitive issues ranging from taxes to foreign policy—in a word, practically everything he was and did—all served to unite his enemies against him, while deterring those who might otherwise have sided with him. The explanation of his fate lies precisely in the very multitude of issues in which Khodorkovsky was perceived by others as having crossed the line. His provocative behavior played into the hands of his enemies. It united against him an otherwise disparate community—the opportunists, the principled and the unprincipled, the conservatives and the more state-minded liberals, the enforcers, and the anti-Semites—people who would not have agreed on anything else.

In the process, Khodorkovsky catalyzed a wave of reaction that went well beyond what his enemies would have been able to achieve without him. The result, I will argue, was a swing in the balance of power, to the advantage of the hard-line fraction of the siloviki in the Kremlin, with far-reaching policy consequences that are still felt today. We turn now to that broader question.

The Role of the Siloviki

The siloviki under Putin are often called a "clan," but that word overstates the unity among them. In actual fact the politics of the Putin era have been marked throughout by bitter internecine warfare among the power structures, as they compete for budgets, rents, power, and Putin's ear. One of Putin's constant preoccupations has been to keep these rivalries within bounds and in balance—and out of sight. Yet every so often fights among the securocrats erupt into the open.[54] One notorious example is the *Tri Kita* ("Three Whales") affair, named after a Moscow furniture chain, a vast smuggling and money-laundering scandal that pitted the FSB and the Procuracy on one side against the MVD and the Customs Committee on the other, with high-level political repercussions that went on for the better part of a decade.[55] In such rare cases, one glimpses, as in a Japanese Kabuki play, the silhouettes of the players and, more dimly, the hands of the puppeteers manipulating them.

There is similar uncertainty surrounding the roles of the various siloviki in the Yukos Affair. One key member of this group, however, was anything but hidden, and his rise, role, and subsequent eclipse constitute a kind of barometer of the shifting politics behind him. That man was the general prosecutor who led the prosecution in the subsequent trials, Vladimir Ustinov.

The Prosecutor from Sochi

Until just a few years before, Vladimir Ustinov had been a small-town figure in southern Russia, the prosecutor of the seaside resort of Sochi and deputy prosecutor general for the surrounding Kuban' region. He had spent his entire working life in the south, and although he was moderately successful, there was little to suggest that his career would end any differently from the way it had begun. But Sochi and the Kuban', once a favorite holiday spot for the vacationing Soviet elite, had become a way station for drug traffic and organized crime emanating from Chechnya after the Russian withdrawal in 1996, and Ustinov had gained a reputation as a forceful prosecutor who was familiar with the problems of the area. A meeting with the personnel chief of the General Procuracy in 1997 led to a promotion to Moscow as deputy general prosecutor overseeing interethnic relations and security in the North Caucasus region. According to the Moscow grapevine, he was recommended by Boris Berezovsky, who at the time was deputy executive secretary of the Security Council while at the same time involved in business in Chechnya and the North Caucasus. Berezovsky reportedly said of Ustinov, "He will be loyal and he will keep his mouth shut."[56]

Ustinov's timing could not have been better. Two years after the southerner's arrival in Moscow, the general prosecutor, Iurii Skuratov, was felled by a high-level intrigue and forced to resign. When Putin came in, in 2000, he wanted his own man as prosecutor general, Dmitri Kozak, a lawyer from Saint Petersburg. But the Yeltsin Family fought to keep Ustinov, whom they perceived as loyal to them, and Putin gave way. Ustinov was duly confirmed by the upper house of parliament in 2000.

Over the next three years, Ustinov successfully transferred his loyalty to the new president and became one of his chief instruments in the campaign to clip back the oligarchs. Ustinov's team in the General Procuracy coordinated the attacks against Boris Berezovsky, Vladimir Gusinsky, Rem Viakhirev and his son Iurii,[57] and others. By 2003, Ustinov had become one of the principal figures in the silovik wing of the leadership and part of their inner social circle. His relationship with Putin's aide Igor Sechin was especially close—and in fact would soon be made closer by the marriage of their children. In the fall of 2003, Ustinov's son Dmitrii, a recent graduate of the FSB Academy, married Inga Sechina, who had recently graduated from the Saint Petersburg Mining Institute.[58] A son was born in July 2005. Both proud grandfathers attended the christening, which was treated by the Russian media as a major event in the Moscow social season.

Born into a family of prosecutors, Ustinov described himself as a "heredi-tary prosecutor." His father had been a prosecutor; his brother was a military prosecutor. "I was born and raised in a family of prosecutors," he told an inter-viewer. "I never imagined a different path for myself."[59] Ustinov's identity was totally bound up in his job. To him the world was full of suspects. "I'm a pros-ecutor even in my sleep," he said. When an interviewer asked him for his opin-ion of Berezovsky and Gusinsky, Ustinov answered shortly, "I don't call them oligarchs, I call them defendants."[60]

As the offensive on Khodorkovsky and Yukos gained momentum through-out 2003 and beyond, Ustinov played the lead role, coordinating the wave of raids, arrests, and investigations that mounted steadily all through the sum-mer. By the early fall of 2003, the Procuracy was running seven separate inves-tigations into Yukos and Menatep, dredging up every possible case against them, including some that had been officially closed over a decade before.

Ustinov presumably felt no particular animus at first against Mikhail Khodor-kovsky. This oligarch was initially no different from the others, and business was business. But as the investigations against Khodorkovsky and Yukos and Menatep expanded and multiplied, Khodorkovsky reacted with extreme and public defiance, which he increasingly directed against Ustinov personally. He launched a campaign to portray Ustinov as a rogue prosecutor, a state official run amok. In July 2003 I visited Yukos's corporate headquarters. In the spa-cious atrium on the ground floor, an extraordinary art exhibit had been set up on Khodorkovsky's orders. It was a collection of famous World War II propa-ganda posters—but each poster had been adapted to the war now going on between Yukos and the General Procuracy. One well-known wartime poster, depicting a fascist serpent with the face of Adolf Hitler being crushed by a handsome square-jawed Red Army soldier, now featured the logo of the Gen-eral Procuracy in place of the swastika on Hitler's helmet. All the other posters in the exhibit, some thirty in all, had been similarly altered.

Clearly Khodorkovsky hoped to split his enemies by pretending to believe that the attacks on him came from the Procuracy rather than the Kremlin. It was a clumsy and disastrous miscalculation. In the eyes of any official and probably most ordinary Russians as well, identifying the Russian government with fascist Germany—in effect calling the General Procuracy the Gestapo—was a direct affront to the state. As for the siloviki themselves, it only redou-bled their determination to bring Khodorkovsky down.

"Werewolves in Uniform"

As Khodorkovsky sensed the trap closing around him over the summer and fall of 2003, instead of moderating his public language he escalated further. He became more and more provocative, openly mocking his enemies, daring them to do their worst, as if words alone could hold off the attack. His relations with Transneft and its chairman, Semyon Vainshtok, had grown increasingly poisonous since Khodorkovsky had mocked Transneft for having a case of "phantom leg"—that is, acting as though the Soviet Union was still alive. At the U.S.-Russia Energy Summit in Saint Petersburg in late September 2003, one month before his arrest, Khodorkovsky infuriated Vainshtok with the following exchange, which was witnessed by Chrystia Freeland of the *Financial Times*:

> At one point in his talk [Khodorkovsky] called for the liberalization of Russia's oil pipeline system. . . . At the lunch after the speeches, Khodorkovsky spotted the head of Transneft, the state-owned oil pipeline company. Smiling broadly, Khodorkovsky called out: "So, how did you like my loyal speech?" [Vainshtok], red-faced and struggling with evident anger, shouted back: "If that was loyal, I'm a trolley bus!" "So where are your headlights?" Khodorkovsky yelled back, miming flashing headlights with his hands cupped round his eyes.[61]

Yet Khodorkovsky continued to hope against hope that the president would rein in the attackers and especially the General Procuracy. On October 20, in a final interview with *Novaia gazeta* only days before his arrest, Khodorkovsky renewed his attack on the General Procuracy, calling those behind the raids "werewolves in uniform" *(oborotni v pogonakh).*[62] He avoided attacking Ustinov by name (evidently having had belated second thoughts about July's poster exhibit, which in the meantime had been taken down) and instead accused unnamed "unscrupulous officers of the Procuracy" of being behind the offensive on Yukos. "I am far from thinking that the entire Procuracy takes this position," Khodorkovsky went on. Rather, he said, "individual officers of the Procuracy are breaking the law." Khodorkovsky tried to draw a line between the good president and the bad prosecutors. "But if after three months no evidence acceptable to an open court exists," then, Khodorkovsky warned darkly, "someone could soon lose his epaulets."

But Ustinov did not lose his epaulets. Instead, his influence and visibility rose higher and higher over the following two and a half years, as he and his principal deputy, Iurii Biriukov, and their team of prosecutors, pursued the cases against Khodorkovsky and his partner Platon Lebedev, who was arrested in July 2003. In the wake of Khodorkovsky's arrest, the campaign against Yukos broadened, as more criminal cases were brought against Yukos personnel in Moscow.[63] Yukos was pushed inexorably toward bankruptcy and breakup, and prosecutors fanned out in every direction, looking for incriminating evidence. No one could tell at that moment how far the Yukos Affair would go or where the siloviki would stop.

The Liberals Pull Away, the Oil Generals Pull Back, Yukos Pulls Apart

Just as Khodorkovsky's visibility and public positions made him an attractive target for his attackers, so also they made him difficult for the business elite and the remaining liberals in the government to defend. Those who spoke out against his arrest and detention did so less out of sympathy or solidarity with Khodorkovsky as an individual than out of alarm over the precedent that his arrest represented and the swing in the balance of political power that apparently lay behind it. The immediate effect of the arrest was to split the liberals. The remaining members of the Yeltsin Family still in high office, mainly the head of the Presidential Administration, Aleksandr Voloshin, and the prime minister, Mikhail Kasyanov, soon left the government (Voloshin resigned, Kasyanov was dimissed). But the leading Petersburg liberals, such as German Gref and Dmitri Medvedev, after initially speaking out against the arrest, remained on board, while Kudrin, who had always been critical of Khodorkovsky, hardened his tone further. Among the business leaders, even fewer spoke up for Khodorkovsky, the one notable exception being Arkadii Vol'skii, the longtime head of the RSPP. Khodorkovsky before his arrest had been an object of envy but also of distrust and disapproval; now he was a source of danger.

The oilmen, who had endured their share of tax raids and other armed interventions in the months leading up to Khodorkovsky's arrest, could not know whether they might be next, and they reacted to the arrest with extreme caution. Vagit Alekperov, as we shall see in the next chapter, had been attentive from the first to the danger signs. Now LUKoil quickly retreated from its restructuring program and returned to a more traditional approach to its West Siberian oilfields.

But it was Roman Abramovich who made the sharpest turn. In the weeks leading up to Khodorkovsky's arrest, Yukos's merger with Sibneft was still progressing smoothly. At the beginning of October the two companies merged their teams and officially began joint operations. Shortly afterward, Sibneft's executives, led by its president, Aleksandr Korsik, moved their offices to Yukos's headquarters. By mid-October the joint teams were already hard at work preparing new organization charts and discussing combined operations for the coming year. But pressure was mounting on Sibneft to cancel the merger. On October 14 Sibneft CEO Evgenii Shvidler was called in by Interior Ministry investigators for questioning about Sibneft's tax optimization practices, a clear warning that the government might bring against it the same tax case as against Yukos.[64] In the weeks following Khodorkovsky's arrest, Abramovich was rumored to be toying with the idea of using the opportunity to take over the combined company for himself. Be that as it may, over the weekend of November 29–30 he suddenly announced that the merger was off. When the Yukos employees came to work on Monday morning, they discovered that the Sibneft people had emptied their desks and vanished.[65]

Khodorkovsky had been Yukos's brain center, but he could not run the company from his jail cell. On November 2, in an effort to protect the company from further attack, he resigned as CEO, but to no avail. Some key officers, particularly those involved in oil trading, had fled abroad overnight, and others followed in a steady stream, as criminal cases were brought against them. The remaining Russian staff began to war against the foreign staff. The board of directors split into quarreling factions. In June 2004 the company's bank accounts were frozen by a Moscow court, and there was no cash to pay pipeline tariffs and to move Yukos's 19,000 tank cars on the Russian rail system. Export revenues collapsed. Over the next two years, the company was drained of its resources by the repeated levies of back taxes and penalties exacted by the government and ceased to function. What remained of the Mach machine dissolved. Funding disappeared; contractors went unpaid; and business stopped. The Yukos Black Belts, the cohort of young reservoir engineers Joe Mach had trained and deployed in the field, began to scatter to other companies. The Field Development Center, the symbolic heart of Joe Mach's operation and the command post for the "Top Twenty" system of well prioritization, was closed in November 2004 when the rent on the building stopped being paid, and the computers and electronics were looted and carried off. Yukos's stock and the stock options that had made up a large part of the compensation packages of the senior officers steadily lost value, ultimately becoming worthless.

All of this followed inexorably from Khodorkovsky's removal. In Russia, property undefended is soon claimed by others. As the Russian proverb goes, "A sacred place never remains empty" ("Sviato mesto pusto ne byvaet").

The Campaign Spreads to the Provinces: Operation Energiia

The campaign against Yukos was not limited to Moscow. In the months following Khodorkovsky's arrest, it appeared as though it might turn into a generalized assault on the private oil companies in the field.[66] One of the principal accusations leveled at them from within the conservative oil establishment, as we have seen, was that they were violating official field development plans, damaging the oilfields, and lowering ultimate recovery. Even before the Yukos Affair began, Putin himself had criticized the oil companies for their "barbaric practices." "The cream is skimmed while the wells go rotten," he had exclaimed in 2002.[67] As the pressure on Yukos mounted in 2003, the call went out to root out "criminality" from the oilfields. Hitherto the General Procuracy had been the main law-enforcement agency in charge of the Yukos case, but in September 2003 the Ministry of Internal Affairs joined the chase. At the instigation of the minister, Rashid Nurgaliev, the MVD launched a vast sweep, dubbed Operation Energiia, through the oil region of West Siberia. Over the next three years, police investigators combed through the local operations of the oil companies. Thousands of people were investigated and hundreds arrested.

The principal targets of the campaign were the heads of the four largest Yukos upstream subsidiaries.[68] Tagirzian Gil'manov had been the general director of Yukos's largest producing asset, Yuganskneftegaz, between 1998 and 2003; Pavel Anisimov was the head of Samaraneftaz; Oleg Vitka, head of Zapadno-Malobalyk (a joint venture between Yukos and the Hungarian oil company MOL); and Sergei Shimkevich, head of Tomskneft. All four were arrested and charged with a variety of offenses related to their management of the oilfields.[69] They were prominent figures in their provinces (both Gil'manov and Anisimov were members of their regional legislatures), local elites supported them, and the local courts were reluctant to convict them. But the Procuracy, under orders from Moscow, stepped up the pressure, and the local judges were forced to give way. Gil'manov was given a three-year suspended sentence;[70] Anisimov was sentenced to two and a half years;[71] Vitka received a three-and-a-half-years' suspended sentence; and Shimkevich was sentenced to twelve years (later reduced to eleven).[72]

Putin Moves to Restore Balance

The two-and-a-half years following Khodorkovsky's arrest marked the high point of the influence of the siloviki in the Kremlin. During this period Putin faced challenges on multiple fronts ("colored revolutions" in Georgia and Ukraine, growing East-West tensions over issues such as Iraq, terrorism in the North Caucasus, intra-elite conflicts at home, etc.), to which he responded with increasingly harsh rhetoric, authoritarian measures, and a growing reliance on the coercive elites for support. This gave the siloviki unprecedented latitude between late 2003 and early 2006, particularly in energy matters.

The drive against the Yukos regional executives culminated in the winter and early spring of 2006.[73] But at this point there occurred an unexpected shift in the political wind in Moscow. Late in the evening of June 1, Vladimir Ustinov was summoned to Putin's dacha at Novo-Ogarevo and summarily dismissed from his post as general prosecutor.[74] The following morning President Putin sent a message to the upper house of parliament, the Council of the Federation, instructing the senators to dismiss Ustinov from his post as general prosecutor. The senators did not hide their astonishment, since they had confirmed him for a second term only a year before,[75] but they dutifully voted him out. Three weeks later came the news that Ustinov had been named minister of justice, trading places with Iurii Chaika, who moved over from Justice to become general prosecutor (which he remains to the present). It was clearly a demotion for Ustinov, since the Ministry of Justice was a much less powerful body. Most of his team of prosecutors, including some of those who had been most prominent on the government side in the Yukos Affair, such as First Deputy Procurator General Iurii Biriukov, were shortly removed as well.[76] Yet Ustinov had not been cast out of the elite circle altogether but simply taken down a notch. It was evidently a signal, but of what?

As Moscow pundits pondered the significance of these moves, they saw connections to the politics of the presidential succession. They noted that in the months before his dismissal, Ustinov had become more and more visible and outspoken. In mid-May, two weeks before his dismissal, Ustinov created a stir with a tough speech at a conference on organized crime (attended by all the top brass of the law-enforcement agencies), in which he asserted that organized crime had become a "national threat," which was being fought "only on paper." He particularly blamed the MVD, whose chief, Rashid Nurgaliev, was sitting in the front row. To some in the audience, it sounded like a campaign speech.[77] It is difficult to believe that Ustinov could have imagined himself a serious contender for the presidential succession, yet that was increasingly how he was seen to be behaving. Ustinov, on this reading, had overreached himself and had to be reminded who was boss.

Ustinov was not the only one for whom the message was intended. The removal of Ustinov from the General Procuracy was followed by a wave of demotions and dismissals between 2006 and 2008 that shifted the balance of power within the silovik clan and weakened the influence of the siloviki overall, restoring something more like the balance of elites that had existed before the Yukos Affair. The General Procuracy and the senior ranks of the FSB were purged of many senior officers. Shortly after Dmitri Medvedev's election as president, several of the leading members of the group that had reached the peak of their influence in the wake of the Yukos Affair lost their jobs. Nikolai Patrushev, head of the FSB; Sergei Ivanov, the first deputy prime minister and Dmitri Medvedev's reported rival for the presidential succession; and Viktor Ivanov, the deputy head of the Presidential Administration in charge of personnel, were all moved to lesser positions. Ustinov was removed from the Ministry of Justice and dispatched back to his home region of the Kuban' as the presidential envoy to the Southern Federal District, and although this was still an important position, for a person of Ustinov's previous eminence and connections it was tantamount to an exile. Igor Sechin was named deputy prime minister for energy, a move that was unclear in its political significance but that some interpreted as part of the overall distancing of the leading siloviki.[78]

However, the dismissal of the general prosecutor and his team did not mean in any sense a softening of the Kremlin's stance against Yukos. There was no letup in the prosecution of cases against people connected to Yukos's financial operations at corporate headquarters in Moscow. Efforts to extradite Yukos executives who had fled to Israel and Great Britain continued unabated. The treatment of Khodorkovsky himself remained harsh and indeed grew harsher. But the campaign in the oil provinces quietly ceased. In November 2006, in a speech before a gathering of high-level law-enforcement officials, Putin declared Operation Energiia a resounding success. There had been 370 suspects arrested, dozens brought before the courts, and "billions of rubles" returned to the state.[79] But a closer look at the actual cases was less impressive. Most of the violations turned out to be cases of small-time theft and fraud, such as tapping crude from pipelines to feed local "moonshine" refineries. Shortly after Putin's speech, the Energiia campaign quietly faded away. It was as though Putin's praise had been a signal to stop.

The logic of the situation by early 2006 suggests why Operation Energiia was no longer useful. By then the major assets of Yukos had already been transferred to Rosneft, and the new owners—CEO Sergei Bogdanchikov and his board chairman, Igor Sechin—had no interest in anything that might disrupt the orderly resumption of growth. Bogdanchikov, in fact, moved quickly to co-opt key members of the Yukos management team into senior positions at Rosneft. Sergei Kudriashov, who had succeeded Gil'manov as general director of Yuganskneftegaz in 2003, was made senior vice president of Rosneft for exploration and production, and Mars Khasanov, head of a key technical institute and a consultant to Yukos in the Joe Mach era, became head of technology. And while Gil'manov and Anisimov no longer have any role in the oil business, Oleg Vitka, following his sentence, was hired by GazpromNeft. Today only Shimkevich remains in jail.

From the Kremlin's perspective, indeed, Operation Energiia had likely achieved its objective. The point had been forcefully made that henceforth the state's rules on oil production had to be taken seriously and that the kinds of practices that had been associated—rightly or wrongly—with Yukos would no longer be tolerated. Yet the wave of prosecutions also generated lasting and harmful side effects. Local law-enforcement officers, having been encouraged to seek out criminals in the oilfields, did not necessarily desist. Today's epidemic of *reiderstvo*—extortion on a mass scale by corrupt law-enforcement officials—has its origins in part in officially sanctioned campaigns such as Operation Energiia. As a result, small oil producers found it increasingly difficult to work independently, and weakened regional authorities were less able to defend them. Larger operators, too, became more cautious in their field practices, for example, focusing on reviving idle wells in order to avoid drawing the attention of regulatory watchdogs and local police. In short, the backlash against Yukos at the local level contributed to a general slowdown in innovation in technology and management in the oilfields, which we discuss in greater detail in Chapters 10–12.

Conclusion

Long-time Moscovites swear that the climate has changed in recent years. "We used to get real winters," they grumble. "Real ones with snow and blue skies. Now we only get the sleet, the slush, and the long nights." On one of those nights, in late 2004, I was walking back to my hotel with a senior foreign executive from Yukos. He had read one of my earlier books, *Russia 2010*, in which my coauthor and I had imagined several contrasting scenarios of the possible future of Russia. One was called *Chudo* ("The Miracle") and was a vision of a free-market capitalist Russia; another, at the opposite extreme, was called "Russian Bear," a Russia of authoritarian reaction.[80] As we reached my hotel, my companion turned to me and said, "For the past three years at Yukos I have lived 'Chudo,' and they have been the most exciting and creative years of my life. But 'Chudo' just met 'Russian Bear.'" Then he walked away into the darkness.

Several years on, how does the Yukos Affair appear to us now? It is hardly surprising that for the participants themselves the arrest of Mikhail Khodorkovsky and the takeover of Yukos felt apocalyptic at the time. But as the years have passed, has it turned out to be the game-changer that it appeared then? Has "Chudo" given way to "Russian Bear"?

Western opinions are still sharply divided. For some, such as the British scholar Richard Sakwa, in his thorough study of the saga, the Yukos Affair marked the definitive end of Russia's experiment with neoliberal capitalism and its replacement by a dirigiste economy.[81] For others, such as the Organisation for Economic Co-operation and Development's William Tompson, it simply underscored what we already knew about post-Soviet Russia, that in a confrontation between illegitimate wealth and arbitrary power, the latter will always win. Consequently, the Yukos Affair was no different in kind from the many other cases of expropriation and abuse of power that have occurred routinely in Russia before and since.[82] Finally, there is a third view, which is that the political trends and events of the Putin era have been driven above all by global developments, particularly the price of oil. On this reading, the Yukos Affair was a symptom of the fever brought on by high oil revenues, with little causal significance of its own. High oil prices and increased oil revenues accelerated trends to which the Russian economy and political system were all too vulnerable, toward corruption and authoritarianism. The Yukos Affair was simply part of the larger story of Russia's decay into petro-statism.[83]

I disagree with all three of these views. First, on the destruction of Yukos as the end of neoliberal capitalism. Yukos's phase as the "model modern corporation" lasted barely five years, and it was never more than part reality, since behind the Western corporate structure there was always a parallel "vertical of power" that was classic Russian and indeed more than a little Soviet. In this respect, Yukos was hardly unique: the other Russian oil companies exhibit similar blends, if to greater or lesser degrees, as do Russian companies throughout the economy. Russian business is hardly neoliberal, and Yukos fits poorly the role of a neoliberal martyr. Where Yukos was truly a entrepreneurial pioneer was in its total commitment to modern management and innovation (meaning the application of "fit-for-purpose know-how," as opposed to new technology) in the search for profits and fast growth. But arguably Sibneft was an equally significant pioneer at the same time; moreover, that role was subsequently played by TNK-BP. In sum, Yukos in its heyday offered a brief glimpse of what a dynamic modern corporation could achieve, but the end of Yukos has not spelled the end of "Chudo" Russian-style, such as it is. We return to this point in a moment.

Next, the Yukos Affair was far more than simply another case of Russian expropriation. It involved, as we have seen, a multitude of critical issues at the interface of the oil industry and the state, ranging from licensing and production policy to oil transportation and the role of foreign companies. Behind all these, the fundamental issue in the Yukos Affair was the role of the oil industry in post-Soviet Russia—not just as a source of wealth for powerful individuals and clans but as a resource for political power and state policy. These, and not simply the ambitions of state-connected elites, were the root causes of the conflict. Without much exaggeration, one could say that the expropriation of

Yukos was the aftereffect of its decapitation, not its premeditated motive. Although the phrase "illegitimate wealth versus arbitrary power" describes a basic truth about property rights in today's Russia, it does not quite capture what was unique about the Yukos Affair, in particular the vindictiveness with which Khodorkovsky and Yukos were attacked and destroyed.

The role of rising oil prices is more interesting, because more complex. The simplest version—that Yukos was expropriated because the leading siloviki saw an opportunity to take it over for themselves—is demonstrably false, as we shall see in the next chapter: the transfer of Yukos's resources to Rosneft came about as the result of a fluke, which was not foreseen by the ultimate beneficiaries themselves. That some individuals profited personally is clear enough, but this was not initially the main motive for the operation.[84] It was only in the second half of the 2000s, as global commodity prices continued their rise, that greed and corruption took on the proportions we see today.

True, there was another factor, the rapid rise in the international valuations of the oil companies after 2000, which made them highly attractive targets for expropriation. What Khodorkovsky had discovered—that he would get richer faster from the rocketing share price of Yukos than from its profits—had not escaped the notice of others as well, including some very powerful state players. But if the hunger for wealth had been their sole motive in the Yukos Affair, it would have made more sense to take over Yukos intact, so as to preserve the company's performance and its share price. The path chosen—years of noisy prosecution followed by a messy breakup of the company—was needlessly destructive of value. If, as is widely believed, key individuals in the political elite already owned sizable equity stakes in other Russian oil companies at the time, one would have expected them to be especially sensitive to this point. Instead, the way the Yukos Affair evolved suggests more improvisation than premeditation, more vengefulness than greed.[85] Yukos was not so much plundered as lynched.

More broadly, however, there is no question but that rising oil prices greatly heightened the stakes in the battle between the oil industry and the government and increased the government's appetite for more oil revenues. Once the new oil-tax system went into effect in 2002, the government went back to the Duma again and again in 2003 and 2004, seeking higher and higher tax rates, while the oil industry's deputies fought a bitter but ultimately futile rearguard action, until finally the oil industry's resistance was swept away in the wake of the Yukos Affair.[86]

Finally, while higher commodity prices amplified the classic symptoms of petro-statism, they also brought the opposite response: the systematic effort by finance minister Aleksei Kudrin and his colleagues to combat resource dependence, by such measures as sterilizing oil and gas revenues (notably by paying off Russia's external debt), broadening the tax base, and reforming fiscal, budgetary, and monetary policy. Throughout the oil boom of the 2000s, the Russian government largely stuck to its cautious macroeconomic policies, and Putin stood by their architect, Aleksei Kudrin. If the patient was losing ground to the disease of petrostatism, it was also fighting against it.

Indeed, Kudrin's very economic orthodoxy caused him to be one of Khodorkovsky's most determined opponents. He was not alone: most of the "liberal Pitertsy"—Kudrin, Gref, and others—stayed on side with Putin and the siloviki throughout the Yukos Affair and indeed were part of the coalition that drove it. The logic was straightforward: for the state to carry out its financial reforms, it had to control the oil revenues, and on this point the liberals were at one with the siloviki. Khodorkovsky's arrest and the dismemberment of Yukos dismayed them, but only a handful left the government. In the end, they were statists first and liberals second. But over the following years they found themselves increasingly uncomfortable partners as Putin embarked on a policy of favoring large state corporations and a dirigiste economy. That policy reflected Putin's own views, but also those of the siloviki, whose influence grew in the wake of the Yukos Affair, until it was partially checked in 2006–2008.

This brings us back to the core point of this chapter. The Yukos Affair was one of those moments when critical issues are poised on a knife edge, when political forces have massed and begun to engage, but to the combatants themselves the day is still in doubt. At such moments, personality and circumstance take control, driving outcomes toward extremes that would not have occurred otherwise. At that decisive moment, the personality and actions of Mikhail Khodorkovsky, as perceived by the oil establishment and the political elite, were all important.

What if, for example, Yukos had been owned by another Mikhail—Mikhail Fridman instead of Mikhail Khodorkovsky? On the eve of Khodorkovsky's arrest, at a major investor presentation in New York that I attended, one financial analyst raised his hand and asked Fridman, "Do you plan to run for president?" Amid laughter from the audience, Fridman hastily replied, "I have no presidential ambitions."[87] The contrast spoke volumes. Khodorkovsky's fellow oil generals knew when to retreat, and they survived with their assets intact.

Without the factor of personality, in short, the contest between the resurgent state and the privatized oil industry would arguably not have descended into such a bitter confrontation among a small group of powerful men, which in turn served as the convenient instrument for one leadership faction to gain the edge in the making of oil policy. The reassertion of state regulation would not have taken the form of a police campaign. There might not have been as strong a reaction against foreign ownership and participation. There might not have been the same extreme shift in the balance between state and private over the ownership of pipelines and export terminals and oil-export policy. All politics is contingent, and Khodorkovsky and Yukos provided precisely the ideal combination of challenge and vulnerability that mobilized its enemies and swung the balance of power in the Kremlin and the political class, making the next phase of oil policy more bitter and confrontational than it might have been without it.

But in longer-term perspective, what difference has the Yukos Affair made? In its wake, some long-standing questions, which had remained unsettled for the previous decade, were permanently closed. The idea of an autonomous oil sector, run as private property for the benefit of private owners, was decisively rejected. Transportation of crude oil, despite a handful of grandfathered exceptions, would henceforth remain a state monopoly. The primacy of the state over the private sector was reasserted, as was the power of state coercion. Corporate strategies such as tax optimization and selective well production, which had existed in a legal limbo before the prosecution of Yukos, were redefined as criminal and made subject to prosecution. The state's tax take increased inexorably over the following years, and although that process had begun before the Yukos Affair, the consequence of the latter was to quell any further attempts at open resistance. Before the Yukos Affair, the oil generals had been on the offensive; after it, they were on the defensive.

On a range of other issues, the Yukos Affair brought resolution on the level of principles, but actual implementation remained a subject of debate and conflict. Thus the Yukos Affair marked the Kremlin's growing commitment to the idea of a state-owned national oil champion, but as we shall see, there followed a bitter battle over which company it would be. Similarly, the Yukos Affair marked the high point of foreign penetration into the Russian oil sector; from that time on, the government's policies grew steadily more nationalistic and exclusive—but the process was marked by constant interagency warfare between the economic ministries and the security agencies. Conflict over oil policy was nothing new, of course, but what was different after the Yukos Affair was that henceforth these battles took place mainly inside the state, rather than between the state and the private sector.

The Yukos Affair lastingly influenced the relations between the state and the oil industry and the overall course of oil policy. The wave of prosecutions and enforcement actions that accompanied the destruction of Yukos intimidated the oil industry and weakened its ability to defend its interests openly and frankly. More broadly, it has aggravated a chronic feature of Russian administration: the strength of coercive institutions and the chronic weakness of regulatory ones. The dominance of "thumbs over fingers" in Russian government, a long-standing legacy, was reinforced by the passions of the Yukos Affair. The level of trust and understanding between the state and the oil industry, never high before, sank to new lows.

Yet "Chudo" was never quite replaced by "Russian Bear." The wave of conservative reaction that accompanied the Yukos Affair produced neither a purge of the oil industry nor a wholesale renationalization. In 2006, as Putin began to prepare the way for his own succession, he readjusted the balance among the Kremlin clans and curtailed the wave of Yukos-related prosecutions in the provinces. By 2008, three key events combined to cause the Russian government to reexamine its policies toward the oil industry: the election of Dmitri Medvedev, the crash and recession of 2008–2009, and the onset of decline in West Siberian oil production. These events have called into question the primacy of the siloviki and partially discredited their policies.

As a result, the atmosphere in Moscow shifted again at the end of the decade, this time in a more positive direction. There have been no further nationalizations. Dialogue has been renewed between the state and the oil industry. Liberals have regained something of their former influence. New ideas are being introduced—in some cases reintroduced—into policy debates.

The tone of relations between the state and the industry, the regulatory and fiscal framework, and policies toward foreign companies and investors have become less harsh. Yet the fundamental system of power established in the wake of the Yukos Affair remains. These are the subjects of the rest of this book.

chapter 8

Russia's Accidental Oil Champion: The Rise of Rosneft

National oil companies (NOCs) are the dominant species in today's oil world. Not long ago, this would have been considered surprising. As recently as 1970, privately owned international oil companies (IOCs) controlled 85 percent of the world's proven oil reserves. Today they control only 10 percent, while the share of the NOCs has increased to over three-quarters. Fourteen of the top twenty oil companies in the world are NOCs, and they are gaining steadily, in their size, their reach, and their ambitions.

Russia in the 1990s went the other way, toward a radical privatization, joining a handful of market economies (notably France and the United Kingdom) that privatized their oil industries at about the same time. But whereas the latter were largely driven by the liberal model then at its height, Russia's privatization was only partly the result of the free-market ideology of the reformers. Rather, it was mainly due, as we have seen, to the collapse of the Soviet planned economy, the disintegration of the Soviet oil sector, the ambitions of the oil generals and the financial oligarchs, and, above all, the weakness of the state. If the Russian state had been stronger in the 1990s, the outcome might have been more similar to the partial privatizations that took place in Italy, Norway, and Brazil, in which the state retained majority control or a golden share. But in Russia there was nothing to stop the tide of privatization. By early 1998, with the planned privatization of the last remaining state-owned entities (Slavneft, Onaco, and Rosneft), the transition to private ownership seemed almost complete.

However, in the early 2000s, as the Russian state began to regain power, the tide began to recede. Rosneft, which had barely survived the 1990s as a state-owned company, emerged as an increasingly powerful national corporation.

Today Rosneft is Russia's largest oil company. It enjoys the Kremlin's favor as its national oil champion, and it is positioned to be the lead player in the next phase of the Russian oil industry in the twenty-first century. None of this could have been foreseen in 1992, or 1998, or even as recently as 2005. The story of this chapter is that of a company whose very existence as a national oil company and its present status as Russia's "oil flagship" are in many respects a quirk of fate.

Yet Rosneft is not a simple reversion to the Soviet past. Even though it occupies the headquarters of the former USSR Ministry of Oil, it is only indirectly its descendant. In many respects it is a new company. But what will be its role in the next phase of Russian oil, and what will be its impact on the rest of the industry? Rosneft today is a company at a crossroads, and its further evolution is an important test of the Russian oil industry's directions, and indeed of those of Russia as a whole.

The Russian Phoenix

It is remarkable that Rosneft exists at all. It almost died even before it was born in 1992. Even after 1995, when it finally gained grudging official recognition by the Kremlin, it barely survived the decade. Oil rivals, traders, gangsters, and assorted politicians raided its choicest assets throughout much of the 1990s, while its managers fought among themselves and made off with bits of their own. Rosneft was almost privatized in 1998—not once but three times—and if in the end it escaped unsold, this was largely because by then there was so little of it left to sell. By the time of the financial crash of August 1998, Rosneft had just lost its last major upstream producer and looked doomed.

Rosneft's survival and current prosperity are due to the tenacity of two men, its founder, Aleksandr Putilov, and his successor, Sergei Bogdanchikov. They each fought to keep a state-owned oil company alive through the 1990s, until the shifting political winds in the new century brought Rosneft back to life, helped along by political oxygen from the Kremlin. The Kremlin, in fact, is the real story behind Rosneft. The saga of Rosneft is above all that of the decline and resurrection of the Russian state and the accompanying transition from the laissez-faire capitalism of the 1990s to Putin's state capitalism in the 2000s.

Yet the trip has not been smooth. The very concept of a national oil company came and went throughout the 1990s, as control of the government seesawed between liberals and conservatives. The decisive turning point came in 2002, when the hard-line silovik wing of the Kremlin—led behind the scenes by Putin's chief assistant, Igor Sechin—joined forces with Sergei Bogdanchikov in the campaign against Mikhail Khodorkovsky and Yukos. By 2003 they had succeeded in gaining the president's support, and the result was the destruction of Khodorkovsky and Yukos, recounted in Chapter 7.

Yet no sooner was Khodorkovsky out of the way and Yukos headed for extinction than Bogdanchikov and Sechin (by now Rosneft's chairman) faced one more threat to Rosneft's survival, this time from a plan by Putin to merge Rosneft into Gazprom, together with the expropriated assets of Yukos. But against all expectations, including their own, Bogdanchikov and Sechin succeeded in capturing Yuganskneftegaz, Yukos's prime asset, while keeping their company independent of Gazprom.

Thus by mid-2005, after a decade and a half of reversals and surprises, Rosneft finally seemed established as Russia's flagship NOC. In 2008–2009 it survived the crash and recession in better shape than any of its competitors, and by 2010 its status seemed secure. With the departure of Bogdanchikov as president and CEO (in September 2010) and the recent appointment of Igor Sechin to the same positions (May 2012), a new period in the company's history has begun, with potentially momentous implications for the Russian oil industry and for Russia as a whole.

The aim of this chapter is to explore two key questions. The first is the influence of Rosneft's history on the company itself; the second is the impact of Rosneft on the rest of the industry. Because of the way it was born and evolved, Rosneft is different from the other Russian companies. Unlike LUKoil and Surgutneftegaz, it is only partly the descendant of Soviet-era ob"edineniia, nor is it controlled by West Siberian neftianiki. Unlike TNK-BP, it is not owned by Yeltsin-era oligarchs or foreign investors, and unlike GazpromNeft, it has not been absorbed by a non-oil parent. The capture of Yukos not only tripled the size of the company but brought to Rosneft some of the leadership and technology and management tools of Yukos. Rosneft has evolved into a company with a mixed personality, or as it likes to style itself in investor presentations, it has "the advantages of an NOC and the discipline of an IOC." Whether it can retain both is, of course, the big question ahead.

Absent-Minded Birth

Rosneft was born out of indecision. We saw in Chapter 3 how President Yeltsin in November 1992 blessed the creation of the first three holding companies— LUKoil, Surgutneftegaz, and Yukos—but left unresolved the question of what to do with the remaining properties inherited from the defunct Soviet Ministry of Oil. For the time being, the best the various players could agree on was a stopgap, a three-year compromise giving formal authority to a state-owned holding company to be called "Rosneft."[1] Vagit Alekperov, who had played a key role in negotiating the arrangement, was offered the position of president. He turned it down, being by this time fully engaged in consolidating LUKoil, but he nominated instead one of his closest allies, Aleksandr Putilov.[2]

Putilov had been the general director of Uraineftegaz (the original "U" in LUKoil) and as such was one of Alekperov's founding partners.[3] He was a core member of the old-boy network of West Siberian oil drillers, a classmate of Sergei Muravlenko at "Indus," the Tiumen' Oil Institute, in the early 1970s. In nominating Putilov to be president of Rosneft, Alekperov was putting forward a friend and partner, someone with whom he had worked well.

For Putilov, Rosneft was a dubious gift. It was less a company than an assemblage of leftovers, the result of the labored compromise that had created it. It had been assigned the state's stake in a wide range of assets, but its largest and best producing properties—Noiabrskneftegaz, Purneftegaz, and the Omsk refinery, as well as Nizhnevartovskneftegaz—were already attracting corporate raiders. Rosneft had only nominal control of these subsidiaries anyway, since their cash and oil flows had passed into the hands of local interests headed by second-tier "oil generals," whose only reason for joining Rosneft was the hope that Putilov could protect them from the larger fish, but they had no intention of surrendering their prerogatives or revenues to a distant entity in Moscow. Rebellion was written into the script from the start.

In any case Rosneft was not viable as a private company on its own. Its upstream assets were scattered across the whole country from West Siberia to the North Caucasus and were poorly aligned with its three antiquated refineries, one on the Black Sea and two in the Far East. As its domestic market it had been assigned some of the hardest-hit agricultural regions of central Russia. It was also responsible for the ministry's scattered remnants, research institutes, design institutes, geophysical laboratories, and the like, employing tens of thousands of people who continued to do things for which there was no longer any call. It was more an assemblage of lifeboats than a company.

Yet Rosneft's most fundamental problem was that under the terms of its founding decree, it was fated to self-destruct within three years. "Rosneft was less a company than a raw material for the creation of other oil companies,"[4] wrote a Russian commentator at the time. Its mandate was to nurture the next generation of private integrated companies, out of its own flesh as it were, and then to go out of existence. Rosneft's built-in lease on life guaranteed that the struggle over its mission and fate would rage continuously over the next three years.

Rosneft was explicitly not called a national company—that had been a key point in the bargaining over the November 1992 decree—but it had been given some of the functions of one just the same, at least on paper, notably channeling state investment, supplying oil and oil products "for state needs," and coordinating oil exports, although no one knew exactly what these grand-sounding tasks meant in a bankrupt state and an oil industry that was rapidly going private.[5]

Putilov could have run Rosneft as a temporary caretaker for the oil generals. He could have presided over its breakup and then returned to a leading position in LUKoil or another one of the private oil companies. Instead, he made a decision that proved in retrospect to be fateful: he chose to try to keep Rosneft together as a national oil company, with himself at the head. There followed six years of struggle, at the end of which Putilov was ejected from Rosneft and lost any significant role in the oil industry, except as a lingering minority shareholder. In the process, he alienated his former classmates and colleagues, particularly Alekperov. But through his dogged persistence in defending an idea that seemed doomed at the time, Putilov kept the idea of a national oil company alive, with Rosneft as its core.

Defending the idea of a state company in the early and mid-1990s, against the liberal tide running at the time, was not as quixotic as it might seem. Privatizing the oil industry was widely unpopular. An undercurrent of statist conservatism ran through the government, and Boris Yeltsin, who used ambiguity as his favorite technique of rule, kept one or two industrial conservatives in high positions throughout the 1990s. The one who lasted longest was Oleg Soskovets, whom we met in Chapter 2. In the mid-1990s Soskovets nearly displaced Chernomyrdin as prime minister, and the palace guard of siloviki then in favor in the Kremlin even thought of Soskovets as a possible successor to Yeltsin.

Conservatives like Soskovets were Putilov's core constituency, but even among them there were few who supported a national oil company out of communist ideology or nostalgia. Rather, there was a mixture of motives and sentiments, which led a variety of people to call for a stronger state role. Some were mainly concerned to keep supplying farms and factories with low-priced oil and gas. Others were alarmed by the spreading chaos in export markets, as Russian traders competed with one another by selling their oil at deep discounts. Law-enforcement officials denounced the spread of criminality in the oil industry, while oilmen grumbled about foreign oilmen skimming profits from joint ventures thanks to special tax privileges. Some, finally, saw an opportunity for a plum job as a reward for their support. Indeed, Putilov himself, to judge from his subsequent behavior after his departure from Rosneft, supported the state-company formula less out of conviction than out of opportunism. The challenge for Putilov was to play on all of these motives and to try to unite them in support of a permanent charter for Rosneft before his three-year mandate ran out.[6]

Putilov's Losing Battle

At the outset, in 1992, Putilov's strategy of casting Rosneft as a national oil company still looked like a possible winning card. But as time went on, Putilov's hand steadily weakened. His efforts to recreate a state-owned oil-export monopoly failed, as did his campaign to act as the government's representative in any future production-sharing ventures with foreign companies.[7] But Putilov was a determined man, and he did not give up. In early 1995 he took his plan for a national oil company to the energy minister, Iurii Shafranik, but that idea too died.[8]

In the meantime, Rosneft's assets were rapidly disappearing, as more and more production associations responded to the three-year ticking clock created by Yeltsin's decree and formed new companies—in 1994 alone, Rosneft lost Slavneft (based on Megionneft), Sidanco (Var'eganneft), Eastern Oil (Tomskneft), ONAKO (Orenburg), and TNK (Nizhnevartovsk), which were all spun off as miniature versions of the three initial integrated companies. Putilov's complaints that many of these companies were too small to be viable fell on deaf ears.[9] By 1996 Rosneft was down to one last big producer, Purneftegaz, and even that was uncertain. Rosneft fought a three-year legal battle with Vladimir Potanin (the head of Oneksimbank, whom we met in Chapter 3) for control, and Purneftegaz swung crazily back and forth until Potanin finally reluctantly surrendered the asset under the government's pressure.[10]

By this time Putilov's plan for a national oil company was long dead. Putilov himself began acquiring personal stakes in Rosneft's remaining subsidiaries, while the two oligarchs, Vladimir Potanin and Boris Berezovsky, fought for control of the corporate headquarters and Rosneft's remaining exports. When the liberal reformers, headed by Anatolii Chubais and Boris Nemtsov, returned to office in the spring of 1997 following Yeltsin's reelection, they attempted to put Rosneft on the auction block. Putilov opposed the plan and was forced out in a boardroom battle.[11] But the planned auction was repeatedly delayed by internal divisions within both the company and the government, and the August 1998 crash put an end to the plan.

The Arrival of Sergei Bogdanchikov

In the wake of the crash, Yeltsin, in one of his signature shifts, replaced the now discredited liberals in the government with a group of Soviet-era technocrats and siloviki, headed by spymaster Evgenii Primakov as prime minister, and the plan to privatize Rosneft was shelved. Primakov, within days of taking office, got rid of the temporary management that had been preparing the company for auction and looked about for someone to take over. After a few weeks of stalemate as contending interests pushed their candidates, Primakov reached out to the other end of the country, eight time zones to the east, and picked a complete unknown, the vice president in charge of Rosneft's operations in far-off Sakhalin and Khabarovsk, a 41-year-old petroleum engineer named Sergei Bogdanchikov.

Bogdanchikov was a newcomer to Moscow. He had spent his entire working life on remote Sakhalin Island, rising through the ranks of the local oil company, Sakhalinmorneftegaz, which in 1995 had become part of Rosneft. By 1993 he was general director of Sakhalinmorneftegaz, and in 1997, a year and a half before he came to Moscow, he had been named vice president for all of Rosneft's operations in the Russian Far East, which included two small refineries and a local distribution and trading system for refined products. His main appeal to Prime Minister Primakov was that he had a good reputation as a manager, and above all he had no ties to any of the contending groups that had fought over the remains of Rosneft for much of the decade.[12]

One might be tempted to say, from today's vantage point, that Primakov's choice was a far-seeing bet on the future. The year 1993, when Bogdanchikov became general director of Sakhalinmorneftegaz, was also the year that Russia's two key production-sharing agreements were signed. Rosneft and its subsidiary, Sakhalinmorneftegaz, held a 40 percent stake in Sakhalin-1, in partnership with Exxon and a consortium of Japanese companies grouped together under the name of Sodeco. By the time he came to Moscow, Bogdanchikov had worked in daily contact with Exxon for over five years and knew more about the practical realities of working within a PSA contract—to say nothing of working with an international major—than any other senior Russian oilman.

But that would be reading the present into the past. In 1998 Sakhalin-1 was still a gleam in the eye, an interesting prospect that at the time looked more like gas than oil, and quite possibly "stranded gas" at that—the term gas people use to mean gas that has no market and is therefore nearly worthless.[13] Sakhalinmorneftegaz itself was a minor company, and despite the "mor" in its name—which means "sea," suggesting offshore work—its operations were entirely on land. Its high point of production, a mere 700,000 tons per year (14,000 barrels per day), had been in 1962, and it had stagnated since. More ominously, Sakhalinmorneftegaz and its parent, Rosneft, were seriously short of money. In the summer of 1998 Rosneft had failed to meet cash calls from its Sakhalin-1 partners, and it might have lost its stake altogether if Exxon and Sodeco had not agreed to carry it through the winter. In the fall of 1998, just before Bogdanchikov's appointment, Rosneft executives spoke of selling out.[14] In short, in 1998 Sakhalin was not yet the world-class oil and gas province it began to appear a decade later, and Bogdanchikov's experience there did not qualify him as the obvious man to lead a national oil champion—even assuming the Russian government was looking for one.

Bogdanchikov the Outsider

Bogdanchikov did not belong to the West Siberian elite of Soviet-era neftianiki, nor was he one of the financial oligarchs. He was an outsider from the remote provinces, someone whom the sophisticated Moscow establishment underestimated, both then and later. But people who dealt with him soon experienced his stubborn willpower. One Western oilman, who played a key role in the Sakhalin PSA projects, recalls:

I first met Bogdanchikov in 1994 when I went up to the headquarters of Sakhalinmorneftegaz in Okha on the northern end of the island. This is truly wild country, far colder and bleaker than the southern end, which is bad enough. What I mainly remember about Bogdanchikov was his piercing blue eyes and tough determination.

Many others have given the same description. A diminutive figure who was always careful about his appearance, Bogdanchikov gave the impression of a man under tight control. He seemed completely without humor. Over time, he acquired a reputation as someone who would not forget a slight and who was proud to the point of vindictiveness. Yet he was also a man of great patience and discipline, who could hide his hand and bide his time. Much of the time, especially in the early years, he kept a low profile, playing the role of the humble hired hand, a mere manager who served the state and whose only ambition was to build a champion for Russia.

But Rosneft, in the early years, hardly looked like a champion of any sort. At the time Bogdanchikov took over as president of Rosneft, the company was practically dead.[15] Like all the other Russian oil companies, Rosneft was suffering from the global downturn in oil prices in 1998, combined with the effects of the financial crash that August. And like all the other oil companies, it was months behind in paying its workers. Its accounts were blocked by the tax collectors because of tax arrears. But there was worse. Its prime producing asset, Purneftegaz, had just been sold off for a pittance to a group of shady creditors,[16] and its other subsidiaries appeared headed the same way. As Bogdanchikov later recalled:

In October 1998 the company had lost management control of 19 out of its 30 subsidiaries. On account of the mother company's debts the accounts of "Sakhalinmorneftegaz," "Krasnodarneftegaz," "Stavropolneftegaz," "Termneft," and the Tuapse refinery had been frozen and controlling shares in them were being prepared for sale. Buyers had already been found for them, just as with "Purneftegaz". . . . A few days more, and they would have been sold. In another ten subsidiaries, Rosneft's controlling stake had been diluted, and the company's representatives were reduced to minorities on their boards.

As a result, a year ago there was absolutely no system of management over the Rosneft subsidiaries; each manager ran his own as he pleased. There was no system for managing physical and financial flows, and there was no investment policy. I couldn't hold anyone accountable.[17]

Rosneft had also lost control of its exports. Its subsidiaries mostly exported their own oil, through "commercial structures" that were presumably controlled by much the same kind of murky interests that Khodorkovsky had contended with at Yuganskneftegaz and Samaraneftegaz. Rosneft's own trading operations were run by personnel affiliated with Sibneft, who sold Rosneft's oil to offshore companies also controlled by Sibneft.[18]

In his first six weeks on the job, Bogdanchikov put on an impressive display of energy. He cut the company's back wages and outstanding debts in half and negotiated a deal with the minister in charge of tax collections, who unfroze the company's bank accounts. He obtained a reprieve, and even a fresh line of credit, from Western banks.[19] As for Purneftegaz, he had some top-level help. The low price of the sale—a mere $10 million—had touched a nerve, even in jaded Moscow. Yeltsin ordered Prime Minister Primakov to recover the lost property "within two weeks."[20] Primakov called in the FSB and the Russian equivalent of the Securities and Exchange Commission and hired three law firms to go to work to get Purneftegaz back. The disputed shares and the shareholder register were frozen, to prevent the new owners from selling on their shares and thus muddying the trail—a common device in those days.[21] Vladimir Putin was head of the FSB at the time, and it seems likely that it was in connection with this affair that Bogdanchikov met him, and possibly Igor Sechin, for the first time.[22] Regaining Purneftegaz, however, took a long battle—nineteen separate court cases, Bogdanchikov later recalled. It was not finally returned until February 1999.[23]

But this was only elementary crisis management. The real job of salvaging Rosneft still lay ahead. It took four more years of constant struggle for Bogdanchikov to gain firm control over the company and its subsidiaries, to centralize oil flows and cash flows, and to begin investing in new production and new ventures—in short, to turn Rosneft from a hulk into a viable company.

Fighting off "Gosneft"

During his first year, Bogdanchikov was still an insignificant figure, widely viewed as a temporary placeholder. The Primakov government was uncertain over what to do with its remaining oil assets. The state still owned three companies, Rosneft (100 percent), Slavneft (75 percent), and Onaco (85 percent). Primakov's energy minister, Sergei Generalov, called for merging the three into a single national oil company, to be called "Gosneft" (i.e., "State Oil").[24] But these were the dying months of the Yeltsin presidency, and the main driver in Russian politics in late 1998 and early 1999 was the Kremlin's desperate search for a suitable successor. As the aging president thrashed about, trying one prime minister after another, oil policy came to a standstill.

The plan had been to unveil Gosneft by the summer of 1999. But the Primakov government was dismissed in May, before the plan could be carried out. Under the short-lived prime ministership of his successor, Sergei Stepashin, the Gosneft idea remained in limbo. Then, when Vladimir Putin came in as prime minister in August, privatization returned to the agenda. Once again the government began shopping for private buyers for its remaining properties. The investment bank Dresdner Kleinwort Benson, which had done the previous assessment of the worth of Rosneft in 1998, was rehired by the Russian Property Fund (the official keeper of state properties) to evaluate the worth of the company.[25] It looked as though Rosneft was about to be put up for sale again, for the fourth time, although this time only a minority stake was involved.[26]

In all these plans there appeared to be no room for Bogdanchikov. There were constant rumors that he was on shaky ground. Over the summer the head of Transneft had been replaced, and Bogdanchikov was said to be next on the list to be dismissed. By October, the Moscow grapevine had him on his way out. Bogdanchikov was summoned to the White House for a meeting with the prime minister. "When I went to see Putin," he later told an interviewer, "I wasn't sure I would keep my job."[27]

But to general surprise, Putin did not fire him. According to Bogdanchikov, Putin said to him simply, "Don't worry—carry on" ("Idi, rabotai spokoino").[28] Neither man has said anything more specific about what kept Bogdanchikov in his job, but two explanations may have been paramount. The first was that Rosneft had emerged nicely from the previous year's crash, and Bogdanchikov had turned a huge loss in 1998 into a small profit in 1999. But that was the result of higher oil prices, and all the other companies were doing similarly well. The other reason was Chechnya.

The Coin of the Realm: Rosneft in Chechnya

Within a month of his appointment as prime minister, Putin had launched a new intervention in Chechnya, and it quickly became the key to his political future. Putin needed all the help he could get there, and Bogdanchikov was in a position to provide it. If Bogdanchikov needed to show that there was a mission for a national oil company, this was it. Very likely, he promised the new prime minister to go into Chechnya, restart oil production there, and use the proceeds to support reconstruction.

Working in Chechnya was difficult, dangerous, and expensive. When Bogdanchikov made a first inspection trip there in January 2000, he found a wasteland. In 1999 Chechnya had produced fewer than 100,000 tons per year (2,000 barrels per day) of oil, compared with 4 million tons (80,000 barrels per day) in 1991. Many wells were burning. The Grozny refinery lay in ruins, and it was well outside the area controlled by the "federals." Even in the supposedly secure zone north of the Terek River, where Rosneft proposed to rehabilitate five fields, its plan called for working under concrete bunkers.

Investing in Chechnya meant borrowing more money and increasing Rosneft's debts, although for this kind of work the Kremlin was prepared to be generous. The state provided loan guarantees and Rosneft was allowed to export 100 percent of its Chechen production, as was its subsidiary Dagneft in neighboring Dagestan. To add further inducement Rosneft's core export quota was also increased. But to export oil from Chechnya, Rosneft had to fix the pipeline to Novorossiisk, which was riddled with hundreds of small taps drilled by the locals. The only oil flowing out of Chechnya at that time was by truck, mostly to neighboring Ingushetiia, and was controlled by local warlords. (According to legend, the Chechen guerilla leader Shamil Basaev had imported a mini-refinery from Germany and operated it with crude oil via a small pipeline that tapped into the main trunk line.) When Rosneft sent out repair crews to plug the holes, they were accompanied by armed convoys of troops.[29]

Bogdanchikov found himself dragged into the murky world of occupation politics. Neither the local warlords nor the local puppet government set up by the Russians wanted to lose control of the meager oil flow and revenues, both of which had a way of disappearing. Nominally, the licenses to the local oil-fields were held by local NGDUs, which were largely inactive, consolidated for a time under a single company called YUNKO, which the Russian authorities regarded as illegitimate. The Ministry of Natural Resources, under the prevailing "two-key system," could not reassign the licenses without the approval of local authorities—who might those have been, anyway?—and in any case it was obviously impossible, given the prevailing chaos, to conduct a meaningful tender.[30] The makeshift solution was to award "temporary licenses" to a joint venture between Rosneft and the Chechen government called Grozneftegaz. Local oilmen, with Rosneft personnel as advisors, produced the oil, while Rosneft acted as an export agent, selecting traders and putting the revenues into a special escrow account to support reconstruction. But security costs ate up most of the profits.[31]

There is no sign that Putin already thought of Rosneft as a national champion at this point, and still less that he was committed to Bogdanchikov as the man to run it. Yet Rosneft's role in Chechnya was the first hint of an answer to a question that had hovered over the oil industry throughout the 1990s, namely, "What is the point of a state-owned oil company?" From the first, Bogdanchikov's strategy for survival was to portray Rosneft as the state oil company and himself as the faithful defender of the state's interest. As the Putin years went on and the doctrine of the resurgent state evolved into its dominant theme, Bogdanchikov and Rosneft rose further in the Kremlin's favor. This became apparent the following year, when Bogdanchikov began to win major victories in battles against key rivals—chiefly LUKoil and increasingly Yukos.

But Bogdanchikov was not out of the woods yet. He still faced the problem of gaining control of his company. His main problem was his predecessor, Aleksandr Putilov.

Conjuring away Putilov's Ghost

Bogdanchikov, with the Kremlin's help, had quickly recaptured Purneftegaz,[32] but the battle to regain control of Rosneft's other wandering subsidiaries lasted another four years. His chief opponent, ironically, was Rosneft's founder and former president, Aleksandr Putilov, who had carved out large personal minority stakes in several of Rosneft's subsidiaries. In early 2000 Putilov still controlled Krasnodarneftegaz and was a minority shareholder in Rosneft-Sakhalin.

In addition, local oligarchs and politicians controlled many of Rosneft's other assets. These were all secondary properties compared with Purneftegaz, but they were all Rosneft had left.

Through a combination of boardroom battles, dilutions, litigation, and buyouts, Bogdanchikov gradually consolidated Rosneft's holdings, essentially repeating the process that the other Russian oil companies had gone through in the mid-1990s. Initially he had little help from the Kremlin. The fact that Rosneft was owned by the state gave it little "administrative resource" (the Russian expression for "political clout"); it was only toward 2002 that Bogdanchikov began to enjoy significant high-level support.

Bogdanchikov's first target was the company's only refinery, located at Tuapse on the Black Sea. On the books it accounted for nearly all of Rosneft's exports of refined products, but the parent company had largely lost control of it. Arguing that the refinery needed additional investment, Bogdanchikov engineered a new share issue, which diluted the local minority shareholders and increased Rosneft's stake from 38 percent to 50 percent.[33] Following that, he began buying out minority shareholders at Sakhalinmorneftegaz, Purneftegaz, and Krasnodarneftegaz. It was an angry battle. Bogdanchikov was widely accused by minority shareholders of deliberately spreading negative rumors to lower the value of the subsidiaries' shares, following which he would buy them up at reduced prices.[34]

By early 2001, Bogdanchikov had managed to gain majority control of Krasnodarneftegaz, by buying up 13 percent of the voting shares on the open market, which gave him a controlling 51 percent stake. Putilov, from the sidelines, mocked Bogdanchikov for spending the state's money to buy shares and offered to sell Rosneft his own for the right price.[35] Even then, however, Bogdanchikov's position was not secure, and he fought on through 2001 to gain majority control of the board of directors and prevent Putilov from splitting off the smaller NGDUs.[36]

And so it went. Even as late as 2002, four years after his arrival, Bogdanchikov was still fighting brush wars all over the country. Krasnodar remained a problem, as minority shareholders clung on. In the spring of 2002 they stormed the company's offices in an attempt to install their own management.[37] Bogdanchikov's efforts to buy out the group were unsuccessful, as the two sides remained deadlocked over price. Yet he was making headway. As oil prices rose and his cash flow improved, he was increasingly able to buy out minority groups instead of fighting with them.

By mid-2002 Bogdanchikov felt strong enough to take the final step, a share swap to replace all the various shares in the subsidiaries with a single Rosneft share. He now controlled the company. But now he found himself faced with a more powerful threat: LUKoil.

The Battle for the Northwest: Rosneft versus LUKoil

Blocked in the South Caspian, Vagit Alekperov had turned his attention in the second half of the 1990s to Northwest Russia, to the oil province known as the Timan-Pechora. A group of geologists there had formed a company called Arkhangel'skgeoldobycha (or AGD), which held most of the exploration licenses to the vast virgin acreage along the coast of the Arctic Ocean but lacked the money or the organization to develop them, leaving them casting about for allies. AGD turned to Rosneft, expecting that it would be the state's representative in any future PSAs with foreign companies. Rosneft under Putilov took a stake in AGD, along with several other plays in the region, but it proved too weak to make good on its strategy.

Starting in the mid-1990s, LUKoil began moving in. It absorbed the main local operator, Komineft, and rolled up the small independents that had proliferated throughout the region in the early 1990s. A key part of LUKoil's strategy was an increasingly close collaboration with Conoco, which had been active in the region since the early 1990s. By 1998, LUKoil had joined Conoco in acquiring a controlling stake in AGD, leaving Rosneft as a minority shareholder, though with a blocking share of 25 percent plus one share.[38] In addition, it blocked Rosneft from taking a 20 percent share in a PSA with the French oil company Total at a nearby field called Khariaga, and it displaced Rosneft in the Timan Pechora Consortium, a group of Western companies headed by Texaco, which was negotiating a PSA to develop the Varandei group of fields on the coast.[39]

By 2001 LUKoil's conquest of the northwest looked all but complete.[40] Indeed, by 2001, having extended his reach up to the coast of the Barents Sea, Alekperov began to look north to the Arctic offshore, where two major prospects had already been found, the Prirazlomnoe oil field and the Shtokman gas condensate field. Gazprom was already active in the area, but in late 2001

LUKoil proposed joining the Shtokman consortium, in which its partner Conoco was already present.[41]

Yet at about the same time, LUKoil began to run into unforeseen obstacles. One came from a group of investors headed by former finance minister Andrei Vavilov, with close ties to the Yeltsin Kremlin (frequently referred to as "the Family"). Alekperov had initially joined with this group to form a company called Northern Oil. But in 2001 the Vavilov group diluted LUKoil's share, effectively forcing it out. Shortly afterward, the same group won a tender for a promising local prospect called Val Gamburtseva. LUKoil had been one of the main bidders and promptly went to court, complaining of fraud. A bitter legal battle broke out over the ownership of Northern Oil and the tender for Val Gamburtseva, which raged on for the next two years.

But soon Alekperov began to realize that he had a larger problem—a resurgent Rosneft. At first, as late as 2000, Bogdanchikov had simply looked like a minor irritant. Yet despite LUKoil's takeover of AGD in 1998, Alekperov had not managed to shake Rosneft loose of its remaining blocking stake in AGD. This was a problem: through its control of the licenses to the promising fields in the northern half of Timan-Pechora, AGD was the key to the future oil development of the northwest, and notably to LUKoil's plans with Conoco to develop the so-called Northern Territories.[42] But Bogdanchikov, with his blocking share in AGD, would not cooperate.

The quarrel soon turned bitter. LUKoil pressured Rosneft to sell its blocking stake in AGD or to exchange its AGD stock for LUKoil stock. But Bogdanchikov vowed not to surrender his stake in AGD. According to Ravil' Maganov, Alekperov's longtime associate and head of LUKoil's upstream operations, Rosneft was using its blocking stake to oppose LUKoil's investment plans in the region. Raising the ante, LUKoil threatened to bankrupt AGD and transfer the licenses to another entity if Rosneft would not agree to accept $40 million in LUKoil stock in exchange for its stake in AGD.[43] But still Bogdanchikov refused, and the result was a stalemate.

There was worse to come. In October 2001 Rosneft and Gazprom announced a joint venture that not only diluted LUKoil's stake in the Shtokman project but effectively blocked it from access to the Barents Sea.[44] As we shall see when we turn to Bogdanchikov's tangled relations with Gazprom, blocking LUKoil was not Bogdanchikov's primary objective in the deal, nor indeed was it Gazprom's—both companies had other purposes in mind—but LUKoil reacted bitterly to the prospect of losing its access to Shtokman and moved to block the transfer.[45] Bogdanchikov, meanwhile, raised the stakes in the AGD dispute, demanding that LUKoil hand over to Rosneft one-quarter of the reserves covered by AGD's licenses (a share corresponding to Rosneft's 25 percent equity stake), an idea that Alekperov rejected.[46]

So far Alekperov might have thought that he could still defeat Rosneft, but the next development convinced him otherwise. In January 2003, Andrei Vavilov, leader of the group that owned Northern Oil, called a surprise press conference to announce he had just sold the company. He would not name the buyer, but he hinted slyly that the new owner was a company that LUKoil would "prefer not to sue."[47] For Alekperov, that one hint was quite enough. The new owner could only be Rosneft.

And suddenly it was equally clear who was backing Bogdanchikov. That became plain three weeks later, during the famous "hockey puck" exchange between Putin and Khodorkovsky in mid-February 2003. When Khodorkovsky accused Bogdanchikov of corruption in the Northern Oil deal, to his face and in front of Putin and the assembled oligarchs, Putin stepped in to defend Bogdanchikov, saying that Rosneft needed additional reserves. That was all Alekperov needed to know. Two days later, he sat down with Bogdanchikov and the two men cut a deal that settled all their outstanding quarrels in a single massive swap.[48]

It was a sudden and astonishing turnaround. Less than two months before, at the end of December, the minister of natural resources, Vitalii Artiukhov, had called in the two oil presidents and attempted to mediate between them, but they would not yield. The year 2003 opened with the prospect of bitter escalation. LUKoil seemed more determined than ever to challenge the transfer of the Barents Sea licenses to the Gazprom-Rosneft joint venture Sevmorneftegaz. In January LUKoil even announced plans to create a new company, called Nar'ianmarneftegaz, to which it meant to transfer all of AGD's licenses, leaving Rosneft with a blocking stake in an empty shell.[49] Bogdanchikov, for his part, maintained his demands. It looked as though Bogdanchikov and Alekperov were gearing up for a battle royal.

Yet only two days after Putin took sides publicly with Bogdanchikov, a deal was done. Also striking was the fact that both sides made roughly equal concessions. Alekperov gave up his claim to the stakes in Shtokman and Northern Oil (including Val Gamburtseva), while Bogdanchikov turned over to LUKoil his blocking share of AGD, thus enabling Alekperov to proceed with his plans for the Northern Territories.

Neither Bogdanchikov nor Alekperov has spoken publicly about their reasons for coming to the table when they did, but there are two plausible inferences: first, that Alekperov understood he could not safely take on the Kremlin; and second, that Bogdanchikov was clearing the decks to pursue the upcoming battle against Yukos. Lastly, there are indirect hints that the deal was brokered by the Kremlin.

The subsequent behavior of both men bears this out. From early 2003 on, Alekperov, who the previous year had conspicuously lined up with Khodorkovsky and Yukos, lowered his profile and began cultivating the image of the "loyal oilman," losing no opportunity to demonstrate his loyalty to the president. In contrast, Bogdanchikov, more and more plainly backed by the Kremlin, became one of the principal leaders of the campaign against Mikhail Khodorkovsky and Yukos.

Thus the summer and fall of 2002 mark the end of one chapter in the evolution of Sergei Bogdanchikov and Rosneft and the beginning of a new one. During his first four years in Moscow, Bogdanchikov and his company were still small players on a stage dominated by the oligarchs and their privatized oil companies. Bogdanchikov's main concern during this period was to arrest the disintegration of Rosneft, regain control of the wandering subsidiaries, restore oil production and exports, and to put Rosneft at the service of the Kremlin. Throughout, he courted Vladimir Putin and the silovik wing of the Kremlin hierarchy. By early 2003 Bogdanchikov had grounds to believe his long campaign was succeeding.

But he was mistaken. His next problem was Gazprom.

Rosneft and Gazprom's Abortive Partnership

From the moment he became president, Putin had encouraged Rosneft and Gazprom to work together. That was the trend worldwide. In contrast to oil, gas had long remained a regional industry; but that was rapidly changing, as technological advances, chiefly the growth of liquified natural gas (LNG), made gas increasingly global. All the major international companies did both oil and gas. In Russia, the inherited Soviet-era separation between oil and gas seemed an anachronism. From the first, Putin showed signs of wanting a single champion, particularly in the north.

But Gazprom and Rosneft were unlikely partners. In the 1990s, under Rem Viakhirev and his associates, Gazprom had hewed to its traditional Soviet-era profile: dry gas from West Siberia, shipped through pipelines to western Russia and Europe. Gazprom had no connection to the eastern half of the country and, despite occasional press releases to the contrary, showed no real interest in it. As for liquids—principally gas condensate—Gazprom had traditionally treated them as a nuisance by-product. Gazprom had inherited no significant oil production and showed no interest in acquiring oil licenses or investing in oil exploration or development. In the 1990s, indeed, Gazprom invested in everything except hydrocarbons, hardly even its own gas resources, let alone oil.

Up to this point, Rosneft and Gazprom had had practically no contact with each other. By 2001 Bogdanchikov was on his way to regaining control of Rosneft's scattered assets, and he had established good relations with the new team in the Kremlin. He now had to show he could grow the company. Oil prices were rising; the other Russian oil companies were booming; and Rosneft by contrast was still a minor player. But where was growth to come from? Production from Sakhalin-1 was still several years away. His top producer and money earner at this time was Purneftegaz. Since regaining control in late 1998, Bogdanchikov had managed to restart production and development there; crude output had grown by 17.4 percent in the previous two years, and Bogdanchikov had obtained more generous export quotas from the government, so that exports from Purneftegaz had quintupled.[50] The area was prospective. Purneftegaz, in short, appeared to be the key to Rosneft's growth for the rest of the decade.

The most promising target for growth at Purneftegaz was a group of five fields collectively called Kharampur. But Kharampur had a problem: it had a large cap of gas sitting above the oil, and the only way to produce the oil economically was to produce the gas simultaneously with the oil. That meant Bogdanchikov could not develop Kharampur unless he could persuade Gazprom to accept the gas from it into its pipeline system.[51]

In October 2001 Bogdanchikov entered into a joint venture with the newly named CEO of Gazprom, Aleksei Miller. Gazprom was looking for help at Prirazlomnoe, whereas Rosneft needed Gazprom to solve its gas problem at Kharampur. It looked like a deal. For a brief time in 2002, Bogdanchikov thought he had gained Gazprom's assent to take his gas. Incautiously, he even began talking about exporting gas to Europe. But by early 2003 it became clear that Gazprom had no intention of allowing gas from Kharampur into its system. At a press conference in March Bogdanchikov vented his frustration: "We need to know where we stand with Gazprom. Or let them simply tell us, 'Over the next 20 years I won't let anybody in.' That too would be a position."[52] By June his patience snapped. For two years he had been trying to get access to Gazprom's system, he said, adding, "If this question can't be worked out very soon at the Gazprom level, we'll get it decided at the government level." Bogdanchikov's threat was greeted with derision in the media; one Russian commentator called Bogdanchikov Miller's "poor relation."[53] The Russian business daily *Vedomosti* commented in an editorial, "Why Bogdanchikov couldn't settle this question over the telephone with Miller is a puzzle for everybody"[54]— and then answered its own question by observing that Rosneft obviously had the losing hand. By the fall of 2003, Gazprom began building a pipeline to a neighboring field of its own, bypassing Kharampur.[55] Kharampur and with it Bogdanchikov's plans for growth at Purneftegaz were stuck.

Bogdanchikov may have thought at this point that his standing with the Kremlin was strong enough that he could enlist Putin's support to overrule Gazprom, but in that he turned out to be mistaken. In fact, as soon became apparent, Putin had a completely different plan in mind: to merge Rosneft into Gazprom altogether.

The Plan to Merge Rosneft and Gazprom

The next chapter in the story begins on a fall day in mid-September 2004, when Prime Minister Mikhail Fradkov and Gazprom CEO Aleksei Miller paid a call on President Putin at his presidential dacha at Novo-Ogarevo. Putin by this time spent most of his working days there and came in to the Kremlin only for official functions. Increasingly, if government top-siders needed to see the president, they had to travel to his dacha—which meant that the Government Road was frequently closed to let the official convoys through.

Fradkov and Miller had brought Putin a draft proposal, on a subject so innocuously technical that it hardly seemed worth a presidential visit. The issue was Gazprom's "ring fence" problem. For years Gazprom and the government had been stumped over how to undo the unforeseen consequences of a law passed seven years before, which limited foreign ownership of Gazprom shares to no more than 20 percent.[56] This led to a situation in which there were, in effect, two classes of Gazprom shares, those that the government had sold on the London and New York stock exchanges and which traded outside Russia, and those that circulated on the domestic market only. At various times since 1997, the domestic shares had been worth as little as 10 percent of the foreign shares. As a consequence, the market worth of Gazprom was far lower than it would have been had Gazprom shares traded freely around the world. But if the ring fence could be removed, Gazprom would suddenly become (in terms of market capitalization) one of the largest companies in the world—not to mention the fact that a number of influential Russians would see their own net worth grow substantially.[57]

But the Putin government did not want to remove the ring fence until it was certain that it had secure majority control of Gazprom. Gazprom and the government by the end of the 1990s controlled only about 38 percent of the company's shares. Aleksei Miller, acting under Putin's orders, had regained control of an additional 17 percent block, giving the government de facto majority control.[58] But the cautious president, wary of a repeat of the past, wanted full legal ownership in the hands of the state itself. The difficulty was, How to pay for it? A commission had been working on the ring fence problem since 2001 but had bogged down amid competing proposals.[59]

The plan that Miller and Fradkov brought to the president was appealing in its seeming simplicity. The Russian state owned 100 percent of Rosneft. All it had to do was swap its Rosneft shares for a block of Gazprom shares of equal value. Gazprom would then own Rosneft, while the state would gain full majority control of the combined Gazprom-Rosneft entity. Miller calculated this would require a little over 10 percent of Gazprom stock. The move would finally make Gazprom "transparent, attractive to investors, and adapted to market conditions," Fradkov told the president.

To Putin the idea was attractive—for several reasons. First, it eliminated the ring fence. But even more important, it created at one stroke the national energy champion that Putin had come to believe was essential. From Putin's point of view it made no sense to have two national champions. Rosneft was still perceived at that time as weak and ineffective. By itself, it was a company with little acreage and a limited future. Equally, Gazprom by itself was only the "West Siberian Pipeline Gas Company," with no presence in the east and no capability to deal with liquids. But if united, Gazprom and Rosneft could provide the kind of unified "total hydrocarbons" approach that appealed to Putin.

None of the trio at Novo-Ogarevo that day appeared to believe the merger would pose any fundamental problem of execution. "It's an operational question," the president told his prime minister, "within the authority of the government. If you consider it advisable, then do it." Speaking to the media later in the day, Fradkov commented, "This will create a very large transnational company." Immediately following the meeting with Putin, Aleksei Miller held a press conference in which he outlined the process by which Rosneft would be absorbed into Gazprom. There seemed to be no doubt in his mind that it was a done deal, and the result would be a total disappearance of Rosneft.[60] Western banks and brokerages greeted the plan warmly and set about calculating how much shareholders would benefit. Gazprom's ADR shares jumped 15 percent overnight to an all-time high.[61]

But two key players had been missing from the meeting with Putin: Sergei Bogdanchikov and Igor Sechin. Bogdanchikov, in fact, seems to have had no warning of Miller and Fradkov's proposal. The morning of the meeting at Novo-Ogarevo he had announced that he planned to fly to the Far East that evening. By midday, however, he had abruptly canceled the trip. Thus while Miller told the press that evening that Bogdanchikov would head a new Gazprom subsidiary, to be called "Gazpromneft,"[62] insiders began quickly leaking to the media that Bogdanchikov was not on board.

In fact, what had seemed at first to be a purely financial maneuver to consolidate state control over a unified energy champion soon turned into a bitter political struggle between the two principal Kremlin clans. Because of the alliance between Bogdanchikov and Sechin in the Yukos Affair, Rosneft had come to be viewed in Moscow as the "silovik oil company," a link that was symbolically confirmed when Putin in July 2004 named Igor Sechin chairman of Rosneft's board of directors. Gazprom, conversely, was viewed as the company of the "Saint Petersburg business elite," with one of the *Pitertsy*'s members, Dmitri Medvedev, as its board chairman. Considered from this angle, the Miller-Fradkov proposal to merge Rosneft into Gazprom was anything but the narrow technical idea it seemed on the surface. To the Moscow media, always inclined to see politics behind every move, it amounted to taking the prime energy asset of the siloviki and turning it over to a rival clan.

To say the least, this would have been an uncharacteristic move for Putin to make. Throughout his first term he had tried to maintain a careful balance among the various groups in his constituency. Medvedev and Sechin, both deputy heads of the Presidential Administration, were among his two closest and most trusted aides, men he had worked with since the early 1990s (although Medvedev was at that time the more junior figure). By 2004, though the balance was visibly tilting in favor of the siloviki (partly as a result of the Yukos Affair), there is no sign that Putin wished to see it tilt further. (Indeed, two years later he came to believe the hard-line siloviki were overreaching themselves and he took steps to right the balance). Instead, it seems more plausible that Putin had intended to give both sides a stake in the merged Gazprom-Rosneft entity. Indeed, there were reports in the press that Putin had designated Sechin to oversee the merger.[63]

Bogdanchikov Fights Back

If cooperation between the clans was Putin's initial hope, it soon foundered on Bogdanchikov's fierce opposition. When the news broke, Bogdanchikov immediately sent a letter to Putin, arguing against the merger. The state did not need to surrender its entire stake in Rosneft, he wrote, in order to gain majority control of Gazprom.[64] Seeing Bogdanchikov's resistance, Gazprom's chairman, Dmitri Medvedev, warned the Rosneft chief, in barely veiled language, against any attempt to unbundle Rosneft assets and make off with them, "as had previously happened in Gazprom itself," he noted. At this time strong pressure appears to have been applied against Bogdanchikov, together with a threat that if he did not agree to Gazprom's terms, he would be replaced altogether.[65]

But there was worse to come. At the end of October the board of directors of Gazprom duly approved the creation of "Gazpromneft," to house Rosneft and Gazprom's own oil assets. Two days later Gazprom announced that Bogdanchikov would head it. Yet in the announcement there was very little that Bogdanchikov could have found much pleasure in. Gazpromneft was to control exploration and production—but crude sales, including the very lucrative export function, would be taken over by Gazprom's export arm, Gazeksport. Gazpromneft was to be located in Saint Petersburg, and Bogdanchikov was to move there, while Gazpromneft's Moscow affairs would be managed by a

Miller protégé, vice chairman Mikhail Sereda, sitting in Gazprom headquarters in Moscow. If Gazprom had deliberately designed the merger as a toad for Bogdanchikov to swallow, it could hardly have been more distasteful. Once again, he was being treated as a hired hand.[66]

Yet it is unlikely that Bogdanichikov was isolated in his struggle; he would hardly have taken such a public stance against the merger (which was backed, after all, by the president) without strong support from powerful people behind the scenes. Igor Sechin, though he remained invisible, was the obvious candidate. As chairman of the board of Rosneft, he too was affected by the planned merger. Throughout the events that followed, Bogdanichikov and Sechin appear to have worked together at every step. And within less than a month, Bogdanchikov's relative setback of October had been erased. The key was Yuganskneftegaz.

The Yuganskneftegaz Auction Changes the Game

It was at this point, in November 2004, that the plot of the Gazprom-Rosneft merger abruptly intersected with the story line of the breakup of Yukos, and the tale took an unexpected turn.

Throughout 2004, as the government's demands for back taxes from Yukos mounted higher and higher, it had became increasingly plain that a forced bankruptcy was not far off. By autumn the Kremlin and the government were already busy orchestrating the sale of Yukos's prime asset, and on November 19 an auction was announced for one month later, December 19.[67]

But who would be the buyer? For weeks Aleksei Miller had repeatedly denied that Gazprom was interested in bidding for Yuganskneftegaz, claiming that there was no provision for the purchase of Yuganskneftegaz in the company's investment plan for 2005.[68] Yet at the same time Gazprom was busy assembling commitments from foreign banks for short-term loans, the only plausible purpose for which was to cover the purchase of Yuganskneftegaz.[69] At the end of November the Gazprom board met and approved a decision to bid.

Thus the script seemed all written out. Gazprom would absorb both Rosneft and Yuganskneftegaz, and the result would be, by some measures, the largest hydrocarbons company in the world—and the Russian national champion that Putin wanted. Such, at least, was the interpretation of the Russian media, which pictured Gazprom under Miller as bent on expansion, with no limits to its appetite, and thus totally behind Putin's plan.[70] On this reading, Miller's denials were nothing but a smoke screen, and Gazprom had intended to bid all along.

In reality, things were more complicated. There are signs that senior leaders in Gazprom had mixed feelings about absorbing a large oil company. The purchase alone would require over $8 billion (the starting price was estimated to be about $8.6 billion), absorbing the bulk of Gazprom's available cash and borrowing capacity. To the barons of Gazprom, with their own ambitions and priorities, this must have been difficult to swallow. There were already lively disagreements inside Gazprom over how the company should invest its resources. The traditional gas professionals, led by the powerful vice chairman for upstream production, Aleksandr Ananenkov, were increasingly worried about the long-term supply position of Gazprom and its deteriorating pipeline system. Ananenkov was pressing hard for an expanded capital spending plan to finance an early beginning of the development of the Yamal Peninsula (which he viewed as the all-important source of the next generation of gas for Gazprom) and a large-scale program to repair and upgrade Gazprom's trunk lines. He can hardly have welcomed the news that Gazprom's resources would be used instead to buy Yuganskneftegaz, any more than the prospect of a strong and unruly Bogdanchikov inside Gazprom, backed by Igor Sechin and the silovik clan of the Kremlin.[71] There were reports that Gazprom's board meeting had been a difficult one.

The more one looks at the events of those few critical days, the more plainly it appears that the driver behind Gazprom's decision to bid for the Yukos assets was not Gazprom but the Kremlin. According to the German press, it was Chancellor Gerhard Schroeder—Putin's personal friend—who was orchestrating the consortium of German banks. The lead player in the consortium was Dresdner Bank, whose managing director in Moscow, Matthias Warnig, had been a friend of Vladimir Putin since the mid-1980s, when both men worked in Dresden in their countries' respective security services.[72] Miller's apparent reversal over whether Gazprom would bid for Yuganskneftegaz is easily explained—he was simply following orders.

But for Bogdanchikov, the prospect that Gazprom would own Yuganskneftegaz changed everything. Suddenly he bounded back onto the stage. It was

Bogdanchikov who announced Gazprom's decision to bid, trumpeting it in triumphant tones that contrasted with his dutiful resignation of one month before. "The task that now stands before the company," he told an international audience, "is to make the gas and oil components of Gazprom equal in size and power."[73] It is not hard to guess the reasons for Bogdanchikov's sudden enthusiasm. Without Yuganskneftegaz, a merged Gazprom-Rosneft remained a gas company with a small oil subsidiary and himself as a minor player. But with Yuganskneftegaz added, the whole chessboard was transformed. Gazprom would become the world's second largest oil company in terms of reserves and the seventh largest in terms of production. Whatever the formal organization chart, Gazpromneft would become the virtual equal of Gazprom, and Bogdanchikov, as the head of it, could no longer be ignored or sidelined.

"A Woman Reshuffles the Cards"

Then came the bombshell.[74] On December 15, lawyers representing Yukos petitioned Judge Letitia Clark of the U.S. Bankruptcy Court for the Southern District of Texas to issue a delaying order to block the planned auction on December 19. Two days later, on December 17, Judge Clark issued a ten-day restraining order while she considered whether to hear the case. This suddenly and radically changed the game. If Gazprom proceeded with its plan, not only could its own officers be held legally liable in the United States, but so could those of the banks that had assembled the package of credits for Gazprom's use at the auction.[75]

Did the Houston court actually have jurisdiction? Yukos argued that it did, on the grounds that it did "significant business" in the United States. The Russians argued vehemently that it did not. Putin, a few days later, reacted angrily at a press conference in Germany. Referring to Judge Clark, Putin snapped, "I'm not even sure she knows where Russia is." The judge's presumption brought back the law student Putin had once been. "Par in parem non habet imperium," he said, quoting a phrase from Roman law, "an equal has no dominion over another equal."[76] Russia was a sovereign foreign power, he said, therefore the court had no jurisdiction. Surely the Houston judge could see that. Yet in recent years U.S. courts had dramatically expanded their reach, claiming jurisdiction over wide swathes of overseas assets. Who knew how far the U.S. court would attempt to go?

On December 16, without waiting for the restraining order from Houston, Gazprom abruptly divested itself of Gazpromneft, the still empty structure it had created to house Rosneft, thus severing itself legally from any role Gazpromneft might play in the upcoming auction.[77] The same day, the foreign banks backed out of the credit agreement, and the consortium assembling the $10 billion loan package for the Yuganskneftegaz auction collapsed.[78]

Yet Miller, still under pressure from the Kremlin, soldiered on. On December 17 Gazpromneft—by now at a safe arm's length from Gazprom—registered for the auction. Gazprom may have assumed that the script remained otherwise unchanged and that behind the front of the now legally separate Gazpromneft it was still the Kremlin's designated bidder. But in fact the entire play was about to be rewritten. On the same day a mystery entrant, called Baikal Finance Group ("Baikalfinansgrup" in Russian), signed up for the auction. This group, supposedly registered in the provincial town of Tver' south of Moscow, was a total unknown. When journalists later went to Tver' to track down the registration address, they found a broken-down wooden shack and a bewildered householder who had no idea what they were talking about. On the day of the auction, December 19, two people claiming to represent Baikalfinansgrup (they were later identified as being employees of Surgutneftegaz[79]) submitted the sole bid for Yuganskneftegaz, at $9.37 billion. The hammer went down, and 76.8 percent of the shares of Yuganskneftegaz had changed hands. Gazpromneft, though present, did not counter.

So who was the new owner? On the day, no one seemed to know. Yuri Petrov, the acting chairman of the Russian Property Fund (which had presided over the sale on behalf of the government), told reporters, "It came as just as much of a surprise for us as it did for you." At first most observers assumed Baikalfinansgrup was a stand-in for Gazprom.[80] Surgutneftegaz, despite the fact that two of its officials had acted on behalf of Baikalfinansgrup at the auction, denied all connection. Government ministers, including Finance Minister Aleksei Kudrin, admitted they were stumped, and the Kremlin refused to comment. The most entertaining reaction came from Vladimir Grabarnik, the governor of the province of Tver', where Baikalfinansgrup was supposedly headquartered. "It is no secret to anyone that this company is purely nominal. And the fact that the office of the company is not located at the registration address is nothing out of the ordinary. It is a normal practice."[81]

Putin, meanwhile, was in Germany. On December 21, two days after the auction, he held a joint press conference with Chancellor Gerhard Schroeder, which only deepened the mystery. Speaking of Baikalfinansgrup, Putin said, "The shareholders of this company, as is well known, are exclusively physical persons, but ones who have done business in the energy sector for many years."[82] That seemed to point toward Surgutneftegaz. But attentive observers noticed two small details. On December 20, Sergei Bogdanchikov had resigned as president of Gazpromneft. On December 21, officials from Rosneft's Purneftegaz had flown in to Nefteiugansk, the main base city of Yuganskneftegaz. The explanation was not long in coming. Late on December 22, Rosneft announced officially it had acquired Baikalfinansgrup.[83]

Rosneft Captures Yuganskneftegaz

This was the turning point in the Gazprom-Rosneft affair, the moment when it became plain that Bogdanchikov meant to use the purchase of Yuganskneftegaz to break free of the forced merger with Gazprom. Bogdanchikov scheduled a press conference for the evening of the December 23. According to advance leaks from Rosneft insiders, he planned to announce that Rosneft's purchase of Yuganskneftegaz was the first step in the creation of a national oil corporation.[84] But Bogdanchikov was unexpectedly forced to backtrack, when it became apparent that the president was not on board. Back from Germany, Putin held a wide-ranging press conference in the Kremlin that afternoon. On the one hand, he vigorously defended Rosneft's purchase of Yuganskneftegaz. But what must have caught Bogdanchikov's ear was the president's words about Gazprom:

> All the largest energy companies, including our company "Gazprom," strive to diversify their activity. You know that the largest global companies—BP, ExxonMobil, Shell, and so on—are involved in electric power, oil, refining, and gas, and LNG. Gazprom too will do the same thing, and is striving in that direction.[85]

There was no mention of a state oil company. In other words, Gazprom was still the president's sole champion. Bogdanchikov hastily canceled his own planned event.[86]

For Russian observers, especially the ever cynical Moscow press corps, the pseudo-auction of Yuganskneftegaz suddenly made everything clear. The entire plot against Khodorkovsky and Menatep had been cooked up from the first by Bogdanchikov and Sechin, with the aim of seizing Yukos. Dmitrii Dokuchaev of *Moskovskie novosti* speculated that

> The motive from the beginning was a banal transfer of property from the oligarch class of the 1990s to the new Petersburg elite. Bogdanchikov and Sechin were able to incline the president to their side by playing on Khodorkovsky's supposed political ambitions. All the other twists and turns of the affair are mere derivatives.[87]

For Dokuchaev and his fellow reporters, the entire merger of Rosneft and Gazprom was a sham, designed to cover the real plot. Nikolai Vardul', economic editor of *Kommersant,* agreed. The plot had been for Gazprom to acquire Yuganskneftegaz through a two-step operation, the first step being the merger of Gazprom and Rosneft, the second the takeover of Yuganskneftegaz. But as in all good mystery stories, wrote Vardul', referring to Judge Letitia Clark, "a woman reshuffled the cards."[88]

Yet the actual plot—if there was one—contained as much improvisation as premeditation. It is clear enough that the Kremlin meant to combine Rosneft and Yuganskneftegaz into a single national energy champion built around Gazprom. It also appears that the president's plan allowed room for Bogdanchikov and Sechin's own ambitions by creating a powerful Gazpromneft inside Gazprom—a second-best solution from their point of view, perhaps, but one that gave them a powerful platform just the same.

The Houston court's temporary restraining order—even though, ironically, Judge Clark ultimately decided not to hear the case—disrupted the Kremlin's plan, but for Bogdanchikov and Sechin it must have come as a blessed break. One can imagine the hurried councils of war in the Kremlin as the players huddled to work out a response. Time was of the essence. Gazprom needed to be kept in the clear and therefore could not bid. Some other entity was needed to stand in and make the down payment to buy Yuganskneftegaz. Surgutneftegaz could provide that. But then how to pay the balance?

It was Bogdanchikov who came up with the solution. Rosneft could do what Gazprom could not—it could parachute experienced oil teams into

Yuganskneftegaz to restore faltering production, it could negotiate an export-backed loan to pay for Yuganskneftegaz, and it could acquire the company with minimal legal risks because it had no exposed assets outside Russia. Rosneft was the answer. It is said that Sechin strode into Putin's office and presented the plan to the president, who readily agreed.

Moscow buzzed with theories that December of how Rosneft had assembled the money, but the full details did not emerge until a year and a half later, when Rosneft published its accounts for 2005.[89] The bulk of the cash came from the Chinese oil company CNPC, in the form of a prepayment against future oil exports by Rosneft to China. (Rosneft took over the bulk of Yukos's existing exports by rail to China.) The prepayment went through Russia's state-owned bank for foreign trade, Vneshekonombank (VEB). In addition, Rosneft received a sizable loan from the other major Russian state-owned bank, Sberbank.[90] At the beginning of January, Bogdanchikov and Energy Minister Viktor Khristenko went to Beijing to negotiate with the Chinese, followed shortly by the announcement of an oil export contract.

Bogdanchikov moved quickly to take charge at Yuganskneftegaz. The company had been adrift for a year and a strong hand was urgently needed. Once the Procuracy had frozen Yukos's bank accounts, all payments had stopped. Yuganskneftegaz's oil workers had received half-pay in November and nothing in December. Contractors and suppliers had been waiting for months; the company owed them between $400 and $500 million. Deliveries of essential supplies had halted. The local electrical utility, Tiumen'energo, had begun shutting off the electricity on which Yuganskneftegaz's well pumps depended.[91] At the turn of the year, as Bogdanchikov later said, "Not a single team was drilling, there was no recovery work going on." Production was about to crash.[92]

At this point, in the middle of the West Siberian winter, Vladimir Bogdanov of Surgutneftegaz once again came to the rescue, strengthening the impression that he had played a key role behind the scenes throughout. He sent drillers and supplies—casing pipe, cement, and the like—and Yuganskneftegaz was able to get operations going again. Bogdanchikov began pouring resources into Yuganskneftegaz, borrowing men wherever he could and cutting back all other commitments.[93] Drilling brigades began arriving from Rosneft's main West Siberian operation, Purneftegaz. Bogdanchikov quickly renewed ties with Schlumberger, which had been severed by Yukos, and Schlumberger resumed fraccing at Priobskoe.

By February 2005 the worst of the crisis had passed. Early that month Bogdanchikov made his first visit to Nefteiugansk, the base city of Yuganskneftegaz, and to Priobskoe. "All the specialists of Yuganskneftegaz are back to work as before," he said in a statement. "All our contractors have returned to work with us."[94] His next stop was a call on Bogdanov in Surgut. "It would have been impolite," he told the media there, "flying back to Moscow out of Surgut airport, not to thank Mister Bogdanov for the help Surgutneftegaz gave Yuganskneftegaz when we first began working there."[95] Asked by a correspondent what the future fate of Rosneft would be, Bogdanchikov hardly bothered with his usual "I'm just a manager" routine, saying simply, "We are proceeding from the assumption that for the time being, Rosneft will work separately."[96]

Putin Soldiers On

Meanwhile, back in Moscow, the stalemate over the fate of Rosneft and Yuganskneftegaz continued. Miller and Gazprom, evidently with the encouragement of Putin himself, continued to insist that the merger was on. Abandoning the merger altogether would have left unsolved the two problems that had led to it in the first place: the Gazprom ring fence and the Kremlin's desire for outright control. It would have meant abandoning the aim of a single state champion for oil and gas. Putin remained bent on his plan. Yet Gazprom and its foreign advisors were nervous about the legal risks of taking over Yuganskneftegaz. There seemed to be no way out of the impasse.

While the government debated, Bogdanchikov was busily binding Yuganskneftegaz ever closer, and with each passing week it was becoming more difficult to undo the web that he was weaving around it. By late March Bogdanchikov was back in Nefteiugansk, announcing that Rosneft planned to increase investment in Yuganskneftegaz by 2.5 times in 2005.[97] Normal production had been restored, he said, and production would reach 54 million tons (1.08 million barrels per day) in 2005. It was clear, however, that this was being achieved through a massive increase in drilling. Whereas previously Yukos had employed ten drilling teams on site, Bogdanchikov had already deployed eleven. There would be sixteen by April and twenty by June, he said, bringing development drilling at Yuganskneftegaz to 500,000 meters for the year. By 2009–2010, Bogdanchikov said, Yuganskneftegaz would be producing 70 million tons (1.4

million barrels per day), up from its 2004 peak of 52 million tons (1.04 million barrels per day) under Yukos.[98]

With the arrival of spring 2005, the awkward deadlock finally broke. The solution was a triangle. The state—by now increasingly solvent as oil prices continued their rise—would simply pay cash for the block of shares needed to consolidate its majority control of Gazprom.[99] Gazprom would then use the proceeds to buy Sibneft, enabling Roman Abramovich to cash out. By mid-July Putin himself confirmed that talks were under way for Gazprom to buy Sibneft, suggesting that he had given his blessing to the arrangement,[100] and at the end of July, Gazprom announced it had received $12 billion to buy Sibneft.[101] There was something for everyone: Gazprom had an oil company, the government had Gazprom (thus enabling it to solve the ring-fence problem), and Bogdanchikov and Sechin had Rosneft.

By August, after nearly a year of battle, the takeover issue had finally been laid to rest. On August 10, on Bogdanchikov's 48th birthday, Putin invited the Rosneft CEO to the presidential dacha at Novo-Ogarevo—fittingly enough, since that was where the merger plan had been launched the previous September. In the public portion of their meeting, neither man mentioned Yuganskneftegaz or Gazprom. Bogdanchikov informed the president that Rosneft was now the second largest oil producer in Russia and would take over first place from LUKoil the following year (as indeed it did). Although both men knew precisely how Rosneft had suddenly grown so large, the president's sole public comment was, "Khorosho" ("Good").[102] With that one word, the Gazprom-Rosneft affair was over. Bogdanchikov and Sechin had won.

Lessons of the Failed Merger

The story of the aborted Gazprom-Rosneft merger puts a rare spotlight on the interplay of power and policy in Putin's office. It showed that Putin's power, formidable as it was, had limits. Plainly, Putin did not get what he had initially wanted: a single state-owned oil and gas company. Instead, after months of conflict, he settled for two companies, a solution he had initially opposed. Sechin and Bogdanchikov never defied the president openly. But they consistently outmaneuvered Gazprom, making the team of Dmitri Medvedev and Aleksei Miller look irresolute and ineffectual. In the end Bogdanchikov and Sechin simply outlasted the other side, if with timely help from Texas.

But seen in broader perspective, the battle over the Rosneft-Gazprom merger and the ultimate creation of two separate hydrocarbon champions was just one episode in the overall trend toward the creation of state corporations that dominated Putin's second term. It was never an orderly or peaceful process; each one of the seven giant state corporations assembled between 2005 and 2008 was marked by improvisation and controversy (some opposed them as boondoggles; others supported them for the same reason).[103] Thus the outcome of the Rosneft-Gazprom affair, while it did not match Putin's initial plan, was still broadly in line with his general industrial policy. As the president might have said, "Khorosho"—good enough.

But the viability of Rosneft as a national oil champion remained to be seen. What would Bogdanchikov do next?

"Strategic Sector": Bogdanchikov at the Apogee

By the beginning of 2006 Bogdanchikov had triumphed over all the odds and survived at the head of what would shortly be Russia's largest and fastest growing oil company. But the next challenges ahead were enormous. The new ex-Yukos assets were different from Rosneft's older ones, in their history, their geology, and their culture. As a result of the acquisition, the combined company was $20 billion in debt. Its reputation in global financial markets was shaky, and so long as Yukos's remaining managers pursued their legal battle against it, Rosneft was viewed as a risk. Lastly, there was the relationship with the Kremlin and with Bogdanchikov's powerful chairman, Igor Sechin. Many expected that Rosneft would evolve into the all-too-familiar caricature of a national oil monopoly—overstaffed, inefficient, and shot through with politics.

Yet Bogdanchikov proved to be an impressive performer. We focus briefly here on four aspects of Bogdanchikov's tenure after 2005: his approach to staffing, his growth strategy, his approach to production, and his relationship to the international financial community.

When he first arrived in Moscow in 1998, Bogdanchikov began building a team in the time-honored Russian way, by bringing in his own people from Sakhalin.[104] Over the next several years, while he fought for control of the company, the veterans from Sakhalin provided a hard core of support.[105] But once he had established control over Rosneft and the company began to expand, he started replacing his former colleagues from Sakhalin with professional managers, hired through Western-style executive-search companies. Particularly in the key areas of finance and investor relations, Bogdanchikov drew talent from banks and investment firms and other Russian oil companies, and he put them in charge.[106] As one senior executive, who worked for both Yukos and then Rosneft told me,

> Unlike Khodorkovsky, whose hiring of foreigners always had something of a public-relations aspect to it and who never really surrendered control to the foreigners he hired, with Bogdanchikov it was a systematic commitment to get the best.[107]

Bogdanchikov's strategy for growth was based now on new production, not further acquisitions. As early as 2003 Bogdanchikov had begun to position Rosneft to move into East Siberia by acquiring the license to a giant field called Vankor, discovered in 1988, but until the absorption of Yukos he had lacked the means to pursue more than a token program of development, along with the completion of field exploration begun in the Soviet era. The addition of Yuganskneftegaz changed everything; it would provide a rapidly growing flow of cash through the end of the decade, and Rosneft began to pour the profits from Yuganskneftegaz into developing Vankor. The field turned out to be a bonanza: as Rosneft continued to explore the site, it discovered more and more reserves, eventually tripling its original estimate of proven reserves to over 195 million tons (1.4 billion barrels).[108]

Vankor was watched closely by the Kremlin, because it was the key to filling the new pipeline to the Pacific, which was already under construction. Bogdanchikov let out all the stops, putting his most trusted Sakhalin veterans in charge of construction and development on site, hiring Western contractors like VECO (with whom Bogdanchikov had worked on Sakhalin) to build camps and roads and SNC Lavalin to develop the engineering. Schlumberger provided a design that telescoped exploration and production into a single continuous process.[109] Using the latest horizontal "smart wells," Rosneft achieved some of the highest flow rates ever attained in Russia.

By 2009 the payoff began to come in, with first production of what would eventually be 25 million tons per year (a half-million barrels per day) from Vankor alone. By 2010 Vankor had become Rosneft's main source of growth.[110] As one looks into the future, Rosneft's investment in East Siberia will power the company's growth for at least another decade, and in this respect Bogdan-chikov deserves credit for having been a pioneer—although, one should add, following in Khodorkovsky's footsteps.

Meanwhile, it was vital that growth be sustained at Yuganskneftegaz for as long as possible. Bogdanchikov had begun pouring money and personnel into Yuganskneftegaz within days of acquiring it, and he continued to invest heavily in his new property over the following years. But his approach was much the same as that of Yukos. Mach and his Black Belts were gone, but his monster fracs continued.[111] The corps of top executives that ran Yuganskneftegaz for Yukos were promoted to Moscow and put to work developing Vankor. Those who remained at Yuganskneftegaz, although they continued fraccing, also fell back on more traditional approaches, above all more drilling. This fit with Bogdanchikov's own views; when an interviewer asked him about his priorities, he answered simply, "Drilling, drilling, drilling." Under Bogdanchikov Rosneft became the largest driller of new wells in Russia, surpassing even Bogdanov's Surgutneftegaz, and Yuganskneftegaz accounted for over 85 percent of Rosneft's share, year after year.[112]

Bogdanchikov passed a major hurdle in 2006 when Rosneft successfully raised $10.6 billion by selling shares in an initial public offering (or IPO), an open sale of shares on the international market. It was a risky exercise, because of the lingering controversies surrounding Rosneft's acquisition of the Yukos assets. Rosneft had the reputation of being one of the least transparent of Russian companies, and the perceived nature of its connections to the Kremlin did not help matters.[113] Bogdanchikov knew what he was up against. He was more knowledgeable about the world outside Russia than most people gave him credit for, and he knew how to take advice, not least from his two sons, who were Western-educated investment bankers working in major international banks. He had also experienced at first hand something of the outside world's suspicions of Rosneft in 2003, when he was stopped and searched and the contents of his briefcase photographed, by British Special Branch officers, as the Rosneft company jet landed at London's Biggin Hill Airport. After just two hours on British soil, Bogdanchikov turned around and flew home in protest.[114]

Bogdanchikov prepared carefully for the IPO, hiring an experienced investment banker, Peter O'Brien, to manage the exercise. O'Brien, a fluent Russian speaker with many years of experience in Moscow, had been vice president of

Morgan Stanley's Russian office and had managed previous share issues for other Russian companies, notably LUKoil. Bogdanchikov gave O'Brien full powers to manage the IPO. The most delicate part was Rosneft's "float prospectus," which by law had to contain a full disclosure of potential risks to investors. The huge document, over four inches thick, described the company in minute detail, but the twenty-five-page section on risks was the test. It did not mince words: it acknowledged "crime and corruption" in Russia, admitted "material weaknesses" in Rosneft's internal controls, and warned prospective investors that lawsuits connected to the Yukos Affair could "expose Rosneft to substantial liability."[115] In the end, the IPO was successful in meeting its $10 billion target; if institutional investors remained somewhat lukewarm (they mainly found the share price too high), Rosneft made up for it by enlisting major international energy companies and prominent Russians, the latter presumably with a little help from the Kremlin. In a Russian first, Rosneft shares were offered to Russian retail investors, some 115,000 of whom took up 7 percent of the offering.[116]

To those observing Rosneft during this period, Bogdanchikov's management of the company appeared professional, suitably cost-conscious, reasonably transparent, and untainted by scandal. Rosneft seemed comparatively free of the classic pathologies of state-owned companies: the corrupt contracting, nepotistic hiring, and politically motivated projects that are all too prevalent elsewhere. Bogdanchikov's approach was more reminiscent of a private-sector CEO than a state functionary. Analysts and markets took note, and if they continued to voice reservations about Rosneft it was not because of Bogdanchikov's overall management of the company but because of the company's heavy debts, high-cost reserves, and huge tax burden.[117]

It is an interesting and important question how Rosneft would have continued to evolve under Bogdanchikov. But the question will remain unanswered. Less than three years after his apparent triumph, he began to lose control of the company.

Exit Bogdanchikov

Soon after the successful IPO of 2006, rumors began to run that Bogdanchikov and Sechin, who had formed such a formidable pair throughout the Yukos Affair and in the successful defense against Gazprom, were increasingly at odds.

The two men disagreed, or so it was said, over Rosneft's role as an international player. Sechin, like Putin, saw Rosneft as Russia's flagship company and a key part of its international diplomacy. But for Sechin, that meant expansion abroad—into the Middle East, Latin America, the Arctic, and wherever else the Kremlin sought to plant a flag. Bogdanchikov was openly disparaging. As he told an interviewer in June 2008:

> We have a strict rule not to buy assets with an internal rate of return of less than 20%. There aren't that many overseas plays that meet that requirement. . . . We have no intention of buying assets that would lower those metrics. We don't need deals that bring nothing except press items.[118]

Yet in the end the battle between the two men was less over specifics than over who would control the company. As the Russian saying has it, "Two bears cannot live in the same cave." In 2008, as Putin moved from president to prime minister, he made Sechin deputy prime minister for energy, which gave Sechin direct authority over Rosneft's day-to-day operations. "He's started to give Rosneft even more attention," Bogdanchikov told *Vedomosti,* with obvious irritation. "In his new job he's already managed to visit our fields. And he's carrying out his duties as chairman with no less energy than before."[119] By 2009, it was increasingly plain that Bogdanchikov had been reduced to ceremonial roles. His protégés were being moved out; his advice was disregarded. When foreign companies came to negotiate, they met with Sechin, not Bogdanchikov. He had fought for a decade to make the company into the powerhouse it had become; his entire identity was bound up in Rosneft; yet now he was being squeezed out. Toward the end, in a rare moment of self-revelation, he confided to a journalist:

> I have a special relationship to the company. Sometimes I can't sleep at nights. I just can't sleep. Then I turn on my computer—I have a special program on it—and I can see the picture from observation cameras set up all over the country. And I just sit there and watch what's going on at Vankor or some other place.[120]

Yet Bogdanchikov fought to the end. There are indications he turned to Gennadii Timchenko and Gunvor as a counterweight to Sechin, but that effort evidently failed. In the final months, he hung on as president, insiders said, only because Timchenko and Sechin were stalemated over the choice of a successor and it took some time before an acceptably neutral stand-in finally was found. In September 2010, as Bogdanchikov accompanied Vladimir Putin on a tour of the Far East, he continued to insist that he would stay. Putin seemed reluctant to part with him; when the final announcement came, it was Dmitri Medvedev who delivered the message.[121]

Conclusion

Two decades after the end of the Soviet Union, Russia's oil industry is once again dominated by a large state-owned company. Rosneft's role as the Kremlin's oil champion is already having a significant impact on the rest of the industry. It is Russia's number-one producer and its output is growing rapidly, thanks to production from a handful of new fields. It has led the way in exploring and developing new prospects in East Siberia. Along with Gazprom, it has a virtual monopoly of the Arctic offshore. It has been given the right (again along with Gazprom) to preempt licenses to new discoveries above a certain size. And thanks to a string of newly concluded strategic alliances with ExxonMobil, GE, Italy's Eni, and Norway's Statoil, Rosneft is poised to play leading roles in Russia's future expansion, not only into its own Arctic waters, but into other offshore plays around the world, such as the Gulf of Mexico, as well as new technological frontiers, most importantly tight oil.

Thus, two decades into the post-Soviet era, the Russian oil industry appears to have settled into a two-tiered structure in which the two state-owned champions, Rosneft and Gazprom (through its oil subsidiary, GazpromNeft), thanks to strong support from the Kremlin, have gained the most attractive opportunities for growth, while the private oil companies share the lesser ones (or at least the ones that presently appear such)—the declining brownfields of West Siberia and the Volga-Urals, the largely gas-prone Caspian offshore, the complex geologies of northwest Russia, and the untested potential of deep shale formations. It is a division of labor that satisfies both the state-owned companies and the Kremlin, not to mention the state's fiscal and regulatory agencies. The private oil companies are understandably not nearly as pleased, but so long as oil prices keep rising and oil output remains steady, there is no particular pressure on the leadership to make a change.[122]

Yet there are several reasons why the present structure could be subject to alteration. The first is coming developments within the oil industry. Sooner or later, the last remaining Soviet-era oil generals will leave the scene, setting off new struggles for ownership and control, which could lead to further renationalizations. Another likely event in the future is a change of leadership in Gazprom, which could be the occasion for a long-awaited restructuring of the gas industry, in which GazpromNeft (Gazprom's oil subsidiary) might be reprivatized as an independent company, or possibly absorbed by Rosneft to form a single giant state-owned oil company, even larger than today.

The likelihood of any of these events depends very much on the overall balance between the state and the private sector in coming years, especially the evolution of the Kremlin's policy toward state corporations. The principle of consolidating Russia's strategic assets into a small handful of giant state-owned companies evidently still appeals to President Putin, and also to Igor Sechin, who has taken strong public positions against a Medvedev-supported plan to privatize stakes in several state-owned energy companies, including Rosneft. But there is growing unease elsewhere in the government over the spread of state corporations. Moreover, the movement to reprivatize may gain momentum from the desire of today's "state oligarchs" to become private owners. The wind has already shifted twice on this question in the past twenty years, and it may well shift again.

Lastly, the fate of the state-owned champions depends very much on their own future performance. There are broadly two possible directions of evolution for Rosneft, the first toward the model of the entrepreneurial high-performance NOC with international exposure and expertise, exemplified by Statoil and Petrobras, and the second toward the model of the politicized, corrupt, and inefficient NOCs seen in some other countries.

But there is a more fundamental question about Rosneft's future performance: Is the model of a giant state-owned company, with near-monopoly control over the major directions of growth, the most appropriate model for the Russian oil industry ahead? Does Rosneft have the management skills and the financial resources to advance on all fronts simultaneously—in the Arctic offshore, in the Gulf of Mexico, in East Siberia, in Venezuela, and in the brownfields of West Siberia? Given the likely challenges to come, will it not turn out that other company models, possibly ranging from a dedicated off-shore specialist for the Arctic to innovative onshore independents for West Siberian tight oil, for example, will turn out to be more appropriate?

We shall come back to these questions in Chapters 12 and 13. But first, we turn to an examination of the fiscal and regulatory environment of the oil industry and discuss its implications for the oil industry's performance and adaptability in the face of new challenges.

chapter 9

Krizis: *The Rude Awakening of 2008–2009 and the Russian Oil-Tax Dilemma*

Every year, at the summer solstice, the cream of Russia's businessmen and politicians, joined by hundreds of high-placed foreign guests, gathers at the Economic Forum in Saint Petersburg for two days of high-level panels, meetings, and garden parties. It is the place to meet and be met, to do deals, to show off Russia's achievements, and, for the Pitertsy, to celebrate the brief summer by the oblique light of the midnight sun.

At the June 2008 edition of the Forum, there was much to celebrate. Russia's economy had grown by 7 percent per year since 1999, nearly doubling in less than a decade. The benefits of growth were spreading throughout Russian society: real incomes had increased by 2.5 times, real wages had tripled, and the unemployment rate and poverty rate had fallen by half. Russians were buying mobile telephones, apartments, vacations abroad, and they were buying more new cars than anyone else in Europe. For most Russians, the decade of the 2000s was the best they had ever known, if only because it was such a welcome contrast to the 1990s, which had been one of the worst.[1]

Vladimir Putin, newly installed at the Russian White House as prime minister while his protégé Dmitri Medvedev moved into the Kremlin as president, could look back on the previous eight years with considerable satisfaction. It was not just the economy that had done well. Putin had overcome most of the political obstacles he faced when he first took office in 2000. Control over key strategic sectors had been recovered; political power had been reunified and the central state restored; and the perceived threat of foreign takeover of Russia's natural resources had been averted. Two national energy companies had been created (even if Putin had initially wanted only one). And the state's strengthened control over Russia's resources supported the Kremlin's ambition to return to the role of a great power on the world stage.

Along the way Putin had managed the considerable exploit of keeping order among the competing elite groups around him and restoring the balance of influence that had been disturbed in the wake of the Yukos Affair. The symbol of this success was the grooming and final selection of Dmitri Medvedev as successor, a choice that the siloviki had opposed right up to the final months, and which Putin had imposed in the end only by demoting or retiring several leading hard-liners.[2] Even as he left the formal office of president to his protégé, thus satisfying the Russian constitution's two-term limit, Putin, then at the height of his power and popularity, remained in power, and not behind the scenes. Stability seemed assured, at least for the next four years.

Much of Russia's success in that decade, to be sure, rested on oil. Oil production had increased by nearly two-thirds since the crash of 1998; and oil prices had risen thirteen-fold. Oil-export revenues in 2007 topped $173 billion, up from $36 billion in 2000.[3] The biggest winner was the state. For every $1 per barrel increase in world oil prices, the combination of export duties and production tax yielded an additional $1.9 billion annually to the state treasury. Oil taxes had risen tenfold, and by 2007 they accounted for nearly 37 percent of Russia's federal budget revenues.[4]

On the face of it, this was a dangerous state of affairs, which exposed the Russian economy and the state to the same overdependence that had exacerbated two previous crashes, in 1989–1990 and 1998. Yet the Russian government, under the steady hand of Finance Minister Aleksei Kudrin, had pursued a prudent fiscal and monetary course throughout the decade. A new Tax Code had been adopted, praised by tax experts as (on paper at least) one of the best in Europe. The budget was in surplus;[5] the state's foreign debts had been paid down; and two sovereign wealth funds had been created to store oil-export revenues, not only as a hedge against any future decline in commodity prices but also as a means of "sterilizing" export revenues, thus helping to protect the economy against inflation and an uncontrolled appreciation of the ruble.[6] By the time of the 2008 Economic Forum, Russia's two funds together held over $180 billion, equivalent to the sixth largest sovereign wealth fund in the world. In addition, the Russian Central Bank held over $550 billion in gold and foreign-exchange reserves, the third largest after Japan and China. With such an umbrella, Russia seemed secure against any storm.

Moreover, the Russian economy, even as it grew, appeared to be starting to diversify away from its extreme reliance on commodities. Only about half of the economic growth of the decade was directly due to commodity revenues; the other half came from a formidable increase in construction and retail trade. This trend, supported by a booming domestic market, was much applauded by foreign banks and analysts. It was fashionable to say that the emerging economies, Russia included, were "decoupling" from the developed ones, which were then going into recession, and this encouraged the Russian policy makers to believe that they were indeed on the right track.[7]

Yet beneath the surface there were worrisome signs. The Russian economy was overheating, as oil-export revenues mounted, and Kudrin's cautious policies of fiscal diversification and budgetary restraint were being overwhelmed by the flood of oil money.[8] Inflation was 14 percent and rising, as productive capacity and labor were stretched to the limit and wages outpaced productivity gains. Faced with an escalating trade-off between inflation and a higher ruble, the Russian Central Bank bought up oil dollars and flooded the economy with rubles. Yet despite this the ruble continued to climb, stimulating imports while squeezing exports—all classic signs of "Dutch Disease."

"Hand Over the Money!"

As money poured in to the government's coffers, the cry went up to spend it. Was it not time to rebuild Russia's ports and roads and factories and to modernize its army and navy? There was no end of good causes. Kudrin found himself besieged from all sides, not least from some of his liberal Pitertsy colleagues, such as German Gref and Gref's protégé El'vira Nabiullina (later his successor at the Economics Ministry), who campaigned for spending the oil dividend. Kudrin denounced the "barbarians" who threatened to crack his precious nest egg and warned that the flood of extra liquidity would set off uncontrollable inflation.[9] Kudrin told an interviewer from the news magazine *Itogi*:

> They are itching to get their hands on that money. You can tell them until you're blue in the face that you mustn't spend it. You see, every ruble in the economy circulates several times and drives up prices. Let's say we inject money from the Stabilization Fund into a factory. If that money is not to have an inflationary effect, the factory must generate four times the investment. But our economy is not capable of doing that. That's the arithmetic. But even after I've explained all that, they still come after me, crying, "Hand over the money!"[10]

Putin on the whole stood by his finance minister. He not only kept Kudrin in charge of finance, but in the fall of 2007, he returned Kudrin to the post of deputy prime minister (where Kudrin had previously served from 2000 and 2004) and eased Gref out of the government.[11] Yet the flood of tax revenues leaked through, despite all of Kudrin's efforts to dam it, and the state budget kept expanding.[12]

Unfortunately, the private sector did not follow Kudrin's example. Even as Kudrin paid off the state's foreign debts, the private sector—companies and individuals alike—was borrowing massively from abroad. External private debt nearly tripled in the last two years before the crash, from $106 billion at the end of 2005 to $275 billion at the end of 2007.[13] In a normally developed economy, the export revenues earned by the commodities sector would have been recycled by private financial institutions (investment banks, pension funds, insurance companies, mutual funds, and the like) that "intermediate" between private capital and investment opportunities; but in Russia, these were still weakly developed. Instead, export earnings were taxed away by the state to support state corporations and the pension and welfare system, thus increasing the weight of the state in the economy. The private sector turned instead to "hot money" from abroad—short-term lending from foreign banks, attracted to Russia by the appreciating ruble and high interest rates. Companies borrowed short money to buy other companies; individuals took out mortgages and credit cards; speculators bought stocks on margin. It was high times—so long as the foreign money remained available.[14] But beginning in 2007, as the repercussions of the U.S. housing crisis spread to Wall Street and from there to the rest of the world, lenders began pulling money back from the emerging economies, and the Russian borrowers were suddenly in trouble.

Meanwhile, the oil industry, the main engine of the economy, had begun to weaken. By 2008, the basic formula that had powered the Russian "oil miracle" of 1999–2004—"a handful of new fields producing more and hundreds losing less"—had faded. Since 2004 the oil industry had been running harder and harder for smaller and smaller gains. Upstream investment, measured in current dollars, had increased nearly 2.5 times in just three years, rising from the equivalent of $9.4 billion in 2004 to $22.9 billion in 2007.[15] But this dramatic increase had not been enough to prevent a slowdown in growth—exactly the same dynamics as in the 1980s.[16] Oil production grew by just over 2 percent per year in 2005–2007, and by 2008 output actually began declining, even as oil prices climbed to record levels. But on July 11, 2008, the price of a barrel of Brent benchmark crude peaked at $147.27—and then broke. By December 21, Brent was trading at $33.87.[17] As oil prices collapsed, they threatened to take the economy down with them.

This chapter tells the story of the crash of 2008–2009—Russia's third in a generation—and its consequences for the oil industry and its relations with the state. At the center of the story is the issue of taxes. The crash forced a wholesale reexamination of the state's tax take from the oil industry. The debate has continued for over four years and, at this writing (summer 2012), is far from over.

The good news is that a constructive dialogue has been engaged between the state and the oil industry on tax matters, marking a considerable improvement from the extreme mistrust and mutual hostility that pervaded the subject in the 1990s and throughout Putin's first two terms as president. Yet at the end of all the analysis and debate over oil taxes, it still comes down to a joust for advantage between the state and the oil companies. More fundamentally, neither side has come to terms with the longer-term problem, which is that even the most carefully wrought oil-tax reform will not solve Russia's growing dependence on oil rents, at a time when the flow of oil rents itself is increasingly vulnerable, both to diminishing returns internally and uncertainties over oil prices externally.[18] The crash and recession of 2008–2009 were an eloquent early warning of the possible consequences.

Russia's Third Crash

When the crash came in 2008 the shock was severe, precisely because the Russians had thought they had learned the lessons of the previous two. Indeed they had—but only partly. The state sector, partially insulated by its currency reserves and its rainy-day funds, held up reasonably well, despite a 14 percent drop in oil-export revenues.[19] But the private sector was badly hurt, as foreign money pulled out and credit disappeared, leaving the indebted private sector gasping for funds.[20] Once again, as in 1998, Russia came to a halt. Markets plummeted; real estate collapsed; stores and hotels and restaurants emptied out. In December 2008, I sat in the grand dining room of the Natsional' Hotel—alone but for the pianist, who played through the evening to an audience of one. When I asked where the other guests had gone, the pianist shrugged and gave the same one-word answer all Russians gave that dark fall, and which explained everything: "Krizis." Extreme optimism gave way overnight to extreme pessimism. Russians took to referring to the first decade of the 2000s as the *nulevye gody*—the "zero years."

As the price of Urals export blend plummeted, the oil companies were suddenly caught in what they called "Kudrin's scissors." The two principal taxes, the export tax and production tax, were keyed to world oil prices but were recalculated only every two months. This lag had actually benefited the companies so long as oil prices were rising, but in the fall of 2008, with prices tumbling by the day, the oil companies' cash flow turned sharply negative. They dared not fall behind on their tax payments—the Yukos Affair was still fresh in their minds—but instead they began cutting back massively on spending. Drilling contracts were suspended; electricity bills went unpaid; wells were shut in. At that rate, oil production would plummet in a matter of weeks.

The government responded with emergency ad hoc tax cuts—in particular, shortening the interval for recalculating the export tax from every two months to every two weeks[21]—and these measures, together with repeated devaluations of the ruble and massive pressure by the companies on oil-service providers, succeeded by the turn of the year in stemming the worst of the companies' red ink. But with oil prices approaching $30 per barrel, the companies insisted this was not enough, and they threatened to cut back investment and production even further in 2009. In February 2009, alarmed by the outlook in the oil sector, Putin called a high-level meeting of top government and industry officials, at the Kirishi refinery near Saint Petersburg.

"Moscow Does Not Believe in Tears"

There was irony in the choice of the setting. The Kirishi refinery, the site of so many battles of the 1990s, the birthplace of some of the largest fortunes of the Putin era—and incidentally the subject of Igor Sechin's *kandidat* dissertation a decade before—was practically a symbol of the Pitertsy and Putin's oil policies. It was not just the setting that was symbolic. The circumstances of the meeting—a classic confrontation of state leaders with the industry—must have reminded the participants of a familiar saying among the red directors of the Soviet era. "Moscow does not believe in tears, only in blood."[22] In other words, if you are not going to make the plan target, comrade, you had better show Moscow you're really bleeding—or else.

That was more or less the mood as the oil generals made a desperate case for more tax concessions to support investment. But Putin, visibly annoyed by the oil generals' pleading, was unyielding. Pointing out that the tax cuts already granted to the industry totaled some 500 billion rubles (or about $17 billion), Putin commented with a touch of sarcasm, "Yes, the oil companies have to work in more difficult conditions. But everyone is having to work in more difficult conditions."[23] The only further concession Putin was willing to make was a temporary exemption to the export tax for new fields in East Siberia. Clearly the oil generals had not shown enough blood.

Indeed, Putin's speech could have been given, with only minor changes, by any Soviet general secretary. "We are entitled to expect," he told the assembled oilmen, "that the monies we leave in the industry's hands will be invested . . . in production, and not spent on bonuses and other things that are far from high-priority given current conditions." It was abundantly clear from the premier's words that he saw no essential difference in this respect between a private and a state-owned oil company.[24] Executives and shareholders, in others words, were expected to do their patriotic duty.

Yet buried in the official minutes—known as the *protokol,* the business end of any official Russian meeting—there was a brief paragraph calling for a detailed study of the entire oil-tax system.[25] This bit was probably little more than diplomatic balm to soothe the oil generals, but it turned out to be highly significant. For the first time, the oil-tax system created in 2000–2002 would be subjected to a rigorous economic analysis, and a systematic set of alternatives would be proposed.

A thoroughgoing analysis was long overdue. Throughout the decade, the issue of oil taxation had been entangled with the larger political agenda of rebuilding state power. The oil-tax system had been adopted in 2000–2002 as much in response to the government's political goals as its budgetary needs and was subsequently enforced by coercion or the threat of it, without much regard for the longer-term consequences for the industry. As designed by Shatalov and Kudrin, the oil-tax system was simple, blunt, and easy to wield. Moreover, when combined with aggressive prosecutorial power, the tax weapon served to strike fear and impose obedience. For the Kremlin, capturing a greater share of the oil rents was not simply a matter of providing funds for the budget; it was a central part of the struggle for political dominance. The debate then had been bitter and confrontational, and complex technical issues had become highly politicized. The result, as one Russian commentator put it, was a "primitivization" of oil policy.[26] The state players—and in this respect the liberals were not much different from the siloviki—tended to discount the oilmen's complaints and warnings as so much crying wolf.

But by 2009 some important things had changed. The bitterness of the Yukos Affair was beginning to fade. In addition, as one consequence of the Affair, a number of high-placed state officials had acquired (or increased) personal stakes in the oil industry. The state's tax-collection bureaucracy had become more professional and competent over the course of the decade and potentially better able to administer a more sophisticated system. Above all, the crash of 2008 and the decline of oil production in that year had concentrated the minds of all the players and demonstrated the negative side effects of the existing tax system. Thus, in the wake of the crash and during the recession that followed, the oil industry had a fresh opportunity to make its case, and key government players appeared somewhat more prepared to listen—at least, so long as the krizis lasted.

2005–2009: Four Years of Debate and Half-Measures

In actual fact, the debate over oil taxation had never really stopped; indeed, it had resumed with fresh urgency as early as 2005, when the performance of the oil industry had begun to falter. The spectacular rise in oil prices had caused the tax take to soar far beyond what its creators had envisioned. As Shatalov acknowledged candidly in a speech late that year:

> When we worked out the formula in 2001, it was next to impossible to imagine that Russian oil prices would reach 50–60 USD per barrel, and its performance was expected to be within an 18–25 USD range. Lucrative prices generated additional revenues for the Government and increased the tax pressure on the oil companies. The resultant taxes grab more than 90% of their additional income earned on the excess of delivery price above the 25 USD per barrel baseline price.[27]

By the end of 2005 Shatalov had come to believe that the tax burden on the industry had become too heavy. "Surely," Shatalov concluded, "we need to find ways to improve oil sector taxation." What was true in 2005, at $50 per barrel, became a steadily more urgent problem as oil prices continued to climb.

The easiest solution, beginning in 2006, was to grant tax holidays to encourage investment in new provinces such as East Siberia. This was essentially a Band-Aid approach, which did not require tinkering with the basic design of the system or threatening the state's oil revenues. The government's main objective was to encourage the companies to develop oil for the high-priority East Siberia–Pacific Ocean pipeline. To this end, the government granted tax holidays for upstream projects in the provinces of Yakutiia (Sakha Republic), Irkutsk, and Krasnoiarsk.[28] In addition the government approved a modest differentiation in the production tax (NDPI), granting a 70 percent reduction for so-called hard-to-recover reserves in selected fields that were more than 80 percent depleted—a measure that Finance Minister Aleksei Kudrin had long opposed as an invitation to corruption. However, the impact of these ad hoc tax reductions proved largely symbolic, amounting to less than a quarter of a billion dollars in 2007, compared with total upstream investment by the Russian majors that year of nearly $16 billion.[29]

In May 2008 Dmitri Medvedev became president, and Putin moved over to the White House as prime minister. He took many of the key officials and functions of the Presidential Administration with him. One of the migrants was Igor Sechin. He had initially been tipped to take over as head of the prime minister's apparatus, the equivalent of his previous spot in the Kremlin, and he was said to want the job—but in a surprise move, Putin named him deputy prime minister instead, with responsibility for the energy sector. Sechin and Medvedev had long been on poor terms, particularly since the Gazprom-Rosneft affair, and keeping Sechin on as Putin's chief of staff would have caused needless friction with the new president.

Sechin into the Breach

At this moment, just weeks before the crash, oil prices were still rocketing upward, but Russia's oil production had already begun to fall. Sechin was given the mission of turning oil production around by the end of the year.[30] For the purpose he was given authority over the Ministry of Energy, plus the Ministry of Natural Resources and a handful of civilian industry departments connected to energy. He had been, in effect, thrown into the breach. At his first press conference, shortly after his appointment, he was asked point-blank by a reporter, "What's to be done about the falling oil production?" to which Sechin answered,

"Do you think it's falling? Let's wait and see until the end of the year. I'm convinced there will be no fall, but an increase."[31]

The deputy prime minister position was something new for Sechin. For nearly two decades he had been, in effect, Putin's chief of staff. He had been the man in the shadows, the "gray eminence of the Kremlin," as the Russian media frequently called him; now he was in the limelight, as the public face of the government for all energy matters. He had never had direct responsibility for managing a large bureaucracy or meeting production targets; now he was directly under the gun, answerable for an industry in difficulty. He was not an oil professional by background, and except for his previous four years as chairman of the board of Rosneft—and his dissertation of a decade before—he had no experience in the oil industry.

Yet Sechin remained a very powerful figure, and by all accounts a man of considerable ability. From the standpoint of the oil companies, he represented a well-placed champion who was likely to be committed to their cause—not only because he was now directly answerable for the success of their sector but also because of his position at Rosneft (which from this time on came to be more like that of a de facto CEO). Moreover, Sechin brought with him some welcome adjustments, in the form of further ad hoc tax concessions aimed at encouraging the oil companies to work harder.[32] Finance Minister Kudrin, ever vigilant, estimated that the new round of concessions were worth an extra 100 billion rubles (then about $3.7 billion) per year to the oil industry.

But the oil companies knew from experience that Sechin was also certain to be a demanding taskmaster, a point that was driven home within two weeks of his appointment, when he toured West Siberia and ordered the oil companies to halt the decline in production in return for the tax breaks he had just brought them.[33] The oil companies were not particularly reassured by this mixture of jam and jawbone, especially when Sechin brought over from the Ministry of Tax Collections a tax lawyer, Anton Ustinov, who had been a leading figure in the tax campaign against Yukos and the other oil companies.[34] The companies, though disturbed by the implied threat, continued to insist loudly that the ad hoc tax concessions were not enough. They were essentially short-term responses to long-term problems; it was the entire structure of the oil-tax system that needed to be reexamined.

The government's energy bureaucracy, however, was poorly equipped to respond. Heading the Ministry of Energy was a new minister, Sergei Shmatko, an economist-turned-businessman whose previous job had been in nuclear power. The ministry had no team of specialists in oil finance and taxation capable of going up against the formidable technical expertise of Aleksei Kudrin's Ministry of Finance.[35] When the crash came, Sechin realized he needed a full-time team of oil professionals at the Energy Ministry with a recognized figure to head them. He reached into Rosneft and drafted an experienced senior oilman, Sergei Kudriashov. (Kudriashov, readers will recall, had been Yukos's last general director at Yuganskneftegaz, whom Sergei Bogdanchikov had promoted to be his senior vice president for exploration and production.) In December 2008, as the crisis deepened in the oil industry, Sechin moved Kudriashov over to the Ministry of Energy as deputy minister.

But Kudriashov had been on the job less than two months when the Kirishi conference took place and the ministry was ordered to review the oil-tax system and propose improvements. The stakes were high: the conference had been an embarrassing failure for the oil industry and there was no room for another mistake. Following the conference, Sechin ordered Shmatko and Kudriashov to produce a tax-reform plan that would hold up against the Finance Ministry and make the industry's case to the prime minister. He gave them six months; instead, it took them two years.

Oil and Taxes

Designing a taxation system for oil is notoriously tricky. The general theory sounds simple. Where the state is the sovereign owner of the oil in the ground, as in Russia, a good oil-tax regime is one that splits oil rents between the industry and the state so that the oil companies make a reasonable return on their capital plus an appropriate reward for the risks taken, while the state receives fair value for its nonrenewable wealth, including a share of any "windfall profits" in periods of high prices. The final test, of course, is whether enough oil is produced and enough oil rent is generated to support the needs of both the industry and the state, however defined.

The difficulty lies, first of all, in those innocent-sounding words, "reasonable," "appropriate," and "fair." But where the devil really lurks is in the word "rent." Defining and measuring rent requires taking into account the stream of costs and returns from an oilfield over its lifetime and making bets on a host of unknowns and unknowables, the most important of the latter being world oil prices. A tax that is "reasonable and appropriate" at the early stages of a field or province may no longer be so toward the end of its life; and similarly, a tax that is "fair" at low prices may not be so at high prices, and so forth. There is often disagreement over what "risk" means. Moreover, costs are not static; tracking and recognizing the increases is another challenge. Despite the sophisticated economic and legal concepts developed by oil-tax experts, actual tax regimes are more the product of negotiation than theory. It is little wonder that Alexander Kemp, a leading authority on petroleum tax systems around the world, concludes in his classic, *Petroleum Rent Collection around the World,* "The great majority of fiscal systems do not perform very efficiently as collectors of economic rents."[36]

But oil-tax systems do more than just collect rents; they are used by states to pursue a multitude of objectives. Taxes provide revenues to the state budget, but they are also used to redistribute wealth (by transferring rents to favored individuals or sectors or causes) and to encourage certain behaviors or discourage others. These objectives are often only poorly compatible with one another, and when the fiscal system is used as a kind of all-purpose tool to advance them all, the result is confusion.

The Russian oil-tax system is a good illustration. As we have seen, it consists essentially of a tax on exports *(poshlina)* and a tax on production (NDPI), both keyed to world oil prices, and thus levied on gross revenues rather than profits. For a number of years, the combined tax rate on crude oil had been set at 65 percent of the Urals export price, and the production tax at 22 percent, for a combined total of 87 percent, levied on the portion of the export price above a threshold of $25/barrel. It is often described as a "super-royalty tax."

Royalty-based systems are not unique to Russia; they have long been used in other oil-producing countries, and they have well-known shortcomings, the main one being that they tend to discourage producers from investing in new fields or in prolonging the lives of old ones. But for the Russian government in the late 1990s and the early 2000s, these minuses had been far outweighed by the pluses. The system was simple to administer, since it did not require knowledge of the oil companies' costs or profits, only of their gross revenues, and it ignored the concept of rent altogether, thus bypassing the whole problem of measurement and information. It had been designed primarily to enable a weak state with a primitive tax bureaucracy to capture quickly a greater share of the export revenues accruing to the oil industry when oil prices started to rise after

1998. It reflected the state of the industry as it was in the early 2000s, when production and transportation costs were low, the ruble was cheap, and the state did not trust the industry to report its growing profits.

In addition, the designers of the Tax Code had had another goal in view: to keep domestic oil prices low. An export tax serves as a "wedge" between the export price and the domestic netback, which has the effect, at least in theory, of keeping down prices to the consumer at home. It is a convenient lever—again, easy to apply and administer—but it comes with a downside: it introduces economic distortions, by favoring overconsumption in the domestic market and thus lowering efficiency of demand; but it also creates potential political mischief, since lowering or removing the export tax, once it is in place, causes domestic fuel prices to spring back up, which is both inflationary and unpopular. Over the years, these nonfiscal issues have made Russian policy makers (and especially the Ministry of Finance) reluctant to part with the export tax.[37]

However, as Shatalov had observed as early as 2005, what had been a rough-hewn but functional system when implemented in the first half of the 2000s gradually became destructive as the starting conditions changed. Oil prices were higher, but so were the companies' costs. Critical inputs such as steel pipes, rigs, electricity, and skilled labor had all doubled in cost over the decade, cutting into the companies' profits—but not cutting their tax bills. By the eve of the 2008 crash, the tax system was taking well over 90 percent of the oil companies' upstream profits at the margin. The companies had little incentive to move out of their traditional provinces to invest in new fields in new areas. A modeling study of twenty-seven major oil prospects in 2008 showed that only one—the Russkoe field, one of the last remaining large new fields in West Siberia—was economic to develop under the existing tax regime at the $65-per-barrel average oil price of that year.[38] Faced with such unfavorable economics, the Russian oil companies redoubled their efforts in older fields already under production, mainly by increasing infill drilling using traditional production methods, while limiting their investment in frontier regions such as East Siberia or in new production technologies.

But high tax rates were not the only problem. In addition, the state began tinkering with the tax system to modify the balance between exports of crude oil and refined products in favor of the latter (a long-standing policy objective of the Putin leadership, as we have seen). The first change came in 2005, with the introduction of lower export-tax rates to encourage the export of refined products instead of crude oil. This reflected the view of the leadership, dating back to the early days in Saint Petersburg, that refined products were more "advanced" than crude, since they required processing and therefore embodied additional value, compared with the "simple" production of crude oil. Thus, encouraging product exports (in this view) contributed to Russia's overall objective of moving up the value chain in the world economy, and the way the tax planners did this was by lowering the export-tax rate on products relative to crude. By 2008, while the export tax rate on crude oil was 65 percent of the Urals export blend oil price (above $25 per barrel), for light products (mainly gasoline, diesel, and jet fuel) the export tax was set at 73 percent of the crude export tax, and for heavy products such as fuel oil it was set at only 38 percent. The system worked as advertised: refined-product exports became far more profitable than crude exports, and product exports, especially of fuel oil, boomed.

The only problem was that this arrangement did not add value; it destroyed it. If a ton of Russian oil in Rotterdam fetched $775 when sold as crude oil, it earned only $750 when sold as products, given the large share of low-value fuel oil in the average Russian refined product barrel. In addition, transporting products to market cost much more than transporting crude. In short, the system was costing a fortune to both the companies and the state budget. Moreover, it was distorting the internal economics of the oil industry, by shifting industry's cash flow downstream, while the upstream became barely profitable. The system of subsidies actually rewarded exports of the least valuable refined products, produced by the oldest and most primitive refineries. This led to a mushrooming of new mini-refineries built for a fast buck, known in Russian as *samovars*.[39] Meanwhile, the companies throttled back upstream investment wherever possible, spending just enough to maintain production, keep their licenses, and stay out of trouble.

Thus a system that had been initially designed to produce revenue (and secondarily to protect domestic consumers, via the wedge) became distorted by the addition of a policy objective essentially based on ideological grounds. But the resulting displacement of value away from the upstream to the downstream amounted by 2008 to some $10–$15 billion per year, or more than half the companies' total upstream investment. Thus the policy starved the upstream, while it also failed to stimulate a modernization of the refinery sector, since it encouraged the oil companies to concentrate on producing low-value heavy products such as fuel oil.[40]

The Goat and the Cabbage

The Ministry of Energy spent 2009–2010 conducting an elaborate study of the oil-tax system. Their findings dramatized the fragility of the Russian production base under the existing system. Most Russian oil came from older Soviet-era wells with production rates of 10 tons (75 barrels) per day or less, the bulk of which were only marginally profitable after taxes, even at record oil prices. Any new well not producing at least 25 tons (180 barrels) per day was not worth drilling, yet such prospects were increasingly few. At existing tax rates, the sum total of new wells that could be drilled each year without loss would add less than 40 million tons per year (800,000 barrels per day) of oil, not enough to sustain Russian output. Findings such as these were eye-openers, because they dispelled the myth, still widespread in the political class, that Russia had unlimited resources of cheap oil.

But the ministry's findings also brought good news: with careful redesign the tax system could be optimized to stabilize oil production, at least for the coming decade. They proposed five key changes: lowering export taxes, eliminating the gap in export-tax rates between crude oil and refined products, abolishing ad hoc regional tax holidays, reducing the production tax for new and small fields, and creating a new profit-based tax for new projects. Beyond the technical details, what mattered was the crucial headline: that by reforming the structure of the oil-tax system the state could simultaneously increase production, stimulate the companies to operate more efficiently, and maintain the flow of oil rents—and all at no loss in state revenues. The proposed reform was a classic win-win proposition, or as the Russians say, it promised to satisfy both the goat and the cabbage. As Aleksey Kondrashov, a noted expert on Russian tax law who had played a key role in the oil-tax review, commented in a series of articles summarizing its recommendations, "The main problem will be solved: The Russian oil-tax system will attract, not repel, investment in Russian oil—our source of wealth and our comparative advantage."[41]

This left two key questions unanswered, however: First, what would happen if the government failed to act on the Ministry of Energy's findings? And second, what would be the broader implications of optimizing the tax structure for the state's other objectives, such as opening up new provinces or optimizing the export mix or keeping down domestic fuel prices? In early 2010 Sechin and Kudriashov ordered a further study to come up with the answers.

The "General Plan"

By late summer they presented a draft "General Plan" (*General'naia Skhema*, often referred to as the *Genskhema*) for the oil industry to 2020. It contained two radical findings. The first was that if the tax regime remained unchanged, oil production would decline sharply after about 2015. Ad hoc tax holidays made little difference; only a thoroughgoing reform would head off a steep drop. Second, the industry needed to shift its focus to where most of the remaining oil reserves still lay—not East Siberia and other frontier regions but the older oil provinces, and above all the industry's traditional core, the Middle Ob' region of West Siberia. Trying to make up the decline in the older regions with production from new ones, through the use of ad hoc tax breaks and subsidies, would fail, because the new regions simply did not have enough ready reserves to fill the gap.

This message challenged several long-standing energy doctrines, which stressed the development of new provinces and the construction of vast new pipeline systems to support them. But there was a further implication: the tax regime needed to be redesigned to encourage the industry to work more efficiently in the brownfields, raising recovery rates through enhanced-recovery techniques while holding back costs.

In October 2010, the Energy Ministry and the companies were summoned to appear again before Putin, Sechin, and Kudrin, this time in the Volga refining town of Samara. Twenty months had passed since the February 2009 meeting in Kirishi, held in the middle of the krizis. This time the Energy Ministry and the companies had done their homework, but would they be heard?

Disappointment in Samara

In Samara the Energy Minister, Shmatko, presented the oil scenarios to Putin. The gathering included most of the players who had been present at Kirishi twenty-one months before. Ninety percent of the reserves of new fields and 30 percent of those of older fields were uneconomic to develop under the existing fiscal regime, the energy minister told Putin. "At this moment, the industry does not have a package of large fields ready to begin production," he said.[42] And the presentation's headline was loud and clear: if there were no changes, Russian oil production would drop by 2020 to less than 400 million tons (8 million barrels per day), 20 percent less than in 2010.

Putin, however, was only partly persuaded. In his closing remarks he chose to focus on the parts of Shmatko's message that promised a basic continuation of the status quo. He repeated his familiar themes: the importance of the development of East Siberia, the strategic expansion of the export pipeline system, the primacy of exporting refined products over crude, and so forth. He acknowledged the key recommendations of the proposed fiscal reform. But when it came to acting on them, Putin temporized. He ordered the Ministry of Finance and the Ministry of Energy to "find a healthy, careful balance, a golden mean, between the investment needs of the oil companies and the task of providing stable funding for the budget." But the specific examples he gave suggested he thought the system of granting ad hoc tax breaks and holidays was perfectly adequate and that no deeper reform was urgently necessary.[43] In sum, Putin's basic response was "Stay the course."

Perhaps the most important reason for his response came from outside the windows of the conference room: global oil prices had been rising steadily all through 2010, sapping the political urgency of the oil-tax reform issue and lessening the appetite for any radical changes. The logic of the *Genskhema,* after all, had been that to preserve the central objective of the oil-tax system— capturing oil rents for the budget—concessions in other policy objectives (East Siberia, "value added" exports, pipelines to the East, and so forth) were needed. But as oil prices headed back above $80 per barrel (which had been the reference price for much of the ministry's modeling), policy makers could reassure themselves that oil investment was profitable again and oil production would keep on growing. Why change anything?

The Search for the Golden Mean

Putin had instructed the Ministry of Energy and the Ministry of Finance to find the "golden mean," but he had offered no guidance on where to find it—he might as well have said "golden fleece." Over the fall months of 2010 the bureaucrats of both sides held meeting after inconclusive meeting, as they argued over competing plans for reform and searched for compromise.[44] But the golden mean proved elusive. The two sides sparred over various compromise export-tax formulas, so arcane in their complexity that they came to be known jokingly as "the telephone numbers."[45] (Commenting on one variant called "60-66-55-86," one participant cracked, "If I dial that number, who will answer?") The first result of their labors, formalized in a decree issued in December 2010, was an ultracautious plan that promised only to equalize the export-tax rates on heavy and light products over a three-year period. It made no provision for lowering the export-tax rate on crude. The Ministry of Finance had stoutly blocked anything more far-reaching.[46]

The Russian media tend to dismiss the Ministry of Finance as a crowd of accountants with green eyeshades and narrow minds, but the team that represented the Finance Ministry on the oil-tax reform debate was of high quality. Kudrin himself took no public part in the debate over oil-tax reform, leaving it to his deputy, Sergei Shatalov, to represent the Ministry of Finance. Shatalov, even though he was considered the father of the oil-tax system, had been one of its earliest critics, but his position at this time could best be described as unhurried. Intellectually, Shatalov knew that the tax rates were too high and that the system needed to be fixed; but as deputy finance minister, he had a budget to balance. Without being precisely obstructive, Shatalov was cautious about backing any sudden changes in the existing system. What would be the consequences for budget revenues? he wanted to know. What about the impact of lower export taxes on domestic fuel prices?

The Ministry of Energy, armed with its numbers, argued for a rapid and complete equalization of tax rates between crude oil and products, thus eliminating the subsidy for product exports. One might have expected the oil companies to line up unanimously in support of this position, but in reality they were divided. Companies that had invested heavily in new refinery capacity (such as Tatneft) or produced large amounts of fuel oil (both Tatneft and Bashneft) wanted a gradual phaseout or none at all.[47] In Bashkortostan, several of the older refineries had recently been taken over by a conglomerate called Sistema, which was rumored to have good connections in Moscow. But even inside each oil company, the upstream (which stood to benefit from the equalization) faced resistance from the downstream (which stood to lose money). Meanwhile, not a few well-heeled Russian influentials were said to have invested in samovars, and they too presumably weighed in against any overhasty changes.

Somewhat lost in all the debate over refined-product exports were the two upstream issues that had prompted the reform effort in the first place, namely, how to encourage more investment in mature areas and frontier provinces. The Ministry of Energy had proposed instituting a new profit-based tax, dubbed a "tax on supplementary income," but the concept was new and unfamiliar, and these talks too bogged down in details.[48] Shatalov, as usual, was ultracautious. The ministry's models were impressive, he conceded, but could such a new system be properly administered? The chief virtue of the existing system was its simplicity. Would the tax collectors have the information needed to monitor a profit-based system or one that took account of fine differences from one oil-field to another?

Meanwhile, as the spring of 2011 arrived, oil prices continued to rise. As they did so, they weakened the government's willingness to grant further tax breaks of any kind. When they hit $100 per barrel, even Sechin, who had fought a steady rearguard battle to salvage the export-tax exemption for Vankor and the other East Siberian fields, finally gave up and declared that there would be no export-tax exemptions for new fields.[49] On May 1, the export-tax exemptions for the three largest East Siberian fields were rescinded. The government would promise only that if the oil price fell back below $95, the question would be reexamined.[50]

Ironically, it was rising oil prices that finally broke the logjam of the endless interagency discussions, by creating a new problem that policy makers had no choice but to react to. The higher oil prices went, the greater the gap between the export tax on crude and the export tax on products, and the more irresistibly profitable product exports became. Fuel oil, diesel, and low-grade gasoline flooded out of the country—and as they did so, gasoline prices soared at the pump inside Russia. Suddenly the politicians remembered they were in an election year (legislative elections were due in December). In some regions local governments slapped price controls on gasoline, which caused the oil companies to withhold supplies to those regions, resulting in localized gasoline shortages. Putin, faced now with a gasoline krizis, muttered darkly about "conspiracy" on the part of the oil companies.[51] In July 2011, he called yet another gathering of the industry, once again at the Kirishi refinery.

Back to Kirishi: "An Absolutely Absurd Situation"

It was the same setting as in early 2009, with mostly the same industry and government players and Putin in the chair. "We are proud of your work and achievements," he began, amiably enough, but from that point on he read them the riot act.[52] The oil companies had deceived him, Putin charged. They had promised to use the "premium" they received from the lower export-tax rates on products to invest in modern refineries. Instead, they had created a unique kind of "technological offshore haven," by exporting fuel oil and paying the proceeds to themselves in the form of dividends. It was, he concluded, "an absolutely absurd situation." "But," Putin glowered at the assembled executives, "I wish to remind you: You work in the Russian Federation." There then followed a blunt restatement of the principles Putin had first enunciated on the campaign trail a decade before: "When you receive a license to use mineral resources, they remain the property of the Russian people, they are our common national property."

Having wielded the *knut,* however, Putin then delivered a bit of cake. He threw out the timid December 2010 decree and substituted for it an immediate leveling of export-tax rates on products, to go into effect October 1. In effect, he sided with the Ministry of Energy against the Ministry of Finance, with Sechin against Kudrin. Under the new formula, whose "telephone number" this time was 60-66-90, the tax on crude exports was lowered from $65 to $60 per barrel, and the export-tax rate was made the same for all refined products at 66 percent of the crude rate—with the exception of gasoline, exports of which would be taxed at 90 percent of the crude rate, to make sure that gasoline stayed inside the country. The implications were substantial. Under the new formula, the incentive to export heavy products such as fuel oil practically disappeared, while crude exports became much more attractive. On balance, it put more money into the hands of the oil companies, available in principle for upstream investment. As one observer put it, "It was the same as an overnight $40 per barrel increase in the world price of oil."[53]

But the relieved oil executives were not yet out of the woodshed. Lest the oil companies take advantage of the new formula to maximize crude exports and cut back on refining, Putin warned, he would hold them to strict targets for investment in advanced refinery capacity. To make sure they met their targets, he would make them sign pledges. If they did not comply, he threatened to cut their crude-export quotas and even to roll back their dividends and confiscate ill-gotten profits.

Russian observers, pondering the significance of Kirishi-2 and the "60-66" decree, were divided between those who hailed the modest progress achieved and those who concluded gloomily that nothing had changed. For the optimists, there had been a breakthrough, and the road to more far-reaching fiscal reforms was now open. For the pessimists, the oil companies would now play it safe, investing only as much in new refinery capacity as would keep them out of trouble, while preserving their margins. The likely outcome, they predicted darkly, was that the flood of fuel oil exports would give way to a flood of diesel.[54]

Still, some money stood to flow back to the upstream. But 60-66 was not quite the win-win that had been advertised. The state stood to lose some revenues—as much as $10 billion per year, estimated a source inside the Ministry of Finance.[55] This was bound to cool the enthusiasm of the Ministry of Finance for further steps.

The main drawback to the present situation is that it is so obviously temporary. The "60-66-90" formula is only a decree, not a law; therefore it can be altered or rescinded at any time. The government has repeatedly changed its mind in the past: why should it not do so again? Given this history of uncertainty, the oil companies are unlikely to respond with higher investment. Yet if they do not, the more likely it is that the government will withdraw even the modest concessions made to date, resorting to coercion instead, as Putin has threatened to do.

Conclusion

Several things are significant about the oil-tax issue. The first is the law of unintended consequences. A tax system whose main virtues were simplicity and ease of application, and which has been highly effective in capturing oil rents for the state, has done its job altogether too well, becoming a serious source of distortions and disincentives as oil prices rose and production costs increased, threatening the future of oil production.

The second significant point is that after the krizis of 2008 policy makers responded with a high-quality debate and a serious effort to find solutions. This was a welcome change from the mistrust and lack of communication that had prevailed between the state and the oil industry in the early 2000s, and which had only worsened in the wake of the Yukos Affair. Both sides, for example, scrutinized closely the cost assumptions used by the oil companies and were able to agree on realistic numbers, which were then used in the modeling that underpinned the *Genskhema*. As a result, a degree of consensus was achieved, particularly on three key conclusions: that subsidizing refined-product exports had turned out to be an expensive mistake; that profit-based taxation was the best way to encourage investment in new fields; and that more attention needed to be given to fiscal means to boost total recovery in older oilfields. Conceptually, the most important of these three is the return to active consideration of profit-based taxation. Its most likely area of implementation may be for large ring-fenced projects, where the flow of profit can be more easily measured.

Yet this improved dialogue between the industry and the state has yet to produce decisive action, other than the placeholder "60-66-90" decree, and this despite the fact that the main message from the *Genskhema* exercise was the urgency of the situation. The facts are now clear, the solutions ready to hand; yet the bureaucracy advances slowly, held back by internal battles over design and implementation and above all by resistance from the Ministry of Finance. Why is progress so slow?

The first reason is revenue. Oil taxes, precisely because they make up such a large part of the state's budget, are too important to take chances with. The temptation is strong to proceed by small steps.

The second is the complex mix of nonrevenue objectives pursued through fiscal policy. Even though there is growing acceptance that tax breaks for refined products or for frontier development are counterproductive, or that the "wedge effect" from export taxes does not actually benefit the consumer, these policies have built up strong constituencies behind them, and the result is resistance to rapid change.

The third reason was the return of high oil prices after the crash of 2008–2009. Falling prices and revenues concentrate the mind, but rising prices dissipate the will. Although far-sighted officials were more worried than ever by the addictive effects of high oil prices, they were a minority. A key event in this connection was the abrupt departure of finance minister Aleksei Kudrin in November 2011. For Kudrin, the state's resumption of breakneck spending, especially the planned increases in military programs, was the last straw, and he rebelled. But for most officials, it was back to business as usual.[56]

For all these reasons, full implementation of the oil-tax reform will likely be slow. But behind this there looms a larger problem, which is that fiscal reform has come to seem to all sides a panacea, obviating the need for other reforms. For the companies, tax reform is the cure-all that will stimulate investment and put the industry back on the road to profitability and growth. For the government, tax policy is the most effective tool for achieving a wide range of objectives, both fiscal and nonfiscal, while avoiding any other changes. Oil-tax reform, in other words, has come to be a substitute for other kinds of reform in oil policy. This is undesirable and counterproductive; fiscal policy is being asked to carry too heavy a load.

One reason this is so, however, is that the other main component of the state's interface with the oil industry, the system of administrative regulation, works poorly. This is the subject of the next chapter.

chapter 10

Strong Thumbs, Weak Fingers: How the State Regulates the Oil Industry

> *In Russia today there are more than twice as many bureaucrats as there were in the Soviet Union, and they make good money. There's not enough shoe-leather to gather all the signatures.*
>
> —Vladimir Bogdanov, CEO, Surgutneftegaz

If the tax system has a reasonably clear primary objective—to produce revenue for the state—the same cannot be said of the other main instrument for state control of the oil industry, the regulatory system. Here the picture looks quite different. In place of one central objective, there is a multitude, which shift over time, with no clear ranking among them. Instead of one principal agency in charge, there are many, which compete with one another for turf and influence. Instead of strong ministers with clear authority, there are weak ones, who preside over divided agencies. The rules they are charged with applying are frequently confused and contradictory. The regulatory system's one great strength is its power to investigate and prosecute, which it does with a will, but to little constructive effect. It is, in short, a system of "strong thumbs and weak fingers."[1]

A common caricature, especially in the Russian media, is that the ills of the bureaucracy are due to incompetence and corruption. This is a rich vein in Russian literature. "Fools and bad roads" was Gogol's famous phrase. "They are all stealing," grumbled Karamzin.[2] Clearly there are problems on both counts, but these by themselves are not adequate explanations. Nor are they universally true. There are many well-trained and hard-working people in the ministries and agencies of the Russian government, people with a strong scientific culture and sincere belief in their work. This chapter will have a number of critical things to say about the Russian bureaucracy, but one should begin by paying tribute to its strengths. One man who symbolized the best of a distinguished tradition of Russian oil science and policy was Nikolai Lisovskii, who served as first deputy head of the formidable Central Commission on Oilfield Development (known as TsKR) until his death in 2009.[3] Let us begin with him.

Nikolai Lisovskii: "One Must Respect the Oil"

I spent an afternoon with Nikolai Lisovskii on a hot summer's day in Moscow, as he reflected on a half century of oil wisdom. As the veteran head of the oil section of the TsKR for the previous two decades, Lisovskii was the man who gave or withheld the state's approval of the oil companies' field development plans (known in the industry as "FDPs"). A dignified-looking gentleman then in his mid-seventies, he had a square jaw and gray eyes that gave him a severe official look on first meeting, but when he unexpectedly smiled, his grin was merry, even slightly impish. His sense of humor was legendary, as was his skill as a geologist. In 2011 a major oil discovery in East Siberia was named after him.[4]

"What makes an oilfield unique is that it is invisible," Lisovskii mused. "A reservoir engineer is like a doctor. He has to make a diagnosis through indirect signs; but unlike the doctor the oilman has no post-mortem to open up the patient and confirm the diagnosis after the fact." After a pause, he went on, "Unlike doctors, oilmen can't bury their mistakes. They're already buried." Lisovskii was smiling broadly now, as he got to his point. "But we can find them."

The TsKR was inherited from Soviet times. Founded in 1963, it is the organ responsible for pronouncing on how much a new field must produce, and by what methods, once an official estimate of reserves has been approved by the State Committee on Reserves, and for monitoring the operator's subsequent observance of the plan. In Soviet times this role put the TsKR in the direct line of fire from political leaders who demanded ever higher production. As an official history of the TsKR ruefully concedes, those pressures were not always successfully resisted.[5] But within their limited power, technical specialists like Lisovskii tried to balance political demands and sound oilfield practice, while championing promising innovations, frequently against the resistance of the industry and its institutes.

After the Soviet Union broke up and the USSR Ministry of Oil disappeared, the TsKR was shunted about, first to the Ministry of Energy, then finally to the Ministry of Natural Resources, where it is located today. In the 1990s it had no funding and no full-time staffing, and its rulings were widely ignored by the new private companies. Lisovskii is widely credited with keeping it alive through the dark days. He was proud of the role of the TsKR as a defender of sound oilfield practice. "Political regimes come and go, but the TsKR remains," he liked to say. Lisovskii was equally philosophical about Russia's return to the market and private enterprise, but it clearly pained him to see oil treated as a mere commodity. "It is absurd," he declared, "that a liter of mineral water costs more than a liter of gasoline. Business is business, but one must respect the oil." At bottom, Lisovskii was an oil romantic.

This basic outlook is not uncommon in the institutes and agencies that regulate the Russian oil industry, particularly among the older generation. A legacy of strong scientific and engineering culture is frequently mixed with a lingering anti-economic bias inherited from Soviet times. This helps to account for one of the most prominent features of the Russian regulatory system, a widespread mistrust of the post-Soviet oil industry, a theme to which we return later on.

Yet Lisovskii was open to new ideas coming from the private sector and from the foreign companies, and he used the TsKR as a means of introducing those ideas to the generally conservative establishment of the oil institutes. In the mid-2000s, in the midst of the Yukos Affair and the politically charged controversy over fraccing and other "barbaric" methods, keeping an open mind required courage. The Russian oil companies, as well as Western oilmen like Joe Mach, respected Lisovskii. He was smart, he was dedicated, and he was honest.

They do not necessarily have the same high opinion, however, of the general run of the TsKR's *eksperty* (Mikhail Khodorkovsky's dismissive remarks about them, quoted in Chapter 7, were unusual only in that he made them in a published interview), and they fume over the TsKR's slowness and general rigidity. There is general agreement that there is a wide gap between the scientific excellence of leading figures like Lisovskii and the conservatism and inefficiency—and increasingly the corruption—of the bureaucracy as a whole.

Yet when Russian oilmen and analysts criticize the poor performance of the regulatory system for oil, it is not corruption or incompetence that they point to as the root causes. There are, in fact, three more fundamental problems: The first is the way the system originated and evolved. The second is the side effects of the recentralization of power. The third is confusion and conflict over goals.

384

The Many-Chambered Nautilus

A bewildering array of state ministries, agencies, committees, commissions, and institutes oversees every aspect of the oil companies' activity. The main regulatory bodies—most importantly, the "Big Three" (the Ministry of Natural Resources, the Ministry of Economic Development, and the Ministry of Energy) but also a dozen other lesser ones—develop outlooks and set policy, license exploration and production, conduct regional surveys, register reserves, conduct tenders and auctions, approve or disapprove production technologies, control access to pipeline transportation and exports, and set transportation tariffs. Other state agencies oversee environment and safety, privatization, competition, labor and welfare, and much more.

The reason the structure of the Russian regulatory system is so complex is that it was not created all at once but evolved without plan, driven by the changing ideologies and politics of the Soviet period, the Yeltsin years, and the Putin era. Each period has added a new set of agencies and missions, without replacing the ones that came before. Thus since the mid-1980s the Russian state has evolved through three stages in its relationship to the economy, from total owner of a centrally planned command economy, to a largely passive player in a laissez-faire "wild east" market economy, and finally to dominant partner in a system of state capitalism. Each of these phases has left its mark on the regulatory system applied to oil and gas. The result rather resembles the multiple chambers of a nautilus shell.

Phase One: The Soviet Foundation

With the collapse of the Soviet system in 1991, the main state agencies charged with planning and allocation—Gosplan, Gossnab (supplies), Gostrud (labor), Gostekhnika (research and development), and others—abruptly disappeared. But many of the more specialized technical offices lived on. Thus the State Commission on Reserves (GKZ) remained responsible for recording new oil and gas discoveries, though in the 1990s there were few to record.[6] The Central Commission on Oilfield Development (TsKR) continued reviewing FDPs.[7] Various state committees remained responsible for mining and industrial safety, including the oil and gas industry (Gosgortekhnadzor),[8] and for environmental protection (Goskomprirody). In the Soviet era these regulatory agencies had operated through networks of technical research and design institutes, mostly subordinated to the industrial ministries or the USSR Academy of Sciences. The institutes worked as consultants (called *eksperty*) to the regulators, supplying much of the staff that performed the actual project reviews *(ekspertizy)*.

Yet though the official nameplates remained, these Soviet-era agencies largely went dormant in the 1990s, for lack of funding, staffing, and enforcement powers. But—and this is the key point—these state functions did not die. The agencies' nominal powers, though temporarily inactive, remained on the books. Only its own weakness forced the bureaucracy to retreat, but without ever surrendering its claims or accepting defeat.

The 1990s: New Regulators and New Regulations

Paradoxically, the 1990s were also a time of great creativity in legislation and policy making. The radical switch to a market economy in the early 1990s called for a no less radical change in the functions and structures of the state. Practically overnight it had to adapt to the new and unaccustomed role of arbiter and regulator of a new private sector. A new system of laws was needed to regulate and defend private property, instead of prosecuting it as before. The state was now expected to develop a "level playing field," with rules on competition, corporate ethics, and transparency, all novel concepts at that time in Russia. Wholly new fields of private activity, such as financial and legal services, insurance, advertising, information technologies, credit rating and bonding, and corporate security—which had not existed in the Soviet Union, or barely—required some sort of state regulation and oversight. Some previously existing functions, such as the gathering and processing of statistics, required radical rethinking.[9] It was a challenge on a grand scale, at a time when the state's resources were at a low ebb, Russians' views and emotions were divided and ambivalent, domestic precedents were nonexistent (or three generations out of date), and relevant skills and experience were in short supply.

The result was a new tier of regulatory bodies and activities, hastily added on alongside the old. In particular, two new regulatory functions appeared that had not existed in Soviet times. The first was licensing. In the old days, a new field was simply turned over to the operator by the parent ministry. But in the 1990s, with the creation of private companies, all that changed. The 1992

Mineral Resources Law mandated the creation of licensing authorities at both the federal and regional levels. Before the oil companies and Gazprom could explore, develop, and produce oil and gas, they now had to obtain a license from the state—which remained the sovereign owner of the resource in the ground—for each field or prospect, granting them a temporary right to explore (five years) or produce (twenty years), subject to the state's oversight.

The second new regulatory function was oversight of "natural monopolies." The term itself was new to Russia. In the Soviet Union the ministries were monopolies as a matter of course, but as they morphed into state corporations (as Gazprom did as early as 1989 and Transneft did in 1992), their monopoly status and their monopoly rents were soon challenged by the reformers. A law on natural monopolies, passed in 1995, led Anatolii Chubais (then first deputy prime minister) to create a Federal Energy Commission (known by its Russian initials as FEK), which had a broad mandate that included not only tariff setting but also rule making on competition (notably, rules for third-party access to pipelines) and oversight over the monopolies' investment plans.[10]

But creating new agencies on paper was one thing; actually making them effective was another. In the 1990s and well into the following decade, the new regulatory bodies remained weak and largely ineffective.

In the early years, the pressure was on the new licensing authorities to issue licenses and get oil and gas resources assigned to the companies as quickly as possible. Rapid privatization was the order of the day, both in Moscow and in the provinces. Thus Gazprom and the oil companies inherited nearly all the properties that had been on their books in the Soviet era, and they were first in line for new properties as these came up for licensing. By the end of the 1990s, 94 percent of the oil resources in West Siberia that were appraised and ready for development had been licensed to the operators. There was no attention to enforcement, only to getting the licenses out the door.[11]

As a result, as late as the first half of the 2000s, there were no real regulatory controls on the production practices of the operators. Indeed, many operating wells were not even on the companies' official books. There were occasional inspections by the Ministry of Natural Resources or by province-level agencies, but at the time these were essentially toothless. Licenses were written in very general terms—basically containing little more than the production profile and the production target—and they were so vague that they could not be enforced in court.[12] Not a single license was lifted at the federal level for nonobservance of license conditions. The only enforcement in practice was at the provincial level, but even there it was weak.

Regulation of the "natural monopolies" remained similarly feeble throughout the 1990s. Applying the concepts borrowed from the West—such as "just and reasonable return" as the basis for setting pipeline tariffs—turned out to be difficult in Russian conditions (owing to the immaturity of the securities market, the lack of long-term credit, the prevalence of speculative interest rates, and so forth). In any case FEK lacked the staff and the skills, let alone the political clout, to discover the monopolies' costs and use them to set tariffs. Transneft was consistently hostile to outside regulation and succeeded in denying FEK any role in setting pipeline tariffs. Gazprom, after initial opposition, became more accommodating so long as it believed that FEK could be a useful ally in its battle to raise domestic gas prices.[13] But when FEK tried to assert jurisdiction over Gazprom's investment plans and capital costs, the would-be regulators found the door shut.

The Regulatory Void of the 1990s

The weakness of the regulatory system, which lasted through the 1990s and well into Vladimir Putin's first term, gave the oil companies considerable latitude to do as they pleased. We have seen how Yukos systematically took advantage of this void, but it was not alone. Much of the increase in brownfield production that took place between 1999 and 2004—and the techniques by which it was achieved—was unauthorized by officially approved field development plans. This was particularly the case with hydraulic fracturing. As two Russian scholars write, "The steady growth of fraccing was due in large part to the absence of an up-to-date and efficient system of state regulation."[14]

The oil companies did not defy the authorities openly, but they did not take them particularly seriously either. Yukos, in particular, found informal ways of getting around the burdensome requirements of the official FDPs approved by the TsKR. One former Yukos executive explains:

> We were careful to report everything we did to the TsKR. But in practice we had a little bit of flexibility. The FDP specifies a certain number of wells to drill and the sequence in which they are drilled. However, because the FDP calls for a great many wells—and since our own doctrine called for

388

drilling the best wells first, regardless of what the FDP said—we would "skip ahead" of the pattern given in the FDP, and we would tell the TsKR that we meant to come back and fill in the pattern later. The TsKR went along.[15]

If the regulatory void was advantageous to the companies, it left a number of fundamental questions unresolved, which later came back to haunt their relations with the state. To whom did the companies answer: the state or their shareholders? The licensing system created by the 1992 Subsoil Law belongs to the realm of administrative law, not civil law. A production license grants the operator only a limited right over the oil it produces, subject to the oversight of the state as the ultimate sovereign owner. In other words, the granting of the license does not extinguish the state's right. But where the state's right leaves off and that of the private owner begins has never been fully clarified, and the confusion is compounded by the fact that the companies' "private" oil is shipped by a state monopoly and exported subject to state quotas.[16]

Russian policy makers in the 1990s dealt with this question mainly by avoiding it. The two prime examples are licenses and reserves. From the standpoint of the state, the grant of a license carries with it an obligation of stewardship, to find and produce all the oil that is technically producible over the lifetime of the field; it is not, in other words, a license to maximize profit. The companies, in contrast, want to develop the best parts first, without necessarily much concern for the long-term development of the field. But as far as the state is concerned, the high profits this produces are a kind of unearned income, bordering on theft.[17]

The ambiguity is even more striking in the case of reserves: the Russian oil companies actually report two sets of reserves numbers. The first follows international practice, based on rules laid down by the Society of Petroleum Engineers (SPE) and the U.S. Securities and Exchange Commission (SEC), and is intended to guide company strategies and to protect the interests of investors.[18] The second, mandated by the Russian state and based on inherited Soviet methods, is aimed at protecting the sovereign interest of the state by cataloguing its mineral wealth. The international standard has no official force in the eyes of the Russian state, so all the Russian companies, including the state-owned Rosneft and Gazprom, use both systems. They report one set of numbers to the international community and the other to the government.

The difference between the two reserves standards is fundamental: the international one defines a reserve by whether it is economic to produce; the Russian standard, inherited from the Soviet era, by whether it is physically producible.[19] The international standard is thus responsive to world oil prices—the higher the price, the larger the reserve—but the Russian standard is not. In the early 2000s this had a politically sensitive consequence: as world prices rose, so did the Russian oil companies' reported "international" reserves, while at the same time the reserves they reported to the Russian government declined, as a result of their limited investment in exploration. Internationally, the Russian oil companies appeared to be going strong and their reserves increasing, and so their share prices shot up, boosting their owners' wealth. But in the eyes of the Russian government, the declining reserves numbers—as measured by the Soviet standard—only reinforced the impression inside Russia that the sector was in crisis and that the companies' failure to find more reserves was evidence of unpatriotic, if not criminal, neglect.[20]

By the end of the 1990s, in sum, the state had not abandoned its claims. But it was too weak to enforce them. The oil industry grew accustomed in those days to living in a regulatory limbo, paying lip service to the state but going its own way. Yet it was only the temporary weakness of the state that made this possible. The stage was set for conflict once the state revived.

Statist Revival under Putin

Under Putin the ministries and regulatory bodies swelled with new life. The revival began as soon as Putin became president and gathered strength throughout his first two terms (2000–2008). Fueled with an increasing flow of money from oil revenues, central state budgets expanded and agency staffs grew. Political fashion shifted as well. "Going to the market" was out; state service was back in. The ambitious and the talented began looking once again to government for their careers. Police, prosecutors, investigators, and judges breathed the new oxygen and set to work with fresh enthusiasm.

The most obvious sign of the revival of the central state was a large increase in the number of federal officials. State employment had begun to swell again as early as the mid-1990s, but mostly at the province and municipal levels, where tax receipts were more resilient and handing out government jobs was a politically popular way of fighting unemployment. Thus ironically, as Russia moved to a market economy, the number of state officials ballooned—although not yet in the straitened federal government, where staffs remained thin, especially at the center in Moscow.

Under Putin it was the turn of the federal bureaucracy to expand. Between 2000 and 2010, total federal employment grew by over two-thirds, reaching a total of nearly 870,000 officials.[21] Most of the new hires were in the regional offices of federal agencies, where the increase was nearly 70 percent.[22] One might suppose that many of those new federal employees had simply moved over from regional and local governments, but these segments continued to grow as well, if much less fast (by 47 percent and 14 percent, respectively[23]). Some of the new federal jobs were located in the seven newly created federal okrugs, a new level of government created by Putin in 2000 between the federal center and the regions. Meanwhile, the size of the central government in Moscow was practically unchanged throughout most of the decade, at about 40,000 officials.[24] In sum, the Russian bureaucracy consists of a small number of officials in the capital and a vast number in the provinces, about thirty-four of the latter for every one of the former. Of the latter, about half work for federal agencies and half for the field offices of the regional and municipal governments.

The growth in the number of federal officials throughout the country had two consequences. The first was an increase in the central state's capacity to investigate and prosecute. The second was a growing problem in control and coordination, as the state struggled to manage an expanded bureaucracy that by 2010 totaled nearly 1.7 million officials. As a result, the main direction of innovation in the regulatory system in the 2000s was not the creation of new functions (as in the 1990s) but rather a series of efforts to reinforce, consolidate, and rationalize the inherited structure—and above all to use it to increase control.

The fundamental problem that Vladimir Putin faced when he became president in 2000 was the lack of an apparatus of loyal and competent cadres to turn his agenda into effective power and the lack of an enforcement system that could command obedience among politicians, bureaucrats, and businessmen, who after a decade of loose government had become accustomed to going their own way. The Communist Party, for all its faults, had provided such an apparatus, but it no longer existed. Putin turned instead to the Federal Security Service (FSB), the most professional and disciplined organization left in the country. In particular, the seven new federal districts (*federal'nye okrugi*) he created in 2000 were staffed predominantly with FSB officers. Their mission was to oversee the regional governments and monitor the local offices of the federal government, and particularly to reestablish central power over the local police, prosecutors, and courts.[25]

This choice was fateful. By relying on a coercive body such as the FSB as his chief instrument, as well as other security organs such as the General Procuracy, Putin opted for a formula that was by definition authoritarian. A professional officer corps necessarily values loyalty over independence and discipline over debate, all the more so if it is one that is closed and secretive. Putin used it to build a vertical chain of command (in Russian, *vertikal' vlasti*) that amounted to a parallel executive branch, running from the Kremlin and the Presidential Administration, down through the newly created federal districts, to a network of federal inspectors in the regions.[26] This system put executive power ahead of legislative and judiciary power, and administrative enforcement ahead of the rule of law. It had no checks and no balances, other than those the Kremlin might impose on itself.

The choice of means was fateful, but it was not accidental. The *vertikal' vlasti* was no more than a translation to the national government of the norms and values of the KGB, the institution in which Putin had spent his most formative years and which he had briefly headed before becoming prime minister. He viewed it as a strong but necessary medicine, to reverse the chaos (as he and many Russians saw it) into which the country had fallen. But in the end the KGB model has engendered powerful and destructive side effects, to which we shall return shortly.

Putin's first target in his campaign to establish control was the system of coercion itself, and after that the regional governments. In the energy sector, as we have seen, he focused first on the gas and pipelines, and he did not turn his full attention to the oil industry until late in his first term. When he did so, the results were dramatic and swift. The goal was to produce fear and awe, and in that it was successful.

But even as elites and underlings hastened to swear obedience to Putin, in reality the recentralization of power did not carry as far as one might suppose, nor was there any noticeable increase in the coherence or effectiveness of government. In public the bureaucrats, regional governors, and oil chieftains bowed low, but in private they remained able to evade or delay the orders of the center. Meanwhile, the reliability of the security apparatus as an instrument of rule deteriorated, as the various clans and families within it began to serve their own private interests.[27] The federal bureaucracy, swollen with new recruits, became increasingly difficult to manage.

It has proved easy, in other words, to expand the federal government and tighten the chain of command, but translating increased size and central power into better policy or more effective capacity has been another matter, and even the establishment of simple control—the Kremlin's primary objective—has proved elusive.

Having sketched the structure and history of the regulatory system, we turn now to two of its chief characteristics—conflicting objectives and mistrust of the oil industry—before examining their consequences for oil production.

Conflicting Objectives

The objectives pursued by the Kremlin in its oil policies grow out of the general aims put forth by Putin and Sechin in the late 1990s and reemphasized many times since. They include, as we have seen, channeling oil revenues to state-sponsored programs; increasing the "value added" from oil by modernized refining; diversifying access to foreign markets through new pipeline construction; developing energy resources in virgin territories; and (increasingly as the decade went on) using oil and the oil industry as instruments of diplomacy. Other goals, such as environmental quality or regional development, though frequently enunciated, clearly rank lower. It is, incidentally, a list of priorities not much different from Soviet times.

Taken singly, each of these objectives has a rationale within the framework of Putin's thinking about energy. The problem is the failure to establish priorities or trade-offs among them. Lacking clear signals from the top, the bureaucracy spends much of its time "coordinating," which in practice means that each agency seeks to advance its "own" goal, while bargaining with other agencies to defend its turf and interests.

Yet there is one exception to this pattern. The one consistent trend in energy policy in the last decade has been a steady increase in state intervention. In other words, if there is a single objective that has clearly driven energy policy in the Putin years, it is the drive for control. One powerful reason for this is the state's mistrust of the oil industry.

So convinced is the state that companies and individuals will cheat that it builds structures designed to preempt malfeasance by hedging them about with prior checks and approvals.[28] A typical Russian oilfield development plan (FDP), for example, contains over sixty mandated performance indicators, including level of production, recovery rate, and the technologies to be used in the project. Each indicator is evaluated year by year, comparing the plan and the actual outcomes. The process of gaining approval of a field development plan takes several years, and there are likely to be several FDPs over the lifetime of a project. Such cumbersome procedures, of course, only raise the temptation to get around them.

Just next door are issues of transparency and secrecy. The oil industry, whether state or privately owned, is increasingly global. Oil companies rely on instantaneous communications between the field and technical centers that may be located halfway around the world. Their capitalization and ability to borrow depend on worldwide financial networks and extensive disclosure of data. All this goes against the grain of a Russian officialdom that even now requires unclassified maps to include deliberate distortions to protect state security from prying foreign eyes,[29] and finds it difficult to understand why oil companies should reveal their reserves to international investors, when reserves are the property of the state and are traditionally regarded as state secrets.[30]

To see what these features mean for the actual content of regulation and its consequences for the oil industry, we turn now to a closer look at the most important principal regulatory body for the oil industry, the Ministry of Natural Resources, known in Russia as Minprirody.

The Case of Minprirody

The Ministry of Natural Resources represents the outcome of a decade of struggle between old-line geologists and reformist environmentalists, who battled one another throughout the 1990s for control of a turf consisting mainly of the decayed buildings of the former USSR Ministry of Geology. At the time, neither constituency had any money or power. In principle, geological exploration was funded through a special levy from the oil companies. When they paid (which was not often), the Finance Ministry seized the funds for the general budget.

Undecided over what to do with either group, the Yeltsin government constantly reshuffled them. This was in fact an old tradition: the Soviet government had done the same thing (as had the tsarist regime before it), and the Putin government has continued since.

In 2000–2001, however, Minprirody began to assume something like its present shape, absorbing functions that had previously belonged to the Ministry of Energy and other agencies.[31] Along the way it has gained in formal authority, and today it is responsible for much of the state's regulatory interface with the oil industry. Licensing, reserves classification, field development plans, exploration policy, tenders and auctions for new prospects, industrial safety, and environmental assessment and oversight are today all controlled by entities that are part of Minprirody.[32]

On the face of it, Minprirody looks like a textbook illustration of the resurgence of central state power in the Putin era. Between 2004 and 2012 the ministry was headed by a tough, well-connected political executive, a former governor of Perm' Province named Iurii Trutnev.[33] Trutnev, who held an advanced black belt in the redoubtable *Kyukushin* form of karate, was an outspoken and colorful individual. At the same time he was a loyal soldier for the Kremlin's causes.

Under Trutnev's leadership the Ministry sharply stepped up its activity as an investigator and enforcer. More ample budgets enabled the Ministry not only to finance more geological exploration but also to buy modern computers and information systems to monitor compliance and support enforcement.[34] At the same time, Minprirody also scaled up its sales of exploration and production licenses, especially for hydrocarbons.[35] On the surface, then, this is an agency that gained steadily in power and funding throughout the 2000s.

Yet a closer look at Trutnev and his ministry reveals a different story. When he took his post in 2004, he vowed to clean up the licensing system and to lift the licenses of nonperforming companies.[36] But despite many investigations, only a handful of licenses were actually canceled. He called for a new Mineral Resources Law that would eliminate the inconsistencies and loopholes that riddled the 1992 law. But by 2007, after four years of interagency warfare, he gave up the attempt and settled for a handful of amendments instead.[37] His campaigns against Gazprom, notably his effort to block the award of fields without tender or auction, were blunted without result.[38] Most recently, his attempts to persuade the government to enact stiff fines for flaring associated gas were watered down. His exhortations to the oil companies to spend more on frontier exploration were routinely ignored.[39] Trutnev in public enjoyed playing the role of the happy warrior, but in reality he lost every major battle he fought, notably his long struggle to enact a new law on mineral resources.

Trutnev's ineffectiveness stemmed not from personal failings, but from factors that were built into the structure of his ministry and that will likely handicap his successor as well. He was never able to establish control, he was always surrounded by stronger players than himself, and he had little support from Putin, even on issues to which Putin appeared strongly committed.

Trutnev's troubles began with the fact that Minprirody is understaffed, especially at the top. Despite the overall expansion of the federal bureaucracy, Minprirody's permanent staffing is too small to cover the wide range of extractive industries in a vast country. It is impossible for the minister and his staff to keep tabs on the performance and behavior of the regional offices. Not surprisingly, the ministry and its subordinate agencies, both under Trutnev's tenure and that of his predecessor Vitalii Artiukhov, were dogged by accusations of corruption, especially at local levels.[40]

A second weakness is that Minprirody's senior leaders under Trutnev had little direct experience in the oil and gas industry or deep knowledge of its technical or economic aspects. None of the main agency heads in Minprirody had a professional background in oil or gas or geology. Though Trutnev's official biography stated that he came from a family of oilmen and was originally trained as a drilling engineer, he had never worked in an oilfield except as a student trainee. Trutnev was essentially a former Komsomol official turned businessman who gravitated into politics and owed his job to his past as a provincial governor and his record as a Putin loyalist.[41] The heads of the three main agencies subordinated to him were likewise political appointees with no background in oil or gas.[42] All three were from the Saint Petersburg area and, to judge from their previous jobs, had personal ties to the Kremlin leadership.[43]

In short, the leadership of Minprirody under Trutnev consisted essentially of political managers chosen for their loyalty—not to the minister, but to the Kremlin.[44] The clear message (not least to their troops in the field) was that these men owed their jobs to their patrons in the various political clans in the Kremlin leadership and that the qualities for which they were appointed were political experience and loyalty, rather than knowledge of oilfield technology or geology.

Finally, the ministry was divided, and is likely to remain so in the future. In 2004, as part of a broad shake-up across the government, Minprirody was split into three quasi-autonomous levels with their own heads and their own budgets, engendering conflict within Minprirody itself. Over the following years Trutnev spent as much time sparring with his own agency as he did with license violators and polluters. Minprirody's family quarrels were legend in Moscow (one young official went so far as to call it a *zheltyi dom*, a "yellow house," the Russian expression for a madhouse). As a recent Russian study noted in a tactful phrase, the "ineffective interaction" between Minprirody and its nominally subordinate agencies was one of the chief problems with project review and licensing.[45]

The coordination problems engendered by the 2004 reorganization were not confined to Minprirody. By the spring of 2008, when Putin handed the presidency to Dmitri Medvedev and named himself prime minister, the problem of conflict between the ministries and their subordinate agencies had grown so severe that Putin, in one of his first acts in his new job, issued a decree giving the ministers power to annul the decisions of agency heads.[46] Yet Trutnev never actually succeeded in gaining any better control of his ministry. Minprirody was—and is likely to remain—reminiscent of a feudal barony in which the king has little real control over his vassals. A colorful but highly revealing case in point is the saga of Oleg Mitvol'.

The Environmental Scourge: Oleg Mitvol'

Mercurial, controversial, by turns disarming and infuriating, Oleg Mitvol' served as the deputy head of Rosprirodnadzor, Minprirody's environmental watchdog, for five action-packed years, from his appointment in April 2004 to his dismissal in April 2009. Mitvol' was always good for a front-page story as he led the charge (often with journalists in tow) against interests he claimed were riding roughshod over the environment. There was no opponent, it seemed, that Mitvol' would not take on, no matter how powerful or well connected. During his tenure at Rosprirodnadzor he went after practically every big player in Russia, from the oligarchs (whom he accused of building luxury dachas in protected areas), to oil companies big and small (whom he denounced as chronic polluters), to foreign investors (notably Shell at Sakhalin-2 and BP at Kovykta), to the authorities of Moscow city and province.[47] Rosneft was a favorite target, but even Gazprom was not spared.

Mitvol' was not an environmental scientist by background (he had a degree as an electronic engineer), nor was he a career government official. Throughout the 1990s he had knocked about the private sector, moving from one business to another. To Miriam Elder, then a journalist at *The Moscow Times,* who followed Mitvol''s career closely over a period of years, he had a dubious reputation in Moscow business circles as a specialist in "greenmail," that is, someone who acquired minority-share positions in privatized businesses and harassed the majority owners until he was bought out.[48] By the mid-1990s he had come into the orbit of Boris Berezovsky, and in 1997 the two men cofounded a liberal newspaper, *Novye izvestiia.* But in February 2003 Mitvol' fell out with Berezovsky, who by this time was in exile in London. Taking sole control of the newspaper, he shut it down. The following year he was named deputy head of Rosprirodnadzor, under Iurii Trutnev, who had taken over the ministry the month before.

Mitvol''s new job was poorly paid and brought only humble perquisites, barely qualifying for an official car and driver (without which no self-respecting Russian official will be seen in public). But the post's seeming modesty was deceptive: a job that involved blowing the whistle (or not) for environmental violations had obvious potential. There was a pattern to his public attacks. Mitvol' would conduct an investigation, announce he had found massive violations, and then the charges would be forgotten or withdrawn. Soon he would be off again, chasing after another prominent target. But in the process the target companies' share prices would fall sharply and then rise again, and it did not go unnoticed in Moscow that there was money to be made on the turns.

But Mitvol' evidently had his higher uses. He spearheaded the campaign against the Sakhalin Energy Company, the license-holder of the Sakhalin-2 LNG project, eventually leading to Shell's sale of a majority stake in the project to Gazprom. Mitvol' likewise led the charge against BP's stake in the Kovykta gas project in Irkutsk Oblast', with the same result. (As a consequence, BP never did develop the Kovykta field.) But these were only the most visible of dozens of cases Mitvol' opened against oil and gas companies, especially foreign ones, charging environmental violations of all sorts and threatening suspension of water-use permits and environmental licenses. Mitvol' became an ever-present gadfly, buzzing about the heads of foreign oilmen.

Mitvol''s eventual downfall came from within his own agency. He did not hide that he thought he should be head of Rosprirodnadzor.[49] But in early 2008, when Mitvol''s superior died of a heart attack, the Kremlin chose a *silovik,*

Vladimir Kirillov, to succeed him. A well-connected former vice-governor of Leningrad Oblast' and therefore an accredited Piterets, Kirillov immediately set about clipping Mitvol"s wings, cutting off his access to the procuracy and other law-enforcement bodies. In the summer of 2008, taking advantage of Trutnev's absence, Kirillov forwarded directly to prime minister Putin's desk an order eliminating Mitvol"s position, which Putin promptly signed.[50] Trutnev, who had attempted to block the order, fought hard over the following months to keep Mitvol', whom he evidently found valuable, but in the end he had to yield.[51] Mitvol's usefulness in higher places had evidently come to an end.

Mitvol"s rise and fall fit into a pattern that became all too familiar in the second half of the 2000s. Under Mitvol', environmental oversight became an exercise in political entrepreneurship, which his superiors were unable or unwilling to rein in. The campaign against Sakhalin-2 coincided with the growing official hostility toward foreign investors and PSAs, and Mitvol"s role further strengthened the impression of a coordinated action in which official concern for the environment was little more than a rhetorical cover for de facto expropriation in favor of well-placed interests. In short, the Mitvol episode not only summed up much that was wrong with the regulatory regime, but also pointed to its deeper causes.

Explaining Minprirody's Weakness

The most striking feature of Minprirody, in sum, is the contradictions between its potential power and its actual weakness, between its broad reach and its modest grasp. This is not, as one might suppose, the result of co-optation by the oil and gas industry. Minprirody's defeats typically come at the hands of other government agencies, or as the result of a direct intervention by the Kremlin (or the prime minister's office during Putin's time there), not as the result of domination by oil and gas interests. Indeed, Minprirody's policies toward the oil and gas industries are as inconsistent as everything else about it—sometimes friendly, sometimes hostile; sometimes progressive, sometimes conservative; but above all unpredictable and changeable.

The most plausible explanation of these mysteries is that they are a by-product of political leadership's policy of divide-and-balance. The only time the potential power of the regulators is fully activated and deployed is when there is a clear will and consensus at the top. But such occasions are rare, because the Kremlin is sensitive to any disturbance in the balance of power and acts to restore it.

This maintenance of checks and balances among the competing elites, and the allocation of rents and power among them, extending deep into the internal structure of each ministry, has increasingly become the hallmark of the Russian state system in the later Putin years. If in 2000–2004 the main objective of the elites that came to power under Putin was to gain control over the regions and the oligarchs, by Putin's second term the emphasis shifted to maintaining a balance of power within the bureaucracy and an equal division of state positions among the clans. In the case of Minprirody, the result is a politically "safe" but weak ministry.

The contrast between words and deeds is striking. In June 2009, at a meeting at Minprirody, Putin called for the creation of a centralized system for resource management. Gazing sternly down a long table crowded with ministers and agency heads, he observed that eight separate agencies were responsible for resource use, and he criticized the many "bottlenecks and systemic problems" in the management of mineral resources, particularly in the licensing process.[52] But his words were not followed by action. As a result, oil regulation by the state suffers from three chronic problems: poor coordination and delays, interagency conflicts, and conservative resistance to change.

Poor Coordination and Delays

Soviet ministries were notorious for their prickly autonomy, and the elaborate structure of horizontal coordinating agencies—the state committees and the party apparatus itself—was never able to overcome the vertical bulkheads that the ministries built around their domains. The very effort to coordinate became part of the problem, as the ministries demanded the right to review and approve every document or initiative. The result was that Soviet bureaucrats spent their time in endless rounds of what the Russians call *soglasovaniia,* the endless dance of multiple sign-offs, followed by equally endless rewrites, or *dorabotki.*

Their post-Soviet successors have not changed much. Policy initiatives, big and small, become caught in the net of interagency coordination and flounder there for what can be years. Much of this behavior has to do with conflicts over turf and precedence. Not only do Russian bureaucrats mistrust the oil companies; they mistrust one another even more. Thus the government's efforts to promote clearer policies on such matters as licensing auctions, exploration, the capture of associated gas, the definition of "strategic" projects, and third-party access to gas pipelines—to cite some recent examples—bog down in interagency battles. In 2009, when Igor Sechin (by this time deputy prime minister for energy affairs) conducted a review of over 150 energy-policy initiatives assigned to the bureaucracy, he was informed that only four had actually reached closure.[53]

In the 1990s regional and local government stepped into the vacuum left by a weak central government. Taking advantage of Moscow's passive acquiescence, they multiplied local taxes, laws, and regulations. Oil companies called for "one-stop shopping"—a single regulatory authority that could spare them the endless quest for licenses and permissions at multiple levels of government. At the same time, in reality they often found it to their advantage to deal with local officials in the oil-producing areas. Thus it was largely because of good relations with local officials that the Sakhalin PSAs came to pass.

Then came Vladimir Putin and the drive to restore central government. In the 2000s the regions lost much of their power to tax and legislate. Their prerogatives and revenues melted away, together with much of their enforcement power.[54] For better or for worse, one might have thought, this was finally the one-stop authority the oil companies had been looking for. But in reality there has been less change than it might appear. The regions and municipalities retain jurisdiction over a wide range of local issues, notably land use, roads, rights-of-way, and licensing for non-energy resources such as building stone, lumber, and water. Thus Aleksandr Reziapov, deputy director general of Surgutneftegaz for capital construction, says that exploration itself takes "much less" time than obtaining the approvals for it, especially at local levels. The cycle of leasing forest areas, obtaining permits for land use in forested areas, and review of seismic shoots takes up to 14 months. Getting a license for disposal of dangerous drilling wastes takes up to 18 months; for water supply for drilling, up to 6 months. Reziapov acknowledges that sometimes the rules are so complex and demanding (requiring a whole new review procedure if there is any minor change in geological conditions) that the company is forced to fake documents.[55]

Oil companies complain about the delays and uncertainties associated with going from an exploration license to a production license. No company will want to make the risky investment in exploration unless there is a reasonable assurance that it will be allowed to produce what it has discovered. Yet in Russia these two stages are often covered by two separate licenses, and there is no guarantee that one will lead to the other. On the contrary, there is a lengthy review process. The State Committee on Reserves must first confirm that a discovery has been made and the reserves properly confirmed through an actual exploration well. This document must then be signed by a deputy minister of natural resources. Only then can the oil company proceed to apply for a production license; this last stage alone can take up to a year.[56]

Interagency Conflicts

Instead of resolving their differences over priorities, the competing interest groups in the leadership institutionalize them in competing bureaucracies. This sets the stage for lengthy interagency conflicts, driven not only by policy differences but by competition for prestige, favor, and turf. Unless the president or the prime minister himself gives them his sustained attention (and sometimes even if he does), policy initiatives bog down in trench warfare.

A good illustration is the long battle over drafting a new mineral resources law. The old 1992 law had long been recognized as inadequate. It had been drafted in haste following the Soviet collapse, and it was riddled with holes and inconsistencies, such as placeholder "forwarding references" (otsylochnye normy) to laws that did not yet exist. For the incoming Putin administration in 2000, its main sin was that it gave too much power to the regional authorities, through its "two-key" provision and its reliance on tenders (konkursy), which could be easily manipulated to the regions' advantage.[57] For the liberals, it had one additional defect: the whole concept of licenses was based on old-style administrative law, instead of contracts based on the new civil law. Not only was this system excessively rigid, but the terms of licensing were exceedingly vague, making their enforcement practically impossible.

Iurii Trutnev, when he came in in 2004, vowed to make a new law his top priority. He saw it as an opportunity to remedy a whole series of ills, ranging from the oil companies' habit of piling up exploration licenses and then sitting on them (Trutnev's proposed remedy was to institute a tax on reserves), to the old law's excessive openness (as he saw it) to foreign companies. Trutnev called for awarding new licenses through transparent auctions rather than the traditional device of tenders, which could be manipulated by regional authorities to force bidders to include all sorts of expensive extras. Trutnev was confident he could prevail, especially since he had Putin's public support.

But by the beginning of 2007, Trutnev and Minprirody had conceded defeat and abandoned the attempt. Over the following year, the government adopted piecemeal a series of amendments dealing with individual issues, but to this day the 1992 law, despite its flaws, remains the basic statute on mineral resources.[58]

What had gone wrong? Suddenly everyone found something to dislike in Trutnev's draft law. Gazprom and Rosneft wanted the offshore closed off to foreigners and found the law insufficiently restrictive.[59] Regional leaders lobbied against it, since it threatened to lessen their influence even further.[60] The oil companies worried that it would make their existing licenses vulnerable and disliked the idea of having their reserves taxed. Legal experts said it was simply too vague and badly written.[61] No one was prepared to fight for replacing tenders with auctions.[62] The Ministry of the Economy had a rival version. By the end, even Putin distanced himself from the Trutnev draft.

In the background to the debate there was stiffening opposition—stoked by active lobbying by Rosneft and Gazprom[63]—to any significant participation by foreign companies. Trutnev's initial position had been a relatively liberal one. He argued that without international competition, the Russian oil and gas industry would have no incentive to become efficient. But step by step, he was forced to retreat, and the definition of "strategic" fields was drawn tighter and tighter, from 150 million tons (1.1 billion barrels) of oil and 1 trillion cubic meters (35.3 trillion cubic feet) of gas in the 2005 draft to 70 million tons (511 million barrels) of oil and 50 billion cubic meters (1.8 trillion cubic feet) of gas.[64] By the end virtually every field of potential interest to a large oil company was effectively reserved to the two state champions.

Resistance to Change

The regulatory system continues to rely on a network of research and design institutes and technical universities, most of them inherited from the Soviet era and still owned by state ministries or the Russian Academy of Sciences. These provide the bulk of the technical expertise on which the regulators draw for project reviews and rule making. On the whole, they are a highly conservative force. In the 1990s, for lack of funding, they lagged behind the technological changes taking place in the industry, and they remain largely isolated from the companies and suspicious of them. In the 2000s, state support revived, but the institutes' curricula and research programs are dominated by senior directors whose administrative positions give them power and control and whose views are traditional and statist. These in turn influence the views of state officials in a conservative direction. In Chapter 6, for example, we saw the role of Vladimir Litvinenko, rector of the Saint Petersburg Mining Institute, in shaping the energy-policy views of the rising Saint Petersburg group—Putin, Sechin, Zubkov, and others—in the mid-1990s. He remains a conservative voice in energy-policy debates today.[65]

The institutes have been a force against change in debates over such issues as reserves classification, exploration policy, production techniques, and the like. Some of the most venomous vocabulary of the Yukos Affair came from the institutes, which condemned the "barbaric" and "destructive" practices of Yukos and Sibneft. The views of the senior figures in the institutes often reflect the experience of the Soviet era, codified in rules and standards that lag decades behind the moving front of oilfield technology. These then become the basis for taboos that bind the industry. One example, discussed earlier, is the ban on producing below bubble point. Another is a rule against stimulating reservoirs through the injection of miscible gas. Such techniques are illegal until they are officially incorporated in field development plans, which typically requires long negotiations with skeptical eksperty from the institutes.

The long debate over changing the method of estimating reserves shows how conservatism can paralyze policy. A strong legacy from Soviet times, enshrined in the institutes, is the habit of putting geology and engineering ahead of economics. The traditional Russian approach to reserves is to ask, "Is it technically feasible to produce?" rather than "Is it economic?" As a former deputy minister of natural resources, Vladimir Mazur, once said, "A recoverable reserve is a technically recoverable reserve. Let the accountants figure out its cost."[66] Thus the traditional Soviet-era approach to reserves, which classifies them as A, B, C1, and C2, according to their technical feasibility but not their economics, is still the official methodology.

Yet the traditional Soviet approach has become increasingly awkward. As we have seen, the oil companies pay it only lip service. Minprirody has been studying and debating proposals for reforming the reserves classification system for the better part of a decade. But rather than simply adopt the SPE-SEC system in use throughout the world (and inside the Russian oil companies themselves), the Russian geological establishment insists on developing its own homegrown system. When asked why, they answer vaguely that any new system should "reflect the specific situation of Russia," without quite spelling out what that means, other than to do things in their own way. But the Ministry's efforts, based loosely on a United Nations methodology, have been cold-shouldered by the oil companies, who call it cumbersome and confusing and have been dragging their feet about recalculating their reserves under the new method. So there the matter rests. "Everyone wants to move to the new system," declared Minister Trutnev hopefully in 2008, calling for it to be officially adopted by the beginning of 2009. But at the end of the year, Minprirody announced that the new classification would be postponed for three more years, until 2013, and it may be delayed even longer.[67] Thus after a decade of debate, the Russian oil companies are still keeping two parallel and noncommunicating sets of reserve numbers. (And even under the new Russian classification system effective January 2012, Russia preserves the A, B, C, and D categories, albeit making more allowance for economic criteria of recoverability.)

Consequences for the Oil Industry

In sum, the Kremlin's effort to restore strong central power has not produced a more unified and coherent regulatory structure. Instead, we see a pattern of delays, obstruction, blocked initiatives, and inconclusive debate. In the end, the regulatory system is unpredictable, arbitrary, and ultimately ineffective. It is a system of rhetoric and half-measures, except in the handful of cases where the Kremlin is directly engaged and employs all its resources to achieve a specific political objective, such as the destruction of Yukos or the takeover of foreign projects—and these are examples not of regulation but of misuse of regulation.[68]

The argument of this chapter has been that these problems are not the result of incompetence or corruption or ingrained bureaucratic culture—although all three are present in varying degrees. Nor are they the product of the multichambered evolution of the regulatory system, although that too is a contributing factor. Rather, at the core, they are consequences of the system itself, which strives for total power while simultaneously dividing it. The normal process of delegation, which relieves the load on higher decision makers, is short-circuited if authority is deliberately divided and subordinates are pitted against one another. No one at lower levels wants to make a move without the Kremlin's approval, yet the leadership in the Kremlin—ultimately Vladimir Putin himself—does not have the time or energy to respond to all the demands on their attention. In the resulting power vacuum, other problems—bureaucratic intrigue, interagency rivalry, politically motivated conservatism, federal-regional divisions, corruption, and ordinary bureaucratic inertia—have free play, defeating the efforts of capable experts and well-intentioned reformers.

There are two main consequences for the oil industry. A system of "strong thumbs and weak fingers" tends to drive the industry toward targets that are simple to define and enforce, especially if in addition they are pushed strongly by the Kremlin. Thus the command "Develop Vankor and all the necessary pipelines to connect it to the main trunk line system" calls forth a strong response by Rosneft, despite the drag of the tax system. By contrast, the slogan "Raise the ultimate recovery rate from existing fields" is not operationalizable to the same extent, because recovery rates are the outcome of many interconnected decisions, technologies, and requirements for information about field performance over an extended period.

Similarly, a simple high-priority command ("Develop Vankor!") tends to force the leadership and the bureaucracy to override other objectives, whereas sound policy would call for striking a more reasoned balance among them. Thus Rosneft, in order to carry out the Kremlin's command to develop Vankor quickly, overrode another mandate ("Use domestic suppliers!"), making extensive use of foreign equipment and service providers, with the apparent blessing of the Kremlin.

Thus, despite its success in forcing action at Vankor (which is administratively part of an East Siberian province but geologically related to West Siberia), the system has been much less successful in generating broad development of East Siberian oil overall. The Kremlin has been able to drive the construction of a new East Siberian pipeline to the Pacific (although final cost is another matter) but has been unable to mandate the exploration and development of enough new reserves to fill it with East Siberian oil. (Instead, it is being filled largely with oil from West Siberia, including Vankor, and this will remain the case for the foreseeable future.) One might say that the power system can force the building of large arteries but not the balanced growth of networks of capillaries.

The same is true of the system's impact on existing fields. If it leans hard enough, the regulators can force the oil companies to obey simple rules ("No more than 10 percent idle wells!"), thus making them spend money on their worst wells instead of their best ones. However, another simple-seeming prohibition ("Recover 95 percent of all associated gas!") turns out to be more complicated to carry out, because it requires expensive equipment to monitor gas flows and heavy investment to dispose of the gas. (Gazprom's stiff resistance to accepting associated gas into its pipeline system, despite stern lectures from the Kremlin, is yet another example of the problems of poor coordination and interagency warfare.) The system can force the companies to spend money but not without limit.

A system of oversimple rules enforced through the threat of coercion tends to drive the oil companies toward safe, near-term solutions while discouraging them from trying new and unproven technologies. Thus in the older established fields, the companies have tended to maintain production mainly by increasing infill drilling and pumping more water, essentially the classic Soviet-era responses. More sophisticated techniques tend to be more expensive (and thus are discouraged by the tax system) and require rewriting FDPs, a lengthy and uncertain process. The knock-on consequence is that the system inhibits the rise of an indigenous high-tech service sector. Such demand as there is for advanced production techniques and equipment tends to be met by foreign service companies, which sell into the Russian oilfields the products of innovations made elsewhere.

Finally, the system tends to perpetuate the big-company structure of the Russian oil industry. Only large companies can carry the additional costs imposed by the regulators. (Thus, under the terms of the fiscal regime in place in 2010, for example, some 30 percent of producing fields operate at a loss.) Only large companies can handle the bureaucracy's burdensome reporting requirements. And only large companies can afford the time and the manpower to work the bureaucracy, securing the revisions, exemptions, and postponements that make the system workable in practice.[69]

The combined effects of the regulatory system can be seen with special force in a policy issue that is vital to the long-range future of Russian oil: investment in exploration in the frontier areas, East Siberia, the Caspian offshore, and the Arctic. The government's designation of larger fields as "strategic" gives the inside track to the state-owned companies. If a private company makes a major discovery, the state can simply designate it as "strategic" and assign it directly to Rosneft or Gazprom, without an auction or even a tender. The law provides for the possibility of compensation, but the companies reject this as highly unsatisfactory—indeed, there has not been a single case of actual compensation to date.

"The problem is not just taxation," says Leonid Fedun of LUKoil. "It is the entire system by which prospects are awarded to the state-owned companies without open competition, and the most attractive prospects are reserved as 'strategic' and kept off-limits."[70]

The result has been a slowdown in exploration in East Siberia. The government's general policy has been to fund the broad regional mapping and geophysical research itself, while leaving to the oil companies the task of identifying and proving up commercially economic fields.

So far, so good, but the problem comes in the passing of the baton from the state's geologists to the oil companies. Trutnev's oft-stated view was that the oil companies should invest 10 rubles in exploration for every ruble spent by the state.[71] But the oil companies didn't see it that way—and this is where the contradictions in the licensing system converge. According to the companies, there was little sense in investing in exploring high-cost regions with unproven potential, that might or may not be economic given the uncertainties in transportation costs, might or might not be rewarded with development licenses, and might or might not be taken away and given to the state-owned companies or assigned to a "state reserve."[72]

As a consequence, the companies have hung back. In response, Rosprirodnadzor deployed its inspectors, uncovered the usual violations, and threatened to lift exploration licenses from companies working in the East Siberian region.[73] In this game of cat and mouse, the oil companies gauge the costs of obeying burdensome regulations against the likelihood of prosecution. So far, their behavior suggests that in the case of East Siberia, the state has nowhere else to turn—giving a new twist to the old Russian saying "Once you're already in Siberia, they can't exile you any farther" (Dal'she Sibiri ne soshliut').[74]

Conclusion: Comparing the Fiscal and Regulatory Systems

In the last two chapters we have examined the two main elements of the state's relationship to the oil industry: taxes and regulation. Comparing the two, one might say that the oil-tax system has the faults of its virtues. It is a blunt instrument that does its job—that of extracting the windfall profits from rising oil prices—but it does it all too well. Over the long run, the fiscal system has aggravated the imbalances of the industry. But in the near term, its goal was to capture rents, and that is precisely what it has done.

The regulatory system is not so easy to sum up. Its main overall mission, we have seen, is to defend the state's interest. But just what that interest is and how it should be protected have been uncertain questions, because of the tremendous changes in the state itself over the last three decades. The system was assembled piecemeal and without plan, from bits left over from the Soviet period, to which were added more bits from the 1990s and finally the statist superstructure of the 2000s. The resulting jumble of agencies is poorly coordinated and internally divided, too often confused in concept and inconsistent in execution.

Yet despite these key differences, the fiscal and regulatory systems share a common fault: they both originated in a policy environment in which state bureaucrats believed the oil industry enjoyed an unlimited resource base and inexhaustible rents and that the central imperative of state policy was therefore to reestablish control—of the rents and of the industry's practices. In both cases, it is a model based on suspicion and conflict, not collaboration.

The problem is that this model of control—in both its fiscal and regulatory aspects—is increasingly out of touch with the rapidly evolving reality on the ground, in which the looming problem is precisely that the resource base is deteriorating and the rents face decline. The sole major exception to date is the constructive dialogue on oil-tax policy that has been engaged since 2009—driven by a recognition that future oil production could be under threat—but even this dialogue, positive as it is, has yet to produce more than marginal results.

Any other picture would have been surprising indeed, given the political, economic, and ideological upheavals in Russia over the last generation. In the best of circumstances, there would have been conflicts over fundamental policy issues, problems in adapting the qualifications of officials to changing requirements, and difficulties from inherited bureaucratic culture and practices.

Over and above these, the greatest challenge of all, the most difficult to deal with for a state bureaucracy, and still largely unresolved, has been where and how to draw the line between the state's interest and that of the private sector. Little wonder that the regulatory system has been a battlefield.

In the middle of that battlefield have been the foreign companies, particularly the international oil companies. We turn now to their experience in the 2000s and their role in the overall evolution of the Russian oil companies and the performance of the industry.

chapter 11

The Half-Raised Curtain: The Foreign Companies as Agents of Change

The Iron Curtain didn't go down: it went up.
    —Valerii Graifer, chairman of the board of LUKoil and RITEK

An old-style Soviet neftianik awakes after a twenty-year sleep. He wanders open-mouthed through the corporate headquarters of one of today's Russian oil giants, gazing in wonder at the gleaming new high-rise office buildings and the expansive boardrooms, the high-tech data centers, and the space-age trading rooms. He concludes that communism has finally arrived. Or—Marx forbid—the capitalist West has triumphed after all. More likely something between the two: Any Russian of a certain age would be irresistibly reminded of the old Soviet-era *anekdot* about the day Leonid Brezhnev proudly shows his mother around the Communist Party Politburo's swank new quarters on Moscow's Old Square. But the old lady is filled with anxiety. "Lyonya," she wails, addressing her son by the familiar form of Leonid, "What will you do when the Reds come back?"

Little fear of that. To the young Russians sitting at their flat-screen workstations in their open-plan offices, the Soviet past is only a childhood memory. In their Friday casuals they could be mistaken for any of their counterparts in Houston or Stavanger, or for that matter Beijing. The corporate headquarters of a Russian oil company look as modern as tomorrow and as determinedly focused on the global market. Television monitors display in real time the company's latest stock price; colorful company websites feature their latest investor presentations; and at the state oil company, Rosneft, the vice president for investor relations—until recently an American—occupies the first office at the head of the grand staircase in the company's refurbished headquarters on Sophie's Embankment, the former building of the USSR Ministry of the Oil Industry, directly facing the Kremlin on the opposite bank of the Moscow River.

Yet appearances are deceiving. On the surface, the Russian oil companies may look and act like their international counterparts. But much of the change is only skin-deep; underneath, the Russian industry remains in transition. Most of its field operations and procedures make as yet only limited use of advanced technology. Its supporting scientific and technical establishment is set in its ways and poorly connected to the fast-moving front of technological advance in the global oil industry. Most young Russian petroleum engineers are still trained using the old curricula. The culture and style of management, heavily hierarchical and authoritarian, are much the same as in the old days.

This is not to understate the enormous changes that have taken place in the Russian oil companies. As we have seen throughout this book, the structure of the industry was turned upside down by the upheavals of the last twenty years, and the companies that have emerged are very different from their Soviet predecessors: vertically integrated, corporatized, and oriented toward making profits, not fulfilling planners' targets. There is wide variety across the industry, and for every one of the judgments above one can cite exceptions. It is a matter of degree. Yet the consensus among oilmen, Russian and foreign, and among informed commentators in the Russian trade media, is that in terms of efficiency and innovativeness the Russian companies still lag behind the rapidly moving front of the international oil industry.

Still Isolated after All These Years

One reason is isolation. The world oil industry today is in the midst of the most far-reaching technological revolution in its history. New knowledge springing from a wide array of fields—imaging, communications, materials science, control systems, and many more—is transforming the ways oil companies find and produce oil and manage their business. These innovations spread quickly. Today's oil industry is a vast web, across which new skills and information flow from company to company and from country to country, through a worldwide network of contractors, consultants, universities and technical centers, and company-to-company partnerships. Companies compete, people move about, nothing remains secret for long.

Yet Russia is not yet closely connected to this fast-moving network of learning and change. International oil companies play only a minor role in Russian oil exploration and development overall and have had relatively little impact on most Russian companies' basic methods of production. Foreign service companies have been more successful, but their market share is limited by their position at the high-tech—and high-priced—end of the services spectrum. Russian oil companies, for their part, have until recently invested little outside the former Soviet Union (with the early and significant exception of LUKoil—see Chapter 3), and when they do, it is seldom with the aim of acquiring new technology.[1] They contribute little to the international oil literature and hold few international patents.[2] Only one Russian technical university—Tomsk Polytechnic—is internationally recognized as meeting the standards of the Society of Petroleum Engineers.[3] Russian oil companies hire few foreign experts as career employees and practically none in upper management (although one will find there a growing number of Russians with foreign degrees and work experience). And although Russian companies make extensive use of foreign consultants as financial and management advisors, it is more often for the purpose of managing their investor relations with the outside world than to upgrade their own internal operations and management (Yukos and TNK-BP have been the two prominent exceptions that underscore the general rule; more about the latter follows). Overall, the divide between the Russian oil industry and the rest of the world is still far from overcome.

Facile Fossils

The other reason is lack of challenge. There is no such thing as "easy oil," yet the dominant fact about the Russian oil industry is that twenty years after the end of the Soviet Union, over 60 percent of Russian production comes from fields that were already in production before 1991. Tens of thousands of Soviet-era wells still flow, if at low rates, requiring little more than maintenance and occasional repairs. The industry's main activity is infill drilling, just as in Soviet times. While basic field techniques such as hydraulic fracturing and horizontal drilling have spread widely, the use of more advanced technologies is limited to a handful of new fields. (Horizontal drilling, for example, remains underused—in 2010 only 11 percent of new wells in Russia used horizontal drilling, compared with 53 percent in the United States. Multistage hydraulic fracturing, to take another example, is not yet in wide use.[4]) Little exploration takes place, because the Russian companies inherited such large portfolios of fields already known and licensed.[5] Up until now, in short, the Russian companies

413

have managed to maintain world-leading levels of production with only about half the upstream investment and little of the innovation required elsewhere.

The Russian companies, for all the talk of innovation at corporate headquarters, are set in their ways when it comes to the local level. To take one concrete example: throughout much of the world, oil companies are moving to "smart" wells, equipped with advanced telemetry equipment, which beam production data directly to headquarters for monitoring and analysis. But most Russian operators in the brownfields still do things the old-fashioned way, sending workers out in trucks to read production data well by well and record the results with paper and pencil. There is, to be sure, a rationale for this behavior. When asked, Russians oilmen will point out that in most established fields there is no need for such advanced tools. The reservoirs are simple; the wells are stable; the oil flows steadily. There is no need for real-time data to provide continuous updates of the state of the reservoir. Besides, even if the data suggested that adjustments were needed in the field development plan, it would take months of hassle to get them approved by the relevant institutes and the regulators. So why spend money to make difficult changes? But that is the point: until now, because of the Soviet legacy, that has been the most rational behavior.

The oil companies' conservatism in turn lessens demand for innovative products and services in supporting industries and institutes. The Russian equipment industry, made up of Soviet-era remnants and a few converted defense plants, does little to renew itself.[6] There is only modest innovation in the domestic service sector, much of which still consists of in-house service divisions of the oil companies (some of them recently spun off as nominally independent but with one preferred client), which spend little on research and development.[7] According to Leonid Fedun, vice-president of LUKoil, Russia accounts for only two percent of the world's production of high-tech equipment for the oil industry.[8] High-tech start-ups, where they exist, suffer from the problems of Russian small business generally and get little encouragement from the oil companies.[9] Russian universities focus on abstract theory and have historically remained aloof from commercial innovation, while industry institutes focus on near-term production problems.

To be sure, for each of these generalizations one can cite exceptions. For example, an innovative start-up company called Novomet, founded in 1991 in the formerly closed city of Perm' in the Urals, uses powder metallurgy (a Soviet-era strength) to make a line of highly regarded down-hole pumps.[10] Another standout is Burintekh, located in Ufa, an innovative producer of high-quality drill bits.[11] A subsidiary of LUKoil called RITEK, founded by LUKoil chairman Valerii Graifer, is expressly dedicated to the development of advanced oilfield technologies. But overall, it remains broadly true that domestic players are not major sources of innovation in the Russian oil industry.

This situation is not sustainable. As the Soviet legacy declines, the Russian oil industry will be under growing pressure to move up to world standards of technology and efficiency. It cannot easily do so alone. Willy-nilly, it will have to break out of its isolation and develop effective ways of learning from global partners.

In principle, there are two ways it can do this—moving out to the outside world, or working with foreign companies inside Russia. The first response—moving out—has not yet gone very far. At a generous estimate, less than one percent of Russian oil production originates outside the Former Soviet Union (and most of that comes from a single company, VietSovPetro, a joint venture of Zarubezhneft with the Vietnamese state oil company). Foreign companies inside Russia account for nearly 12 percent of Russia's production at home. But such numbers give little clue to the actual interaction that may be taking place. The more fundamental question is how mutual learning actually takes place, and what changes happen as a result.

It Takes Two to Innovate

The issue here is what drives "technology transfer," that is, the process by which new skills and technology are communicated and absorbed across national and corporate boundaries. The most effective mechanisms for change are ones that involve real people, working together on common projects, and the most effective driver is shared interest. In contrast, mechanisms that separate the recipient of new knowledge from its human source hinder the process of transfer. The most effective mechanism of innovation is people to people, where both sides agree on the objective and both stand to gain.

It takes two to innovate: a source of "supply," of new ideas, new practices, new equipment, and so forth; and "demand," that is, receptiveness and motivation on the receiving side to put them to work—in short, a perceived need to innovate. But there must also be suitable "vehicles," that is, individuals, teams, joint projects, or mixed companies, that serve as transmission belts through which supply meets demand and the spark passes.

Chapters 4 and 5 described the initial contacts between foreign and Russian companies in the 1990s and their difficult first steps in overcoming decades of isolation. The main vehicle of technology transfer in that first phase was the joint ventures, most of which were absorbed early in the next decade. This chapter picks up the story since 2000. In this second phase, the principal vehicles were the IOCs and the international service companies. By the end of the decade of the 2000s a handful of foreign companies had established niches in the Russian industry and channels of technology transfer had begun to function on a broader scale than in the previous decade. Yet the image of "worlds in collision" remains in many respects as valid for the 2000s as it was for the 1990s.

In this chapter I will argue two key points: first, that in the Russian oil industry the chief obstacles to externally generated change and innovation have been on the demand side. The problem is not so much resistance or hostility to foreigners per se—although that has been a factor—but resistance to change generally, together with a lack of incentives to change.

Second, despite problems with the state's policies toward the oil industry (discussed in the last two chapters), the resistance to foreign presence and influences is due at least as much to the Russian oil companies themselves. It is only now, at the beginning of the third post-Soviet decade, that the pressures for change are beginning to alter the Russian companies' balance of incentives, opening up new possibilities for communication and technology transfer. But whether a third phase, radically different from the first two, is about to open, remains to be seen.

The experience of two companies, BP and Schlumberger, stands out as especially significant. Of all the foreign companies in Russia since the late 1990s, these two have arguably had the broadest impact on the Russian oil industry as a whole. What were the reasons for their successes, and what are the lessons of their setbacks? Will their experiences be relevant for the future, or will they be superseded by new models of interaction, involving different companies?

1998–1999: The Tantalizing Turn

The crash of 1998 had caused a mass exit of much of the expatriate community—a Western banker famously said at the time that he "would sooner eat nuclear waste than invest in Russia again." The foreign IOCs mostly stayed on, although with slimmer staffs. But the turnaround in oil prices and production that followed the crash soon brought the foreigners flooding back. Within a few more years, Russia was once more "the place you couldn't afford not to be." Indeed, pretty soon you couldn't afford to be there either, at least if you were a Westerner. Moscow and Saint Petersburg burgeoned with new office buildings, upscale hotels, and expensive theme restaurants, which quickly filled with newly wealthy Russians, while the sticker-shocked Westerners nervously checked their wallets and ordered mineral water.

Behind these surface changes there was a new reality in the oil industry, both in Russia and outside. The Russian oil industry by this time was largely in private hands. The new owners were beginning to discover that the royal road to wealth lay less through growing oil production per se than through growing their share prices, which meant reshaping their companies to make them more attractive to global markets. In addition, as they consolidated their control over their companies, the new owners—whether finansisty or neftianiki—began to lengthen their horizons (at least compared with the ninety-day time frame of the earlier 1990s) and look to the next generation of opportunities. Thus their motivation in their dealings with foreign companies underwent a significant change. In the early 1990s they had reluctantly accepted the participation of foreign oilmen as a source of emergency help, and subsequently they had learned to deal directly with foreign service companies and banks. But by the end of the 1990s, as their control over their companies began to stabilize, they had begun to think in terms of strategic alliances and longer-term partnerships. Some of them, the finansisty at any rate, even appeared receptive in principle to selling stakes in their companies to foreign partners. A window of opportunity for the foreign companies appeared to be opening.

The world oil industry too was changing. For the IOCs, the price collapse of 1997–1998 brought to a head a crisis that had been latent in the industry since the mid-1980s. Oil prices had never really recovered from the previous decade and company profits had remained low. With oil seemingly more plentiful than ever before, energy in the 1990s remained out of favor with investors, and capital flowed toward more fashionable sectors. The IOCs, strapped for funds, cut back even further on investment in R&D, exploration, and development.[12] Yet they could see trouble ahead: new oil was becoming tougher and more expensive to find. The IOCs needed to find and book more reserves, but most conventional areas were closed to them, as oil-rich states increasingly favored their own national oil companies.[13] The places still open, mainly the deepwater or unconventional plays such as heavy oils or tar sands, would require larger resources to explore and develop than all but the two or three largest IOCs could command. As the IOCs sized up the situation, they all reached the same conclusion: the only answer was further consolidation.[14]

But who would take over whom? Some IOCs had emerged strengthened from the trials of the previous decade, but others had been lastingly weakened. The price crash of 1998 touched off a first wave of mergers, as the weak were absorbed by the strong. Exxon took over Mobil. Amoco and ARCO were absorbed by BP. Texaco was bought by Chevron. Phillips merged with Conoco, and Total acquired Elf. Over four years, between 1999 and 2002, the number of international majors dropped by half. Of all the majors, only Shell seemed unaffected.

Russia was not a significant factor in the disappearance of the weaker companies, but it is striking that all six of the IOCs that were absorbed between 1999 and 2002 (Texaco, Mobil, Amoco, Conoco, Elf, and ARCO) had tried hard to establish onshore beachheads in Russia and had spent much time and money in the process, to little return (although Conoco and Amoco did have some significant successes to point to). In contrast, most of the surviving majors had been more cautious. Exxon and Shell had focused on the offshore periphery and BP and Chevron on the non-Russian Caspian, while Phillips, up to the time of its merger with Conoco, had avoided the former Soviet Union altogether. Their common view, distilled from their first decade of experience, was that the only acceptable way to manage "Russia risk" was through PSAs, and they redoubled their lobbying efforts to win more of them, while delaying big spending commitments in the meantime.

But one major had decided not to wait. In 1997, BP took a stake in one of the new Russian companies. Six years later, after a roller-coaster ride of accidents and adventures, BP found itself co-owner of what is today the third largest oil company in Russia. In so doing, it broke ranks with the other IOCs' cautious insistence on PSAs and ventured instead into new and uncharted territory, one filled with both rewards and perils, that have shaped both BP and the Russian oil industry since.

BP: From Chickens and Eggs to Elephants

Like many other oil giants, BP had diversified in the 1980s into a wide range of businesses outside oil, including food—it was said at the time that BP produced one of every three chickens in Britain and one of every five eggs. A company that prided itself on its skill in exploration, BP was still smarting over its failure to find oil at Mukluk in Alaska in 1983—the "biggest dry hole in history." With too many small stakes in too many countries, BP had lost focus, and it had fallen into debt. In the City of London, BP was perceived as a company that had lost its way. Inside the company, morale was at a low ebb.

At this point the company reached into its own ranks for a new leader, a Cambridge-educated physicist turned petroleum engineer named John Browne. Browne, whose courtly manner masked a fierce will and a gambler's love of a good bet, fit the mood of the times perfectly. He had served in Alaska and the North Sea and had built a reputation as a skilled manager. By 1995, when he was named CEO, Browne was already widely regarded as one of the most innovative figures in the oil world.[15]

Hunting for Elephants

A key part of Browne's strategy was to take BP back to its historic strength— finding big fields. The objective, he said, was "to hunt for elephants." Over nearly two decades, from 1989 to 2007, Browne personally led his company to every region of Russia. His initial search for elephants did not yield the first-class prospects he was looking for, however, and after a first foray in 1990–1991 BP withdrew from the Russian upstream to concentrate on the South Caspian.

Its return, six years later, began, of all places, in China, and initially it was not even about oil. In the summer of 1997, on a visit to Beijing, John Browne was struck by the Chinese leaders' growing interest in natural gas. Browne recalled that six years earlier BP's Russia team had looked at a gas field called Kovykta in East Siberia near Lake Baikal—and local Russian environmentalists were then promoting gas as a clean alternative to coal. BP had studied the field at the time but had decided it was not economic. "It probably contained as much gas as the whole Norwegian continental shelf," Browne recalled. "But at the time we had neither the right technology to produce it at a profitable rate nor the pipelines to get the gas to a market."[16] Yet in the last half-dozen years the China economy had doubled yet again, and there was no end in sight. Perhaps a gas pipeline from Russia could be profitable after all.

Back in London, Browne learned that the license to Kovykta had passed into the hands of a Russian company called Sidanco, which had recently been acquired by a fast-rising Russian banking group, Oneksimbank, and its industrial arm, Interros. Within days Browne was on a plane to Moscow to meet the bank's young president, Vladimir Potanin. Potanin, then just 36, came from a prominent family in the Soviet foreign-trade ministry. He had grown up in foreign posts all over the world, spoke good English, and his style was polished and urbane. For a brief time until March of that year he had been first deputy prime minister. Soon the two men were talking about collaborating in projects ranging far beyond Kovykta, including, notably, a joint bid for Rosneft. In November 1997 BP purchased a 10 percent stake in Sidanco for $571 million.[17]

What Browne learned too late was that he had just stepped into a minefield. Potanin had acquired Sidanco jointly with Alfa Group, led by Mikhail Fridman, in a shares-for-loans agreement with the government, similar to the one for Yukos. Fridman's Alfa Group was fast emerging as a major player in the oil industry, as the owner of the Tiumen Oil Company, known as TNK. Potanin had put up $200 million for two-thirds of the company, and Fridman $100 million for the remaining third. When Potanin then sold off pieces of Sidanco at much higher prices—including BP's stake—Fridman felt cheated and began planning revenge.[18] The stage was set for a battle royal between oligarchs, Fridman's TNK versus Potanin's Interros, and BP was caught in the middle.

The Battle for Sidanco

Sidanco was one of the weaker of the new oil companies. It had been created in 1994 on the model of the other integrated oils, but from the beginning it was an awkward assemblage. By mid-1998 Sidanco was looking anything but secure. TNK's chief weapon in the war against Potanin was a new bankruptcy law that gave a lopsided advantage to creditors.[19] Anyone who held even a minimal amount of a company's debt—or could buy it on the secondary market—could go to court and have the debtor placed in receivership. Provided the court was compliant, the receiver (who was typically the creditors' man) was soon in control. Once in possession of the director's office, his safe, and his official seal, the receiver could carve up the victim and sell it off to front companies belonging to the creditor. The 1998 bankruptcy law touched off an epidemic of corporate raiding throughout Russia.

TNK's strategy was to buy up the debt of the subsidiaries on the secondary market and to force them into bankruptcy, thus peeling them away from the parent company, Sidanco. Their chief target was one of Sidanco's more attractive subsidiaries, Chernogorneft. TNK soon succeeded in placing its own man in charge as receiver and began diluting or removing Chernogorneft's other creditors so as to gain sole control. In a parallel action, other oil groups went after other Sidanco subsidiaries, Varyogannneft and Kondpetroleum.[20] By late 1998 Sidanco was on the verge of becoming an empty shell.

BP was slow to recognize the danger. Focusing on Kovykta, it had initially played no role in the management of Sidanco, which may have led TNK to believe that BP would not try to hold on to Chernogorneft. By the fall of 1998, TNK was on the verge of having Chernogorneft declared bankrupt. Browne later recalled:

> It seemed unreal. Not only had we lost Chernogorneft, but it had been sold for one-tenth of its value. The company's so-called "debts" could easily have been settled by BP, or one of the other investors. The company could have been refinanced. A lot of people were clearly in cahoots. It emerged that the subsidiary's general manager had already become employed by TNK. Now Sidanco was little more than a skeleton with hardly any assets. We were a naive foreign investor caught out by a rigged legal system. I had signed the deal in front of Blair, BP had been made to look ridiculous.[21]

Browne vowed to fight back. The battled raged for over a year, from the fall of 1998 to the end of 1999. BP and a group of other foreign creditors attempted to work through the courts, but found them mysteriously biased in favor of the other side. By September 1999 it appeared that TNK had won; its receiver prepared to sell off Chernogorneft at auction—an auction that TNK would make sure it won.[22]

But at this point BP found a weak point in TNK—outside Russia. TNK had recently obtained a loan guarantee from the U.S. Export-Import Bank to redevelop an antiquated refinery in Riazan'. The Sidanco affair by this time was drawing major media attention, and in the wake of Russia's massive default the previous summer it was not difficult to mobilize anti-Russian sentiment in New York and Washington against TNK and its parent, Alfa Group. BP, arguing its case at the highest levels in Washington, was able to have TNK's Export-Import Bank loan guarantee canceled.[23] The final showdown came in December 1999. One of Browne's deputies met Mikhail Fridman in Moscow. "I told him he could beat us up inside Russia," the deputy later recalled, "but we could beat him up outside Russia."[24] The government, with Putin now installed as prime minister, quietly signaled to the oligarchs that it was time to settle. The two sides agreed to make peace.[25]

The details took nearly two more years to wrap up.[26] TNK returned Chernogorneft, in exchange for a blocking share of Sidanco. In the end, everyone seemed to have won something. TNK won a stake in Sidanco, practically free. Potanin turned a $300 million investment into a total return of over $1.5 billion. BP won vindication—as well as a measure of respect from the Russians for having fought the good fight. BP put in its own man as CEO of Sidanco, and TNK and BP joined forces in managing the company. Within two more years, Sidanco had turned profitable, creating a platform for a sustained push into the Russian upstream.[27]

For BP, the consequences of the Sidanco affair were far-reaching. From its vantage point inside Sidanco, BP was one of the first foreign companies to grasp the potential "Soviet dividend" that could be realized from the legacy brownfields of West Siberia. From there to the idea of an alliance with its former opponent was but a step. By 2001 Browne and Fridman were discussing merging Sidanco and TNK into a single company. After two years of warfare, from bitter enemies BP and the Russian owners of TNK were about to become allies. In 2003 BP formed a joint venture with a consortium of three Russian partners, Alfa Group, Access Industries, and Renova, which came to be known as AAR. The key players in the consortium, Mikhail Fridman of Alfa and his deputy, German Khan, and the head of Renova, Viktor Vekselberg, played active roles alongside BP in the management of TNK-BP.

From Quarrel to Marriage

The prize seemed irresistible. Thanks to unforeseeable accident and circumstance—but also because it had fought and prevailed—BP now had an opening to do what no other IOC had been allowed to do, namely, to move into the brownfield heartland of West Siberia and reap the "Soviet dividend" as Yukos and Sibneft were doing. But it was no automatic ticket to easy revenues. BP's challenge was to prove that it could bring advanced know-how and management skills to the rehabilitation of the aged Samotlor field, whose collapse in the late 1980s had been the very symbol of the crisis of the Soviet oil industry. But with 466 million tons (3.4 billion barrels) of proven reserves remaining, Samotlor had plenty of life left. BP engineers saw attractive parallels to BP's Prudhoe Bay field in Alaska and were confident Samotlor would respond to the same methods BP had used there. Bob Dudley, the soon-to-be CEO of the prospective joint venture (and today the CEO of BP), called it "a petroleum engineer's dream."[28]

On the face of it, the acquisition of TNK-BP was a relatively modest investment. At $8 billion it was dwarfed by the $48 billion John Browne had paid for Amoco five years before. But in the context of his strategy of "elephant hunting," it was a major move indeed. At one stroke BP added 11 percent to its proven oil and gas reserves and 15 percent to its production.[29] Overnight TNK-BP became the largest of BP's six profit centers worldwide. Samotlor alone was suddenly BP's largest field.[30] Since the core assets were already developed, the joint venture promised immediate dividends, adding considerably to BP's cash flow. But equally appealing was the long-term strategic perspective: if successful, BP would have a broad platform for the development of new onshore assets in Russia, many of them already licensed to the company, and beyond that beckoned the prospect of natural gas production, including John Browne's original dream, the long-sought Kovykta project with its potential market in China. In short, the TNK-BP joint venture would put BP well ahead of any other international company.

But the risks were equally sizable. BP's recent experience of the war over Sidanco had shown that legal remedies were of little help. (As one BP executive put it to me, "We lost every court case we fought.") Consequently, success depended on a close alignment of interests with BP's partners—and the goodwill of the Kremlin. To ensure that the Russian partners would have every incentive to stay on board, BP agreed to a 50–50 ownership split and an equal division of power on the board. "I tried to push for 51 per cent," Browne later wrote, "but both Putin and Fridman told me we could not have it. I knew if we had 49 percent we would have no power whatsoever. So in the end the only option was to go for a 50–50 deal."[31] Putin approved the joint venture personally, giving his blessing at various points. But he disapproved of the 50–50 arrangement. In a private aside to Browne, Putin warned, "It's up to you. But an equal split never works."[32] In light of subsequent events, Putin's warning was not only prophetic but revealing: it suggested that Putin was making no commitment to step in in case of trouble.

At the same time, BP was determined to make sure that it would have operating control of the new entity, which it had never quite achieved with Sidanco. This led to an elaborate division of duties in the management of the company: BP executives had primary responsibility for the management of strategy, technology, and finance, while the Russian partners took charge of political relations, legal affairs, and security. This arrangement proved to be two-edged. On the one hand, it enabled TNK-BP to pursue an aggressive strategy of applying advanced technology and know-how, which over the following five years made TNK-BP the most innovative and successful of all the Russian oil companies. Yet it resulted in a perception of lopsided dominance by the foreign side that was soon resented by the Russians, and the political resources the latter controlled turned out to be decisive.

The Second BP-TNK War—and the Third

For the first several years the joint venture thrived. To lead TNK-BP, John Browne chose an Amoco veteran with Moscow experience, Bob Dudley, who had spent the crucial years 1994–1997 in Amoco's Moscow office. Few foreign oilmen had the intimate knowledge of Russia that Dudley had as he returned to Moscow in 2003, bringing with him a large team of BP specialists that included so many former Amoco hands with U.S. brownfield expertise that for a time TNK-BP became known jokingly as "Amoco's revenge."[33]

TNK already had a reputation for aggressive innovation. (Russians had quickly dubbed TNK the *"tankisty"*—the "tank drivers"—which was both a play on their initials and a comment on their straight-ahead corporate culture). Horizontal drilling, for example, had already migrated to TNK in 2002 when the chief geologist of Noiabrskneftegaz, Iurii Krasnevskii, moved to TNK, bringing with him the new art that had been introduced at Sibneft the year before.[34]

The result was a burst of production and a steep growth curve that lasted about three years, from 2003 through 2005.[35] This strong growth phase was strikingly similar to the earlier pattern at Yukos and Sibneft, and was achieved by much the same combination of measures—"pumps, fracs, and floods"—and like them, it could only be sustained for so long. Predictably, after 2005 the growth in production subsided, as the techniques that had worked so spectacularly at first gradually lost their punch. Hydraulic fracturing, for example, which had yielded over 50 million tons (1 million barrels per day) of incremental production in 2004 at a cumulative cost of about $170 million, by 2007 yielded only 45 million incremental tons (0.9 million barrels per day) at a total cost nearly three times higher.[36]

Maintaining production was now a matter of holding off the decline of the established fields (especially Samotlor)—and of settling in for the long haul. In 2005 TNK-BP began implementing a five-year program to optimize water-flood patterns at Samotlor, based on a state-of-the-art visualization of liquid flows using three-dimensional seismography (known in the industry as "3-D seismic").[37] Through this and other innovative measures, TNK-BP succeeded in slowing the rate of decline at the field, but reversing it was no longer possible. Over the following years, Samotlor continued its steady decline.[38] At the same time, TNK-BP was hampered in the development of new fields by the lack of pipeline connections and the discouraging oil-tax regime, which made most new fields unprofitable.

This slowdown did not sit well with the Russian partners. Beginning in about 2006 rumors began to circulate inside TNK-BP of stormy sessions between CEO Bob Dudley and AAR's German Khan, who as the company's executive director was broadly responsible for strategy. Khan demanded to know why BP's numerous expatriates were unable to maintain the previous rapid rate of growth. But for Dudley this was simply not realistic. In the fall of 2007, unveiling a five-year plan for TNK-BP, he warned that output would be flat until the next generation of fields came online. Investment needs would cut into profits and dividends, and shareholder returns would be 4 percent, less than half the levels of previous years. For the Russian partners, who had come to rely on a steadily growing flow of revenues from TNK-BP to finance investments in their other businesses, this slowdown was unacceptable, and the boardroom quarrels worsened. As German Khan put it in an interview in late 2010:

> There were two key issues. The first was the development of the company as an independent entity, not as a subsidiary of BP. Our partners unfortunately had illusions on that score. The second was the optimization of management costs.[39]

Control and management costs were not the only subjects of discord. AAR from the first had seen TNK-BP as a means of expanding beyond Russia; but for BP, TNK-BP was strictly a Russian venture, and thanks to its veto power on the board, it was able to block AAR's proposals to invest outside. In addition, BP made little secret that it was looking beyond TNK-BP to the next generation of plays at the Russian frontier and that AAR was not part of its plans. There was much discussion in the Russian media that BP might sell its stake in TNK-BP as part of a larger deal. In Russia there are few secrets, and rumors of BP approaching Gazprom and Rosneft reached the AAR partners. "I got the whole information the next day," Fridman claimed later.[40] As the months went by, mistrust and rancor only grew.

Beginning in March 2008, in what had all the appearances of an orchestrated campaign, pressure mounted on the British side in TNK-BP from several quarters at once. Over the next two months, FSB officers raided TNK-BP's offices, arrested a TNK-BP employee (who though a Russian was a British citizen), and hauled away computers and documents. The environmental agency, Rosprirodnadzor (led by the ever-helpful Oleg Mitvol'), announced a probe of TNK-BP's environmental practices at Samotlor. TNK-BP was forced to withdraw 148 of its expatriate staff from Russia when their visas were not renewed. Minprirody hinted that TNK-BP might be stripped of its license at Kovykta. The Ministry of Tax Collections launched a claim for back taxes. Although government officials denied that there was any intent to harass TNK-BP, it was nevertheless a classic display of what Russians euphemistically call "administrative resource."

By May 2008, the conflict between the foreigners and the Russians in TNK-BP had burst into the open, each side denouncing the other for obstructionism and bad faith. The Russian partners demanded Dudley's resignation and turned up the pressure on him both inside and outside the company. A direct appeal to Putin and Sechin by BP's CEO, Tony Hayward, who had succeeded John Browne the year before, produced no letup.[41] By the end of June, Dudley abruptly left Russia, reportedly in fear of personal actions against him. Soon afterward, he was forced to resign.[42]

The Russians had made their point. Yet remarkably, the two sides then proceeded to make peace one more time, with carefully balanced representation for both sides, plus a trio of independent directors—as one insider put it, "one chosen by BP, the second by AAR, and the third—former German chancellor

Gerhard Schroeder—chosen by Putin." Membership in other key bodies, such as the management committee and the shareholders' committee, was shared between the two sides. BP won one important concession, the power to name directors to the key subsidiaries, giving it a measure of oversight over local operations.

Yet the Russian side now effectively dominated the company. Mikhail Fridman became acting CEO, and the number of expatriates was sharply reduced. Although foreigners continued to play key management roles, it was no longer as BP secondees but as employees of TNK-BP. Yet BP remained heavily dependent on income from the joint venture, which by now accounted for one-quarter of its production. It was a vulnerable position.

BP now redoubled its efforts to build a strategic alliance with one of the state-owned giants, and Rosneft soon appeared the likelier candidate. Even as its relations with AAR deteriorated, BP and Rosneft intensified their talks. By early 2010 the main lines of a deal had been worked out. The two companies would explore a large swath of virgin acreage in the Kara Sea, off Russia's Arctic island of Novaya Zemlya. BP would assist Rosneft in developing Arctic skills through joint training programs. The two companies would create a joint Arctic research center in Saint Petersburg. In short, the foundations of an alliance between BP and Rosneft were largely in place.

Then in the spring of 2010 came the Deepwater Horizon disaster in the Gulf of Mexico. In the wake of the giant spill and the crisis that enveloped BP, Bob Dudley, who replaced Tony Hayward as CEO, began the daunting task of rebuilding the company and diversifying its portfolio. Russia was not initially at the top of his list. BP was already heavily invested in Russia, and other opportunities beckoned around the world. But Putin gave a sympathetic reception to the beleaguered company, and appeared ready to support the Rosneft alliance. Moreover, the agreement was practically ready to go. Dudley was persuaded. At the beginning of 2011 the two companies announced their alliance, which was made even broader when, reportedly at Igor Sechin's last-minute suggestion, the two sides agreed to swap minority shares of their stock. For a brief moment it seemed as though BP had pulled off another coup in Russia, sealing its position as the leading foreign oil company.

But AAR angrily charged that the BP-Rosneft agreement violated the terms of the joint venture's founding agreement, and it threatened to take BP to court. After several frantic months, during which the various parties tried to find a compromise, the case went to litigation. The High Court of Justice in

London issued a temporary injunction, which was subsequently upheld by an arbitration panel; and while neither body ruled on the merits of the case, the delay alone was fatal.[43] Rosneft, still eager to find a strategic partner, turned to talks with other candidates. In August 2011 came the coup de grâce, when ExxonMobil and Rosneft announced an even more sweeping strategic alliance (but minus the share swap.) As the *Financial Times*'s influential Lex column commented mercilessly, referring to ExxonMobil's CEO, "Rex Tillerson has eaten Bob Dudley's lunch."

The setback left BP without the long-term strategic relationship it had been hoping for, or access to the Arctic offshore, the key to its long-term strategy in Russia. Moreover, by the following year it had become plain that the latest patch-up between BP and AAR had failed to work. The partners were again at loggerheads, the board was paralyzed, and dividends were going unpaid. The partnership appeared to have run its course, and both sides began looking for an exit.

Nevertheless, BP's experience in Russia stands out as a unique case in the relationship of the foreign companies and the Russian oil industry to date. No other foreign company has ever gained such broad access to the Russian brownfield heartland; no other foreign oil company has ever gained such a degree of operational control over a Russian major; no other foreign company has ever harvested so much of the upside of the venture. It is probably safe to say that no other foreign company ever will again. But BP was rewarded for its daring; it is arguably the only IOC to have made really serious money in Russia. As of 2012 BP had reportedly made over $19 billion in dividends from its investment in TNK-BP, and TNK-BP remains a major source of profits.

In broader perspective, BP's impact on the Russian oil industry, through the vehicle of TNK-BP, has been substantial. TNK-BP between 2003 and 2008 was the leading edge of technology transfer into Russian oilfield practice. In key respects it picked up where Yukos and Sibneft had left off, as the most innovative company in Russia's legacy fields, and in the process it turned TNK from an accidental assemblage of assets into Russia's most modern oil company. Moreover, TNK-BP has hardly said its last word. In recent years it has moved on to major greenfield projects in northern and eastern Siberia, even as it continues to find and produce new oil in West Siberia and in the brownfields of the Urals.[44] As the tight-oil revolution comes to Russia, TNK-BP will very likely play a leading role in it.

At the same time, the TNK-BP story also underscored—yet again—the inherent instability of partnerships and the unreliability of political connections as a basis for investment, in an environment where legal protections are weak. "BP gets into trouble because it tries to play the politics," an influential Russian businessman told a Western audience shortly after the collapse of the BP-Rosneft alliance. "No foreign company can possibly understand Russian politics—it's too complicated." The businessman was Mikhail Fridman.[45]

Yet what, one might reasonably ask, is the alternative? The standard answer is the old standby, the production-sharing contract. But as we saw in Chapter 4, PSAs were viewed with suspicion by both the Russian government and the companies, and as a result, by the end of the 1990s, they had made only limited headway. In the next section we look at what happened.

Chasing the Holy Grail: The Elusive Promise of PSA

Despite the passage of a framework law in 1994, PSA in practice remained an unsatisfactory vehicle. At Sakhalin-2, despite its "grandfathered PSA," over 1,700 authorizations of various kinds (decrees, licenses, approvals) were required before the first oil was produced in 1999.[46] The other two grandfathered PSAs, Sakhalin-1 and Khariaga, found the road similarly bumpy. Meanwhile, further PSA deals remained frustratingly out of reach. The framework law required a raft of enabling legislation to bring it into conformity with other Russian laws, but the enabling legislation had been stuck in the works for half a decade. Meanwhile, over two dozen other projects, slated for PSAs, waited in line for approval.

When Vladimir Putin became president in 2000, there were high hopes for reforms of all sorts, and the foreign oil companies renewed their attempts to establish PSA as the standard vehicle for new projects involving IOCs. Initially the new president appeared receptive. He put his new minister of economics, German Gref, in charge of PSA and instructed him to push through the long-stalled enabling legislation. At a special conference on PSA in September 2000, convened on Sakhalin Island and attended by the top Russian ministers and oil and gas leaders, together with the CEOs of several foreign companies who had flown in specially for the occasion, Putin gave what seemed to be a ringing endorsement to PSA. Calling it "an effective and widely used mechanism" and "an important part of our investment policy," Putin acknowledged that PSA had become bogged down in politics, and he promised that the new government would smooth the way forward.[47]

But looked at more closely, Putin's remarks at Sakhalin were less encouraging than his listeners thought at the time. He rejected the idea of a special new government body—German Gref's Ministry of Economics was sufficient, he said. He insisted on the principle of equal access for Russian and foreign companies and also on the importance of using Russian personnel and equipment. When it came to specific measures, Putin was unsupportive or vague.

Over the following two years, it became clear that Putin simply did not like PSA. In June 2001, at a press conference in Ljubljana, Slovenia, following the U.S.-Russian summit with President George W. Bush (the one where Bush famously declared he had "looked the man in the eye . . . and got a sense of his soul"), Putin spoke far more candidly:

> You know that I meet regularly with Russian business leaders. Some of the government's plans in the area of PSA make them uneasy, and it would be wrong not to pay attention to them. Their point is very simple. "Well, if you're offering foreign investors some kind of preferential terms, let's say, on taxes, then how are we worse than they?"[48]

He went on to say that oil and gas investment should be governed by "the normal tax regime," which the government was working on improving. He did not rule out the need for preferential terms in the case of high-risk frontier projects, but he added, "We cannot put our own companies in a worse position than the foreign ones. The terms on production sharing must be universal; they must be available to Russian businessmen as well."[49]

But mostly Putin ignored PSA altogether. Over the next several years, particularly on foreign trips, Putin's official remarks included ritual one-line references to it, but that was all. Sensing the lack of enthusiasm from his boss, German Gref went about other business, and work on the enabling legislation for PSA slowed back down to a crawl. It was not until 2003, two years later, that the government's bill finally reached the Duma. Meanwhile, the foreign companies continued to negotiate deals and projects, some of which involved spending substantial sums on preliminary exploration—in the tens and sometimes hundreds of millions of dollars—but before they would commit billions for full-scale development they insisted on having an acceptable legal base, and as far as they were concerned, PSA was it. By 2003, there were over twenty-five projects waiting in the queue, involving twenty-eight companies holding sixty-five licenses.[50] They had received preliminary approval of eligibility for PSA, but without the all-important enabling legislation, they could not go forward.

But the government was not the only problem; the Russian companies were unenthusiastic as well. Indeed, there was one Russian oilman who was more than just "uneasy" about PSA—he was determined to kill it. Mikhail Khodorkovsky of Yukos between 2001 and 2003 made it a personal crusade to block PSA. Khodorkovsky's motive was quite clear: by killing PSA he meant to prevent foreign companies from gaining independent access to Russian resources and reserves. Their only means of access would be through buying stakes in Russian companies—especially his own—thus driving up their market value. Khodorkovsky was playing a double game. In public he affected to believe that there was no need for new investment in frontier projects, and consequently no need for foreign companies either. As he told a reporter:

> For the next 30 years there are enough low-cost fields in Russia to sustain production of 9 million barrels a day, and more than that no one will buy. And by then the more inaccessible fields will have become "normal," since their costs will have come down substantially.[51]

But in private—and in frequent meetings with the foreign companies themselves—Khodorkovsky was quite candid about his real aim. From 2002 on, as we have seen, he was negotiating actively with ExxonMobil and Chevron to sell or swap a controlling block in Yukos.[52] We have seen in earlier chapters how Khodorkovsky had gained virtual veto power over tax legislation in the Duma, and placing one of Menatep's senior shareholders, Vladimir Dubov, in the key position of chairman of the key subcommittee on taxes. From that vantage point Dubov was able to act as a gatekeeper over all tax legislation initiatives, particularly on PSA.[53] By the time the long-awaited enabling legislation finally reached the floor of the Duma in the spring of 2003, Khodorkovsky's people had loaded it with killer amendments that were designed to make it totally unpalatable to the foreign companies.

Old Russia hands in the foreign companies blame Khodorkovsky for killing PSA. ("Brilliant and ruthless" is how one sums up his campaign.) But the reality was more complex. The other private Russian oils did not like PSA either (except for themselves), and for much the same reasons as Khodorkovsky, but they were content to let Khodorkovsky be their stalking horse in the Duma.

The government, as we have seen, was mostly opposed or at best lukewarm. While Putin was distant and Gref was dilatory, the Ministry of Finance actively opposed any expansion of PSA. Thus the private oil companies and the government, though for different reasons, combined to smother further progress on PSA.[54]

Thus by 2003–2004 the only vehicle left for foreign companies wishing to invest in Russian oil projects was the joint venture. BP, as we have seen, had been the first to reach this conclusion, when it negotiated TNK-BP as a joint venture with its Russian AAR partners. Several other foreign companies, having concluded that PSA would never happen, also fell back on the joint venture as the only way to hold on to their positions in Russia. Shell held out for a decade for a PSA for its project at Salym in West Siberia, but when threatened with the loss of its license it decided to take a chance on a joint venture with its partner Evikhon, a small independent with connections to various second-tier oligarchs and the city government of Moscow.[55] It was that or nothing, and Salym was too attractive to pass up; though a relatively small project, its complex geology offered an opportunity to showcase Shell's capabilities. Conoco (by this time ConocoPhillips), which had waited an equally long time for a PSA for its Northern Territory project, entered into a strategic alliance with LUKoil. The two companies formed a 50–50 joint subsidiary, Nar'ianmarneftegaz, to develop the South Khylchuiu field near the Arctic Sea coast. It was this very proximity to the sea that made the field prospectively economic and the risk worth taking: by building a pipeline directly to a floating terminal located just offshore, the partners avoided paying pipeline tariffs to Transneft. But ConocoPhillips went further, buying a 20 percent stake in LUKoil itself, essentially forming a strategic relationship with Vagit Alekperov's company.

Thus by 2003 a decade of effort to establish PSA as the preferred investment vehicle in Russia came to an end, defeated by hostility from both politicians and oilmen. Its advocates could never quite overcome its negative image in Russia, and as the country stabilized and the fiscal regime evolved, the Russians could argue that PSA was not needed. What the Russians' rejection of it for the IOCs in Russia really meant, as subsequent events were about to prove, was that they did not want the IOCs in controlling roles. Indeed, this became abundantly clear over the following years, when even the grandfathered PSAs came under attack.

The Wind Shifts against the Foreign Companies

Despite the disappointment over PSA, 2003 was a year of breakthroughs in the international oil companies' involvement in the Russian oil industry. All three grandfathered PSAs were moving forward, as Shell made a final investment decision at Sakhalin-2. Three newly formed joint ventures (TNK-BP, Salym, and Nar'ianmarneftegaz) appeared promising. It even seemed briefly possible, in the spring and summer of that year, that the IOCS might acquire majority stakes in the two leading Russian companies, Yukos and Sibneft.

But in the wake of the Yukos Affair, the atmosphere changed radically. Instead of opening the door wider to foreign oil investment, the Russian government shut it. In the spring of 2005, in his annual address to the parliament, the president called for new legislation to regulate foreign investment. He justified it on the grounds that private investors needed clear guidelines on which sectors were open to outside capital and which were not. Read in context, his intent seemed relatively liberal. In the same speech he also called for a statute of limitations on prosecution of tax cases; for more favorable conditions to encourage repatriation of Russian offshore capital; and for new regulations to reach closure on outstanding taxes and penalties. All of these had been prominent issues in the Yukos Affair, and the business community had been vocal in its criticism of the way the government had handled them. Putin's words gave the impression he was responding to their complaints. "The tax organs do not have the right," he said, "to 'terrorize' business by returning repeatedly to the same problems." Thus Putin's call for legislation on foreign investment could reasonably have been interpreted at the time as part of an attempt by the president to draw a line under the Yukos Affair, but in a way that was not necessarily unfriendly to private investors, including foreign ones.[56]

At first this benign interpretation appeared confirmed by events. Iurii Trutnev, the minister of natural resources, was initially given the lead role in drawing up the new legislation Putin had called for. His approach was to fold it into a revised mineral resources law *(Zakon o nedrakh),* a draft of which had already been approved by the government in March 2005.[57] In this draft, the restrictions on foreign investment were relatively mild: foreign participation in "strategic" projects was limited to companies registered in Russia and at least 51 percent owned by Russian entities. At this early stage, the government was still vague about its definition of "strategic." The general impression was that

Trutnev intended to keep the list short and that the new rules being pro-posed by Trutnev's ministry would have relatively little impact on foreign investors.[58]

Yet by the summer of 2006 the entire tone of the discussion inside the Russian government had hardened. First, the MVD and the FSB openly entered the fray. Their view of "strategic" was much more extensive, essentially covering any sector that could be construed as having any significance for national security. Over the following two years the FSB became an active player in the battle over the new law, drafting its own versions of the legislation and gaining a de facto veto power over the process.

Second, the steady rise of global oil and gas prices generated euphoria in Russia. Russian officials and businessmen became enthusiastic believers in the "new thinking" that said as global oil demand increased and oil production neared its peak, prices could only go up. The commodity cycle was a thing of the past.

Third and perhaps most important, Putin's enthusiastic support for the concept of "national champions" gave the state-owned companies, chiefly Gazprom and Rosneft, steadily higher status and political clout. Both companies were keen to prevent competitors—whether foreign or Russian—from gaining access to frontier areas, and especially to the Arctic offshore, which loomed as the next generation of Russian oil and gas. As the debate over the legislation on "strategic fields" went on, it underwent a subtle shift: whereas initially it had been aimed primarily at foreign investors, by the time the final draft was approved it had turned into a weapon directed against all nonstate players.

Thus Trutnev's original liberal draft of the investment law was displaced by more restrictive versions, more focused on excluding foreign investors than on regulating them and indeed, it seemed, on shutting out private players altogether. The resulting law, as signed by Putin shortly before he stepped down as president in May 2008, was a sweeping piece of legislation that covered forty-two separate sectors of the economy now designated as strategic, ranging from military-industrial factories to TV and radio broadcasting, space exploration, printing, weather forecasting, fisheries, and just about everything in between.[59]

By the time Putin stepped aside as president in the spring of 2008, the Russian government's policies on foreign investment had become so restrictive that they practically shut off any possibility of meaningful foreign participation in new oil and gas projects, except in the lesser role of service providers.

Foreign companies that wished to acquire even so much as a 10 percent stake in an oil or gas property "of strategic significance" (defined as any oilfield with reserves of more than 70 million tons [511 million barrels] or a gasfield with more than 50 billion cubic meters [1.8 trillion cubic feet]) were required to go through an elaborate approvals procedure, culminating in a review by a commission chaired by the prime minister—who after May 2008 happened to be Putin himself, wearing his new hat. The Russian government appeared determined to reserve all future oil and gas of any significance to domestic companies, and especially to its "national champions," Gazprom and Rosneft.

At the same time, the word "privatization" practically disappeared from the government's lexicon. Instead, Putin's second term was notable for the steady concentration of key assets in an ever smaller circle of state-owned companies, most of them controlled by individuals close to the Kremlin and indeed to Putin himself. Former KGB officers and former officials of the Saint Petersburg mayoralty were prominently represented. In parallel with this trend at the top, there was a wave of takeovers of businesses all across the country (most of them hostile, a phenomenon known in Russian as *reidy*—"raids"), many of them instigated by business groups with ties to the siloviki.[60] This new redivision of property (quickly dubbed by Russians the "second *peredel*," in comparison with the first *peredel* of the 1990s[61]), created a new generation of well-connected oligarchs.[62] In contrast to the first generation of oligarchs, who owed their fortunes to the dissolution of the state under Yeltsin, the second generation owed theirs to its reconstitution under Putin. But in both cases the source was the same: the state.

The Grandfathered PSAs as Vehicles of Innovation

Even as PSA faded as a model for new projects, the three "grandfathered PSAs," Sakhalin-1, Sakhalin-2, and Khariaga, carried on. What was their role as agents of technology transfer? This is a timely question, in view of the recent conclusion of a strategic alliance between ExxonMobil and Rosneft, the two principal partners in the Sakhalin-1 PSA.

The significant fact about the Sakhalin PSAs is that they were frontier offshore projects located in territory where Russian companies had not worked before on any significant scale. Consequently, Exxon and Shell had virtually sole control of both projects' design and execution, such as the long-reach wells that were the centerpiece of Sakhalin-1. Much of the actual work was also done by foreign contractors because there were practically no Russian companies with the necessary skills and experience. The local-content rules under which the PSA operated required identifying and hiring potential Russian contractors where possible, but this did not lead to the kind of intimate collaboration and mutual learning that were the norm, say, in TNK-BP. (Exxon, for example, never seconded its executives into the top management of Sakhalinmorneftegaz, much less Rosneft itself.) Therefore the impact of the Sakhalin projects as vehicles of technology transfer and learning was relatively minor. The most important legacy of Sakhalin-1 for Rosneft may have been on the level of senior management. When Sergei Bogdanchikov moved from Sakhalin to Moscow, he staffed Rosneft's senior positions with his core team from Sakhalinmorneftegaz—people who had long worked with Exxon in jointly running the Sakhalin-1 PSA. However, most of the Sakhalinmorneftegaz veterans have since left the company, a potentially significant point in the new alliance.

If ExxonMobil was fortunate in its choice of partners, Shell at Sakhalin-2 was not nearly so lucky. Its main backer in Russia had been the regional government of Sakhalin Island, and especially its charismatic governor, Igor Farkhutdinov. But the regions rapidly lost influence when Putin became president, and after Farkhutdinov was killed in a helicopter crash in August 2003, Shell and the other foreign shareholders in the Sakhalin Energy Investment Company found themselves without a Russian partner. Thus they were hostages to fortune, all the more since they had decided not to wait further for the long delayed enabling legislation to accompany the 1994 PSA Law, but instead took their final investment decision on the strength of a "comfort letter" provided by then prime minister Mikhail Kasyanov.[63]

But a would-be partner soon stepped forward: Gazprom. The gas giant had given little attention to the eastern half of the country in the 1990s, but that changed after 2001, reflecting Putin's own growing strategic interest in eastern Russia and the Pacific rim. Under a new CEO, Aleksei Miller, and a new management team, Gazprom signaled that it wished to join the Sakhalin-2 consortium, and for the next several years, the two companies negotiated without result. Finally, in June 2005, Shell and Gazprom announced a memorandum of understanding (MOU), under which Shell would gain a half interest in Gazprom's Zapoliarnoe field, while Gazprom would take a 25 percent stake (plus one additional share) in Sakhalin-2.

Barely a week after the MOU had been signed, however, Shell announced that the costs of Sakhalin-2 were expected to come in at double the initial 2003 estimate of $10 billion (which was long out of date by 2006). This could hardly have been news to the Russian side, and least of all to Gazprom (which had presumably done a careful review before the MOU was signed), but the timing was awkward to say the least because it gave the Russian government a convenient bludgeon to use against Shell. The announcement was followed by a wave of angry reactions on the Russian side. Multiple government agencies launched investigations into the cost overruns and reported environmental violations. All through 2006 pressure mounted on Shell and its Japanese partners. In December, Oleg Mitvol', the Ministry of Natural Resources' environmental regulator, announced that the government intended to sue Sakhalin Energy in foreign courts for over $30 billion in environmental damages, and the General Procurator's office announced it was considering criminal charges against the company's executives. For Shell and its Japanese partners, it was clear the game was up. On December 21, 2006, they signed an agreement to turn majority control over to Gazprom, for a price of $7.45 billion in cash.

The Sakhalin-2 affair is repeatedly cited in the international media as the classic illustration of the insecurity of foreigners' property rights in Russia, but for the purposes of this chapter what is equally important is the significance of Sakhalin-2 for what it tells us about technology transfer and learning between the foreign partners and the Russian companies. The impact was mixed. The design and construction of the offshore platforms was a great engineering achievement; but the cost overruns and environmental violations associated with the pipeline project pointed to problems of management, in particular in the oversight of Sakhalin Energy's principal Russian contractor. In short, the chief comparative advantage claimed by the IOCs—their supposed superiority in managing large and sensitive projects—was undermined by this case.

Yet the most important test of the long-term significance of Sakhalin-2 may still lie ahead. In acquiring majority control of Sakhalin-2, Gazprom has entered a partnership with one of the leading global players in the liquified natural gas (LNG) business. LNG, though made from gas, is in fact a radically different product, both in its engineering and in its commerce. Gazprom is a latecomer to it and is still in an early learning phase. Through Shell, Gazprom now has a platform through which to train a cadre of engineers and executives in the production, transportation, and marketing of a new industry, working with the people who pioneered it. Only time will tell how Gazprom will take advantage of the opportunity.

Service Companies as a Channel of Transfer: The Case of Geophysics and Schlumberger

Yet another channel of technology transfer to the Russian oil industry is the service sector. The most successful foreign company in this sector has been the Franco-American giant Schlumberger. While the service sector attracts less attention in the media than the IOCs, from the standpoint of the transfer of technology the impact of Schlumberger and other foreign service companies has arguably been the most powerful of all,

In today's oil business, much of the actual work of exploration and development, drilling and repairing wells, and so on, is outsourced to specialized service companies. In the Soviet industry, however, most services were traditionally performed by in-house service departments directly subordinated to the NGDUs, and the levels of efficiency and technological sophistication applied to the fields were on the whole quite low. This situation only worsened in the 1990s. The emerging Russian companies were too poor, and too busy with more urgent matters, to spend much money on advanced technologies. Most of the joint ventures that sprang up at the time, as we saw earlier, focused on well repair and rehabilitation. The only foreign technique that was adopted widely in the industry in that decade was hydraulic fracturing.

The large international service companies, such as Schlumberger, Halliburton, and Baker-Hughes, opened offices in Russia soon after the Soviet Union fell but mainly with the strategy of providing services to the IOCs once, as expected, PSAs were concluded and actual projects began. However, as we have seen, with the exception of the three grandfathered projects, the hoped-for PSAs never materialized. The service companies found work at Sakhalin and the small handful of other locations where foreign companies were active, but overall, business remained modest. As Andrew Gould, Schlumberger's longtime CEO, recalls,

> Our initial beginnings were difficult. We could not get substantial business with the Russian oil companies, and the attempts of the international oil companies to penetrate the Russian oil market were small and slow. Logistics were complex and operating practices different.[64]

The first big breakthrough came in 1998, when Schlumberger concluded its strategic agreement with Yukos. Schlumberger took over the hydraulic fracturing equipment left behind by Canadian Fracmasters after the crash of 1998 and put it to work on a much larger scale, while installing one of its employees, Joe Mach, in charge of oilfield technology inside Yukos. Between 1998 and 2002, Schlumberger became the chief conduit for innovation at Yukos, not only revolutionizing its approach to production but also introducing modern financial and human-resources management. "Much of Yukos's incentive system was copied from Schlumberger," the head of Schlumberger Russia told me later. "It relied heavily on promoting young talent. Movement upward was a key part of the incentive system." If one considers Yukos to be Russia's first "Western-style" oil company, it was partly thanks to Schlumberger's role as a channel of learning and innovation in the initial years under Khodorkovsky.

One of Khodorkovsky's planned innovations was to split away the service departments of the Yukos subsidiaries and amalgamate them into a single company controlled jointly by Yukos and Schlumberger as partners. This structure would have given Schlumberger practically monopoly control of Yukos's services, but the plan foundered, partly on Joe Mach's opposition but probably also Khodorkovsky's second thoughts, before it could be implemented. By this time Yukos's relationship with Schlumberger had cooled, and in 2003 the strategic relationship was terminated, leaving Schlumberger's leadership with the challenge of finding a new strategy to expand their base in Russia.

Schlumberger was founded early in the twentieth century by two French brothers, Conrad and Marcel Schlumberger, who had pioneered the revolutionary approach of "seeing" through formations of solid rock by passing electrical currents through them. They took their novel technique to the United States and applied it there to logging wells in the nascent Texas oil industry. From these early origins Schlumberger has retained a uniquely international management style: wherever it works, it hires and trains local nationals and then moves them throughout its worldwide organization.[65] From the moment it arrived in Russia, Schlumberger set about doing the same.

It found no lack of local talent, given the strong traditions of geology, geophysics, materials science, and computer software that had been nurtured by the Soviet regime. Here we focus particularly on geophysics as an example. A

439

network of R&D institutes in geophysics had been created under the aegis of the USSR Ministry of Instrument-Building, which was one of the nine ministries belonging to the so-called *oboronka,* the military-industrial complex. These institutes mainly supported the vast oil-exploration program of the Soviet era (which was mostly carried out by the Ministry of Geology), although a few also oversaw the development of production plans. But the system fell apart in the 1990s when the Soviet Union ended, and the geophysicists suddenly had to fend for themselves.

One of those struggling outfits was the Oil and Gas Geophysical Research Institute (VNIIneftepromgeofizika), which had been created in 1970 to provide well logging and other services to the oil and gas industry. In 1991, left to its own devices, the institute was privatized under the name of "Geofizika" and survived the dog years of the 1990s by providing whatever services it could to the new oil companies, for example, applying acoustic methods to testing the soundness of cement casings. When Schlumberger arrived in Russia, it formed a partnership with Geofizika to develop computerized logging stations. Thanks to this early business with Schlumberger, Geofizika developed a line of advanced oilwell applications, which enabled it to grow as an independent company.

Today, Geofizika has become a major competitor to Schlumberger for the Russian market in geophysical equipment. By the beginning of the 2000s, indeed, competition from Russians was rapidly rising all across the spectrum of oilfield services, as Russian start-ups took advantage of the accelerating oil boom and the increasing willingness of the Russian oil companies to spend money for services—basic to the world industry but new to Russia—like hydraulic fracturing, logging, management of drilling fluids, advanced perforation and high-quality cementing, and the like, but also, increasingly, more expensive and sophisticated technology, such as 3-D seismic and its applications to field development.[66] New techniques such as "measurement while drilling," which enable drillers to guide their drill bits to their targets with great precision while obtaining real-time information about the structures they are crossing, began to find a market with the Russian oil companies, at least in the newer fields. At the beginning of the decade, the foreign service companies had been the only ones to offer these services; but by the second half of the 2000s they had begun to spread to Russian service providers.[67]

With its alliance with Yukos at an end and competition increasing, Schlumberger set a bold course: expansion by acquisition. Its business plan for Russia aimed at quickly capturing a dominant position by buying out the emerging private companies all across the spectrum of Russian geophysics services. Between 2003 and 2007 Schlumberger acquired a broad swath of Russian start-ups. Many of these acquisitions retained their own brands, even though they were owned by Schlumberger.[68] By 2007, Schlumberger had 14,000 employees in Russia (both directly and through its owned brands) and by some estimates held one-third of the market for oilfield services and a dominant position in the most advanced high-end applications.

Whereas Schlumberger's main entry ticket into Russia had been hydraulic fracturing, by 2005 this market was beginning to fill with Russian competitors, and Schlumberger branched out into newer techniques, such as horizontal drilling and integrated project management, meaning the application of advanced technologies to the management of the entire reservoir through digital data processing and modeling. In addition, Schlumberger set up factories and began producing equipment—submersible pumps, perforating equipment, and equipment for fracturing fleets (most of these by now operated by Russian companies). Much of this business represented a departure for Schlumberger, in that it was relatively standard compared with its more high-tech services, but there was a substantial market for it. By 2006 Schlumberger had expanded well beyond its initial niche and was realizing over $1 billion in annual revenues in Russia.[69] As Andrew Gould put it,

> Their technology is fit for purpose and their knowledge of the problems associated with production in Western Siberia is far superior to ours. . . . This has helped tailor our service delivery to the high-volume nature of West Siberian operations.[70]

However, Schlumberger's expansion into the Russian market and its buyouts of smaller players raised fears that Schlumberger would soon become the only significant player in high-end services. In 2004 a coalition of Russian investors and companies, with the discreet backing of the oil companies and the Russian government, formed a holding company called Integra. Its CEO was a young entrepreneur, Feliks Liubashevskii, who was the son-in-law of Russian oligarch Viktor Vekselberg, one of the co-owners of TNK-BP. Throughout

2005–2007, with backing from foreign partners, Integra pursued essentially the same acquisitions strategy as Schlumberger, buying up smaller Russian companies in the drilling and geophysics business. In parallel, another holding company, Geotek, also co-owned by Vekselberg, grew rapidly by the same means. Schlumberger and a handful of foreign providers retained their dominant positions as the chief providers of high-end technologies, but the Russians were learning how to compete by creating conglomerates of their own.[71]

The crash of 2008 caused a severe shake-out of the Russian oilfield services market. In the brownfields the Russian oil companies scaled down their orders, focusing selectively on services that would maintain production at the least cost, while putting intense pressure on the service companies to cut their prices and accept longer payment schedules. Only in the highest-priority greenfield projects, such as Rosneft's Vankor field, did the Russian companies continue to buy the most advanced equipment and services, and when they did so it was primarily from the leading foreign companies. However, such frontier business was limited by the unfavorable tax regime, which caused the Russian companies to hold back on new greenfield projects.[72]

The result was an extensive restructuring of the geophysics market, which is still ongoing today. One-third of the Russian geophysics companies, chiefly the smaller ones, went under in 2008–2009.[73] Many of the remaining ones, including some of the in-house service departments of the Russian oil companies, are once again being absorbed by the foreign companies, particularly Schlumberger.[74] The Russian geophysics companies complain that they are being pushed back down to the low end of the market by the Russian oil companies, which they accuse of being willing to pay top dollar to a foreign company but not to a Russian one. As a result, the Russian service companies say they do not have the resources to finance large-scale R&D and consequently are falling farther and farther behind the rapidly moving front of technological advance worldwide.[75]

At the same time, the foreign service companies too have felt constrained by the lack of new business in greenfield projects, and this has caused them to adjust their strategies. In 2010 Schlumberger created a joint venture with Integra, which by this time had become its principal Russian competitor. Not surprisingly, the joint venture has touched off speculation that it is the prelude to yet another acquisition, but both companies have denied any such plans.[76] It remains that the joint venture with Integra is a direct extension of

Schlumberger's strategy in Russia, especially West Siberia, over the past decade.

Schlumberger, meanwhile, continues to consolidate its position as the Russian market leader for advanced oilfield services. In 2010 it opened a state-of-the-art "operations support center" in Tiumen' City, which provides remote monitoring and modeling of the oil companies' drilling operations, to support advanced techniques such as horizontal drilling. This is the most up-to-date such facility in Russia and as such seems certain to widen the gap between the sophisticated support Schlumberger can provide and the more modest support available from the Russian companies.[77]

Thus, next to BP, Schlumberger has been to date the single most successful and profitable foreign company in the Russian oil sector. The chief reason is undoubtedly Schlumberger's determined effort to "look Russian, hire Russian, and act Russian." By 2005, Schlumberger had 4,500 employees in Russia, 95 percent of them Russian. As Andrew Gould said at the time, "Russia is no different from the development of Schlumberger in any other country. . . . But nowhere in the last few years have we applied this formula more successfully than in Russia."[78]

Thus, service companies like Schlumberger provide yet another channel between the global oil industry and its Russian counterpart. Schlumberger draws on Russia as a major source of talent and ideas for Schlumberger's operations worldwide. As early as 2005, Schlumberger had recruited over 500 Russian engineers, many of them from its joint program with Gubkin University, and assigned them to its international operations. The following year, it opened its first training center in Russia, to support both its own operations in-country and its international recruitment.[79] But the most striking example of Schlumberger's role in creating bridges between Russian and global technology is its appointment of the rector of the Moscow Institute of Physics and Technology ("Fiztekh"), Nikolay Kudryavtsev, to Schlumberger's board of directors.

Schlumberger's R&D in Russia, unlike that of most Russian institutes and companies, has been translated into patents and applications worldwide. According to former CEO Andrew Gould, Schlumberger has filed over 234 patents for inventions originating from research at Schlumberger's centers in Russia, including a proppant for hydraulic fracturing that is now widely used in the United States.[80] This is far more than the combined total of foreign patents filed by all of the Russian oil companies combined.

The impact of Schlumberger and the other foreign service companies on the interconnectedness of the Russian oil industry with the global industry is less clear. On the one hand, it all comes down to people, and here Schlumberger's contribution has been immense. Over the last fifteen years, Schlumberger has trained tens of thousands of Russians in its culture and techniques, and it has rotated several thousand of them in and out of its international operations worldwide. This represents a huge potential source of new experience and knowledge for Russia, some of which has undoubtedly migrated horizontally into other service companies and into the Russian majors.

What is less obvious is the impact on the Russian upstream overall. Insofar as these employees migrate to other Russian service companies, they find themselves subject to the same general indifference of their clients, and they lack the means to maintain the R&D activity that they experienced inside Schlumberger. Insofar as they move to the Russian upstream companies themselves, it is not clear what impact they have yet had on the companies' procurement practices, which remain for the most part conservative and near-term. In sum, the impact of the foreign service companies on people is undoubtedly large, probably indeed the largest single source of technology transfer and learning, yet its overall effect on the industry is not yet fully visible.

Meanwhile, the danger, as the market share of the foreign companies expands, is the possibility of political reaction. It is surprising, indeed, that there has not been more pushback to date. This may be due to the extreme deconcentration of the Russian services industry (particularly in the geophysics area, which accounts for only about 15 percent of the total services market) or to counterpressure from the Russian oil companies, who for all their rhetoric about "buying Russian" are not keen to see government regulators interfere with their traditional dominance over the service sector. The last thing the oil companies want to hear is the kind of procurement regime proposed recently by one spokesman for the domestic geophysics companies: "The Russian companies must have preference in getting orders, and agreements should be structured on a long-term basis and mutually acceptable financial terms."[81] To an oil company, that will sound like "captive market and fixed prices and prepayment."

The government too has largely ignored the calls of the domestic oil-service industry for a more protectionist policy, except in the more politically visible

444

area of procurement for the large PSAs.[82] But the political atmosphere may be changing, for three reasons. First, the Russian equipment suppliers are coming under growing competition from Chinese manufacturers. The traditional dominance of Uralmash as a supplier of drilling rigs, for example, is being rapidly eroded by cheap rigs from China. The Russian service companies have been quick to point out that the Chinese oil companies have blocked any significant penetration of foreign companies into their home market and invoke Chinese policy as a model for Russia. Second, the "modernization and diversification" campaign is putting the political spotlight on all domestic sources of innovation, and on small business in particular, which may stimulate government agencies to take a more active role in supporting it. Third, and perhaps related, is the growing visibility of some well-placed investors, notably Gennadii Timchenko, who recently bought a stake in Geotek. All in all, the position of the foreign service suppliers may soon come under challenge.

However, the real obstacle to more efficient transfer of advanced technology via the service companies remains the weakness of demand for innovation from the oil companies themselves. Until now, it has been the lack of a determined push by the Russian oil industry into new areas of activity—the Arctic offshore, East Siberian exploration, enhanced recovery in West Siberia, and unconventional liquids of all kinds—that has limited the market for advanced services to the oil industry. The comfortable cocoon of the Soviet-era legacy and the flow of rents it provides still envelop both the industry and the government and constrain the demand for advanced services.

Conclusion: On the Edge of a New Era?

The proposition of this chapter is that the Russian oil industry has not yet emerged from the isolation of the Soviet era; it is not yet well connected with the revolutionary changes taking place in the global industry; and consequently it lags behind the leading global players (a category that includes the private-owned IOCs but also an emerging cohort of increasingly competitive NOCs as well as the top service companies) in efficiency, innovativeness, and entrepreneurship. This lag, in turn, leaves the Russian oil industry poorly prepared for the coming challenges of the next generation of oil—higher costs, tougher conditions, and, ultimately, the threat of lower rents.

The Russian oil industry's continuing isolation is not accidental but the result of a systematic pattern. The argument of this chapter (and of Chapter 4, on the 1990s) is that the main channels by which cross-border transfer of skills and experience normally take place—joint ventures, PSAs, strategic alliances, international partnerships, service contracts, individual secondments and study abroad, exchange programs, and so forth—have been blocked, impeded, or neglected. All have been tried; some have succeeded; but with one or two exceptions (which underscore the general pattern) they have been marginal in their impact on the Russian industry and on the Russian government, compared with the larger and more transformative flows of learning and change that have taken place in other countries such as Norway and Brazil.

Why is this so? History is an important factor. For the first decade after the Soviet collapse, the Russians and the foreigners struggled to find a common language. They were united by a common set of technical skills but separated by everything else. Throughout the 1990s, the extreme instability of Russia hampered the effort to identify suitable projects, find appropriate partners, or focus on common interests. But the relative stabilization that occurred after 2005, both in Russian politics and in the oil industry, did not improve the situation—indeed, in some respects it made it worse.

There are, I have argued in this chapter, three fundamental obstacles: (1) an inadequate legal and regulatory structure, which provides only weak protection for the property rights of investors and little basis for taking long-term risks; in the 2000s these problems were compounded by the adoption of an extreme tax regime; (2) a deep-seated resistance to the presence of foreigners in strategic sectors, especially in oil, where the Russians have traditionally excelled on their own; this was exacerbated after 2004 by a systematic tightening of the rules governing access by foreigners, on national-security grounds; and (3) a lack of demand for the skills and resources that foreign companies and individuals might bring, because of the rich legacy of low-cost conventional resources lying within traditional Russian capabilities. All three have been serious obstacles, but it is the third that is ultimately the most important, and it drives the other two. For this state of affairs the state bears part of the blame, but it is not alone—the oil industry is also responsible.

Russia is not the only resource-rich country to set up barriers to the flow of global investment and participation by foreigners. Over the last four decades, in a growing number of oil-producing countries, foreigners have been excluded or at best tightly restricted, barred from access to reserves, forbidden to own controlling stakes in local companies or to take operatorship of major projects, and increasingly held at arm's length in favor of state-owned national champions. But here we are talking about something different. Resource nationalism does not imply isolationism; it does not imply sheltering oneself from outside presence or influences. On the contrary, the drive to be independent has led many countries to reach out to foreign sources of advice, to send their staffs overseas for training, to hire foreign nationals, and to learn from experience wherever they can find it. Thus Norway's Statoil, seeking to turn itself into a global player, formed a strategic alliance with BP in the 1990s, sending joint teams all over the world, from Siberia to Venezuela. Petrobras, Brazil's national oil company, has systematically sent its technical experts and executives on secondment to other companies. The Chinese oil companies, though they restrict access to their domestic market, work with foreign companies and service providers as they expand overseas. But perhaps the ultimate example is Saudi Arabia, whose national oil company, Saudi Aramco, is an Arab American corporation in which the working language is English and most senior executives, though Saudis, are graduates of top U.S. engineering schools. There are, so far at least, no similar examples involving Russian companies, except TNK-BP, between 2004 and 2008.

Change is difficult. Large organizations, even more than individual human beings, change only when they have to, and even then they try to limit change, wherever possible, to what is consistent with established practices and values and power structures. But powerful forces are building, which even now are pushing the Russian industry more strongly toward the world outside and toward greater openness within. One is the inexorable deterioration of the legacy of Soviet-era conventional oil. The second is the continuing technological revolution in the global energy industry. The third is the accumulated effect of such technology transfers as have, despite the obstacles, taken place to date.

There are signs that the Russian leadership and the industry are responding. Several new initiatives are under way. The Kremlin is stepping up the priority of the Arctic offshore and onshore tight oil, backed by new tax holidays to stimulate both. With the president's direct support, Rosneft has concluded strategic alliances in quick succession with ExxonMobil, Eni, and Statoil. The oil companies have increased their activity outside the former Soviet Union. And they have substantially increased spending on research and development.[83] In short, a new chapter may be opening in the relationship of the Russian oil industry to the global mainstream of the hydrocarbons industry. I explore these propositions, and their possible implications, in the concluding chapters.

chapter 12

Three Colors of Oil: The Coming Crisis of Oil Rents

The Siberian Veteran and the Novice President

"Sixty percent of our reserves have already been produced." Vladimir Bogdanov, the CEO of Surgutneftegaz, is briefing president Dmitri Medvedev and a high-powered group from Moscow. Outside, it is Siberian spring, the temperature still well below zero. Bogdanov's voice grows more urgent. "Three-quarters of our oil comes from low-grade reserves. Ninety percent of what we produce is water. Our costs are rising twice as fast as world oil prices."[1] Bogdanov is talking about his own company, but his words have a larger import. The news is bad. West Siberia, the oil province that still produces two-thirds of Russian oil, is declining.[2]

It is 2010, two decades after the fall of the Soviet Union, but there is an eerie resemblance here, which is presumably not lost on the veteran Bogdanov, to similar inspection tours of earlier Russian leaders, of Mikhail Gorbachev and Leonid Brezhnev before him, and to previous West Siberian oil crises. Bogdanov is no longer the young firebrand he was in the early 1980s, when he was promoted to head Surgutneftegaz (then a Soviet "production association") at the age of 32. His face is deeply lined; his hair is streaked with gray, but he is still as thin as a drill pipe. After nearly thirty years at the head of his company, the onetime driller from the nearby village of Suerka is now one of the elder statesmen of Russian oil. He has survived it all—the breakup of the Soviet oil industry, the rise of the privatized oil companies, the brief "oil miracle" of the early 2000s, the Yukos Affair, the oil-price fever of the late 2000s, and the subsequent crash of 2008–2009. Now in his early sixties, loaded with praise and honors, Bogdanov shows no sign of retiring.[3] Yet even so, his time is passing; within the next several years he will be gone, along with the other oilmen and politicians who have held the stage since the fall of the Soviet Union.

Yet for the present Bogdanov and Surgutneftegaz still represent the persistence of a certain Soviet way of oil. All through the 1990s and into the 2000s, he focused his company's energies on essentially the same patch of West Siberia as in Soviet times, exploring every nook and cranny, discovering and developing smaller and smaller fields, and maintaining production by drilling twice as much as any other Russian company, as well as applying a good deal of modern know-how.[4] It was only with the greatest reluctance, beginning in the mid-2000s, that Bogdanov began expanding outside West Siberia, first to Sakha in the far northeast, and then to other frontier regions of Russia, but the core of his production remains in West Siberia. He has never operated outside Russia;[5] he has never formed a joint venture; and although he is not averse to adopting new technologies and employing foreign service companies, he has never taken a foreign strategic partner. He buys Russian whenever he can. These traits, needless to say, have made Bogdanov highly popular with the Kremlin. Igor Sechin calls Bogdanov "a legend of the Russian oil industry."[6]

If Bogdanov is the last Soviet generation, the men facing him on that early spring day—Medvedev and his advisors and aides—were the latest new Russians. The contrast could hardly be greater, between the hard-bitten engineer who came up from the drill floor, who fed the Siberian mosquitoes in summer, the bedbugs in winter, and the party functionaries all year round—and the young president, the son of a comfortable middle-class Saint Petersburg family, trained as a lawyer, at home in the world and advised by economists with foreign degrees. And the president's visit to West Siberia was not in fact a Soviet-style crisis-driven inspection tour of the oilfields but the latest meeting of Medvedev's Commission on the Modernization and Technological Development of the Economy of Russia, the spearhead of Medvedev's campaign to lead Russia into the high-tech future. It was all about innovation and efficiency, computers, nanotechnology, nuclear power, and space. Its chief aim was precisely to escape from Russia's dependence on oil, an addiction that Medvedev called "shameful" and "humiliating." The two men represent not only two separate, but nearly opposite poles of experience and viewpoint.

Bogdanov's plea to the president for help and Medvedev's obvious skepticism symbolize Russia's growing dilemma, as it faces the decline of the Soviet oil legacy. It is oil, more than ever, that feeds Russia, just as it was oil that kept Russia going through the dark 1990s and oil again that fueled Russia's revival in the 2000s. Oil remains the essential engine of the economy, and to men like Bogdanov, there is no choice but to soldier on. But Medvedev and the

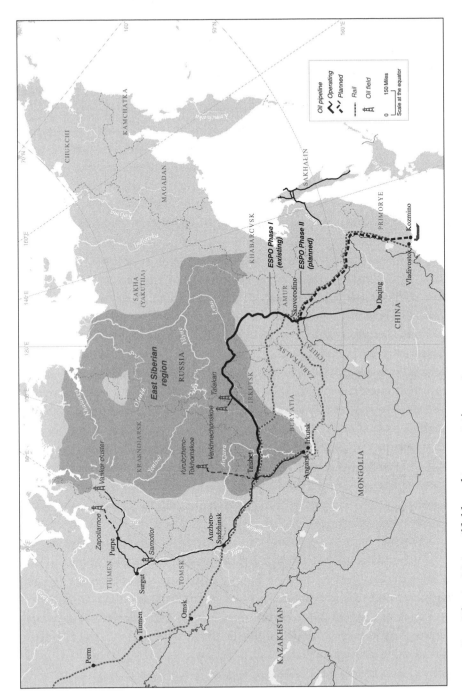

MAP 3 *East Siberia: Major oilfields and transportation routes.*

"modernizers" behind him, it is essential to make a radical break. But the dilemma is that the modernization they propose, even assuming it succeeds, will take time and vast amounts of money—which can only come from oil.

Medvedev's reelection campaign ended unsuccessfully a year and a half later, with Putin's decision in September 2011 to reoccupy the presidential post himself. To the disappointed liberals who had placed their hopes in him, the outcome represented not just a personal defeat for Medvedev, as he moved to the lesser post of prime minister, but also that of his entire modernization agenda. As Putin settled back into the Kremlin for what seemed likely to be a lengthy new lease,[7] Russia appeared headed back to business as usual; indeed, since Putin had continued to hold the reins of power throughout Medvedev's brief term, it had never left.

Yet no one, not even Putin, can step into the same river twice. Over a decade has passed since he was first elected president in 2000. During that time Russia produced over 35 billion barrels (or nearly 5 billion tons) of oil—the nonrenewable cream of the Soviet oil legacy. The burst of prosperity and growth it engendered cannot be repeated.[8] Indeed, as I shall try to show in a moment, the rents from oil are unlikely to be sustained, unless a determined effort is made to reform the oil sector itself and its relationship to the state.[9] Of all the sectors in the Russian economy, it is above all the oil industry itself that needs to become more modern, innovative, and efficient—in a word, to become the high-tech sector that it has become in the rest of the world. Ironically, the modernization campaign, by drawing attention and funds away from this basic point, becomes part of the problem. But there is also another problem: can any modernization of the oil industry, no matter how successful, satisfy the constantly growing thirst of the economy and the political system for more oil revenues?

This chapter begins by focusing on the outlook for Russian oil production, against the backdrop of the accelerating changes in the world of energy. I look first at the structure of Russian oil supply, to see just what makes it different from the rest of the world today. Then I examine the recent trends in the Russian oil industry, to understand why production growth is slowing down while costs are going up and what this is doing to oil rents. Lastly, I focus on the challenges of change, in particular the unexpected rise of tight oil in the United States and its possible implications for Russia.

Russian Oil Supply in Global Perspective: A Unique Architecture

Because of Russia's unique endowment and history, the structure of its oil supply today is strikingly different from that of the global oil industry as a whole.[10] To see this, we will need to look briefly at some concepts and numbers. Oil analysts distinguish among four different categories of fields and prospects: fields in production (FIP); fields under development (FUD); fields under appraisal (FUA); and yet to find (YTF) resources. Figure 12.1 summarizes the sharp differences between the Russian and the global supply structure. The left-hand bar in each pair shows the situation in 1988, on the eve of the Soviet collapse; the right-hand bar shows the picture in 2008, at the peak of the latest oil boom.

Compared with the global supply structure, the Russian oil industry has a unique signature. Its most significant features are described below.[11]

Production. Worldwide production of liquids has grown steadily over the past quarter century, from 2.94 billion tons (58.7 million barrels per day [mbd]) in 1988 to 4.10 billion tons (82.1 mbd) in 2010. In contrast, Russian production declined by 47 percent through 1996 before recovering in the 2000s, reaching 505.1 million tons (10.2 mbd) in 2010. However, Russian oil production has not yet returned to the Soviet-era peak of 569.5 million tons (11.4 mbd), reached in 1987. As a result, Russia's share of global oil production has dropped sharply over the past quarter century, from about 19 percent in the late 1980s to 12 percent in 2010.

Discoveries. Between 1988 and 2008, 537 large fields (defined as fields with proved and probable reserves greater than 14 million tons [100 million barrels]) were discovered worldwide, of which 222 were developed by 2008, adding 785 million tons per year (or 15.7 mbd) to global production in 2008. During that same period, thirty-four large fields were discovered in Russia, of which only thirteen had begun production by 2008, adding 16.1 million tons per year (0.3 mbd) to production. In addition, smaller fields made a substantial contribution to the worldwide total during this period, but much less in Russia. All told, fields discovered and developed between 1988 and 2008 (YTF in Figure 12.1) added 865 million tons per year (17.3 mbd) to worldwide production by 2008 but only 38.6 million tons per year (0.8 mbd) to production in Russia.

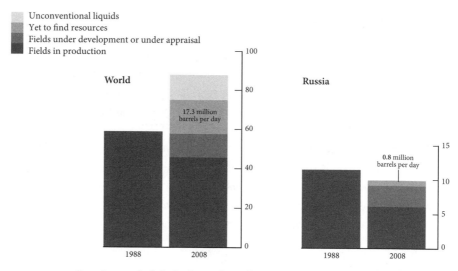

FIGURE 12.1 *Russian and global oil supply architecture, in millions of barrels per day. All production in 1988, by definition, comes from FIP. Production in 2008 is built up from fields that were already in production in 1988 (FIP) and fields that were discovered and undergoing appraisal (FUA) or in development (FUD) in 1988 and began production afterward. The YTF category designates fields that were discovered after 1988 and entered production before or during 2008. (Sources: Russian Statistical Committee and Russian Ministry of Energy.)*

The modest contribution of new discoveries to 2008 Russian production was due to the sharp falloff in spending on exploration after 1991 but also to a decline in the average size of new discoveries. In particular, only five new giant fields (i.e., with reserves of more than 68 million tons [500 million barrels] or more) were discovered in Russia between 1988 and 2008—of which only one, Vankor, has begun production.[12] One reason for the decline of the average size of new discoveries is the continuing concentration of exploration in West Siberia, where there are few if any large fields left to discover.[13]

New Field Development. Worldwide, the development of fields known before 1988 but only developed after that year (i.e., FUD and FUA) added 650 million tons per year (13 mbd) to production by 2008, that is, less than the contribution of newly discovered fields. In Russia, in contrast, fields discovered before 1988 but developed between 1988 and 2008 made a major contribution to the recovery of oil production in the 2000s, adding 158.7 million tons (3.2 mbd) to production by 2008.

These differences reflect that the Soviet Union had been explored extensively prior to 1988. Indeed, in economic terms it was overexplored, because most oil exploration in Soviet times was conducted by an independent Ministry of Geology, supported as a separate line in the state budget. As a consequence, Russia emerged from the Soviet period with a large overhang of undeveloped fields, which enabled it to avoid spending scarce capital on exploration. By the end of the 2000s, however, the overhang had largely dissipated. What is left, particularly the stock of unexplored prospects in the state's "undistributed fund" (i.e., not yet licensed to producing companies), consists for the most part of much lower-quality resources.

Production from Existing Fields. Worldwide, fields that were already producing before 1988 (FIPs) have declined slowly, at about 1.5 percent per year between 1988 and 2003, thanks to a strong focus on new technologies and efficient management. In Russia, the history of the 1988 FIPs has been more complex: their output at first declined sharply through 1996; they then led the recovery of the 2000s (especially during 1999–2004, when the decline of the mature fields was temporarily reversed). But after 2005 the decline of the 1988 FIPs resumed, and by 2008 their output had dropped to 291.3 million tons (5.8 mbd), or about 60 percent of total output that year.

Thus the significance of "legacy production" (the 1988 FIPs) is quite different in Russia from the rest of the world. In the global industry, production from the 1988 FIPS is basically stable; their declining share of total production (currently about half) is due to strong growth in the other categories. In Russia, the 1988 FIPS still account for about 60 percent of total output, but in absolute terms their production has declined by nearly half since 1988, and in recent years it has dropped markedly. As I discuss below, these numbers suggest the possibility of a crisis ahead in the Russian mature fields, especially in West Siberia, but also conceivably the potential for a turnaround.[14]

Nontraditional Liquids. In 1988–2008 so-called nontraditional liquids (e.g., deepwater offshore, natural gas liquids, heavy oils, oil from oil sands, and so forth) contributed significantly to the global supply picture, adding 700 million tons per year (14 mbd) to global capacity. Since then, the contribution of nontraditional liquids has soared, thanks notably to the unexpected advent of tight oil (chiefly so far in the United States) but also to a continuing stream of large deepwater discoveries, primarily in West Africa, the Gulf of Mexico, and Brazil. In contrast, the Russian oil industry remains largely focused on conventional liquids, with only minor additions from heavy oil, very little from offshore, and none from the newer unconventional sources, such as tight oil. (The only significant exception is natural gas liquids, which originate as a by-product of gas production.) Lastly, the Russian oil industry has only recently taken its first steps into deepwater plays and is not yet producing these.[15]

In sum, compared with the global oil industry, the Russian oil industry has maintained production essentially by working the legacy assets discovered and developed in Soviet times, using the infrastructure inherited from the Soviet Union. Having little need to explore new prospects, especially outside established areas, it has made relatively few discoveries, especially large ones. Most of its additions to reserves have come from in-place upgrades in established areas. Endowed with ample conventional resources onshore, the Russian industry has made little effort to expand offshore or to find and develop unconventional liquids.

Given the circumstances of the Russian industry, this approach to production has been sensible, appropriate, and successful. Although it has recorded no net growth in production since the end of the Soviet period, the Russian oil industry has overcome the collapse and stagnation of the first half of the 1990s and is once again the world's largest oil producer. Thanks to its legacy assets, it has achieved this performance with a much lower level of capital investment per barrel than the global industry as a whole, and Russian production costs remain competitive in world markets, despite Russia's relative isolation from major terminals and consequent long transportation distances and high pipeline tariffs.

However, Russia's Soviet inheritance in oil has now reached a turning point of sharply higher costs and lower returns, signaling that the Soviet legacy chapter is nearing an end.

The Soviet Legacy Runs Down

By the second half of the 2000s, the oil industry began showing signs of growing stress. The most eloquent indicator was a sharp slowdown in the growth of production, despite a rapid rise in investment. In the first half of the 2000s (i.e.,

2001–2005), output grew by 35 percent; in the second half (2006–2010), by only 5 percent; yet over the same period, annual investment increased over fourfold, from \$6.7 billion in 2001 to \$23.7 billion in 2010.[16]

Trends in drilling, which accounts for about 40 percent of upstream investment, tell the same story of diminishing returns. Producing the 35 percent production increment of the first half of the decade took 42.2 million meters of development drilling; in contrast, the 5 percent increment of the second half of the decade took 70.6 million meters, or 40 percent more. Even more striking was the declining effectiveness of hydraulic fracturing, the most important single technique responsible for the "oil miracle" phase of the early part of the decade. By the end of the 2000s the impact of each "frac job" had declined to less than one-third of what it had been in the peak year of 2002, and despite a hefty increase in the total number of treatments performed, the contribution of hydraulic fracturing to total oil production was only about half of what it had been in 2002.[17]

In other words, by the end of the 2000s the Russian oil industry was having to work very much harder to keep oil production growing. The older fields, where decline had been briefly halted between 1999 and 2004) began falling again in the second half of the decade. The decline was offset by the development of a handful of new fields, located mainly in East Siberia, as discussed below. But in both cases the bottom line was a sharp decline in the impact of each dollar invested.

No one, incidentally, could accuse the Russian companies of not stepping up their efforts. But not only do they face diminishing returns from each meter drilled and each well fracced, their unit costs are going up all across the board, for manpower, steel, electricity, and all other inputs, the result of inflation, an appreciating ruble, and steady tariff increases. One meter of development drilling, for example, cost \$126 in 2000; by 2010 it cost \$481.

The Russian story is hardly unique. Oil companies worldwide are working harder and spending more. The Russian oil industry faces the same forces that are driving up costs everywhere. The more oil one produces, the more one must spend to keep the base from declining, while adding increments of new oil that cost steadily more. Oil is a wasting asset, and there is ultimately no escape from the law of diminishing returns.

But although this is broadly true, technological and scientific breakthroughs can add whole new tiers of profitable production, pushing out what economists call the "production possibility frontier" and postponing the onset of diminishing returns. That is what has happened in the global oil industry in the last two decades, in a revolution that is continuing to unfold before our eyes. The ceaseless worldwide search for reserves and production has driven the global oil industry into previously inaccessible locations and nontraditional sources of liquids. At the same time, the life of existing fields is being dramatically extended through the application of advanced imaging, computing, and communications. As a result, the world's "oil peak" is being continually postponed. While production of conventional oil may indeed be nearing its maximum, possibly as early as midcentury, the rapidly growing prospects of unconventional oil, especially tight oil, are pushing back the peak in total liquids by decades, possibly well into the next century.[18]

In contrast to the oil industry worldwide, Russia has concentrated mainly on simply doing more of what it did before, producing conventional oil in conventional locations with largely conventional methods. Yet the next generation of oil will have to come from plays that are farther out on the perimeter of difficulty in every dimension—deeper, tighter, colder, more sour, more remote, and above all more costly. The capital required to find and produce it and transport it will weigh much more heavily on the companies and on the state than it has in the past two decades. Thus there will be, as oil people like to say, a "bend in the trend," as much more investment is required to maintain existing production as well as to find and develop new oil in harsher environments.

A Back-of-the-Envelope Calculation

To see where these trends might lead, let us perform a back-of-the-envelope calculation, using a simplified model of the Russian oil industry. Think of Russian oil production today as a balance between a large stock of mature fields, declining at an average of 2 percent per year, and a small number of new fields (chiefly three East Siberian fields, Vankor, Talakan, and Verkhnechonskoe, plus a handful of others), whose growing output just offsets the decline. This picture accounts for the slow but reasonably steady net growth of recent years.

But owing to today's punitive tax regime, as well as declining reserve quality, the oil companies have not prepared the next generation of new fields. As a result, as Energy Minister Shmatko informed Putin in his Samara presentation in late 2010, oil output could decline to 388 million tons (7.7 million barrels per day) by 2020, down from its 2010 level of 505 million tons per year (10.1 million barrels per day), unless major policy changes take place, chiefly in the tax regime.[19]

Confronted with the reality of a decline, the political leadership would undoubtedly react as it has repeatedly in the past, with the usual mixture of carrots and sticks, and the oil companies might well succeed in squeezing production upward again, at least for a short time, with yet more infill drilling in the mature fields and accelerated development of the lesser fields remaining in inventory.

Yet it is an increasingly formidable challenge. Let us say that the mature fields account for 80 percent of total oil production, or about 400 million tons per year (or 8 million barrels per day). To offset two percentage points of annual decline in the brownfield provinces (mainly West Siberia and the Volga-Urals), the Russian oil industry must add some 8 million tons per year (160,000 barrels per day) of new production from frontier provinces,[20] just to keep total oil production at its present level. Over the decade from 2011 to 2020, that means developing 80 million tons of annual capacity (1.6 mbd), from a stock of undeveloped fields that is of much poorer quality than in the 1980s.

The real issue here is not output but cost and its implications for the flow of rents. The prime symptom of the problem is the inexorable rise of the investment required just to maintain today's level of production. In round numbers, developing 8 million tons per year (160,000 barrels per day) of new-field production currently requires about $5 billion per year (not counting transportation).[21] Meanwhile, holding back the decline of Russia's mature provinces takes about $20 billion per year. In other words, the greenfields presently take about one-fifth of upstream capital spending, while the mature fields take the remaining four-fifths.

Over time, two things are going to happen. First, the stock of mature fields will increase, as today's new fields become "mature." Therefore the capital required to hold back their decline will increase also. But even if the overall decline rate remains the same, the absolute volume of decline will grow, requiring even more new oil each year to offset it. Therefore the capital requirements of the new fields will grow as well. In both cases, each successive barrel, whether "old" or "new," will be more difficult and more costly.

The implication is that whereas the oil industry today invests around $25 billion per year upstream, by 2020 it could well require some $50 billion per year or more just to produce the same amount of oil as now.[22] These are the

459

conditions under which, if the export price of Russian oil remains roughly at its present level, the share of capital spending in a barrel of Urals export crude would rise from its present level of about 10 percent to as much as 25 percent.[23] To that must be added the higher operating costs of production. As a result, the total flow of rents available to other claimants will shrink correspondingly. But this process will not stop, of course, in 2020. With each passing decade the slope of rising costs will grow steeper, and the pressure on oil rents will increase.[24]

In sum, the Russian oil industry is coming under mounting pressure to move out its present "comfort zone" and to progress in the same directions as the global mainstream. It will have to explore more. It will have to reach for nontraditional or unconventional opportunities such as the Arctic deepwater. It will require more advanced technologies, both for brownfield recovery and new-field development. It will need to develop customized approaches to deal with the complexity and variability of mature-field situations. And it will need to become more integrated with the global oil industry, particularly through strategic alliances, to develop these frontier opportunities.

In the next section, we look at these challenges in more detail. It will be clear that responding to them will require major changes in the structure and behavior of the oil companies, as well as fundamental changes in oil policy.

Three Colors of Oil

In shorthand, it helps to think of Russian oil in three colors: brown, green, and blue. "Brown" refers to mature fields already in production; "green" to new on-shore fields not yet developed; and "blue" to offshore fields in frontier areas.[25] Each color of oil poses different challenges and requires different approaches. Without too much exaggeration one can think of the three colors as representing three separate oil industries.

The "Brownfields"—the Mature Onshore. So-called mature fields are defined as fields in which half of the original reserves have already been produced. The heart of the brownfields is the Khanty-Mansiisk okrug of West Siberia, centered on the Middle Ob' basin, which still produces over half (51 percent in 2011) of total Russian oil production and of explored reserves.[26] This is the region where Vladimir Bogdanov was born and raised and where he has spent his entire life. It is still the core asset of the Russian oil industry. Yet of Khanty-

Mansiisk's 230-odd producing fields, all but eighty-six are in decline, and within a few more years most of the latter will start downhill too.[27] The same is broadly true of the other Russian brownfield areas, such as the Volga-Urals basin or the fields of the North Caucasus.

This decline is ineluctable in the long run, but it can be slowed, or even temporarily reversed, as it was in the early 2000s. From a century of experience in brownfields all over the world, operators have developed ingenious techniques, variously called "secondary" and "tertiary" recovery, some of which we have seen at work in earlier chapters.[28] These have grown increasingly powerful as they are combined with advanced technologies. Whereas most of the surge in Russian oil production between 1999 and 2004 came from improving the performance of individual wells, the latest techniques increasingly enable operators to focus on entire reservoirs.[29] The potential for application of these advanced techniques to Russia is still substantial.

The challenge is controlling costs. Operators in mature fields work a wafer-thin margin of profit, and as they decide on a new production technique they must make constant choices between yield and cost to prevent their margins from disappearing altogether. But the returns from each new technique soon diminish, forcing still more choices. In West Siberia as in every other mature province, the industry is constantly deploying a moving front of new tricks: high-precision and long-reach horizontal drilling, sidetrack and multilateral wells, underbalanced drilling,[30] advanced reservoir modeling, waterflood optimization, multistage hydraulic fracturing—and the list goes on. Yet the front does not move forward; it is a rearguard action against diminishing returns, despite occasional reversals when new technologies are deployed.

In this business there are no free gifts. Most enhanced-recovery techniques—such as waterflooding or gas injection—themselves consume energy. This is true worldwide but especially so in West Siberia, where advanced techniques consume as much as 10 percent of the energy value produced, the equivalent of a "mature fields tax" that only grows heavier as the field is produced.[31] One example is electricity. The familiar quip that the "Russian oil companies are the largest water companies in Europe," because of the large volumes of water used in waterflooding, implies that they are also among the largest consumers of the electricity needed to pump water into the oilfields. Over time, as the "water cut" in the West Siberian oilfields has grown, the electricity consumed per ton of oil has risen also; and with the sharp increase in power tariffs in recent years, the oil operators' electricity bills have skyrocketed.[32] As other enhanced-recovery techniques are implemented, the "mature-field tax" from them will rise also.

The only counter to declining yields and rising costs is constant innovation and attention to efficiency. But this is only partly a matter of technology; above all, it is a matter of focus and know-how. Increasing recovery rates in a mature field requires developing an intimate knowledge of each field, something that can be achieved only over a period of years and sometimes decades, and by finding the custom blend of approaches that will get the best long-term yield from each field. It is what the Russians call *iuvelirnaia rabota*—"jeweler's work."

By continuously measuring and improving their knowledge of their fields, by carefully choosing which "fit for purpose" techniques to apply, skilled and motivated operators can squeeze out more oil from a mature field than would have seemed possible when its life began and still make a profit. But making money from the mature fields, whether in West Siberia or West Texas or in the North Sea, requires obsessive attention to finding and cutting costs.

This is not something that large companies do well; instead, it is the domain of smaller specialist companies, whose skills and culture are focused on extracting every last drop of value from a declining play. The international oil industry resembles an ecological system, in which different kinds of companies occupy different parts of the food chain. The majors find and develop the big new prospects, and then, as the fields mature, they sell them on to the smaller independents, who are better adapted to finding the lowest-cost solutions to extract the next few points of recovery. This has been the single most important cause of the continuing viability of the upstream oil industry in the Lower 48 of the United States, and of its recent tight oil revival.

But in Russia the independents are largely missing from the ecosystem. Russia today badly needs the smaller companies, the brownfield specialists, that it allowed the giants to swallow up in the 2000s. But unfortunately the trend is still moving in the wrong direction: each year the ranks of the small companies decline further, and their share of total oil production, already below 5 percent, is still dropping. Only in the Volga-Urals do they still play an important role—and significantly, it is Tatarstan and Bashkortostan, the most mature provinces in the Russian oil portfolio, that have the best record in stabilizing their output over the last decade.[33]

462

Russian leaders, though they recognize in rhetoric the importance of small business as a force for innovation and efficiency in a modern economy, do little to protect it in practice, whether from predatory companies or grasping bureaucrats and policemen.[34] The same is true of the smaller independent oil-service companies, which are quickly absorbed by the larger ones. In the 1990s, independents and joint ventures benefited from the support of the regional governments. This was particularly the case in Tatarstan, where former president Mintimer Shaimiev made it a policy to support smaller companies, and there the performance of the mature fields has been surprisingly strong. But the weakening of the regions under Putin in the 2000s has lessened local support for the independents.

Expanding the role of independents in the Russian brownfields faces many obstacles. In the United States, Canada, and the British continental shelf, mature oil properties can be readily bought and sold, and companies routinely practice what they call "portfolio optimization," that is, selling off their "used" properties to specialists. For example, the fabled Forties Field in the North Sea, the jewel in BP's crown in the 1980s, continues to produce profitably in the 2000s under Apache, an American independent. This cycle is characteristic of industry operations in North America and in the North Sea, and it is central to their dynamics.

But in Russia licenses cannot be transferred in this way; they must be returned to the state and re-auctioned; consequently, the large companies have no incentive to divest themselves of them.[35] An alternative approach might be leasing, but the large companies are reluctant to allow smaller operators into their properties, and in any case such an arrangement would leave the independents exposed to many risks, while offering them little upside.[36]

In any case, state policy favors the larger companies working in greenfield areas, not the smaller ones in the brownfields. The tax exemptions granted in recent years apply mainly to East Siberia (Sakha, Irkutsk, and Krasnoiarsk) and to new oil in the North Caspian and the Timan-Pechora Province in the northwest, but not the mature fields and provinces of West Siberia and the Volga-Urals, where the handful of surviving independents mostly work. Similarly, the smaller companies, since they own no refineries, do not benefit from the tax breaks given to exports of refined products. Lastly, the independent companies have little access to credit, whether from foreign or domestic banks or government programs. As a result, the smaller companies were hit particularly hard during the 2008–2009 recession, and a number of them went bankrupt, further reducing their ranks. Thus raising recovery rates in the mature fields would require a massive change in state policy but, even more important, in entrenched attitudes. At this writing, there is little evidence of that.

The remarkable "tight-oil" revolution sweeping the United States illustrates the crucial importance of an industry structure that favors innovation and entrepreneurship. The artful combination of horizontal drilling, hydraulic fracturing, and seismic imaging has enabled U.S. operators to "crack the code" (as they like to say) of low-permeability formations that were previously unproductive or uneconomic. The tight-oil phenomenon did not stem from any one technological breakthrough, but rather from the extension and integration of the latest advanced versions of known techniques. But just as important were the "above-ground" factors—competition among small and medium-sized independents, learning from trial and error, strong relations between operators and service companies, and support from a favorable regulatory and fiscal environment.

The landscape of liquids production in North America has been turned upside down. In just a few years, North Dakota—previously an insignificant producer—has surged to second place in U.S. output, ahead of Texas and second only to Alaska. But tight-oil production is spreading rapidly to other states as well. As a result, the outlook for U.S. oil production has been transformed. Tight oil has added about 7 billion tons (50 billion barrels) to U.S. reserves in the last five years alone, and by 2020 production of tight oil could exceed 250 million tons per year (5 million barrels per day)—nearly half of Russian production—up from essentially nothing as recently as 2008.

The obvious question is whether a similar revolution could take place in Russia. Geology is not likely to be the obstacle: tight oil is simply oil from low-porosity, low-permeability rock, the hard-to-produce stuff that lies alongside conventional formations. In the United States, tight oil is now being produced not only from new fields, but also from the impermeable margins of conventional fields located all over the Lower 48—fields that had been considered depleted or in decline. Tight oil is the ultimate brownfield revival.

The implications for the Russian brownfields, and especially for West Siberia, have not gone unnoticed, particularly by President Putin, who recently announced a tax holiday aimed at encouraging the oil companies to increase their focus on tight oil. The president speaks of adding between 40 and 100 million tons per year (0.8 to 2 million barrels per day) to Russian production after 2020.[37] However, the new measure is unlikely to have such a sweeping effect, or at any rate not soon. To begin with, it applies only from the start of the commercial production phase, thereby excluding most already-producing fields by definition, whereas the U.S. experience suggests that it is precisely in established fields, where accumulated knowledge is greatest and infrastructure is already in place, that the potential for quick results may be best. In addition, the tax holiday applies only to the production tax (the so-called NDPI, discussed in Chapter 9), not to the export tax, which is far larger. In short, the Russians are still at the beginning of what could be a long road.

This brings us to the second color of Russian oil, the "greenfields."

The "Greenfields"—the Remote Onshore. Over the next two decades, the most likely source of the new oil needed to offset the decline of the mature fields will be new fields mostly located in remote onshore regions. The most promising onshore locations are at the periphery of the Russian land mass, in the northwest and the vast Russian east. The latter comprises two large regions, East Siberia and the Russian Far East. Compared with the traditional core of the Russian oil industry in West Siberia and the Volga-Urals, fields in these areas are smaller and more widely scattered, their geology is more complex, the oil quality is often not as good, and above all they lack infrastructure. The consequence is longer lead times and higher cost. This is particularly true of East Siberia, which has two particular liabilities: remoteness and extreme cold.

In East Siberia cold reaches a whole new dimension. It is a frigid fact of Russian geography that if you start from Saint Petersburg on a winter's day and proceed due east along the 60th parallel, it will get steadily colder, even though you have not changed latitude. By the time you cross the Yenisei River into East Siberia, January temperatures average 30 degrees below zero Celsius and lower.[38] At those temperatures, "cranes fail, tractor shoes break, ball bearings shatter, circular saws stop, and standard steels and structures rupture on a mass scale."[39] Special equipment must be used, and ordinary tasks typically take between two and four times as long to complete as they would under normal conditions. Initial investment costs, operating costs, maintenance costs, and labor costs all run much higher.[40]

On the map, East Siberia looks impressively huge. But geologically it is a very different place from West Siberia, and it is most unlikely to contain anywhere near the same abundance of oil and gas.[41] West Siberia was an oilman's dream—deep stacks of permeable sandstone laid down in large ancient seabeds fed by the Ob' River, which has flowed with little change for hundreds of millions of years. The best resources were concentrated in a handful of supergiants over a small area. East Siberia, by contrast, is an oilman's nightmare. Ancient volcanoes covered two-thirds of the area, the so-called Tungusska Plateau, with thick shields of lava, preventing the rocks beneath from being seen or studied. Most of the discoveries to date lie around the edges of this volcanic shield, in what Russian geologists call the "oil-bearing belt": carbonate formations that are fractured and folded in complex patterns, difficult to explore and produce. The oil there is among the oldest on earth. In most places around the world, such oil has long since seeped away or turned to gas.[42]

How much of this ancient oil may still lie buried and undiscovered in East Siberia is anyone's guess. But finding out will take time and money, to explore some of the most rugged and remote environments anywhere. Russians call East Siberia "a cat in a bag" (kot v meshke), an expression meaning that one pays one's money without knowing what one may get for it.

Despite the government's urgings, the Russian oil generals have been reluctant to spend much money on that cat. One of the few exceptions is Vladimir Bogdanov, who in keeping with his good-citizen policy has invested some of his company's considerable cash reserve in heeding the state's call to move east. Between 2004 and 2010 Surgutneftegaz invested over 20 billion rubles (or about $700 million) in exploration in East Siberia, mainly in the far northeastern province of Yakutiia, now known as Sakha. The results so far have been modest—only five new fields discovered to date, all smallish. By 2020, based on present trends, Surgutneftegaz will have discovered and developed enough in East Siberia to support only about 10 million tons (200,000 barrels per day) of production per year, at a total capital cost of over $10 billion. Surgutneftegaz had hoped that East Siberia would offset its declining reserves in West Siberia. But the results to date appear disappointing.[43]

The difficulties of developing East Siberia can also be seen at another of the discovered "hot spots" of the region, the Yurubchen complex. Discovered in 1983, Yurubcheno-Tokhomskoe (the main field in the complex) was acquired in the 1990s by Yukos, which scripted it as one of the main sources for its planned pipeline to China. It is a very large prospect, with recoverable proved and probable reserves estimated at about 135 million tons (984 million barrels). But the more Yukos worked on the field, the more it grew discouraged by its geological complexity and the prospective costs of development. Rosneft, which acquired the field as part of its takeover of Yukos assets in 2005, has likewise been deterred by the field's difficulty and has moved it to the back of its portfolio. Yurubcheno-Tokhomskoe may not be producing before the 2020s.[44]

Thus the future of East Siberia is far from clear, but it is very unlikely to be the bonanza that West Siberia was.[45] In the view of Aleksei Kontorovich, one of the pioneers of the petroleum geology of East Siberia,

> East Siberia will never be comparable to West Siberia. With luck, it will supply the eastern region's own needs plus a small amount of exports to the Asia-Pacific region. . . . If it is correctly managed it may provide 85–90 million tons a year [1.7–1.8 million barrels per day]. . . . But West Siberia, and especially Tiumen' Oblast', will remain the country's main oil-producing region at least through the middle of the century.[46]

Other experts are even less optimistic. Valerii Kriukov, a leading specialist on Siberian oil and gas, points out that while a number of large fields have been found in East Siberia, there has been no single "crown jewel" comparable to Samotlor in West Siberia and Romashkino in the Volga-Urals. Since the general history of most oil provinces around the world is that the largest fields are commonly among the first discovered, Kriukov is pessimistic about the chances of ever finding a similar supergiant in East Siberia. Adding up the modest proven reserves of the large East Siberian fields discovered to date, Kriukov concludes that East Siberia is unlikely to produce more than 30 to 40 million tons per year (600,000 to 800,000 barrels per day), that is, less than half of Kontorovich's estimate.[47]

Fortunately, the Russian oil companies do not need to take the plunge into East Siberia all at once. There exists a kind of bridge, located at the extreme northeastern corner of West Siberia. Administratively it spills over from West Siberia's Yamal-Nenetsk okrug (YaNAO) into East Siberia's Krasnoiarsk Krai, but geologically it is an extension of the West Siberian basin. Thus it is a kind of gateway to the east but with some of the attractive features of West Siberia. In 2008 Putin hailed what he called the "YaNAO-Krasnoiarsk cluster" as a major new oil and gas province, describing it as the main source of new Russian oil production to 2020. By 2020, according to Putin, the region will be producing up to 115 million tons of liquids per year (or 2.3 million barrels per day).[48] Other estimates, however, are considerably more cautious.

The centerpiece of the YaNAO-Krasnoiarsk region is the giant Vankor field, which began production in 2008. Vankor is being developed with some of the most advanced technology in Russia, including so-called smart wells (which in Russian are called "intellectual wells"—*intellektual'nye skvazhiny*), equipped with wireless transmitters that send real-time information about the wells' performance back to data centers that can be located anywhere on the globe. Working alongside Rosneft is an army of service contractors, including the leading international service companies. Vankor, which is expected to peak at 25 million tons of oil per year (or about 500,000 barrels per day) by 2013, is currently the most important single source of growth of Russian oil production.

One of the main challenges of developing the remote greenfields is building pipelines, and this is particularly true of the YaNAO-Krasnoiarsk cluster. Geologically speaking, as noted, Vankor could almost be considered the last of the great West Siberian giants, yet its oil is being shipped thousands of kilometers to the east to fill Russia's new pipeline to the Pacific, called the ESPO (East Siberia to Pacific Ocean) line. Since the October 2011 start-up of a new Transneft pipeline link, oil from Vankor travels in a vast semicircle, first flowing south to link up with the existing West Siberian system at Samotlor and then continuing on to connect to the new eastern pipeline at Taishet.[49] This long circuitous route is needed because oil from East Siberia proper will not be available in sufficient quantity to fill ESPO before 2020. Even then, each of the major field groups in East Siberia will need its own feeder pipeline to connect to the ESPO artery, a striking illustration of the additional costs imposed by the scattered distribution of oil in East Siberia.

The greenfields' remoteness and lack of infrastructure have two unavoidable implications. First, the demanding environment favors large integrated companies. East Siberia is actually the playing field to which the present structure of the Russian oil companies is best suited. Drilling wells and laying pipe in remote locations and extreme conditions and building infrastructure in virgin territory were precisely the tasks at which the Soviet industrial giants excelled in their day, and they are still what the large Russian companies do best. The greenfields are their core competence and the basis of their corporate culture. Smaller companies, by contrast, are at a disadvantage. Independents are few and far between in East Siberia, and their ranks were further thinned by the oil-price crash and recession of 2008–2010.[50] Likewise there are few locally based service companies. The local governments no longer have the power or the resources to be effective patrons. In short, the greenfields favor precisely the kind of large centralized companies that evolved from the Soviet past and dominate the industry today.

The other consequence of East Siberia's remoteness and wilderness conditions is that the Russian central state is inevitably involved, just as it was in Soviet times, because of what the Russians call the "region-forming" significance of large greenfield projects, that is, the large-scale infrastructure they require (roads, pipelines, cities, towns) and their impact on the economies of the regions in which they are located. The state's involvement, however, inevitably multiplies the costs of the greenfields. Western commentary tends to focus on state ownership as the principal cause of high costs, but in the Russian setting the form of ownership is less important than the fact that these projects are command performances commissioned by the state and executed by agencies whose costs, in the Russian manner, are an important source of their profits.

To be sure, that is the sovereign's prerogative. If the Russian state chooses to invest its resources to develop the eastern half of the country, that is a political choice, driven by priorities that lie beyond oil and gas—goals such as maintaining the unity of the country, slowing out-migration, forestalling penetration by Pacific powers, rewarding supporters, and the like. But using oil and oil companies as the chief instruments for regional development is problematic. The oil fields are far from existing industrial and population nodes in the region. The resources used to develop them—the manpower, the equipment, the technology—all come from elsewhere and will eventually move on. A sounder plan for developing East Siberia and the Russian Far East would focus instead on the region's locational advantages, mainly on the Pacific seaboard. The fuel required should logically come from Sakhalin, not from high-cost oil from the hinterlands that has to travel thousands of kilometers to the coast.

The result of the present arrangement is to turn the oil companies into state instruments. In these circumstances the Russian companies—whether private or state owned—have little incentive to work more efficiently in the greenfields. The state's political stress on developing the frontier and its statist choice of means amount to a reenactment of the Soviet model, but with oil and gas as the lead sectors instead of hydropower and aluminum as in the old days.

The story of the East Siberian pipeline (ESPO) illustrates this point. The concept of a pipeline to the east originated with Yukos in the late 1990s. The Yukos version was carefully designed to be a profitable investment. Compared with ESPO, it was far shorter and cheaper. It was focused on a specific commercial market—China—and it was to be filled initially from existing production from Tomsk in West Siberia. As production from successive East Siberian fields came on stream, the pipeline would gradually be filled from local sources. In short, it was a phased project, focused on markets and economics.

In contrast, ESPO is a strategic project in the grand Soviet tradition, built by a state-owned monopoly. The key point is that the oil industry is footing the bill for the state's objectives and for the rent-distribution system it supports. The strategic project drives the investment priorities, rather than the other way around. It amounts to taking the rents from oil and reallocating them by state fiat, but in an inefficient and often corrupt way. Yet the state is not the sole problem here. So long as the oil companies' culture favors large-scale green-field projects while the state's policies favor oil as a means of frontier development, there is a tacit marriage of convenience between the two, matching the inclinations of both. The only question then is the terms of the state's tax subsidy. Hence the vigorous fiscal bargaining we see today, which stands in lieu of a more comprehensive reform.

Finally, the next category, the "bluefield" Arctic offshore, raises challenges of a whole new order.

The "Bluefields"—the Final Frontier? Last on the list come the "bluefields," the Arctic offshore that lies all along the northern and eastern continental shelf of Russia.[51] To get a sense of the challenges involved, a good place to begin is Sakhalin Island, the site of two of Russia's three PSAs. Although technically Sakhalin Island is not "Arctic," in that it lies well south of the Arctic Circle, it is certainly cold and harsh enough to qualify. "The biggest challenge," said an ExxonMobil engineer, remembering his five years on Sakhalin Island, "was the moving ice. The whole ice pack drifts along, and if you haven't built for it, it will drag your whole platform away." Sakhalin Island—hitherto known to Westerners, if at all, as the prison colony Anton Chekhov described in *A Journey to Sakhalin*—was Russia's first major Arctic offshore venture. The setting is one of wild and austere beauty. Temperatures fall below 50 degrees Celsius in winter, while spring and fall storms whip up waves over thirty feet high.

Sakhalin Island is the beginning of the final Russian frontier. By 2030, according to the government's long-range energy program, 20 percent of Russian oil and gas production will need to come from offshore plays like Sakhalin.[52] And by midcentury, the growth of Russian oil and gas could depend largely on the bluefields.

But today the Russian oil and gas industry does not yet have the skills, institutions, and policies or the industrial and technological support needed to tackle the Arctic offshore.[53] Sakhalin Island, where a new oil and gas province was created in less than two decades, was almost entirely the work of the international companies. It was the site of many technological firsts, such as some of the world's longest "extended-reach" horizontal wells, extending more than 10 kilometers out to sea from shore-based drill pads. Another key innovation was the design of special ball bearings placed between the concrete foundations and superstructure of drilling platforms, to isolate the platform from the effects of earthquakes, which are frequent in the area.[54] But although Sergei Bogdanchikov, in his days as chief of Sakhalin's local oil company, Sakhalinmorneftegaz, had experimented with shore-based long-reach wells, the Russians played only minor roles in developing and implementing the solutions deployed in the Sakhalin PSAs or in supplying the advanced equipment and personnel used there. At the time the Sakhalin PSAs got under way, there were too few qualified Russian manufacturers and skilled specialists to meet the projects' requirements; and even though Russian law required that 70 percent of the matériel and personnel be provided from Russian sources, in practice the definition of "Russian content" was interpreted very loosely.

Yet the greatest challenge at Sakhalin was management. A large offshore project brings together thousands of skilled specialists from hundreds of contractors and subcontractors all over the world. The job of the operator is to bring this vast armada into focus, coordinating the multitude of moving parts to execute a job that oilmen compare with a moon shot in its complexity and technological sophistication. Arctic conditions add a further layer of danger and difficulty. "Any fool can launch a rocket," says another Sakhalin veteran. "But imagine assembling it in the middle of a heaving ocean, surrounded by icebergs."

The international companies like to say that their comparative advantage lies in the ability to execute such complex projects safely, on time, and on budget. Yet no human organization is immune to human imperfection or plain bad luck. As the size and complexity of construction projects increases, cost overruns, delays, and unforeseen incidents multiply, and this is true around the world.[55] But in the deepwater offshore, despite recent headlines, the international oil companies have a remarkably good record of safety and effectiveness, and accidents are uncommon. At Sakhalin their performance, though not perfect—witness the huge cost overruns in the construction of the Sakhalin-2 gas pipeline—was nevertheless outstanding. The Sakhalin PSAs were management exploits of the first magnitude.

It is precisely in the area of management, say international oilmen with experience in Russia, that the Russian oil companies have the most to learn. The Russians are no strangers to large projects, and in Soviet times Russian engineers and skilled workers realized extraordinary exploits under unbelievably harsh conditions. But in those days cost was no object. In today's global economy, cost is critical—not to mention safety and environment. On these dimensions the present generation of Russian companies has yet to demonstrate the new capabilities needed, particularly in the Arctic offshore, where they have only just begun to work.

Russian policy on the Arctic offshore is still hardly more than embryonic.[56] Until very recently the Arctic offshore has played almost no role in Russian oil policy, and Russia's two major state-owned champions, Rosneft and Gazprom, even though they have been granted a virtual monopoly of Arctic offshore licenses, have traditionally given them low priority, except for a small handful of special projects, notably Shtokman and Sakhalin, as well as Gazprom's Prirazlomnoe field in the Pechora Sea in Russia's northwest. At this point the one Russian major with the most actual offshore experience is LUKoil, which is developing several offshore projects in the Russian zone of the Caspian Sea, and through its subsidiary, LUKoil Overseas, has formed a partnership with a foreign independent, Vanco, to explore the deep offshore off the coasts of Ghana, Ivory Coast, and Sierra Leone.[57] However, LUKoil as yet has no Arctic offshore experience.

Hence the potentially pathbreaking importance of the recently concluded strategic alliance between ExxonMobil and Rosneft. For Rosneft, the alliance serves three objectives at once—to gain experience in the Arctic offshore, to expand outside Russia, and to learn the skills needed for tight-oil development. But the Arctic offshore component is likely to be the centerpiece. Together with Rosneft's recent agreements with Statoil and Eni, the relationship with

ExxonMobil appears to signal a fresh chapter in Russia's relations with foreign partners.

The best model is the experience of Norway. In the late 1960s, when the potential wealth of the North Sea was just being realized, Norway had no oil-related capability. Its two great assets, however, were a highly developed private shipping industry and a stable political system with a strong tradition of state support for a mixed economy, together with an honest and competent bureaucracy.[58] These enabled Norway to build not only a world-class NOC, but also a diversified network of high-tech suppliers and service companies. The most critical aspect of Russia's new strategic alliances, therefore, will be their success in fostering the transfer of technology, the development of skills, and the spread of high-tech entrepreneurship. This will not happen overnight. Perhaps the main lesson from Norway's experience is that it takes a long time to develop a broad-based offshore expertise, together with the supporting industrial and technological structure. Norway, despite its initial assets, took twenty years to develop a world-leading capability in all the key specialties, particularly in the most important part of the business, the management of large projects. The more recent experience of Brazil and Petrobras in the 1990s and 2000s tells the same story. Igor Sechin describes the ExxonMobil-Rosneft alliance in the same long-range perspective:

> This will be a giant leap forward on a scale comparable to the development of the oilfields of West Siberia in the 1960s and 70s of the last century.... It's more ambitious than man's first walk in space or sending man to the moon, and it will require a comparable amount of investment.[59]

In sum, the three colors of Russian oil—brown, green, and blue—pose different challenges and call for different strategies. But they have one thing in common: addressing them successfully will require both the oil industry and the state to make major changes in priorities, structures, and policies. We begin with the companies, then turn to the state.

Strategic Choices for the Russian Oil Industry

Since the end of the Soviet Union, the Russian oil companies have focused primarily on two challenges: during the decade of the 1990s, survival; and during the decade of the 2000s, recovery. Both challenges tended to push the industry toward short horizons and near-term decision making. Long-term strategy took a back seat to the pressures and opportunities of the moment, whether they stemmed from political and economic turbulence (as in the 1990s) or from the near-term opportunities offered by high prices (as in 1999–2008).

Now, as the Soviet legacy winds down, the Russian oil companies face more fundamental challenges. Confronted with many of the same pressures as the global oil industry a generation ago, the Russian oil companies must now prepare to move in similar directions—toward high-tech solutions, nontraditional sources, greater international involvement, and more efficient management. They will need to rethink inherited structures and practices. All this boils down to four strategic choices.

The first choice is what to do about the brownfields. International experience shows that as fields mature, the large companies need to move on. At this moment, the brownfields absorb the bulk of the capital and talent of the large companies, in a losing battle against diminishing returns. Present industry policy toward the brownfields, largely because of state pressure, is to maintain production at the expense of profitability; a recent modeling exercise has found that up to 30 percent of current production from the Russian brownfields loses money. The clearest example of this is the companies' high priority on repairing idle wells. By law the proportion of idle wells in a field may not exceed 10 percent of the total well stock. The resulting administrative pressure to maintain and repair idle wells causes the companies to invest selectively in their worst producers instead of their best ones. But the state is not the only source of the problem; many companies continue to focus on their existing well stock because it is the easiest thing to do and because there are regulations against "selective development."

A shift in brownfield policy toward profitability, instead of volume at all costs, would cushion the decline in rents from the brownfields for both the companies and the government, as well as freeing up the companies' resources for more productive uses. But realizing this potential requires a change in the organization of the industry to encourage smaller specialist companies that are familiar with local conditions and focused on limiting costs. The large companies, instead of seeking to absorb or squeeze out the smaller ones, should encourage them instead, by selling off marginal properties, leasing well blocks, creating specialist subsidiaries on the model of RITEK—and incidentally, welcoming back small and medium-sized foreign operators as partners in the brownfields.

If the large companies begin divesting themselves of the brownfields, they will need to increase their efforts to find new oil in the greenfields as well as the remaining outlying areas of West Siberia. The latest *World Energy Outlook* of the International Energy Agency puts the case starkly: "One third of the crude oil produced in 2035 will need to come from new fields that have yet to be proven or discovered."[60] This will require a far larger investment in exploration than the Russian companies have made until now—indeed, reversing the steady decline in exploration that has taken place throughout the 2000s.

The second strategic choice is how to address the ongoing high-tech revolution in production technologies. For the past two decades the large companies have taken an ad hoc approach, selectively adopting new techniques as they were introduced into Russia, mainly by foreign operators and service companies—hydraulic fracturing, horizontal drilling, and the like. These did not require fundamental changes in the companies' traditional cultures or organization of work. But the next generation of technologies—tomorrow's "digital oilfield"—will require the companies themselves to change. They must be able to analyze complex streams of data, to remeasure continuously as they produce, to disseminate information in real time, to combine multiple techniques in a single task, and to make rapid adjustments in development strategies. Operating the digital oilfield successfully will require integrating teams across disciplines and overcoming departmental and professional barriers, a perennial Russian problem. It is necessary for the Russian oil companies not to reinvent the wheel by maintaining large R&D facilities of their own (as is sometimes urged) but to take a longer-range view of what technologies to acquire and to do a better job of procuring and managing them, in particular by continuing the process of divesting themselves of in-house service departments, an inefficient Soviet holdover, while giving more business to domestic high-tech providers.

The third strategic choice is how to change the Russian industry's relationship with the global oil industry. At present the Russian industry makes little use of the most efficient vehicles for technology transfer and change. The contrast with Norway and Brazil is striking. Where the latter make aggressive use of partnerships, secondments, overseas training, international hires, and the like, the Russian industry remains largely isolated. This is crucial as the Russian

475

industry prepares to work in the Arctic offshore, to expand production of non-traditional liquids, and to master new sources, such as tight oil. The recently concluded strategic alliances are a critical start, but they are only a start.

Lastly, the Russian companies need to take a tough look at their own structures. The Russian companies took shape in the early to mid-1990s, as the pieces of the Soviet oil industry came down in the aftermath of the breakup. The resulting assemblages are the product not of planning but of chance and circumstance. In particular, the companies' upstream portfolios tend to fit awkwardly with their downstream assets and distribution networks. The Russian companies cling to what they have, partly because of the difficulty of transferring licenses, as well as (in some cases) because of relationships that go back to Soviet times, particularly the long-standing ties of the companies to the oil towns that depend on them. But a thoroughgoing rationalization of the companies' portfolios is long overdue, including a rethink of the prevailing doctrine of tying the upstream to the downstream within a single corporate structure.

In short, the Russian oil companies need to lengthen their horizons and reexamine many of the comfortable arrangements and practices that have been made possible by the Soviet legacy. This will necessarily be a challenging process, since these are a matter not simply of habit and culture but of long-standing relationships and networks of rent distribution. Above all, the companies presently have little incentive to change. There is also the relationship with the state.

The Prospects for Reform in State Oil Policy

The Russian state's oil policy in the 2000s has been dominated by two objectives: to capture oil rents and to establish secure control over the oil industry. By mid-decade, both of those aims had been largely achieved. Putin in his first five years was extremely effective in capturing the windfall profits from the massive run-up in oil prices in the 2000s and at the same time in imposing his will on the oil industry. Since then, the industry has played the role of a subordinate partner to the state, surrendering much of the rent from high oil prices while operating under increasingly pervasive regulation and intervention, as the state pursues an expanding range of goals through its control of oil. In return, the present owners of the oil companies have gained a degree of stability and security, so long as they play by the rules.

One may argue that it is the state's prerogative, as the sovereign owner of the country's natural wealth, to dispose of its resources as it sees fit. Indeed, as one looks across much of the oil world, the state is the dominant partner nearly everywhere. Seen from that perspective, the latitude enjoyed by the Russian oil industry through the mid-2000s was an anomaly, the product of the collapse of the Soviet system and the temporary weakness of the Russian state. As the state regained strength, it was inevitable that it would act to recover revenues and power.

But that is not the question here. Rather, what the preceding two chapters have argued is that the system of taxation and regulation built in the 2000s is defective. It removes most of the companies' incentive to respond aggressively and creatively to the decline of the Soviet oil legacy. As a result, both partners—the state and the industry—now face the prospect not only of a near-term decline in production but, more fundamentally, a long-term decline in oil rents. How should they respond?

Clearly, the first task is to press on with rationalizing the tax system. As we have seen, the dialogue engaged in over the past three years has led to a broad consensus among the players over the way forward. It consists, first, of doing away with the misplaced bias in favor of the downstream over the upstream. Second, the taxation of gross revenues must give way to a system based on taxation of profits, initially applied to large new fields. Third, export taxes, with their distorting effects on domestic prices, must be eliminated. The underlying premise of the tax reform, which creates the basis for consensus and early action, is that a properly redesigned tax system will allow a "win-win solution," that is, an increase in the cash available for reinvestment at no cost to the state budget. The first steps have been taken; the next ones are under study.

Despite the good beginning, however, further progress on the tax front is likely to be slow. The fiscal imbalance between crude oil and product exports will not be righted until 2015 at the earliest, and profit-based taxation will probably not be widely adopted before 2020, if then. That is a long time to wait, given the rapidly mounting pressures on the industry. But at least the way forward is clear.

The problem with the tax-reform debate, however, is that it has come to be a substitute for consideration of other needed reforms. The regulatory system that has grown so constrictive in the second half of the 2000s is the product of an unplanned layering of Soviet-era and post-Soviet structures, the whole bound to the Kremlin via an inefficient *vertikal'* of power. The system promotes a confusing array of uncoordinated and frequently contradictory objectives. The rhetoric of high-tech modernization clashes with the ideology of Soviet-style frontier development, symbolized by high-priority pipeline projects in virgin territories. The goal of maximizing export revenues competes with that of manipulating the export mix to move up to "valued-added" exports, regardless of whether they actually add value or not. The oil companies are urged to "fly the flag" by investing abroad, yet are criticized for capital flight when they do so. A rhetoric of welcome to foreign investment contrasts with a policy of limiting access by actual foreigners. Politicians debate over where to draw the line between private and state and wobble unpredictably between the two. "National security" wars with economic efficiency as a policy goal.

These contradictions are not new. In the 1990s they contributed to further paralyzing an already weak government, and the result was effectively no oil policy at all or, rather, oil policy by default, as the oil industry followed the path of least resistance toward breakup and privatization. In the 2000s, in contrast, oil policy swung in favor of state control, resource nationalism, and rent extraction. Longer-range challenges such as modernization of the oil sector, the encouragement of efficiency, international integration, and the renewal of the reserve base have been effectively smothered.

Addressing the broader problem of regulatory control will be very much more difficult than reforming the tax system, because of the many interests that have grown up around it and because regulatory reform is much more of a zero-sum game. The centralization of power around the Kremlin and the systematic division of that power to prevent any one actor from acting independently appear to suit the Kremlin's purposes and the influential interests behind it. Consequently, the most likely outlook is that the government will tinker cautiously around the edges but that the present arrangements will remain much the same.

That may be enough to maintain oil production at something like today's roughly 500 million tons per year (10 million barrels per day), or at least to avert a sharp decline over the next decade.[61] But it will not be enough to maintain an expanding flow of oil rents—unless world markets oblige with a continued rise of oil prices. This means that in coming years Russia will be more hostage than ever to world energy trends and to the increasingly radical developments that are driving them.

What might some of those developments be, and how will Russia's future depend on them? That is the subject of the concluding chapter.

chapter 13

Looking Ahead: Oil and the Future of Russia; Russia and the Future of Oil

As they look back over the last twenty years since the Soviet breakup, the veterans, people like Vladimir Bogdanov of Surgutneftegaz, know better than anyone how much has turned on chance and personality, and how easily the outcomes could have been different. What if Bogdanov had not managed to close the airport to Surgut and prevent his company from being auctioned off to a financial oligarch during the "Sale of the Century" in the mid-1990s? What if he had lost his battle for the Kirishi refinery and not formed early alliances with the then obscure Vladimir Putin and Gennadii Timchenko? What if he had not managed to persuade Putin to leave Surgutneftegaz alone as an independent company, rather than absorb it into the national oil company Rosneft? There were so many ditches one could have run into, so many side roads leading to other places. Chance and personality—and luck. All of today's surviving winners know their story is the same. Such is the wheel of fortune.

The Logic of Fate and Circumstance

Yet at the same time, there is a deep logic to the path followed by the Russian oil industry over these past twenty years. On the surface, it might seem circumstance that the Soviet-era oil-related ministries broke up and their assets passed into private hands. The gas industry, after all, remained a state monopoly. A strong figure at the head of the oil industry, comparable to Viktor Chernomyrdin, might have used the state's control over the transportation system to force the oil generals into line and keep the oil industry in state hands. But there was no such strong figure for oil, and the barons in the industry, seeing opportunity for themselves, favored breakup and privatization instead, because oil could be conveniently exported and turned into money, while gas could not. For the same reason, it was much more difficult to stop them. Keeping the oil industry together and preventing it from going private would have required a far stronger state with more determined statist leadership, and that did not come until a decade later. Given the players and the circumstances as they were, any other outcome than breakup would have been surprising indeed. For all practical purposes, the breakup and privatization of the oil industry were inevitable.

The rise of Yukos and Sibneft and the radical pioneering roles they played in the "oil miracle" phase of 1999–2004 likewise appear at first to be almost matters of chance, yet they too obeyed the same deep logic. It was circumstance that the Yeltsin government handed some of the best oil properties to the finansisty in the shares-for-loans auctions, while only two neftianiki—Alekperov and Bogdanov—managed to hang on to theirs. Yet given the bankrupt condition of the state and the mushrooming fortunes of those who soon came to be known as the "oligarchs," it was predictable that financial operators would succeed somehow in penetrating the oil industry. Indeed, the penetration was already far advanced by the time of the shares-for-loans affair. Similar battles took place between the Soviet-era "generals" and the new financial oligarchs in every part of the Russian commodity sector, particularly in the metals industry, and the outcome was broadly the same: those Soviet-era managers who learned fast survived, while the others were swept away.

It might also seem to be circumstance that Mikhail Khodorkovsky's unique combination of business genius and hubris would offer such a perfect target for the ambitions of Igor Sechin and Sergei Bogdanchikov, and that these two, thanks to the opportunity unwittingly presented to them by a judge in far-off Texas, would capture the assets of Yukos for Rosneft. Indeed, the very existence of Rosneft as a state-owned company was itself largely a matter of chance, owing to the state's repeated failures to sell it off. It had survived as a rump state-owned company because of Aleksandr Putilov's stubbornness and opportunism and subsequently because its assets were considered nearly worthless. But it was quite predictable that the extreme weakness of the Russian central state would not last and that as it regained strength after 2000 (thanks in no small part to rising oil prices) the stage would be set for a showdown with the oligarchs. In that conflict, coercion would very likely win out over money (at least in any frontal contest), and the siloviki would get their turn. But the more street-smart among the oil-company owners—Bogdanov, Alekperov, Bogdanchikov, Abramovich, and Fridman and his colleagues—never forgot what country they lived in, and so they survived.

Despite the accidents of personalities and events, what stands out above all is the logic of the mutual dependence of the oil industry and the state. From the crisis of the late 1980s through the decline of the 1990s, and from the revival of the 2000s to the crash of 2008 and beyond, the fortunes of oil have determined those of the state, while the strength or weakness of the state has shaped the fortunes of the oil industry.

This was not always so. The tight intertwining of oil and politics, in which oil has been both provider and prize for the state and its politicians, is a phenomenon of the final Soviet decade and the post-Soviet transition. But once that dependence entered its present phase in the early 1990s—as the Russian economy and polity became increasingly addicted to oil—it became the central feature of Russian politics. The Soviet Union was not a petro-state; but post-Soviet Russia is increasingly taking on the characteristics of one.

Yet this book has argued that Russia's "petro-statism" is due not to oil per se but rather to three deeper causes, which have been the central subjects of this book: the consequences of the Soviet legacy in all its facets, the cycle of collapse and rebirth of the central state, and the impact of Russia's exposure to an increasingly unstable global economy. In all of these, oil played an important part, but it was not by itself the driver.

The real driver of events in Russia has been a more fundamental set of issues, which affect oil along with everything else. It is the unresolved conflict among Russians over the principles by which society and the economy should be run. There is no consensus among Russians about the most basic issues in economic and political life. There is no common view that capitalism is better; on the contrary, two decades on, many Russians—although not all—prefer a Russian brand of populist socialism largely unchanged from Soviet times. There is no agreement over who should own and run the essential assets of the country or which goods should be public or private. There is no unanimity among Russians about their place in the world or their relationship to the global economy and international players in it. At most there is a vague nostalgia for the Soviet past—not for communism as an ideology but rather for an era in which Russia was powerful and the central state provided.

This basic ambivalence has hindered the rethinking of the state and held back the development of effective new institutions. Despite the impressive effort to create new codes and procedures, the Russian state remains only half "re-formed," halfway between its previous Soviet-era roles as owner of a centrally planned economy and its new ones as referee of the market, private property, and civil society. Instead of progressing toward the formal rules, impartial procedures, and public outcomes that characterize (at least in aspiration) a modern, developed state, Russia has not escaped from rule by personalities and coteries, backroom bargaining, and hidden deals. The picture is not uniformly bleak, to be sure. One can point to significant advances, such as the creation of the Tax Code and vastly improved institutions for monetary, budgetary, and fiscal administration. Yet the overall story is one of a failure of consensus over the way ahead.

The oil industry mirrors this indecision: Should it be private or state-owned? Should it be run on free-market principles or state-capitalist ones? Should it be integrated with the outside world or stand alone? Who should get the rents, and what should they be used for? What are the respective property rights of the companies and the state? On these fundamental points Russians are at odds, and as a result the oil industry has drifted, pulled this way and that by opposing forces with conflicting goals. So long as they have not been resolved, the logic of the future points to continuing conflict and instability.

Yet even so, thanks to the oil assets inherited from the Soviet Union, the oil industry has managed to rebuild production back to the Soviet level, generating enough rent to sustain its three main stakeholders: the Russian consumers, the owners and managers, and the state. But as this book has argued, the Soviet legacy is now at the point of diminishing returns. As costs rise, the flow of oil rents will depend above all on one remaining variable: oil prices.

What, then, can we expect oil prices to do in the decade or two ahead?

Russia and the Future of Oil: Two Scenarios

There is no more uncertain enterprise than trying to guess the future of oil prices. Compounding the difficulty today is that both the supply and demand for oil worldwide are increasingly driven by new and unprecedentedly powerful forces. Surprises in technological innovation, shifts in patterns of economic growth, changes in the structure of oil markets, aggravated political and military conflict, and many other factors besides are making oil prices more volatile than ever before.

Yet nothing so closely predicts the future of Russia as oil prices. In round numbers, oil and gas (the prices of the latter being still largely linked to oil) together account for about 30 percent of Russian GDP. Since about 2000, the steady rise in oil and gas prices has explained about half of GDP growth. In contrast, the sharp drop in average annual oil prices from $95 per barrel in 2008 to $60 per barrel in 2009 cost Russia 9 to 16 percentage points of annual GDP growth.[1] However one looks at it, the pattern of oil prices is crucial for Russia.

But what about the future? As one peers into the crystal ball, two opposite images appear. One is a world of high and rising oil prices, the other a world of lastingly lower ones. Both turn out to be plausible; but how could they both be true?

Let us take the high-price scenario first. It is not difficult to construct a narrative in which oil prices continue to rise for another decade and beyond. The first element is high and rising demand from Asia and the Middle East, driven by strong economic growth and rising incomes, reinforced by state subsidies to oil consumers. The second is continuing steady increases in the costs of finding and producing oil; and the third is growing political threats to oil supplies from instability in key oil-producing countries (Nigeria, the Middle East, and others). These three drivers have been the chief forces behind the spectacular rise in global oil prices since the late 1990s, and they could well remain in command for the indefinite future, pushing oil prices higher and higher. This is a widespread view; for example, the U.S. Government's Energy Information Administration, in its reference-case projection, sees oil prices rising to nearly $150 per barrel by 2035.[2]

Yet a lower-price scenario is also plausible, but based on very different drivers: (1) a major expansion of hydrocarbon supply, based on the spread of shale gas and tight-oil technology from North America to the rest of the world, including especially China; (2) large-scale substitution of natural gas for oil in transportation and other uses (both directly and indirectly, by way of gas-generated electricity); (3) continuing decline in oil consumption in the countries of the Organisation for Economic Co-operation and Development (OECD), owing to slow economic growth coupled with consumer reaction to high oil prices; and finally, (4) a slowdown in economic growth in Asia, especially China.

This lower-price scenario is based on several increasingly powerful propositions. First, the production of shale gas and tight oil in North America is

484

gathering speed at an astonishing rate, far outstripping all forecasts. As it spreads to the rest of the world, it will change sharply the outlook for global oil production in the decades ahead. China, in particular, combines large-scale shale and tight-oil resources with the political will to develop them, and although it is unlikely to become self-sufficient in oil, its production of hydrocarbons will grow rapidly, slowing the growth of its oil imports. Second, an unprecedented price gap has opened up—so far mainly in North America but likely to spread elsewhere—between cheap natural gas and expensive oil, creating a strong incentive to displace oil in such applications as trucking and railroads and industry.

The biggest changes are likely to come from the demand side. Oil demand has already peaked in the OECD countries, chiefly in Europe and the United States, and today's oil prices (which remain historically high) are only accelerating that trend. Finally, economic growth is slowing in many of the so-called emerging economies, particularly in China, where accumulating imbalances in the Chinese economy, after three decades of breakneck growth, may cause the rate of increase of oil demand to moderate.

A broad shift is taking place in the world's demand for oil. The "oil intensity" (i.e., the consumption of oil per unit of GDP) of the economies of the developed world has declined steadily since the 1970s—a trend set off by the first "oil shocks" of 1973 and 1980 and further stimulated by the price boom of the last ten years.[3] In many countries, oil has already been largely displaced by other fuels in most of its traditional uses, such as power generation and home heating. The one remaining place where oil has no real competition is transportation, where at present it is the only practical fuel for passenger cars and trucks. But even there oil's supremacy is coming under challenge. The steady progress of battery technology is gradually making the electric car a reality; and if the electric car becomes a mass-market vehicle, it will eventually make oil vulnerable in its last redoubt.

The signs are clear: the age of oil is slowly passing, not because of a peak in supply but because of a coming peak in demand. This will not happen immediately, nor will it happen smoothly. The price of oil, as with all commodities, swings with every change in the balance of supply and demand and in response to passing events and changes in market sentiment. Indeed, the frequency and amplitude of swings in oil prices has increased in recent years, owing to the growing "financialization" of oil, meaning the growing role in oil markets of non-oil players, investing through derivatives and exchange-traded funds and other new financial instruments, going "long" or "short" on oil contracts from trading floors and work stations all over the world. In decades to come, oil prices are likely to be more unstable than ever.

Short-term events can produce dramatic price spikes, but they are not necessarily long lasting. It is only when a long-term change occurs in the forces driving supply and demand that the "playing field" of oil prices shifts decisively for a decade or more, whether from low price to high price (as after 1973) or high price to low price (as after 1986).

Ultimately the most powerful depressive force pushing toward a lower-price scenario is simply the impact of today's high prices themselves. The higher oil prices go, the greater the drag on consumption, the stronger the stimulus to displacement of oil by natural gas and renewables, and the more powerful the incentive to invest in unconventional hydrocarbons like shale gas and tight oil. In other words, the price level itself is a major causal factor: the higher oil prices go, the more likely a shift to a lower-price playing field becomes.

"Demand destruction" (as economists call it), once it has occurred, tends to be long lasting. The effects of the oil shocks of 1973 and 1980 are still with us; the trend line of per-capita oil consumption in the OECD countries has never returned to pre-1973 levels. Moreover, in the process oil has been permanently displaced from nearly all its previous applications except transportation. The point here is that oil's place in the global energy balance is potentially fragile.

A scenario is not a forecast. It is, at best, an attempt to broaden the mind or, as Daniel Yergin writes, "to peer around the corner of history."[4] For the moment, the forces pushing toward higher prices are still dominant, and they are made even stronger by the tendency of markets to overshoot. Political risks, especially in the volatile Middle East, are continuing to push prices toward the upside. The costs of finding and producing oil are rising rapidly. But the forces behind a lower-price scenario are becoming stronger; the drag on consumption from higher prices is increasing; and as the saying goes, when something cannot continue, it eventually stops.

But what would the consequences of a lower-price scenario be for Russia?

Implications of a Lower-Price Scenario for Russia

A lower-price scenario for hydrocarbons would be very disruptive for Russia, for obvious direct reasons (lower export revenues from oil and gas) but also for less obvious indirect ones. To see why, let us look first at Russia's place in the global energy economy.

In its overall energy profile, Russia remains very much in the Soviet mold, locked in the patterns of the late twentieth century. Its energy supply consists largely of conventional fossil fuels, with a minor contribution from nuclear power and hydropower. Its energy consumption is dominated by inefficient Soviet-era factories and power plants, and the energy intensity of its economy is still one of the highest in the world. Russia has taken almost no part in the multiple revolutions that are transforming the world's definitions of energy, energy markets, and energy security. It plays no significant role in solar power, wind, hybrid and electric cars, battery research, smart grids, biofuels, or carbon sequestration.[5] Its only entry in the race for new energy forms is an old one—nuclear power—and most of its nuclear power plants, like the rest of its generating stock, date from the Soviet era.[6]

Russia's influence in global energy matters is modest compared with the scale of its energy resources. In oil markets it is a passive price taker, and it has shown little desire to join with other oil producers to influence output levels or prices. In gas markets it has leverage only in Europe, and even that is limited by the high degree of interconnectedness of the European gas market and the availability of storage, together with the growing role of LNG. The only real sense in which Russia is a great power in energy is in its ability to put pressure on its near neighbors, and even there, as the examples of Azerbaijan, Kazakhstan, and Turkmenistan show, there is little that Russia can do when those countries decide to diversify their outlets.

In a world of lower-priced oil and gas, Russia, with its conventional energy signature and its declining legacy, would be squeezed between higher-cost production at home and lower prices for its oil and gas exports. (The same would also be true for its exports of "embodied" hydrocarbons, that is, commodities using oil and gas in their production, such as steel, petrochemicals, and fertilizers.) In a lower-price world there would be less interest from outside investors for Russia's costly resources along its Arctic shelf and its eastern interior. Russian oil companies, with their present conventional-oil skill set, would be even less competitive outside their own borders than they are today. Russian pipeline gas would face increased competition from shale gas and LNG in Europe and China, while the "shale gale" has already shut the door to Russian LNG in North America.

In short, Russia is potentially highly vulnerable to any long-term shift from the present high-price scenario to a lower-price one, and all the more so if the shift coincides with the higher costs stemming from the winding down of the Soviet oil legacy.

But how do Russian policy makers perceive the problem, and if so, how do they propose to address it?

Escaping from Oil Addiction: Three Visions of Russia's Future

In Russia, the theme of natural-resource dependence has been around for a long time. It was popular in the Soviet era. "Only third-world countries export raw commodities" was a common refrain in Soviet literature. "We do not want to be a natural-resource dependency [*resursnyi pridatok*]." The Soviet government constantly urged industry to export more manufactured goods, without much success. Throughout its existence, the Soviet Union remained a raw-materials exporter.

Yet in the post-Soviet period, as Russia has become more dependent than ever on exports of oil and gas and other natural resources, while failing to develop the sectors that might export higher-tech goods and services (except for weapons), thoughtful Russians have grown increasingly dispirited. As Andrei Klepach, deputy minister of economic development, put it in a memorable phrase, Russia has become "a country that exports oil, girls, and future Nobel Prize laureates."[7]

In the wake of the 2008 crash, a remarkable debate began—one of those periodic self-examinations for which the Russians are famous—on the evils of natural-resource dependence and the ways to escape from it. But although the goal was clear, there was no consensus on how to achieve it—illustrating once again the seeming inability of post-Soviet Russia to agree on fundamentals. Instead, three competing visions of Russia's future are on offer: "high-tech modernization," "return to market reform," and "stay the course." Each one is identified with a prominent public figure: the former president (now prime minister) Dmitri Medvedev, the former finance minister (now in opposition) Aleksei Kudrin, and the president-reelect Vladimir Putin.

Dmitri Medvedev's Vision: High-Tech Modernization

Dmitri Medvedev's four-year term as president of Russia seems fated to go down in history as a brief filler between Vladimir Putin's first two terms and his third. As Medvedev took office there was an immediate mass migration of aides and bureaucrats from the Kremlin to the White House, where Putin, as prime minister, remained very much in charge. Medvedev himself, in his first public appearances as president, appeared uncertain and ill at ease.[8]

But Medvedev gained in self-assurance as time went by, and the crash and recession of 2008–2009 gave him an opening to identify himself with the cause of liberal reform. Liberals gravitated to him as their patron, as he put forward a new agenda of economic modernization and diversification, amounting to a tacit critique of the policies of the previous decade. Medvedev proved surprisingly effective in using the latest technologies of political communication— websites, blogs, streaming video, phone apps, social networks, and the rest—to dominate the public space (or at least that growing portion of the Russian public space that is online and wired in), to the point of overshadowing his patron (even though the latter clearly retained the reality of power). Medvedev was unfortunately less successful in getting results, partly because he got only tepid support from Putin. Now that Medvedev has left the presidency, the fate of his modernization program is uncertain, but he deserves credit for introducing a wide range of new ideas into public currency, thus contributing to the demands for change that are now challenging the political system.

Medvedev's modernization program was all about high-tech innovation and efficiency—computers, nanotechnology, advanced medicine, nuclear power, and space. "For centuries," he declared early in his modernization campaign, "we have shipped our raw materials abroad, and imported all the 'smart' products."[9] The spirit and thrust of his modernization program could almost be summed up as "anywhere but hydrocarbons, anything but oil and gas." Energy played an important part in Medvedev's vision, but the focus was not on increasing supply but on limiting consumption. Meanwhile, the revenues from oil should be invested in high-tech manufacturing, while putting as little as possible into the oil sector itself.

The oil industry too was part of the problem. Medvedev was openly disparaging of the industry's backwardness and complacency:

> We commonly think of the fuel sector as conservative. The industry, in this view, has settled so completely into its own role that in essence it has become part of the paternalistic mindset. It embodies the state of mind that says that nothing needs to be changed, everything's fine as it is, there's plenty of oil and gas left, and that therefore we can continue to grow without technological improvements.[10]

This kind of talk brought an indignant pushback from the oil and gas establishment. Viktor Orlov, the former Soviet-era minister of geology and lately the chairman of the committee on natural resources and environment of the upper house of parliament, criticized the modernizers' "ignorance of the high scientific content and innovative significance" of the natural-resource sector.[11] Leonid Fedun, vice president of LUKoil, commented acidly:

> Let's say we have a dairy farm. We go around the cowshed putting in energy-saving lightbulbs, and we're thinking about changing the windowpanes to new ones with nanocoating. But nobody is worrying about raising the milk yield of the cows, which is actually what feeds us.[12]

Iurii Shafranik, the former energy minister, put his finger on the central weakness of the modernization program: even if successful, he pointed out, it will require at least two or three decades to make a real difference. In the meantime, the economy will continue to rely on oil.

For many Russians, the Medvedev program, in its ambition and sweep, was disturbingly reminiscent of the Soviet five-year plans. It was the same top-down modernization by political mandate, the same drive to overcome decades of lag in one giant leap.

In contrast, former Finance Minister Aleksei Kudrin's vision marks a return to the agenda of market-oriented reform. Kudrin is now "in de facto opposition," as he describes it, but his views remain influential, not least within the government.[13]

Aleksei Kudrin's Vision: Back to the Basics

Russia owes much to Aleksei Kudrin. As finance minister throughout Putin's first decade, he pursued a cautious fiscal and budgetary strategy, while presiding over a sweeping modernization of Russia's tax system and the state's finances. If Russia weathered the 2008–2009 crisis without a cataclysmic economic collapse, it was largely due to him. But by 2010, oil prices were rising again, and Kudrin saw the same old devils returning—excessive optimism and complacency, the all-too-familiar syndrome of "irrational exuberance" Russian style.

But this time something seemed broken. As oil prices passed quickly through the $70, $80, and $90 marks, breaking $100 per barrel by the late winter of 2011, Kudrin noted that economic growth was not responding in proportion. Before the crash, he observed, $60 oil had been enough to generate 8 percent GDP growth; now, oil at nearly twice the price barely produced half as much impact.[14] Much of the problem stemmed from weak investment. Instead of generating growth at home, capital was fleeing Russia, on a scale not seen even in the chaotic 1990s.[15]

More and more of the oil revenues were being absorbed by the state, to feed a ballooning budget. Once again the barbarians were at the gates, Kudrin warned, clamoring to spend the windfall. Once again, bureaucrats were pushing for increases in their budgets. Once again, ministries and local governments were allowing costs to run out of control. Three years after the crash, Kudrin saw Russia on the same roller-coaster as in 2004–2008, cranking inexorably uphill toward higher deficits and greater instability, setting up the crazy ride to follow. The result was more and more dependence on oil prices. "If this year it takes oil at $115 a barrel to balance the budget," he warned, "next year it will take about $122 a barrel."[16]

Yet Kudrin did not believe that oil prices would keep on rising; on the contrary, he predicted that by 2014 oil prices would be back down to $60 per barrel. He believed that they were being driven by a worldwide credit bubble, centered on China. The bubble would soon pop, he thought, taking the world economy down with it.[17] In any case, Kudrin believed that the Russian oil industry's days of rapidly increasing production were over. As the combined result of stagnant production and lower prices, Kudrin predicted that the share of the oil and gas sector in Russia's total GDP would shrink by 2020.[18] The oil industry, Kudrin argued, had become a brake on the Russian economy, and the inevitable result would be a fiscal disaster.[19] By this time, in early 2011, Kudrin had turned into virtually a one-man opposition. He was openly critical of Medvedev's modernization program and of the Kremlin's plans to increase military spending. He was especially scathing toward the Ministry of Economic Development's aim to fund Russia's modernization through annual deficits. The state should strive to create the best possible investment climate, Kudrin argued, and stop trying to channel investment through large state corporations, which led only to corruption and capital flight. Low inflation, a stable currency, and strong property rights were the three key prerequisites. Only if these three were present would long money become available for investment and entrepreneurs have an incentive to take risks. Kudrin's formula represented in many ways a revival of the liberal market-reform program of the early 2000s, which Putin in his first term appeared to support.

But Kudrin was increasingly isolated, discounted by the rest of the leadership as a cranky Cassandra. The end came in September 2011. Angered by Putin's decision to take back the presidency and name Dmitri Medvedev prime minister, Kudrin, in a dramatic press conference in Washington, announced he would not serve under Medvedev. Back in Russia the next day, Kudrin was publicly dressed down by Medvedev and expelled from the government, to faint praise but no support from Putin, the man Kudrin had served for a decade.

Kudrin's departure removed from the leadership the one person who had the stature and the determination to stand against the growing pressures to spend. Over the following year, budgetary restraint disappeared as election-year politics took over. Campaigning for reelection in the spring of 2012, Putin multiplied promises to wage raises for teachers and doctors and to increase pensions. According to a recent report by Citigroup Russia, funding Putin's campaign commitments will require oil prices at $150 per barrel or higher to keep the budget in balance.[20]

But Putin is not just about spending. Putin too has a vision.

Putin's Vision: Trust the State and Stay the Course

Putin is the one Russian leader (together with Igor Sechin) who has paid the most sustained attention to the details of energy policy over the years, and especially since the 2008 crash. In general he remains committed to a traditional conception of the oil industry, founded on four propositions. First, oil is still abundant in Russia; one must simply look harder for it. Second, the first obligation of the oil companies is to the state and the state budget, not to their shareholders. Third, the preferred vehicle for finding, producing, and transporting oil is a large, preferably state-owned, integrated company. Lastly, the aim of such a company should be to provide "value added," which in Putin's mind still means exports of refined products in preference to crude. In short, the state remains the engine of growth and progress. The job of the oil industry is to provide the fuel for it.

Putin denounces Russia's dependence on oil just as Medvedev and Kudrin do. But his view is tempered by his belief that oil has an indispensable role to play for decades to come, not only as a source of revenue but also as an important instrument of regional development at home and geopolitical influence abroad. Unlike Medvedev and his team, Putin praises the oil industry as potentially a technological leader—but it is clear that in his mind it takes second place to more "advanced" sectors like the military industry. His basic view, that revenues from oil should be channeled by the state to support Russia's other strategic industries, remains essentially unchanged from those views he first expressed in the late 1990s when he first came to power.

Igor Sechin expresses much the same view, as indeed he has since Saint Petersburg days. As deputy prime minister from 2008 to 2012 he tended in his public pronouncements to emphasize sectors other than oil; and even within the oil sector he put the needs of the refining and petrochemical sector for advanced machinery and equipment ahead of those of the upstream.[21] That was perhaps not surprising, given his broad responsibility for both energy and industry as a whole. However, over time, as we saw in Chapter 9, Sechin became increasingly concerned about the outlook for oil production, and he called for greater attention to technology and training for the upstream industry. In his parallel role as chairman of the board and de facto head of Rosneft, Sechin in 2008 launched a new Oil and Gas Institute in Krasnoiarsk, funded partly by Rosneft and conceived as a combined research and training center for the next generation of the oil industry. Two years later Putin and Sechin traveled together to Krasnoiarsk to inaugurate it.[22]

Sechin played a key role (as we saw in Chapter 11) in creating Rosneft's new strategic alliances with ExxonMobil, Eni, and Statoil. Now back at Rosneft as president and CEO (May 2012), Sechin sees Rosneft as a vehicle for the modernization not only of the oil industry but also of related sectors. For example, at the signing ceremony in New York in April 2012 for Rosneft's strategic alliance with ExxonMobil, Sechin said, "The new framework will also help reindustrialize Russia, with the construction of new airports, pipelines and seaports."[23] He can be expected to stress the importance of technology transfer and domestic content, especially through staff exchanges and joint training programs. Significantly, one of the key components of the alliance with ExxonMobil is a planned Arctic research center to be located in Saint Petersburg.

Russia's Modernization Dilemma

As Putin begins his third term, his vision appears, more than ever, to be the dominant one. One might suppose, indeed, that with Medvedev's move to the premiership and Kudrin's departure from the government their views have lost influence. Yet in reality all three remain strongly represented in the refashioned leadership, and the actual direction of policy is likely to reflect a continuing competition, but also dialogue, among them. The composition of the new government, announced in May 2012, suggests as much.[24]

Despite their apparent differences, all three visions have some points in common. All three see oil as a bridge leading to somewhere else, a way station to the high-tech future and the knowledge economy; but they do not view oil itself, or the oil industry, as a major source of high-tech innovation. This view is broadly shared throughout the policy-making elite, but it is especially pronounced among the market reformers.[25]

More generally, however, all three visions share the faith that Russia has the capacity to compete in the global economy as a leading producer of high-tech products and services. But this is, to put it mildly, a brave bet. Russia, with its diminished human and physical capital, will be hard-pressed to keep up with the emerging economies of Asia, as well as the mature knowledge economy of the United States, which continues to be a world leader in innovation and entrepreneurship.

This is a reality that Russians, understandably, find difficult to accept. To their discomfort, they now find themselves lumped together with countries they only recently looked down upon as underdeveloped compared with themselves. To Russian ears, to be called a "BRIC" is not necessarily a compliment.[26]

They still regard Western Europe and the United States (despite their problems) as the relevant models of technological progress and look upon themselves as members of that same advanced league. The Russian modernizers still travel to MIT and Silicon Valley and Düsseldorf, not (or, at any rate, not as often or as enthusiastically) to Bangalore, Shanghai, or Saõ Paulo. They have still not quite adjusted to the fact that it is the other BRICs that are now Russia's real competition.

Each of the other BRICs has comparative advantages that Russia does not. India has its huge internal market. Brazil has, in addition to oil, a wealth of natural resources, such as ethanol derived from sugar. All three have dynamic and entrepreneurial private sectors. China's low costs, entrepreneurship, R&D capabilities, and financial might are a special challenge. China is bankrupting competitors everywhere, and Russia is no exception. (A recent example is drilling rigs, where competition from Chinese producers has virtually wiped out the near monopoly once enjoyed by Uralmash.)

China and India are obviously vastly different from Russia, but lately Brazil has attracted the curiosity of Russian liberals, who detect interesting parallels—and key differences—with themselves. To Russian eyes, Brazil is a country that successfully combines modernization and natural-resource development, generating high levels of growth in a diversified and increasingly high-tech economy. Petrobras, the Brazilian national oil company, has become a world leader in deep-water oil exploration and production. But it is the way Petrobras has achieved this that particularly interests the Russians. Petrobras has succeeded where Russia has barely begun, drawing on international partners for training and technology to develop homegrown skills. Moreover, Brazilian oil policy has combined private ownership and state leadership in a way that seems—to far-off Moscow at least—to be constructive and successful. To Russian eyes, Brazil has somehow managed over the past two decades to marry growth, stability, and democracy, in a way that Russia has struggled to do. As one Russian critic, commenting ironically on the Brazilian national motto, "Order and Progress," recently wrote: "They got the progress, we got the order."[27]

But Russia's comparative advantage is still oil and gas, whether the Russian modernizers like it or not. One key difference between Russia and Brazil is that the Brazilians embrace oil, viewing it as a symbol of progress and a catalyst for the development of homegrown technology,[28] whereas many Russian policy makers view it as a symbol of backwardness. Yet Russia has little choice but to follow a similar path. For now and for the foreseeable future, hydrocarbons will remain Russia's chief comparative advantage in an increasingly competitive world economy.

This is a not a popular message in Russia, and indeed it runs counter to the universal conventional wisdom about the "curse of oil." Can a country as dependent on natural resources as Russia be competitive in the world economy? According to Michael Porter, the global guru of competitiveness to two generations of Harvard Business School students, being competitive comes down to a few simple rules: It's not what you do; it's how you do it. All industries are potentially high-tech and can be world leaders. All one needs is the right blend of foreign and domestic investment, management, and technology. Russia has the human and technological assets to achieve this. In short, Russia should go with what it's got, only do it better.[29]

So far, so good. But at this point Porter's argument takes a sharp turn. There are two kinds of prosperity—inherited and created. Natural resources are inherited, and that's bad. Inherited prosperity collapses when the natural resources run down. In the meantime, rent-seeking interest groups compete with one another for a share of the inherited wealth, each trying to get a bigger share of the pie. The state plays too large a role, both as owner and principal distributor. That's a suggestive description of today's Russia. In contrast, created prosperity is self-renewing and therefore unlimited. On this reasoning, Russia should move away from inherited prosperity (i.e., oil) and seek to create new sources of wealth. This is precisely the Medvedev program.[30]

It is true that Russia's present oil wealth is inherited. But that is a temporary feature of the last twenty years. In Soviet times oil and gas were anything but "inherited." The Soviet Union developed excellent schools of geology and engineering. It encouraged mapping of natural resources and systematic exploration of the mineral base of the country. It developed pioneering techniques for exploration and production. In short, the basis for today's Russian oil and gas legacy was definitely a "created" knowledge industry, and it is in large part because such a base existed that the Russian oil industry was able to recover so quickly from the trauma of the 1990s and to return to nearly the Soviet level of production in the 2000s.

The Soviet experience precisely matches that of another major natural-resource producer, the United States. As a study of the history of the U.S. oil industry concludes, the United States in the early twentieth century owed its

496

success not only to its favorable geological endowment but also to the systematic application of knowledge in a favorable institutional environment. Again: It's not what you have, it's what you do with it.

This is, to say the least, a different take on the "curse of oil." The study's conclusion is worth quoting as a message to Russia's modernizers:

> Minerals themselves are not to blame for problems of rent-seeking and corruption. Instead, it is largely the manner in which policy makers and businesses *view* minerals that determines the outcome. If minerals are conceived as fixed stocks, and mineral abundance as a "windfall" unconnected to past investment, then the problem becomes one of divvying up the bounty rather than creating more bounty. Minerals are not a curse at all in the sense of inevitability; the curse, where it exists, is self-fulfilling.[31]

The history of the global oil industry over the past twenty years demonstrates its importance as a high-tech knowledge industry. The latest and most spectacular illustration of this is the renaissance of oil and gas production in the United States from shale gas and tight oil, the products of entrepreneurship and innovation. But as I suggested in the preceding chapter, there is every bit as much potential for a similar renaissance in Russia, in the very center of the Soviet oil and gas industry, the Volga-Urals and West Siberia.

The challenge for the Russian oil industry, in short, is to return to its roots as a knowledge industry, as a source of created, not inherited, prosperity, and to use the oil industry as a stimulus for innovation and entrepreneurship throughout the economy. One important vehicle of progress is the development of innovation "clusters," that is, locations in which scientific and technological excellence, entrepreneurship, and finance coexist and interact, forming a synergistic network that drives growth. Clusters have caught on among Russia's modernizers (indeed, the word has been adopted into the Russian language as *klaster*), and it has led to the ambitious plan to create a Russian Silicon Valley near Moscow, at a location called Skolkovo. But it is symptomatic that Skolkovo is modeled on San Jose and Boston's Route 128 complex. The Russians should be looking as well at Aberdeen and Stavanger—major innovation centers, but for the oil industry—and above all Houston, for thirty years a model of diversified high-tech progress based on oil.[32] The Russian *klastery* with a future may be where they are already forming today, without fanfare, in oil centers like Tiumen, Almet'evsk, Tomsk, and Murmansk.

To sum up, the argument of this chapter is that it is energy, and principally oil and gas, that constitutes Russia's fastest ticket to the high-tech future, if the opportunity is correctly perceived and seized. But will Russia take up the challenge? Indeed, can it do so, if oil prices decline and Russia's flow of oil rents fails?

Decay Meets Decline: What Happens Then?

In the fall of 2011 and the winter of 2012, the surface calm of Russian politics was suddenly broken by a wave of mass demonstrations, which began in Moscow but soon spread all over Russia, as a new middle class, born of the hydrocarbon-based prosperity of the last decade, turned out to voice its opposition to the perceived corruption of the political class, especially the "party of power," United Russia. For a time, as the protest movement gained momentum, the very foundations of the regime appeared to shake.

Notwithstanding, in the presidential election of March 2012, Putin won comfortably in the first round, and despite widespread evidence of manipulation even the opposition conceded that Putin had won a convincing victory. There was no credible alternative. The opposition as yet had no leader, no program, and no unity, and it was still largely confined to the middle class of Moscow. The main lesson of the election was that the rest of the country failed to follow the capital. At the time of this writing (summer 2012) Russia appears to be settling in for a third term under Putin (this time for six years), until the next scheduled election in 2018, when—according to the letter of the Constitution—Putin could run yet again.

It will not be as easy the next time around. By 2018 Putin will have been president for fourteen years and the de facto head of the country for nearly nineteen. The opposition will be better organized, and given the rapid spread of the Internet and social networking in Russia, it will have gained strength and depth outside the capital. New leaders will have emerged, possibly from the regions, where political life is already showing signs of revival. They will find increased support from a population grown even more alienated than today by the perceived excesses of the favored elites. If the regime is showing signs of wear today, they will be all the greater by the end of the decade.

Yet so long as the Kremlin is able to retain the loyalty of the business and political elites and to support the welfare system on which the majority of the population depends, the system is likely to remain fundamentally stable. This, then, is the key question—how much longer can the flow of commodity rents support the elites' and the population's steadily growing expectations?

Seen from this perspective, the past decade was altogether anomalous. Between 2001 and 2011, the state budget grew ninefold and wages tripled (both in real terms), while trade surpluses totaled nearly $800 billion. What made this possible was a doubling of oil production and a quadrupling of oil prices, generating a tidal wave of rents, of which the state was able to capture the lion's share. That is not simply unlikely to happen again—it is impossible.

It is here that the political story and the oil story intersect. Sometime in the coming decade—just when is impossible to predict, because it hinges on so many variables—the flow of Russian oil rents could well decline, even as Russia's reliance on them grows. Even if world oil prices were to double again in the next decade (itself a doubtful proposition, as discussed), Russia's budget and trade balance surpluses will shrink, and the rising tide of money that enabled the Kremlin to meet everyone's rising expectations for a decade will vanish. Then, and only then, will the "objective preconditions" (as the Russians like to say) for the end of the Putin era be present.

What will happen then? It does not follow that Russia will be thrown into crisis overnight. Thanks to a decade of prudent fiscal and monetary management, the government has plenty of room to borrow (external debt is currently at an ultralow 15 percent of GDP). The ruble can be allowed to devaluate (which will curtail imports and make exports more competitive). Russia can spend from its foreign-currency reserves (at over $500 billion, they are the third largest in the world). Yet these are only expedients. Major spending programs will have to be cut back, including socially sensitive ones such as pensions and subsidies. The state's rainy-day funds will be depleted. Inflation will eat away the population's savings. The myth of endless prosperity, which has sustained the popularity and legitimacy of the present regime for so long, will erode.

In the midst of all this, the state will also be driven to confront head-on the difficult choice it has avoided since 2005, namely, the need to lessen its tax take from oil, so as to enable the oil industry to invest in the next generation of oil. What it was unwilling to do more than marginally in 2010–2011, it will be forced to do on a much larger scale after 2015—when it will no longer have the comfortable surpluses it has today. In this and other ways, the politics of the expanding pie will give way to the much more painful politics of the shrinking one.

One can visualize two possible responses, one destructive and the other constructive. Oil will be at the center of both.

Houdini's Choice

The destructive scenario appears all too plausible. A peak in oil rents toward the end of the decade coincides with the passing of the post-Soviet leadership in several of the leading oil companies, and the predictable result is a new round of conflict for control. Until now the profits from oil have been divided among three main groups: the shareholders, the consumers, and the state. As the flow shrinks, the temptation grows for state players to squeeze out the remaining private owners, and the result is further renationalizations. The main issue then is the division of spoils among the state-based clans, and a weakened Kremlin is increasingly unable to keep order among them in the conflicts that follow. Despite lower oil revenues, policy makers are reluctant to cut welfare payments to the population, and budget deficits grow. The tax take from the oil companies remains prohibitively high, and despite state ownership, the oil industry responds by cutting back investment, leading to lower production. The result is a downward spiral of crisis, as oil revenues shrink and Russia sinks into debt.

There is, however, a constructive scenario. It requires two things: first, on the demand side, the state must reduce its dependence on oil revenues. This means coming back to the main points of the Kudrin program: pension reform,[33] redirection of subsidies, privatization, curtailment of military expenditures, and restoration of budgetary discipline. Second, on the supply side, the state must complete the task of rationalizing the oil-tax system, reshaping it for the needs of the decades ahead. In addition, it must improve the regulatory system and stimulate changes in the structure of the industry itself, so as to encourage the innovation and entrepreneurship that will bring about the renaissance of West Siberia and other opportunities at the knowledge frontier of oil and gas.

The combination of the two is crucial. It is only if Russia addresses both the oil addiction and the decline of the oil legacy together that it will be able to manage the coming crisis.

Will it do so? Over the past two decades, Russia has revolutionized its economy, rewritten its laws, and reentered the world. In the process, talented and determined people have laid valuable foundations for a modern state, rethinking the state's roles and creating the necessary means to carry them out. At the same time, the Soviet past continues to hold both people and institutions in its grip. The attempt to recreate a "vertical of power," using the remnants of the old order, has impeded progress and led to an increase of corruption. But that formula is now leading to a dead end.

Russia, once again, is at a crossroads. Whichever path it chooses, oil will be a central part of the choice—whether as prize in a new division of the spoils or as the catalyst of a renaissance of reform.

Notes

Note: This book follows the transliteration system recommended by the Library of Congress, except where a name appears frequently in the Western media under a different spelling [for example, Khodorkovsky or Yuganskneftegaz]. In the case of Russian authors appearing in both Russian-language and Western sources, I have followed Library of Congress rules for the Russian works, while the Western works are cited as published. Thus I have used Valerii Kriukov in Russian sources, but Valeriy Kryukov [or Valery Kryukov] in Western ones.

Introduction

1   OPEC refers to the Organization of Petroleum Exporting Countries. Oil statistics frequently distinguish between "OPEC production" and "non-OPEC production," the latter being a measure of diversification of production outside the OPEC cartel.

2   Source: *BP Statistical Review of World Energy 2011,* http://www.bp.com/sectionbody copy.do?categoryId=7500&contentId=7068481.

3   Although the peak daily price of oil reached in July 2008 has yet to be exceeded, the average price of oil through the year 2011 marked a new record, which at this writing (summer 2012) might be broken again in 2012, despite the global economic slowdown. (In contrast, the peak price of oil in 1981, measured in 2010 dollars, was $90.)

4   Thane Gustafson, *Crisis amid Plenty: The Politics of Soviet Energy under Brezhnev and Gorbachev* (Princeton, NJ: Princeton University Press, 1989).

5   In 2010, Russian oil output was 505.2 million tons (10.1 million barrels per day), while gas output was 532.2 million tons (10.6 million barrels per day) of oil equivalent. The contribution of gas to Russia's primary energy supply has been greater than that of oil throughout the 1990s. (Note: Here and throughout the book, all references to tons are to metric tons. The conversion rate to barrels for crude oil is taken to be 1 ton = 7.3 barrels.)

6   There is a running debate among economists—and also, not coincidentally, between Russia and the European Union—over which is the appropriate basis for pricing Russian gas, "export netback parity" or "long run marginal cost." For the Europeans, the former benchmark is the correct one, and anything lower represents an unwarranted subsidy to Russian domestic consumers and manufacturers. Many Russians, however, argue that the second benchmark simply recognizes the value of Russia's abundant gas resources, which Russian consumers should legitimately be allowed to enjoy. In any case, Russian domestic gas prices, while still well below netback parity, have risen substantially over the last decade and are now arguably in the range of long-run

marginal cost. Thus the remaining "gas subsidy," if there still is one, is far smaller today than in the past. The case is clearer for oil: domestic oil prices are kept well below world oil prices by the device of a large export tax, which acts as a wedge between the two. The export tax on gas, though it has the same effect, is much smaller.

7   To this one must add that many of Russia's non–energy commodity exports, such as metals, fertilizers, and basic petrochemicals, are produced using natural gas and thus represent "exports of embodied gas."

8   The best study of the Russian gas industry, though unfortunately now somewhat out of date, is Jonathan Stern, *The Future of Russian Gas and Gazprom*, copublished by the Oxford Institute for Energy Studies (Oxford: Oxford University Press, 2005). Stern has updated the Russian gas story in "The Russian Gas Balance to 2015: Difficult Years Ahead," in Simon Pirani, ed., *Russian and CIS Gas Markets and Their Impact on Europe*, copublished by the Oxford Institute for Energy Studies (Oxford: Oxford University Press, 2009), pp. 54–92.

9   McKinsey Global Institute, *Lean Russia: Sustaining Economic Growth through Improved Productivity* (Moscow: McKinsey, 2009). In a broad study conducted in 1999, the McKinsey Global Institute found that labor productivity averaged 18 percent of the U.S. level across the ten sectors it analyzed. In the follow-up study conducted in 2007, McKinsey found that labor productivity had increased to 26 percent of the U.S. level in the five sectors it analyzed—still low but considerably improved.

10 Anders Aslund and Andrew C. Kuchins, *The Russia Balance Sheet* (Washington, DC: Petersen Institute for International Economics and Center for Strategic and International Affairs, 2010).

11 Resource rents from Russian oil are primarily of two sorts: "legacy rents" arising from capacity developed in the Soviet era and "scarcity rents" arising from high price of oil in global markets, as transmitted to Russia from its exports. See the more extended discussion of rents later in this chapter.

12 Vladimir Putin, "Ezhegodnoe Poslanie Prezidenta Rossiiskoi Federatsii Federal'nomu Sobraniiu Rossiiskoi Federatsii," April 3, 2001. This is the Russian-language version of Putin's annual "State of the Federation" speech to the Russian parliament, accessed at http://www.archipelag.ru/agenda/povestka/message/message-2001/.

13 Sources: Goskomstat for oil-export and total export revenues; International Monetary Fund and Ministry of Economic Development for tax revenues. The tax numbers include natural gas, but the share of oil is considerably larger than that of natural gas.

14 I am very much in agreement here with the analysis of Clifford Gaddy and Barry Ickes, as published in a series of important articles since 2005. See Clifford G. Gaddy and Barry W. Ickes, "Resource Rents and the Russian Economy," *Eurasian Geography and Economics* 46, no. 8 (2005), pp. 559–583; "Russia's Declining Oil Production: Managing Price Risk and Rent Addiction," *Eurasian Geography and Economics* 50, no. 1 (2009), pp. 1–13; and "Russia after the Global Financial Crisis: Prospects for Reforming a

Crucial Sector," *Eurasian Geography and Economics* 51, no. 3 (2010), pp. 281–311. A summary and update of their analysis appears in "Russia's Dependence on Resources," in Michael V. Alexeev and Shlomo Weber, eds., *The Oxford Handbook of the Russian Economy* (Oxford: Oxford University Press, 2012), pp. 1–34. Dr. Gaddy points out that the main thing that happened at the end of the Soviet era was less a "collapse" in real terms than the fact that the introduction of market prices revealed the true state of affairs. Manufacturing had never been value adding. The "circus-mirror effect" of Soviet pricing had undervalued the commodities sectors and overvalued manufacturing (private communication to the author).

15 Video of Kudrin speech in Krasnoiarsk, February 19, 2011, http://www.youtube.com /watch?v=gn5z6FaQJII.

16 The "resource curse" issue has generated a vast literature since the late 1980s. Some of the major early works include William Ascher, *Why Governments Waste Natural Resources* (Baltimore, MD: Johns Hopkins University Press, 1999); Richard Auty, *Resource-Based Industrialization: Sowing the Oil in Eight Developing Countries* (New York: Oxford University Press, 1990); Jeffrey Sachs and Andrew Warner, "Natural Resource Abundance and Economic Growth," National Bureau of Economic Research, Working Paper No. 5398 (1995); Terry Lynn Karl, *The Paradox of Plenty: Oil Booms and Petro-States* (Berkeley: University of California Press, 1997).

   More recently there has been a skeptical "counterliterature," which criticizes some of the earlier work on empirical and methodological grounds and argues that the existence and severity of the "resource curse" are above all a function of the strength and quality of institutions. See, for example, Michael Alexeev and Robert Conrad, "The Elusive Curse of Oil," *Review of Economics and Statistics* 41, no. 3 (2009), pp. 599–616; H. Mehlum, K. Moene, and R. Torvik, "Institutions and the Resource Curse," *Economic Journal* 116, no. 508 (2006), pp. 1–20; and Gavin Wright and Jesse Czelusta, "Why Economies Slow: The Myth of the Resource Curse," *Challenge* 47, no. 2 (March 2004), pp. 6–38.

   Applied to Russia, the "resource curse" literature focuses on both the economic and political aspects. R. M. Auty prefers to call Russia a "mineral economy." See his "Russia: The Political Economy of Transition in a Mineral Economy," in S. Mansoob Murshed, ed., *Issues in Positive Political Economy* (London: Routledge, 2002), pp. 39–56. An excellent analysis, which also emphasizes the importance of institutions and property rights, is Pauline Jones Luong and Erika Weinthal, *Oil Is Not a Curse: Ownership Structures and Institutions in Soviet Successor States* (Cambridge: Cambridge University Press, 2010). A wide-ranging political analysis, which includes a thoughtful analysis of the "resource curse," is M. Stephen Fish, *Democracy Derailed in Russia: The Failure of Open Politics* (Cambridge: Cambridge University Press, 2005), chapters 5 and 6.

   Russian scholars and policy makers too have written on the "resource curse." Among many useful sources one might name A. Arbatov and V. Smirnov, " 'Resursnoe prokliatie' Rossii: Ekskurs v istoriiu i nyneshnie problemy," *Obshchestvo i ekonomika,* December 31, 2004, pp. 137–157; and Sergei Guriev, Andrei Plekhanov, and Konstantin Sonin, "Development Based on Commodity Revenues," European Bank for Reconstruction and Development (EBRD), Working Paper No. 108 (November 2009).

17 On this point I agree with Marshall Goldman in his *Petrostate: Putin, Power, and the New Russia* (Oxford: Oxford University Press, 2008), pp. 12–13.

18 See Yegor T. Gaidar, *Gibel' imperii: Uroki dlia sovremennoi Rossii* (Moscow: "Rossiis-kaia politicheskaia entsiklopediia," 2006); translated as *Collapse of an Empire: Lessons for Modern Russia* (Washington, DC: Brookings Institution Press, 2007). Most of the retrospective commentary on the Soviet Union's dependence on oil exports focuses on the revenues from exports to the West; but in actual fact most Soviet oil exports until a late date went to the Soviet bloc. In other words, it wasn't simply the economy that was being propped up with oil but the imperial system as well.

19 Cliford G. Gaddy and Barry W. Ickes, *Russia's Virtual Economy* (Washington, DC: Brookings Institution Press, 2002).

20 The classic analysis of the "curse of oil" as applied to a developing economy is Karl, *Paradox of Plenty,* which is based on a case study of Venezuela and the Venezuelan state oil company PdVSA.

21 For data on the educational levels of the Russian civil service, see Robert J. Brym and Vladimir Gimpelson, "The Size, Composition, and Dynamics of the Russian State Bureaucracy in the 1990s," *Slavic Review* 63, no. 1 (Spring 2004), pp. 90–112.

22 Russia has been a net donor of capital to the outside world throughout the 1990s and again since 2008, for a total of over $500 billion over the period. (Source: Russian Central Bank.)

23 Gaddy and Ickes, *Russia's Virtual Economy.*

24 See, among many other works, Vagit Alekperov, *Oil of Russia: Past, Present, and Future* (Minneapolis, MN: East View Press, 2011).

25 The definitive analysis of the state of the Soviet oil industry in its final decade is John D. Grace, *Russian Oil Supply: Performance and Prospects,* copublished by the Oxford Institute for Energy Studies (Oxford: Oxford University Press, 2005).

26 Mikhail Khodorkovskii and Leonid Nevzlin, *Chelovek s rublem* (Moscow: LITRU.RU, 1992).

27 Author's interview with Valerii Graifer, June 22, 2010.

28 Author's notes, May 2011.

29 To name just a few, Strobe Talbott, *The Russia Hand: A Memoir of Presidential Diplomacy* (New York: Random House, 2002) and Martin Gilman, *No Precedent, No Plan* (Cambridge, MA: MIT Press, 2010), tend to stress how much was done to support Russia. In contrast, Daniel Treisman, in *The Return: Russia's Journey from Gorbachev to Medvedev* (New York: Free Press, 2011), pp. 313–315, is highly critical of the West's efforts.

30 For a recent summary, see Aslund and Kuchins, *Russia Balance Sheet,* chapter 7.

31 A remarkable survey underscores how deeply Russian opinions had changed since the early 1990s, even before the 2008 crash: Irina Denisova, Markus Eller, and Ekaterina Zhuravskaya, "What Do Russians Think about Transition?," *Economics of Transition* 18, no. 2 (2010), pp. 249–280.

32 Richard Sakwa, *The Quality of Freedom: Khodorkovsky, Putin, and the Yukos Affair* (Oxford: Oxford University Press, 2009), pp. xiv and 2.

33 I am grateful to Robert Mabro of the Oxford Institute of Energy Studies for emphasizing this point to me over the years.

34 "The term *"siloviki"* denotes members of the coercive elites *(silovye struktury)*, principally the FSB, the uniformed police, and the military. The significance of the distinction between "liberals" and "siloviki" is discussed in "The Brothers from Saint Petersburg" in Chapter 7.

35 My thinking on this point has been much influenced by the excellent doctoral thesis of Adnan Vatansever of the Carnegie Endowment for International Peace: Vatansever, "The Political Economy of Countering the 'Resource Curse': The Case of Russia under Putin (1999–2005)" (PhD diss., Johns Hopkins School of Advanced International Studies, 2008).

36 The definition used here is less rigorous than the strict definition of rent as "economic profit" (i.e., the difference between revenue and cost, both being understood from the standpoint of opportunity cost). That is the definition used by Gaddy and Ickes in their pathbreaking work on Russian oil and gas rents, cited in note 14 above. Defining rents as "unearned profits" as I do here is somewhat closer to the original concept of rent as enunciated by the nineteenth-century economist David Ricardo, based on differences in natural endowment.

37 In other words, the industry's required "normal return" will increase. The "normal" return consists of three components: the prevailing return from alternative investments, expected inflation, and a "risk premium." In the oil industry worldwide, the latter two components are clearly on the rise, and particularly so in Russia. Needless to say, the state and the industry will disagree over what constitutes a "normal" rate of return, particularly over the definition of the risk premium, which in the industry's view will include a substantial (and possibly growing) element of political risk.

38 I am in full agreement here with this key insight from the work of Gaddy and Ickes (see note 14 above).

39 On the causes of decay of political regimes, see Francis Fukuyama, *The Origins of Political Order: From Prehuman Times to the French Revolution* (New York: Farrar, Straus, and Giroux, 2011), especially chapter 29, "Political Development and Political Decay."

1. The Breakup

1   Author's interviews with Valerii Graifer and Gennadii Bogomiakov, spring 1992. Graifer's life and family background are recounted in a volume published in honor of his eightieth birthday. Mariia Slavkina, ed., *Valerii Graifer: Vremia ne zhdet* (Moscow: "Tsentr," 2009).

2   The chain of command in West Siberia ran from the Main Administration for Tiumen Oil and Gas (Glavtiumenneftegaz) through the seven "production associations" *(proizvodstvennye ob"edineniia)* to the local "oil and gas production administrations" *(neftegazovye proizvodstvennye upravleniia,* or NGDU). The general directors of the production associations were commonly referred to as the "oil generals." For a more detailed description of the administrative structure and how it functioned, see Thane Gustafson, *Crisis amid Plenty: The Politics of Soviet Energy under Brezhnev and Gorbachev* (Princeton, NJ: Princeton University Press, 1989). At the end of the Soviet period there were thirty-two production associations in the Russian oil industry, which oversaw 111 NGDUs. Arild Moe and Valeriy Kryukov, "Observations on the Reorganization of the Russian Oil Industry," *Post-Soviet Geography* 35, no. 2 (1994), p. 89, n.2.

3   The distribution and sale of refined products was under the administration of the State Committee for Petroleum Products Supply (Goskomnefteprodukt), which was organized on a territorial basis, with each union-republic having its own committee. These were the actual operators of the terminals and depots, the refined-product pipelines, and the retail filling stations.

4   Ed A. Hewett, *Energy, Economics, and Foreign Policy in the Soviet Union* (Washington, DC: Brookings Institution, 1984). For the oil industry specifically, see Matthew J. Sagers, Valeriy A. Kryukov, and Vladimir V. Shmat, "Resource Rent from the Oil and Gas Sectors and the Russian Economy," *Post-Soviet Geography and Economics* 36, no. 7 (1995), pp. 389–425.

5   In 1989, energy exports outside the Soviet bloc accounted for 43 percent of export revenues. By 1993 the share had risen to 46.3 percent. Gosudarstvennyi komitet Rossiiskoi Federatsii po statistike (hereafter Goskomstat Rossii), *Sotsial'no-ekonomicheskoe polozhenie Rossii,* various years, cited in Sagers, Kryukov, and Shmat, "Resource Rent," p. 389. It has fluctuated widely since then, depending mainly on variations in world energy prices.

6   In this respect the Soviet oil industry was not so different from the structure of an international oil company, where executives at all but the top positions can spend an entire career in the upstream or the downstream or at a trading desk.

7   Equipment for the oil industry was the province of three major industrial ministries, all of them independent of the oil industry. Drilling rigs and other heavy equipment came from the Ministry of Heavy and Transport Machine-Building (Mintiazhmash). Most domestically produced pipe came from the Ministry of Ferrous Metallurgy (Minchermet). Oilfield equipment came mainly from the Ministry of Chemical and

Petroleum Machine-Building (Minkhimmash), whose oil equipment subsidiary, Glavneftemash, was responsible for two-thirds of the oil tools produced in the Soviet Union, mainly through a network of factories located in Azerbaijan. For a detailed discussion of the structure and operations of this support system, together with its mounting problems in the 1980s, see Gustafson, *Crisis amid Plenty,* chapter 6.

8   There were other "private" phone systems as well; Gazprom, for example, had one that ran wire down all pipeline right-of-ways.

9   The classic treatment of the functions of the Soviet obkom first secretary is Jerry F. Hough, *The Soviet Prefects: The Local Party Organs in Industrial Decision-Making* (Cambridge, MA: Harvard University Press, 1969).

10   Mariia V. Slavkina, *Triumf i tragediia: Razvitie neftagazovogo kompleksa SSSR v 1960–1990 gg.* (Moscow: "Nauka," 2002), p. 193. What Kosygin meant was that more oil was needed for export, to pay for unexpectedly high imports of wheat that year. As time went by, the dependence of the Soviet economy on imported wheat steadily grew, requiring higher oil exports.

11   V. P. Karpov, "Neftegazovyi profil' industrializatsii Tiumenskoi oblast'i 1960–80-e gody," *Nalogi, Investitsii, Kapital* (Tiumen), nos. 5–6 (2004), http://nic.pirit.info.

12   For details see Gustafson, *Crisis amid Plenty,* p. 105; and Slavkina, *Valerii Graifer,* pp. 171–175.

13   Author's interview with Bogomiakov, June 1991. After his career in the party apparatus, Bogomiakov in the 1990s became a local banker, as chairman of Tiumenenergobank. Bogomiakov celebrated his eightieth birthday in 2010.

14   The word "enterprise" has a slightly jarring sound to Western ears. It is the closest English translation of the standard Soviet term *predpriiatie,* which was the basic legal-administrative unit of Soviet industry. It was more than a factory *(zavod),* since a predpriiatie could include many factories, and some were actually large complexes. At the same time, a predpriiatie was less than an *ob"edinenie,* the next higher administrative unit, commonly translated as "association," which was actually more akin to a corporate division.

15   See Clifford G. Gaddy and Fiona Hill, *The Siberian Curse: How Communist Planners Left Russia Out in the Cold* (Washington, DC: Brookings Institution Press, 2003). In fairness to the central planners, they were not unaware of the problem, and they did try to restrain the Ministries of Oil and Gas from establishing large cities, urging them instead to rotate temporary workers in and out, as is the practice in the West. In the end, the oil and gas industries employed a mixture of both. But one of the endemic features of the Soviet system was the determination of each ministry not to depend on other ministries for help—in this case air support—and in the end the planners went along with the large permanent settlements that resulted, since their common goal was to meet the all-important output target. See Gustafson, *Crisis amid Plenty,* pp. 174–179.

16   World crude prices reached their Soviet-era peak in 1980 at $87.65 (in 2005 dollars) and then declined steadily to $25.63 in 1986. From 1986 through 1992 they hovered between

the mid-20s and the mid-30s before starting another long slide to a low of $15.71 in 1998. Source: *BP Statistical Review of World Energy 2011,* http://www.bp.com/sectionbodycopy .do?categoryId=7500&contentId=7068481.

17   There were fierce debates in Moscow and West Siberia in the 1970s and 1980s over how much oil remained to be discovered and how much money should be spent on finding it. As John Grace rightly observes, although better funding of exploration would have slowed the fall of production, it would not have changed the basic trend. See John D. Grace, *Russian Oil Supply: Performance and Prospects,* copublished by the Oxford Institute for Energy Studies (Oxford: Oxford University Press, 2005), pp. 39–41.

18   Three careful Western analyses have focused on the rise and fall of oil rents. They all come to much the same conclusions, even though their methodologies and the numbers they produce are different. See Grace, *Russian Oil Supply,* pp. 89–98; Clifford G. Gaddy and Barry W. Ickes, "Resource Rents and the Russian Economy," *Eurasian Geography and Economics* 46, no. 8 (December 2005), pp. 559–583; and Sagers, Kryukov, and Shmat, "Resource Rent," pp. 389–425. See also Egor T. Gaidar, *Gibel' imperii: Uroki dlia sovremennoi Rossii* (Moscow: "Rossiiskaia politicheskaia entsiklopediia," 2006); translated as *Collapse of an Empire: Lessons for Modern Russia* (Washington, DC: Brookings Institution Press, 2007).

19   Grace, *Russian Oil Supply,* p. 95.

20   The many ways, mostly invisible, in which the rent was collected are described in Sagers, Kryukov, and Shmat, "Resource Rent," especially pp. 390–397.

21   For a review of the situation as it appeared around 1988, see Gustafson, *Crisis amid Plenty,* especially chapter 4.

22   In contrast, prison laborers were farmed out in large numbers to the power industry, particularly hydropower. In 1952 a division of Gulag was created to supply labor to oil refinery construction but does not appear to have played a major role in the development of that sector. For an exhaustive study of the role of prison labor in the power industry, see Anatolii B. Chubais, ed., *Zakliuchennye na stroikakh kommunizma: GULag i ob"ekty energetiki SSSR* (Moscow: "Rossiiskaia politicheskaia entsiklopediia," 2008).

23   Farman K. Salmanov, *Kto tolkaet Rossiiu k energeticheskoi katastrofe* (Moscow: Izdatel'stvo "Pressa," 1997), quoted in Slavkina, *Triumf i tragediia,* pp. 90–91.

24   An interview with Alekperov's mother, Tat'iana Bocharova, appears in Nikolai Chernikov, *Vertikal' "LUKoila": Vagit Alekperov i ego komanda: Geroi dvukh epok* (Moscow: Smena, 2000).

25   Alekperov had already been made the de facto head of Kogalym the year before. As one of the measures taken by Gorbachev to allocate more resources to West Siberia, the Bashkir oil company Bashneft was put in charge of developing Kogalym as a division of Bashneft, separate from Glavtiumenneftgaz. The general director of Bashneft, Sergei Stoliarov, recognized Alekperov's leadership qualities and made him his first deputy,

in charge of Kogalym, in 1985. The following year Graifer regained control of Kogalym and raised it to a "production association" under Glavtiumenneftgaz, with Alekperov as general director (Slavkina, *Valerii Graifer,* p. 191).

26 The Tiumen Industrial Institute was founded in 1963. In 1994 it was renamed the Tiumen State Oil and Gas University. Its present rector, Vladimir Karnaukhov, is a 1971 graduate of the Institute and thus a classmate or contemporary of many of the leading oil generals of West Siberia.

27 "Khoroshii paren'. My eshche s ego ottsom vmeste v tundre komarov kormili."

28 Gosudarstvennyi Komitet Rossiiskoi Federatsii po Statistike (Goskomstat Rossii), *Rossiiskii Statisticheskii Ezhegodnik* (Moscow, various years).

29 In the first half of the 1970s the average field discovered in West Siberia had 76.7 million tons (560 million barrels) of $A + B + C_1 + C_2$ reserves in the traditional Russian methodology, whereas by the first half of the 1980s the average had dropped to 34.2 million tons (250 million barrels), and by the second half of the 1980s to 17.9 million tons (130.7 million barrels) Source: *Vestnik Tiumenskoi Oblast'noi Dumy,* no. 9 (2002), p. 53, cited in V. A. Kriukov and A. N. Tokarev, *Neftegazovye resursy v transformiruemoi ekonomike: O sootnoshenii realizovannoi i potentsial'noi obshchestvennoi tsennosti nedr* (Novosibirsk: "Nauka-Tsentr," 2007, p. 171). See the book's foreword for a discussion of the differences between the Russian and the Western reserve classification systems.

30 See Grace, *Russian Oil Supply,* pp. 47–49.

31 See ibid., chapter 3; also Gaidar, *Gibel' imperii.*

32 Just where one puts the Soviet-era peak depends on whether one is looking at the peak rate at any given moment or the peak rate for the year as a whole. In annual terms, the peak was reached in 1987; in quarterly terms, the peak was reached in 1988.

33 The best and most comprehensive description of the Gorbachev perestroika and its impact on the command economy is Anders Aslund, *Gorbachev's Struggle for Economic Reform,* updated ed. (Ithaca, NY: Cornell University Press, 1991).

34 Graifer interview in Slavkina, *Valerii Graifer,* p. 194. The election of managers was reversed in 1990, but by then the central ministries and the party apparatus had lost all power.

35 Slavkina, *Valerii Graifer,* p. 193.

36 Five decrees authorizing various kinds of cooperatives were issued by the Council of Ministers in 1987. The real breakthrough came in May 1988, with the passage of the "Law on Cooperatives in the USSR." Aslund, *Gorbachev's Struggle,* pp. 157–158 and 167–171.

37 See the excellent analysis of Gorbachev's reform of the banking system and its consequences in Joel S. Hellman, "Breaking the Bank: Bureaucrats and the Creation of Markets in a Transitional Economy" (PhD diss., Columbia University, 1993). See also Juliet Johnson, *A Fistful of Rubles: The Rise and Fall of the Russian Banking System* (Ithaca, NY: Cornell University Press, 2000).

38 Slavkina, *Valerii Graifer*, p. 195.

39 The differential between the world price of crude and the domestic price fluctuated widely between the late 1980s and the early 1990s. In December 1991, as the Soviet Union collapsed, the differential reached its maximum at 100 to 1. Subsequently, with the gradual liberalization of the domestic oil market and the slow stabilization of the ruble, the differential decreased. In September 1992 it was only 3 to 1. By the mid-1990s the domestic price of crude stabilized at between 55 percent and 60 percent of world levels. See Matthew J. Sagers, "Russian Crude Oil Production in 1996: Conditions and Prospects," *Post-Soviet Geography and Economics* 37, no. 9 (1996), p. 537.

40 There was little point for small-time gangsters to drill into pipelines and steal crude oil by truck. Such "help yourself" thievery was more common in south Russia and the North Caucasus, where the pipelines were smaller and there were more roads, and in any case such cases mostly involved refined-product pipelines. This remains a major problem in the North Caucasus, especially along the main trunk line that crosses Chechnya, but isolated cases are still reported in other parts of Russia, such as the discovery of a gang of tappers in Samara Oblast'. See *Samarskoe obozrenie,* no. 89 (November 20, 2006), p. 15. The most notorious case involved the Caspian Pipeline Consortium, which was systematically tapped through an underground network of offtake pipes placed during the pipeline's construction.

41 A profile of Andrei Pannikov appears in Iuliia Govorun, "Vybor rezidenta," *Forbes-Russia,* no. 3 (2008). Further background on Pannikov's partners from the Kirishi refinery appears in the next chapter.

42 As early as 1990, for example, the chief procurator of the oil city of Nizhnevartovsk, Vladimir Rogachev, left his state job to launch a private trading company called "Delta." Sometimes he and his partners bought oil on their own account, sometimes they insured oil loans made by others. See the profile of Rogachev by Igor Lur'e, "Oburenie iskopaemykh: neft' omyvaet nizhnevartovskuiu prokuraturu," *Novaia gazeta,* no. 19 (May 15, 2000).

43 Joint ventures are discussed in more detail in Chapter 4.

44 Author's interviews with Golubev, Calgary, 1995–1996.

45 Cooperatives in the upstream oil industry were limited to services and auxiliary production. The only producing NGDU that managed to break away and turn itself into a "leased enterprise" was Chernogorneft', which broke away from its parent, Nizhnevartovskneftegaz, in 1989 (Sagers, Kryukov, and Shmat, "Resource Rent," p. 400); see also Matthew J. Sagers, "Review of Soviet Energy Industries in 1990," *Soviet Geography* 32, no. 4 (April 1991), pp. 251–290.

46 The former general director of Nizhnevartovskneftegaz, Viktor Palii, was dogged for years by stories that he had opened illegal bank accounts abroad. Palii has always vigorously denied the charges. In December 2001 two local television stations in Nizhnevartovsk aired a documentary called "Criminal Russia." The picture of private sales of oil recounted in that source corresponds in broad outline to other accounts of the way

oil and oil revenues leaked out of the system as early as 1992. Palii sued the two television companies, and the case was fought out in the courts through 2003, when Palii was awarded symbolic damages. See *Mestnoe Vremia* (a local newspaper in Nizhnevartovsk that was published between 1999 and 2003), September 28, 2002, http://www.nvart.wsnet.ru/~company/mv/about.asp?d=28.09.2002. See also Anfisa Voronina, "Palii stal kinogeroem," *Vedomosti*, August 2, 2002. At the time, Palii was general director of Slavneft-Nizhnevartovsk and a deputy of the oblast' parliament.

47 In the far downstream, the national-level State Committee for Petroleum Products Supply was abolished in 1990 and its responsibilities transferred to the republic-level committees. However, in the three largest republics (Russia, Ukraine, and Kazakhstan), the distribution and supply of refined products was further decentralized to province (oblast') supply organizations, the so-called *oblnefiesnaby*. See Matthew J. Sagers, Igor A. Didenko, and Valeriy A. Kryukov, "Distribution of Refined Petroleum Products in Russia," *Post-Soviet Geography and Economics* 40, no. 5 (1999), pp. 408–409.

48 Gaidar, *Collapse of an Empire*, p. 133.

49 Matthew J. Sagers, "News Notes: Review of Soviet Energy Industries in 1990," *Soviet Geography* 32, no. 4 (1991), p. 252.

50 Matthew J. Sagers, "News Notes: Special Regional Development Program for Tyumen' Oblast' Established by RSFSR Government," *Soviet Geography* 32, no. 9 (1991), p. 633.

51 In 1990 Soviet oil production declined by 37.6 million tons (752,000 barrels per day). Of this, 94 percent was concentrated in West Siberia. See Sagers, "News Notes: Special Regional Development Program," p. 633.

52 The commission was headed by Deputy Prime Minister L. Riabev and conducted extensive hearings on location in Tiumen. Source: *Tiumenskaia pravda*, April 16, 1991, cited in Valerii Kriukov, *Institutsional'naia struktura neftegazovogo sektora: Problemy i napravleniia transformatsii* (Novosibirsk: Institut ekonomiki i organizatsii promyshlennogo proizvodstva SO RAN, 1998), p. 96.

53 See Aslund, *Gorbachev's Struggle*, pp. 127–128 (on state orders) and 139–141 (on foreign-trade reform).

54 Sagers, "News Notes: Review of Soviet Energy Industries in 1990," pp. 255–257. Subunits that were performing well agitated for independence from their parent production associations; thus Urai broke away from Krasnoleninsk, effective January 1, 1991.

55 Matthew J. Sagers, "Soviet Commodity Exchanges Trading in Oil," *Soviet Geography* 32, no. 7 (September 1991), p. 514.

56 It was in 1991 that the squeeze on Russian oil exports was the greatest: oil production was dropping sharply, but consumption was still high. Exports of crude through the Transneft system reached their lowest point in 1991 at 47.8 million tons (956,000 barrels per day). The drop seems to have been pretty much uniform across all the export outlets, not just through the Druzhba, suggesting that the drop was mainly supply driven, not driven by a decline in East European offtakes.

57 For a detailed analysis, see Matthew J. Sagers, "News Notes: Russian Crude Oil Exports in 1992: Who Exported Russian Oil?," *Post-Soviet Geography* 34, no. 3 (March 1993), pp. 207–211.

58 Matthew J. Sagers, "News Notes," *Soviet Geography* 30, no. 4 (1989), p. 310. Similar quotas were granted to other oil-producing regions in 1989 and 1990, ranging from 5 percent to 20 percent of "above-plan" output.

59 Slavkina, *Valerii Graifer,* pp. 196–197.

60 An *oblast'* is a Russian administrative unit that is roughly equivalent to a province. In some instances the Russians use the word *krai* instead of oblast' (as in "Krasnoiarsk krai"), but the meaning is essentially the same. An *okrug* is a subentity within an oblast' or a krai.

61 For an overview of events in Tiumen in the first half of the 1990s, see Carnegie Endowment for International Peace, Moscow office, "Tiumenskaia oblast'," *Sotsial'no-ekonomicheskie portrety regionov,* Book 2 (Moscow: Carnegie Endowment for International Peace, 1998), pp. 943ff.

62 Shafranik had previously served a tour in 1985–1987 as a party functionary, first as secretary and then second secretary of the Langepas city apparatus of the party, before being named general director of Langepasneftegaz. Interview with Iurii Shafranik, "O kar'ere nikogda ne dumal," *Sibirskii posad,* February 27 2002, http://2mus.ru/read.php ?id=1522. In the same interview Shafranik hints that he felt his position as general director of Langepasneftegaz had become a dead end.

63 By tradition the speaker of the Tiumen oblast' Soviet (i.e., province-level parliament) sat as an ex officio member of the oblast' committee of the party (obkom). Significantly, following his election as speaker, Shafranik refused to join the obkom. Source: Carnegie Endowment, "Tiumenskaia oblast'," p. 943.

64 The *banya* is a core part of Russian culture. It consists of a hot sauna, followed by vigorous beating with dried birch leaves, and concludes (preferably) with a running jump into the nearest snowdrift or Siberian pond.

65 Timothy J. Colton, *Yeltsin: A Life* (New York: Basic Books, 2008), pp. 196–202.

66 Interview with Iurii Shafranik by Sergei Zemlianoi, "Formuly napolnennoi zhizni: Iurii Shafranik o svoikh trudakh i dniakh," *Nezavisimaia gazeta,* March 15, 2001.

67 *Sovetskaia Rossiia,* October 29, 1991, p. 1.

68 In November 1991 Boris Yeltsin named Yegor Gaidar deputy prime minister for economic policy and simultaneously finance minister and minister of the economy. Gaidar quickly assembled a team of economic reformers, which included such key figures as Anatolii Chubais (former CEO of Unified Energy System and now CEO of Rusnano) and Petr Aven (now president and chairman of Alfa-Bank). By the end of November 1991 Gaidar unveiled a list of high-priority measures to put the economy on a fast track to the market.

69 Yegor T. Gaidar, *Days of Defeat and Victory* (Seattle: University of Washington Press, 1999) [in Russian: *Dni porazhdenii i pobed* (Moscow: "Evrasiia," 1997)].

70 Approximately 90 percent of consumer goods prices and 80 percent of industrial goods prices were decontrolled at the federal level in January 1992. Oil, gas, and electric power prices were not.

71 For a detailed discussion of inflation in the first half of the 1990s, see Andrei Shleifer and Daniel Treisman, *Without a Map: Political Tactics and Economic Reform in Russia* (Cambridge, MA: MIT Press, 2000), chapter 3.

72 Sagers, "News Notes: Review of Soviet Energy Industries in 1990," p. 255.

73 Ibid., pp. 255–257.

74 Iu. K. Shafranik and V. A. Kriukov, *Neftegazovye resursy v kruge problem* (Moscow: "Nedra," 1997), pp. 108ff.

75 The decree created a "Program for the Development of Tiumen Province," with broad powers over mineral development and production. Carnegie Endowment, "Tiumenskaia oblast'," p. 944.

76 In October 1990 the legislature of Yamal-Nenets actually declared the okrug an independent republic. Khanty-Mansiisk limited itself to declaring economic autonomy. For a brief history of the emergence of the Khanty-Mansiisk *okrug* as an autonomous entity in the first half of the 1990s, see Carnegie Endowment for International Peace, Moscow office, "Khanty-Mansiiskii Avtonomnyi Okrug," *Sotsial'no-ekonomicheskie portrety regionov*, Book 2 (Moscow: Carnegie Endowment for International Peace, 1998), pp. 1053–1064.

77 Shafranik interview, "O kar'ere nikogda ne dumal."

78 *Za Yuganskuiu Neft'*, November 11, 1991, cited in *Russian Petroleum Investor* 1, no. 1 (January 1992), p. 31.

79 Lev Churilov, from an interview cited in Li-Chen Sim, *The Rise and Fall of Privatization in the Russian Oil Industry* (London: Palgrave Macmillan, 2008). See also Churilov's memoir, *Lifeblood of Empire: A Personal History of the Rise and Fall of the Soviet Oil Industry* (New York: PIW Publications, 1996).

80 "Rebirth of Rosneftegaz?," *Russian Petroleum Investor*, May 1992, pp. 7ff.

81 One of the drivers behind Rosneftegaz's proposal was the acute problem of what to do with the many tens of thousands of employees of the former ministry, organized in innumerable—and then penniless—institutes and academies. Even now, two decades later, this legacy has not been entirely resolved.

82 *Russian Petroleum Investor*, March 1993, p. 5.

83 Source: Russian Federation Ministry of Energy, Russian Statistical Committee (Goskomstat). By 2010 the share of natural gas in primary energy consumption had reached 56.1 percent.

84 To be more precise, while natural gas plays only a minor role in the sparsely settled eastern two-thirds of Russia, where Gazprom's pipeline system does not reach, the western third of the country, where most of the country's population and wealth are concentrated, depends on natural gas.

85 On money, see David Woodruff, *Money Unmade: Barter and the Fate of Russian Capitalism* (Ithaca, NY: Cornell University Press, 1999); on crime and protection and the

regression of the state, see Vadim Volkov, *Violent Entrepreneurs: The Use of Force in the Making of Russian Capitalism* (Ithaca, NY: Cornell University Press, 2002); on banking, see Johnson, *Fistful of Rubles*; on the judiciary and the administration of justice, see Todd S. Foglesong and Peter H. Solomon, *Courts and Transition in Russia: The Challenge of Judicial Reform* (Boulder, CO: Westview Press, 2000).

86 The phrase "virtual economy" was coined by Clifford G. Gaddy and Barry W. Ickes, initially in their article "Russia's Virtual Economy," *Foreign Affairs* 77, no. 5 (September/October 1998), pp. 53–67. Their argument was further developed in the authors' subsequent book, *Russia's Virtual Economy* (Washington, DC: Brookings Institution Press, 2002).

87 In 1988 total drilling by the oil industry (exploratory and development combined) had been 41.4 million meters. In 1990 drilling dropped to 36.2 million meters, in 1991 to 31.4 million, and in 1992 to 21.4 million meters. Source: Russian Federation Ministry of Industry and Energy.

2. Riding Chaos

1 Lopukhin had a degree in economics from Moscow State University and had worked as an academic researcher at the prestigious Institute for the World Economy and International Relations (IMEMO), where for a time he had worked in the same department as Gaidar. Lopukhin had no experience in politics and had never served in government.

2 Andrew Hill, "Russia Considers Fuel Clawback," *Financial Times,* December 18, 1991, p. 2.

3 Author's interview with Valerii Cherniaev, May 2007. Eduard Grushevenko, in fairness, was no newcomer to government or to the oil sector. Already in his mid-fifties at the time of these events, Grushevenko was an expert on oil refining with a long career in the Ministry of Oil Refining and Petrochemicals. After Lopukhin's dismissal, Grushevenko stayed on as acting minister, reporting to Deputy Prime Minister Viktor Chernomyrdin, until Iurii Shafranik took over as energy minister in January 1993. In 1993 Grushevenko joined Yukos as vice president. In 1995–1996, on the eve of Menatep's takeover of Yukos, he was responsible for "social and economic supply," that is, Yukos's deliveries of fuel to farms and municipal governments in exchange for tax credits.

4 By 1991 fifteen out of 140 NGDUs had turned themselves into quasi-autonomous "state enterprises." Yet in the end, the "revolt of the NGDUs" turned out to be more threat than substance. The only NGDU that actually became an independent "leased enterprise" *(arendnoe predpriiatie)* was Chernogorneft', which had been an NGDU under the Nizhnevartovskneftegaz production association. See Arild Moe and Valeriy Kryukov, "Observations on the Reorganization of the Russian Oil Industry," *Post-Soviet Geography* 35, no. 2 (1994), p. 92.

5   Ibid., p. 96.

6   "Who Is Walking Out?," *Russian Petroleum Investor,* June 1992, pp. 13ff.

7   One of the most enterprising oil generals was Viktor Palii, general director of Nizh-nevartovskneftegaz. Between 1991 and 1993 Nizhnevartovskneftegaz was a founder stakeholder in a local oil exchange, a small producer (Sinko), an investment bank (NI-PEK), a distributor of refined products (Kedr), a joint venture with a refinery (Sunrise), and a bank (Yugorskii). See Valerii Kriukov, *Institutsional'naia struktura neftegazo-vogo sektora: Problemy i napravleniia transformatsii* (Novosibirsk: Institut ekonomiki i organizatsii promyshlennogo proizvodstva SO RAN, 1998), p. 98.

8   A detailed description, drawn from police reports, is "Zapadno-sibirskie OPG: Spravka po linii liderov prestupnoi sredy," www.compromat.ru/main/mafia/zapsibirskie.htm, originally posted July 2, 2000.

9   Interview with Viktor Palii, "Ia khotel by imet' svoego cheloveka v pravitel'stve," *Kommersant-Daily,* October 5, 1996.

10 "Watch Out for Geologists," *Russian Petroleum Investor,* March 1993, p. 45. See also the interview with Viktor Orlov, "The Orlov Offensive," in the same issue, pp. 41–45.

11 According to Andrei Konoplianik, who was deputy minister of energy under Lopukhin, there were two competing drafts before the Duma, the geologists' and the oilmen's (author's conversation with Konoplianik, May 2007). However, see also Iu. K. Shafranik and V. A. Kriukov, *Neftegazovye resursy v kruge problem* (Moscow: "Nedra," 1997), pp. 147ff. According to Shafranik and Kriukov, Lopukhin's Ministry of Fuel and Power was not actively engaged in the battle. Instead, the "battle of the drafts" in-volved, in addition to the State Geology Committee, two competing legislative com-mittees of the Supreme Soviet, the Committee for Industry and Energy (which repre-sented the interests of the oil industry), and the Committee on Ecology and Protection of the Environment (where the geologists and the regions were stronger).

12 The regulatory system and its strengthening in the hands of the state in the following decade are discussed in Chapter 10.

13 According to some sources, the reformers were not won over, and the battle between them and the oil generals continued until Viktor Chernomyrdin became deputy prime minister in June 1992. See Sergei P. Peregudov, *Korporatsii, obshchestvo, gosudarstvo: Evoliutsiia otnoshenii* (Moscow: Nauka, 2003), citing A. B. Vasilenko, *Rossiiskie nef-tianye kompanii i politika v perekhodnyi period* (Moscow, Lesar, 1997), pp. 26–29.

14 Lopukhin interview with Li-Chen Sim, quoted in her book, *The Rise and Fall of Privatization in the Russian Oil Industry* (London: Palgrave Macmillan, 2008), p. 146, fn.44.

15 Despite the modest-sounding title, an *instruktor* in the apparatus of the Central Com-mittee was a powerful individual, typically responsible for overseeing an entire minis-try as the eyes and ears of the party leadership. Chernomyrdin had already had experi-ence in a similar role in Orenburg, having worked as an instruktor in the city party apparatus of Orsk in Orenburg from 1967 to 1973.

16 "My khoteli kak luchshe, no poluchilos' kak vsegda." Russians collect Chernomyrdin sayings the way Americans collect Yogi Berraisms, and there are many websites and blogs devoted to them. See for example http://echo.msk.ru/blog/echomsk/723455 -echo/.

17 Sergei Emel'ianov, "Eksport rossiiskogo gaza: istoriia, sostoianie, perspektivy," *Neftegazovaia Vertikal'*, no. 6 (2003). Gorbachev had begun loosening the Ministry of Foreign Trade's monopoly control of foreign trade as early as 1988, and it is likely that Soiuzgazeksport had begun drifting under Gazprom's influence well before the actual incorporation occurred in 1991.

18 Elena Chernova and Leonid Skoptsov, "Moroz po kozhe ot reformy v gazovoi otrasli," *Moskovskie Novosti*, no. 6 (1992), p. 4.

19 "Problemy i perspektivy TEK glazami vedushchikh rossiiskikh politikov," *Neft' i Kapital*, no. 11 (1995), p. 11.

20 Ibid.

21 Spontaneous privatization of large industry by nomenklatura insiders was already well advanced by the late 1980s. The main legal cover for it was a decree that allowed enterprise directors to lease their enterprises' assets to a private cooperative. This subsequently was broadened into "leasing with the right to buy" *(arenda s vykupom)*. See Petr Mostovoi, "V poiskakh pravovogo polia," in Anatolii Chubais, ed., *Privatizatsiia po-rossiiski* (Moscow: "Vagrius," 1999), pp. 37–38, as well as Chubais's own comments on leasing (pp. 28–31).

22 Chubais, *Privatizatsiia po-rossiiski*, pp. 74–80.

23 Interview with Vagit Alekperov, "The Future Belongs to Us," *Russian Petroleum Investor*, May 1992, pp. 23ff.

24 Interview with Vagit Alekperov, "My ne khotim teriat' sviaz' s gosudarstvom," *Kommersant-Daily*, February 6, 1996, p. 10.

25 The general director of Kogalymneftegaz at that time was Vitalii Shmidt, who subsequently played a major role in LUKoil managing the company's foreign investments until his death in 1997. Ralif Safin also had an important part in LUKoil's early development, initially as head of its downstream sales and distribution in Russia (1993–1998) and then as head of its expansion into downstream refining and distribution in Eastern and Central Europe (2001–2002).

26 Aleksandr Putilov, in an interview with the author in 2007, confirmed this story.

27 But significantly, even at this early date, the proposed association included a foreign-trade joint venture, a Soviet-Dutch trader called "Urals," as well as the Kirishi refinery, which was already actively exporting refined products.

28 Alekperov interview, "My ne khotim teriat' sviaz' s gosudarstvom."

29 Quoted in Iuliia Govorun, "Vybor rezidenta," *Forbes-Russia*, no. 3 (2008), http://www .forbes.ru/forbes/issue/2008-03/11824-vybor-rezidenta.

30 Petr Mostovoi, "Kak raskruchivalsia makhovik privatizatsii," in Anatolii B. Chubais, ed., *Privatizatsiia po-rossiiski* (Moscow: "Vagrius," 1999), p. 124.

31 "To Strike or Not to Strike," *Russian Petroleum Investor,* July 1992, pp. 23ff.

32 Anatoly Sivak's article criticizing Lopukhin and the Ministry of Fuel and Power was originally carried by the *Federal News Service* on April 22, 1992, then reprinted in "Sivak Speaks Out," *Russian Petroleum Investor,* May 1992, pp. 34ff.

33 Valerii Paniushkin, Mikhail Zygar', and Irina Reznik, *Gazprom: Novoe russkoe oruzhie* (Moscow: "Zakharov," 2008), pp. 21–25, gives a dramatic minute-by-minute account of Lopukhin's dismissal and Yeltsin's on-the-spot replacement of him with Viktor Chernomyrdin, for which Lopukhin and Gaidar were given no advance warning.

34 Boris Yeltsin, *The Struggle for Russia* (New York: Times Books, 1994), pp. 165–168. Yeltsin offers some additional reasons for his action. He had been under pressure from deputies of the Congress of People's Deputies to dismiss four liberal ministers, of whom one was Lopukhin. Gaidar, at that time acting prime minister, resisted strongly, even going to the length of publicly submitting the resignation of the entire cabinet. In the end, however, Yeltsin insisted. "There was a very concrete reason for Lopukhin's dismissal," Yeltsin writes. "Using him as a battering ram, Gaidar was putting pressure on me to release prices on energy resources simultaneously with other prices without restrictions."

35 The position of head of the Ministry of Fuel and Power (Mintopenergo) remained officially vacant until January 1993, when Iurii Shafranik was named energy minister.

36 "Secret Visit to Tiumen," *Russian Petroleum Investor,* July 1992, pp. 17ff. Despite the sensational title of the article, the visit was far from secret.

37 Presidential decree No. 1403, dated November 17, 1992. Given the fact that a portion of the total shares of the three companies was issued in the forms of nonvoting preferred shares, the 45 percent state stake represented well over a majority of the voting shares. Similarly, a 38 percent stake in the remaining ob"edineniia was turned over to Rosneft for a three-year period, but this stake likewise represented a majority of the voting shares.

38 On the broader theme of the victory of the "gradualists" over the "shock therapists" and the "restorationists," see M. Steven Fish, *Democracy Derailed in Russia: The Failure of Open Politics* (Cambridge: Cambridge University Press, 205), pp. 160–169.

39 Anatolii B. Chubais, "Rozhdenie idei," in Anatolii B. Chubais, ed., *Privatizatsiia porossiiski* (Moscow: "Vagrius," 1999), p. 25.

40 The transformation of Boris Yeltsin from Communist Party functionary to the reformist leader of a democratic Russia is the central theme of Timothy J. Colton's magnificent biography, *Yeltsin: A Life* (New York: Basic Books, 2008).

41 Schetnaia Palata Rossiiskoi Federatsii, *Analiz protsessov privatizatsii gosudarstvennoi sobstvennosti Rossiiskoi Federatsii za period 1993–2003 gody* (Moscow: "Olita," 2004), p. 9.

42 On the key role of pipelines—and Rockefeller's belated recognition of their strategic importance—see Ron Chernow's biography of Rockefeller, *Titan: the Life of John D.*

Rockefeller, Sr. (New York: Random House, 1998), especially pp. 171–172, 197–198, and 206–212.

43 For an elaboration on this point, together with a discussion of the impact of the Soviet breakup on the gathering and processing of crude oil statistics, see Matthew J. Sagers, "Russian Crude Oil Production in 1996: Conditions and Prospects," *Post-Soviet Geography and Economics* 37, no. 9 (1996), p. 524, fn. 3.

44 *Komsomol'skaia Pravda,* December 1991, cited in *Russian Petroleum Investor* 1, no. 1 (January 1992), p. 31.

45 Russian Television, November 15, 1991, 1940 GMT.

46 TASS World Service in Russian, November 17, 1991.

47 *Rossiiskaia gazeta,* November 28, 1991, p. 2.

48 Lopukhin press conference, January 13, 1992, quoted in *Russian Petroleum Investor* 1, no. 1 (January 1992), p. 11. See also Andrew Hill, "Russia Considers Fuel Clawback," *Financial Times,* December 18, 1991, p. 2.

49 The state still controlled Transnefteprodukt, the pipeline system for refined products, but this moved only about one-tenth of the Russian total. In 1994, for example, according to Transnefteprodukt figures, 82.5 percent of all refined products moved by rail, 7.6 percent by river barge and tanker, and only 9.9 percent by pipeline. Cited in Oleg Bakhmet'ev, "'Transneft'iu' i 'Gazpromom' spetssluzhby poka zanimat'sia ne budut," *Neft' i Kapital,* no. 6 (1995), p. 12.

50 A profile of Davyd Aleksandrovich Cherniaev appears in the house journal of Transneft, *Truboprovodnyi transport nefti,* no. 6 (2004), pp. 42–44.

51 Author's interviews with the consultants in 2007.

52 Chapter by Cherniaev in Iurii P. Batalin, ed., *Neftegazostroiteli Zapadnoi Sibiri,* a volume in the series *Stroiteli Rossii XX. Veka* (Moscow: Soiuz neftegazostroitelei, 2004).

53 The next two paragraphs are drawn from "Soviet Union: Central Control of Exports Fragments," *Weekly Petroleum Argus,* June 17, 1991.

54 Yegor Gaidar, *State and Evolution: Russia's Search for a Free Market* (Seattle: University of Washington Press, 2003), p. 59, cited in Li-Chen Sim, "The Changing Relationship between the State and the Oil Industry in Russia (1992–2004)" (D.Phil. thesis, St. Antony's College, University of Oxford, March 2005), p. 101.

55 In 1987 the Kirishi refinery (then officially known as Kirishinefteorgsintez) formed its own export subsidiary, Kirishin'eftekhimeksport.

56 According to a report in the weekly *Ogonek,* in 1982 Timchenko began work at the Leningrad representative office of the Ministry of Foreign Trade, where he became acquainted with Andrei Katkov and Evgenii Malov, colleagues in the same office. When on January 1, 1987, Gorbachev broke up the USSR Ministry of Foreign Trade and authorized seventy large enterprises to conduct foreign-trade operations on their own, the three men succeeded in having the Kirishi refinery included on the list. This was the start of Kirishin'eftekhimeksport, which subsequently became Kineks. Vsevolod Bel'chenko and Natal'ia Shergina, "Kuznets svoego 'Gazproma'," *Ogonek,* March 29, 2010.

57 On the early history of Kirishineftekhimeksport and Urals, see also (with caution) Denis Kirillov and Valerii Vaisberg, "Svoi sredi chuzhikh, chuzhoi sredi svoikh," *Russkii fokus,* March 1, 2004, http://www.compromat.ru/page_14523.htm.

58 Paul Klebnikov, "Hostile Takeover, Russian-Style," *Forbes,* November 21, 1994, pp. 74–79.

59 Maksim Poliakov and Aleksei Makarov, "Pravitel'stvo Rossii prinialo predlozhenie merii Sankt-Peterburga," *Kommersant-Daily,* October 24, 1992, http://www.kommersant.ru/doc/27719. The interests behind this group subsequently came into conflict with the mayoralty of Saint Petersburg when the latter attempted to create a company called "Golden Gates" to expand the oil terminal (see Chapter 6). (Note: Here and elsewhere I have not provided barrel equivalents for refined products because the conversion rate varies depending on which products are involved.)

60 Matthew J. Sagers, "News Notes: Russian Crude Oil Exports in 1992: Who Exported Russian Oil?," *Post-Soviet Geography* 34, no. 3 (March 1993), p. 208.

61 The Russian Ministry of Foreign Economic Relations (*Ministerstvo Vneshnikh Ekonomicheskikh Sviazei,* or MVES) was created by the Russian Federation government in July 1990 under Prime Minister Ivan Silaev as a rival to the increasingly symbolic USSR Ministry of Foreign Trade. Its first minister, named in February 1992, was Petr Aven, who had been an academic researcher in the Institute of Systems Research. Aven, however, left the ministry in December 1992 to become a private consultant. In 1994 he was named president of the newly created private Alfa Bank, today part of the Alfa Group. Aven was succeeded at the ministry by his protégé, Sergei Glaz'ev, who was replaced in September 1993 by Oleg Davydov, who served until 1997, and then by Mikhail Fradkov.

62 For an account of Abramovich's beginnings, see—with caution—Dominic Midgley and Chris Hutchins, *Abramovich: The Billionaire from Nowhere* (London: HarperCollins, 2005). Russian sources include Vladimir Sumarokov, "Chernoe zoloto Romana Abramovicha," *Tribuna,* no. 24 (June 11, 1999); and A. Lazarev and S. Sorokin, "Roman Abramovich i ego sledy v Komi," *Molodezh' severa,* June 10, 1999, both cited in *Lentapedia,* http://lenta.ru/lib/14161457/full.htm.

63 Colton, *Yeltsin,* p. 337.

64 A review of these events appears in Andrei Bagrov, "MVF—glavnyi borets s korruptsiei v Rossii," *Kommersant-Daily,* March 4, 1999.

65 There were several categories of special exporters. As of June 1994 there were eighty-four special exporters for refined products and nineteen special exporters for crude oil. *Interfax Petroleum Report,* June 24–July 1, 1994, p. 9.

66 For useful background on the origins and functions of the *spetseksportery* system, see Sergey Verezemskii, "Torgovyi kapital gotov vlozhit' sebia v neftedobychu," *Neft' i Kapital,* no. 1 (1995), pp. 45–47. A useful follow-up article by the same writer is "Neftianye treidery ischezli iz eksportnykh svodok," *Neft' i Kapital,* no. 5 (1995), pp. 52–54. See also Sergey Verezemskii, "Kto budet meniat' neft' na sakhar?," *Neft' i Kapital,* no. 6 (1995), pp. 50–52.

67 MES, which stands for *Mezhdunarodnoe Ekonomicheskoe Sotrudnichestvo,* or International Economic Partnership, was an oil-trading company owned by the Moscow Patriarchate of the Russian Orthodox Church. Founded in 1990, by the mid-1990s it was one of the largest oil-trading *spetsy* in Russia. See http://warrax.net/82/church business.html.

68 *Russian Petroleum Investor,* June 1995, p. 34. This estimate came from the "Union of Special Exporters," a lobby group supported by MVES. Official government figures put the actual total of crude exports at 1.78 million barrels per day (89.0 million tons).

69 Quoted in *Interfax Petroleum Report,* November 4–11, 1994, p. 7.

70 For the reformers' own account of the origins of privatization, see Anatolii B. Chubais, ed., *Privatizatsiia po-rossiiski* (Moscow: "Vagrius," 1999).

71 The full text of the government order *(postanovlenie)* No. 1446, December 31, 1994, "O vyvoze neft i nefteproduktov...," can be accessed at http://www.referent.ru:4005/1 /6625. The government order implemented Yeltsin's July 1, 1994, decree, No. 1385.

72 Interview with Anatolii Chubais, "Dlia ekonomicheskoi katastrofy predposylok net," *Izvestiia,* January 14, 1995.

73 "For Members Only," *Russian Petroleum Investor,* April 1995. Total Russian exports of crude oil were 126.8 million tons (2.5 million barrels per day) in 1994.

74 Ibid.

75 "Hard to Kill," *Russian Petroleum Investor,* June 1995, pp. 33–36.

76 Ibid., p. 34.

77 Sergei Verezemskii, "Kontrasty neftianogo eksporta 1995 goda," *Neft' i Kapital,* no. 1 (1996), p. 60.

78 The oil-trading specialists in Alfa-Eko shortly migrated into TNK and Sidanco, while Alfa-Eko itself evolved away from the oil business toward more diversified roles. Thus German Khan, the director of oil exports for Alfa-Eko in 1993–1994, shortly afterward became a member of the board of directors of Sidanco, and after 1996 became a senior manager of TNK. See "For Members Only."

79 Verezemskii, "Kontrasty," p. 60.

80 "Think Again," *Russian Petroleum Investor,* April 1995, pp. 2–4. See also Verezemskii, "Kvoty," pp. 57–59. For an elaboration of this point, see Georgii Topuridze, "Neftedobyvaiushchie SP: Vyzhyvaet sil'neishii," *Neft' i Kapital,* no. 0 (1994), pp. 11–12.

81 The geologicals had guaranteed exports and priority in the Transneft system, but their main problem was getting physical access to the trunk line, since they were typically in remote locations. From 1995 on, the geologicals tended to be absorbed by the nearest vertically integrated companies, although in some cases they were absorbed by traders such as Alfa-Eko. See Mikhail Grigor'ev, "Geologi opiat' poluchili eksportnuiu kvotu, i opiat' dumaiut, kak ee ispol'zovat'," *Neft' i Kapital,* no. 6 (1995), pp. 59–62.

82 Interview with Roskomnedra chairman Viktor Orlov, in *Interfax Petroleum Report* 4, no. 15 (April 7–14, 1995), pp. 16–17.

83 According to Sagers, oil production in 1996 was operating at 53 percent of its 1988 capacity: 301.2 million tons (6.0 million barrels per day), compared with 568.8 million tons (11.4 million barrels per day) in 1988. Oil investment in 1995 was only 30 percent of the 1988 level. Investment in new fields was still practically at a standstill: between 1991 and 1995, only twenty to twenty-five new fields were added in all of West Siberia, as were perhaps an equal number in other regions of Russia. Sagers, "Russian Crude Oil Production in 1996," pp. 524–525.

3. The Birth of the Russian Majors

1 Sergei Kolchin, "Gonki po neftianoi vertikali," *Neft' i Kapital,* no. 1 (1996), p. 42. LUKoil itself, not surprisingly, agreed. See V. I. Alekperov, *Vertikal'no integrirovannye neftianye kompanii v Rossii* (Moscow: "Autopan," 1996), p. 189.

2 Source: Ministry of Fuel and Power (Mintopenergo), *Infotek* (monthly bulletin), no. 1 (2000) and no. 1 (2003).

3 Chrystia Freeland, *Sale of the Century: The Inside Story of the Second Russian Revolution* (Boston: Little, Brown, 2000); David E. Hoffman, *The Oligarchs: Wealth and Power in the New Russia,* rev. ed. (New York: Public Affairs, 2011); Peter Reddaway and Dmitri Glinski, *The Tragedy of Russia's Reforms* (Washington, DC: Institute of Peace Press, 2001).

4 See the report of the Russian Duma's Accounting Chamber (Schetnaia Palata) in S. V. Stepashin, ed., *Analiz protsessov privatizatsii gosudarstvennoi sobstvennosti v Rossiiskoi Federatsii za period 1993–2003 gody* (Moscow: "Olita," 2004).

5 For a careful retrospective review of the loans-for-shares episode, which attempts to place it in the context of the times and against the yardstick of privatization auctions elsewhere, see Daniel Treisman, "'Loans for Shares' Revisited," *Post-Soviet Affairs* 26, no. 3 (2010), pp. 207–227.

6 Petr Mostovoi, "Kak sozdavalas' programma," in Anatolii B. Chubais, ed., *Privatizatsiia po-rossiiski* (Moscow: "Vagrius," 1999), p. 68.

7 Dmitri Vasil'ev, "Kak my provodili chekovuiu privatizatsiiu," in Anatolii B. Chubais, ed., *Privatizatsiia po-rossiiski* (Moscow: "Vagrius," 1999), pp. 138–139.

8 See Valerii Kriukov, *Institutsional'naia struktura neftegazovogo sektora* (Novosibirsk: Institut ekonomiki i organizatsii promyshlennogo proizvodstva SO RAN, 1998), p. 101.

9 There is no simple way to translate the confusing welter of Soviet and post-Soviet administrative terms. I have chosen to stick with the Russian term, *ob"edinenie,* as the most straightforward rendition. In the literature the most common name for the upstream producing units was "production association," or *proizvodstvennoe ob"edinenie,* which I have shortened to *ob"edinenie.* In the plural, the final "e" changes to "ia."

10 In late 1991 and early 1992, a number of attempts by ob"edineniia to register as joint-stock corporations were turned down on the grounds that there was no provision for them in the legislation. Kriukov, *Institutsional'naia struktura neftegazovogo sektora,* pp. 99–101.

11 Indeed, in several places NGDUs exercised their legal right to exit from the ob"edineniia: thus Chernogorneft from Nizhnevartovskneftegaz, Yugraneft from Yuganskneftegaz, and Var'eganneftegaz from its parent of the same name. Ibid., p. 100. For a short overview in English, see Arild Moe and Valeriy Kryukov, "Observations on the Reorganization of the Russian Oil Industry," *Post-Soviet Geography* 35, no. 2 (1994), pp. 89–101.

12 For a summary description of voucher privatization against the background of the privatization policy as a whole, written by a group of Westerners who were consultants to the State Property Committee, see Joseph R. Blasi, Maya Kroumova, and Douglas Kruse, *Kremlin Capitalism: Privatizing the Russia Economy* (Ithaca, NY: Cornell University Press, 1997), pp. 41–46.

13 The activity of the exchanges and the beginnings of trade in vouchers on the Moscow exchanges are described in "Birzhevaia torgovlia v proshlom godu: Utrachennye illiuzii," *Kommersant-Daily,* January 9, 1993. Articles from *Kommersant-Daily* and other *Kommersant* publications can be accessed through *Kommersant*'s online archive at http://www.kommersant.ru/search.

14 Vasil'ev, "Kak my provodili chekovuiu privatizatsiiu," pp. 130–143.

15 Komi's strategy was to hold voucher auctions as quickly as possible, seeing in them a means of maintaining local control over its regional oil industry. Thus Komineft conducted the first oil-company voucher auctions in August 1993.

16 Anatolii Chubais, "Kak dushili privatizatsiiu," in Anatolii B. Chubais, ed., *Privatizatsiia po-rossiiski* (Moscow: "Vagrius," 1999), pp. 171–179.

17 Author's interview, November 24, 2004.

18 Ibid.

19 Specifically, the Russian Federal Property Fund, as custodian of the shares in the oil companies, turned over to the parent holding companies 38 percent of the initial stock of the underlying joint-stock companies. Since a portion of the stock consisted of nonvoting preferential shares, this was the equivalent of 51 percent of the voting shares.

20 Viktor Palii, then general director of Nizhnevartovskneftegaz, reportedly acquired 9 percent of the company in this way, operating through Western front organizations registered in the names of family members. But other oil generals were doing similar things. (In December 2001 a television documentary called "Palii's Gold" was broadcast on local television in Nizhnevartovsk, quoting extensively from court records.

21 Some of the key figures in these early advisory relationships subsequently migrated into the LUKoil management structure. Aleksandr Matitsyn, for example, today LUKoil's vice president for corporate finance, began working in the early 1990s in the Moscow office of KPMG. (See note 60.)

22 Of the original members of the LUKoil management team in the early 1990s, only Sergei Kukura and Liubov' Khoba had prior training in economics or accounting. But neither, for obvious reasons, had had any exposure to modern finance or securities. (Kukura is today LUKoil's first vice president for economics and finance, and Khoba is chief accountant.) In addition, Anatolii Barkov, vice president for security

and corporate communications since 1993, has two advanced degrees in economics with a focus on strategic decision making, but these were acquired later, in 1999 and 2003.

23 Brief biographies of Leonid Fedun can be found at http://www.viperson.ru/wind .php?ID=7678.

24 Interview with Leonid Fedun in Roman Streshnev, "Kaspii—element natsional'noi bezopasnosti," *Krasnaia zvezda,* August 23 2002.

25 "Samym bogatym russkim okazalsia Vagit Alekperov," *Ekonomicheskie novosti,* July 26, 2002. Articles from *Ekonomicheskie novosti* and many other Russian publications can be obtained via East View Information Services (Online) at http://eastview.com /Online/OnlineDB.

26 Quoted in Streshnev, "Kaspii."

27 Ol'ga Kryshtanovskaia, *Anatomiia rossiiskoi politicheskoi elity* (Moscow: "Zakharov," 2005), pp. 264–272.

28 From a profile of Alekperov, "Chelovek igraet na trube," *Profil',* July 17, 2000.

29 This biographical material on Tsvetkov comes from Natal'ia Aliakrinskaia, "Izmenil nebu," *Moskovskie novosti,* March 26, 2004.

30 "Samym bogatym russkim okazalsia Vagit Alekperov." This source lists Alekperov with 10.38 percent of the company; Nikolai Tsvetkov, chairman of Nikoil (today Uralsib), as number two, with 5.26 percent (in addition to a block of 6.88 percent of LUKoil owned by Nikoil); and Leonid Fedun as number three, with 4.62 percent.

31 A good treatment of LUKoil's early management of financial matters is Valery Kryukov and Arild Moe, "Banks and the Financial Sector," in David Lane, ed., *The Political Economy of Russian Oil* (Lanham, MD: Rowman and Littlefield, 1999), pp. 47–74, especially pp. 55–56.

32 An overview of Russian banking through the financial crash of 1998 is Juliet Johnson, *A Fistful of Rubles: The Rise and Fall of the Russian Banking System* (Ithaca, NY: Cornell University Press, 2000). For developments since 1998, see Timothy Frye, "Governing the Banking Sector," in Timothy J. Colton and Stephen Holmes, *The State after Communism: Governance in the New Russia* (Lanham, MD: Rowman and Littlefield, 2006), pp. 155–186.

33 Kryukov and Moe, "Banks and the Financial Sector," pp. 55–56.

34 For a brief account of the debate over privatization, see Thane Gustafson, *Capitalism Russian-Style* (Cambridge: Cambridge University Press, 1999), chapter 2. For a more detailed description of the development of the privatization program, see Anders Aslund, *How Russia Became a Market Economy* (Washington, DC: Brookings Institution, 1995), chapter 7.

35 Of the 22 percent reserved for voucher auctions, 18.25 percent were to be made available for exchange at open auctions, 3.75 percent at closed ones reserved for related employees. See "Vaucher kak tragicheskii geroi: Apogei pered konchinoi," *Kommersant-Vlast',* no. 14 (April 19, 1994), kommersant.ru/doc/9796/.

36 "Games Generals Play," *Russian Petroleum Investor,* March 1994, p. 30. Such episodes were widely reported in the Russian press in the first half of 1994.

37 "Vaucher kak tragicheskii geroi."

38 The new majors were entrusted with 38 percent of the total shares, but after allowing for nonvoting shares this was equivalent to a narrow 51 percent majority of the voting shares.

39 The companies that were not yet included in one of the new majors, but had been grouped loosely into Rosneft, privatized first. Thus two refineries, Angarsknefteorgsintez and the Riazan' refinery, held their voucher auctions as early as March 1993, more than a year before LUKoil. Arkadii Klimov and Irina Pil'man, "Giganty pererabotki vnov' na auktsione," *Kommersant-Vlast',* no. 7 (March 1, 1994), http://kommersant.ru/doc/9628.

40 Interview with Leonid Fedun, then general director of LUKoil Consulting (described as the "business advisory unit" of LUKoil), "LUKoil on the Block," *Russian Petroleum Investor,* October 1993, pp. 60–63.

41 "LUKoil-Fond otdaet predpochtenie 'neftianym' aktsiiam," *Kommersant-Daily,* December 7, 1993. By mid-1995 LUKoil-Fond was the seventh largest voucher investment fund (the second largest was the infamous MMM Fund, a pyramid fund created by Sergei Mavrodi in the early 1990s), right behind Alfa-Kapital. But whereas Alfa-Kapital invested widely, focusing particularly on the food industry, LUKoil-Fond invested primarily in oil properties. At this time it even owned an 7 percent stake in the Omsk Refinery. Vlad Vdovin, "Chekovye investitsionnye fondy: Optimisticheskaia epitafiia," *Kommersant-Den'gi,* July 26, 1995; Aleksandr Tutushkin, "Sobranie aktsionerov 'LUKoil-Fonda': Pribyl'iu v 36.8 mlrd podelilis' s paishchikami," *Kommersant-Daily,* July 27, 1996.

42 Vologdanefteprodukt, one of LUKoil's sixty-six "daughter" companies, attempted in December 1993 to go ahead with its own privatization auction and arranged for the local privatization committee to transfer a "certificate" to the local property fund, authorizing the latter to release shares for the auction. LUKoil's parent company and GKI stepped in quickly to halt the revolt. Aleksandr Kovalev, "Denatsionalizatsiia prodolzhaet sil'no otdavat' neft'iu," *Kommersant-Daily,* December 10, 1993.

43 Aleksandr Kovalevskii and Aleksandr Tutushkin, "Investorov zakhlestnet potok aktsii neftianykh kompanii," *Kommersant-Daily,* February 19, 1994.

44 Alekperov press conference, reported in *Interfax Petroleum Report* 3, no. 27, July 1–8, 1994, p. 11. See also Aleksandr Tutushkin, "'LUKoil' khochet prodat' sebia kak mozhno bol'she," *Kommersant-Daily,* April 12, 2004; and Aleksandr Kovalev and Aleksandr Tutushkin, "V rossiiskoi neftianoi promyshlennosti net nichego dorozhe 'LUKoila'," *Kommersant-Daily,* May 13, 1994.

45 By the spring of 1994, the government, after initial reluctance, had given permission for foreigners to acquire oil company shares.

46 Alekperov press conference. LUKoil was apparently not the only one to be startled. According to a widely repeated story in Moscow at the time, the CSFB traders in Moscow had conducted their operations in their own names, accumulating a large tax liability for the company. In the fall of 1994, after an internal audit, the home office of CSFB

suspended its office's trading in Moscow, removing such a large player that the infant Moscow stock market promptly crashed.

47 Arkadii Klimov and Mikhail Repnin, quoting from a statement by Leonid Fedun, in "Vyvodok 'LUKoila' na chekovom auktsione," *Kommersant-Daily,* April 5, 1994.

48 The operation of FK-LUKoil is described in Aleksandr Tutushkin, "'LUKoil nadeetsia na uspekh novoi tsenovoi politiki," *Kommersant-Daily,* March 3, 1994.

49 Aleksandr Tutushkin, "Neftianiki nadeiutsia operedit' infliatsiiu," *Kommersant-Daily,* December 7, 1993, http://kommersant.ru/doc/66595. At that time, in 1993, the main problem was that three-quarters of all settlements took longer than three months. In view of the prevailing high inflation, this cost the creditors a fortune.

50 Aushev was elected a deputy in the Duma in late 1995 and left LUKoil in early 1996. He became deputy chairman of the committee on security and subsequently deputy chairman of the Duma committee on credit institutions and financial markets. He left the Duma in 2007, and today he is a private investor. In December 1998 he was briefly in the news for having called for independence for Chechnya. *Svobodnaia Gruziia,* December 4, 1998.

51 According to Vitalii Lesnichii, who was one of the original members of the LUKoil board of directors established in January 1992, the original government decree creating LUKoil (Decree of the RSFSR Council of Ministers No. 18, November 25, 1991) authorized the company to set internal prices, but this was not implemented at the time since there was no legal basis for it. Vitalii Lesnichii, "Nachalo," *Neft' Rossii,* no. 1 (2001), http://www.oilru.com/nr/80/768/. The conventional system up to that time was cost-plus pricing. The crude producers were allowed to add a 50 percent margin to their costs, the refiners 20 percent, and the wholesale distributors *(neftebaza)* 35 percent. LUKoil's system was to have the various participants in the chain sign an agreement *(dogovor)* under which the profits would be shared in proportion to the costs of each in the chain. Tutushkin, "Neftianiki nadeiutsia operedit' infliatsiiu," and "LUKoil nadeetsia na uspekh novoi tsenovoi politiki," *Kommersant-Daily,* March 3, 1994.

52 *Tiumenskaia pravda,* January 25, 1994, cited in Moe and Kryukov, "Observations on the Reorganization of the Russian Oil Industry," p. 94.

53 Stephen O'Sullivan, *LUKoil: Leader of the Pack* (London: MC Securities, September 1995), p. 63.

54 *Interfax Petroleum Report* 14, no. 17 (April 21–28, 1995), p. 9. Alekperov set the price of the LUKoil shares at the peak market value reached to that point, the value of the shares on the eve of the April 1 presidential decree authorizing the swap. This guaranteed that the minority shareholders would feel well treated. See Sergei Savushkin, "Edinaia aktsiia po-surgutski," *Neft' i Kapital,* no. 4 (1996), p. 14. One share of LUKoil-Kogalymneftegaz, for example, was swapped for eight shares of LUKoil, and the other subsidiaries were swapped at similarly advantageous ratios.

55 Savushkin, "Edinaia aktsiia po-surgutski."

56 Alekperov apparently had to be persuaded to shut down FK-LUKoil; for some reason he was reluctant. "I very much did not want to abolish the Finance Company, but after

lengthy arguments within the management board *(pravlenie)* I was nevertheless per-suaded to replace it with territorial sales units, subordinated to the central management structure. Although now we see that that wasn't the very best approach either." Interview with Vagit Alekperov, "My ne khotim teriat' sviaz' s gosudarstvom," *Kommersant-Daily,* February 6, 1996, p. 10.

57 At the same time, LUKoil announced that the state had approved the plan. The bonds were backed by shares from the state's remaining stake. According to Russian commen-tators, this was a compromise between those who wanted to raise capital by selling the state's stake and those who wanted to retain state control as long as possible. Sergei Sa-vushkin and Sergei Kokolev, "Za investitsiiami—na fondovyi rynok," *Neft' i Kapital,* no. 5 (May 1995), pp. 15–19. In the end, when the actual presidential decree authorizing the sale was issued, it allowed only an 11 percent share of LUKoil's charter capital to be sold. Government decree No. 269, March 22, 1995. See Alekperov, *Vertikal'no-integrirovannye neftianye kompanii v Rossii,* p. 179.

58 Aleksei Sukhodoev, "Kompaniia ozabochena poiskom luchshego prodavtsa svoikh aktsii," *Kommersant-Daily,* July 27, 1994.

59 KPMG had been advising LUKoil informally since 1992. This began a long association between LUKoil's management team and KPMG's Moscow director, Aleksandr Matit-syn. In 1997 Matitsyn joined LUKoil as a vice president for financial affairs. Today Matitsyn is LUKoil's vice president for treasury and corporate finance, one of the few "outsiders" to penetrate LUKoil's original inner circle in the company's first decade. See http://lukoil.com/back/staff__head_6_5dep_20_.html.

60 *Interfax Petroleum Report,* November 4–11, 1994, p. 6.

61 "Strategicheskie investory prikhodiat s Aliaski," *Neft' i Kapital,* no. 10 (1995), pp. 31–33. ARCO's stake in LUKoil was subsequently passed on to BP when ARCO was absorbed in 2000. BP sold its stake in LUKoil on the open market in 2001, reportedly for a hand-some profit.

62 For a colorful account of oil and oil politics in the Caspian Basin in the 1990s, see Steve Levine, *The Oil and the Glory: The Pursuit of Empire and Fortune on the Caspian Sea* (New York: Random House, 2007).

63 ITAR-TASS, January 21, 1994. Daily bulletins since 1987 can be accessed by subscrip-tion at http://info.itar-tass.com/.

64 Interfax, October 14, 1994. Interfax daily bulletins can be accessed at http://archive.org/details/interfax.ru.

65 Interfax, June 16, 1995.

66 OMRI (Open Media Research Institute) Daily Digest (in Russian), October 19, 1995, http://fa.osaarchivum.org/ft?col=208&i=116.

67 After a brief time as general director of CPC, Stanev became deputy minister of energy, a position he held from 1998 to 2004.

68 "Ne nado pitat' illiuzii naschet 'LUKoila'," *Zerkalo* (Baku), January 11, 1997, p. 14.

69 Interview with Vagit Alekperov, *Interfax Petroleum Report* 3, no. 27 (July 1–8, 1994), p. 3.

70 Interview with Alekperov, "My ne khotim teriat' sviaz' s gosudarstvom," p. 10.

71 Cited in Aleksei Sukhodoev and Aleksandr Tutushkin, "Neftianoi marafon finishi-roval. Samochuvstvie uchastnikov neodnoznachno," *Kommersant-Daily,* October 12, 1995.

72 Bogdanov has little time for the media and has always kept the tightest controls over Surgutneftegaz's contacts with them. When he gave a press conference in Moscow in February 1995, on the eve of the company's first voucher auctions, it was the first time in nearly three years that he had been seen in the capital, and the rare event drew a crowd of reporters. Aleksei Sukhodoev, "Kompaniia stanet narodnoi, esli ne pomes-haiut," *Kommersant-Daily,* February 21, 1995. As a result, there are few firsthand descriptions of the man or the company and a correspondingly large amount of specu-lation. For samples of the latter, see the coverage of Bogdanov and Surgutneftegaz at www.kompromat.ru.

73 Iulia Latynina, "Mikhail Khodorkovskii: Khimiia i zhizn'," *Sovershenno sekretno,* Au-gust 1999, http://www.sovsekretno.ru/magazines/article/376.

74 Aleksei Sukhodoev, "Surgutskie neftianiki raschityvaiut tol'ko na sebia," *Kommersant-Daily,* May 3, 1995.

75 Sergei Kolchin, "Gonki po neftianoi vertikali," *Neft' i Kapital,* no. 1 (1996), p. 42.

76 Mariia Ignatova, "Surgutskii pas'ians," *Forbes* (Russian ed.), April 2004, http://www.forbes.ru/forbes/issue/2004-04/2365-surgutskii-pasyans.

77 The complete archive of the Russian government's Federal Chamber of Accounts *(Schetnaia Palata)* for the years since 2002 is available at http://www.ach.gov.ru in searchable format.

78 Biulleten' Schetnoi Palaty Rossiiskoi Federatsii, "Ob ekonomicheskiom i finansovom sostoianii estestvennykh monopolii (analiticheskaia zapiska)," no. 8 (68), 2003, http://www.ach.gov.ru/ru/bulletin/126/.

79 Alone of all the Russian oil majors, Surgutneftegaz is incorporated in Khanty-Mansiisk, which has the effect of increasing the share of Surgutneftegaz's oil-tax pay-ments going directly to the okrug government.

80 Natal'ia Alekseeva, "Galushki sami v rot ne prygnut," *Izvestiia,* April 30, 2004.

81 An enterprising reporter, however, managed to reach Bogdanov on the company's closed internal telephone line. Natal'ia Kalinichenko and Aleksandr Privalov, "Bor'ba za aktsii tol'ko nachinaetsia." *Kommersant-Vlast',* November 22, 1993.

82 Thus the Kirishi refinery held its own separate voucher auction, and Credit Suisse First Boston acquired a 5.78 percent stake, becoming one of the largest minority sharehold-ers in Kirishi. See Savushkin, "Edinaia aktsiia po-surgutski."

83 This can be seen from the way production was reported in the official statistics. Unlike the other companies, whose producing subsidiaries continued to report separately all through the 1990s, Surgutneftegaz reported as a single entity from the beginning. See A. M. Mastepanov, ed., *Toplivo i energetika Rossii* (Moscow: "Energiia," various years).

84 Kryukov and Moe, "Banks and the Financial Sector," p. 57.

85 Natal'ia Ol'shanova in the early 1990s was the head of Surgutneftegaz's department of financial securities. See Sukhodoev, "Surgutskie neftianiki raschityvaiut tol'ko na

sebia." In the second half of the 1990s she became a vice president of Surgutneftegaz. By 2000 Ol'shanova had retired and was advisor to Bogdanov (Praim-TASS, March 28, 2000). An archive of daily news bulletins is available online for 2006 and after at http://www.1prime.ru/news/archive.aspx. To my knowledge there is no electronic archive for earlier years.

86 "'Surgutneftegaz': Chuzhie zdes' ne khodiat," *Kommersant-Vlast'*, October 17, 1995.

87 For background on the origins and early years of Vladimir Potanin and Oneksimbank, see Hoffman, *The Oligarchs*, pp. 303–307. A biographical sketch of Vladimir Potanin is available from V. Pribylovkii's website, http://www.scilla.ru/works/raznoe/potanin .html.

88 Surgutneftegaz's success in avoiding loans and credits was only relative. As Bogdanov himself said in October 1995, "Half of our working capital is our own," which implies that the other half was borrowed. But even that much was an achievement. "'Surgutneftegaz': Chuzhie zdes' ne khodiat."

89 Kryukov and Moe, "Banks and the Financial Sector," pp. 57–58.

90 Sergei Savushkin, "GKI podgotovil bol'shuiu sezonnuiu rasprodazhu," *Neft' i Kapital*, no. 11 (1995), pp. 22–23.

91 Sergei Savushkin, "'Rosneft' ne stala strategicheskim investorom," *Neft' i Kapital,* no. 12 (1995), pp. 17–19.

92 Author's interview, December 2004.

93 Kirishineftekhimeksport was renamed Kineks in 1995. See Denis Kirillov and Valerii Vaisberg, "Svoi sredi chuzhikh, chuzhoi sredi svoikh," *Russkii fokus,* March 1, 2004.

94 Vadim Somov, a 1975 Gubkin graduate who had previously been the deputy head of economics and planning at the refinery, was named general director of the Kirishi refinery (officially called Kirishinefteorgsintez, or Kinef) in May 1994, where he remains today. (Source: Company website, www.kinef.ru.) According to a 2000 profile, Somov, who was backed by Surgutneftegaz, was elected general director by the Kirishi "workers' collective" in a competitive election against eight other candidates. See Konstantin Zborovskii, "Metry s Baltiki," *Profil',* February 14, 2000.

The export arm of the Kirishi refinery, Kirishineftekhimeksport (subsequently renamed Kineks), had privatized on its own in 1993 and was independent of the Kirishi refinery, even though it continued to handle the bulk of the refinery's exports. The original four founders of Kirishineftkhimeksport (Adol'f Smirnov, Andrei Katkov, Evgenii Malov, and Gennadii Timchenko) stayed on as shareholders in the privatized Kineks. Over the next several years, through a series of recombinations, ownership in Kineks remained essentially in the hands of its four founders. It is plausible to assume that they were shareholders in the Kirishi refinery as well and that they formed one of the main groups that Bogdanov had to negotiate with as he consolidated control over the refinery. It is possible that understandings were reached and shares were exchanged at that time that left the four founders with a minority interest in Surgutneftegaz (Kirillov and Vaisberg, "Svoi sredi chuzhikh, chuzhoi sredi svoikh"). According to one recent account, an arranged divorce of the four founders of Kineks took place in 2003, as a result of which Timchenko was left with sole control over exports from Surgutneft-egaz (Irina Reznik and Irina Mokrousova, "Pervyi vozle Putina," *Vedomosti*, March 19, 2012, p. 1).

95 The beginnings of the takeover of the Saint Petersburg fuels business by the *Tambovtsy* are described in a first-person interview with Vladimir Kumarin-Barsukov, one of the cofounders of the Tambov gang and subsequently the principal shareholder in the Petersburg Fuel Company. See Andrei Konstantinov, *Banditskii Peterburg*, 2 vols. (Saint Petersburg: "Neva," 2005), 1:553–554.

96 Vladimir Putin's possible involvement in the creation of PTK and the battles for control of the Saint Petersburg fuels market are discussed separately in Chapter 6. By the time of these events, Sobchak, who was notorious for his hands-off style and his frequent travels out of town, had delegated much of the day-to-day business of running the city to Putin.

97 Marina Latysheva, "Post-modern nefteproduktoobespechaniia," *Neft' i Kapital*, no. 3 (1995), pp. 34–37. For the official history of the Petersburg Fuels Company, see its website at www.ptk.ru. According to Latysheva, the competing refineries were induced to offer refined products to Saint Petersburg without prepayment by the offer of the city's support for the refineries to gain access to the more profitable end of the fuels business, such as service stations.

98 Latysheva, "Post-modern nefteproduktoobespechaniia." Makarov was replaced in that position by Vadim Glazkov.

99 Quoted in "Problemy 'Surgutneftegaza' v Peterburge: 'Surgutneftegaz' v Sankt-Peterburge glazami Vladimira Bogdanova," *Kommersant-Daily*, November 28, 1995. The controversial lease agreements are also described in Aleksandr Shvets, "Kreiseru 'Avrora' takoe i ne snilos'," *Neft' i Kapital*, no. 9 (1997), pp. 26–30.

100 Official PTK history, www.ptk.ru.

101 Svetlana Azarova, "Kto poseet veter," *Neft' i Kapital*, no. 11 (1996), p. 35.

102 "LUKoil Challenges Surgutneftegaz in Northwest Russian Gasoline Market," *Interfax Petroleum Report*, April 5–12, 1996, p. 7.

103 Shvets, "Kreiseru 'Avrora' takoe i ne snilos'," p. 27.

104 Ibid., p. 28. Manevich was a key member of the business group surrounding Vladimir Putin at the time. At the time of his death he was chairman of the oversight board of a Russian-German business group called SPAG, which invested in real estate in the Saint Petersburg area, and as head of the city property committee he sat on the board of directors of PTK. In his campaign interviews published as *First Person* in 2000, Putin pays tribute to Manevich and recalls that he persuaded Manevich to stay on as deputy mayor after the defeat of Anatolii Sobchak in the 1996 mayoral election. Putin was shaken by the death of Manevich, who was evidently a good friend and ally, to judge by Putin's comments. Vladimir Putin, *First Person* (New York: Random House, 2000, p. 114. For a portrait of Manevich at the time of his murder, see Konstantin Smirnov and Dmitrii Liukaitis, "V Peterburge soversheno politicheskoe ubiistvo goda," *Kommersant-Daily*, August 27, 1997.

105 Sergei Kolchin, "Bor'ba za rynki v supertiazhelom vese," *Neft' i Kapital,* no. 3 (1997), p. 43.

106 This picture of the end of 1997 comes from Aleksandr Shvets, "Za chto borolis'," *Neft' i Kapital,* no. 9 (1998), pp. 64–66.

107 Shvets, "Kreiseru 'Avrora' takoe i ne snilos'," p. 28.

108 Shvets, "Za chto borolis'," pp. 64–66.

109 Kumarin even briefly became vice president of PTK, although his tenure lasted only until 1999. In 2000, the role of Kumarin and the *Tambovtsy* became a political issue in the mayoral race, and the incumbent mayor, Vladimir Yakovlev, sought to distance himself from Kumarin and the management of PTK. But even though he stepped down as vice president, Kumarin appears to have retained de facto control of PTK.

110 There are reports—to be treated with the usual caution—that Bogdanov's withdrawal from the Saint Petersburg retail market was part of a larger negotiated settlement, in which Bogdanov gained full legal recognition of Surgutneftegaz's ownership of the Kirishi refinery in exchange for abandoning claims to monopoly control of the distribution market in the city. Sergei Sobianin, today the mayor of Moscow but then the deputy governor of the Khanty-Mansiisk oblast, is said to have mediated the conflict at Bogdanov's request. See Konstantin Gaaze, Iuliia Taratuta, Nadezhda Ivanitskaia, and Mikhail Fishman, "Oblechen doveriem," *Russkii Newsweek,* no. 43 (October 18, 2010), http://www.compromat.ru/page_29979.htm.

111 Thane Gustafson, *Crisis amid Plenty: The Politics of Soviet Energy under Brezhnev and Gorbachev* (Princeton, NJ: Princeton University Press, 1989), chapter 4, especially pp. 105–107.

112 Muravlenko's brief biography appears in *Russian Petroleum Investor,* March 1994, p. 67.

113 Ekaterina Zapodinskaia, "Istets obvinil Roskomnedra v nezakonnoi vydache litsenzii," *Kommersant-Daily,* November 12, 1993.

114 From a 1996 report on Yukos's downstream by a group of Western consultants, Bain and Company. The largest of the three refineries in the Samara area, Novokuibyshev, took most of its crude from a local upstream producer; Yuganskneftegaz supplied the two smaller refineries, Kuibyshev and Syzran'.

115 In the early 1990s, the combined capacity of the three Samara refineries was about 75 percent of Yuganskneftegaz's crude production.

116 Between 1990 and 1996, production at Yuganskneftegaz declined by 55 percent, versus 43 percent for Russia as a whole. Only one company, Nizhnevartovskneftegaz, the site of Samotlor, had a worse collapse. Matthew J. Sagers, "West Siberian Oil Production in the Mid-1990s," *International Geology Review* 36 (1994), p. 1004.

117 Mastepanov, *Toplivo i energetika Rossii.*

118 All the Russian oil companies were cutting back on drilling at this time, but Yuganskneftegaz did so more slowly than the industry as a whole. In 1994, whereas the Russian industry had cut development drilling by two-thirds, Yuganskneftegaz was still drilling at nearly half its 1990 level. This state of affairs lasted until the end of 1995,

when Yukos, with the help of Energy Minister Iurii Shafranik, managed to replace the local management of Yuganskneftegaz. From that point on, Yuganskneftegaz drastically curtailed its investment in drilling. Mastepanov, *Toplivo i energetika Rossii.*

119 Two leading analysts write, "The first years of YUKOS, 1993–95, were characterized by the often antagonistic relationship between the holding company, YUKOS, and its main production unit, Yuganskneftegaz. . . . The leadership of the holding company could not prevent resistance from Yuganskneftegaz to its policies; nor was the holding company able to control the main material and financial flows within the larger integrated organization." Kryukov and Moe, "Banks and the Financial Sector," pp. 56–57.

120 *Interfax Petroleum Report,* December 1–8, 1995, p. 12, and January 19–26, 1996, p. 9. See also Aleksandr Tutushkin, "Smotrite, kto prishel!" *Kommersant-Daily,* February 21, 1995. Guliaev was replaced by another local oilman, Vladimir Parasiuk, who had been general director of one of Yuganskneftegaz's NGDUs, Maiskneft'. Parasiuk had graduated from "Indus" in 1979 and risen through the ranks at Yuganskneftegaz. He went on to become executive vice president of Yukos EP, responsible for upstream production.

121 The story of Yuganskfracmaster and the first joint ventures in Russia is told in Chapter 4. In 1994, its high point, Yuganskfracmaster produced 2.7 million tons (54,000 barrels per day) of crude, of which 1.7 million tons (34,000 barrels per day) was credited as its "exclusive" contribution and was therefore eligible for 100 percent export to the "Far Abroad," that is, outside the former Soviet Union. See Sagers, "West Siberian Oil Production," p. 1012. This compares with only 4.0 million tons (80,000 barrels per day) in Far Abroad exports credited to Yukos in that year, most of which was actually exported by Yuganskneftegaz.

122 Ol'ga Bolmatova, "Gospredstaviteli vmeshalis' v protsess upravleniia 'YUKOSom'," *Neft' i Kapital,* no. 4 (1995), pp. 6–8.

123 Press statement by Yuganskneftegaz Vice President Eduard Grushevenko, *Interfax Petroleum Report,* December 1–8, 1995, p. 12.

124 Yukos press service, quoted in *Interfax Petroleum Report,* December 15–29, 1995, p. 19. See also *Ekspert,* no. 11 (October 24, 1995), p. 52. The other top five tax debtors were all oil companies as well.

125 An account of Misiurin's takeover of Petroplast and the sequel up to Misiurin's death three years later appears in "Problemy torgovtsev neft'iu," *Kommersant-Daily,* November 1, 1995.

126 The story that follows is based mostly on "Delo 'Nefsama'," *Moskovskii komsomolets,* June 3, 1998.

127 Li-Chen Sim, "The Changing Relationship between the State and the Oil Industry in Russia (1992–2004)" (D.Phil. thesis, St. Antony's College, University of Oxford, March 2005), p. 100.

128 "Zaderzhany podozrevaemye v ubiistve krupnogo biznesmena," *Kommersant-Daily,* October 26, 1995. See also Paul Klebnikov, "Russia's Robber Barons," *Forbes,* November 21, 1994, pp. 75–82.

129 Tarkhov served as mayor from 2006 to 2010.

130 "Look Before You Leap," *Russian Petroleum Investor,* October 1993, pp. 55–56.

131 Sergei Verezemskii, "Samara mozhet stat' 'vtorym serdtsem' 'YUKOSa," *Neft' i Kapital,* no. 1 (1995), pp. 67–68.

132 *Interfax Petroleum Report,* February 9–16, 1996, p. 9.

133 "Nasledstvo 'Papy' otoshlo k Rossii," *Kommersant-Daily,* March 21, 2002.

134 Iurii Siun, "Neftianoi triller s desiatkami trupov," *Kommersant-Daily,* November 26, 1998.

135 Interview with Sergei Muravlenko, "Betting on Yukos," *Russian Petroleum Investor,* March 1994, p. 67.

136 Ibid.

137 *Interfax Petroleum Report,* April 19–26, 1996, p. 178.

138 "Interv'iu s 'general'nym generalom'," *Kommersant-Daily,* April 27, 1995.

139 Tutushkin and Sukhodoev, "Neftianye kompanii splotilis' v bor'be za svoi interesy."

140 This account is drawn mainly from Freeland, *Sale of the Century,* pp. 177–178; and Hoffman, *The Oligarchs,* pp. 315–318 and 361–362. There were actually two separate auctions, held on the same day. In the first, the "loan-for-shares" auction, Laguna took a 45 percent stake for $159 million; in the second, an investment tender, Laguna took an additional 33 percent stake in exchange for a commitment to invest just over $150 million in Yukos.

141 Rustam Narzikulov, "'Menatep' rastvoriaetsia v 'Yukose'," *Nezavisimaia gazeta,* April 13, 1996.

142 The paragraph that follows is drawn largely from Hoffman, *The Oligarchs,* chapter 5; and Freeland, *Sale of the Century,* pp. 114–121.

143 On the significance of the Komsomol (Communist Youth League or YCL) as a source of "within-system entrepreneurship" in the 1980s, see Stephen Solnick, *Stealing the State: Control and Collapse in Soviet Institutions* (Cambridge, MA: Harvard University Press, 1998), chapter 4.

144 Ekaterina Zapodinskaia, "Razoruzhili nachal'nika sluzhby bezopasnosti 'Yukosa'," *Kommersant,* October 24, 2006. In the state's subsequent prosecution of Yukos and Menatep officials, the spotlight focused on the role of Aleksey Pichugin, the head of security at Yukos, who was arrested in June 2003 and convicted in November for a double homicide committed in 2002. In addition, in 2006 Pichugin was charged and convicted for the murder of the mayor of Nefteiugansk, Vladimir Petukhov. However, in the late 1990s Pichugin was not primarily responsible for security in Yukos but reported to Leonid Nevzlin on matters concerning Rosprom and Menatep rather than Yukos. The central security role at Yukos in those years, according to this source, was played by Shestopalov. Shestopalov currently lives in Israel.

145 "Lovlia ryby v mutnoi vode s posleduiushchim ischeznoveniem," February 20, 2004, http://kompromat.flb.ru/material.phtml?id=5641. The author of the source claims to have obtained biographical information on Shestopalov from the security department of the Most Group.

146 Aleksandr Tutushkin, "Zasedanie soveta direktorov 'Yukosa': Bankiry priobshchilis' k neftianym problemam," *Kommersant-Daily,* April 23, 1996.

147 Narzikulov, "'Menatep' rastvoriaetsia."

148 Interview with Khodorkovsky, "Mikhail Khodorkovskii: Krupnyi biznes ne mozhet sushchestvovat' vne gosudarstva," *Kommersant-Daily,* April 16, 1996.

149 Narzikulov, "'Menatep' rastvoriaetsia."

150 Aleksandr Tutushkin, "'Yukos' sozdaet sistemu bezopasnosti: Neftianaia kompaniia vziala sebia pod kolpak," *Kommersant-Daily,* April 16, 1996.

151 Ibid.

152 Ibid.

153 Ibid.

154 Ibid. The acronym OMON stands for "special-purpose police units" *(otriady militsii osobogo nuzncheniia)*. In the 1990s these were largely under the authority of the regional governors.

155 Samaraneftegaz was a latecomer to Yukos. It was joined to the company by a government decree issued in September 1995.

156 The meeting is described in Aleksandr Tutushkin, "Neftianaia kompaniia i bank ne obidiat oblast'," *Kommersant-Daily,* March 28, 1996.

157 Rustam Narzikulov, "Dobyvat' neft' na Priobskom—ne v kukly igrat'," *Nezavisimaia gazeta*, November 12, 1996, p. 4.

158 "Metamorfozy 'krasnogo direktora' Petra Romanova," *Segodnia,* October 29, 1996.

159 Maksim Isaev, "Dobrovol'naia ssylka Mikhaila Khodorkovskogo," *Profil',* no. 19 (May 1997).

160 Mikhail Sidorov, "Estestvennyi otbor," *Profil',* no. 32 (September 2, 2002), http://www .profile.ru/items_7749. As usual, the Russian media reporting on organized crime must be treated with caution. For example, Sidorov writes that several of the traders in Nefteiugansk were connected to the notorious Moscow gang lord Otari Kvantrishvili. But by the time of Khodorkovsky's trip to Nefteiugansk, Kvantrishvili had already been dead for three years.

161 This estimate is based on an average of exchange rates between 1993 and 1996.

162 Briefing by Yukos spokesman A. Krasnov in "Strategicheskim partneram nuzhna stabil'nost'," *Ekonomika i zhizn',* no. 6 (February 10, 1996).

163 *Interfax Petroleum Report,* January 28–February 2, 1996.

164 Cited in ibid., p. 178.

165 Aleksandr Tutushkin, "Zasedanie soveta direktorov 'Yukosa'."

166 Rustam Narzikulov, "Nikuda ia ot Yukosa ne uidu," *Nezavisimaia gazeta,* June 4, 1996; Aleksandr Tutushkin, "Neftianaia kompaniia ugodila v trast," *Kommersant-Daily,* June 5, 1996. In an interview in April 1996, Khodorkovsky estimated that Yukos represented 70 percent of Rosprom's total assets at the time. "Mikhail Khodorkovskii: Krupnyi biznes ne mozhet sushchestvovat' vne gosudarstva," *Kommersant-Daily,* April 16, 1996.

167 Interview with Khodorkovsky, "Mikhail Khodorkovskii."

168 Author's interview with Valerii Graifer, June 2, 2009.

169 Rosneft under Aleksandr Putilov and Sergei Bogdanichikov was another exception, but via a very different path, which is discussed in Chapter 8.

4. Worlds in Collision

1 Matthew J. Sagers, "Joint Ventures in the Soviet Energy Sector," *PlanEcon Report* 5, no. 40 (October 6, 1989), pp. 1–11.

2 For background on the origins of the Russian oil industry in the Caucasus and its subsequent evolution in the 1920s, see Daniel Yergin, *The Prize: The Epic Quest for Oil, Money, and Power*, rev. ed. (New York: Free Press, 2008),pp. 220–226; Robert W. Tolf, *The Russian Rockefellers: The Saga of the Nobel Family and the Russian Oil Industry* (Stanford, CA: Hoover Institution Press, 1976); Anthony C. Sutton, *Western Technology and Soviet Economic Development, 1917 to 1930* (Stanford, CA: Hoover Institution Press, 1968); and Marshall I. Goldman, *The Enigma of Soviet Petroleum: Half-Full or Half-Empty?* (London: Allen & Unwin, 1980).

3 A chronology of Shashin's travels appears in M. N. Gaikazov's recent biography *Valentin Dmitrievich Shashin: Blistatel'nyi strateg neftianoi promyshlennosti* (Moscow: Izdatel'stvo 'Neft' i gaz' RGU nefti i gaza im. I. M. Gubkina, 2006), pp. 384–386.

4 I am grateful to George Helland for background information on this period. George Helland played a key role in leading several international service companies into Russia and served as Deputy Assistant Secretary of Energy for International Affairs at the time of the Soviet breakup.

5 The Soviet media were not at all reticent about covering these problems, and Soviet oil officials themselves appeared frequently in print with denunciations of the poor quality of oilfield equipment, much of which was produced in Azerbaijan. See Thane Gustafson, *Crisis amid Plenty: The Politics of Soviet Energy under Brezhnev and Gorbachev* (Princeton, NJ: Princeton University Press, 1989), chapter 6.

6 Soviet imports of Western oilfield equipment generally ran under 100 million rubles per year (then approximately $125 million at official exchange rates) and often much less. Only once, in 1978, did the annual figure top 300 million rubles. *Vneshniaia torgovlia SSSR*, various years, cited in M. V. Slavkina, *Triumf i tragediia: Razvitie neftagazovogo kompleksa SSSR v 1960–80-e gody* (Moscow: "Nauka," 2002), figure 5.23, p. 158. My own analysis of the Soviet foreign-trade figures through 1988 in *Crisis amid Plenty*, pp. 196–202, broadly agrees with that of Slavkina.

7 Thus the USSR in the 1980s regularly imported between 100,000 and 150,000 tool joints, 300,000 to 400,000 blowout preventers, 10,000 to 30,000 tricone bits, and a rapidly growing number of pumping jacks. Most of these items, however, were imported from Romania. For details, see Gustafson, *Crisis amid Plenty*, table 6.9, drawn from USSR Goskomstat, *Vneshniaia torgovlia SSSR*, various years.

8 Soviet upstream oil investment rose steadily throughout the 1970s and 1980s, from 15.7 billion rubles in 1971–1975 to 74.1 billion in 1986–1990. If one assumes that Soviet

oilfield equipment imports from the West ran at roughly 100 million rubles per year, then their share of total oilfield equipment actually fell throughout this period. For Soviet upstream oil investment, see R. W. Campbell, "Recent Trends in the Soviet Upstream Oil Industry (Investment, Drilling, and Well Completions): Soviets Run Faster and Faster Just to Stay in Place," *PlanEcon Soviet Energy Outlook* March 1991, p. 49.

It is difficult to compare official Soviet statistics on imports (denominated in foreign exchange rubles) with statistics on domestic investments (denominated in domestic rubles). In addition to conversion issues, the various categories into which the statistics are grouped do not allow precise comparisons. On the exchange-rate conversion question, see Vladimir G. Treml and Barry L. Kostinsky, *Domestic Value of Soviet Foreign Trade: Exports and Imports in the 1972 Input-Output Table,* Foreign Economic Report No. 20 (Washington, DC: U.S. Department of Commerce, Bureau of the Census, October 1982).

9   Slavkina, *Triumf i tragediia,* p. 155. For background on U.S. oil-control policy and technology transfer to the Soviet Union in the 1970s, see Thane Gustafson, *Selling the Russians the Rope? Soviet Technology Policy and U.S. Export Controls,* R-2649-ARPA (Santa Monica, CA: Rand, 1981).

10 See Franklyn Holzman, *Foreign Trade under Central Planning* (Cambridge, MA: Harvard University Press, 1974), and *The Economics of Soviet Bloc Trade and Finance* (Boulder, CO: Westview Press, 1987).

11 On this point, see Egor T. Gaidar, *Gibel' imperii: Uroki dlia sovremennoi Rossii* (Moscow: "Rossiiskaia politicheskaia entsiklopediia," 2006), translated as *Collapse of an Empire: Lessons for Modern Russia* (Washington, DC: Brookings Institution Press, 2007).

12 The Soviet Union's financial collapse in the second half of the 1980s and the role of oil in it are described in Gaidar, *Gibel' imperii,* passim.

13 Spears and Associates, *Petroleum Equipment and Service Needs of the CIS* (Tulsa, OK: Spears and Associations, April 1992).

14 Ibid., p. 42.

15 Ibid. The comparison is not entirely fair, since the Western rig drilled along a much more controlled well path, which took more time and gathered valuable geological information along the way.

16 This was a general pattern throughout the Soviet science and technology structure: the Russians tended to be strongest at the theoretical end and weaker at the experimental and applied end. As Westerners soon discovered, on the level of broad theory the Russian geologists were among the best in the world.

17 Spears and Associates, *Petroleum Equipment,* p. 37.

18 Ibid., p. 44.

19 Ibid., pp. 67–72.

20 John D. Grace, *Russian Oil Supply: Performance and Prospects,* copublished with the Oxford Institute for Energy Studies (Oxford: Oxford University Press, 2005), pp. 36–41,

and especially table 1, p. 38. A giant oilfield is defined in the international industry as one with initial reserves of 70 million tons (500 million barrels) or more. Most of the West Siberian giants had been discovered by the end of the 1970s; only thirteen more were discovered in the 1980s. I am indebted to Dr. John Webb, research director of IHS CERA in Moscow, for this information.

21 Joseph A. Pratt, *Prelude to Merger: A History of Amoco Corporation, 1973–1998* (Houston, TX: Hart Publications, 2000), p. 175.

22 In contrast, those who had been in the outer orbits of the Soviet oil world, or not part of it altogether, had less pride to swallow and saw more opportunities in the foreigners' presence. Thus the geological ekspeditsii such as Arkhangel'skgeoldobycha, breakaway NGDUs such as Chernogorneft, the okrugs who rebelled against their former parent oblasti (such as the Nenets okrug in Timan-Pechora or the two "rebel" okrugi of Tiumen Oblast'), were all more favorably disposed to the presence and activities of the foreigners. Similarly, the handful of local startup oil companies, such as Magma and Sinco, which were connected to Iurii Shafranik and the oblast government of Tiumen or to the oblast' government of Arkhangel'sk, were likewise inclined to welcome foreign companies.

23 Sagers, "Joint Ventures in the Soviet Energy Sector."

24 Matthew J. Sagers and Jennifer Nicoud, "Russia's Upstream Oil Industry: Derailed but Not Dead Yet." *PlanEcon Energy Outlook* (June 1996), pp. 89–90.

25 Source: Russian Ministry of Energy and Russian Committee on Statistics (Goskomstat). To be precise, these were the volumes that were officially "credited" to the joint ventures. As is explained below, most joint ventures worked "brownfields," that is, mature fields that had already been developed in Soviet times. They were credited with any increase that resulted from their efforts.

26 A Russian overview of the status of the various types of joint ventures in existence in the mid-1990s is Nikita Dvorets and Aleksey Kocheshkov, "Sovmestnye predpriiatiia v neftedobyche: Chto god griadushchii im gotovit," *Neft' i Kapital*, no. 1 (1996), pp. 10–12.

27 By 1992, 45 percent of the oil credited to joint ventures was produced through hydraulic fracturing, compared with 30 percent by a variety of rehabilitation techniques. International Energy Agency, *Energy Policies of the Russian Federation: 1995 Survey* (Paris: International Energy Agency, 1995), p. 120, fn. 28. The technique is explained in the next chapter.

28 Vadim Kravets, "'Frakmaster v Rossii—vser'ez i nadolgo," *Neft' i Kapital*, no. 6 (1997), pp. 92–93.

29 See Allen L. Hammond, "Bright Spot: Better Seismological Indicators of Gas and Oil," *Science* 185 (August 9, 1974), pp. 515–517.

30 "Benton Oil and Gas Company," *International Directory of Company Histories,* http://www.encyclopedia.com/doc/1G2-2845100019.html.

31 For an account of the origins and development of Geoilbent, see Sergei Verezemskii, "Vtoroe dykhanie 'Geoilbenta'," *Neft' i Kapital,* no. 4 (1999), pp. 32–35.

32 On Levinzon's remarkable career see Natal'ia Grib, "Iosif Levinzon vernulsia k Leonidu Mikhel'sonu v sostav NOVATEKa," *Kommersant,* December 12, 2009. Levinzon was general director of Purneftegazgeologiia from 1987 to 1996.

33 A conventional drill column is rotated by a drive located at the top of the rig; thus the entire column rotates and the drill bit itself turns passively. A turbodrill, in contrast, has its own motor located next to the drill bit at the bottom of the column; thus the drill rotates at high speed but the drill column does not. The advantage of this arrangement is that it does not require high-quality steels for the drill pipe and tool joints. This was an important adaptation, since high-quality steels were reserved for the military sector. The drawback of the rotary drill, however, was that it is difficult to control, and Russian wellbores were notoriously nomadic. As one Russian oilman once told me with a smile, "We invented horizontal drilling long before the West did—all our wells were more or less horizontal."

34 The Russian Federation's Law on Foreign Investment, passed in July 1991, at a time when the Russian government under Boris Yeltsin was seeking to weaken the parent Soviet government under Mikhail Gorbachev by denying it tax revenues, imposed only two taxes on joint ventures: an income tax of less than 1 percent and a profits tax of 25 percent. Matthew J. Sagers and Jennifer Nicoud, "Joint Ventures and Foreign Investment in Russia's Upstream Oil Industry: Derailed but Not Dead Yet." *PlanEcon Energy Outlook* (June 1996), p. 83. The same law (Article 25) granted joint ventures the right to export 100 percent of their crude production without restriction (ibid., p. 76).

35 For detailed numbers on the reported production and exports of the joint ventures in 1992–1995, see ibid., pp. 110–113.

36 Ibid., p. 93.

37 Tamara Trunilina is today a senior officer of Rosneft.

38 For a detailed account of the changing rules of the game on export quotas and the multiplication of taxes between 1993 and 1995, see Sagers and Nicoud, "Joint Ventures and Foreign Investment," pp. 77–79.

39 Ibid., pp. 98–100.

40 Ibid., p. 74. Dvorets and Kocheshkov, in "Sovmestnye predpriiatiia v neftedobyche," using data from the Ministry of Fuel and Power, put the average at between $40 and $50 million, that is, not essentially different from the estimate by Sagers and Nicoud.

41 Sagers and Nicoud, "Joint Ventures and Foreign Investment," p. 73.

42 Staff Appraisal Report, Second Oil Rehabilitation Project, June 13, 1994.

43 In researching the role of the World Bank and other international financial institutions in financial upstream oil investment in Russia in the first half of the 1990s, I have benefited from the excellent doctoral thesis of Andrew B. Seck, "Financing Upstream Oil and Gas Ventures in the Transitional Economies of the Former Soviet Union: A Study of Foreign Investment and Associated Risks" (PhD thesis, Centre for Energy, Petroleum, and Mineral Law and Policy, University of Dundee, Scotland, August 1997).

44 There has been a vigorous debate, much of it conducted inside the World Bank itself, over whether the oil rehabilitation loans were successful in promoting the bank's larger objective of creating an investment environment that would support efficient growth and attract international capital. A review in 2002 by the bank's Operations Evaluation Department (OED) concluded, "In the first half of the 1990s, under pressure from shareholders, the Bank approved many technical assistance and investment projects that were overly ambitious, far from ready for implementation, and in sectors with a weak commitment to reform" (p. 30). "The two completed oil rehabilitation projects contributed to significant increases in production and modest improvement in the taxation of the sector. However, the outcome of both projects was rated unsatisfactory by the Region and OED because of failure to make sufficient progress on policy and institutional reform objectives" (p. 27). *Russian Federation Country Assistance Evaluation,* Report No. 24875, September 23, 2002. The bank's management, in its response to the OED's evaluation, vigorously defended its record: "The two oil rehabilitation loans failed to introduce needed institutional reforms, but they did improve productivity and finance essential rehabilitation which allowed production to be maintained. Technical assistance alone to the oil sector likely would have produced neither institutional reforms nor improved productivity" (p. 61).

45 Olga Vinogradova, "Desiat' let spustia: inostrannye kompanii v Rossii," *Neftegazovaia Vertikal',* no. 7 (2002), pp.9–22.

46 They were also, in their day, one of the most important channels of foreign direct investment, not only for the oil industry, but for the entire Russian economy. According to an estimate by Vladimir Solomin, then head of the oil and gas department of the Ministry of Fuel and Power (Mintopenergo), joint ventures in the oil industry accounted for nearly one-quarter of the foreign direct investment in the Russian economy as a whole between 1992 and 1998. See Vladimir Solomin, "Sovmestnye predpriiatiia eshche nuzhny rossiiskoi 'neftianke'," *Neft' i Kapital,* no. 4 (1999), pp. 29–32.

47 A Russian summary of the technological innovations brought by the joint ventures included, in addition to hydraulic fracturing, enhanced-recovery techniques using polymer injection (Tatolpetro—a joint venture of Tatneft and Total); more powerful well perforations (Chernogorskoe—a joint venture of Anderman Smith and Chernogorneft'); steam injection (Nobeloil); and acid treatment (Yuganskfracmasters)—all conventional applications in the West at that time. See Sergei Khrulev, "Sovmestnye predpriiatiia kak polygon dlia novoi tekhniki," *Neft' i Kapital,* no. 6 (1997), pp. 90–91.

48 Several of the major international companies also experimented with joint ventures, mainly as a means of forming relationships and learning the terrain, but even these ended up looking much like the other joint ventures, and for the same reason—the economics were perceived as too risky to justify major spending. (BP and Statoil, for example, joined Purneftegaz in a joint venture at a West Siberian field called Tarasov, but it was a typical rehabilitation project.)

49 Quoted in Richard W. Stevenson, "Oil Companies Tread Warily into Russia's Decrepit Fields," *New York Times,* November 26, 1993, p. D17.

50 In parallel, they were also looking at the Caspian Basin, beginning with Tengiz in the Kazakh Soviet Socialist Republic. See Steve Levine, *The Oil and the Glory: The Pursuit of Empire and Fortune on the Caspian Sea* (New York: Random House, 2007).

51 Thus while the first two PSAs (Khariaga and Sakhalin Energy) began producing commercially in 1999, their first big buildup occurred in 2000. The third PSA, Sakhalin-1, had its first significant production in 2006. In contrast, joint ventures of various types produced over 4 million tons (80,000 barrels per day) as early as 1992. Source: *Infotek*, January issues, various years.

52 The impact on the oil industry of the difficult low-price environment of the 1980s, particularly in the United States, is described in Yergin, *The Prize*, chapters 35 and 36.

53 Autobiography of John Browne, *Beyond Business: An Inspirational Memoir from a Visionary Leader* (London: Orion Books, 2010). Browne related that he initially turned to a local consultant in Anchorage, Millett Keller, who had started up a small computer services company to create statements for the local bank.

54 This trend began in the 1980s and continued steadily throughout the 1990s and into the 2000s. According to a study by Judson Jacobs of IHS Cambridge Energy Research Associates, spending on upstream R&D by exploration and production companies in the United States declined from a peak of $1.6 billion in 1982 to just over $0.4 billion in 2003, while that of oilfield equipment and service companies increased steadily, from under $0.8 billion in the early 1990s to $1.9 billion in 2007. During that period, six R&D centers maintained by U.S. majors were closed.

55 Pratt, *Prelude to Merger*, pp. 97–99 and 110.

56 Ibid., p. 170.

57 Ibid., p. 171.

58 Yet characteristically, Exxon's entry into Russia was not led personally by the CEO (Lee Raymond in 1993 and after) but initiated by lieutenants such as Sid Reso, a senior vice president of the former Exxon Company International, who made the first contacts concerning joining the Sodeco consortium, and Robert Olsen, now executive vice president of ExxonMobil Production Company, who was the principal contact with Sakhalinmorneftegaz general director Sergei Bogdanchikov in the negotiations that led to the Sakhalin-1 PSA. See the official history of Sakhalin-1 produced by Exxon Neftegaz Limited, *Sakhalin 1: A New Frontier* (PennWell Custom Publishing, 2008).

59 Author's interview, August 5, 2009.

60 For an analysis of the Soviet Arctic exploration program, see Helge Ole Bergesen, Arild Moe, and Willy Ostreng, *Soviet Oil and Security Interests in the Barents Sea* (New York: St. Martin's Press, 1987). The early history of Sodeco and the beginnings of Russian-Japanese collaboration at Sakhalin are described in Peter Egyed, "Western Participation in the Development of Siberian Energy Resources: Case Studies," Carleton University (Ottawa, Canada), Institute of Soviet and East European Studies, East-West Commercial Relations Series, report no. 22 (December 1983). The Soviet offshore program,

contrasting the Caspian and Arctic programs, is discussed in Gustafson, *Crisis amid Plenty,* pp. 212–218.

61 In the large literature on the state of Russia's regions in the depressed 1990s, one little gem stands out, a remarkable portrait from an unusual perspective: Fen Montaigne, *Reeling in Russia: An American Angler in Russia* (New York: St. Martin's Griffin, 1999). The title is a rare example of a perfect triple pun.

62 The leading example was the giant Vankor field, which although located in the Taimyr okrug of Krasnoiarsk Krai is geologically part of the West Siberian basin. It initially appeared that the most cost-effective route for the evacuation of oil from Vankor was via the Arctic Ocean at a coastal location called Dikson. Several foreign companies, notably Shell, studied this route.

63 Exxon Neftegas Limited, *Sakhalin 1.*

64 For an excellent account of the efforts—all ultimately unsuccessful—by Shell and Gazprom between 1995 and 2005 to create a strategic alliance, and subsequently to arrange a share swap of two key gas assets, see Rawi Abdelal, *Journey to Sakhalin: Royal Dutch Shell in Russia.* Harvard Business School Case Study (Cambridge, MA: Harvard Business School, Part A, June 2, 2006; Part B, February 6, 2007; Part C, February 8, 2007). I am grateful to Professor Abdelal for sharing this case study with me.

65 In rare instances a foreigner might be caught in the line of fire. But the number of foreign businessmen actually killed in business disputes in the 1990s could be counted on the fingers of one hand. Groznyi, the capital of Chechnya, was to be sure an exception, but the local oil industry, though important in the 1930s and 1940s, was by the 1990s of little interest to foreigners.

66 *Biulleten' SD,* no. 98, 1997, p. 22, quoted in Paul Chaisty, *Legislative Politics and Economic Power in Russia* (Basingstoke, UK: Palgrave, 2006), p. 188.

67 Chaisty, *Legislative Politics,* p. 177.

68 The government was concerned with avoiding the scandals of the previous round of auctions and at the same time with ensuring that the government received actual cash in exchange for its stake. Allowing foreign bidders to participate was intended to serve both purposes. For a Russian commentary, see Sergei Savushkin, "Privatizatory priotkryvaiut 'zheleznyi zanaves'," *Neft' i Kapital,* no. 10 (1997), pp. 5–6.

69 Russian oil production hit bottom in 1996 at 301.2 million tons (6.0 million barrels per day) and increased slightly to 305.6 million (6.1 million barrels per day) in 1997. Source: InfoTEK ezhemesiachnyi neftegazovyi zhurnal (Moscow: "Izdatel'skii dom InfoTEK," 1996, 1997).

70 Platts Urals CIF Mediterranean First Month Daily.

71 Russian State Statistical Committee (Goskomstat), *Rossiiskii statisticheskii ezhegodnik* (Moscow: "Goskomstat," various years).

5. The Russian "Oil Miracle"

1   By the summer of 2000, a staff report of the IMF concluded, "Real GDP has more than recovered from the recession that followed the 1998 crisis." International Monetary Fund, "Russian Federation: Staff Report," IMF Staff Country Report No. 00/145 (Washington, DC: International Monetary Fund, November 2000).

2   The recovery of the Russian economy after 2000 can be conveniently tracked, year by year, through the semiannual reports of the Moscow office of the World Bank. See *Russian Economic Report,* various issues beginning in October 2001, available at http://siteresources.worldbank.org/INTRUSSIANFEDERATION/Resources/305499 -1094736798511/518266-1097661221042/rer1_102401_eng.pdf.

3   This is true of natural gas, too, but the export prices of natural gas are tied to a "reference basket" of energy prices, most of which consist of oil and oil products. Therefore, the export prices of natural gas follow the movements of oil, although with a lag of about nine months.

4   John D. Grace, in his admirable book on the Russian oil industry, has done a careful reconstruction of the economics of the Russian oil industry from 1983 through 2002 and concludes that the industry lost money every year between 1985 and 1999. John D. Grace, *Russian Oil Supply: Performance and Prospects,* copublished by the Oxford Institute for Energy Studies (Oxford: Oxford University Press, 2005), appendix, pp. 89–99. There is no doubt that in a broad sense the energy sector subsidized the rest of the economy, but one may question whether the new owners, or even the corporate headquarters, actually lost money in cash-flow terms. There were many ways of not paying receivables and taxes in those years, and the companies received export income not only from crude oil but also from refined products (which Grace does not include in his reckoning). As Clifford Gaddy and Barry Ickes point out in their insightful essay on the "virtual economy" of 1992–1998, in the noncash economy of those years, anyone with cash was making money, and the owners of the oil holding companies definitely had cash. See Clifford G. Gaddy and Barry W. Ickes, "Russia's Virtual Economy," *Foreign Affairs* 77, no. 5 (September/October 1998), pp. 53–67. The argument was further developed in the authors' subsequent book, *Russia's Virtual Economy,* Brookings Institution Press, 2002.

5   Ministerstvo promyshlennosti i energetiki, *Toplivo i energetika Rossii* (Moscow: Energiia, 2005 and 2007). Upstream investment dropped from 16.9 billion rubles in 1991 (about $9.9 billion at the average annual exchange rate of that year) to 29.54 billion rubles in 1998 (about $3.0 billion at the average annual exchange rate of that year). Over the next six years through 2004, investment in upstream oil production recovered to 264.8 billion rubles (or $9.2 billion at the average annual exchange rate of that year).

6   From 1998 through 2004, world oil production increased from 3.55 billion to 3.87 billion tons (73.59 million to 80.26 million barrels per day [mbd]), a growth of 321.9 million tons (6.67 mbd). Russian oil production grew over the same period from 304.3

million tons (6.17 mbd) to 458.7 million tons (9.29 mbd), an increase of 154.4 million tons (3.11 mbd). Thus Russia accounted for 47 percent of the net growth of world oil production during this period. Source: BP, *Statistical Review of World Energy 2005*, http://www.bp.com/ genericsection.do?categoryId=92&contentId=7005893.

7   These numbers include both crude oil and refined products and are limited to exports outside the former Soviet Union. Sources: Russian Energy Ministry (Ministerstvo energetiki), www.minenergo.gov.ru, and Russian Statistical Service (Goskomstat), www.gks.ru.

8   Russian Statistical Committee (Goskomstat), *Rossiiskii Statisticheskii Ezhegodnik v 2005g.* (Moscow: "Statistika," 2006).

9   Source: International Monetary Fund.

10 Money power and coercive power clearly reinforced one another, as Putin rebuilt the power of the central coercive apparatus. For a description of the ways in which this was achieved, see Nikolai Petrov, "The Security Dimension of the Federal Reforms," in Peter Reddaway and Robert W. Orttung, eds., *The Dynamics of Russian Politics: Putin's Reform of Federal-Regional Relations,* 2 vols. (Lanham, MD: Rowman and Littlefield, 2005), 2:7–32.

11 Grace, *Russian Oil Supply,* p. 85.

12 IHS, *World Petroleum Trends—1994 to 2003* (Denver, CO: IHS, October 2004).

13 Some idea can be had by comparing Russian numbers for reserves in production or under development (i.e., so-called A and B reserves) against proven reserves not under development (so-called C1 reserves). At the end of the 1990s, total Russian C1 reserves were about 12 billion tons (87.6 billion barrels), compared with A + B reserves of nearly 4.5 billion tons (32.9 billion barrels)—in other words, almost triple. Most of that overhang consisted of fields already licensed to the Russian companies. This measure is not the same thing as discovered but undeveloped fields, since the C1 category includes the remaining undeveloped reserves of fields already in production or under development. Nevertheless, it gives a general idea of the dimensions of the overhang. Source: Russian Ministry of Natural Resources.

14 The four large fields are Priobskoe (Yukos), Tianskoe (Surgutneftegaz), Sugmut, and Sporyshev (both Sibneft). A fifth large field, Tevlinsko-Russkinskoe (LUKoil) has not been included since it began development in Soviet times and grew only slightly during the period 1999–2004. Data on annual production from these fields comes from the IHS EDIN (Energy Data Information Navigator) database. See also Grace, *Russian Oil Supply,* p. 83.

15 Data on new well development and production can be found in the annual year-end reports of the Ministry of Industry and Energy, *TEK Rossii: Itogi proizvodstvennoi deiatel'nosti otraslei.* The numbers for 1999–2004 come from the 2005 edition (Moscow: RIA TEK, 2005), p. 14.

16 IHS EDIN database.

17 Ibid. See also the valuable profile of the production history of Samotlor in Grace, *Russian Oil Supply,* pp. 47–49. An account of the politics of production policy at Sa-

motlor will be found in Thane Gustafson, *Crisis amid Plenty: The Politics of Soviet Energy under Brezhnev and Gorbachev* (Princeton, NJ: Princeton University Press, 1989), chaps. 3 and 4. For a valuable Soviet-era source, see S. N. Starovoitov, *Problemy razvitiia Zapadno-Sibirskogo neftegazovogo kompleksa* (Novosibirsk: "Nauka," 1983), especially pp. 64 and 65.

18 Oil professionals informally distinguish between brownfields, which are fields already under development, and greenfields, which are prospects awaiting development. Some even speak of bluefields, which are areas considered prospective but as yet unexplored.

19 IHS EDIN database. In 2005 the field produced about 31.2 million tons (624,000 barrels per day) of crude oil and condensate, which has been the post-Soviet peak to date. (In 2010 Samotlor produced about 28.4 million tons [540,000 barrels per day].)

20 For a profile of Ron Bullen, see Gail Gravelines, "The Master of Frac," *University of Alberta Engineer Magazine,* Spring 2007, http://www.uofaengineer.engineering.ualberta .ca/article.cfm?article=61250&issue=61230. The other side of the story is worth noting as well. In the late 1980s the head of the Soviet oil ministry's science and technology department was an outstanding figure named Aleksandr Dzhavadian. Above him was the first deputy minister, an experienced and capable executive named Vladimir Filanovskii-Zenkov, who had previously headed Gosplan's oil and gas department. Both of these men decided to back the Canadian Fracmasters experiment—which was not only proof of the desperation of the industry at that time but also testimony to the fact that there were some Soviet officials who were willing to try something new. Filanovskii-Zenkov, in particular, subsequently became an enthusiastic supporter of hydraulic fracturing. After the fall of the Soviet Union he founded a private company to do fraccing in the Orenburg area. His company subsequently partnered with the Austrian service company CAT to form KatKo, one of the largest players in the Russian frac market today.

21 The Russians credit a distinguished academic geologist from the Gubkin Institute, Iu. P. Zheltov, with the first experiments in hydraulic fracturing in the 1950s and 1960s. See G. K. Maksimovich, *Gidravlicheskii razryv neftianykh plastov* (Moscow, 1957); and Iu. P. Zheltov, *Deformatsii gornykh porod* (Moscow, 1966). Over the course of a long career that extended into the 1990s, Zheltov continued his research and writing on the theory of hydraulic fracturing. With all due respect to Zheltov, however, he was not the first to use hydraulic fracturing to boost the flow of hydrocarbons. The first documented commercial frac job was performed by Stanolind (now part of BP) in 1946 at the Hugoton gas field in Kansas. See Belgacem Chariag, "Maximize Reservoir Contact," *E&P Magazine,* January 2007, pp. 11–12.

22 Quoted in Gravelines, "The Master of Frac."

23 Valentin Gavrin, "Chuzhogo nam ne dano," *Neft' i Kapital,* no. 6 (1996), pp. 55–56.

24 Much of this process of diffusion and adaptation took place spontaneously, as Russians who had learned fraccing techniques in the joint ventures struck out on their own,

combining Russian components with foreign-made ones to create their own fraccing fleets. In contrast, a high-level government-sponsored effort to enlist military-industrial companies to develop a wholly Russian frac truck resulted in a frustrating failure. See Boris Ignat'ev, "Zatianuvsheesia ozhidanie—seriinoe proizvodstvo otechestvennykh kompleksov otkladyvaetsia," *Neft' i Kapital,* no. 6 (1997), pp. 88–89.

25 For a description of the Soviet system of technology espionage and its limited efficiency, see Thane Gustafson, *Selling the Russians the Rope? Soviet Technology Policy and U.S. Exports Controls,* R-2649-ARPA (Santa Monica, CA: Rand, 1981).

26 One veteran Western hydraulic fracturing expert, who participated in the initial joint ventures in West Siberia in the early 1990s, recalls that local oilmen initially resisted the reintroduction of hydraulic fracturing, because they thought it was a repeat of the disastrous Soviet experiments of the 1970s, in which nuclear explosives had been used (in Kazakhstan and in Timan Pechora Province of Northwest Russia) to fracture oil reservoirs. The heat and pressure generated by nuclear explosives, however, only fused the sandstone into glass and prevented any oil from flowing.

27 BP had this experience in the early 1990s at a field called Tarasov, part of a joint venture BP formed with Purneftegaz to gain experience on the ground.

28 Export prices of Russian crude vary widely, depending on the grade of crude and the export location. Export prices for various locations are reported in Russian customs statistics. The Ministry of Energy publishes monthly averages for Urals Mediterranean and Urals Rotterdam in its journal *InfoTEK,* which are used here.

29 Statement by Yukos deputy chairman Viktor Kazakov, quoted in Aleksandr Tutushkin, "YUKOS budet trekhglavym," *Vremia MN,* September 2, 1998. The electronic archive of *Vremia novostei* (http://www.vremya.ru/) only begins in 2000. Earlier issues may be accessed via Eastview Universal Databases (by subscription). Yukos's delivered costs appear to have been much higher than the average for the industry at this time. In August 1998, for example, Sidanco was reporting costs of only $4.90 per barrel, although it is not clear that the definition is the same. Petr Sapozhnikov, "YUKOS uvolit tret' upravlentsev," *Kommersant-Daily,* September 2, 1998.

30 Interview with Yukos deputy chairman Viktor Kazakov, "Pora ukrupniat'sia," *Moskovskie novosti,* December 22, 1998. It is not clear whether these quoted numbers correspond to "lifting costs" or "total operating costs." A typical definition of lifting costs as reported in Russia includes costs of labor, repairs, maintenance, materials, supplies, and fuel consumed during the oil production process, as well as property and severance taxes and insurance costs. A wider definition of upstream operating costs includes the following key components in addition to lifting costs (in the fairly typical case of Rosneft): costs of gathering, treating, processing, and storing crude oil and (associated) gas in the fields and of delivering crude oil and gas to a main pipeline (e.g., a Transneft trunk pipeline transshipment point).

31 *Russkii telegraf,* June 17, 1998. A shareholders' meeting held in June 1998 canceled the company's annual dividend, even though the previous year had been profitable.

32 *Vedomosti*, September 8, 1999. According to Ivan Mazalov of Troika-Dialog, Yukos investment in current rubles was only 4 billion rubles in 1998, compared with 6 billion the previous year. Allowing for inflation of nearly 30 percent that year, the purchasing power of the 1998 rubles was much diminished.

33 Development drilling by Yukos was 987.8 thousand meters in 1997 but dropped to 538.0 thousand the following year.

34 For the fuel industry as a whole (which includes gas and coal as well as oil), unpaid taxes *(nedoimki)* in 1998 reached 48 percent of total taxes paid. By 1999 the crisis had eased: in 1999 the fuel industry's unpaid taxes dropped to 28 percent of its tax payments, and by 2000 to 13 percent. Source: Ministerstvo promyshlennosti i energetiki, *Toplivo i energetika Rossii* (Moscow: Energiia, 2002), p. 26.

35 For a brief account of the way Khodorkovsky handled the impact of the 1998 crash on Menatep Bank, see Andrew Jack, *Inside Putin's Russia: Can There Be Reform without Democracy?* (Oxford: Oxford University Press, 2004), pp. 208–210.

36 Between August 1998 and December of that year, the ruble dropped from 6.8 to the dollar to 20. Source: Central Bank of Russia website, http://www.cbr.ru/currency_base /dynamics.asp.

37 Interview with Kazakov, "Pora ukrupniat'sia."

38 The real effective exchange rate (which corrects for inflation) declined from 13 rubles to the dollar in August 1998 to 8 in December 1998 but did not bottom out until February 1999, at a little over 7. Source: World Bank, *Russian Economic Report*, no. 1 (Washington, DC: World Bank, October 2001), figure 7. In nominal terms, the exchange rate went from 6.3 rubles to the dollar on the eve of the crash to 23.1 in early February 1999, after which the nominal exchange rate settled down to a slow decline that lasted until the end of 2002. Source: Central Bank of Russia, http://www.cbr.ru /currency_base/dynamics.asp.

39 In September 1999, for example, LUKoil's vice president for strategic planning, Leonid Fedun, assured the press that oil prices were certain to drop again the following year. *Vedomosti*, September 10, 1999. To be sure, the oil companies' public pronouncements on oil prices must be taken with caution, since they were part of the bargaining with the government over setting the export tax rate.

40 Yukos was not the only oil company trying to cut costs. The others did so with varying degrees of aggressiveness. By and large, the neftianik companies (LUKoil and Surgutneftegaz) limited layoffs and maintained their tax payments to the West Siberian municipalities. In contrast, in Noiabrsk, the "home" city of Sibneft, the oil company's share of the city's budget plummeted from 70 percent in 1996 to 28 percent in 1998, although this was partly offset by an increase in Gazprom's contribution. See Vladimir Shmyganovskii, " 'Sibirskim emiratam' predstoit bor'ba za vyzhivaniem," *Izvestiia*, March 20, 1998.

41 Interview with Yukos deputy chairman Viktor Kazakov, "Bol'shoi i krepkoi 'YUKSI' poka ne poluchilos'," *Russkii telegraf*, May 22, 1998.

42 Soviet planners had never intended to build permanent cities in the far north of East Siberia. Their idea was to fly in *vakhtoviki*—temporary workers on rotation. But the

workers flew in—and stayed. Willy-nilly, the oil industry had to provide for them, and by the end of the Soviet era the private oil companies had inherited whole cities, complete with housing, bus lines, water mains, clinics, and day care centers. See Gustafson, *Crisis amid Plenty,* pp. 174–176.

43 Katy Daigle, "Yukos Chief Faces Workers' Wrath," *Moscow Times,* May 30, 1998.

44 Aleksei Makarin, "Kto raspravilsia s merom Nefteiuganska?," *Komsomol'skaia pravda,* June 30, 1998.

45 Daigle, "Yukos Chief Faces Workers' Wrath."

46 Ibid.

47 As we shall see in Chapter 7, the Petukhov affair resurfaced in 2004–2005, when murder charges were brought against Yukos's former chief of security, Aleksei Pichugin.

48 Oleg Chernitskii, " 'YUKOS izbavliaetsia ot ubytochnykh predpriiatii," *Russkii telegraf,* August 25, 1998.

49 In Tomsk Province, for example, the implementation of the scheme was blocked by the province government. As one source within the province government said, "We have serious doubts that the operators will be profitable even after all local taxes have been lifted; and in that event the responsibility for laying off workers will fall on us, and not on Yukos." Yet despite this, Yukos managed to negotiate an amicable settlement of its tax debts with the Tomsk government and halt a bankruptcy proceeding against the company. Oleg Chernitskii, " 'Tomskneft' ostanetsia za 'YUKOSom'," *Russkii telegraf,* September 11, 1998.

50 The journalist Valerii Paniushkin, in his sympathetic biography of Khodorkosvky, gives a vivid description of the atmosphere during and after the crash of 1998, which he sees as the critical turning point for Khodorkovsky and Yukos. *Mikhail Khodorkosvkii: Uznik tishiny* (Moscow: "Sekret Firmy," 2006), p. 108.

51 Author's interview, March 22, 2006.

52 Interview with Don Wolcott, then Yukos vice president, May 14, 2004.

53 Inna Ermishina, "Nadezhdy na deval'vatsiiu ne opravdalis'," *Neft' i Kapital,* no. 11 (1998), pp. 22–23; Vadim Kravets, "Akh, 'Samaraneftegaz,' bespokoinaia ia," *Neft' i Kapital,* no. 11 (1998), pp. 28–30.

54 Thane Gustafson, *Capitalism Russian-Style* (Cambridge: Cambridge University Press, 1999), chapter 9.

55 Dowell had been a 50–50 joint venture between Schlumberger and Dow Chemical. In 1993 Schlumberger bought out Dow Chemical's share and Dowell became a division of Schlumberger.

56 "Putting Yukos on top of Russia's oil tree," *Upstream,* January 3, 2003.

57 Nodal analysis was the joint creation of Tenneco and Johnson Testers, working as a team in the mid-1970s. The principal originator was Kermit Brown at the University of Tulsa, where Mach had been a student. Among the early leaders were Lisa Stewart (now CEO of El Paso) and Carl Joseph Granger. At Tenneco nodal analysis was first programmed for computers. Mach's role was key in developing nodal analysis as a com-

mercial product for Dowell. Johnson Testers, by that time, had been absorbed into Dowell, and from there passed into Schlumberger.

58 The basics of nodal analysis are explained in Steve Bartz, Joe M. Mach, et al., "Let's Get the Most out of Existing Wells," *Oilfield Review,* Winter 1997, pp. 1–21. For a more technical discussion of the principles involved, see M. J. Economides, A. D. Hill, and C. Ehlig-Economides, *Petroleum Production Systems* (Englewood Cliffs, NJ: Prentice Hall, 1997).

59 DESC stands for Design and Evaluation Services for Clients.

60 For a description of the DESC approach in operation, which recognizes its sensitive "cross-cultural" implications, see "The DESC Engineer Redefines Work," *Oilfield Review,* Summer 1995, pp. 40–50.

61 F. M. Eaton and G. J. Decker, "Digital Transmission of Well Logs by Radio and Telephone," *Journal of Petroleum Technology* 18 (February 1966), pp. 151–154.

62 Interview with Joe Mach, Moscow, March 17, 2004.

63 For the basics on ESPs, see Kate Van Dyke, *A Primer of Oilwell Service, Workover, and Completion* (Austin: Petroleum Extension Service, University of Texas at Austin, 1997), pp. 40–41.

64 V. A. Dinkov, *Neft' SSSR 1917–1987* (Moscow: "Nedra," 1987), p. 159.

65 According to a Western report, at the beginning of the 1990s there were 80,450 ESPs installed worldwide, of which 52,350 were located in the Soviet Union, compared with only 11,600 in the United States. Source: Spears and Associates, *Petroleum Equipment and Service Needs of the CIS* (Tulsa, OK: Spears and Associates, April 1992), p. 57.

66 *Tekhicheskii progress v neftianoi promyshlennosti v desiatoi piatiletke* (Moscow: "Nedra," 1981), p. 106.

67 Dinkov, *Neft' SSSR 1917–1987,* p. 158.

68 Interview with Mikhail Khodorkovsky, "Mikhail Khodorkovskii: Milliardy lezhat pod nogami," *Moskovskii komsomolets,* July 24, 2002, p. 3.

69 By the beginning of 2005 there were approximately 50,000 ESPs operating in Russia alone. The process of upgrading and replacing Soviet-era ESPs generated a thriving market, which has remained strong over the years. This is a market that has long been dominated by Russian producers, who typically hold between 85 and 90 percent of the total market. For a report, see the website of the Russian Association of Oil and Gas Equipment Producers, http://www.derrick.ru/index.php?f=n&id=8329& page=0.

70 Interview with Joe Mach.

71 Ibid.

72 "U neftianikov khotiat otniat' dobychu," *Neft' i Kapital,* no. 3 (2002), pp. 68–71.

73 Author's interview, May 20, 2006.

74 James A. Lewis, *History of Petroleum Engineering* (New York: American Petroleum Institute, 1961), pp. 849–873.

75 "Chronicle—60 Years of Tatarstan Oil," http://www.tatneft.ru/eng/history.htm. There had been earlier experiments with waterflooding in the 1950s, notably at the Tuimazinskoe field.

76 Official Russian statistics appear to confirm this story, at least for Yuganskneftegaz. According to the yearly handbook of the Ministry of Industry and Energy, the average producer at Yuganskneftegaz was available 91 percent of the time in 1998 but declined steadily to only 83 percent by 2003. Source: Ministerstvo promyshlennosti i energetiki, *Toplivo i energetika Rossii* (2005), pp. 248–249.

77 Mach's numbers on shutdowns are cited in Iurii Beilin and Joe Mach, "Russia's Desolate Oil Future," *Energy Tribune,* February 2006, p. 6.

78 No laws were actually broken. There were creative ways, especially in those days, of avoiding outright illegality, as described in Chapter 10.

79 Two classic statements on these themes are Ed A. Hewett, *Reforming the Soviet Economy: Equality versus Efficiency* (Washington, DC: Brookings Institution, 1988), chapter 4; and Alena V. Ledeneva, *Russia's Economy of Favors: Blat, Networking, and Informal Exchange* (Cambridge: Cambridge University Press, 1998).

80 SCADA is just one of many digital techniques increasingly available to oil companies. For a survey see IHS Cambridge Energy Research Associates, *Digital Oil Field of the Future: Lessons from Other Industries* (Cambridge, MA: IHS Cambridge Energy Research Associates, 2004) and *Lessons of the DOFF: A Global Assessment of Potential Oil Recovery Increases* (Cambridge, MA: IHS Cambridge Energy Research Associates 2005). (DOFF stands for Digital Oilfield of the Future.)

81 Interview with Joe Mach.

82 "Joe Mach Shares the Secrets of Yukos's Success," *Yukos Review,* January–February–March 2003, pp. 16–23.

83 Interview with Mikhail Khodorkovsky, "Milliardy lezhat pod nogami," *Moskovskii komsomolets,* July 24, 2002, p. 3. On the art of the four-letter word in male Russian culture, see the essay by Viktor Erofeev, "The Unique Power of Russia's Underground Language," *The New Yorker,* September 13, 2003, pp. 42–48.

84 Author's interview, May 22, 2006.

85 These could not be converted and sold for five years, however, so that many senior executives ended up taking heavy losses when Yukos stock started falling in 2003, and most of the stock options ended up being worthless.

86 Yukos presentation at CERA Week (annual energy conference of IHS Cambridge Energy Research Associates), Houston, February 2001.

87 In 1997, Yukos's average flow rate was 8.0 tons per day (58.4 barrels); by 2002 it had increased to 15.9 tons per day (116.1 barrels). For the industry as a whole, it increased from 7.3 tons per day (53.3 barrels) in 1997 to 8.3 tons per day (60.6 barrels) in 2002. More detailed statistics on flow rates can be found in the annual statistical publication of the Ministerstvo promyshlennosti i energetiki, *Toplivo i energetika Rossii*. However, those numbers are not directly comparable, since they report company well flows by ob"edinenie, not by company. It is apparent from those numbers, however,

that most of Yukos's increase took place at Yugneftegaz and not at Samaraneftegaz or Tomskneftegaz.

88 Ministerstvo promyshlennosti i energetiki, *Toplivo i energetika Rossii,* various years.

89 Ibid. The industry average, of course, includes Yukos, which biases the average upward.

90 Source: "YukosSibneft: Greater Opportunities to Build Value," Yukos presentation at
Lehman Brothers Energy/Power Conference, New York, September 2, 2003.

91 Ibid.

92 By February 2003 the capitalization of Yukos had reached nearly $33 billion.

93 For a candid Russian assessment of the controversy, and of the different approaches
of the more "traditional" Russian companies—on the whole favorable to Yukos and
Sibneft—see "Ratsional'noe, effektivnoe, i prochie filosovskie kategorii neftedobychi v
Rossii," *Neft' i Kapital,* no. 4 (2002), pp. 47–51.

94 Sibneft's core division, Noiabrskneftegaz, rested on four older fields that had been producing since the 1980s (Vyngapur, Sutormin, Vyngayakhin, and Muravlenko). These
fields had considerable remaining potential, as evidenced by the follow-on production
strategy that the Andrei Matevosov-Iskander Diyashev team put in place in 2003 following the peak of production at Sugmut and Sporyshev.

95 The best brief account in English of the maneuvering by Berezovsky and Abramovich
to create Sibneft, based on extensive interviews with many of the actual participants, is
Paul Klebnikov, *Godfather of the Kremlin: The Decline of Russia in the Age of Gangster
Capitalism* (New York: Harcourt, 2000), pp. 194–197, 205–208. According to Klebnikov,
Berezovsky secured Chernomyrdin's support by promising to coordinate the financing
of the "Our Home Is Russia" party's campaign in the 1995 legislative elections and to
provide favorable coverage on Berezovsky's ORT television channel.

96 Aleksandr Korsik, Shvidler's executive vice president for production, was 42 in 1998;
Andrei Matevosov, vice president for upstream production, was 36; Mikhail Stavskii,
general director of Noiabrskneftagaz, was 37.

97 Shvidler himself had spent six years in New York, studying for a master's in business
administration at Fordham University, then working at Deloitte and Touche's offices in
New York, specializing in international tax matters. His CFO, Tatyana Breeva, was also
a veteran of Deloitte and Touche, although from its Moscow office. Korsik, although he
had an engineering degree from Bauman, had graduated from the Diplomatic Academy
and had begun a diplomatic career at the time he switched to the oil industry in 1995.

98 *Ekonomicheskie novosti,* December 11, 1998. The four fields were Muravlenko, Sutormin, Vyngapur, and Vyngaiakhin.

99 *Ekonomicheskie novosti,* October 19, 1999.

100 Interview with Iskander Diyashev, January 8, 2006. According to the Gazpromneft
website, the first horizontal well at Romanov field, in January 2001, flowed at 1,550 barrels per day. See http://www.gazprom-neft.com/press-center/news/3635/.

101 Dick Ghiselin, "Technology and Brotherhood at the New Frontier," *Hart's E&P,* November 2003, http://www.epmag.com/EP-Magazine/archive/Technology-brotherhood
-the-frontier_2698. See also http://www.gazprom-neft.com/press-center/news/3530/.

102 Between Abramovich and Diyashev were Evgenii Shvidler (CEO), Aleksandr Korsik (executive vice president), and Andrei Matevosov (vice president for upstream production). The chain of command from headquarters to field production ran from Matevosov to Stavskii. Diyashev, as chief engineer, reported to Matevosov, with whom he worked closely. It would probably be more accurate to think of Matevosov and Diyashev jointly as the catalysts of Sibneft's upstream growth.

103 See the brief portrait of Surgutneftegaz's performance in Grace, *Russian Oil Supply,* pp. 134–138. A longer analysis of Surgut's operations and use of technology in the first half of the 2000s is Ronald Smith's excellent and detailed report, *Surgutneftegaz: Drilling Power* (Moscow: Renaissance Capital, 2005). Surgutneftegaz today remains one of the technological leaders of the Russian industry. By 2010, 60 percent of Surgutneftegaz's oil was produced by so-called advanced methods, compared to 24 percent for LUKoil and only 16 percent for Rosneft. ("Advanced methods" is a Russian catch-all term that includes most categories of well stimulation and enhanced recovery, as well as horizontal drilling and sidetracking, but not waterflooding.) "KINa ne budet?," *Neftegazovaia vertikal',* no. 2 (2012), pp. 60–63.

104 Paul Collison, "Russian Oils: Standing Out from the Crowd," *Russia Equity Research Report,* April 29, 2002, p. 8.

105 *Interfax Petroleum Report* 11, no. 14 (April 5–11, 2002), p. 9.

106 *Interfax Petroleum Report* 11, no. 15 (April 12–18, 2002), p. 12.

107 *Interfax Petroleum Report* 11, no. 17 (April 26–May 2, 2002), pp. 9–10.

108 *Interfax Petroleum Report* 11, no. 12 (March 22–28, 2002), p. 22.

109 Quoted in Oleg Chernitskii, "LUKoil pokaialsia. On budet prodavat', sokrashchat', uvol'niat' i bol'she zarabatyvat'," *Vremia novostei,* April 23, 2002, p. 7. Note the interesting turns of phrase, which suggests that Fedun, the former intelligence officer turned financial expert, was identifying himself with the oilmen rather than the oligarchs.

110 Overall LUKoil production increased by about only 2 percent in 2002 (due largely to the Komi acquisition); it then declined in 2003. LUKoil–West Siberia output went from about 45.1 million tons (902,000 barrels per day) in 2001 to 45.3 million tons (906,000 barrels per day) in 2002 and 46.5 million tons (930,000 barrels per day) in 2003 (so an increase of only approximately 3 percent in two years). The main LUKoil spurt in terms of organic growth came in 2004, when overall LUKoil output went from 72.2 million tons to 84.1 million tons (or from 1.4 to 1.7 million barrels per day), an increase of 16.5 percent (LUKoil–West Siberia's output amounted to 52 million tons (1.04 million barrels per day) in 2004, an increase of 11.9 percent); overall LUKoil growth in 2005 was about 4.5 percent. I am grateful to my colleague John Webb for this detailed analysis.

111 Attending LUKoil's April 22 press conference were two key government officials, Aleksandr Braverman, first deputy minister for property relations, and Vladimir Malin, chairman of the Russian Property Fund. Significantly, they were not regulators but rather belonged to the part of the government that was preparing the sale of LUKoil stock on the London market and was therefore likely to be sympathetic to any reforms

that would bring up LUKoil's share price. See Mariia Ignatova, "Igra v dogonialki. LUKoil nachal pogoniu za konkurentami," *Izvestiia,* April 23, 2002, p. 5.

112 This point is well developed in John Grace, *Russian Oil Supply.* For a discussion of the high-level decision making involved, see Gustafson, *Crisis amid Plenty.*

6. The Brothers from Saint Petersburg

1 See the reminiscences of Aleksey Uliukaev, now first deputy chairman of the Central Bank of Russia, in Natal'ia Kalashnikova, "Vos'midesiatniki," *Itogi,* no. 12 (March 22, 2010), pp. 32–40. Not all the Pitertsy in high government positions in Moscow in the 1990s were by origin young liberal academics. For example, Il'ia Klebanov, who had been a leading industrial executive in Leningrad and a former first deputy governor of Saint Petersburg, was already deputy prime minister in the Stepashin government, which immediately preceded Putin's appointment as prime minister.

2 With the approach of the 2012 presidential election, the references to this group became more explicit and detailed, as individual members occasionally went public with stories that were carried in the mainstream Russian press. Thus in late 2010 a Saint Petersburg businessman, Sergei Kolesnikov, accused his former partners of corrupt involvement in building a palace in south Russia, which, according to Kolesnikov, had been intended for Putin's use. The ensuing scandal shed a sharp light on the origins of the "Bank Rossiya" and some of its principal stockholders. See in particular Rinat Sagdiev and Irina Reznik, "Troe iz dvortsa," *Vedomosti,* April 4, 2011. The story was then picked up and investigated by Western journalists, who added further details on the claimed offshore connections of the Russian players. See notably Catherine Belton, "A Realm Fit for a Tsar," *Financial Times,* December 1, 2011.

3 Source: Aleksandr Gol'ts, "Vulkanicheskii ostrovok," *Itogi,* no. 23 (June 8, 1999), accessed via Eastview Universal Databases (by subscription) at http://o-dlib.eastview.com.library .lausys.georgetown.edu/browse/doc/3031336. According to Vladimir Kozhin, who has headed the influential Administration of Affairs *(Upravlenie delami)* of the Presidential Administration since 2000 and was one of the earliest arrivals among Putin's Pitertsy, "For the last eight years there has existed a small informal club of people whom you might call 'the President's team' in the narrow sense of the word, people who came in 1999–2000 and who now work in various positions. We try to get together at least once a month, simply in order to see one another, drink beer and shoot a little pool, and just talk without touching on work or politics." See Andrei Kamakin's interview with Vladimir Kozhin, "Kolybel' Konstitutsii," *Itogi,* no. 49 (December 1, 2007), www.itogi.ru/archive /2007/49/10641.html. I have no information on whether this informal practice continued after Medvedev became president in 2008.

4 Prominent Pitertsy among the Putin-era siloviki include Nikolai Patrushev (FSB chairman from 1999 to 2008) and Patrushev's high school classmate, Boris Gryzlov (subsequently chairman of the "United Russia" Party from 2005 to 2008 and speaker of the Duma through the end of 2010); Sergei Ivanov (former defense minister and deputy

prime minister, currently head of the Presidential Administration); Evgenii Murov (head of the Federal Protection Service); and Viktor Cherkesov (former head of the Federal Narcotics Service)—all from roughly the same generation of high officials who originated in the security apparatus (or in the case of Gryzlov, defense industry) of Leningrad. This group also includes Viktor Ivanov and Igor Sechin, who are introduced later in the chapter.

5 Thus "liberals" and "siloviki" have at times switched policy stances with no apparent discomfort when it suited their group interests. See for example the analysis by Tat'iana Stanovaia of the competing tax-legislation initiatives backed by the "liberals" and the "siloviki" in the wake of the Yukos Affair in 2005 ("'Liberaly' i 'siloviki': Ideologiia i apparatnye interesy," *Politkom.Ru*, February 7, 2005, www.politcom.ru /2005/pvz601.php).

6 It has become convention in the Western media to refer to the Russian marketeers as "liberals," but the word is problematic because of the very different understandings of it on the U.S. and European sides of the Atlantic. Throughout this book I use "liberal" in its European sense rather than its U.S. sense. A Russian "liberal," in other words, is someone who favors private ownership, strong property rights, and a market economy, supported by rule of law, sound state regulation, and orthodox macroeconomic policy.

7 See Nikolai Petrov, "The Security Dimension of the Federal Reforms," in Peter Reddaway and Robert W. Orttung, eds., *The Dynamics of Russian Politics: Putin's Reform of Federal-Regional Relations,* 2 vols. (Lanham, MD: Rowman and Littlefield, 2005), 2:7–32.

8 This account comes from Putin's self-portrait in *First Person,* trans. Catherine A. Fitzpatrick (New York: Random House, 2000), pp. 125–127 (published in Russian as *Ot pervogo litsa;* see note 36). This was actually Putin's second job-seeking trip to the Kremlin. He had initially been offered the position of deputy head of the Presidential Administration by its then chief, Nikolai Egorov. But the offer was rescinded when Egorov was unexpectedly replaced by Anatolii Chubais, who eliminated the position Putin had been offered. Kudrin then invited Putin to Moscow for a second visit and introduced him to Chubais, but Chubais offered Putin only the much more modest position of head of the Directorate for Public Liaison. Thus Putin was ultimately helped less by Chubais than by behind-the-scenes support from two other Kremlin influentials, Pavel Borodin (head of the Kremlin's powerful Administration of Affairs) and Aleksei Bolshakov (first deputy head of the Presidential Administration under Chubais). Bolshakov was a veteran former official of the Leningrad city government. Thus there is no evidence of a KGB network. It is worth noting that Aleksei Kudrin rose to the Kremlin independently of Putin, mainly, it seems, thanks to a long-standing friendship with Chubais. Chubais, when he was named head of the Presidential Administration in 1996, appointed several Pitertsy as his deputies. See Stepan Kiselev, "Kremlevskie kadry: Zemliaki, privatizatory, i byvshii chekist," *Izvestiia,* August 3, 1996. A digital archive to *Izvestiia* is available by subscription via Eastview Universal Databases: see http://www.eastview.com/Files/EVIzvestiiaDA.pdf.

9   Quoted by Timothy Colton in his biography of Yeltsin, *Yeltsin: A Life* (New York: Basic Books, 2008), p. 431. "I waited for a new general to appear, unlike any other general. . . . Time passed, and such a general appeared . . . Vladimir Putin" (p. 587). To be sure, the memoir was written after Putin was already president. One man who played a key role behind the scenes was Aleksandr Voloshin, then head of the Presidential Administration, who though often classified as a "liberal" and a member of the Yeltsin "Family," had come to believe that the central government needed to be strengthened and the power of the regions cut back, and that Putin could be the right man for that job.

10 In March 1999 Putin was named secretary of the Security Council, a post that he held concurrently with his job as FSB chairman.

11 The *fin de règne* atmosphere of the Kremlin in the summer of 1999 is nicely captured in Timothy Colton's biography of Yeltsin, based on extensive interviews with Yeltsin himself and most of the major players in his entourage at the time. Colton argues that although Putin had influential sponsors, the wily president, despite his failing health and increasingly erratic mind, remained the controlling force in the game of intrigue surrounding his succession and made the key choices, including that of the dark horse, Putin. In particular, Colton discounts the role of Boris Berezovsky. See Colton, *Yeltsin*, chapter 16. For more conspiratorial accounts, see Peter Baker and Susan Glasser, *Kremlin Rising: Vladimir Putin's Russia and the End of Revolution* (New York: Scribner, 2005); and Andrew Jack, *Inside Putin's Russia* (Oxford: Oxford University Press, 2004).

12 See Timothy J. Colton and Michael McFaul, *Popular Choice and Managed Democracy: The Russian Elections of 1999 and 2000* (Washington, DC: Brookings Institution, 2003).

13 From a large literature, see in particular Peter Reddaway, "Will Putin Be Able to Consolidate Power?," *Post-Soviet Affairs* 17, no. 1 (2001), pp. 23-44; Lilia Shevtsova, *Putin's Russia* (Washington, DC: Carnegie Endowment for International Peace, 2003).

14 Petrov, "The Security Dimension."

15 For a lively account of the politics surrounding Gazprom in that period, based on extensive interviews with most of the participants, see Valerii Paniushkin, Mikhail Zygar', and Irina Reznik, *Gazprom: Novoe russkoe oruzhie* (Moscow: "Zakharov," 2008).

16 The term "self-interest" can be understood in multiple ways. On one level, the phrase captures Putin's very different approach to the treatment of cadres, compared with Yeltsin's. In contrast to Yeltsin's temperamental hirings and firings, which created anxiety and resentment among senior officials, Putin's personnel policy emphasized "respect for cadres." He raised salaries and perks, restored Soviet-era ranks, privileges, and sinecures for dismissed and retired officials, and was generally measured and cautious in his personnel policy. See the excellent analysis by Ol'ga Kryshtanovskaia, *Anatomiia rossiiskoi elity* (Moscow: "Zakharov," 2005), chapter 3.

17 The phrase "coalition of discontent" comes from Adnan Vatansever, whose fine doctoral thesis analyzes the fiscal policies of the Putin administration through 2005. Adnan

Vatansever, "The Political Economy of Countering the 'Resource Curse': The Case of Russia under Putin (1999–2005)" (PhD diss., Johns Hopkins School of Advanced International Studies, 2008).

18 Kryshtanovskaia, *Anatomiia rossiiskoi elity*, pp. 277–278.

19 Ibid., p. 278.

20 See Fiona Hill and Clifford Gaddy, "Putin and the Uses of History," *The National Interest*, January–February 2012, http://nationalinterest.org/article/putin-the-uses-history -6276?page=show.

21 Putin interview with Mikhail Leont'ev on ORT Television, February 7, 2000.

22 There are unfortunately few general histories of Leningrad and none, to my knowledge, of post-Soviet Saint Petersburg. An excellent study of Leningrad politics and policy making is Blair Ruble's *Leningrad: Shaping a Soviet City* (Berkeley: University of California Press, 1989). The early years of post-Soviet Saint Petersburg are recounted in Robert W. Orttung, *From Leningrad to Saint Petersburg: Democratization in a Russian City* (New York: Saint Martin's Press, 1995).

23 Peter Almquist, *Red Forge: Soviet Military Industry since 1965* (New York: Columbia University Press, 1990).

24 Two other "first deputy" mayors were named at the same time: Vladimir Yakovlev (who subsequently succeeded Sobchak as mayor) and Aleksei Kudrin. Somewhat later Valerii Malyshev joined the group as a fourth first deputy. But Putin was treated by Sobchak as "first of the firsts," as evidenced by the fact that Putin was entrusted with the city's affairs during Sobchak's frequent trips abroad.

25 For Putin's own account of his earlier service in Germany and his years in the Saint Petersburg mayoralty, see Putin, *First Person*, chapters 5 and 6. Sobchak himself bylined two memoirs, *Khozhdenie vo vlast'*, 2nd ed. (Moscow: "Novosti," 2001), and *Zhila-byla kommunisticheskaia partiia* (Saint Petersburg: "Lenizdat," 1995). Neither book, however, contains any information about the period when Putin was deputy mayor.

26 The privatization of state assets had actually begun a number of years earlier, as powerful Soviet institutions with international connections took advantage of the Gorbachev reforms and the loosening of the state's foreign-trade monopoly to shelter their assets overseas. For a description of this process on the eve of the collapse of the Soviet Union, see Iurii Schekochikhin, "Rassledovaniia: Oni vozvrashchaiutsia," *Novaia gazeta*, April 15, 2002. Thus a part of the "foreign economic relations" activity of the Committee for Foreign Economic Relations (KVS) presumably included assisting offshore Russian interests reinvesting assets in the Saint Petersburg area.

27 Putin, however, in the interviews published as *First Person*, stressed that KVS, as a municipal authority, did not deliver foreign-trade licenses and did not itself conduct foreign trade (p. 99).

28 The "Bank Rossiya" was created in 1990 at the initiative of the Leningrad province committee of the Communist Party and was initially capitalized from party funds. See the bank's homepage at http://web.abr.ru/sankt-petersburg/.

29 Petromed was subsequently much in the news two decades later, as the starting point for the fortunes of Dmitri Gorelov and Nikolai Shamalov, both subsequently major shareholders in "Bank Rossiya" and frequently mentioned as members of Putin's wider circle of business friends.

30 Much of my information concerning the business elite of Saint Petersburg, KVS, and Putin's role in it comes from the research of a Russian journalist, Vladimir Pribylovskii. See in particular Vladimir Pribylovskii, "Proiskhozhdenie putinskoi oligarkhii," *Polit. ru,* October 19 and 27, 2005 (part 1: polit.ru/analytics/2005/10/19/oligarhi_print.html; part 2: polit.ru/analytics/2005/10/17/oligarhi_print.html). Pribylovskii is a Russian journalist with a good record of reliability, the author over the years of several reference books on Russian elites. Pribylovskii's articles and books, as well as his website, antikompromat.ru, are based in part on a KVS database, listing the companies registered by the committee between 1991 and 1994. I am indebted to Peter Reddaway for bringing this source to my attention.

31 A good account is Jack, *Inside Putin's Russia,* pp. 67–79.

32 *Wall Street Journal,* February 23, 2005; *Moscow Times,* February 25, 2005. In the mid-1980s Warnig had been an officer in the East German security service, the Stasi. Subsequently, after Putin became president, Warnig headed Dresdner Bank's Moscow subsidiary and served on Gazprom's board of directors.

33 Viktor Cherkesov, who subsequently served as first deputy director of the FSB under Putin in 1998–1999, was head of the FSB's Saint Petersburg Directorate during the Putin years. Aleksandr Bortnikov, now the director of the FSB, was coming up the ranks of the FSB in Saint Petersburg and Leningrad Province during the same period, as was Sergei Ushakov, who became head of security at Gazprom from 2003 to 2007.

34 See the Russian edition of Vladimir Pribylovskii's book, coauthored with Iurii Fel'shtinskii, *Korporatsiia: Rossiia i KGB vo vremena Prezidenta Putina* (Moscow: "Terra," 2010), http://www.corporation-kgb.org/. (The English-language version of the book is unfortunately less reliable.)

35 Aleksei Makarkin, "Vladimir Iakunin: Pravoslavnyi chekist, kandidat v preemniki," *Politkom.ru,* June 30, 2005, http://politcom.ru/286.html.

36 Mayor Sobchak's widow, Liudmila Narusova, recalls that her husband was amused by his first deputy's abstemious dress and before official receptions offered to lend him one of his own ties. Il'ia Zhegulev, "Sozdanie preemnika," *Smart Money,* April 21, 2008, http://www.vedomosti.ru/smartmoney/article/2008/04/21/5410.

37 Vladimir Putin, with N. Gevorkian, N. Timakova, and A. Kolesnikov, *Ot pervogo litsa: Razgovory s Vladimirom Putinym* (Moscow: "Vagrius," 2000), p. 121. An online version is available at http://bookz.ru/authors/gevorkian-natalia/gevorkiannato1 /1-gevorkiannato1.html. After their dacha burned down in the summer of 1996, the Putins used a government dacha in Arkhangel'sk until 1998, by which time Putin was chairman of the FSB.

38 Andrew Osborn, "Putin Place: Lakeside Residents Clash with Russia's Power Elite," *Wall Street Journal*, September 25, 2007, http://andrewosborn.co.uk/article/78/. There have been repeated rumors, however, that at this time Putin and Sobchak both owned villas in Spain, financed with federal subsidies intended to build housing in Saint Petersburg. These rumors have never been confirmed, but in recent years they have become more pointed and detailed. See, for example, an interview with former police investigator Andrei Zykov, "Nam skazali, chto v otnoshenii prezidenta ugolovnoe delo ne vedetsia," *Zaks.ru*, September 6, 2011, http://www.zaks.ru/new/archive/view /83713.

39 The single most controversial *affaire* involving Putin concerns a food-for-oil barter deal in 1992 that went wrong (the oil was exported, but no food arrived in return) and was investigated by a committee of the city's legislature (then still known as the Leningrad City Soviet). For a retrospective account that seeks to put the matter in the context of the times, see an interview with the former chairman of the Leningrad Soviet, Aleksandr Beliaev, "Aleksandr Beliaev o piterskoi kar'ere Putina," *Radio Svoboda*, March 23, 2010, http://www.svobodanews.ru/articleprintview/1990526.html. For a summary of Putin's rumored business connections in the early 1990s, see (with caution) "Ten' Prezidenta," January 28, 2000, http://www.flb.ru/info/3570.html. This article asserts that Vladimir Yakunin played a discreet but indispensable role as Putin's representative in a wide range of businesses.

40 The City Property Committee owned a 14.5 percent share in PTK; various other bodies connected to the city and oblast' governments were also shareholders. Pribylovskii, *Korporatsiia*, pp. 85–86.

41 According to Pribylovskii, in August 1994, Putin, on behalf of the mayoralty, signed the decree authorizing the creation of the Petersburg Fuel Company (PTK). See *Korporatsiia*, p. 85.

42 Ibid. Friends and associates of Putin's remained actively involved in the affairs of the Saint Petersburg fuels market after his departure for Moscow. Vladimir Smirnov, a leading financial and real estate entrepreneur, head of the oil trading company Nevskii Dom, and president of PTK from its creation in 1994 until 2000, briefly joined Putin in the Presidential Administration in 2000–2001; until 2009 he was general director of Tekhsnabeksport, a state company that specializes in export of nuclear fuels. He was succeeded as general director of PTK (and subsequently as president) by Vadim Glazkov, a former KGB officer and previously head of the fuels department of the city government between 1992 and 1994, where he knew Putin. Glazkov had been deputy head of the northwest department of Surgutneftegaz between 1994 and 1999, conceivably as part of an accommodation between Surgut and the city government. (Glazkov remained at the head of PTK until 2007.) Lastly, Mikhail Manevich remained as deputy mayor and head of the city's Property Committee until he was murdered in August 1997.

43 In 2000 Glazkov replaced Vladimir Smirnov as general director of PTK, becoming president in 2001 (*Leningradskaia pravda*, July 19, 2001), while Kumarin-Barsukov was

persuaded to step down as vice president, though he retained his stake as PTK's principal shareholder until his arrest in 2007.

44 Maksim Poliakov and Aleksei Makarov, "V Pitere budet novaia neftebaza: Pravitel'stvo Rossii prinialo predlozhenie merii Sankt-Peterburga," *Kommersant-Daily,* October 24, 1992.

45 Catherine Belton and Neil Buckley, "On the Offensive: How Gunvor Rose to the Top of Russian Oil Trading," *Financial Times,* May 15, 2008, p. 9. In a letter to the *Financial Times,* Gennadii Timchenko acknowledged that Kirishineftekhimeksport had been a shareholder in Golden Gates but asserted that his own connection had been "so insignificant as to be practically nonexistent."

46 Andrei Sinitsyn and Viktor Mel'nikov, "Vozrozhdenie torgovogo porta poka otkladyvaetsia," *Kommersant-Daily,* January 25, 1995.

47 According to another source, Golden Gates was included in the overall plan. See "Porty i ikh stroiteli," *Kommersant-Daily,* March 23, 1996. But if so, it was likely a diplomatic afterthought.

48 Sinitsyn and Melnikov, "Vozrozhdenie torgovogo porta poka otkladyvaetsia."

49 Ibid.

50 In 1996 Surgutneftegaz was granted a special 10 million ton (73 million barrel) export quota to finance the construction of the new terminal. See *Interfax Petroleum Report* 6 (November 8–15, 1996), p. 4; and 6 (January 31–February 7, 1997), p. 3. The federal government and the local government of Leningrad oblast' promised tax breaks and loan guarantees. Igor' Fedorov, "Raznye sud'by domashnykh portov," *Kommersant-Daily,* June 26, 1996. See also Inna Ermishina, "Novyi terminal v Sankt-Peterburge nachal rabotat'," *Neft' i Kapital,* no. 1 (1998), p. 33.

51 In the fall of 1995 the terminal was reported to be under construction, and by the end of 1997 it was even announced that the first phase, with a capacity to export 7.5 million tons of refined products per year, was nearly complete. Source: Ermishina, "Novyi terminal." But in reality the work on the ground appears to have been limited to an approach road and some preliminary foundation work. In June 1997 the government held another cornerstone ceremony to celebrate the beginning of construction, complete with a message from Boris Yeltsin, which was buried in a capsule at the site, but no actual work followed. *Interfax Petroleum Report* 6, no. 25 (June 20–27, 1997), p. 4. Since then the project has generated an occasional press release but appears no closer to actual construction.

52 Gennadii Timchenko co-founded the "Yavara-Neva" judo club with Putin's former judo trainer Arkadii Rotenberg. Putin is the club's honorary president.

53 For background on Gunvor's oil-trading operations, see "Riddles, Mysteries, and Enigmas," *The Economist,* May 5, 2012, pp. 58–61.

54 Belton and Buckley, "On the Offensive."

55 The Russian press reports regularly on Gennadii Timchenko's expanding assets in Russia. See, for example, "Chem vladeet Gennadii Timchenko," *Kommersant,* October 4, 2011.

56 For example, the weekly *Ogonek,* part of the *Kommersant* stable of publications, has made a virtual hobby of investigating Timchenko's activities and assets. See especially the issues of November 30, 2009, and March 29, 2010.

57 See the widely circulated pamphlet by Boris Nemtsov and Vladimir Milov, *Putin. Itogi. 10 let,* available on Boris Nemtsov's website, at http://nemtsov.ru/?id=706211. See also V. Milov, B. Nemtsov, V. Ryzhkov, and O. Shorina, eds., *Putin. Korruptsiia. Nezavisimyi ekspertnyi doklad,* 2nd ed. (Moscow, 2011), http://www.putin-itogi.ru/f/Putin-i -korruptsiya-doklad.pdf.

58 The workings of the Administration of Affairs under Yeltsin, as well as the rest of the complex structure of the Presidential Administration, are nicely analyzed in Eugene Huskey, *Presidential Power in Russia* (Armonk, NY: M. E. Sharpe, 1999), esp. pp. 43–97. Borodin's successor, Vladimir Kozhin, is a *Piterets* who has held this key position since 2000. See Mikhail Rostovskii, "Putinburg na Moskva-reke," *Moskovskii komsomolets,* February 2, 2000.

59 Vladimir V. Putin, *Strategicheskoe planirovanie vosproizvodstva mineral'no-syr'revoi bazy regiona v usloviiakh formirovaniia rynochnykh otnoshenii (Sankt-Peterburg i Leningradskaia oblast'),* dissertation in satisfaction of requirements for the degree of *Kandidat* in economics (Saint Petersburg, 1997), electronic copy available (to library cardholders) from the Russian State Library, 2002, http://diss.rsl.ru/diss/02/0000 /020000840.pdf, pp. 116–117.

60 When the Putin thesis first became available in the West, there was a flurry of commentary over the fact that a portion had been excised from a Western source, and more generally doubts were expressed that Putin had written the thesis himself. See David Sands, "Researchers Peg Putin as Plagiarist over Thesis," *Washington Times,* March 25, 2006; and "It All Boils Down to Plagiarism," *Washington Profile,* March 31, 2006. The story was picked up by several Russian newspapers. See Maksim Shishkin et al., "The President as Candidate: Creative Method," *Kommersant Online,* March 2006, http:// www.kommersant.com/pda/doc.asp?id=662935; "Putin Faces Plagiarism Accusation," *Saint Petersburg Times,* March 28, 2006. The reaction from the Kremlin was relaxed. For an entertaining Russian commentary on the industry of thesis writing for senior officials, see Igor' Dmitriev, "Vashe stepenstvo!" *Nasha versiia,* no. 16 (April 23, 2007), pp. 10–11.

61 Indeed, there are suggestions in the Russian media at the time that he had his hands full, fighting to gain control of an organization that regarded him, for all of his past uniform, as a political parvenu and a threat.

62 Zubkov (whom we met earlier in this chapter) by this time headed the Saint Petersburg tax administration (with the rank of deputy head of the federal tax administration). The following year Putin named him to head a newly created Financial Intelligence Service within the Ministry of Finance (with the rank of first deputy minister of Finance). The role this key agency played in the Yukos Affair is described in Chapter 7. Zubkov, who went on to become prime minister, is today the chairman of the board of Gazprom.

63 Their paths diverged only briefly in 1998 and 1999, when Putin was named chairman of the FSB and of the Security Council, while Sechin served in the Presidential Administration and then in the Secretariat of the first deputy prime minister, conceivably as Putin's eyes and ears in those institutions. In August 1999, when Putin was named prime minister, Sechin became the head of his secretariat. For a biographical sketch of Sechin's career, see Lentapedia, http://www.lenta.ru/lib/14160890/. A detailed biographical essay on Sechin appears in Irina Reznik and Irina Mokrousova, "Pervyi vozle Putina," *Vedomosti*, March 19, 2012, accessed via Eastview Universal Databases (by subscription) at http://0-dlib.eastview.com.library.lausys.georgetown.edu/sources /article.jsp?id=26773899.

64 Elena Liubarskaia, "V teni Putina," *Demokratiia.ru,* July 27, 2004. Putin recounts that he first met Sechin on a goodwill tour to Brazil. Sechin, who had returned from service as a military interpreter in Portuguese-speaking Africa and was working as an instructor at the Foreign Department of Leningrad University, was the Russian delegation's interpreter and coordinator.

65 Vladimir V. Putin, "Mineral'no-syr'evye resursy v strategii razvitiia rossiiskoi ekonomiki," in *Problemy toplivno-energeticheskogo kompleksa,* a special issue of *Zapiski gornogo instituta,* tom 144 (1) (1999), pp. 3–9. An English translation, with an introduction by Harley Balzer, appears in *Problems of Post-Communism* 53, no. 1 (January/February 2006), pp. 48–54.

66 On the contrary, Putin was named FSB director partly to reverse the policies pursued by his predecessor Nikolai Kovalev, who had used the two economic-intelligence departments of the FSB to gain leverage over the oil industry and control over oil revenues. Putin abolished the two departments and conducted a wholesale purge of the senior ranks of the FSB officer corps, replacing them with KGB officers from Saint Petersburg, many of them former fellow officers. See (with caution) Fel'shtinskii and Pribylovskii, *Korporatsiia.*

67 Putin, on the eve of his appointment as prime minister, described his work as secretary of the Security Council in the following words: "Look at the agenda of our meetings and sessions for the first and second halves of this year: air defense, the development of the navy, nuclear deterrence." Aleksandr Gamov, "Vladimir Putin: Gosudarstvennyi perevorot Rossii ne grozit," *Komsomol'skaia pravda,* July 8, 1999. In press interviews during this period, Putin does not mention energy even once. See, for example, his interview in *Itogi,* June 8, 1999, cited in note 3.

68 Vladimir V. Putin, "Rossiia na rubezhe tysiacheletii," *Nezavisimaia gazeta*, December 30, 1999.

69 Ibid.

70 A transcript of Putin's speech in Surgut is available on the presidential website, http://archive.kremlin.ru/appears/2000/03/03/0003_type63374type63378_28480.shtml.

71 German Gref headed an expanded Ministry of Economic Development and Trade. A liberal economist, Viktor Khristenko, was named deputy prime minister with authority over energy and industry. Aleksei Kudrin took over as minister of finance.

72 Even though much of his subsequent career has been spent in the area of economic and financial policy, it was only in 2011, after he was chairman of Sberbank, that Gref defended a kandidat dissertation in economics at the Academy of the National Economy. The dissertation defense can be seen on video at http://video.ane.ru/index.php?live=0 &cat=diss&fn=diss-2011-02-18.

73 At the time he succeeded Manevich, the media asked Gref "whose man he was." Gref gave a diplomatic answer that prefigured his subsequent political flexibility: "You may consider me Chubais's man and Yakovlev's man and Nemtsov's man—they're all for reforms and I'm for them." Natalia Samoilova, "Peterburg kormit MGI kadrami," *Kommersant-Daily,* August 12, 1998. A biographical sketch of German Gref appears at http://www.whoswho.eu/biografie_russia.php?lan=eng.

74 The Center for Strategic Projects was created at the initiative of the new prime minister, who in a speech in the Russian Far East in October 1999 called for an institute that would be capable of turning broad strategic goals into detailed policy plans. Although it has receded somewhat from public view since the Ministry of Economic Development took over much of this function, it remains active as a think tank on various government initiatives such as financial and land reforms. The Center's website is http://www.csr.ru.

75 *Interfax,* March 1, 1999.

76 Pavel Felgenhauer, "Defense Dossier: A New Thousand-Year Reich?," *Moscow Times,* March 2, 2000. After the appointment of Putin's first government, its members, while giving the Center for Strategic Projects' program lip-service support, began distancing themselves from it. "Programma, kotoruiu razrabatyvaet TsSR Germana Grefa posle ee rassmotreniia v pravitel'stve ne preterpit printsipial'nykh izmenenii," *Ekonomicheskie novosti,* May 22, 2000.

77 The traditional meaning of the word *poslanie* is "epistle." Consequently, it connotes a ceremonial quality that is missing from the mere word "speech."

78 All of Putin's major speeches are available on the presidential website, http://kremlin.ru.

79 Most of the speech had been written by El'vira Nabiullina, a Gref protégée who was then the Center for Strategic Projects' deputy director (and was subsequently economics minister under both Putin and Medvedev). Gref served as economics minister throughout Putin's two terms before becoming chairman of Sberbank in 2007. Nabiullina replaced him as minister in that year.

80 Putin, "Rossiia na rubezhe tysiacheletii."

81 For a description of Aleksei Kudrin's early years in Saint Petersburg, see a profile from the *Saint Petersburg Times* at http://petersburgcity.com/city/personalities/kudrin/; and "Tikhii udarnik Kudrin," *Profil',* October 23, 2000, http://www.profile.ru/items_5075. See also Oleg Moroz, "Portret-Dos'e. Kudrin," *Literaturnaia gazeta,* June 7, 2000.

82 For a detailed analysis of Kudrin's main policy innovations between 2000 and 2011, see Dmitri Butrin, Petr Netreba, and Oleg Sapozhkov, "Krupneishie dostizheniia

Alekseia Kudrina," *Kommersant Online,* October 7, 2011, http://www.kommersant.ru /doc/1789469.

83 An excellent description of the Soviet fiscal system and its post-Soviet evolution as applied to the oil and gas sector is V. A. Kriukov and A. N. Tokarev, *Neftegazovye resursy v transformiruemoi ekonomike* (Novosibirsk: "Nauka-Tsentr," 2007), chapter 10.

84 Sergey Shatalov, "Tax Reform in Russia—History and Future" (Economic Policy Distinguished Lecture, presented at the London School of Economics and Political Science, November 10, 2005), available on the website of the International Tax and Investment Center, http://www.iticnet.org/Public/other_publications.aspx#divYear2006, February 2006, p. 4.

85 For an overview of the tax system on the eve of the crash, see Thane Gustafson, *Capitalism Russian-Style* (Cambridge: Cambridge University Press, 1999), chapter 9; and Gerald Easter, "Building Fiscal Capacity," in Timothy J. Colton and Stephen Holmes, eds., *The State after Communism: Governance in the New Russia* (Lanham, MD: Rowman and Littlefield, 2006), pp. 21–52. See also Andrei Shleifer and Daniel Treisman, *Without a Map: Political Tactics and Economic Reform in Russia* (Cambridge, MA: MIT Press, 2000), chapter 6. A firsthand account is Martin Gilman, *No Precedent, No Plan* (Cambridge, MA: MIT Press, 2010).

86 See an interview with Aleksandr Pochinok, then minister for tax collections, "Chetyre udara Pochinka," *Ekspert,* December 1, 1997. Useful background will be found in *Russian Economic Trends,* "Special Report: Taxes in Russia" (Monthly Update, December 1997).

87 Bulat Stoliarov, "Tvorchestvo neftianykh baronov," *Novaia gazeta,* August 7, 2000.

88 For a history and review of the Financial Action Task Force's relationship with Russia, see http://www.fatf-gafi.org/dataoecd/31/6/41415981.pdf.

89 For a biographical essay on the career of Viktor Zubkov, which includes references to the major media stories on him over the years, see Lentapedia, lenta.ru/lib/14174946 /full.htm. Having served as head of the Federal Monitoring Service from November 2001 to September 2007, Zubkov was briefly prime minister to May 2008. He then served concurrently as first deputy prime minister during Medvedev's term as president, and as chairman of the board of Gazprom, as well as chair of the government's interagency working group on money laundering. See http://lenta.ru/news/2012/01/12 /zubkov/.

90 Open letter to President Putin from the economics minister German Gref and the tax minister Gennadii Bukaev, published in *Kommersant,* December 22, 2000.

91 See, for example, Kudrin's speech to the Association of Russian Banks, "Aleksei Kudrin snizit nalogi," *Novye izvestiia,* May 24, 2000, and his address to an All-Russian conference of the regional offices of the federal treasury, "Dokhody do narastaiushchei," *Rossiiskaia gazeta,* May 12, 2000.

92 "Vladimir Putin toropit priniatie nalogovogo kodeksa," *Vremia-MN,* May 24, 2000. A first part had already been enacted into law late in Yeltsin's second term.

93 This relatively accommodating opening stage in the battle for oil taxes is captured by Pauline Jones Luong and Erika Weinthal in an important article, "Contra Coercion:

Russia Tax Reform, Exogenous Shocks, and Negotiated Institutional Change," *American Political Science Review* 98, no. 1 (February 2004), pp. 139–152. It is now clear in retrospect that this first stage was followed by a much more conflictual one; the key question is when the first stage ended and the second one began. Adnan Vatansever ("The Political Economy of Countering the 'Resource Curse'") concludes that the turning point came well before the adoption of the oil chapter of the Tax Code in 2001 and its implementation in January 2002—indeed, as early as the summer of 2000. My own research leads me to agree with him. The implication is that the stage of "negotiated change" proved very short.

94 Natal'iia Ivanova and Viktor Kuz'min, "Vlast' demonstriruet sistemnyi podkhod—teper' vzialis' za LUKoil. Gon na oligarkhov," *Nezavisimaia gazeta,* July 12, 2000.

95 Aleksei Germanovich, "Trebuetsia novoe slovo," *Vedomosti,* July 31, 2000.

96 Aleksandr Tutushkin and Elizaveta Osetinskaia, "Den'gi zaberut," *Vedomosti,* December 4, 2000.

97 Interview with Kudrin by Aleksandr Budberg, "Ukrotitel' deneg," *Moskovskii komsomolets,* February 9, 2001.

98 Natal'ia Neimysheva, "Kudrin odoleet neftianikov," *Vedomosti,* November 24, 2000.

99 "Nalog na dobychu poleznykh iskopaemykh," or Tax on Production of Natural Resources.

100 Vatansever, "The Political Economy of Countering the 'Resource Curse,'" table 3.2, based on O. Berezinskaia and V. Mironov, "Otechestvennyi neftegazovyi kompleks: Dinamika konkurentnosposobnosti i perspektivy finansirovaniia," *Voprosy ekonomiki,* no. 8 *(*2006), p. 143.

101 Ibid.

102 Vitaly Yermakov, "New Russian Oil Taxes: A World of the Second Best?," Cambridge Energy Research Associates Decision Brief, December 2001. Also author's conversation with Yermakov, December 2008.

103 Galina Liapunova, "Nachalas' reshaiushchaia stadiia bor'by za 'prezidentskii paket,'" *Kommersant,* May 16, 2001.

104 "Russian Oil Export Tariff to Be Cut to 23.4 Euros per Ton," *Interfax Petroleum Report* 10, no. 32 (August 10–16, 2001), p. 4.

105 "Russian Government Places New Export Tariff on Oil," *Interfax Petroleum Report* 10, no. 23 (June 8–14, 2001), p. 10. Of course, the oil price could go down as well as up, and in the summer of 2001, as oil prices briefly dipped, the commission accordingly revised the export tax downward. *Interfax Petroleum Report* 10, no. 32 (August 10–16, 2001), p. 4.

106 The evolution of Gazprom in the 1990s is recounted in many sources, of which the best is Jonathan P. Stern, *The Future of Russian Gas and Gazprom* (Oxford: Oxford University Press, 2005).

107 It was only during Putin's second term that Putin began to allow other interests, notably those connected with Gennadii Timchenko and some of the leading shareholders

of Bank Rossiya, to take growing roles in the gas sector, and Gazprom's monopoly began once more to weaken.

108 This section is based on the author's own interaction with the reformers in the early 1990s, including conversations with then economics minister German Gref and his principal deputy in charge of the restructuring program at that time, Andrei Sharonov.

109 This was much to the chagrin of Energy Minister Viktor Kaliuzhnyi, who wanted to divert the funds being collected from the oil companies to finance the BPS to a new pipeline to bypass Chechnya, but complained that the prime minister was adamant in his support for the BPS. Source: *Russia Today*, October 8, 1999, p. 1, and October 20, 1999, p. 1.

110 Elizaveta Osetinskaia, "Tumannyi BTS," *Vedomosti*, February 11, 2000; and Vasilii Verbin and Vera Kuznetsova, "Gosudarstvennyi podkhod k trube," *Vremia-MN*, February 11, 2000. For further background on the alignments of interests at this time, see Petr Fadeev, "Syr'evye voiny," *Izvestiia*, February 9, 2000.

111 Ol'ga Korabel'nikova, "Primorsk dozhdal'sia prezidenta," *Trud*, December 28, 2001, p. 1.

112 A brief account of Vainshtok's prior career at LUKoil can be found in Maksim Kashulinskii, "Nastoiashchii direktor," *Vedomosti*, September 21, 1999; and "Korotko," *Segodnia*, February 4, 1997. Vainshtok had proved his toughness and skill as a manager by taking LUKoil-West Siberia through the crisis years 1997–1998, partly by instituting a tight system of security and discipline. For press accounts of the situation in LUKoil's West Siberian fields in those years, see Vladimir Shmyganovskii, "'Sibirskim emiratam' predstoit bor'ba za vyzhivaniem," *Izvestiia*, March 20, 1998; and Vasilii Shchurov, "Energiia Rossii: Sotsial'nyi rakurs; na kogo Sibir' molitsia," *Trud*, September 17, 1999.

113 On October 19, at a conference on energy development in Leningrad Oblast', Vainshtok endorsed the construction schedule for BPS. ITAR-TASS (daily bulletins since 1987 can be accessed by subscription at http://info.itar tass.com/); in English, *BBC Summary of World Broadcasts*, October 29, 1999.

114 After some deliberation, Putin ordered in July 2000 that the BPS corporation would be 100 percent state owned. Whereas earlier it had been discussed that the oil companies would gain equity stakes in exchange for helping to finance the project, in the end they were assessed a special tariff, while Transneft remained the sole owner of the pipeline, on behalf of the state (*Petroleum Economist*, August 2000, p. 40). In September 2000 the corporation was liquidated, since there was no further need for it, and BPS was reorganized as a subsidiary of Transneft. See *Interfax Petroleum Report* 9, no. 36 (September 1–7, 2000), p. 13. Miller was promoted to deputy energy minister in Moscow. The following year he was named CEO of Gazprom.

7. "Chudo" Meets "Russian Bear"

1   The story of Khodorkovsky's arrest has become part of the political folklore of the Putin era. It was closely followed by the Russian press at the time. See, in particular, Dmitrii Vinogradov and Sergei Kez, "Prervannyi polet," *Nezavisimaia gazeta*," October 27, 2003, p. 2; Tat'iana Vitebsakaia et al., "Yukos—eto poslednii boi," *Izvestiia*, October 27, 2003, p. 1 (which contains Khodorkovsky's last interview before his arrest); Andrei Sharov and Vladislav Kulikov, "Vzlet i posadka oligarkha—podrobnosti," *Rossiiskaia gazeta*, October 28, 2003, p. 1; Iuliia Bushueva et al., "Yukos obezglavlen," *Vedomosti*, October 27, 2003, p. 1. Richard Sakwa's thorough account of the Yukos Affair, *The Quality of Freedom: Khodorkovsky, Putin, and the Yukos Affair* (Oxford: Oxford University Press, 2009), includes a detailed reconstruction of the arrest. Another detailed narrative is Martin Sixsmith's book *Putin's Oil: The Yukos Affair and the Struggle for Russia* (London: Continuum Books, 2010), based on interviews with several unnamed eyewitnesses.

2   The interested reader will find an excellent overview of the legal issues involved in the charges against Khodorkovsky and Yukos in the series of articles written by Peter Clateman, which appeared in Johnson's Russia List, http://www.cdi.org/russia/johnson/default.cfm, between December 2003 and March 2006.

3   Gosudarstvennyi komitet po statistike Rossiiskoi Federatsii (Goskomstat Rossii), *Konsolidirovannyi biudzhet Rossiiskoi Federatsii,* various years, available on the website of the Russian Statistical Committee, http://www.gks.ru/wps/wcm/connect/rosstat/rosstatsite/main/publishing/catalog/statisticCollections/doc_1138717651859.

4   For a review of the declining capacity of the federal government to raise revenue in the 1990s, see Thane Gustafson, *Capitalism Russian-Style* (Cambridge: Cambridge University Press, 1999), chapter 9. On the abrupt turnaround in tax receipts and its consequences, see the doctoral dissertation by Adnan Vatansever, "The Political Economy of Countering the 'Resource Curse': The Case of Russia under Putin (1999–2005)" (PhD diss., Johns Hopkins School of Advanced International Studies, 2008). On the use of FSB officers as cadres for the recentralization, see Nikolai Petrov, "The Security Dimension of the Federal Reforms," in Peter Reddaway and Robert W. Orttung, eds., *The Dynamics of Russian Politics: Putin's Reform of Federal-Regional Relations,* 2 vols. (Lanham, MD: Rowman and Littlefield, 2005), 2:7–32.

5   Interview in *Novaia gazeta*, November 13, 2003.

6   Ibid.

7   Putin was inaugurated on May 7. On May 13 he signed a decree creating seven "federal districts" *(federal'nye okrugi),* a new layer of government between the federal center and the regions; less than a week later he named the seven federal envoys who would head them. See Nikolai Petrov, "How Have the Presidential Envoys Changed the Administrative-Political Balance of Putin's Regime?," in Reddaway and Orttung, *Dynamics of Russian Politics,* 2:33–63.

8   Author's interview with Iurii Golubev, Calgary, Alberta.

9   For a detailed description of the press conference at which Leonid Fedun announced the LUKoil plan, and of Khodorkovsky's reaction, see *Interfax Petroleum Report* 11, no. 17 (April 26–May 2, 2002), pp. 9–12.

10 An excellent portrait of Surgutneftegaz's adoption of "Western" production methods in the first half of the 2000s is Ronald Smith, "Surgutneftegaz: Drilling Power," *Renaissance Capital,* March 2005.

11 Here also Yukos differed not in kind but in degree. Data on investment in exploratory drilling from *Neftegazovaia Vertikal'* show Yukos higher than the industry average in 1999 but lower than the industry average during 2000–2004.

12 *Company* magazine, reproduced in *UBS Warburg Daily News,* February 17, 2004, p. 2.

13 The behavior of Menatep's partners contrasted unfavorably with that of the Alfa Group, which stood by its debts. Menatep Bank was officially shut down in February 2001. A final partial compensation to its creditors was paid in December 2002. See *Gazeta.ru,* December 18, 2003.

14 Interview with Valerii Graifer, June 2, 2009.

15 Interview with Mikhail Khodorkovsky, "Mikhail Khodorkovskii: Milliardy lezhat pod nogami," *Moskovskii komsomolets,* July 24, 2002, p. 3.

16 From the author's survey of the relative frequency of references in the Russian central press, using the search function of Eastview Universal Databases (by subscription) at http://www.eastview.com.

17 ADR stands for "American Depositary Receipt," a kind of stock that represents a certain number of shares in a foreign company. ADRs are traded on American markets like regular stocks. Companies issuing "Level 3 ADRs" are allowed to raise capital on U.S. markets through public offerings but are required to provide correspondingly more information about their ownership structure and operations.

18 News reports in *Neftecompass,* June 27, 2002, p. 7.

19 Brunswick UBS Warburg, *Corporate Governance Analyzer,* August 16, 2002.

20 Dmitrii Sivakov, interview with Mikhail Khodorkovsky, "Vlast' bol'shoi nefti," *Ekspert,* no. 4 (February 3, 2003), pp. 29–34.

21 *Interfax Petroleum Report* 11, no. 17 (April 26–May 2, 2002), p. 11.

22 For a valuable analysis of the structure and history of the tax havens and the changing Russian government policy toward them, see Vladimir Samoilenko, "Special Report: Government Policies in Regard to Internal Tax Havens in Russia" (Moscow: International Tax and Investment Center, December 2003), http://www.iticnet.org/Public/other _publications.aspx#divYear2003. An abbreviated version appears as Vladimir Samoylenko, "Government Policies for Internal Tax Havens in Russia," *Tax Notes International,* April 5, 2004, pp. 84–85. I have benefited from the thorough analysis of Russian tax havens and the uses made of them by the oil companies in Adnan Vatansever's doctoral dissertation, "The Political Economy of Countering the 'Resource Curse,'" chapter 3.

23 Samoilenko, "Special Report," p. 6.

24 Institut Finansovykh Issledovanii, *Otsenka nalogovoi nagruzki rossiiskikh kompanii v 2001–2003 godakh* (Moscow: Institut Finansovykh Issledovanii, February 2004).

25 In actual fact, however, most of the free economic zones had never been covered by legislation. Consequently, the tax breaks that developed in them were in a legal gray zone, although the government was perfectly well aware of them. For a well-informed discussion of the technical issues involved, see Joel M. McDonald, *Business Operations in Russia,* Tax Management Publication 981, Foreign Income Portfolio Series (Washington, DC: Bureau of National Affairs, 2005), pp. A-82–83.

26 Quoted in Samoilenko, "Spetsial'nyi otchet," p. 2.

27 Interview with Sergei Shatalov, *Vedomosti,* October 30, 2003.

28 Petr Netreba, "'Iukosu my vsego lish' nachali vydvigat' pretenzii'," *Kommersant-Daily,* May 5, 2004, p. 1.

29 "Kudrin Tells Businesses to Pay Taxes," *Moscow Times,* June 2, 2005.

30 Dmitrii Sivakov, interview with Mikhail Khodorkovsky., "Vlast' bol'shoi nefti."

31 Presentation by Ray Leonard, then Yukos vice president for exploration, "Strategy and Perspectives of Yukos Projects in East Siberia and the Far East," at the World Petroleum Congress, Shanghai, September 20, 2001. The further development of Yukos's strategy in the Far East was presented to an investors' conference in London (April 22, 2002) by Ted Gorton, then head of Foreign Projects with Yukos Exploration of Yukos E&P. What is striking about these presentations is Yukos's apparent confidence that it would secure a dominant position in East Siberian production to support the China pipeline in its later stages.

32 Svetlana Babaeva et al., "Neft' poidet drugim putem," *Izvestiia,* December 9, 2002, http://www.izvestia.ru/news/270557.

33 Mariia Ignatova, "O dvukh golovakh," *Izvestiia,* March 4, 2003, http://www.izvestia.ru/news/273773.

34 Sivakov interview with Khodorkovsky, "Vlast' bol'shoi nefti," p. 33.

35 At the end of August 2002, Kasyanov met with Chinese Prime Minister Zhu Rongji in Shanghai, and Kasyanov said that the project should be approved as soon as possible (*Neftecompass,* August 29 2002, p. 2). For a detailed analysis of the history of the discussions around the competing pipelines, see Shoichi Itoh, "The Pacific Pipeline at a Crossroads: Dream Project or Pipe Dream?," working paper of the Economic Research Institute for Northeast Asia, Niigata City, Japan. I am grateful to Dr. Itoh for making this working paper available to me.

36 Sivakov interview with Khodorkovsky, "Vlast' bol'shoi nefti."

37 An abbreviated version of the president's opening remarks is available at http://archive.kremlin.ru/appears/2000/07/28/0000_type63376_28808.shtml. The full quote from Putin comes from Sakwa, *The Quality of Freedom,* p. 79.

38 The "hockey puck" exchange between Khodorkovsky and Putin was immediately perceived as significant and was widely reported in the Russian press over the following days. See Elena Evstigneeva, "Kazhdomu o svoem," *Vedomosti,* February 20, 2003; also Andrei Kolesnikov, "Sobranie: Vladimir Putin vzial ostroe interv'iu u oligarkhov," *Kommersant,* February 20, 2003; Andrei Reut, "Mamut zabolel," *Gazeta.ru,* February

20, 2003; and for a commentary, Denis Pinchuk, "Shaiboi v trubu," *AKS News,* February 20, 2003.

39 Viktor Gerashchenko, "Oni unichtozhili Yukos," *Novaia gazeta,* July 10, 2008, http://www.novayagazeta.ru/data/2008/49/00.html.

40 *Literaturnaia gazeta,* September 9, 1992.

41 See Sergey Pravosudov, "Lobbisty v Gosdume: Chto pochem i kto zakazyvaet muzyku," *Russkii fokus,* September 15, 2003.

42 Quoted from the record of Duma proceedings, in Arkadii Izotov, "Sergei Ivanovich, chego vy priniali, kakoi krov'iu?," *RusEnergy,* May 20, 2003. The episode was widely reported in the Russian press at the time. For useful background on the legislative issues, see Sergey Shtogrin's website, http://www.shtogrin.ru, which archives numerous newspaper articles on the tax issues, going back to 2003.

43 "Stenograficheskii otchet o press-konferentsii v Kremle dlia rossiiskikh i zarubezhnykh SMI," formerly available on the presidential website.

44 The phrase is so commonly used in Russian that it is more a figure of speech than a literary reference (a Google search for the phrase yields over 20,000 hits). The citation is from Pushkin's *Evgenii Onegin* (book VIII, stanza 51).

45 The text of the report appeared on May 26, 2003, in the nationalist newspaper *Utro,* under the title "V Rossii gotovitsia oligarkhicheskii perevorot."

46 On July 4, the website compromat.ru published the transcript of a supposed phone conversation linking Stanislaw Belkovskii, Sergei Bogdanchikov, and a voice that the source claimed was that of Igor Sechin: http://www.compromat.ru/main/bogdanchikov/prosl.htm. The authenticity of the supposed phone taps cannot be confirmed.

47 *Der Spiegel,* April 24, 2003, cited in Sakwa, *The Quality of Freedom,* p. 120.

48 *Financial Times,* October 3, 2003.

49 Iuliia Bushueva and Vladimir Karpov, "Sdelka zakryta," *Vedomosti,* October 3, 2003.

50 Sergei Topol' and Marina Lepina, "Delo Yukosa: Prishli za sirotami," *Kommersant-Daily,* October 4, 2003, p. 1.

51 *New York Times,* October 4, 2003.

52 Ivan Sas, "Khodorkovskii uezzhaet: Glava IuKOSa obeshchaet vernut'sia," *Nezavisimaia gazeta,* October 7, 2003, p. 1.

53 Sakwa, *The Quality of Freedom,* p. 158, fn. 46, citing his interview with Russian journalist Andrei Kolesnikov.

54 The term "securocrat" is said to have been coined by Australian diplomats in Moscow, searching for a translation of the Russian "silovik."

55 For background on the multiple twists and turns in the "Tri Kita" affair, see Alek Akhundov and Iurii Senatorov, "Chistka mundirov," *Kommersant,* June 28, 2006; Boris Reznik, "Na trekh kitakh," *Novye izvestiia,* July 18, 2006; and especially the reporting of Roman Shleinov in *Novaia gazeta* over the years, particularly "Gnutye spinki," *Novaia gazeta,* no. 25, June 19, 2006. I am grateful to two graduate students in my research

seminar on Russian politics at Georgetown University, John Yi and Leonid Godunov, for their excellent research on this and related affairs, using the numerous published sources available in the Russian language.

56 Reported by Inga Rostovtseva, "Prokuror i iudei," *Profil'*, no. 24, June 26, 2000, http://www.profile.ru/items_4746.

57 Irina Reznik, "Viakhirev ukhodit v otstavku," *Vedomosti*, January 29, 2002.

58 Maksim Brezhnev, "Deti izvestnykh roditelei. Bez prikras," *Kto est' kto*, no. 6 (2006), http://www.whoiswho.ru/old_site/russian/Curnom/62006/deti1.htm.

59 Inna Luk'ianova and Natal'ia Shcherbanenko, "Chelovek na vershine kar'ery," *Profil'*, no. 27, July 15, 2002, p. 92, http://www.profile.ru/items_7564.

60 Ibid.

61 Chrystia Freeland, "A Falling Tsar," *Financial Times Weekend Magazine*, November 1, 2003.

62 "Kto-to mozhet poteriat' pogony," *Novaia gazeta*, no. 78 (October 20, 2003). The expression "werewolves in uniform," although it was used by Khodorkovsky in the *Novaia gazeta* article, was not original with him. It had first been used in a popular Soviet-era television serial about the police. Later it was used to refer to a group of rogue police officers, led by Lieutenant-General Vladimir Ganeev, who ran an extortion racket directed against private businessmen in Moscow between 1997 and 2003. The expression has remained widely used in journalism and popular culture, most recently in the context of former president Medvedev's efforts to combat police extortion.

63 To date, some four or five dozen people associated with Yukos have been arrested and charged, while others, including most of the top officers of Yukos and Menatep, have escaped abroad to Israel and Great Britain. In September 2004 the General Procuracy launched a criminal case against Iurii Beilin, the senior vice president responsible for exploration and production, for exceeding production quotas; in July 2005 Beilin left for London. Alek Akhundov and Alena Miklashevskaia, "Iurii Beilin ukrylsia v London ot obvinenii," *Kommersant-Daily*, July 20, 2005.

64 *Interfax*, October 14, 2003. (Shvidler had been called to the Ministry the day before, on October 13.)

65 Source: Conversations with Yukos and Sibneft executives.

66 Dmitrii Simakin, "Delo 'Yukosa' ukhodit v provintsiiu," *Nezavisimaia gazeta*, January 26, 2004.

67 "Putin kritikuet pravitel'stvo Rossii za nedostatochnuiu zashchitu otechestvennykh proizvoditelei," *Interfax*, July 8, 2002.

68 A few senior executives of Yukos's downstream operations were targeted as well. In January 2004, Rafail Zainullin, chairman of the board of the Kuibyshev Oil Refinery (KNPZ), a subsidiary of oil giant Yukos, was arrested and charged with evading payment of 67 million rubles ($2.3 million) in oil excises in 1999, when he was the refinery's general director. Dmitrii Simakin, "Delo 'Yukosa' ukhodit v provintsiiu," *Nezavisimaia gazeta*, January 26, 2004; Elena Naumova, "Rafail' Zainullin pytaetsia

osvobodit'sia pod nalog," *Kommersant,* January 27, 2004. However, in February 2004 he was granted amnesty and released. Aleksei Nikol'skii and Vladimir Shtanov, "Menedzher 'Yukosa' priznal vinu," *Vedomosti,* February 2, 2004. Amnesties were also granted in cases brought by the Procuracy against two other former directors of Yukos refineries, Semen Mikhailov of the Novokuibyshev Refinery and Nikolai Liadin of the Syzran' Refinery. Andrei Bondarenko, "V Samare pytaiutsia otprotestovat' amnestiiu," *Nezavisimaia gazeta,* April 28, 2004. In all three of these cases the Procuracy attempted to challenge the amnesty decisions handed down by the local courts but without success.

69 Gil'manov was charged with understating the amount of oil produced at Yuganskneftegaz, with the result that taxes were underpaid. Mariia Cherkasova and Iurii Dorokhov, "Nalogovyi terror. Prigovorchiki v stroiu," *Kommersant-Daily,* April 27, 2005, p. 1.

70 Dmitri Vasil'ev, "Tagirziana Gil'manova osudili so vtoroi popytki uslovno," *Kommersant-Daily,* February 7, 2006, p. 5. The local court, in suspending Gil'manov's sentence, noted Gil'manov's "excellent record." In the end, the Procuracy did not insist on actual jail time.

71 Pavel Anisimov, general director of Samaraneftegaz, and the company's former chief accountant, Elena Marochkina, were charged with the same offense as Gil'manov. In both cases the defendants argued that they had acted under orders from Yukos headquarters. When the local judge and prosecutor called for a suspended sentence, they were replaced, and both Anisimov and Marochkina were sent to jail. In addition, the local procuracy accused Anisimov of exceeding official production quotas. See Pavel Sedakov and Liliia Abdulina, "Upravliaiushchemu 'Samaraneftegaza' ne zachli raskaiane," *Kommersant-Daily,* May 20, 2006, p. 3.

72 The Shimkevich case appears to have been somewhat different from the others. Shimkevich was arrested in 2007, after Operation Energiia had effectively ceased. Moreover, he is the only local oil official to have been sentenced to a lengthy jail term, which he is still serving. See Elena Bogdanova and Petr Pintusov, "Shimkevich arestovan," *Vedomosti,* January 18, 2007.

73 There were also some cases brought against other oil companies in other regions, for example, in Bashkortostan, where Bashneft was accused of having exceeded the production levels specified in field development plans. In Tomsk, a case was brought against Rosneft on the same grounds. See G. Khanianova and D. Skorobogat'ko, "'Bashneft' dokachalas' do prokuratury," *Kommersant,* December 17, 2004; and T. Egorova and R. Levinskii, "'Bashneft' perestaralas'," *Vedomosti,* December 17, 2004.

74 This surprise development caused a sensation in Moscow and was much discussed in the liberal media. See in particular the analysis of the usually well-informed commentator for *Moskovskii komsomolets,* Aleksandr Budberg, "Otstavka. General'naia uborka," *Moskovskii komsomolets,* June 3, 2006, p. 1.

75 The vote on April 13, 2005, had been nearly unanimous, with only one dissenting vote out of the 150 cast. Alla Barakhova, "Sovet Federatsii utverdil genprokurora aplodismentami," *Kommersant-Daily,* April 14, 2005.

76 The career of Iurii Biriukov, the first deputy prosecutor general and the leader of the prosecution throughout the first Khodorkovsky trial, had been closely associated with Vladimir Ustinov for at least the previous decade. In 1999, when Ustinov became acting prosecutor general, Biriukov succeeded him as head of the Procuracy's department for the North Caucasus ("Kadry," *Profil'*, no. 22, June 12, 2000). Biriukov was dismissed from the General Procuracy in 2006, officially for having prematurely closed the "Tri Kita" affair, the investigation of which was revived at this time (Aleksei Nikol'skii and Alek Akhundov, "Oborotni s mikrofonami," *Vedomosti,* October 4, 2007). Dmitrii Shokhin and Kamil' Kashaev, Biriukov's two principal deputies, were also demoted from the General Procuracy at about the same time (*Kommersant-Daily,* September 20, 2006). When Ustinov returned to the south, some of his former team may have followed him. In 2010 Kashaev was the prosecutor in a murder case in Dagestan. Natal'ia Krainova, "Protsess bez zakazchikov: Poterpevshii obviniaet genprokuratora," *Novoe Delo* (Dagestan), May 21, 2010.

77 Aleksandr Zheglov, "Soveshchanie v Genprokurature: Vladimir Ustinov rasstroil vertikal' prestupnosti," *Kommersant-Daily,* May 16, 2006, p. 3.

78 Vladimir Milov has written the most detailed exposition of this view. See his two-part article, "Zakat kar'ery Igoria Sechina," in specletter.com, April 7, 2011, http://www.spec letter.com/politika/2011-04-07/print/zakat-karery-igorja-sechina.html.

79 "Militseiskaia 'Energiia,'" *Lenta.ru,* November 28, 2006, http://lenta.ru/articles/2006 /11/28/energy/.

80 Daniel Yergin and Thane Gustafson, *Russia 2010 and What It Means for the World* (New York: Random House, 2004) [translated into Russian as *Rossiia: Dvadtsat' let spust'ia* (Moscow: "Mezhdunarodnye otnosheniia," 1995)].

81 Sakwa, *The Quality of Freedom,* p. xiv.

82 William Tompson, "Putting Yukos into Perspective," *Post-Soviet Affairs* 21, no. 2 (2005), pp. 159–181, especially p. 161: "The Yukos case . . . is hardly unique. The Yukos affair was exceptional only in its scale and visibility, and because the victim did not capitulate rapidly. In other respects, it is all too typical." The phrase "illegitimate wealth facing arbitrary power" was originally coined by Martin Wolf, editorialist for the *Financial Times.*

83 This is a widespread view, skillfully expressed by Steven Fish, in *Democracy Derailed in Russia* (Cambridge: Cambridge University Press, 2005), chapter 5.

84 Richard Sakwa, in his recent book, *The Crisis of Russian Democracy* (Cambridge: Cambridge University Press, 2011), writes, "Property redistribution was a consequence rather than a cause" (p. 146).

85 I agree with the assessment of Richard Sakwa, who writes, in *The Quality of Freedom,* "Putin's administration did not enter into this struggle with clear intentions, let alone a grand design, but stumbled from event to event, torn by the factional fights that were characteristic of his presidency" (p. 92).

86 Between 2000 and 2005, the state's share of oil industry revenues rose from 25.2 percent to 57.9 percent, while its share of oil company profits shot up from 45.1 percent to 83.8

percent. O. Berezinskaia and V. Mironov, "Otechestvennyi neftegazovyi kompleks: Dinamika konkurentnosposobnosti i perspektivy finansirovaniia," *Voprosy Ekonomiki*, no. 8 (2006), p. 143, cited in Vatansever, "The Political Economy of Countering the 'Resource Curse,'" table 3.2.

87   Author's notes, October 17, 2003.

8. Russia's Accidental Oil Champion

1   A good account of the early days of Rosneft, from its creation in 1992 to its near privatization in 1998, is found in Li-Chen Sim, *The Rise and Fall of Privatization in the Russian Oil Industry* (London: Palgrave Macmillan, 2008), chapter 5. For an analysis that runs through mid-2006, see Nina Poussenkova, *Rosneft: Novoe litso rossiiskogo neftianogo biznesa*, Series "Stat'i i interv'iu" (Moscow: Carnegie Endowment for International Peace, 2007). A version of this essay was published under the title "Lord of the Rigs: Rosneft as a Mirror of Russia's Evolution" (Houston, TX: Baker Institute for Public Policy, Rice University, 2007).

2   Alekperov did, however, accept the position of head of the organizing committee of Rosneft in February 1993. *Russian Petroleum Investor*, March 1993, p. 5.

3   A brief biography of Putilov appears in *Russian Petroleum Investor*, July 1993, p. 9. I first met Putilov in the spring of 1991 on a visit to Wytche Farm, when he was part of a delegation led by Alekperov.

4   Aleksey Galochkin, "'Rosneft v poiskakh utrachennogo," *Neft' i Kapital*, nos. 7–8 (2000), pp. 48–49.

5   Stepan Avdeev, "Preobrazovanie neftianogo kompleksa: Neft' vziata pod goskontrol' novym sposobom," *Kommersant*, November 14, 1992.

6   An excellent analysis of Rosneft in the 1990s is Nina Poussenkova, *Rosneft: Novoe litso rossiiskogo neftianogo biznesa* (Moscow: Moscow Center of the Carnegie Endowment for International Peace, 2006), http://www.carnegie.ru/ru/print/75155-print.htm.

7   Pavel Kunanev, "Neftianomu kompleksu ne nravitsia proekt upravleniia im," *Neft' i Kapital*, no. 1 (1995), pp. 13–15; and Mikhail Grigor'ev, "Na kacheliakh," *Neft' i Kapital*, no. 2 (1995), pp. 6–7.

8   Nikolai Lavrov, "Ideia natsional'noi neftianoi kompanii pretenduet na status 'nepotopliaemoi,'" *Neft' i Kapital*, no. 3 (1995), pp. 53–54. In February 1995 Putilov and Shafranik organized a quasi-conspiratorial meeting in Serpukhov—out of sight of the large VICs—at which they discussed creating a national oil company with Shafranik as chairman and Putilov as president. The "second-tier" oil generals who had been invited—Viktor Gorodilov of Noiabrskneftegaz and Viktor Ageev of Purneftegaz—failed to show up. The main attendees were players from the refining and distribution ends of the business, the smaller local producers, and a handful of provincial politicians.

9   Aleksei Sukhodoev and Aleksandr Tutushkin, "Neftianoi marafon finishiroval," *Kommersant-Daily*, October 12, 1995.

10 A detailed chronology of the battle, from its inception in July 1994 to its final conclusion in October 1997, appears in *Neft' i Kapital,* no. 11 (November 1997), p. 5.

11 For an account of the multiple intrigues swirling around the oil sector in the spring of 1997, see Sergei Aleksandrovich, "Doroga bez kontsa," *Neft' i Kapital,* no. 6 (1997), pp. 5–7.

12 Interview with Bogdanchikov by reporter Mikhail Klasson, "Putin skazal mne, 'Idi, spokoino rabotai,'" *Vedomosti,* January 13, 2000.

13 At the time, Exxon's plan for Sakhalin-1 called for an undersea pipeline from Sakhalin to Japan, but the idea ran into opposition from environmental and fishing groups in Japan, as well as from Japanese utilities, which were wedded to LNG. In the end, Exxon was forced to drop the plan—but by that time the prospects for oil production at Sakhalin-1 had become more central than the gas.

14 Sergei Savushkin, "Na myse dobroi nadezhdy," *Neft' i Kapital,* no. 11 (1998), p. 12.

15 For the flavor of that moment, see Aleksandr Davydov, "V 'Rosnefti' novyi prezident," *Vremia MN,* October 19, 1998.

16 Inna Ermishina, "Nadezhdy na deval'vatsiiu ne opravdalis'," *Neft' i Kapital,* no. 11 (1998), pp. 22–24.

17 Klasson interview, "Putin skazal mne."

18 *Neftecompass,* March 21, 2002, pp. 1–2.

19 Aleksandr Savel'ev, "'Rosneft' skoree zhiva, chem mertva," *Trud,* December 5, 1998.

20 "V oktiabre na neftianykh aktsiiakh mozhno bylo zarabotat'," *Neft' i Kapital,* no. 11 (1998), pp. 20–21. See also Nikolai Poluektov, "V 'Rosnefti'—novyi prezident," *Kommersant-Daily,* October 17, 1998; and Sergei Zamkov, "Kto stoit za aferoi s 'Purneftegazom,'" *Rossiiskaia gazeta,* October 22, 1998.

21 Zamkov, "Kto stoit za aferoi s 'Purneftegazom.'"

22 Ibid.

23 The details of the case can be found in Aleksandr Vladimirov, "Kadrovaia chekharda v 'Rosnefti,'" *Nezavisimaia gazeta,* February 11, 1999. See also Nikolai Poluektov, "'Purneftegaz' vernulsia," *Kommersant-Daily,* February 16, 1999; and Oleg Korzunskii, "'Purneftegaz': Koshmar pozadi?," *Rossiiskaia gazeta,* February 10, 1999.

24 Savushkin, "Na myse dobroi nadezhdy," p. 12.

25 Andrei Ivanov, "Bogdanchikova staviat vperedi Teleginoi," *Finansovye Izvestiia,* October 20, 1999.

26 Jeanne Whalen, "Russia Aims to Sell Stakes in Oil Firms, Probably to Insiders," *Wall Street Journal,* October 27, 1999. According to Whalen, Dresdner Kleinwort Benson recommended a price of $305 million for a 25 percent stake, whereas the previous year the same firm had recommended $2.1 billion for a 75 percent stake, before lowering their recommendation to $1.6 billion.

27 Interview with Sergei Bogdanchikov by Nikolai Ivanov, "Idi rabotat'," *Segodnia,* October 20, 1999.

28 Ibid.

29 "Chechenskaia neft' iz betonnykh bunkerov," *Vedomosti,* January 18, 2000.

30 Oleg Chernitskii, "Konkurs na Chechniu," *Vedomosti*, February 9, 2000.

31 A brief report on Grozneftegaz and Rosneft's role in Chechnya appears in *Neftecompass*, October 25, 2001, p. 3.

32 The battle was not finally won until February 1999, when the arbitration court of Yamal-Nenets okrug approved a settlement *(mirovoe soglashenie)* between Purneftegaz and its creditors that finally put an end to the bankruptcy case that had led to the take-over in the first place. Nikolai Poluektov, " 'Purneftegaz' vernulsia," *Kommersant-Daily*, February 16, 1999.

33 Elizaveta Osetinskaia, " 'Rosneft atakuet," *Vedomosti*, April 18, 2000.

34 Elizaveta Osetinskaia, " 'Rosneft vstrevozhila investorov," *Kommersant*, December 25, 2000.

35 Iuliia Bushueva, "Krasnodarskii revansh," *Vedomosti*, February 1, 2001.

36 Ibid.

37 Ibid.

38 *Interfax Petroleum Report* 10, no. 36 (September 7–13, 2001), p. 7.

39 In the mid-1990s a consortium of Western investors, led by Texaco, had formed to ne-gotiate a PSA to develop the most attractive northern prospects, of which the largest was the Varandei field. Initially the Russian member of the consortium had been Ros-neft. But in 1998, at the low point of Rosneft's fortunes, LUKoil pushed it out of the consortium and stepped in.

40 For a review of LUKoil's activities in the Timan-Pechora region in 2001 and its plans for 2002, see "LUKoil to Invest 3.78 Billion Rubles in Arkhangelskgeoldobycha in 2002," *Interfax Petroleum Report* 10, no. 26 (June 29–July 5, 2001), p. 11.

41 Statement by LUKoil vice president Leonid Fedun, *Neftecompass*, November 8, 2001, p. 3, also reported in *Interfax Petroleum Report* 10, no. 45 (November 9–15, 2001), p. 12. According to the *Interfax* story, LUKoil had submitted a proposal to Gazprom to take a 25 percent share in the Shtokman development project, on the strength of AGD's 16 percent share in Rosshelf. Fedun said that LUKoil aimed to become the number two gas producer in Russia.

42 For a description of Conoco's plans at this time, in late 2001, see "Conoco Plans to In-vest $2–2.5 Billion in Russia over Next Few Years," *Interfax Petroleum Report* 10, no. 52 (December 28, 2001–January 3, 2002), p. 5.

43 Aleksandr Tutushkin, " 'LUKoil' opolchil'sia na 'Rosneft,' " *Vedomosti*, December 28, 2000.

44 *Neftecompass*, December 6, 2001, and January 10, 2002. See also "Rosneft meniaet kontseptsiiu," *Neft' i Kapital*, no. 11 (2002), pp. 50–53.

45 A detailed discussion can be found in "Vremia razdela: LUKoil ne stanet monopolis-tom v Timan-Pechore," *Neft' i Kapital*, no. 4 (2003), pp. 6–8.

46 Bogdanchikov interview, *Vedomosti*, February 20, 2003. Following his acquisition of Northern Oil, Bogdanchikov reframed his demand: LUKoil should hand over the licenses to a group of fields located near Val Gamburtseva, which Rosneft now owned as part of Northern Oil. Bogdanchikov's idea was to create a complex around Northern

Oil that would be capable of producing 20 million tons per year (400,000 barrels per day).

47 "Northern Sale: LUKoil on Guard as Vavilov Sells Northern Oil," *Neftecompass*, January 23, 2003, p. 3; and "Closing In: Rosneft Sea's Controversial Northern Oil Deal," *Neftecompass*, February 20, 2003, p. 3.

48 Elizaveta Osetinskaia et al., "Obidy zabyty," *Vedomosti*, February 25, 2003. Only a week before, LUKoil's head of public affairs, Aleksandr Vasilenko, had vowed that LUKoil would fight on. Aleksandr Tutushkin and Aleksandr Bekker, "Vavilov stal bogache na $600 mln," *Vedomosti*, February 13, 2003.

49 "Polar Bears: LUKoil and Rosneft in Arctic Dispute," *Neftecompass*, January 9, 2003, p. 3.

50 Exports credited to Purneftegaz in 1999 were only 0.7 million tons (14,000 barrels per day); by 2001 they had leapt to 3.6 million tons (72,000 barrels per day). (Source: Rosneft.)

51 A good description of the Kharampur group and its early history to 2002 is Svetlana Azarova, "Unesennye vetrom: Litsenzii 'Purneftegaza' sgoraiut na fakelakh," *Neftegazovaia Vertikal'*, no. 13 (2001), pp. 81–84. A detailed update from early 2004, with more description of the difficult geology of the field, is "V tupike: 'Purneftegaz' ne mozhet nachat' promyshlennuiu dobychu gaza na Kharampure," *Neft' i Kapital*, no. 1 (2004), pp. 36–39.

52 Transcript of Bogdanchikov press conference, March 11, 2003, Federal News Service.

53 Aleksei Grivach, "Bednyi rodstvennik: Sergei Bogdanchikov napomnil 'Gazpromu,' chto 'Rosneft' tozhe goskompaniia," *Vremia novostei*, June 11, 2003.

54 "Sor iz izby," *Vedomosti*, June 11, 2003.

55 "V tupike."

56 The Gas Supply Law of 1999 sets an outer bound of 20 percent foreign ownership. However, two presidential decrees of the late 1990s set tighter limits. Presidential Decree No. 529 of May 28, 1997, limited foreign ownership to 9 percent of Gazprom. Presidential Decree No. 943 of August 10, 1998, loosened the limits somewhat by allowing sale to foreigners of another 5 percent.

57 In March 2003 Gazprom board member Boris Fyodorov said in an interview with *Interfax* that a full liberalization of Gazprom's shares would make it possible to "at least double" the company's market capitalization within a year. *Interfax Petroleum Report* 12, no. 10 (March 14–20, 2003), p. 16. Since in the event full liberalization took two years longer than anticipated, Fyodorov's prediction was not realized until 2005.

58 *Interfax Petroleum Report* 12, no. 10 (March 14–20, 2003), p. 16.

59 See Varvara Aglamish'ian and Aleksei Tikhonov, "El'tsin poterial 'Gazprom,' a Putin ego vernul," *Izvestiia*, September 15, 2004.

60 The September 14 press conference is not (or is no longer) available on the Gazprom website, but summaries appeared in the media, notably in Nikolai Gorelov and Andrei Denisov, "Privatizatsiia 'Rosnefti' obernulas' natsionalizatsiei 'Gazproma'," *Vremia novostei*, September 15 2004, http://neftegaz.ru/press/view/876.

61 The reference here is to Gazprom's foreign-traded shares.

62 Here and throughout this chapter, "Gazpromneft" refers to the holding structure created in 2004 to house Rosneft's and Yukos's oil assets inside Gazprom. It is not the same as the present-day GazpromNeft (usually spelled with a capital "N"), which is the renamed Sibneft, purchased by Gazprom in 2005 after the attempt to acquire Rosneft failed. These events are described in detail in this chapter.

63 This item occurs in an otherwise plausible and well-informed narrative of the internal debates leading up to the September 2004 proposal: Liudmila Romanova and Nikolai Makeev, "Syr'evaia vertikal' vlasti," *Gazeta*, September 15, 2004.

64 *Kommersant*, October 4, 2004. In a November 9 interview in *Vedomosti*, Bogdanchikov confirmed that he had written a letter to Putin.

65 This at least is the reconstruction of *Vremia novostei*'s commentators, usually well informed about gas matters. See Nikolai Gorelov, "Priobretenie litsa: 'Rosneft ofitsial'no kupila 'Yuganskneftegaz,'" *Vremia novostei*, December 24, 2004, p. 1.

66 "'Gazpromneft': Zarodysh giganta, sozdavaemogo politicheskoi volei?," *RosBiznesKonsalting*, November 1, 2004.

67 The chief orchestrator may have been Viktor Ivanov, who was responsible for overseeing the judiciary, rather than Igor Sechin, who oversaw the Procuracy. The process was launched by the Ministry of Justice (part of Ivanov's domain), which sent a directive to the Russian Property Fund (RFFI) to sell off the shares in Yuganskneftegaz that the government had seized. The announcement of the date of the auction was delayed while the two agencies exchanged drafts, but the Justice Ministry was clearly in charge of the process, at least to judge from a statement from the chairman of RFFI, Vladimir Zelentsov, that "We need to find out from the Justice Ministry the price, the form of the auction and the date." *Interfax Petroleum Report*, vol. 13, no. 41 (October 14–20, 2004), p. 11. The actual date of the auction was announced by the bailiffs' service of the Russian Federal Property Fund and posted on the website of the government daily *Rossiiskaia gazeta* on November 19, 2004. See also *Interfax Petroleum Report*, vol. 13, no. 46 (November 18–November 24, 2004), pp. 5–10. By Russian law, there had to be a month between the announcement and the auction, so the auction was set for December 19.

68 For a direct quote of Miller's words, see Aleksei Grivach, Andrei Denisov, and Denis Rebrov, "'Gazprom,' kak i bylo skazano...," *Vremia novostei*, December 1, 2004, http://www.eprussia.ru/pressa/articles/376.htm.

69 According to the German daily *Berliner Zeitung*, around this time Chancellor Gerhard Schroeder was helping to assemble a consortium of German banks to support Gazprom's purchase. By early December, Deutsche Bank and ABN AMRO were reported to be leading a pool of banks prepared to extend an unsecured short-term loan of $10 billion to Gazprom, and Gazprom had earmarked an additional $5 billion of its own funds. The total of $15 billion represented the sum thought to be necessary to cover the cost of Yuganskneftegaz itself (approximately $8.6 billion), its tax liabilities ($5 billion for the years 1999 through 2003), and $1.5 billion in other debts. See Irina Reznik and

Anna Nikolaeva, "Bogdanchikov priznalsia," *Vedomosti,* December 1, 2004. One week later, eleven days before the auction, the process was reported to be well along. The consortium had assembled a one-year loan package at 1.3 percent above LIBOR (London Interbank Overnight Rate). See Irina Reznik et al., " 'Gazprom' idet na rekord," *Vedomosti,* December 8, 2004.

70 The Russian media made much of the fact that in late November Gazprom's advisor Deutsche Bank had submitted a report to Gazprom, recommending an aggressive strategy of acquisition. According to news accounts, Deutsche Bank advised Gazprom not only to bid for Yuganskneftegaz but to buy Surgutneftegaz and Sibneft as well. The latter quickly objected that they were not for sale, but an anonymous source from the Presidential Administration was quoted as saying approvingly that the idea was "entirely logical." Irina Reznik and Iuliia Bushueva, "Pokupaite vse: Deutsche Bank sovetuet 'Gazpromu' 'Iugansk,' 'Sibneft" i 'Surgut,'" *Vedomosti,* November 29, 2004.

71 Some prominent members of the Gazprom management board were whispered to be loyal to the siloviki, not to Miller and Dmitri Medvedev. There was a past history. The silovik faction had tried in the past to put its people inside Gazprom—the ex-CFO Boris Iurlov was cited as an example. When Iurlov left Gazprom in April 2004 to become deputy head of the Atomic Energy Agency, it was rumored that Ananenkov had played a role in removing him. (There were, however, other possible explanations, such as a report that Andrei Kruglov, Iurlov's deputy and subsequently his successor, was Miller's brother-in-law. See Aleksei Grivach and Nikolai Gorelov, "Stroitel' finansovykh sistem," *Vremia novostei,* April 14, 2004, http://www.vremya .ru/2004/64/8/96249.html.)

72 The *Wall Street Journal* reported that Matthias Warnig, then a major in the East German Stasi, had worked closely with Putin in Dresden in the late 1980s and remained a close personal friend of the Russian president. Guy Chazan and David Crawford, "In From the Cold," *Wall Street Journal,* February 23, 2005, p. A1. See also a follow-up article in *Manager-Magazin.de,* "Der Präsident, die Stasi und der Banker," February 23, 2005, http://www.manager-magazin.de/unternehmen/artikel/0,2828,343332,00.html and http://www.manager-magazin.de/unternehmen/artikel/0,2828,343332-2,00.html.

73 "Ob uchastii v auktsione po prodazhe 'Iuganskneftegaza' zaiavil glava kontserna 'Gazpromneft,'" *FK-Novosti* (Russian version), November 30. See also Fedor Chaika, " 'Gazprom' priznalsia: On kupit 'Iuganskneftegaz,'" *Izvestiia,* December 1, 2004.

74 Catherine Belton, "Yukos Files for Bankruptcy in Houston," *Moscow Times,* December 16, 2004, p. 1; also Arkady Ostrovsky, Peter Thal Larsen, and Patti Waldmeir, "US Court Move Fuels the Mixture," *Financial Times,* December 18, 2004, http://www.ft.com/cms/s /0/218163a8-5099-11d9-b551-00000e2511c8.html.

75 Petr Sapozhnikov et al., "SOS-menedzhment: YUKOS sdalsia soiuznikam," *Kommersant-Daily,* December 16, 2004, p. 1.

76 Press conference transcript, December 23, 2004, available on the presidential website at http://www.president.kremlin.ru/appears/2004/12/23/1414_type63380type82634_81691 .shtml.

77 This emerged from a press conference by Gazprom spokesman Sergei Kuprianov, as reported by Tat'iana Chaplygina in *Russkii kur'er*, December 24, 2004, p. 9. See also Dmitrii Butrin, "Rasprodazha 'Gazproma': Nadezhda umiraet pervoi," *Kommersant-Daily*, December 22, 2004, p. 1.

78 "Prodazhnaia khronika," *Kommersant-Daily*, December 21, 2004, p. 14; Catherine Belton, "Gazprom Loan Put on Hold," *Moscow Times*, December 17, 2004, p. 1.

79 According to *Gazeta*, Baikalfinansgrup was registered in Tver' on December 6, 2004, by Valentina Davletgareeva, a partner in two Surgut-based investment companies affiliated with Surgutneftegaz. She was accompanied at the auction by Igor' Minibaev, a department head at Surgutneftegaz, who submitted the actual bid. Oksana Shebel'kova and Nikolai Makeev, "'Surgutneftegaz' pereekhal v Tver'," *Gazeta*, December 21, 2004, p. 1. It was later reported that Surgutneftegaz had advanced the $1.7 billion deposit to enable Baikalfinansgrup to register at the auction. Petr Sapozhnikov, "'Rosneft' prostilas' s shel'fom," *Kommersant-Daily*, December 29, 2004, p. 5.

80 Guy Falconbridge, "Mystery Bidder Wins Yugansk for $9.4 Billion," *Moscow Times*, December 20, 2004, p. 1.

81 Quoted in Valeria Korchagina, "Auction Leaves Yukos in Chaos," *Moscow Times*, December 21, 2004, p. 1.

82 Press conference transcript, December 21, 2004, http://www.president.kremlin.ru/appears/2004/12/21/1943_type63380_81545.shtml. (This link appears to be no longer active.)

83 Dmitrii Butrin, "Natsionalizatsiia: Neftianoe pererozhdenie," *Kommersant-Daily*, December 24, 2004, p. 1. Rosneft raised the funds for the purchase by selling Gazprom its 70 percent stake in their joint venture Sevmorneftegaz. This sum was then transferred to the Surgut-based companies that nominally owned Baikalfinansgrup, which in turn repaid Surgutneftegaz, the original source. The amount of the deposit required to register for the Yuganskneftegaz auction was $1.7 billion. See Sapozhnikov, "'Rosneft' prostilas' s shel'fom," p. 5.

84 Gorelov, "Priobretenie litsa: Rosneft," p. 1.

85 Presidential press conference transcript, December 23, 2004.

86 Butrin, "Natsionalizatsiia."

87 Dmitri Dokuchaev, "Kupilis'," *Moskovskie novosti*, December 24, 2004, p. 4.

88 Nikolai Vardul', "Replika: Nefterpezh," *Kommersant-Vlast'*, January 17, 2005, p. 38.

89 Ekaterina Derbilova, "Vsia pravda 'Rosnefti,'" *Vedomosti*, May 17, 2006, p. 1.

90 The main lines of the financing arrangements had already been revealed in a joint press conference by Finance Minister Aleksei Kudrin and the head of the Russian Energy Agency, Sergei Oganesian, in early February 2005. See *FK-Novosti* (Russian version), February 2, 2005.

91 Tat'iana Egorova and Rodion Levinskii, "'Rosneft' spasla 'Yuganskneftegaz' ot otkliucheniia elektrichestvo," *Vedomosti*, December 29, 2004.

92 Petr Sapozhnikov, "Dobycha nefti: My prodolzhaem konstruktivnoe sotrudnichestvo s YUKOSom," *Kommersant-Daily*, February 7, 2005, p. 13.

93 Passing through Khabarovsk in February, Bogdanchikov informed the governor of the province, Viktor Ishaev, that he was pulling out of a joint project to build a gas pipeline from Sakhalin-1 to Khabarovsk. He was quoted in the press as saying the following blunt words: "A few years ago, Rosneft was a different company, and since we had no access to new assets or new reserves, we decided to diversify our company's activity, and to try to make money in other sectors—coal production and participation in pipeline projects. Today the situation has changed. The quantity and quality of our reserves are such that taking part in building a gas pipeline is unprofitable." Quite clearly for Bogdanchikov the acquisition of Yuganskneftegaz changed everything. Oksana Shebel'kova and Nikolai Makeev, "Zimovka: 'Rosneft' zamorozili," *Gazeta*, February 7, 2005, p. 17.

94 A video clip of Bogdanchikov's visit to Yugansk was formerly available on the website of the state *Vesti* television news program, http://www.vesti.ru/comments.html?id=33175, but the link appears to be no longer active. For newspaper coverage, see Sapozhnikov, "Dobycha nefti," p. 13. See also Shebel'kova and Makeev, "Zimovka," p. 17. This last source mentions the detail that Bogdanchikov had earlier planned to go to Yugansk on January 18, but the trip had been postponed.

95 Sapozhnikov, "Dobycha nefti."

96 Ibid.

97 Bogdanchikov press conference, text formerly posted on Rosneft website: http://www .rosneft.ru/infocenter/press/press_29-03-05-1.html (link no longer active). In 2004, amid considerable turmoil, Yuganskneftegaz had invested (according to Bogdanchikov) 11–11.5 billion rubles. This would now be increased to 28 billion rubles.

98 In the event, Yuganskneftegaz barely exceeded 66 million tons (1.32 million barrels per day) in 2009 and 2010, and although it reached a record 66.7 million tons (1.33 million barrels per day) in 2011, that may be close to a peak. (Source: *Infotek*, January issues for 2009, 2010, and 2011.)

99 *Neftecompass*, May 5, 2005, citing an article in *Vedomosti*.

100 *Neftecompass*, July 14, 2005, p. 3.

101 *Neftecompass*, July 28, 2005, p. 5.

102 See http://www.kremlin.ru/text/appears/2005/08/92314.shtml.

103 The controversies surrounding the creation of the state corporations are perceptively analyzed by Tat'iana Stanovaia, political commentator of the Center for Political Technologies in Moscow, who writes regular columns for the online periodical Politkom.ru. See especially "Sud'ba goskoporatsii v Rossii," February 23, 2009, http://www.politcom .ru/7834.html; and "Vozvrashchenie Vladimira Putina—revansh goskorporatsii?," February 13, 2012, http://www.politcom.ru/13301.html.

104 I am grateful to my former Georgetown student, Ilya Breyman, for the analysis of Bogdanchikov's staffing policy, on which the subsequent description is based.

105 In 1998 Nikolai Borisenko became first vice president; Sergei Oganesian was named vice president for foreign projects; Antonina Kim became chief accountant. All three had worked under Bogdanchikov at Sakhalinmorneftegaz. The following year Bogdan-

chikov added a new tier of vice presidents drawn from Sakhalinmorneftegaz: Evgenii Terpugov (first deputy director of SMNG), Aleksandr Fratkin (supplies and transportation at SMNG), Dmitri Shulman (head of security).

106 Bogdanchikov initially looked to ABN-AMRO, with which he had worked in Sakhalin, as his principal financial advisor. In 2003 he recruited Sergei Alekseev from ABN-AMRO and put him in charge of investor relations and corporate finance.

107 In actual fact, Bogdanchikov continued to place people with Sakhalin backgrounds into other senior Rosneft positions, in a style reminiscent of the Soviet tactic of placing loyal commissars alongside technical specialists. Thus Igor Pavlov and Antonina Kim, who had previously worked at Sakhalinmorneftegaz, were both transferred from Purneftegaz into Rosneft's management. Pavlov was appointed deputy general director for economic questions and Kim was named chief accountant. Ramil' Valitov was transferred from general director of Sakhalinmorneftegaz to head supplies and equipment. Even as late as 2006 Bogdanchikov continued to draw from Sakhalin, as in the appointment of Sergei Karaganov as head of personnel and Ivan Chernov as head of strategic and foreign projects. Chernov had played a role in relations with Exxon in the early days of the Sakhalin-1 PSA. Broadly, the division of labor that took shape inside Rosneft was that Sakhalin veterans continued to control the sensitive rent-connected and political functions, such as capital construction, corporate management, personnel and social services, and downstream, while "outsider professionals" handled upstream, refining, finance, legal matters, and investor relations. Finally, as in other state-owned corporations, a representative from the security services rounded out the picture.

108 See John C. Webb and Thane Gustafson, *Bridge to the East: The Yamal-Nenets-Krasnoyarsk Oil Cluster* (Cambridge, MA: IHS Cambridge Energy Research Associates, March 2011). For Russian sources, see Andrei Meshcherin, "Nash parovoz vpered letit?," *Neftegazovaia Vertikal'*, no. 7 (April 20, 2010).

109 Vladimir Baidashin, "Vankorskii proekt: Samye peredovye tekhnicheskie resheniia," *Nefteservis*, no. 1 (2008), pp. 74–76.

110 Presentation by Peter O'Brien, Rosneft vice president for finance and investment, at the Credit Suisse Energy Summit, Vail, Colorado, February 2011, accessed on the Rosneft website at http://www.rosneft.com/attach/0/62/26/Rosneft_Vail_Feb_2011.pdf.

111 See an interview with Andrei Smarovozov, business development manager for Schlumberger Russia Well Services, in *Neftegazovaia Vertikal'*, no. 4 (March 13, 2007).

112 Presentation by Peter O'Brien at CERA Week (annual energy conference of IHS Cambridge Energy Research Associates), Houston, February 2009. Annual production drilling at Yuganskneftegaz more than doubled between 2005 and 2009, from 0.83 million meters to 1.85 million (Rosneft analyst data book, posted on its website at http://www.rosneft.com/Investors/results_and_presentations/analyst_databook/). Only in 2009, as production drilling began to ramp up at Vankor, did Yuganskneftegaz's place in the company's development drilling begin to slip.

113 For an example of the international press coverage in the run-up to the Rosneft IPO, see Arkady Ostrovsky, "Reserves and Reservations," *Financial Times,* April 19, 2006, p. 13.

114 Valeria Korchagina, "Rosneft: Brits Copied BP Deal," *Moscow Times,* April 4, 2003, p. 7.

115 Joanna Chung, "Rosneft Rolls Out Litany of Risks," *Financial Times,* June 27, 2006, p. 1.

116 Joanna Chung and Nikki Tait, "Rosneft Raises $10 Billion in Biggest Russian Offering," *Financial Times,* July 15, 2006, p. 15; also Poussenkova, *Rosneft,* citing figures from the Russian State Statistical Service.

117 See, for example, an analyst report from Troika Dialog, "Rosneft: Poised to Become the Top Oil producer, but Is It a Top Stock?," *Troika Dialog Oil and Gas,* January 10, 2007.

118 Ekaterina Derbilova and Irina Malkova, "Nashe delo—burit', burit', burit'," *Vedomosti,* June 6, 2008.

119 Ibid.

120 Iurii Peredonov, "Kreslo-kachalka," *Kompaniia,* July 12, 2010, http://ko.ru/articles /22348.

121 In May 2012 Putin named Sechin president and CEO of Rosneft. (At this writing Aleksandr Nekipelov remains chairman of the board.)

122 LUKoil's Vagit Alekperov, for example, has campaigned vigorously against what he calls "discrimination" in favor of the state-owned companies. He argues instead for recognizing the private majors as "national" companies, with equal rights and privileges, especially equal access to the Arctic offshore. See for example his interview in *Vedomosti,* December 22, 2011.

9. Krizis

1 Sergei Guriev and Aleh Tsyvinski, "Russian Economy in Crisis: Strategy of Growth and Reforms," in Anders Aslund, Sergei Guriev, and Andrew C. Kuchins, eds., *Russia after the Global Economic Crisis* (Washington, DC: Peterson Institute for International Economics and Center for Strategic and International Affairs, 2010), pp. 9–38. See also World Bank, *Russia Economic Report,* No. 16 (Washington, DC: World Bank, June 2008), http://siteresources.worldbank.org/INTRUSSIANFEDERATION/Resources /rer16_eng.pdf.

2 For an excellent account of the "silovik wars" that broke out over the 2008 succession, see Richard Sakwa, *The Crisis of Russian Democracy: The Dual State, Factionalism, and the Medvedev Succession* (Cambridge: Cambridge University Press, 2011), chapters 5 and 6. I have also had the benefit of Peter Reddaway's insightful research on the same subject, as well as many hours of enlightening conversation.

3 Source: *Rossiiskii statisticheskii ezhegodnik 2007* (Moscow: Goskomstat, 2008).

4 Source: RF Ministry of Finance, http://www1.minfin.ru/common/img/uploaded /library/2011/07/ONBP_2012-2014.doc.

5 Although, once oil revenues were stripped out, the balance was actually negative by 2.9 percent of GDP. (Source: World Bank, *Russian Economic Report,* No. 15, p. 12, http://siteresources.worldbank.org/.)

6 Shinichiro Tabata, "The Russian Stabilization Fund and Its Successor: Implications for Inflation," *Eurasian Geography and Economics* 48, no. 6 (2007), pp. 699–712. The "Stabilization Fund" by 2007 had been split into a Reserve Fund (capped at 10 percent of GDP) and a National Welfare Fund, into which further oil revenues were placed, available for priority investment and social programs.

7 See the discussion in Guriev and Tsyvinski, "Russian Economy in Crisis."

8 World Bank, *Russian Economic Report,* No. 16.

9 Thane Gustafson, *Cracking the Nest Egg? The Growing Battle over Russia's Oil Stabilization Fund* (Cambridge, MA: IHS Cambridge Energy Research Associates, November 2004). The debate over cracking the Stabilization Fund to support various spending projects is well told in Adnan Vatansever's doctoral dissertation, "The Political Economy of Countering the 'Resource Curse': The Case of Russia under Putin (1999–2005)" (PhD diss., Johns Hopkins School of Advanced International Studies, 2008), chapter 7. Kudrin frequently invoked the Norwegian investment fund as a model (Andrei Lavrov, "MinFin prizyvaet variagov," *Gazeta,* December 14, 2006, p. 11). He was convinced that if the Stabilization Fund were tapped, most of it would be wasted or stolen, but even more important (in Kudrin's eyes) that the resulting flood of liquidity would set off an uncontrollable inflationary spiral.

10 Aleksandr Chudodeev, "Iz pervykh ruk: Stabilizirui eto . . . ," *Itogi,* no. 42 (October 19, 2004), p. 30.

11 Andrei Lavrov et al., "Kabinet kamikadze," *Gazeta,* September 26, 2007, p. 7. Gref was named head of the state-owned Sberbank.

12 In 2001 general government expenditures (i.e., the so-called consolidated budget) absorbed 26.6 percent of GDP. In 2005 they were 31.5 percent of GDP; by 2007 they stood at 34.1 percent. World Bank, *Russian Economic Report,* No. 4 (March 2003), p. 12; No. 20 (November 2009), p. 12; http://siteresources.worldbank.org/.

13 World Bank, *Russian Economic Report,* No. 16 (June 2008), p. 12.

14 See Erik Berglof and Alexander Lehmann, "Sustaining Russia's Growth: The Role of Financial Reform," *Journal of Comparative Economics* 37, no. 2 (2008), pp. 198–206.

15 Source: IHS Cambridge Energy Research Associates, derived from official Russian government sources and company reports. For a comprehensive discussion of sources and conventions on upstream oil investment in Russian statistical reporting, see Matthew J. Sagers, Thane Gustafson, Sergej Mahnovski, and John C. Webb, *How Much Is Enough? How Much Tax Relief Will It Take to Restore Growth in Russian Oil Production?* (Cambridge, MA: IHS Cambridge Energy Research Associates, November 2008), pp. 4–11.

16 John D. Grace, *Russian Oil Supply: Performance and Prospects,* copublished by the Oxford Institute of Energy Studies (Oxford: Oxford University Press, 2005), especially chapter 4.

17 The Urals crude marker, which trades at a discount to Brent, peaked on July 11 at $147.47 per barrel and bottomed out on December 24 at $34.21.

18 The sources of this erosion and the policy dilemmas that follow are the central subject of Chapter 13.

19 Total oil-export revenue (from crude and products combined) actually rose from $173.7 billion in 2007 to $241 billion in 2008, reflecting the surge of world oil prices on the eve of recession, but fell to $148.7 billion in 2009 due to the subsequent price crash. Source: *Rossiiskii statisticheskii ezhegodnik 2010* (Moscow: Goskomstat, 2010).

20 Aleksei Kudrin and O. Sergienko, "Posledstviia krizisa i perspektivy sotsial'no-ekonomicheskogo razvitiia Rossii," *Voprosy ekonomiki,* no. 3 (March 2011), pp. 4–19.

21 Additional new measures, which took effect in January 2009, raised the threshold of the production tax from $9 per barrel to $15 and expanded the number of regions eligible for "holidays" from the production tax.

22 In the last decade of the Soviet Union, a romantic film, *Moscow Does Not Believe in Tears,* was briefly popular on screens in the West. Most Western viewers were unaware that the movie's title was a sly reference to the full version of the saying given here.

23 A transcript of Putin's remarks is available on the prime minister's web site at http:// www.government.ru/gov/priorities/docs/3379/. For fuller accounts of the Kirishi meeting, see Aleksandr Bergelis, "Sud'ba rossiiskoi 'neftianki' reshalas' v Kirishakh," *Vesti,* February 14, 2009; and (in a more colorful vein) Andrei Kolesnikov, "Vladimir Putin vyrazil nematerial'nuiu blagodarnost' neftianikam," *Kommersant,* February 13, 2009.

24 See http://www.government.ru/gov/priorities/docs/3379/print/; a video can be downloaded from http://www.government.ru/gov/priorities/docs/3379/video.html.

25 The official protocol of the Kirishi meeting can be found at the website of the Union of Oilfield Equipment Producers, http://www.derrick.ru/?f=z&id=15505.

26 The phrase comes from an informative review of oil-tax policy, "Nalogooblozhenie: 'Nozhnitsy Kudrina' i prianiki dlia izbrannykh," *Neftegazovaia Vertikal',* no. 5 (2010), pp. 16–23.

27 Sergey Shatalov, "Tax Reform in Russia—History and Future" (Economic Policy Distinguished Lecture, presented at the London School of Economics and Political Science, November 10, 2005), http://www.iticnet.org/Public/other_publications.aspx#divYear2006.

28 Matthew J. Sagers and John C. Webb, *From East Siberia to the Pacific: Putin's Oil Pipeline "Project of the Century"* (Cambridge, MA: IHS Cambridge Energy Research Associates, March 2008).

29 The oil industry stands to benefit less from the tax breaks for depleted fields under the Russian (i.e., Soviet) reserve classification system, in which 80 percent of technically recoverable reserves must be depleted in order to qualify a field for fiscal relief, compared with the Western reserve classification systems, which are based on economic criteria of recoverability.

30 Natal'ia Timakova, "Liberaly ponevole: Igor'iu Sechinu i Minenergo porucheno uder-zhat' dobychu nefti," *RusEnergy,* July 3, 2008.

31 Evgenii Strel'tsov, "Vitse-prem'er Igor Sechin: 'Budet uvelichenie dobychi'," *Izvestiia,* May 15, 2008, p. 2.

32 Timakova, "Liberaly ponevole." Timakova's article gives details on the ad hoc tax breaks Sechin obtained for the oil industry after his first meeting with the oil industry in May 2008, three days after the new ministry was announced. He not only obtained new tax holidays for the companies but also took an active hand in accelerating con-struction of the East Siberia–Pacific Ocean pipeline. The threshold at which the extrac-tion tax (MRET) was levied was raised from $9 to $15 per barrel, and the number of regions eligible for MRET holidays was expanded.

33 Sergei Antonov and Dmitri Butrin, "Vitse-prem'er osmatrivaet dobychu," *Kommersant-Daily,* May 29, 2008, p. 14.

34 Filipp Sterkin and Nadezhda Ivanitskaia, "Ustinov pomozhet Sechinu," *Vedomosti,* May 28, 2008.

35 Natal'ia Timakova, "Minenergo ukrepliaet 'neftegazovoe krylo,'" *RusEnergy,* June 4, 2009.

36 Alexander Kemp, *Petroleum Rent Collection around the World* (Halifax, Nova Scotia: Institute for Research on Public Policy, 1987), p. xxxix.

37 As visitors to Russia will notice, retail gasoline prices at the pump are not much differ-ent from the United States. Where the de facto subsidy created by the export-tax wedge may be going, and whom it is benefiting, are interesting questions, but it is not the re-tail consumer. Therefore, in practice, the wedge may not add much to domestic con-sumption after all.

38 Sagers, Gustafson, Mahnovski, and Webb, *How Much Is Enough?,* pp. 25–28. The thresh-old definition of "economic" is a 15 percent internal rate of return. To be sure, most of those same fields were profitable at $100 per barrel, but such high prices would have to prevail over much of the early life of the field to provide a decent return.

39 According to Igor Sechin and GazpromNeft CEO Aleksandr Diukov, responding in early 2010 to a question from then-president Medvedev on the state of the refinery sec-tor, 196 such "mini-refineries" had been built over the previous decade and a half, of which only 80 were officially registered. The others were unlicensed, unregistered, and, according to Sechin, operating illegally. For the verbatim exchange, see http://news .kremlin.ru/transcripts/6856.

40 In the fall of 2008, as oil prices headed downward, Moscow-based analysts for UBS published a study, one of the first to focus on the issue, showing the costs to the compa-nies and the government of the tax subsidies for refined-product exports. UBS Invest-ment Research, *Russian Oil and Gas: A Paradigm Shift Is Needed* (Moscow: UBS Global Equity Research, September 29, 2008), www.ubs.com/investmentresearch.

41 An overview of the ministry's findings, as well as a valuable background discussion of the whole oil-tax issue, appears in a series of articles by Aleksei Kondrashov, Ernst and Young partner in Moscow, in *Vedomosti.* See "Nalogooblozhenie neftianoi otrasli: Pervyi

shag k reforme," *Vedomosti,* September 14, 2011; "Dorozhnaia karta reformy" and "Kak pravil'no izvlech' rentu," *Vedomosti,* October 5, 2011. See also (by the same author) "Strane nuzhny effektivnye nalogi," *Neft' Rossii,* no. 2 (2012), pp. 82–85.

42 Presentation by then-Energy Minister Sergei Shmatko to Prime Minister Putin, "Doklad po voprosu General'noi skhemy razvitiia neftianoi otrasli na period do 2020g," October 28, 2010. Putin's opening speech and response are accessible on the prime minister's website at http://premier.gov.ru/events/news/12784/. A useful summary and commentary on the *Genskhema*'s main points (although based on an earlier, preliminary version) appear in Sergei Savushkin, "Prizadumalis'," *Neft' i Kapital,* no. 11 (2011).

43 Thus Putin praised the four-month extension of reduced export-tax rates recently granted to Vankor. But this, of course, was precisely the sort of Band-Aid approach that the advocates of reform were most critical of.

44 "Zhertva dobychi: Novaia sistema nalogooblozheniia mozhet destimulirovat' nefterererabotku," *RusEnergy,* November 25, 2010.

45 Thus in the December 2010 decree, the export-tax rate scheduled to go into effect in 2011 for "light products" (such as gasoline and diesel) was set at 67 percent of the rate for crude oil, while that of "dark products" (such as fuel oil) was 46.7 percent. The Ministry of Energy proposed to lower the marginal crude-oil export tax rate to 60 percent, while that of all refined products would be 66 percent of the crude rate. This formula came to be known as "60-66." Above $90, the rate for crude oil would drop to 55 percent, while refined products would be taxed at 86 percent of the crude rate. This proposal came to be known as "60-66-55-86." See Filipp Sterkin et al., "Dvoinaia stavka," *Vedomosti,* May 5, 2011, p. 1.

46 The twists and turns of the negotiations over various oil-tax formulas are nicely summarized in "60-66-90 ≠ 90-60-90: Ideal'nykh nalogov ne byvaet?," *Neftegazovaia Vertikal',* no. 17 (September 2011), pp. 60–68.

47 The new Nizhnekamsk refinery in Tatarstan, which began operations in 2011, was built by Taneko, in which Tatneft is the majority shareholder. Construction of the plant represented a risky bet by Tatneft that refined product-export tax breaks would continue indefinitely. In contrast, the other Russian oil companies limited their refinery investment programs during the same period to upgrades at existing plants.

48 Anastasiia Bashkatova, "Neftianiki dobivaiutsia nalogovykh poslablenii," *Nezavisimaia gazeta,* February 22, 2011, p. 4.

49 Reported in RusEnergy, *Dobycha i razvedka,* no. 19 (2011), p. 6.

50 Dmitri Kaz'min et al., "Tsena l'goty," *Vedomosti,* May 20, 2011, p. 3.

51 Tat'iana Zamakhina, "Putin obvinil neftianikov v sgovore," *Moskovskii komsomolets,* May 6, 2011, p. 3.

52 The transcript of the July 2011 meeting at Kirishi is available on the prime minister's website at http://premier.gov.ru/events/news/15842/. The accompanying video is accessible at http://premier.gov.ru/events/news/15842/video.html.

53 Kondrashov, "Dorozhnaia karta reformy" and "Kak pravil'no izvlech' rentu."

54 "60-66-90 ≠ 90-60-90."

55 Ibid. See also "Biudzhet 2012: Nasos dlia neftedollarov," *Neftegazovaia vertikal'*, no. 2 (2012), pp. 22–30.

56 This episode is discussed in Chapter 13.

10. Strong Thumbs, Weak Fingers

1 This nice phrase was originally coined by Yale political scientist Charles E. Lindblom in his classic book *Politics and Markets: The World's Political-Economic Systems* (New York: Basic Books, 1977).

2 Prince Nikolai Karamzin (1766–1826), Russian historian and essayist, is famous among Russians for this one phrase, uttered by Karamzin during a visit to western Europe in 1789–1790.

3 Nikolai Lisovskii spent much of his career in the Bashkir oil industry. In 1980 he was promoted to chief geologist of the USSR Ministry of Oil, and he was in charge of all geological work in the Ministry until it was dissolved in 1992. He served continuously on the Central Commission on Oilfield Development (TsKR) from 1978 until his death in 2009. A brief biography appears in *Neftianoe khozisiatvo* at http://www.oil-industry .ru/images/upload/pozdravlenija/2007/126_Lisovskiy_pozdr.pdf.

4 Rosneft website, http://www.rosneft.ru/printable/news/news_in_press/14022011.html.

5 V. F. Baziv et al., eds., *U rulia razrabotki neftianykh mestorozhdenii (35 let TsKR Minto-penergo RF)* (Moscow: VNIIOENG, 1998).

6 www.gkz-rf.ru. The State Commission was founded in 1927. It is currently part of Rosnedra, the agency responsible for coordinating exploration and licensing of the Ministry of Natural Resources.

7 The Central Commission was founded in 1963, initially under the USSR Ministry of the Oil Industry. After the end of the Soviet Union, it was housed in the Ministry of Fuel and Power (Mintopenergo). Today it is part of the Ministry of Natural Resources (MPR). For a history of the TsKR, see Baziv et al., *U rulia razrabotki neftianykh mestorozhdenii*.

8 http://www.gosnadzor.ru/. In 2004 the agency took its present form, bringing together the functions of overseeing industrial and mining safety, ecological impact, and radiation hazards. As such it covers the entire energy sector.

9 See Yoshiko M. Herrera, "The Transformation of State Statistics," in Timothy J. Colton and Stephen Holmes, eds., *The State after Communism: Governance in the New Russia* (Lanham, MD: Rowman and Littlefield, 2006), pp. 53–86.

10 Sergei Verezemskii, "Spokoino, zdes' vse svoi," *Neft' i Kapital,* no. 10 (1996), pp. 10–13. In 2004 FEK was abolished and its tariff-setting functions were taken over by a newly created Federal Tariff Service (Federal'naia Sluzhba po Tarifam).

11 V. A. Kriukov and A. N. Tokarev, *Neftegazovye resursy v transformiruemoi ekonomike: O sootnoshenii realizovannoi i potentsial'noi obshchestvennoi tsennosti nedr* (Novosibirsk: "Nauka-Tsentr," 2007), pp. 50–51.

12 Indeed, a broad review of over 20,000 licenses by MPR in 2001 found that in about 1,000 cases the license conditions were totally disregarded. Even so, only forty licenses were singled out for cancellation—but those were recommendations only, and the cancellations were not acted upon. Kriukov and Tokarev, *Neftegazovye resursy v transformiruemoi ekonomike,* p. 53. See also an interview with then minister Vitalii Artiukhov by Aleksandr Tutushkin, "Obespechit' prikhod bol'shikh deneg v bol'shuiu geologiiu," *Vedomosti,* January 16, 2002, http://www.vedomosti.ru/newspaper/article/2002/01/16 /39792#ixzz1dhQuKf2k.

13 Sergei Verezemskii, "Pribyl' 'Transnefti' mozhet stat' 'razumnoi i spravedlivoi'," *Neft' i Kapital,* nos. 6–7 (1998), pp. 49–52; Vadim Kravets, "Regulirovanie monopolii prokhodit pod zhestkim kontrolem samikh monopolii," *Neft' i Kapital,* no. 4 (1997), pp. 20–23.

14 See I. Mishchenko, "Primenenie GRP trebuet kraine ostorozhnogo i izbiratel'nogo podkhoda," *Neft' i Kapital,* no. 9 (2005), pp. 50–51.

15 Author's interview, March 8, 2006.

16 Rather than describe the Russian oil companies as "owners" of the oil they produce under license, it is perhaps more appropriate to compare them to "lessees." In other words, they stand in roughly the same position relative to the state as producers in many other countries, including the United States, where oil companies operating on federal lands or in federal waters are subject to regulations imposed by the state. Even in the onshore United States, where mineral rights can be individually owned, there is a wide variety of state regulations that apply to producers and transporters.

17 Kriukov and Tokarev, *Neftegazovye resursy v transformiruemoi ekonomike,* p. 53. The same issues arise, as we shall see in a later chapter, over the disposition of the oil. The Russian state under Putin considers itself entitled to dictate whether oil, even produced by a private company, is exported as crude or passed through a refinery, and if the latter, what slate of products and product exports is appropriate.

18 However, the SPE and SEC systems serve different purposes, and the SEC standard of reserves is more conservative. See John D. Grace, *Russian Oil Supply: Performance and Prospects,* co-published by the Oxford Institute for Energy Studies (Oxford: Oxford University Press, 2005), pp. 256–260. In 2007, the Society of Petroleum Engineers adopted a new system, called the Petroleum Resources Management System, or PRMS, aimed at bringing into closer alignment the different systems in use in various countries. But the essence of the revised SPE system (now known as SPE-PRMS) remains focused on the individual project and its commerciality.

19 For two useful overviews of the differences between the Russian and international systems of reserves classification as they were to the late 2000s, see John D. Grace, "Molecules and Money: True Value in Oil and Gas Reserves," *Petroleum Intelligence Weekly,* May 3, 2004, p. 6; and V. I. Poroskun, A. M. Khitrov, O. V. Zaborin, M. Y. Zykin, S. Heiberg, and E. Sondenå, "Reserves/Resource Classification Schemes Used in Russia and Western Countries: A Review and Comparison," *Journal of Petroleum Geology* 27, no. 1 (January 2004), pp. 85–94. The Grace essay is an enlightening reflection on the nature of an oil reserve; the Poroskun article is more technical. In addition, a useful

primer written for investors is Paul Collison, Maxim Moshkov, and Andrei Matchans-kis, "The Russian Hydrocarbon Resource Base" (Moscow: Brunswick UBS Global Equity Research, March 9, 2004).

20 Thane Gustafson and Konstantin Kovalenko, *The Controversy over Oil Exploration and Reserves in Russia* (Cambridge, MA: IHS Cambridge Energy Research Associates, May 2005).

21 Source: State Statistical Committee (Rosstat), *Rossiiskii statisticheskii ezhegodnik 2008*, section 2.3, http://www.gks.ru/bgd/regl/B10_13/IssWWW.exe/Stg/d1/02-03.htm. These numbers group together the three branches of government (executive, legislative, and judiciary, of which the executive is by far the largest component) but do not include law enforcement officials (FSB, MVD) or the military. See also Andrei Dolgikh and Mikhail Kalmatskii, "Apparat raspukh: Kolichestvo chinovnikov v strane postoianno uvelichivaetsia," *Novye izvestiia*, April 29, 2008, quoting Lev Iakobson, a prominent expert on the state apparatus at the Higher School of Economics and formerly a member of the government's commission on administrative reform.

22 The swelling of the federal bureaucracy at regional levels has been especially controversial. See Mikhail Vorob'ev, "Suslik federal'nogo podchineniia," *Vremia novostei*, November 20, 2006, http://www.vremya.ru/2006/213/4/165816.html. In absolute numbers, the regional offices of the federal government increased from 483,700 in 2000 to 821,400 in 2010.

23 The total regional and local bureaucracy (as opposed to regional offices of federal agencies) grew steadily through 2008 but shrank slightly in 2009 and 2010 to 272,600 regional-level and 507,000 municipal and local employees.

24 Note, though, that the size of the central bureaucracy (defined as employees of federal agencies working in the central apparatus in Moscow) went through a spurt in 2008–2010, from 41,100 to 47,500 in 2010.

25 Peter Reddaway, "Historical and Political Context," in Peter Reddaway and Robert W. Orttung, eds., *The Dynamics of Russian Politics: Putin's Reform of Federal-Regional Relations,* 2 vols. (Lanham, MD: Rowman and Littlefield, 2004), 1:1–19. See also Nikolai Petrov, "The Security Dimension of the Federal Reforms" and "How Have the Presidential Envoys Changed the Administrative-Political Balance of Putin's Regime?," both in Reddaway and Orttung, *The Dynamics of Russian Politics*, 2:7–32 and 2:33–64.

26 On the relations of power between the FSB and the regional federal inspectors, see an interview with the federal inspector for Perm' Oblast', the home province of then governor Iurii Trutnev, lately minister of natural resources. The interview makes clear that the federal inspectors were under the supervision of the FSB. Nikolai Fadeev, "Tret'ii chelovek," *Zvezda*, December 20, 2002.

27 The most detailed revelations on this point came in a 2007 interview with Oleg Shvartsman, the manager of an investment fund called *Finansgrup*, whose major clients, the manager claimed, were the families of high-ranking siloviki. "Partiiu dlia nas olitsetvoriaet silovoi blok, kotoryi vozglavliaet Igor' Ivanovich Sechin," *Kommersant*,

November 30, 2007, http://www.kommersant.ru/doc-rss/831089. For an interpretation of the Shvartsman interview as part of the increasingly tense politics of the presidential succession at that time, see Richard Sakwa, *The Crisis of Russian Democracy: The Dual State, Factionalism, and the Medvedev Succession* (Cambridge: Cambridge University Press, 2011), pp. 205–207.

28 In framing this chapter I have profited from the writing of Vladimir Pastukhov, a well-known lawyer and professor at the Moscow School of Economics, in particular his article, "Law under Administrative Pressure in Post-Soviet Russia," *East European Constitutional Review* 11, no. 2 (Summer 2002), pp. 66–74.

29 Andrew Kramer, based in part on interviews with former TNK-BP employees Bruce Morrow and Frank Rieber, "Mapmakers and Mythmakers," *New York Times*, December 1, 2005. As Kramer observes, there is also a commercial motive involved, since the oil companies pay "scores of FSB-licensed cartographers" to encode and decode maps. "Oil companies either outsource the work of stripping and restoring coordinates to independent institutes," Kramer writes, "or employ Russians with security clearances to do the work, as TNK-BP does."

30 Russian law makes a distinction between disclosure of reserves data on individual fields, which is legal, and reserves data on whole provinces or Russia as a whole, which are secret. That at least is the interpretation of the Ministry of Natural Resources, based on a government resolution, No. 210 of April 2002. See statement by Deputy Natural Resources Minister Ivan Glumov, quoted in *Interfax Petroleum Report* 11, no. 23 (June 7–13, 2002), p. 5. However, at the time of the Yukos Affair there were reports that the FSB was investigating the disclosure of reserves data to nonresident employees of oil companies, notably TNK-BP. See "TNK-BP Seeks Changes to Russian Law on Information Disclosure," *Interfax Petroleum Report* 13, no. 21 (May 27, 2004); and Andrei Panov et al., "FSB skryvaet podrobnosti: Inostrantsam zapreshcheno pristal'no razgliadyvat' Rossiiu," *Vedomosti*, October 24, 2005. As recently as 2005, regional offices of the FSB reportedly threatened to shut down operations at some sites operated by TNK-BP, on the grounds that foreign operators were barred by secrecy rules from seeing maps with a resolution finer than 1/2500 (i.e., 1 centimeter = 25 meters).

31 This did not happen without conflict. In 2001 the then minister of energy, Igor' Yusufov, attempted to take over the licensing and oversight function from MPR and place it in Mintopenergo. This was partly motivated by the perception that MPR, under its then minister Vitalii Artiukhov, was hostile to the interests of the energy sector. See Natal'ia Melikova, "Ministerskii peredel," *Nezavisimaia gazeta,* October 23, 2001.

32 In particular, as a result of the 2004 reorganization of the executive branch, the Central Commission on Oilfield Development (TsKR) was transferred from the Ministry of Energy (Minenergo) to the Ministry of Natural Resources (Minprirody), under the authority of Rosnedra, which oversees exploration and licensing. Rosnedra claimed

that TsKR had become too sympathetic to the oil companies and was trespassing on the regulatory responsibilities of the Ministry of Natural Resources. There was indeed a basis for conflict of interest, in that the various expert studies carried out by specialized institutes at the request of the TsKR were financed by the oil companies. It is not clear that this conflict of interest has disappeared, however, as a result of the transfer.

33 In May 2012, as part of a general reshuffling of government ministers following Dmitri Medvedev's assumption of office as prime minister, Trutnev was replaced by a former deputy, Sergei Donskoi (http://www.mnr.gov.ru/mnr/minister/biography.php). Trutnev, along with a number of the replaced ministers, was named an assistant to President Putin in the Presidential Administation.

34 *Interfax Oil and Gas Report,* no. 26 (June 22–28, 2006), p. 17.

35 See "Nedra ne v mode," *RusEnergy,* March 10, 2011.

36 See, for example, an *Interfax* report in May 2004, "Most Subsoil Licenses in Russia Drawn up Improperly," *Interfax Petroleum Report* 13, no. 21 (May 27–June 2, 2004), p. 31.

37 Anna Gorshkova, "Kamennyi tsvetok: Razrabotka novogo zakona 'O nedrakh' okazalas' pravitel'stvu nc po zubam," *Vremia novostei,* no. 40 (March 7, 2007), http://www.vremya.ru/2007/40/4/173089.html. See also two valuable Western studies: Stephen Fortescue, "The Russian Law on Subsurface Resources: A Policy Marathon," *Post-Soviet Affairs* 25, no. 2 (2009), pp. 160–184; and Yuko Adachi, "Subsoil Law Reform in Russia under the Putin Administration," *Europe-Asia Studies* 61, no. 8 (October 2009), pp. 1393–1414.

38 He was eventually defeated by Gazprom's vigorous lobbying and the Ministry of Industry and Energy, which conveniently created a list of fields "of federal significance," enabling Gazprom to claim that under the Law on Gas Supply it was entitled to take them over. Two government orders signed by Prime Minister Viktor Zubkov, in April and May 2008, finally transferred the fields to Gazprom: "'Gazprom' poluchil, chto khotel: 9 mestorozhdenii bez konkursa," *Polit.ru,* May 14, 2008, http://www.polit.ru/news/2008/05/14/bez_konkursa/.

39 Despite a steady stream of grumpy press releases from Minprirody and Trutnev over the years, there is little sign that Trutnev was able to influence the companies' level of spending for exploration. Yet he did not give up. In 2009, in response to the crash in oil prices and the economic recession, Trutnev vowed, "The government is taking all necessary measures so that exploration work in 2009 is not cut back by even one ruble. . . . We don't plan to relax licensing requirements. . . . Those will entail penalties just as they have in the past." Source: "Russian Oil Majors to Cut Back Exploration Work in 2009—Trutnev," *Interfax Russia and CIS Oil and Gas Weekly,* no. 6 (February 12–18, 2009), p. 14. But these proved to be empty threats.

40 See for example (with caution) Oleg Aleksandrov, "'Korruptsionnoe tsarstvo' Iuriia Trutneva," *Moscow Post,* March 29, 2012, http://moscow-post.ru/politics/korruptsionnoe_tsarstvo_jurija_trutneva8774/.

41 Indeed, Trutnev presumably owed his initial appointment to the fact that he was seen as a provincial governor who would be effective in carrying out a policy of curtailing the powers of other provincial governors.

42 Anatolii Ledovskikh, the head of Rosnedra until his retirement in May 2012, was a longtime agricultural official and rural district executive from Leningrad Oblast' who was originally trained as a veterinarian. (In what may mark a welcome change of policy, he was replaced by Aleksandr Popov, an "Indus" graduate with a degree in oil and gas drilling, who previously headed Severneftegazprom and Vostokgazinvest, and most recently served as an aide to Igor Sechin.) Vladimir Kirillov, the chairman of Rosprirodnadzor, is a former KGB officer who retired from the service in 1991 and built a second career in the government of the Vyborg District of Saint Petersburg. By 2000 he was the head of administration of Vyborg, and from 2000 to 2007 he was first vice governor of Leningrad Oblast'. Nikolai Kut'in, the head of Rostekhnadzor, is likewise a former official from Saint Petersburg, originally trained as a jurist, who served in the Saint Petersburg Property Committee.

43 In contrast, the only one of the agency heads with ties to Perm'—and who thus might have been regarded as a Trutnev protégé—was Iurii Podturkin, the head of the State Commission on Reserves (GKZ), who was also the only one of the group with significant career experience in oil. Podturkin's professional biography appears on the website of the GKZ at http://www.gkz-rf.ru/index.php?option=com_content&view=article&id=48&Itemid=60.

44 At the time of Ledovskikh's appointment at the head of Rosnedra, it was rumored that Trutnev himself had wanted his ally Aleksei Varlamov to get the position, but Ledovskikh was recommended directly to the president by a personal friend, the head of Rosrezerv Aleksandr Grigor'ev. See Mikhail Fedorov, "Ministr i ego nedrugi," *Russkii kur'er*, no. 50 (December 18, 2006), p. 8.

45 Kriukov and Tokarev, *Neftegazovye resursy v transformiruemoi ekonomike*, p. 58.

46 Evgeniia Pis'mennaia et al., "Putinskaia vertikal'," *Vedomosti*, May, 14, 2008.

47 A biographical essay, complete with abundant footnotes to press sources, has been compiled in *Lentapedia* from the massive media coverage on Mitvol' over the years. See http://lenta.ru/lib/14159313/full.htm. See also the lengthy 2007 interview with Mitvol' in *Moskovskie novosti*, April 6, 2007, p. 34.

48 From the coverage by the *Moscow Times* over the years, see Miriam Elder, "The Mysterious Influence of Inspector Mitvol," *Moscow Times*, December 12, 2006, p. 1; Elder, "Mitvol Facing Official Rebuke," *Moscow Times*, December 15, 1996, p. 1; Elder, "A Little Oil Firm Playing a Big Game," *Moscow Times*, December 21, 2007, p. 1; Elder, "Mitvol's Agency to Probe TNK-BP," *Moscow Times*, March 24, 2008, p. 1; Elder, "Mitvol's Boss Seeks His Ouster," *Moscow Times*, February 21, 2008, p. 7.

49 Konstantin Smirnov, "Minprirodnyi kataklizm," *Gazeta*, December 15, 2006, p. 13.

50 Dmitrii Butrin and Ol'ga Mordiushenko, "Rosprirodnadzor ishchet na sebia upravu," *Kommersant-Daily*, July 15, 2008, p. 2; Kirill Mel'nikov, "Minus Mitvol'," *Vremia no-*

vostei, August 6, 2008, p. 1; and Kirill Mel'nikov, "Mitvolevoe reshenie," *Vremia novostei,* July 15, 2008, p. 1. For background on Kirillov, see note 42.

51 Strictly speaking, the order did not dismiss Mitvol', but merely reduced the number of deputy heads of Rosprirodnadzor from four to three, which left Mitvol' as the odd man out. Trutnev attempted to dismiss another deputy head instead, but Kirillov was evidently able to defeat this maneuver as well. News report in Lenta.ru, http://lenta.ru/lib /14159313/full.htm.

52 For a transcript of the prime minister's remarks, see the government's official website at http://www.premier.gov.ru/events/news/4351.html.

53 Irina Malkov et al., "Chetyre iz 150 i eshche 46," *Vedomosti,* January 22, 2009.

54 For a thorough review of center-regional relations in the 1990s and an overview of Putin's centralization policies, see Kathryn Stoner-Weiss, "Resistance to the Central State on the Periphery," in Colton and Holmes, *The State after Communism,* pp. 87–120. For a more detailed book-length study, see also Reddaway and Orttung, *The Dynamics of Russian Politics.*

55 Ivan Egorov-Tismenko, "Beg po krugu," *RusEnergy,* September 19, 2008.

56 Aydyn Dzhebrailov and Iurii Kravchenko, "Nagrada za investitsii: O problemakh preobrazovaniia geologicheskoi litsenzii v ekspluatatsionnuiu," *Neft' i Kapital,* no. 11 (2003).

57 In contrast to an *auktsion* (auction), which favors the highest bidder (all other things being equal), the *konkurs* (tender) is won by the company offering the overall field development program preferred by the tender committee. By definition, the criteria of success in investment tenders are less transparent than in the case of auctions, and tenders are more easily won by companies affiliated with political elites (at the regional or central levels) represented on the committees.

58 See the coverage in *Neft' i Kapital* throughout 2007, notably in "Litsenzii—prodlit', s bureniem—ne speshit'," no. 6, www.indpg.ru/nik/2007/06/3879.html; Sergei Bogdanchikov, "Platsdarm dlia Arktiki," no. 7, www.oilcapital.ru/analytics/2007/07/241155_111963.shtml; and "Uspeli! Prezident podpisal Zakon o prodlenii sroka GRR na shel'fe, a pravitel'tsvo utverdilo perechen' strategicheskikh mestorozhdenii," no. 12, www.oilcapital.ru /company/154922.html. The government extended the duration of exploration licenses on the shelf from five years to ten and created by decree a list of "strategic" fields in which foreign companies would not be allowed to be operators. However, it failed to deal with the problem of "full-cycle" licensing and did not address the problem of moving from tenders to auctions. See interview with Viktor Orlov, "Uchastie inostrannykh kompanii v osvoenii shel'fa neizbezhno," *Neft i Kapital,* no. 6 (2007), www.indpg.ru/nik/2007/06 /3871.html.

59 Denis Rebrov, "Nedra natsional'noi bezopasnosti," *Vremia novostei,* June 23, 2005, www .vremya.ru/2005/110/8/128204.html.

60 Viktor Somov, "Nikto ne khotel ustupat': Regiony i federal'nyi tsentr soshlis' v skhvatke za nedra," *RusEnergy,* September 21, 2005. Ironically, the fact that the regional governors were no longer elected locally but appointed by the center caused them

to reassert the prerogatives of the regions, on the grounds that the center had already won its battle for central control and therefore further centralizing measures (such as the draft mineral resources law) were uncalled for. See the remarks by Sergei Mironov, speaker of the Council of the Federation, during hearings on the draft law in March 2005, http://www.council.gov.ru/inf_ps/chronicle/2005/03/item2905 .html.

61 E. V. Novikova, "O problemakh reformirovaniia zakonodatel'stva o nedrakh," *Gosudarstvo i pravo,* no. 4 (April 2007), pp. 18–24.

62 A scandal over a patently rigged tender in 2001, in which the Val Gamburtseva field was awarded to the Severnaya Neft' (Northern Oil) Company, gave the temporary advantage to those who wanted to eliminate tenders in favor of auctions. But by 2006–2007 the state companies had come to realize that tenders favored their interests. By 2008 the issue had become moot, since the law on investment in strategic sectors, passed in that year, made direct awards to the state companies legal. For background on tenders versus auctions, see Iurii Kogtev, "Prozrachnye konkursy: V Rossii vozrozhdaiutsia davno zabytye formy litsenzirovaniia nedr," *RusEnergy,* May 8, 2009.

63 See, for example, "Sobaka laet—karavan idet," *Neft' i Kapital,* no. 6 (2007), www.indpg .ru/nik/2007/06/3877.html.

64 The evolution of the debate can be conveniently followed on Trutnev's personal website. See in particular his June 19, 2006, interview with *Interfax,* available at http://www .trutnev.ru/smi/view/64.html.

65 Throughout 2005–2006, for example, Litvinenko campaigned against Trutnev and the draft law, attempting to enlist the support of the regional governors against it. In August 2005, together with the former USSR minister of geology Evgenii Kozlovskii, Litvinenko published a detailed critique of Trutnev's draft law. Evgenii Kozlovskii and Vladimir Litvinenko, "Novyi zakonoproekt 'O nedrakh' skvoz' prizmu obshchenatsional'nykh interesov," *Promyshlennye Vedomosti,* no. 8 (August 8, 2005), http://www.pv.derrick.ru /articles/article.phtml?id=543&nomer=21.

66 "Izvlekaemyi zapas—eto tekhnicheski izvlekaemyi zapas, a stoimost' pust' bukhgal'tery schitaiut." Cited in Mikhail Krutikhin, "V trekhmernom prostranstve: Rossiia gotovitsia priniat' novuiu klassifikatsiiu zapasov," *RusEnergy,* July 16, 2008. This source gives a useful overview of the proposed new system.

67 Kirill Mel'nikov, "Gosudarstvo ne dobralos' do zapasov," *Kommersant,* January 30, 2012.

68 In some cases political pressure is to bend the regulations, in others to further them. An example of the former—very much a continuation of Soviet-era practices—was the pressure put on TsKR to give early approval to Rosneft's production plan for Vankor, despite the fact that only 62 percent of the reserves identified to that point had been confirmed to the C1 level. It was widely believed among Russian geologists that TsKR was under pressure to give its approval so Rosneft could go ahead quickly and begin developing Vankor in parallel with its exploration program. But this carried a higher

risk that Rosneft could get the reserves number wrong or develop the wrong places. Natal'ia Timakova, "Vankkorskoe chudo," *RusEnergy,* June 8, 2007. At the other extreme is Putin's campaign to compel the oil companies to cut back flaring of associated gas, which aims to enforce existing regulations that mandate 95 percent utilization of associated gas but had been widely ignored by the companies until Putin decided to make the issue a political priority. But even then progress has been slow.

69　Thus despite official rhetoric in support of smaller operators, the regulatory system does very little to accommodate their special needs and circumstances. One of the few exceptions is a measure adopted in 2010 allowing operators of small fields (i.e., producing less than 25,000 tons per year, or 182,500 barrels), to deviate from the production levels specified in the FDP by as much as 50 percent, whereas fields producing over 25 million tons per year (or 182.5 million barrels) may not deviate by more than 7.5 percent.

70　Author's interview with Leonid Fedun, May 2009.

71　Transcript of Trutnev presentation to a meeting of the Cabinet, March 27, 2008, http://www.mnr.gov.ru/files/part/3131_yupt_tek_itogi_27_marta.doc.

72　At the time of this writing, the "state reserve" is still a tentative proposal that may or may not be realized, but in the meantime has added to the general atmosphere of uncertainty and mistrust between the state and the companies. By one interpretation, the state reserve is yet another device for reserving promising acreage to the state-owned companies. Another and more benign view is that the companies' failure to participate in auctions is leaving the state with an excess of undistributed properties, and the proposed state reserve is little more than a temporary parking lot. But the private oil companies have been outspoken in their opposition to the plan, particularly LUKoil. See Aleksandr Gudkov, "Gosrezerv budet sozdan iz nedobytoi' nefti," *Kommersant-Daily,* April 28, 2009, p. 2.

73　*RIA Novosti,* March 20, 2009, http://www.rian.ru/business/20090320/165477180.html.

74　Andrei Chernobylets, "Era geologicheskikh zakrytii," *Ekspert Sibir',* February 9, 2009, expert.ru/siberia/2009/04/sokreschenie_grr/.

11. The Half-Raised Curtain

1　LUKoil is an exception to this pattern, mainly no doubt because of the non-Russian background of its founder and CEO, Vagit Alekperov, and perhaps also because of the influence of its longtime chairman of the board (and Alekperov's onetime patron), Valerii Graifer. Graifer is simultaneously the founder and CEO of RITEK, a high-tech start-up affiliated with LUKoil that has acquired subsidiaries in the United States since the early 1990s. For a Russian commentary on LUKoil's external activity in the wake of the 2008–2009 crisis and recession, see "Gde trava zelenee," *RusEnergy,* January 27, 2010. A useful survey of the overseas activity of all the Russian oil companies in Africa, Latin America, and Asia appears in Ol'ga Vinogradova, "Rossiiskii apstrim," *Neftegazovaia Vertikal',* no. 11 (2011), pp. 26–38.

2   A survey of 33,000 technical papers added to the library of the OnePetro website over the decade 2000–2010 found only 240 contributed by identifiably Russian authors working in Russian institutions. (In addition, a further 131 papers came from Russian authors working for Schlumberger and Halliburton.) Most of the "Russian" papers came from Russian oil companies and only a small number from Russian research institutes or R&D and engineering firms. Russian universities were practically unrepresented. By way of contrast, the petroleum engineering department of Texas A&M contributed 783 papers over the same period. (I am indebted for this information to Dr. Iskander Diyashev of the Independent Resource Development Corporation in Moscow.)

3   The SPE Education and Accreditation Committee lists 71 universities worldwide as meeting industry-recognized standards. The petroleum engineering program at Tomsk Polytechnic was revived in the late 1990s and funded by Yukos, in association with Herriot-Watt University of the United Kingdom. Tomsk Polytechnic's program is also supported by several other Russian oil companies, notably by Surgutneftegaz.

4   Goldman Sachs Equity Services, "Russia Energy: Oil Services" (Moscow: Goldman Sachs, August 19, 2011), p. 11. Data sourced from company data, compiled by Goldman Sachs.

5   Thane Gustafson, John C. Webb, and Paulina Mirenkova, *The Russian Oil Industry in Global Perspective: The Challenges Ahead* (Cambridge, MA: IHS Cambridge Energy Research Associates, April 2011).

6   A stark example is the Uralmash complex in Ekaterinburg, which was the Soviet Union's leading producer of heavy drilling rigs.

7   For example, Surgutneftegaz, although it spends over $1 billion per year acquiring new designs and equipment, spends only about $45 million per year on internal research and development. Presentation by CEO Vladimir Bogdanov to the President's Commission on Modernization and Technological Development of the Economy of the Russian Federation, Khanty-Mansiisk, March 2010, http://www.i-russia.ru/sessions/10.html.

8   Interview with Leonid Fedun in Andrei Vin'kov, Ivan Rubanov, and Dmitrii Sivakov, "Zametit' korovu v korovnike," *Ekspert*, no. 12 (March 28, 2011), pp. 36–44.

9   See, for example, the analysis of the problems of the Russian software industry in Keith Crane and Artur Usanov, "The Role of High Technology Industries in the Russian Economy," in Anders Aslund, Sergei Guriev, and Andrew C. Kuchins, eds., *Russia after the Global Economic Crisis* (Washington, DC: Petersen Institute for International Economics and Center for Strategic and International Affairs 2010), pp. 95–124.

10   See the Novomet website at www.novomet.ru. Powder metallurgy was a highly developed branch of materials science in Soviet times, with many applications in military industry.

11   See the Burintekh website at http://burinteh.ru/rus/about/me/.

12   These trends are detailed in the extensive annual reports prepared by IHS Herold and Harrison Lovegrove and Co., *Global Upstream Performance Review.*

13 On the national oil companies, see *The Changing Role of National Oil Companies in International Energy Markets* (Houston, TX: James A. Baker III Institute for Public Policy, Rice University, and Japanese Petroleum Energy Center, 2007). The report contains individual chapters on most of the leading NOCs, as well as an overall assessment of their performance. The report is available online at http://bakerinstitute.org/programs/energy -forum/publications/energy-studies/nocs.html.

14 Daniel Yergin, *The Quest: Energy, Security, and the Remaking of the Modern World* (New York: Penguin Press, 2011), chapter 4.

15 Background on BP in the 1970s and 1980s will be found in Daniel Yergin, *The Prize: The Epic Quest for Oil, Money, and Power* (New York: Simon and Schuster, 1991). Browne's own account appears in his autobiography, *Beyond Business. The Inside Story: Leadership and Transformation in BP* (London: Weidenfeld and Nicholson, 2010).

16 Browne, *Beyond Business*, p. 135.

17 The agreement was signed by Vladimir Potanin and John Browne on November 18, 1997, in the presence of British prime minister Tony Blair. It was seen by both sides as a preliminary step toward a joint bid by BP and Oneksimbank for the government's stake in Rosneft, for which an auction was expected to take place at the end of 1997. See Aleksandr Tutushkin and Gleb Baranov, "Odnim vystrelom Potanin ubil trekh zaitsev," *Kommersant-Daily*, November 19, 1997.

18 Iuliia Latynina, "Zakhvat po-russki: Dva zelenykh krokodila i odin britanskii lokh," *Sovershenno sekretno*, no. 11 (1999), p. 12. German Khan interview in *Vedomosti*, "Na samom dele ia nezhnyi i pushistyi," *Vedomosti*, January 18, 2010.

19 For an analysis of the 1998 bankruptcy law, which went into effect in March 1998, see *Ekspert*, no. 5 (1998), pp. 19–33. Data on the bankruptcy cases that come before the commercial courts each year can be tracked in the monthly journal of the High Commercial Court, the *Vestnik Vysshego Arbitrazhnogo Suda*.

20 Kseniia Iastreb, "Vtoroe dykhanie Var'egannefetegaza," *Neftegazovaia Vertikal'*, no. 15 (2001), pp. 38–40.

21 Browne, *Beyond Business*, p. 140.

22 A useful source for Russian coverage of the blow by blow as TNK's takeover of Chernogorneft approached its climax is the reporting of Oleg Chernitskii in *Vedomosti* between September 10 and 20, 1999. See in particular "BP Amoco podtalkivaiut k peregovoram s TNK," *Vedomosti*, September 10, 1999; "'Chernogorneft' prodadut TNK," *Vedomosti*, September 13, 1999; "Pravitel'stvo ne pomozhet sokhranit' Sidanco," *Vedomosti*, September 14, 1999, and "Aktivy 'Sidanco' k prodazhe gotovy," *Vedomosti*, September 20, 1999.

23 In parallel, another group of shareholders brought suit against TNK and Alfa under the RICO Act.

24 Conversation with Ralph Alexander, September 5, 2001.

25 The above account in based on public sources and on the author's interviews with several of the key participants.

26 Iuliia Bushueva, "'Chernogorneft' vernulas'," *Vedomosti,* November 27, 2001.

27 On this point, see Svetlana Azarova, "TNK zaplatit za vse," *Neftegazovaia Vertikal',* no. 11 (2001), pp. 38–40.

28 Bob Dudley, "TNK-BP Overview," PowerPoint presentation at a meeting with the financial community at the Pierre Hotel in New York, October 17, 2003. Also "TNK-BP Data Book," prepared for the same event.

29 These numbers are based on BP's 50 percent share of TNK-BP. Source: Presentation by Tony Hayward, then chief executive of BP Exploration and Production, New York, October 17, 2003.

30 Ibid. Samotlor's proven reserves are quoted here on an SPE basis.

31 Browne, *Beyond Business,* p. 146.

32 Ibid.

33 Amoco was known for its brownfield expertise. At the time BP acquired Amoco in 1998, BP had only about 1,000 wells worldwide, whereas Amoco had about 20,000, many of which were produced using waterflooding, an Amoco specialty (author's interview, May 20, 2006).

34 A twenty-year veteran at Sibneft-Noyabrskneftegaz, Iurii Krasnevkii was chief geologist and deputy general director of the company when Iskander Diyashev pioneered the new technique of horizontal drilling at Sibneft. Krasnevskii became an early and enthusiastic supporter of the new technology, which he then applied successfully at TNK when he moved there in 2002, one year before the alliance with BP. He stayed with TNK-BP for nearly a decade, rising to director of new technology in the E&P business group before moving to Bashneft in 2011. See http://www.bashneft.ru/press -centre/news/detail.php?id=3399.

35 It is open to question, indeed, how much of the initial burst in production growth was due to BP's entrance, since the first year or two of strong growth was presumably the result of plans and contracts that were already in place at the time the joint venture began, which was not until late in 2003.

36 Source: Richard Herbert, then executive vice president for technology, presentation at the 2008 SPE conference, Moscow, October 2008. The scorpion plots presented by Herbert suggest that it took some time for corporate decision makers to adjust to the deteriorating economics of fraccing. Even though by 2007 the most costly frac jobs accounted for nearly one-third of the total spend, they yielded no significant increase in production.

37 Author's interviews with Larry McVay, then chief operating officer of TNK-BP, 2006.

38 Between 2006 and 2010, production from Samotlor declined from 31.6 million tons to 27 million tons (0.6 million barrels per day to 0.5 million).

39 Interview with German Khan, "Na samom dele ia nezhnyi' i pushistyi'," *Vedomosti,* January 18, 2010.

40 Quoted in Dmitri Zhdannikov, interview with Mikhail Fridman, *Reuters,* June 24, 2008.

41 According to a story in the *Wall Street Journal,* Sechin, then newly named deputy prime minister for energy, summoned German Khan to a joint meeting with BP and heard both sides of the dispute, following which he reportedly told them that "they were big boys and would have to sort it out." Gregory L. White and Guy Chazan, "Boardroom Brawl Roils BP's Russia Venture," *Wall Street Journal,* June 12, 2008, p. A1.

42 For a time Dudley attempted to run TNK-BP from an undisclosed location in Western Europe, but it was clearly an untenable arrangement. A Russian description of the resulting paralysis in decision-making appears in Irina Reznik and Irina Malkova, "Ni shagu vpered," *Vedomosti,* August 11, 2008.

43 Following the temporary injunction granted by the High Court of Justice in London, an arbitration panel was established, per the shareholders' agreement. The panel operates under the rules of the Stockholm Chamber of Commerce (UNCITRAL), but it is made up of three English barristers and has only met in London. At this writing (summer 2012) there has not yet been a finding on the merits of the case.

44 TNK-BP's finding and development costs, at $3.80 per barrel of oil equivalent ($27.75 per ton) in 2010, are well below TNK-BP's international peers as well as its competitors in Russia. Its 74 percent exploration success rate in the same year, which speaks to its use of advanced technology, is likewise the best in the Russian industry. (Source: TNK-BP company website, www.tnk-bp.com.)

45 Fridman later commented to a television interviewer, "Sechin said to me, 'I think you were mistaken not to support that deal. It would have been profitable for you, but I acknowledge your right to challenge it.'" (Source: Praim News Agency, reported in *Vedomosti,* April 13, 2012.)

46 *Moscow Times,* February 13, 2001, p. 10. Shell and its partners at Sakhalin-2 decided to develop their license area in two phases. The first phase aimed at developing the oil from the Piltun-Astokhskoe fields, using a converted platform, called Moliqpak, brought from Alaska. This yielded first oil in 1999 and provided an early cash flow to pay for the second phase, as well as tax payments to the regional and central governments. The second phase focused on the gas resources at the Lunskoe field. The final investment decision for the second phase was not taken until 2003.

47 "Stenogramma vystupleniia Prezidenta Rossiiskoi Federatsii V. V. Putina na mezhdunarodnoi prakticheskoi konferentsii SRP-2000," September 3, 2000. The text of Putin's remarks is available on the presidential website at http://www.kremlin.ru/appears/2000/09/03/0002_type63376type63378_28850.shtml.

48 Putin press conference following the U.S.-Russian summit in Ljubljana, Slovenia, June 18, 2001, available on the presidential website at http://www.kremlin.ru/text/appears/2001/06/28569.shtml.

49 Ibid.

50 Viktor Somov, "Razdel produktsii v deistvii," *RusEnergy Praim-Onlain,* April 4, 2003.

51 Quoted in Viktor Somov and Mariia Braslavskaia, "Novyi povorot: Kompaniia YU-KOS pri podderzhke deputatov Gosdumy dobivaetsia fakticheskoi likvidatsii rezhima SRP," *RusEnergy Praim-Onlain,* January 22, 2003.

52 Another of Khodorkovsky's motives was that he did not want Rosneft to become an equity holder in PSAs on behalf of the state, on the model of Kazmunaigaz in Kazakhstan. Rosneft had been named the state's "authorized agent" for PSAs, and by 2002 was involved in some fifteen PSAs that had been approved in principle by the government at that time. It was pushing to expand its role beyond that but failed to get the government's support. In the end, the issue became moot when PSAs faded after 2003. See "Downer: Rosneft Gets Reduced PSA Role," *Neftecompass* 11, no. 1 (April 11, 2002), p. 5.

53 Aleksei Nedogonov, "YUKOS vs. SRP: Chem prodiktovana bor'ba Mikhaila Khodorkovskogo s rezhimom razdela produktsii," *RusEnergy Praim-Onlain,* February 12, 2003. In December 2002 Khodorkovsky spoke at a meeting of the deputies of the Otechestvo-Vsia Rossiia fraction of the Duma to argue the case against PSA, while simultaneously conducting a blitz of media interviews as well as commissioned articles.

54 Ironically, the state-owned companies, Rosneft and Gazprom, saw advantages in PSA as a vehicle for large offshore projects, and they lobbied to have them included on the PSA list. Even more striking is the fact that when the Russian companies invested in projects outside Russia, particularly in the former Soviet Union, PSA was their preferred vehicle. Sauce for the goose was not sauce for the gander.

55 Shell in 2009 published a commemorative history of the project with the title *Salymskii proekt: Liudi, partnerstvo, uspekh,* which traces the origin and evolution of the project. In 1993 Shell won a tender to form a partnership with the license holder, Evikhon. The final joint venture was concluded ten years later, in September 2003, on the eve of Khodorkovsky's arrest. In 2009 GazpromNeft acquired an 81 percent share of Evikhon's parent company Sibir Energy, thus becoming Shell's 50–50 partner in Salym Petroleum Development. As of this writing, however, Shell remains the operator. *Neft' i Kapital* news release, July 2, 2009, http://www.oilcapital.ru/news/2009/07/020909_141162.shtml.

56 V. V. Putin, "Poslanie Federal'nomu Sobraniiu," http://archive.kremlin.ru/appears/2005/04/25/1223_type63372type63374type82634_87049.shtml.

57 Trutnev speech to the Duma, February 10, 1995; a video is available at www.1tv.ru/news/polit/97272. An initial draft of the new mineral resources law was approved "in general" by the government on March 17, 2005. Plans to limit access by foreigners to strategic fields had been under discussion since the first draft mineral resources law appeared in July 2004.

58 Konstantin Kovalenko and John C. Webb, *Russia's New Subsoil Licensing Rules: Closing the Door on Foreign Investment in Future Big-Ticket Oil Projects?* (Cambridge, MA: IHS Cambridge Energy Research Associates, March 23, 2005). Among the most likely candidates as seen at the time for designation as strategic were the

Sakhalin-3 offshore block, four blocks of the Central Khoreiverskoye structure and the Titov and Trebs fields in the Timan-Pechora Basin, and three Barents offshore blocks.

59 For a detailed description and analysis of the "Law on Procedures of Making Foreign Investment in Business Entities of Strategic Importance to National Defense and Security of the State," see Organisation for Economic Co-operation and Development, *Russian Federation: Strengthening the Policy Framework for Investment,* OECD Investment Policy Reviews (Paris: OECD, 2008), pp. 24–28.

60 For additional perspective on the "reprivatization" issues, see, for example, http://www .polit.ru/article/2007/12/29/zakharov/.

61 The term *peredel,* or "redistribution," refers to the massive transfer of property from state to private ownership that took place in the first half of the 1990s.

62 Daniel Treisman, "Putin's Silovarchs," *Orbis* 51 (January 2007), pp. 141–153.

63 Rawi Abdelal, *Journey to Sakhalin: Royal Dutch/Shell in Russia,* Harvard Business School Case Study (Cambridge, MA: Harvard Business School. Part A, June 2, 2006; Part B, with Irina Tarsis, February 6, 2007; Part C, with Marina N. Vandamme, February 8, 2007).

64 Presentation by Andrew Gould at the Goldman Sachs BRICs Conference in London, May 11, 2010, available at http://phx.corporate-ir.net/External.File?item=UGFyZW50S UQ9NDY5MTF8Q2hpbGRJRDotMXxUeXBlPTM=&t=1.

65 Schlumberger was one of the first non-Anglo-American companies to adopt English as its internal language of communication.

66 The use of 3-D seismic in onshore surveys grew from 9,600 square kilometers in 2000 to 27,700 square kilometers in 2008. Source: VNIGNI, reported in Sergei Chernyshov, "Tishina v pole," *Nefteservis,* no. 1 2009, p. 15.

67 Sergei Glazkov, "Russian Oilfield Services: Before and after the Crisis," *Russian Petroleum Investor* 18, no. 6 (June–July 2009), pp. 42–49. Spending by the Russian companies for geophysics applications to support production followed a similar trend.

68 Between 2003 and 2007 Schlumberger acquired Siberian Geophysics Company (the former services department of YuganskNG), PetroAlliance, Tiumenpromgeofizika, Krasnoiargeofizika, Geofit, Pomorneftegeofizika, and several others. Source: Vladimir Laptev, "Otechestvennyi geofizicheskii servis: Strategicheskii prioritet inostrannykh kompanii," *Neftegazovaia Vertikal',* no. 7 (2011), pp. 30–36.

69 Presentation by CEO Andrew Gould, 34th Annual Howard Weil Conference, New Orleans, March 20, 2006, http://library.corporate-ir.net/library/97/975/97513/items/188718 /Howard_Weil_200306.pdf.

70 Presentation by Gould at the Goldman Sachs BRICs Conference.

71 For a candid assessment of the situation, and the uphill battle faced by Integra and the Russian service providers, see a 2005 interview with Feliks Liubashevskii, "My ne prodadimsia Schlumberger i Halliburton," *Neft' i Kapital,* no. 12 (2005), pp. 42–46.

72 In the recession that followed in 2009–2010, there was an initial boost to the Russian companies from the devaluation of the ruble, but it was short-lived. As oil prices

recovered, the ruble began to appreciate, as it always tends to do in commodity-exporting countries. This always favors foreign imports over domestic ones, and as a result the foreign companies have regained a competitive advantage over the domestic ones, which partially offsets the higher prices they charge.

73 Dmitri Liutiagin, Veles Kapital, cited in Maia Nobotova, "Rasprodazha," *Neftegazovaia Vertikal'*, nos. 13–14 (2010), pp. 62–64.

74 Thus in the summer of 2009 Weatherford acquired TNK-BP's remaining service assets; Schlumberger purchased Smith International, which had itself previously acquired smaller Russian geophysics companies.

75 Laptev, "Otechestvennyi geofizicheskii servis."

76 Interview with Chris Einchcomb, then executive vice-president of Integra's geophysics division: "Esli v seismorazvedku, to s nami," *Neftegazovaia vertikal'*, no. 22 (2010), pp. 52–55. (Einchcomb has since moved to TNK-BP as Executive Vice President for International Projects and Geological Exploration.)

77 "Schlumberger: Tsentr udalennogo monitoringa i kontrolia teper' v Rossii," *Neftegazovaia Vertikal,'* no. 13 (2010).

78 Presentation by CEO Andrew Gould, 33rd Annual Howard Weil Conference, New Orleans, April 4, 2005, http://media.corporate-ir.net/media_files/irol/97/97513/presentations/howard_weil_040405.pdf.

79 Schlumberger's employment of Russians dwarfs its employment of nationals from Brazil, China, and India—over 12,000 compared with roughly 2,000–3,000 each for Indians, Chinese, and Brazilians. At the same time, Russia has not become the dominant source of international talent for Schlumberger that it might have seemed it would become in the mid-2000s. The numbers of Russians employed by Schlumberger outside Russia have remained roughly constant since then, while the numbers of Indians and Chinese have raced ahead. Presentation by Gould at the Goldman Sachs BRICs Conference.

80 Presentation by Gould at the Goldman Sachs BRICs Conference.

81 Laptev, "Otechestvennyi geofizicheskii servis." Since 2007 there has been growing concern in various parts of the Russian government over the share of foreign companies in the oil and gas service sector, though so far no significant action. See also Vladimir Laptev, "Budet li integrirovan neftegazovyi servis Rossii? *Neftegazovaia Vertikal'*, no. 17 (2011), pp. 74–79; and "Nefteservis ne nuzhdaetsia v monopolii," *Rusenergy*, April 3, 2012.

82 For example, in the exhaustive review of the oil industry prepared in 2010 for Prime Minister Putin by the Ministry of Energy (the so-called *General'naia skhema*), there is no particular attention given to the services sector.

83 Aleksei Grivach and Irina Kezik, "Kto platit dvazhdy," *Moskovskie novosti*, May 4, 2012, http://mn.ru/business_oilgas/20120504/317096873.html. The increase followed sharp public criticism from Medvedev in 2010. For Medvedev's criticism, see http://www.i-russia.ru/sessions/reports/8.html.

12. *Three Colors of Oil*

1   The transcript of the meeting, including the full text of Bogdanov's presentation, is available at "Stenograficheskii otchet o zasedanii komissii po modernizatsii i tekhno-logicheskomu razvitiiu ekonomiki Rossii," Khanty-Mansiisk, March 23, 2010, available on the presidential website at http://news.kremlin.ru/transcripts/7198.

2   Statistics on oil production in West Siberia's two okrugs are available from the Russian Statistical Service (Rosstat), in the monthly publication *Sotsial'no-ekhonomicheskoe polozhenie Rossii,* within the regional appendix (*Prilozhenie*). The latest issues of this publication can be accessed at the following section of the Rosstat website: http://www .gks.ru/wps/wcm/connect/rosstat/rosstatsite/main/publishing/catalog/periodicals /doc_1140086922125.

3   Bogdanov turned 60 in May 2011, and his contract as general director of Surgutneft-egaz was extended for a further five years. A summary of his life and career appeared in *Neft' i Kapital,* May 2011, http://www.indpg.ru/nik/2011/05/42435.html.

4   In 2010 Surgutneftegaz accounted for 25 percent of all development drilling and 30 percent of all exploratory drilling.

5   For a brief time Surgutneftegaz took a minority stake in the Hungarian oil company MOL, but it was a purely passive investment and Surgutneftegaz was never involved in MOL's operations in the field.

6   Although Bogdanov's high official standing with the leadership has not deterred re-peated attempts to absorb his company into Rosneft. In recent years, such attempts, having consistently run up against Bogdanov's determined resistance, appear to have died away.

7   Under the 1993 constitution, he can be elected to two consecutive terms, both now ex-tended to six years, which means he could serve to 2024.

8   This was the central point of former finance minister Aleksei Kudrin's critique of the direction of policy under Putin and Medvedev at the time of his resignation/dismissal in September 2011.

9   For a similar view by two well-known Russian energy experts, see Leonid Grigor'ev and Valerii Kriukov, "Mirovaia ekonomika na perekrestke dorog: Kakoi put' vybrat' Rossii?," *Voprosy ekonomiki,* no. 12 (2009), pp. 22–37. They write: "There is no prospect of continuing to obtain resource rents over the long term" (p. 24).

10 This section is an abbreviated and updated version of an analysis written by the author with the assistance of two colleagues and published as Thane Gustafson, John C. Webb, and Paulina Mirenkova, *The Russian Oil Industry in Global Perspective: The Challenges Ahead* (Cambridge, MA: IHS Cambridge Energy Research Associates, April 2011). Academic researchers may obtain the original report by contacting the author at Thane.Gustafson@ihs.com.

11 In the discussion that follows, the term "liquids" means "oil and condensate." Occa-sionally I use the word "oil" alone as a shorthand, but it is understood to include condensate, as is generally the case in oil statistics.

12 The five fields are Vostochno-Messoyakhskoe (1989), Vankor (1991), Medyn-More (1997), Dolginskoe (1999), and Filanovskoe (2005). In addition Rosneft made three major discoveries in 2010–2011 in East Siberia, which could eventually turn out to be giants: Sevastyanovo, Sanarskoe, and Lisovskoe. All three fields are located in Irkutsk Oblast, in the same general area as the Verkhnechonskoe field. None of the three is yet under development.

13 In the second half of the 1980s, the average field discovered in West Siberia had 17.9 million tons (131 million barrels) of proven, probable, and possible reserves, whereas by the mid-2000s the average field discovered had less than 2 million tons (14.6 million barrels).

14 A mature field can be defined as one in which either of two criteria has been met: (1) over 50 percent of reserves has been produced, or (2) the field has been producing for over twenty-five years.

15 However, LUKoil has lately begun partnerships with international independents to explore off the coasts of West Africa and India, and Rosneft has concluded a strategic alliance with ExxonMobil, about which more below.

16 The production and drilling numbers in this paragraph and the next one are from the Russian Federation Ministry of Energy; the investment numbers are derived from series published by Goskomstat, the Russian Federation Statistical Committee.

17 John C. Webb and Thane Gustafson, *Why Is Russian Oil Output Slowing Down? What Fraccing Trends Show* (Cambridge, MA: IHS Cambridge Energy Research Associates, April 2008).

18 On "peak oil," see Daniel Yergin, *The Quest: Energy, Security, and the Remaking of the Modern World* (New York: Penguin Press, 2011), chapter 11.

19 Presentation by Energy Minister Sergei Shmatko to Prime Minister Putin, "Doklad po voprosu General'noi skhemy razvitiia neftianoi otrasli na period do 2020g," October 28, 2010. Putin's opening speech and response are accessible on the prime minister's website at http://premier.gov.ru/events/news/12784/.

20 In 2008, in the wake of oil shock and the recession, the decline rate in West Siberia surged above 3 percent; in 2009 it returned to about 2 percent. These estimates are necessarily imprecise, since they are based on the output trends in broad regions rather than a buildup field by field. Therefore they include not only production from mature fields but also a certain amount of new production from smaller new fields in otherwise mature areas. The annual decline rate of older fields alone is more likely between 5 and 8 percent.

21 This is a purely back-of-the envelope estimate, based on the rule of thumb that developing one barrel per day of new greenfield capacity in Russia requires about $30,000 of capital investment. To this must be added the capital investment required for pipelines to evacuate the new oil to market. The pipelines are built by Transneft and financed through a levy added to the transportation tariffs paid by the operators.

22 It does not take a very large annual increase in capital spending to yield a doubling over the space of a decade—7.2 percent per year, to be precise. These estimates are in

2010 dollars. If one reckons in current dollars, that is, "dollars of the day," the 2020 total goes still higher. This exercise assumes that the level of production remains about what it is today, that is, about 500 million tons per year (10 million barrels per day). Raising net production by another 50 million tons per year (1 million barrels per day) to 550 million tons per year (11 million barrels per day) might require another $20–$30 billion per year. These numbers do not include investment in transportation.

23 One way to visualize the growth of the "investment burden" is to look at the share of capital expenditure in the price of a barrel of Urals export crude. Since 2005 the share of capital expenditure in the Urals price has more than doubled, from 4.9 percent in 2005 to about 10 percent in 2010. If one assumes that the real price of oil in 2020 remains the same as today, but capital expenditure doubles in real terms (not an unreasonable expectation given the trends of the last decade), then the share of capital expenditure in the price of an export barrel of crude would rise from about 10 percent today to over 20 percent.

24 This is true unless the world price of oil keeps rising in proportion. We return to this point in the concluding chapter.

25 To be sure, this is an oversimplification; in reality, the three categories overlap considerably. For example, even in a mature area, new fields are constantly being discovered and developed, although usually they are smaller satellites and "step-outs" located near the larger mature fields. Thus the vast majority of new fields discovered in Russia between 1988 and 2008 contain less than 1.4 million tons (10 million barrels) and are located near existing fields. For all practical purposes these can be grouped with the "mature" fields. (Source: IHS EDIN database.)

26 In 2011 the Khanty-Mansiisk okrug produced 261 million tons (5.2 million barrels per day) out of total Russian production of 511.4 million tons (10.3 million barrels per day).

27 Igor' Tolstolytkin, "Glavnaia zadacha Iugry," *Nefteservis*, no. 4 (Winter 2009), pp. 12–15. To refer to the entire Khanty-Mansiisk okrug as "brownfield" is another oversimplification. In Khanty-Mansiisk some 450 fields have been discovered to date, of which 220 have not yet been developed. These are by and large smaller and less attractive fields, but ultimately some of them will be produced. In addition, a handful of new fields are discovered every year. Thus the production statistics for Khanty-Mansiisk include a certain amount of "new oil." But "mature fields" account for 85–90 percent of production in Khanty-Mansiisk.

28 Oil people distinguish between two broad types of techniques: those that maintain or increase reservoir pressure ("improved" or "secondary" recovery), as opposed to any other technique resulting in increased production ("enhanced" or "tertiary" recovery). A useful survey of techniques used in mature oil fields and their application around the world is T. Badabagli, "Mature Field Development—A Review," a paper prepared for presentation at the SPE Europec/EAGE Annual Conference held in Madrid, Spain, June 13–16, 2005, Paper No. 93884-MS, http://www

.onepetro.org/mslib/app/Preview.do?paperNumber=SPE-93884-MS&soci
etyCode=SPE.

29 Hydraulic fracturing ("fraccing"), which was the single technique most responsible for the surge of 1999–2004, is not considered an "enhanced recovery technique" but is traditionally classified as well stimulation. Increasingly, however, the advent of controlled hydraulic fracturing, in which the direction of fractures can be directed under the guidance of seismic models, is turning hydraulic fracturing into a reservoir optimization technique.

30 Underbalanced drilling (in Russian, *burenie na depressii*) is a procedure used in drilling wells in which the pressure in the wellbore is kept lower than the pressure in the formation being drilled. In traditional drilling operations, "underbalancing" was considered dangerous, since it could lead to a blowout. But given adequate techniques to measure and manage pressure, underbalanced drilling has a number of advantages, such as increased drilling speed and added reserves. Interestingly, Surgutneftegaz, despite its reputation as a conservative company, is the leading user of underbalanced drilling in Russia.

31 Paul Markwell, *Mature Oil Fields: An Energy Intensity Dilemma.* (Cambridge, MA: IHS Cambridge Energy Research Associates, September 2009).

32 Thus for a typical production unit in West Siberia, electricity consumption has increased 50 percent between 2005 and 2010, but tariffs per kilowatt-hour have increased 2.5 times. Figures for Pokachevneft', cited in Mikhail Ignat'ev, "Energosberezhenie i energoeffektivnost'," *Neftegazovaia Vertikal'*, no. 12 (2010), pp. 62–71.

33 The relative stabilization of output in Tatarstan is less surprising than it might seem. Mature fields and provinces decline more slowly at the end of their lives, once over 80 percent of their reserves have been produced, than fields and provinces that have recently come off their peaks, as is still the case in West Siberia.

34 There are about 150 small oil-producing companies in Russia. In 2008 they produced 24 million tons of crude oil (480,000 barrels per day), or 5 percent of Russian production. They range widely in size: half produced less than 50,000 tons per year (1,000 barrels per day); the four largest, over 500,000 tons (10,000 barrels per day). Nearly half of the small companies are located in three provinces: Tatarstan, Komi, and Orenburg. For an overview of the status of the small companies, see an interview with the president of the Association of Small and Medium Oil Producers (ASSONeft), Elena Korzun, in *Infotek,* no. 1 (2009), pp. 2–5.

35 Under current legislation a license holder is allowed to transfer a license to its subsidiary. One possible solution, then, is to form a joint venture with the company one wishes to transfer the license to. It is, however, a cumbersome procedure compared with a straight sale.

36 Mikhail Ignat'ev, "Sam ne am, a drugim ne dam," *Neftegazovaia Vertikal'*, no. 2 (2010), pp. 40–44. The local operators in the large companies tend to view the smaller companies as bothersome "small fry." In addition, as operators they answer to the state for the execution of field development plans; consequently, they are liable for the actions of the

smaller operators within their license areas. As a result, the operators have little incentive to support independents on "their" territory.

37 Address by Vladimir Putin to a meeting of ministers, May 4, 2012, http://premier.gov.ru /events/news/18865. For a brief commentary, see Oksana Gavshina, "Trudnye zapasy," *Vedomosti*, May 4, 2012, http://www.vedomosti.ru/newspaper/article/280260/trudnye _zapasy#ixzz1tt8rvj2G. The measure establishes three levels of tax holiday, depending primarily on the permeability of the formation and the viscosity of reserves.

38 At such temperatures it does not matter whether one is speaking of Celsius or Fahrenheit, since the two scales meet at minus 40 degrees.

39 Quoted from Fiona Hill and Clifford Gaddy, *The Siberian Curse: How Communist Planners Left Russia Out in the Cold* (Washington, DC: Brookings Institution Press, 2003), p. 43.

40 Ibid., chapter 3, esp. pp. 41–51. As one illustration, at the Vankor field, located in the northern part of Krasnoiarsk Krai, three to four support workers are required for every oilfield worker, a far higher proportion than is typical farther south. Vladimir Baidashin, "Vankorskii proekt: Samye peredovye tekhnicheskie resheniia," *Nefteservis*, no. 1 (2008), pp. 74–76.

41 For overviews of the oil and gas potential of East Siberia, see James W. Clarke, "Petroleum Habitat of East Siberia," *International Geology Review* 36 (1994), pp. 238–249.

42 Prior to the 1980s most Russian geologists were skeptical that any significant oil would be found in East Siberia at all. In 1979, the Communist Party leadership ordered a step-up in funding and effort to explore the rim of the volcanic plateau. The result was the discoveries that make up the core of the known oil resources of East Siberia today. For a brief account of the history of oil exploration in East Siberia, see an interview with Academician Aleksei Kontorovich, "O glavnom poiase neftenosnosti Vostochnoi Sibiri," *Baikal-24*, February 13, 2010, http://baikal24.ru/page.php ?action=showItem&type=article&id=8750.

43 Nadezhda Sergeeva and Viacheslav Chirkov, "Vostochnyi front 'Surgutneftegaza'," *Neft' i Kapital*, no. 3 (2010), pp. 30–32. The prospects identified by Surgutneftegaz total "probable and possible" ($C_1 + C_2$) reserves of 150 million tons (1.1 billion barrels). The company projects adding a further 75 million tons (about 550 million barrels) more of $C_1 + C_2$ reserves of oil between 2010 and 2015, despite spending twice as much as in 2004–2010. (Everything depends, of course, on the proportion of C_1 to C_2, and the rate C_2 is moved to C_1.)

44 "Za shirokoi spinoi Vankora: Real'nye sroki nachala polnomasshtabnogo osvoeniia Iurubcheno-Tokhomskoi Zony po-prezhnemu neizvestny," *Neft' i Kapital*, no.3 (2010), pp. 34–38. Everything depends, of course, on the tax regime and on pipeline capacity. If Rosneft is able to negotiate ad hoc tax relief for Yurubchenskoe, then it could become a priority, especially because the necessary pipeline for evacuating oil from the complex has recently been approved for construction.

45 A useful review of the state of play in East Siberia as of 2010 is "Uskol'zaiushchii Klondaik," *RusEnergy*, April 22, 2010. For context, see an earlier overview on the same topic,

just as the 2008 crash in oil prices hit the industry, "Truba ne pomozhet," *RusEnergy*, September 25, 2008.

46 "Akademik Kontorovich: Nikogda Vostochnaia Sibir' ne sravnitsia s Zapadnoi," *Rosinvest.com*, February 6, 2006, http://www.vsluh.ru/news/oilgas/73913. This is also the official view of the government, as expressed in the official outlook to 2030. Of new oil reserves, between 2010 and 2030 50 percent (6.2 billion tons, or 45.3 billion barrels) will come from West Siberia, 20 percent (2.6 billion tons, or 18.7 billion barrels) from East Siberia, and 5 percent (0.6 billion tons, or 4.5 billion barrels) from the Timan-Pechora in Northwest Russia. These numbers presumably include in-field additions as well as new discoveries.

47 Interview with Valerii Kriukov, *Ekspert-Sibir'*, no. 35 (September 25, 2011), pp. 20–22. According to Kriukov, the three main East Siberian fields—Talakan, Verkhnechonskoe, and Yurubcheno-Tokhomskoe—currently have a total of 370 million tons of proven and probable reserves.

48 A useful overview of the YaNAO-Krasnoiarsk program as of 2010 is Andrei Meshcherin, "Nash paravoz vpered letit," *Neftegazovaia Vertikal'*, no. 7 (2010), pp. 10–16.

49 "Na pereput'e," *Neft' i Kapital*, no. 4 (2010), discusses the policy issues involved in the transportation of oil from the YaNAO-Krasnoiarsk region to the East Siberian Pipeline system.

50 Georgii Semenev and Aleksandr Shved, "'Nezavisimye' v Vostochnoi Sibiri," *Mintop* (a monthly publication of the Ministry of Energy), no. 5 (2010), pp. 11–14. Urals Energy, the largest independent license holder in East Siberia on the eve of the crash of 2008, went bankrupt and its assets were passed into the hands of Sberbank's investment bank, Sberbank-Kapital. Another local player, Irkutskaia Neftianaia Kompaniia, was more fortunate. It survived thanks to a timely loan from the European Bank for Reconstruction and Development, granted on the eve of the crisis and a joint venture with the Japan Oil, Gas and Metals National Corporation.

51 Useful background on the oil and gas potential of the Arctic offshore worldwide, and specifically on the Russian continental shelf, can be found on the website of the U.S. Geological Survey's Circum-Arctic Resource Appraisal, at http://energy.usgs.gov /arctic/.

52 Ministry of Energy of the Russian Federation, *Energy Strategy of Russia for the Period up to 2030* (Moscow: "PAC Energiya," 2010), pp. 66–73.

53 A detailed critical review of the state of Arctic offshore policy as of 2010 is Ol'ga Vinogradova, "Skazhi shel'fu net," *Neftegazovaia Vertikal'*, no. 2 (2010), pp. 28–33. The lack of skilled personnel for the offshore is discussed in "Kadry dlia shel'fa," *RusEnergy*, June 10, 2010. At this writing, the Russian educational system graduates only seventy to eighty specialists per year in all the various specialties relevant to offshore oil and gas. Foreign and Russian corporations, particularly from Norway, are developing their own programs in Russia to take up the slack. See also "Kto razburit shel'f? V Rossii rastet spros na vypolnenie podriadnykh operatsii v ramkakh morskikh proektov," *RusEnergy*, December 16, 2010.

54 The geographer Michael Bradshaw, an authority on the Russian Far East and a long-time observer of Sakhalin developments, gives an overview of the history of the Sakhalin projects in "A New Age in Pacific Russia: Lessons from the Sakhalin Oil and Gas Projects," *Eurasian Geography and Economics* 51, no. 3 (May–June 2010), pp. 330–359. Something of the drama of the engineering innovations in the Sakhalin projects is captured in a commemorative volume published by Shell, "Sakhalin-II: A Venture Like No Other" (The Hague: Royal Dutch Shell, 2009), together with a companion DVD.

55 According to Bruce Grewcock, CEO of Kiewit, one of the world's largest general contractors for large transportation and energy projects, the record of the international power and energy industry in large project construction is "only so-so." The biggest cause of cost overruns and delays is "friction" at the interface among the various organizations and specialties involved. In other words, the challenge is management, and particularly the allocation of risk and responsibility among the separate players. Presentation at CERA Week (annual energy conference of IHS Cambridge Energy Research Associates), Houston, March 12, 2010.

56 In October 2011 the Ministry of Natural Resources announced a draft long-term program to 2030 for exploration of the Russian continental shelf. See http://www.mnr .gov.ru/news/detail.php?ID=127745&sphrase_id=67277. The plan calls for a major expansion of spending on exploration and development, and projects production of between 40 and 80 million tons per year (0.8 and 1.6 million barrels per day) of oil by 2030. The ministry's program, which had been in gestation for several years, was at last report still undergoing review by other ministries and has not yet been adopted as official state policy.

57 According to LUKoil vice-president Leonid Fedun, LUKoil plans to invest up to $900 million in its West African offshore projects in 2012 (*Russia Today,* December 14, 2011). For a Russian commentary on LUKoil's West African deepwater program, see "Afrikanskii posrednik LUKoila," *Rusenergy,* January 11, 2012.

58 Petter Nore, "The Norwegian State's Relationship to the International Oil Companies over North Sea Oil, 1965–75" (PhD diss., School of Social Sciences, Division of Economics, Thames Polytechnic, June 1979), especially chapter 7.

59 ExxonMobil Corporation Strategic Cooperation Agreement with Rosneft Conference Call, April 18, 2012.

60 International Energy Agency, *2011 World Energy Outlook* (Paris: International Energy Agency, 2011), p. 300. This edition of the *Outlook* contains a valuable analysis of the long-term outlook for Russian energy production and consumption (chapters 7–9).

61 The International Energy Agency (IEA), in its latest world energy outlook, projects a gradual downward drift in Russian oil production, from about 522.5 (10.5 million barrels per day) in 2010 to 495 million tons (9.9 million barrels per day) in 2020 and 483 million tons (9.7 million barrels per day) in 2035. That projection is based on a scenario that the IEA calls "New Policies," which assumes as its main feature continued progress in oil-tax reform, with a consequent increase in greenfield exploration and development,

and the beginnings of a more active offshore policy, both in the Caspian and in Arctic waters. See International Energy Agency, *2011 World Energy Outlook,* chapter 8, especially table 8.3, p. 295.

13. Looking Ahead

1 A good discussion of the literature and the various methodologies used to derive these estimates will be found in Sergei Guriev and Aleh Tsyvinski, "Russian Economy in Crisis: Strategy of Growth and Reforms," in Anders Aslund, Sergei Guriev, and Andrew C. Kuchins, eds., *Russia after the Global Economic Crisis* (Washington, DC: Peterson Institute for International Economics and Center for Strategic and International Affairs, 2010), pp. 9–38.

2 U.S. Energy Information Administration, *Annual Energy Outlook 2012* (Washington, DC: U.S. Energy Information Administration, April 2012).

3 Daniel Yergin, *The Quest: Energy, Security, and the Remaking of the Modern World* (New York: Penguin Press, 2011).

4 For an example of scenario-writing applied to Russia, see Daniel Yergin and Thane Gustafson, *Russia 2010 and What It Means for the World* (New York: Random House, 1993).

5 There are pilot projects in all of these areas, but little concrete to point to so far. Revealingly, the agency in charge of Russia's wind program is Rosatom, the nuclear power agency. Atomenergomash, Rosatom's subsidiary for nuclear engineering, is responsible for developing Russia's first wind parks, which so far remain on paper. For the comments of Atomenergomash's general director, Vladimir Kashchenko, see http://www.i -russia.ru/energy/media/2011/.

6 About 83 percent of Russia's nuclear capacity dates from the Soviet era. Only one entirely new plant (at Rostov) has been completed since the end of the Soviet era, although a number of units have been added to existing plants. There are elaborate official plans to increase nuclear capacity, but IHS's baseline projection is that by 2020 it will remain roughly where it is today, at about 25 gigawatts. I am indebted to Christopher DeVere-Walker, IHS Energy's research director for FSU power, for this update.

7 Cited in Elena Kukol, "Ne podelili dokhody ot nefti," *Rossiiskaia gazeta,* December 13, 2010, p. 1.

8 A streaming video of Medvedev's first *Poslanie* in November 2008 is available on the presidential website at http://news.kremlin.ru/video/185.

9 These examples are taken from Medvedev's second annual address to the parliament, "Poslanie Federal'nomu Sobraniiu Rossiiskoi Federatsii," November 12, 2009, available on the presidential website at http://news.kremlin.ru/transcripts/5979.

10 Transcript of the March 2010 session of the Commission on Modernization and Technological Development of the Economy of Russia, held in Khanty-Mansiisk, March 23, 2010, http://news.kremlin.ru/transcripts/7198. Medvedev went on to add

that he had become persuaded otherwise by his visits to local facilities of Surgutneft-egaz and Rosneft. But in subsequent meetings of the Commission over the following two years, those were virtually Medvedev's last words on the oil industry as a source of innovation.

11 V. P. Orlov, "Syr'evoi sektor ekonomiki v usloviiakh modernizatsii," *Mineral'nye resursy Rossii. Ekonomika i upravlenie*, no. 1 (2010), pp. 3–10.

12 Interview with Leonid Fedun in Andrei Vin'kov, Ivan Rubanov, and Dmitrii Sivakov, "Zametit' korovu v korovnike," *Ekspert*, no. 12 (March 28, 2011), pp. 36–44.

13 Kudrin appears frequently in the media and has founded a nongovernmental organization called the Committee for Citizen Initiatives. See the transcript and video of his appearance on Fin-Am radio (Moscow), http://finam.fm/archive-view/6057/.

14 Speech by Aleksei Kudrin to the Russian Union of Producers and Industrialists (RSPP), April 21, 2011, formerly available on the site of the Ministry of Finance. Much the same concerns were expressed in the World Bank's semiannual reports on the Russian economy. See, for example, World Bank, *Russian Economic Report*, No. 26 (Moscow: World Bank, September 2011), http://siteresources.worldbank.org/INTRUS SIANFEDERATION/Resources/305499-1245838520910/6238985-1316082024531 /RER26_ENG.pdf.

15 Between 1994 and the first quarter of 2012, Russia has been a net capital donor of $377.8 billion to the rest of the world. But whereas the total net outflow was only $161.6 billion for the period 1994–2005, the net outflow was $339.4 billion between 2008 and the first quarter of 2012. Throughout the entire period there have been only two years, 2006 and 2007, when the net flow was inward. Source: Russian Central Bank, http://www.cbr.ru/eng/statistics/print.aspx?file=credit_statistics/capital_e.htm &pid=svs&sid=cvvk.

16 Kudrin, speech to the RSPP.

17 Kudrin never spelled out in detail his reasons for this bleak forecast, but they had mainly to do with his belief that high commodities prices were the result of loose monetary policies. Since these could not be sustained indefinitely, and because governments would sooner or later be forced to rein in their deficit spending, Kudrin believed that the decades ahead would be characterized by a general shrinkage of credit and by low growth—and therefore by low oil prices. According to Kseniia Iudaeva, an increasingly influential Russian economist who heads the Center for Macroeconomic Analysis at Sberbank, the process is already well advanced. See the interview with Iudaeva by Andrei Susarov, "Mezhdu puzyriami," *Moskovskie novosti*, February 2, 2012, p. 8.

18 Cited in Tat'iana Zykova, "Kudrin vkliuchil shchetchik," *Rossiiskaia gazeta*, December 10, 2010, p. 1.

19 Kudrin, speech at the Gaidar Forum, March 16, 2011, as reported in *RIA Novosti*. The proceedings of the Forum are available at http://www.iep.ru/ru/konferencii -seminary-kruglye-stoly/mezhdunarodnaya-konferenciya-rossiya-i-mir-v-poiska -innovacionnoi-strategii.html. A video of Kudrin's remarks at the Forum can be found

at http://www.youtube.com/watch?v=5g3bQK-9BII. Kudrin made the same point in a number of other public addresses in the spring of 2011. See, for example, his remarks to the RSPP.

20 Report by Kingsmill Bond of Citigroup Russia, cited in Andrew Kramer, "Putin Needs Higher Oil Prices to Pay for Promises," *New York Times*, March 17, 2012, p. B1. A more recent analyst's report from Morgan Stanley puts the break-even price even higher, at $160 by 2015. See Margarita Liutova, "$80 za barrel' poschitali stressovoi situatsiei," *Vedomosti*, May 12, 2012, http://www.vedomosti.ru/finance/news/1731335/shok_za_80 #ixzz1udq1po1m.

21 See for example Sechin's speech at the March 2010 meeting of Medvedev's Modernization Commission in Khanty-Mansiisk, available at http://news.kremlin.ru/transcripts /7198.

22 See http://lenta.ru/news/2010/09/01/putin/. The new Oil and Gas Institute is part of the Krasnoiarsk Federal University. The website of the new institute is http://oil.sfu -kras.ru/.

23 Angel Gonzalez, "Russian Energy Czar Sees Key Role for Foreign Firms," *Wall Street Journal*, April 18, 2012, http://online.wsj.com/article/SB1000142405270230342550457735 2062867437978.html.

24 Thus for example Arkadii Dvorkovich, Dmitri Medvedev's principal economic advisor during his presidency and one of the chief supporters of the modernization campaign, is now deputy prime minister with broad responsibility for energy and industry.

25 It is symptomatic that in the annual conferences called the "Gaidar Lectures," organized by the Gaidar Institute, one searches in vain for any papers addressing the challenges of the global hydrocarbons revolution.

26 The term "BRIC" refers to Brazil, Russia, India, and China.

27 Vladislav Inozemtsev and Viktor Krasil'shchikov, "Modernizatsiia.ru: Ordem vs. Progresso," *Vedomosti*, March 23, 2010.

28 For comprehensive coverage of the implications of Brazil's oil boom for technology and innovation throughout the rest of the Brazilian economy, see the special issue of *Upstream* devoted to "Brazil's Gold Rush," August 19, 2011, pp. 23–67. Follow-up coverage will be found in the *Upstream* issues of September 9 (pp. 29–31) and September 30, 2011 (pp. 32–35). I am grateful to George Helland for bringing these articles to my attention.

29 For background see the website of Michael Porter's Institute for Strategy and Competitiveness, Harvard Business School, Harvard University, www.isc.hbs.edu.

30 It is also the central argument of a 2008 report on the Russian economy written by Michael Porter and Christian Ketels, *Competitiveness at the Crossroads: Choosing the Future Direction of the Russian Economy,* report available on the website of the Institute for Strategy and Competitiveness, Harvard Business School, Harvard University, http://www.isc.hbs.edu/pdf/Russia_Competitiveness_Crossroads_Dec2007 .pdf.

31 Gavin Wright and Jesse Czelusta. "Mineral Resources and Economic Development," unpublished paper prepared for the Conference on Sector Reform in Latin America, Stanford Center for International Development, November 13–15, 2003, www-siepr .stanford.edu/workp/swp04004.html.

32 Houston has long been one of Michael Porter's favorite illustrations of the power of a cluster to catalyze diversified high-tech development. But despite the diversification of Houston's economy into health and computers, the core of the city's economy remains the oil industry, which has undergone a renaissance in the last decade as the result of deepwater exploration and production in the Gulf of Mexico.

33 The Ministry of Finance's "Strategy 2020 document" recommends, among other measures, raising the retirement age to 63, according to Kseniia Iudaeva, the Sberbank economist who also cochairs the Ministry's Group on Pension Reform. See Ol'ga Kuvshinova, Filipp Sterkin, Evgeniia Pis'mennaia, and Natal'ia Kostenko, "Nashli chto sokratit'," *Vedomosti*, February 16, 2012. For a fuller statement of Kudrin's views on the budgetary implications of Russia's aging population, see A. Kudrin and E. Gurvich, "Starenie naseleniia i ugroza biudzhetnogo krizisa," *Voprosy ekonomiki*, no. 3 (2012), pp. 52–79.

Bibliography

General Works

Blanchard, Olivier, and Michael Kremer. "Disorganization." *The Quarterly Journal of Economics* 112, no. 4 (November 1997), pp. 1091–1126.

Bressand, Albert. "Foreign Direct Investment in the Oil and Gas Sector." In Karl P. Sauvant, ed., *Yearbook on International Investment Law and Policy 2008–2009.* Oxford: Oxford University Press, 2009, pp. 117–211.

Fukuyama, Francis. *The Origins of Political Order: From Prehuman Times to the French Revolution.* New York: Farrar, Straus, and Giroux, 2011.

Gaines, Susan M., Geoffrey Eglinton, and Jürgen Rullkötter. *Echoes of Life: What Fossil Molecules Reveal about Earth History.* Oxford: Oxford University Press, 2009.

Huntington, Samuel P. *Political Order in Changing Societies.* New Haven, CT: Yale University Press, 1968.

Lindblom, Charles E. *Politics and Markets: The World's Political-Economic Systems.* New York: Basic Books, 1977.

McPhee, John. *Annals of the Former World.* New York: Farrar, Straus, and Giroux, 1998.

North, Douglass C. *Institutions, Institutional Change, and Economic Performance.* Cambridge: Cambridge University Press, 1990.

North, Douglass C., et al. "A Conceptual Framework for Interpreting Recorded Human History." National Bureau of Economic Research, Working Paper No. 12795 (December 2006). www.nber.org/papers/w12795.

Porter, Michael E. *The Competitive Advantage of Nations.* New York: The Free Press, 1990.

———. *On Competition.* Cambridge, MA: Harvard Business School Press, 1998.

Scott, James C. *Seeing Like a State: How Certain Schemes to Improve the Human Condition Have Failed.* New Haven, CT: Yale University Press, 1998.

Economics and Politics

Economy: Russia

Aslund, Anders. *Gorbachev's Struggle for Economic Reform.* Updated ed. Ithaca, NY: Cornell University Press, 1991.

Aslund, Anders, Sergei Guriev, and Andrew C. Kuchins, eds. *Russia after the Global Economic Crisis.* Washington, DC: Petersen Institute for International Economics and Center for Strategic and International Affairs, 2010.

Aslund, Anders, and Andrew C. Kuchins. *The Russia Balance Sheet.* Washington, DC: Petersen Institute for International Economics and Center for Strategic and International Affairs, 2010.

615

Barnes, Andrew. "Russia's New Business Groups and State Power." *Post-Soviet Affairs* 19, no. 2 (April–June 2003), pp. 154–186.

Blasi, Joseph, Maya Kroumova, and Douglas Kruse. *Kremlin Capitalism: Privatizing the Russian Economy.* Ithaca, NY: Cornell University Press, 1997.

Block, Alan A. "Banking, Fraud, and Stock Manipulation: Russian Opportunities and Dilemmas." In Sami Nevala and Kauko Aromaa, eds., *Organized Crime, Trafficking, Drugs.* Selected papers presented at the Annual Conference of the European Society of Criminology, Helsinki, 2003. Publication Series No. 42. Helsinki, Finland: European Institute for Crime Prevention and Control HEUNI, 2004, pp. 1–16. http://www.heuni.fi/uploads/v2t9skuki.pdf.

Chubais, A. B., ed. *Zakliuchennye na stroikakh kommunizma: GULag i ob"ekty energetiki SSSR.* Moscow: "Rossiiskaia politicheskaia entsiklopediia," 2008. http://www.rao-ees.ru/ru/info/history/show.cgi?history_zak.htm, or on the personal website of Anatolii Chubais, http://www.chubais.ru/cgi-bin/cms/smi.cgi?sect=0005.

Denisova, Irina, Markus Eller, and Ekaterina Zhuravskaya. "What Do Russians Think about Transition?" *Economics of Transition* 18, no. 2 (2010), pp. 249–280.

Gilman, Martin. *No Precedent, No Plan.* Cambridge, MA: MIT Press, 2010.

Gosudarstvennyi Komitet po Statistike Rossiiskoi Federatsii (Goskomstat Rossii). *Konsolidirovannyi biudzhet Rossiiskoi Federatsii.* Moscow, various years.

Gosudarstvennyi Komitet Rossiiskoi Federatsii po Statistike (Goskomstat Rossii). *Rossiiskii Statisticheskii Ezhegodnik.* Moscow, various years.

Gosudarstvennyi Komitet Rossiiskoi Federatsii po Statistike (Goskomstat Rossii). *Sotsial'no-ekonomicheskoe polozhenie Rossii.* Moscow, various years.

Gustafson, Thane. *Cracking the Nest Egg? The Growing Battle over Russia's Oil Stabilization Fund.* Cambridge, MA: IHS Cambridge Energy Research Associates, November 2004.

Hewett, Ed A. *Reforming the Soviet Economy: Equality versus Efficiency.* Washington, DC: Brookings Institution, 1988.

Hill, Fiona, and Clifford Gaddy. *The Siberian Curse: How Communist Planners Left Russia Out in the Cold.* Washington, DC: Brookings Institution Press, 2003.

Holzman, Franklyn. *The Economics of Soviet Bloc Trade and Finance.* Boulder, CO: Westview Press, 1987.

———. *Foreign Trade under Central Planning.* Cambridge, MA: Harvard University Press, 1974.

Johnson, Juliet. *A Fistful of Rubles: The Rise and Fall of the Russian Banking System.* Ithaca, NY: Cornell University Press, 2000.

Khodorkovskii, Mikhail, and Leonid Nevzlin. *Chelovek s rublem.* Moscow: LITRU.RU, 1992.

Kudrin, Aleksey. "Mekhanizmy formirovaniia neftegazovogo balansa biudzheta Rossii." *Voprosy ekonomiki*, no. 8 (2006), pp. 4–16.

———. "Stabilizatsionnyi fond: Zarubezhnyi i rossiiskii opyt." *Voprosy ekonomiki*, no. 2 (2006), pp. 28–45.

Ledeneva, Alena V. *Russia's Economy of Favors: Blat, Networking, and Informal Exchange.* Cambridge: Cambridge University Press, 1998.

McDonald, Joel M. *Business Operations in Russia.* Tax Management Publication 981, Foreign Income Portfolio Series. Washington, DC: Bureau of National Affairs, 2005.

McKinsey Global Institute. *Lean Russia: Sustaining Economic Growth through Improved Productivity.* Moscow: McKinsey, 2009.

Organisation for Economic Co-operation and Development. *Russian Federation: Strengthening the Policy Framework for Investment.* OECD Investment Policy Reviews. Paris: OECD, 2008.

Pappe, Iakov Sh. *"Oligarkhi": Ekonomicheskaia khronika 1992–2000.* Moscow: Vysshaia Shkola Ekonomiki, 2000.

Samoilenko, Vladimir. "Special Report: Government Policies in Regard to Internal Tax Havens in Russia." Moscow: International Tax and Investment Center, December 2003. http://www.iticnet.org/Public/other_publications.aspx#divYear2003.

Shleifer, Andrei, and Daniel Treisman. *Without a Map: Political Tactics and Economic Reform in Russia.* Cambridge, MA: MIT Press, 2000.

Sutton, Anthony C. *Western Technology and Soviet Economic Development, 1917 to 1930.* Stanford, CA: Hoover Institution Press, 1968.

Treisman, Daniel. "Loans for Shares Revisited." *Post-Soviet Affairs* 26, no. 3 (2010), pp. 207–227.

Treml, Vladimir G., and Barry L. Kostinsky. *Domestic Value of Soviet Foreign Trade: Exports and Imports in the 1972 Input-Output Table.* Foreign Economic Report No. 20. Washington, DC: U.S. Department of Commerce, Bureau of the Census, October 1982.

USSR State Statistical Committee (Goskomstat SSSR). *Vneshniaia torgovlia SSSR.* Moscow: "Statistika," various years.

World Bank. "From Transition to Development: A Country Economic Memorandum for the Russian Federation." Moscow: World Bank, April 2005. http://go.worldbank.org /Y9YXEF31H0.

———. *Russian Economic Report.* Washington, DC: World Bank, published annually from 2001 to the present.

———. *Russian Federation Country Assistance Evaluation.* Report No. 24875. Washington, DC: World Bank, September 23, 2002.

Literature on Market Reforms and the Evolution of the Russian Economy

Adachi, Yuko. "The Ambiguous Effects of Russian Corporate Governance Abuses of the 1990s." *Post-Soviet Affairs* 22, no. 1 (2006), pp. 65–89.

Boycko, Maxim, Andrei Shleifer, and Robert Vishny. *Privatizing Russia.* Cambridge, MA: MIT Press, 1995.

Carnegie Endowment for International Peace, Moscow office. *Sotsial'no-ekonomicheskie portrety regionov,* Book 2. Moscow: Carnegie Endowment for International Peace, 1998.

Chubais, Anatolii B., ed. *Privatizatsiia po-rossiiski.* Moscow: "Vagrius," 1999.

Foglesong, Todd S., and Peter H. Solomon. *Courts and Transition in Russia: The Challenge of Judicial Reform.* Boulder, CO: Westview Press, 2000.

Freeland, Chrystia. *Sale of the Century: Russia's Wild Ride from Communism to Capitalism.* New York: Crown Publishers, 2000.

Gaidar, Yegor T. *Days of Defeat and Victory.* Seattle: University of Washington Press, 1999. [In Russian: *Dni porazhdenii i pobed.* Moscow: Evrasiia, 1997.]

———. *State and Evolution: Russia's Search for a Free Market.* Seattle: University of Washington Press, 2003. [In Russian: *Gosudarstvo i Evoliutsiia.* Moscow: Evraziia, 1997.]

Gilman, Martin. *No Precedent, No Plan.* Cambridge, MA: MIT Press, 2010.

Goldman, Marshall I. *Lost Opportunity: What Has Made Economic Reform in Russia So Difficult.* New York: Norton, 1996.

———. *Petrostate: Putin, Power, and the New Russia.* Oxford: Oxford University Press, 2008.

———. *The Piratization of Russia: Russian Reform Goes Awry.* New York: Routledge, 2003.

Grigor'ev, Leonid, ed. *Sovremennye tendentsii v mirovoi ekonomike.* Moscow: Vysshaia Shkola Ekonomiki, 2012.

Guriev, Sergei, and Ekaterina Zhuravskaya. "Why Russia Is Not South Korea." *Journal of International Affairs* 63, no. 2 (Spring/Summer 2010), pp. 125–139.

Gustafson, Thane. *Capitalism Russian-Style.* Cambridge: Cambridge University Press, 1999.

———. *Selling the Russians the Rope? Soviet Technology Policy and U.S. Export Controls.* R-2649-ARPA. Santa Monica, CA: Rand, 1981.

Hellman, Joel S. "Breaking the Bank: Bureaucrats and the Creation of Markets in a Transitional Economy." PhD diss., Columbia University, 1993.

Hoffman, David E. *The Oligarchs: Wealth and Power in the New Russia.* 2nd ed. New York: Public Affairs, 2011.

Jack, Andrew. *Inside Putin's Russia: Can There Be Reform without Democracy?* Oxford: Oxford University Press, 2004.

Klebnikov, Paul. *Godfather of the Kremlin: The Decline of Russia in the Age of Gangster Capitalism.* New York: Harcourt, 2000.

Kokh, Alfred. *The Selling of the Soviet.* New York: S.P.I. Books, 1998.

Kolesnikov, Andrei. *Anatolii Chubais: Biografiia.* Moscow: "AST Moskva," 2008.

———. *Neizvestnyi Chubais: Stranitsy iz biografii.* Moscow: "Vagrius," 2003.

Konstantinov, Andrei. *Banditskii Peterburg.* 2 vols. Saint Petersburg: "Neva," 2005.

Kornai, Jànos, Bo Rothstein, and Susan Rose-Ackerman, eds. *Building a Trustworthy State in Post-Socialist Transition.* New York: Palgrave MacMillan, 2004.

Kotkin, Stephen. *Armageddon Averted: The Soviet Collapse, 1970–2000.* Oxford: Oxford University Press, 2001.

Kryshtanovskaia, Ol'ga. *Anatomiia rossiiskoi politicheskoi elity.* Moscow: "Zakharov," 2005.

Lieven, Anatol. *Chechnya: Tombstone of Russian Power.* New Haven, CT: Yale University Press, 1998.

Midgley, Dominic, and Chris Hutchins. *Abramovich: The Billionaire from Nowhere.* London: HarperCollins, 2005.

Paniushkin, Valerii. *Mikhail Khodorkovskii: Uznik tishiny.* Moscow: "Sekret firmy," 2006.

Peregudov, Sergei P. *Korporatsii, obshchestvo, gosudarstvo: Evoliutsiia otnoshenii.* Moscow: Nauka, 2003.

Petrakov, Nikolai Iakovlevich. *Russkaia ruletka: Ekonomicheskii eksperiment tsenoiu 150 millionov zhiznei.* Moscow: "Ekonomika," 1998.

Reddaway, Peter, and Dmitri Glinski. *The Tragedy of Russia's Reforms.* Washington, DC: Institute of Peace Press, 2001.

Reteium, Aleksei Iu. *Dvenadtsat' let iz zhizni strany.* Moscow: "Khorion," 2004.

Schetnaia Palata Rossiiskoi Federatsii. *Analiz protsessov privatizatsii gosudarstvennoi sobstvennosti Rossiiskoi Federatsii za period 1993–2003 gody.* Moscow: "Olita," 2004. Available on the website of the Schetnaia Palata, www.ach.gov.ru.

Sedaitis, Judith B. "Spinoffs versus Startups under Market Transition: The Development of Post-Soviet Commodity Exchange Markets." PhD diss., Columbia University, 1994.

Shatalov, Sergey. *Tax Reform in Russia: History and Future.* Economic Policy Distinguished Lecture delivered at the London School of Economics, November 10, 2005. Published as a Special Report of the International Tax and Investment Center, February 2006.

Troika Dialog. *Corporate Governance: Russia's Evolution.* Moscow: Troika Dialog, November 2001.

Volkov, Vadim. *Violent Entrepreneurs: The Use of Force in the Making of Russian Capitalism.* Ithaca, NY: Cornell University Press, 2002. [In Russian: *Silovoe predprinimatel'stvo.* Saint Petersburg: Letnii Sad, 2002.]

Woodruff, David. *Money Unmade: Barter and the Fate of Russian Capitalism.* Ithaca, NY: Cornell University Press, 1999.

Russian Politics and the Evolution of the Russian State

Al'bats, Evgeniia. *Mina zamedlennogo deistviia.* Moscow: "Russlit," 1992.

Almquist, Peter. *Red Forge: Soviet Military Industry since 1965.* New York: Columbia University Press, 1990.

Baker, Peter, and Susan Glasser. *Kremlin Rising: Vladimir Putin's Russia and the End of Revolution.* New York: Scribner, 2005.

Brym, Robert J., and Vladimir Gimpelson. "The Size, Composition, and Dynamics of the Russian State Bureaucracy in the 1990s." *Slavic Review* 63, no. 1 (Spring 2004), pp. 90–112.

Chaisty, Paul. *Legislative Politics and Economic Power in Russia.* Basingstoke, UK: Palgrave, 2006.

Chung, Han-Ku. *Interest Representation in Soviet Policymaking: A Case Study of a West Siberian Energy Coalition.* Boulder, CO: Westview Press, 1987.

Colton, Timothy J. *Yeltsin: A Life.* New York: Basic Books, 2008.

Colton, Timothy J., and Stephen Holmes, eds. *The State after Communism: Governance in the New Russia.* Lanham, MD: Rowman and Littlefield, 2006.

Colton, Timothy J., and Michael McFaul. *Popular Choice and Managed Democracy: The Russian Elections of 1999 and 2000.* Washington, DC: Brookings Institution, 2003.

Fel'shtinskii, Iurii, and Vladimir Pribylovskii. *Korporatsiia: Rossiia i KGB vo vremena prezidenta Putina.* Moscow: "Terra," 2010.

Felshtinsky, Yuri, and Vladimir Pribylovsky. *The Age of Assassins: The Rise and Rise of Vladimir Putin.* London: Gibson Square, 2008.

Fish, Stephen. *Democracy Derailed in Russia: The Failure of Open Politics.* Cambridge: Cambridge University Press, 2005.

Hough, Jerry F. *The Soviet Prefects: The Local Party Organs in Industrial Decision-Making.* Cambridge, MA: Harvard University Press, 1969.

Huskey, Eugene. "From Higher Party Schools to Academies of State Service: The Marketization of Bureaucratic Training in Russia." *Slavic Review* 63, no. 2 (Summer 2004), pp. 325–348.

———. *Presidential Power in Russia.* Armonk, NY: M. E. Sharpe, 1999.

Mendras, Marie. *Poutine: L'Envers du Pouvoir.* Paris: Editions Odile Jacob, 2008.

Milov, V., B. Nemtsov, V. Ryzhkov, and O. Shorina, eds. *Putin. Korruptsiia. Nezavisimyi ekspertnyi doklad.* 2nd ed. Moscow, 2011. http://www.putin-itogi.ru/f/Putin-i-kor ruptsiya-doklad.pdf.

Montaigne, Fen. *Reeling in Russia: An American Angler in Russia.* New York: St. Martin's Griffin, 1999.

Mukhin, A. A. *Piterskoe okruzhenie prezidenta.* Moscow: "Tsentr politicheskoi informatsii," 2003.

Nemtsov, Boris, and Vladimir Milov. *Putin. Itogi. 10 let.* Moscow: "Solidarnost," 2010. http://nemtsov.ru/?id=706211.

Orttung, Robert W. *From Leningrad to Saint Petersburg: Democratization in a Russian City.* New York: Saint Martin's Press, 1995.

Pastukhov, Vladimir. "Law under Administrative Pressure in Post-Soviet Russia." *East European Constitutional Review* 11, no. 2 (Summer 2002), pp. 66–74.

Petrov, Nikolai. "How Have the Presidential Envoys Changed the Administrative-Political Balance of Putin's Regime?" In Peter Reddaway and Robert W. Orttung, eds., *The Dynamics of Russian Politics: Putin's Reform of Federal-Regional Relations,* 2 vols. Lanham, MD: Rowman and Littlefield, 2004, 2:33–64.

———. "The Security Dimension of the Federal Reforms." In Peter Reddaway and Robert W. Orttung, eds., *The Dynamics of Russian Politics: Putin's Reform of Federal-Regional Relations,* 2 vols. Lanham, MD: Rowman and Littlefield, 2004, 2:7–32.

Pribylovskii, Vladimir. "Proiskhozhdenie putinskoi oligarkhii," *Polit.ru,* October 19 and 27, 2005 (part 1: polit.ru/analytics/2005/10/19/oligarhi_print.html; part 2: polit.ru/analytics/2005/10/17/oligarhi_print.html).

Putin, Vladimir, with with N. Gevorkian, N. Timakova, and A. Kolesnikov. *First Person,* trans. Catherine A. Fitzpatrick. New York: Random House, 2000. [In Russian: *Ot pervogo litsa: razgovory s Vladimirom Putinym.* Moscow: "Vagrius," 2000.] An online version is available at http://bookz.ru/authors/gevorkan-natalia/gevorkiannato1/1 -gevorkiannato1.html.

Reddaway, Peter. "Historical and Political Context." In Peter Reddaway and Robert W. Orttung, eds., *The Dynamics of Russian Politics: Putin's Reform of Federal-Regional Relations,* 2 vols. Lanham, MD: Rowman and Littlefield, 2004, 1:1–19.

———. "Is Putin's Power More Formal Than Real?" *Post-Soviet Affairs* 18, no. 1 (2002), pp. 31–40.

———. "Will Putin Be Able to Consolidate Power?" *Post-Soviet Affairs* 17, no. 1 (2001), pp. 23–44.

Reddaway, Peter, and Robert W. Orttung, eds. *The Dynamics of Russian Politics: Putin's Reform of Federal-Regional Relations.* 2 vols. Lanham, MD: Rowman and Littlefield, 2004.

Ruble, Blair. *Leningrad: Shaping a Soviet City.* Berkeley: University of California Press, 1989.

Sakwa, Richard. *The Crisis of Russian Democracy: The Dual State, Factionalism, and the Medvedev Succession.* Cambridge: Cambridge University Press, 2011.

———. *The Quality of Freedom: Khodorkovsky, Putin, and the Yukos Affair.* Oxford: Oxford University Press, 2009.

Shevtsova, Lilia. *Putin's Russia.* Washington, DC: Carnegie Endowment for International Peace, 2003.

Sobchak, Anatolii. *Khozhdenie vo vlast'.* 2nd ed. Moscow: "Novosti," 2001.

———, *Zhila-byla kommunisticheskaia partiia.* Saint Petersburg: "Lenizdat," 1995.

Solnick, Stephen. *Stealing the State: Control and Collapse in Soviet Institutions.* Cambridge, MA: Harvard University Press, 1998.

Talbott, Strobe. *The Russia Hand: A Memoir of Presidential Diplomacy.* New York: Random House, 2002.

Treisman, Daniel. *The Return: Russia's Journey from Gorbachev to Medvedev.* New York: Free Press, 2011.

Yeltsin, Boris. *The Struggle for Russia.* New York: Times Books, 1994.

Yergin, Daniel, and Thane Gustafson. *Russia 2010 and What It Means for the World.* New York: Random House, 2004. [Translated into Russian as *Rossiia: Dvadtsat' let spust'ia.* Moscow: "Mezhdunarodnye otnosheniia," 1995.]

The State and Its Policies

The Rentier State and International Competitiveness

Ahrend, Rudiger. "Can Russia Break the 'Resource Curse'?" *Eurasian Geography and Economics* 46, no. 8 (December 2005), pp. 584–609.

Alexeev, Michael, and Robert Conrad. "The Elusive Curse of Oil." *Review of Economics and Statistics* 41, no. 3 (2009), pp. 599–616.

Arbatov, A., and V. Smirnov. " 'Resursnoe prokliatie' Rossii: Ekskurs v istoriiu i nyneshnie problemy." *Obshchestvo i ekonomika,* December 31, 2004, pp. 137–157.

Aslund, Anders. "Russian Resources: Curse or Rents?" *Eurasian Geography and Economics* 46, no. 8 (December 2005), pp. 610–617.

Auty, R. M. "Russia: The Political Economy of Transition in a Mineral Economy." In S. Mansoob Murshed, ed., *Issues in Positive Political Economy*. London: Routledge, 2002, pp. 39–56.

Birdsall, Nancy, and Arvind Subramanian. "Saving Iraq from Its Oil." *Foreign Affairs* 83, no. 4 (July/August 2004), pp. 77–89.

Bradshaw, Michael. "Observations on the Geographical Dimensions of Russia's Resource Abundance." *Eurasian Geography and Economics* 47, no. 6 (2006), pp. 724–746.

Breach, Alastair. "Expanding Horizons: Russia's Route to Prosperity in a Post-Industrial World." *Brunswick UBS Warburg Global Equity Research*, January 31, 2003.

Ellman, Michael, ed. *Russia's Oil and Natural Gas: Bonanza or Curse?* London: Anthem Press, 2006.

Frankel, Paul H. *Essentials of Petroleum: A Key to Oil Economics*. London: Chapman and Hall, 1946.

Gaddy, Clifford G., and Barry W. Ickes. "Resource Rents and the Russian Economy." *Eurasian Geography and Economics* 46, no. 8 (December 2005), pp. 559–583.

——. "Russia after the Global Financial Crisis: Prospects for Reforming a Crucial Sector." *Eurasian Geography and Economics* 51, no. 3 (2010), pp. 312–329.

——. "Russia's Declining Oil Production: Managing Price Risk and Rent Addiction." *Eurasian Geography and Economics* 50, no. 1 (2009), pp. 1–13.

——. "Russia's Dependence on Resources." In Michael V. Alexeev and Shlomo Weber, eds., *The Oxford Handbook of the Russian Economy*. Oxford: Oxford University Press, 2012, pp. 1–34.

——. "Russia's Virtual Economy." *Foreign Affairs* 77, no. 5 (September/October 1998), pp. 53–67. [The argument was further developed in the authors' subsequent book, *Russia's Virtual Economy*. Washington, DC: Brookings Institution Press, 2002.]

Gaidar, Yegor T. *Gibel' imperii: Uroki dlia sovremennoi Rossii*. Moscow: "Rossiiskaia politicheskaia entsiklopediia," 2006. [Translated as *Collapse of an Empire: Lessons for Modern Russia*. Washington, DC: Brookings Institution Press, 2007.]

Guriev, Sergei, Andrei Plekhanov, and Konstantin Sonin. "Development Based on Commodity Revenues." European Bank for Reconstruction and Development (EBRD), Working Paper No. 108 (November 2009).

Karl, Terry Lynn. *The Paradox of Plenty: Oil Booms and Petro-States*. Berkeley: University of California Press, 1997.

Lam, Ricky, and Leonard Wantchekon. "Political Dutch Disease." Unpublished manuscript, posted on the web page of Professor Leonard Wantchekon at http://www.nyu.edu/gsas /dept/politics/faculty/wantchekon/research/lr-04-10.pdf, April 10, 2003.

Luong, Pauline Jones. "The 'Use and Abuse' of Russia's Energy Resources: Implications for State-Society Relations." In Valerie Sperling, ed., *Building the Russian State: Institutional Crisis and the Quest for Democratic Governance*. Boulder, CO: Westview Press, 2000, pp. 27–45.

Luong, Pauline Jones, and Erika Weinthal. "Contra Coercion: Russia Tax Reform, Exogenous Shocks, and Negotiated Institutional Change." *American Political Science Review* 98, no. 1 (February 2004), pp. 139–152.

Luong, Pauline Jones, and Erika Weinthal. *Oil Is Not a Curse: Ownership Structures and Institutions in Soviet Successor States*. Cambridge: Cambridge University Press, 2010.

Mahdavy, Hossein. "The Patterns and Problems of Economic Development in Rentier States: The Case of Iran." In M. A. Cook, ed., *Studies in the Economic History of the Middle East*. London: Oxford University Press, 1970, pp. 37–61.

Mehlum, H., K. Moene, and R. Torvik. "Institutions and the Resource Curse." *Economic Journal* 116, no. 508 (2006), pp. 1–20.

Sachs, Jeffrey D., and Andrew M. Warner. "The Curse of Natural Resources." *European Economic Review* 45, nos. 4–6 (May 2001), pp. 827–838.

———. "Natural Resource Abundance and Economic Growth." National Bureau of Economic Research, Working Paper No. 5398 (1995).

Shields, David. *Pemex: Un futuro incierto*. Mexico City: Editorial Planeta, 2003. [See the review in English by George Baker in *Energy Press Americas*, January 27, 2004.]

Volkov, Vadim. "The Selective Use of State Capacity in Russia's Economy: Property Disputes and Enterprise Takeover, 1998–2002." In J. Kornai and S.-R. Ackerman, eds., *Trust in Post-Socialist Economies*. Budapest, 2003.

Weinthal, Erika, and Pauline Jones Luong. "Combating the Resource Curse: An Alternative Solution to Managing Mineral Wealth." *Perspectives on Politics* 4, no. 1 (March 2006), pp. 35–53.

Wright, Gavin, and Jesse Czelusta. "Mineral Resources and Economic Development." Unpublished paper prepared for the Conference on Sector Reform in Latin America, Stanford Center for International Development, November 13–15, 2003. www-siepr.stanford .edu/workp/swp04004.html.

———. "Why Economies Slow: The Myth of the Resource Curse." *Challenge* 47, no. 2 (March 2004), pp. 6–38.

Evolution of Russian Energy and Investment Policy

Balzer, Harley. "The Putin Thesis and Russian Energy Policy." *Post-Soviet Affairs* 21, no. 3 (2005), pp. 210–225.

Baziv, V. F., et al., eds. *U rulia razrabotki neftianykh mestorozhdenii (35 let TsKR Mintopenergo RF)*. Moscow: VNIIOENG, 1998.

Gaddy, Clifford G., and Andrew C. Kuchins. "Putin's Plan." *The Washington Quarterly* 31, no. 2 (Spring 2008), pp. 117–129.

Hewett, Ed A. *Energy, Economics, and Foreign Policy in the Soviet Union*. Washington, DC: Brookings Institution, 1984.

International Energy Agency. *Energy Policies of the Russian Federation: 1995 Survey*. Paris: International Energy Agency, 1995.

———. *Energy Policies of the Russian Federation: 2002 Survey*. Paris: International Energy Agency, 2002.

Konoplianik, Andrei. *Rosssiia na formiruiushchemsia evroaziatskom prostranstve: Problemy konkurentosposobnosti*. Moscow: Nestor Academic Publishers, 2004.

Konoplianik, Andrei, and Mikhail Subbotin. *Tiazhba o razdele (Diskussiia vokrug zakona "O soglasheniiakh o razdele produktsii")*. Moscow: VNIIOENG, 1996. http://www.yabloko.ru/Publ/Srp-ks/srp-ks.html#1.

Kriukov, Valerii. "Neftegazovyi sektor Rossii: Resursnye vozmozhnosti i institutsional'nye ogranicheniia." In Leonid Grigor'ev, ed., *Sovremennye tendentsii v mirovoi ekonomike*. Moscow: Higher School of Economics, 2012.

Moe, Arild, and Valeriy Kryukov. "Observations on the Reorganization of the Russian Oil Industry." *Post-Soviet Geography* 35, no. 2 (1994), pp. 89–101.

———. "Oil Exploration in Russia: Prospects for Reforming a Crucial Sector." *Eurasian Geography and Economics* 51, no. 3 (2010), pp. 312–329.

Putin, Vladimir V. "Mineral'no-syr'evye resursy v strategii razvitiia rossiiskoi ekonomiki." In *Problemy toplivno-energeticheskogo kompleksa* (a special issue of *Zapiski gornogo institute*), tom 144 (1) (Saint Petersburg, 1999), pp. 3–9. [An English translation, with an introduction by Harley Balzer, appears in *Problems of Post-Communism* 53, no. 1 (January/February 2006), pp. 48–54.]

———. "Rossiia na rubezhe tysiacheletii." *Nezavisimaia gazeta*, December 30, 1999.

———. *Strategicheskoe planirovanie vosproizvodstva mineral'no-syr'revoi bazy regiona v usloviiakh formirovaniia rynochnykh otnoshenii (Sankt-Peterburg i Leningradskaia oblast')*. Dissertation in satisfaction of requirements for the degree of *Kandidat* in economics (Saint Petersburg, 1997). Electronic copy available (to library cardholders) from the Russian State Library, 2002, http://diss.rsl.ru/diss/02/0000/020000840.pdf.

Sechin, Igor Ivanovich. *Ekonomicheskaia otsenka investitsionnykh proektovtranzita nefti i nefteproduktov (na primere nefteproduktovoda Kirishi-Batareinaia)*. Dissertation in satisfaction of requirements for the degree of *Kandidat* in economics. Saint Petersburg:

G. V. Plekhanov State Mining Institute, 1998. Electronic copy available (to library card-holders) from the Russian State State Library.

Solov'eva, Evgeniia A., and Viktor A. Zubkov. "O kontseptsii nalogovoi reformy v mineral'no syr'evom komplekse Rossii." *Zapiski gornogo instituta*, tom 145 (1), pp. 19–29.

Starovoitov, S. N. *Problemy razvitiia Zapadno-Sibirskogo neftegazovogo kompleksa.* Novo-sibirsk: "Nauka," 1983.

Zubkov, Viktor A. *Nalogooblozhenie v mineral'no-syr'evom komplekse Rossii.* Saint Peters-burg: Saint Petersburg Mining Institute, 1999.

Energy

General

Ascher, William. *Why Governments Waste Natural Resources.* Baltimore, MD: Johns Hop-kins University Press, 1999.

Auty, Richard. *Resource-Based Industrialization: Sowing the Oil in Eight Developing Coun-tries.* New York: Oxford University Press, 1990.

Baker, Ron. *A Primer of Oilwell Drilling.* 5th ed. revised. Austin: Petroleum Extension Ser-vice, University of Texas, 1996.

Bergin, Tom. *Spills and Spin: The Inside Story of BP.* London: Random House Business Books, 2011.

Bower, Tom. *The Squeeze: Oil Money and Greed in the Twenty-First Century.* New York: HarperPress, 2009.

BP. *Our Industry: Petroleum.* London: The British Petroleum Company Limited, 1977.

———. *Statistical Review of World Energy,* various years. http://www.bp.com/sectionbody copy.do?categoryId=7500&contentId=7068481.

Bressand, Albert, et al. *Shell Global Scenarios to 2025.* London: Shell International, 2005.

Browne, John. *Beyond Business. The Inside Story: Leadership and Transformation in BP.* London: Weidenfeld and Nicholson, 2010.

Chernow, Ron. *Titan: The Life of John D. Rockefeller.* New York: Random House, 1998.

Chevalier, Jean-Marie. *Les Grandes Batailles de l'Energie: Petit Traité d'une Economie Vio-lente.* Paris: Gallimard, 2004.

Chevalier, Jean-Marie, and Jacques Percebois. *Gaz et Electricité: Un Défi pour l'Europe et pour la France.* Paris: Conseil d'Analyse Economique, La Documentation Française, 2008.

Deffeyes, Kenneth S. *Hubbert's Peak: The Impending World Oil Shortage.* Princeton, NJ: Princeton University Press, 2001.

Eller, Stacy L., Peter Hartley, and Kenneth B. Medlock III. *Empirical Evidence on the Op-erational Efficiency of National Oil Companies.* Houston, TX: James A. Baker III Insti-tute for Public Policy, Rice University, March 2007.

Fox-Penner, Peter. *Electric Utility Restructuring: A Guide to the Competitive Era.* Vienna, VA: Public Utilities Reports, 1998.

Grace, John D. "Molecules and Money: True Value in Oil and Gas Reserves." *Petroleum Intelligence Weekly*, May 3, 2004, pp. 6–9.

Hunt, Sally. *Making Competition Work in Electricity*. New York: John Wiley & Sons, 2002.

IHS. *Digital Oil Field of the Future: Lessons from Other Industries*. Cambridge, MA: IHS Cambridge Energy Research Associates, 2004.

———. *Lessons of the DOFF: A Global Assessment of Potential Oil Recovery Increases*. Cambridge, MA: IHS Cambridge Energy Research Associates, 2005.

———. *World Petroleum Trends, 1994 to 2003*. Denver: IHS, October 2004.

IHS Herold and Harrison Lovegrove and Co. *Global Upstream Performance Review*, various years.

International Energy Agency (IEA). *World Energy Outlook*. Paris: IEA, various years.

Jackson, Peter M., and Keith M. Eastwood. *Finding the Critical Numbers: What Are the Real Decline Rates for Global Oil Production?* Cambridge, MA: IHS Cambridge Energy Research Associates, September 2007.

Kasim, Farouk al-. *Managing Petroleum Resources: The "Norwegian Model" in a Broad Perspective*. Oxford Institute for Energy Studies monograph No. 30. Oxford: Oxford University Press, 2006.

Kemp, Alexander G. *Petroleum Rent Collection around the World*. Halifax, Nova Scotia: Institute for Research on Public Policy, 1987.

Klett, T. R., and J. W. Schmoker. "Reserve Growth of the World's Giant Fields." In M. T. Halbouty, ed., *Giant Oil and Gas Fields of the Decade 1990–1999*, AAPG Memoir 78. Tulsa: American Association of Petroleum Geologists, pp. 107–122.

Lewis, James A. *History of Petroleum Engineering*. New York: American Petroleum Institute, 1961.

Link, Peter K. *Basic Petroleum Geology*. Tulsa, OK: Oil and Gas Consultants International Publications, 1982.

Markwell, Paul. *Mature Oil Fields: An Energy Intensity Dilemma*. Cambridge, MA: IHS Cambridge Energy Research Associates, September 2009.

Marcel, Valerie. *Oil Titans: National Oil Companies in the Middle East*. London: Chatham House, 2006.

McKinsey Global Institute. *Curbing Global Energy Demand Growth: The Energy Productivity Opportunity*. San Francisco: McKinsey, May 2007.

National Petroleum Council. *Hard Truths: Facing the Hard Truths about Energy*. Washington, DC: U.S. Department of Energy, 2007.

Neal, W. Howard (team leader). "Oil and Gas Technology Development." Topic Paper No. 26, Working Document of the 2007 National Petroleum Council Global Oil and Gas Study. Unpublished document, released July, 18 2007. http://www.npchardtruthsreport.org/topic_papers.php.

Nore, Petter. "The Norwegian State's Relationship to the International Oil Companies over North Sea Oil, 1965–75." PhD diss., School of Social Sciences, Division of Economics, Thames Polytechnic, June 1979.

Noreng, Øystein. *The Oil Industry and Government Strategy in the North Sea*. London: Croom Helm, 1980.

Olcott, Martha Brill. *Kazakhstan: Unfulfilled Promise*. Washington, DC: Carnegie Endowment for International Peace, 2002.

Pratt, Joseph A. *Prelude to Merger: A History of the Amoco Corporation, 1973–1998*. Houston, TX: Hart Publications, 2000.

van Dyke, Kate. *A Primer of Oilwell Service, Workover, and Completion*. Austin: Petroleum Extension Service, University of Texas at Austin, 1997.

Yergin, Daniel. *The Prize: The Epic Quest for Oil, Money, and Power*. Rev. ed. New York: Free Press, 2008.

———. *The Quest: Energy, Security, and the Remaking of the Modern World*. New York: Penguin Press, 2011.

Yergin, Daniel, David Hobbs, and Richard Ward. *Modernizing Oil and Gas Reserves Disclosures*. CERA Special Report. Cambridge, MA: IHS Cambridge Energy Research Associates, February 2006.

Soviet Union and Russia

Abdelal, Rawi. *Journey to Sakhalin: Royal Dutch/Shell in Russia*. Harvard Business School Case Study. Cambridge, MA: Harvard Business School. Part A, June 2, 2006; Part B, with Irina Tarsis, February 6, 2007; Part C, with Marina N. Vandamme, February 8, 2007.

Bradshaw, Michael. "A New Energy Age in Pacific Russia: Lessons from the Sakhalin Oil and Gas Projects." *Eurasian Geography and Economics* 51, no. 3 (2010), pp. 330–359.

Chernikov, Nikolai. *Vagit Alekperov i ego komanda: Geroi dvukh epokh*. Moscow: Smena, 2000.

Chumalov, Mikhail Iur'evich. *Kaspiiskaia neft' i mezhnatsional'nye otnosheniia*. Moscow: Russian Academy of Sciences, Institute of Ethnology and Anthropology, 2000.

Clarke, James W. "Petroleum Habitat of East Siberia, Russia." *International Geology Review* 36 (1994), pp. 238–249.

Eliseev, Iu. B., and L. G. Kiriukhin. "Neftegazovye resursy Vostochnoi Sibiri: Real'nost', problemy, resheniia." *Geologiia nefti i gaza*, no. 1 (2002), pp. 17–20.

Gustafson, Thane. *Crisis amid Plenty: The Politics of Soviet Energy under Brezhnev and Gorbachev*. Princeton, NJ: Princeton University Press, 1989.

Gustafson, Thane, and Vadim Eskin. *Russia's Gazprom Turns Inward: Can It Bring the Domestic Gas Market under Control?* Cambridge, MA: IHS Cambridge Energy Research Associates, March 1997.

Gustafson, Thane, John C. Webb, and Paulina Mirenkova. *The Russian Oil Industry in Global Perspective: The Challenges Ahead*. Cambridge, MA: IHS Cambridge Energy Research Associates, April 2011.

Kriukov, V. A., and A. N. Tokarev. *Neftegazovye resursy v transformiruemoi ekonomike: O sootnoshenii realizovannoi i potentsial'noi obshchestvennoi tsennosti nedr.* Novosibirsk: "Nauka-Tsentr," 2007.

Levine, Steve. *The Oil and the Glory: The Pursuit of Empire and Fortune on the Caspian Sea.* New York: Random House, 2007.

Russian Federation Ministry of Industry and Energy. *TEK Rossii: Itogi proizvodstvennoi deiatel'nosti otraslei.* Moscow: Russian Federation Ministry of Industry and Energy, various years.

Shafranik, Iu. K., and V. A. Kriukov. *Neftegazovye resursy v kruge problem.* Moscow: "Nedra," 1997.

Sim, Li-Chen. "The Changing Relationship between the State and the Oil Industry in Russia (1992–2004)." D.Phil. thesis, St. Antony's College, University of Oxford, March 2005.

———. *The Rise and Fall of Privatization in the Russian Oil Industry.* London: Palgrave Macmillan, 2008.

Vladimirov, A. N., and V. Ia. Kershenbaum. *Konkurentosposobnost' i problemy neftegazovogo kompleksa.* Moscow: NP "Natsional'nyi institut nefti i gaza," 2004.

Voronov, V. N., et al. "Novye perspektivnye neftegazopoiskovye ob"ekty Zapadnoi Sibiri." *Geologiia nefti i gaza,* nos. 5–6 (1999), pp. 7–14.

RUSSIAN OIL

Ahrend, Rudiger, and William Tompson. *Realizing the Oil Supply Potential of the CIS: The Impact of Institutions and Policies.* OECD Economics Department Working Papers, No. 484. Paris: OECD, 2006.

Alekperov, Vagit. *Oil of Russia: Past, Present, and Future.* Minneapolis, MN: East View Press, 2011.

Alekperov, Vagit Iu. *Vertikal'no integrirovannye neftianye kompanii v Rossii.* Moscow: "Autopan," 1996.

Alexeev, Mikhail, and Robert Conrad. "The Russian Oil Tax Regime: A Comparative Perspective." *Eurasian Geography and Economics* 50, no. 1 (2009), pp. 93–114.

Amirov, Anvar. *LUKOil: Obzor deiatel'nosti.* Moscow: "Panorama," 2001.

Batalin, Iurii P., ed. *Neftegazostroiteli Zapadnoi Sibiri.* A volume in the series *Stroiteli Rossii XX. Veka.* Moscow: Soiuz neftegazostroitelei, 2004.

Bergesen, Helge Ole, Arild Moe, and Willy Ostreng. *Soviet Oil and Security Interests in the Barents Sea.* New York: St. Martin's Press, 1987.

Bradshaw, Michael. "A New Energy Age in Pacific Russia: Lessons from the Sakhalin Oil and Gas Projects." *Eurasian Geography and Economics* 51, no. 3 (2010), pp. 330–359.

Campbell, R. W. "Recent Trends in the Soviet Upstream Oil Industry (Investment, Drilling, and Well Completions): Soviets Run Faster and Faster Just to Stay in Place." *PlanEcon Soviet Energy Outlook* (Washington, DC) (March 1991).

Chadwick, Margaret, David Long, and Machiko Nissanke. *Soviet Oil Exports: Trade Adjustments, Refining Constraints, and Market Behavior.* Oxford: Oxford University Press, 1987.

Churilov, Lev. *Lifeblood of Empire: A Personal History of the Rise and Fall of the Soviet Oil Industry.* New York: PIW Publications, 1996.

Clarke, James W. "Genesis of the West Siberian Basin and Its Petroleum Geology: A Recent Interpretation." *International Geology Review* 36, no. 11 (1994), pp. 985–996.

Collison, Paul, Maxim Moshkov, and Andrei Matchanskis. "The Russian Hydrocarbon Resource Base." Moscow: Brunswick UBS Global Equity Research, March 9, 2004.

Dixon, Sarah. *Organizational Transformation in the Russian Oil Industry.* Northampton, MA: Edward Elgar, 2008.

Douglas-Westwood. *The Onshore Russian Oilfield Services Market Report, 2009–2013.* 2nd ed. Canterbury, UK: Douglas-Westwood, 2009.

Egyed, Peter. *Western Participation in the Development of Siberian Energy Resources: Case Studies.* Carleton University (Ottawa, Canada), Institute of Soviet and East European Studies, East-West Commercial Relations Series, report no. 22 (December 1983).

Exxon Neftegaz Limited. *Sakhalin 1: A New Frontier.* Tulsa, OK: PennWell Custom Publishing, 2008.

Flemming, William. "Business-State Relations in Post-Soviet Russia: The Politics of Second Phase Privatization, 1995–1997." M.Phil. thesis, St. Antony's College, University of Oxford, 1998.

Gaikazov, M. N. *Valentin Dmitrievich Shashin: Blistatel'nyi strateg neftianoi promyshlennosti.* Moscow: Izdatel'stvo 'Neft' i gaz' RGU nefti i gaza im. I.M. Gubkina, 2006.

Goldman, Marshall I. *The Enigma of Soviet Petroleum: Half-Full or Half-Empty?* London: George Allen & Unwin, 1980.

Gorst, Isabel. "LUKoil: Russia's Largest Oil Company." Houston, TX: James Baker Institute for Public Policy, Rice University, March 2007.

Grace, John D. *Russian Oil Supply: Performance and Prospects.* Copublished by the Oxford Institute for Energy Studies. Oxford: Oxford University Press, 2005.

Graifer, V. I., and M. A. Danilenko. *Malyi i srednii biznes v neftianoi promyshlennosti Rossii.* Moscow: RITEK, 2000.

Gustafson, Thane, and Konstantin Kovalenko. *The Controversy over Oil Exploration and Reserves in Russia.* Cambridge, MA: IHS Cambridge Energy Research Associates, May 2005.

Institut Energeticheskoi Politiki. *Novaia struktura rossiiskogo neftianogo sektora: Nekotorye itogi.* Moscow: Institut Energeticheskoi Politiki, July 2004.

Institut Finansovykh Issledovanii. *Otsenka nalogovoi nagruzki rossiiskikh kompanii v 2001–2003 godakh.* Moscow: Institut Finansovykh Issledovanii, February 2004.

Karpov, V. P. "Neftegazovyi profil' industrializatsii Tiumenskoi oblasti 1960–80-e gody." *Nalogi, Investitsii, Kapital* (Tiumen), nos. 5–6 (2004), http://nic.pirit.info.

Kovalenko, Konstantin, and John C. Webb. *Russia's New Subsoil Licensing Rules: Closing the Door on Foreign Investment in Future Big-Ticket Oil Projects?* Cambridge, MA: IHS Cambridge Energy Research Associates, March 23, 2005.

Kriukov, Valerii. *Institutsional'naia struktura neftegazovogo sektora: Problemy i napravleniia transformatsii.* Novosibirsk: Institut ekonomiki i organizatsii promyshlennogo proizvodstva SO RAN, 1998.

Kryukov, Valery, and Arild Moe. "The Changing Structure of the Russian Oil Industry." *Oil & Gas Law and Taxation Review*, no. 12 (1991), pp. 367–372.

———. "Russia's Oil Industry: Risk Aversion in a Risk-Prone Environment." *Eurasian Geography and Economics* 48, no. 3 (May–June 2007), pp. 341–357.

Lane, David, ed. *The Political Economy of Russian Oil.* Lanham, MD: Rowman and Littlefield, 1999.

Loukashov, Dmitry, et al. "Russian Oils: Upstream Is Down, Downstream Is Up." *UBS Global Equity Research* (Moscow), December 14, 2007.

Maksimovich, G. K. *Gidravlicheskii razryv neftianykh plastov.* Moscow, 1957.

McKinsey Global Institute. *Unlocking Economic Growth in Russia.* Moscow: McKinsey, October 1999, chapter 3, "Sector Case Study of Oil," pp. 132–171.

Ministerstvo energetiki Rossiiskoi Federatsii. *Toplivo i energetika Rossii: Spravochnik spetsialista toplivno-energeticheskogo kompleksa.* Moscow: Energiia, various years.

Moe, Arild, and Valeriy Kryukov. "Joint Management of Oil and Gas Resources in Russia." *Post-Soviet Geography and Economics* 39, no. 10 (1998), pp. 588–605.

———. "Observations on the Reorganization of the Russian Oil Industry." *Post-Soviet Geography* 35, no. 2 (1994), pp. 89–101.

Moser, Nat, and Peter Oppenheimer. "The Oil Industry: Structural Transformation and Corporate Governance." In Brigitte Granville and Peter Oppenheimer, eds., *Russia's Post-Communist Economy.* Oxford: Oxford University Press, 2001, pp. 314–319.

O'Sullivan, Stephen. *LUKoil: Leader of the Pack.* London: MC Securities, September 1995.

Peterson, James A., and James W. Clarke. *West Siberian Oil-Gas Province.* U.S. Geological Survey, Open-File Report 89-192. Washington, DC: Department of the Interior, 1989.

Proskun, Vladimir I., et al. "Reserves/Resource Classification Schemes Used in Russia and Western Countries: A Review and Comparison." *Journal of Petroleum Geology* 27, no. 1 (January 2004), pp. 85–94.

Pusenkova, Nina. *Rosneft: Novoe litso rossiiskogo neftianogo biznesa.* Moscow: Moscow Center of the Carnegie Endowment for International Peace, 2006, http://www.carnegie.ru/ru/print/75155-print.htm.

Renaissance Capital. *Surgutneftegaz: Drilling Power.* Moscow: Renaissance Capital, March 4, 2005.

———. *West Siberia: Stronger for Longer.* Moscow: Renaissance Capital, October 30, 2002.

Royal Dutch Shell. *Salymskii proekt: Liudi, partnerstvo, uspekh.* Moscow: Royal Dutch Shell, 2009.

Sagers, Matthew J. "Joint Ventures in the Soviet Energy Sector." *PlanEcon Report* 5, no. 40 (October 6, 1989), pp. 1–11.

———. "News Notes." *Soviet Geography* 30, no. 4 (1989), pp. 310–311.

———. "News Notes: Russian Crude Oil Exports in 1992: Who Exported Russian Oil?" *Post-Soviet Geography* 34, no. 3 (March 1993), pp. 207–211.

———. "News Notes: Special Regional Development Program for Tyumen' Oblast' Established by RSFSR Government." *Soviet Geography* 32, no. 9 (1991), pp. 633–634.

———. "Oil Pipeline Rupture in Komi Republic: Magnitude and Potential Impact." *Post-Soviet Geography* 35, no. 7 (September 1994), pp. 431–432.

———. "The Regional Dimension of Russian Oil Production: Is a Sustained Oil Recovery in Prospect?" *Eurasian Geography and Economics* 47, no. 5 (2006), pp. 505–545.

———. "Review of Soviet Energy Industries in 1990." *Soviet Geography* 32, no. 4 (April 1991), pp. 251–290.

———. "Russian Crude Oil Production in 1996: Conditions and Prospects." *Post-Soviet Geography and Economics* 37, no. 9 (1996), pp. 523–537.

———. "Soviet Commodity Exchanges Trading in Oil." *Soviet Geography* 32, no. 7 (September 1991), pp. 513–515.

———. "The Status of Foreign Investment in Russia's Upstream Oil Industry." *PlanEcon Energy Outlook* (Washington, DC), May 1994, pp. 67–86.

———. "West Siberian Oil Production in the Mid-1990s." *International Geology Review* 36 (1994), pp. 997–1018.

Sagers, Matthew J., Igor A. Didenko, and Valeriy A. Kryukov. "Distribution of Refined Petroleum Products in Russia." *Post-Soviet Geography and Economics* 40, no. 5 (1999), pp. 407–439.

Sagers, Matthew J., and John D. Grace. "Observations on the Russian Oil Sector in 1992 and 1993." *International Geology Review* 35 (1993), pp. 855–877.

Sagers, Matthew J., Thane Gustafson, Sergej Mahnovski, and John C. Webb. *How Much Is Enough? How Much Tax Relief Will It Take to Restore Growth in Russian Oil Production?* Cambridge, MA: IHS Cambridge Energy Research Associates, November 2008.

Sagers, Matthew J., Valeriy A. Kryukov, and Vladimir V. Shmat. "Resource Rent from the Oil and Gas Sectors and the Russian Economy." *Post-Soviet Geography and Economics* 36, no. 7 (1995), pp. 389–425.

Sagers, Matthew J., and Jennifer Nicoud. "Joint Ventures and Foreign Investment in Russia's Upstream Oil Industry: Derailed but Not Dead Yet." *PlanEcon Energy Outlook* (June 1996), pp. 65–116.

Sagers, Matthew J., and John C. Webb. *From East Siberia to the Pacific: Putin's Oil Pipeline "Project of the Century."* Cambridge, MA: IHS Cambridge Energy Research Associates, March 10, 2008.

Seck, Andrew B. "Financing Upstream Oil and Gas Ventures in the Transitional Economies of the Former Soviet Union: A Study of Foreign Investment and Associated Risks." PhD thesis, Centre for Energy, Petroleum, and Mineral Law and Policy, University of Dundee, Scotland, August 1997.

Simonov, Konstantin. *Russkaia neft': Poslednii peredel.* Moscow: "Algoritm," 2005.

Sixsmith, Martin. *Putin's Oil: The Yukos Affair and the Struggle for Russia.* London: Continuum Books, 2010.

Slavkina, Mariia Vladimirovna. *Triumf i tragediia: Razvitie neftagazovogo kompleksa SSSR v 1960–1990 gg.* Moscow: "Nauka," 2002.

———. *Valerii Graifer: Vremia ne zhdet.* Moscow: "Tsentr," 2009.

Spears and Associates. *Petroleum Equipment and Service Needs of the CIS.* Tulsa, OK: Spears and Associates, April 1992.

Tolf, Robert W. *The Russian Rockefellers: The Saga of the Nobel Family and the Russian Oil Industry.* Stanford, CA: Hoover Institution Press, 1976.

Tolstolytkin, Igor'. "Glavnaia zadacha Iugry." *Nefteservis*, no. 4 (Winter 2009), pp. 12–15.

Tompson, William. "Putting Yukos into Perspective." *Post-Soviet Affairs* 21, no. 2 (2005), pp. 159–181.

UBS Investment Research. *Russian Oil and Gas: Paradigm Shift Is Needed.* Moscow: UBS Global Equity Research, September 29, 2008. www.ubs.com/investmentresearch.

U.S. Government, Central Intelligence Agency. *The International Energy Situation: Outlook to 1985.* ER77-10240. Washington, DC: Central Intelligence Agency, April 1977.

———. *Prospects for Soviet Oil Production.* ER77-10270. Washington, DC: Central Intelligence Agency, 1977.

———. *Prospects for Soviet Oil Production: A Supplemental Analysis.* Washington, DC: Central Intelligence Agency, August 1977.

U.S. Government, Department of Energy, Energy Information Administration. *Oil and Gas Resources of the West Siberian Basin, Russia.* Washington, DC: Energy Information Administration, 1997. http://www.eia.doe.gov/oil_gas/natural_gas/analysis _publications/oil_gas_resources_siberian_basin/siberian.html.

Vatansever, Adnan. "The Political Economy of Countering the 'Resource Curse': The Case of Russia under Putin (1999–2005)." PhD diss., Johns Hopkins School of Advanced International Studies, 2008.

Webb, John C., and Thane Gustafson. *Bridge to the East: The Yamal-Nenets-Krasnoyarsk Oil Cluster.* Cambridge, MA: IHS Cambridge Energy Research Associates, March 2011.

———. *Why Is Russian Oil Output Slowing Down? What Fraccing Trends Show.* Cambridge, MA: IHS Cambridge Energy Research Associates, April 2008.

Yenikeyeff, Shamil M. *The Battle for Russian Oil: Corporations, Regions, and the State.* Oxford: Oxford University Press, 2008.

Zheltov, Iu. P. *Deformatsii gornykh porod.* Moscow, 1966.

RUSSIAN GAS

Estrada, Javier, and Ole Fugleberg. "Price Elasticities of Natural Gas Demand in France and West Germany." *Energy Journal* 10, no. 3 (1989), pp. 77–90.

Golubkin, V. K. "Povyshenie effektivnosti raboty gazodobyvaiushchikh organizatsii v uslo-viiakh padaiushchei dobychi." *Gazovaia promyshlennost. Seriia: Ekonomika, organizatsiia i upravlenie proizvodstvom v gazovoi promyshlennosti*, no. 2 (2002), pp. 9–13.

Il'chenko, V. P., L. Iu. Timonina, and O. A. Marshaev, "Usloviia obvodneniia senomanskoi zalezhi Yamburgskogo mestorozhdeniia." *Gazovaia promyshlennost'*, no. 4 (2002), pp. 51–53.

Illarionov, Andrei. "Povyshat' li tarify 'estestvennykh monopolii?" Unpublished working paper, January 2002.

Kleiner, Vadim. "How Should Gazprom Be Managed in Russia's National Interests and the Interests of Its Shareholders?" PowerPoint presentation. Moscow: Hermitage Capital, June 2005.

Kosolobenkova, L. N. "Energeticheskii potentsial gazovoi promyshlennosti." *Gazovaia promyshlennost. Seriia: Ekonomika, organizatsiia i upravlenie proizvodstvom v gazovoi promyshlennosti*, no. 1 (2002), pp. 3–9.

Lohmann, Heiko. *The German Path to Natural Gas Liberalization: Is It a Special Case?* Oxford: Oxford Institute for Energy Studies, 2006.

Paniushkin, Valerii, Mikhail Zygar', and Irina Reznik. *Gazprom: Novoe russkoe oruzhie.* Moscow: "Zakharov," 2008.

Remizov, V. V., N. A. Krylov, and N. G. Ivanova. "Zapasy mestorozhdenii, ozhidaemykh k otkrytiiu v senomanskom komplekse Zapadnoi Sibiri." *Gazovaia promyshlennost'* (January 2002), pp. 77–81.

Rezunenko, V. I., et al. "Problemy i perspektivy dobychi i utilizatsii nizkonapornogo gaza." *Gazovaia promyshlennost'*, no. 5 (2002), pp. 46–49.

Sahlawi, Mohammed A. al-. "The Demand for Natural Gas: A Survey of Price and Income Elasticities." *Energy Journal* 10, no. 1 (January 1989), pp. 77–90.

Stern, Jonathan P. *The Future of Russian Gas and Gazprom.* Copublished by the Oxford Institute for Energy Studies. Oxford: Oxford University Press, 2005.

———. "The Russian Gas Balance to 2015: Difficult Years Ahead." In Simon Pirani, ed., *Russian and CIS Gas Markets and Their Impact on Europe.* Copublished by the Oxford Institute for Energy Studies. Oxford: Oxford University Press, 2009, pp. 54–92.

Steward, Dan B. *The Barnett Shale Play: Phoenix of the Fort Worth Basin, A History.* Fort Worth, TX: The Fort Worth Geological Society and the North Texas Geological Society, 2007.

Tarr, David, and Peter Thomson. "The Merits of Dual Pricing of Russian Natural Gas." Unpublished internal paper. Washington, DC: World Bank, July 19, 2003.

Journals and Periodicals

General

East European Constitutional Review
EKO

Ekspert
Financial Times
Finansovye izvestiia
Forbes Russia
Gazeta.ru
Izvestiia
Kommersant
Kommersant-Daily
Kommersant-Vlast'
Komsomol'skaia pravda
Moscow Times
Moskovskie novosti
Moskovskii komsomolets
New York Times
Nezavisimaia gazeta
Novaia gazeta
Ogonek
Post-Soviet Affairs
Post-Soviet Geography (subsequently renamed *Post-Soviet Geography and Economics*, and
     more recently *Eurasian Geography and Economics*)
Profil'
Rossiiskaia gazeta
Segodnia
Sovetskaia Rossiia
Trud
Vedomosti
Voprosy ekonomiki
Vremia novostei (also *Vremia MN*)
Wall Street Journal

Energy

Infotek
Interfax Russia and CIS Oil and Gas Weekly
Interfax Russia Petroleum (also at various times published as *Interfax Petroleum Report*)
Itogi
Neftecompass
Neftegazovaia Vertikal'
Nefteservis
Neftianoe khoziaistvo
Neft' i Biznes
Neft' i Kapital

Neft' Rossii
Petroleum Economist
Petroleum Intelligence Weekly
RusEnergy (also at times called *RusEnergy Praim-Onlain*)
Russian Petroleum Investor
Truboprovodnyi transport nefti
Weekly Petroleum Argus

Acknowledgments

This book is based on my academic research and my work as a consultant on Russian energy since the mid-1980s. In the course of that work I have made over a hundred trips to Russia, traveled all over Russian oil country, and worked alongside many of the people described here. During that time I have developed deep respect and admiration for the men and women who work in the oil industry, both Russian and international. The oil industry rests on a foundation of rigorous scientific and engineering disciplines, and I would like to thank the many oil professionals who took the time and interest to tutor me in the basics. This book, in the end, is about these very real people, to whom I express my gratitude.

I have many people to thank from the decade I have worked on *Wheel of Fortune*. But I have drawn particular inspiration from four, without whom it would not exist. Daniel Yergin and Angela Stent, my close friends and colleagues of many years, have been a constant source of encouragement and advice. Matthew Sagers, my teammate for over a decade, has given unstintingly of his knowledge and wisdom, not only on this book but in the many projects we have done together. And last but not least, I would like to pay tribute to the memory of the late Dr. Vadim Eskin of the Russian Academy of Sciences, my friend and mentor up to his untimely death in 2006, who taught me all that is best and admirable about Russia. This book is dedicated to him and to his family.

The book also could not have been written and completed without the extraordinary help and advice of John Webb, who has drawn on his unique expertise on Russia and the Russian oil industry in reviewing every line in the manuscript, correcting maps and charts, finding and checking statistics, and applying throughout his rare common sense and sound judgment.

Many friends and colleagues have given patiently of their time in reading and critiquing drafts of the book over the years and offering me the benefit of their advice. Iskander Diyashev and Valeriy Kryukov read and commented on the whole manuscript, as did Peter Charow, John Grace, Charles King, Peter Reddaway, and Philip Vorobyov. I am also grateful to the many other

637

friends and colleagues who read chapters or groups of chapters, often more than once: Harley Balzer, Simon Blakey, the late Sarah Carey, Timothy Colton, Cliff Gaddy, Andrey Gaidamaka, Loren Graham, George Helland, Jeremy Huck, Barry Ickes, Craig Kennedy, Ray Leonard, Arild Moe, David Moore, Paul Musgrave, Petter Nore, Peter O'Brien, Robert Otto, Andrew Seck, Christine Telyan, Levi Tilleman-Dick, Adnan Vatansever, Grigorii Vygon, and Julian West.

This book is based on countless interviews and conversations over the last two decades with many of the players themselves, Russians and Westerners who have shaped the Russian oil industry since Soviet times. Many have spoken to me on condition of anonymity. I thank them, and I hope I have protected their confidence.

I have been fortunate to listen and learn from the many talented professionals working in international companies, government bodies, and universities in Russia and around the world. I particularly want to thank Tim Adams, John Barry, Larry Bates, Sam Bennett, Mark Bilsland, Ilya Bourtman, Natasha Braginsky, Albert Bressand, John Browne, Pius Cagienard, Paul Chaisty, Howard Chase, Peter Davies, Maurice Dijols, Bob Dudley, Frank Duffield, Chris Einchcomb, Hugo Erikssen, Rondo Fehlberg, Jean Gerin, Andrew Gould, Tom Hamilton, Richard Herbert, Richard Hildahl, Chris Hopkinson, Simon Kukes, Daniel Lefebvre, Robert Mabro, Ian MacDonald, Joe Mach, Larry McVay, James Pearson, Jean Riboud, Frank Rieber, Howard Rogers, Jerry Rohan, Andrew Seck, Martyn Smith, Michel Soublin, John and Richard Spears, T. Don Stacy, Gregory Stoupnitsky, Bernie Sucher, David Tournadre, Don Wolcott, Glenn Waller, Thomas Wolf, and Gary Yamamoto.

Among the many Russian oilmen, bankers, journalists, analysts, and others whose views have informed this book, I would particularly like to mention Aleksandr Afanasenkov, Aleksandr Berezikov, Gennadii Bogomiakov, Valerii Cherniaiev, Pavel Fedorov, Tagirzian Gil'manov, the late Iurii Golubev, Valerii Graifer, German Gref, Aleksei Grivach, Sergei Guriev, Aleksei Kondrashov, Andrei Konoplianik, Sergei Kudriashov, the late Nikolai Lisovskii, Aleksandr Matevosov, Petr Mostovoi, Nina Poussenkova, Aleksandr Putilov, Iurii Shafranik, Andrei Sharonov, Rair Simonian, Tamara Trunilina, Dmitrii Vasil'ev, Vladimir Vyssotskii, and Vadim Yakovlev.

My colleagues at IHS have generously supported this project from the beginning. I'm grateful to Jerre Stead, Scott Key, Arshad Matin, Jonathan Gear,

Atul Arya, Slavo Pastor, David Hobbs, Jamey Rosenfield, and Pete Stark, as well as Jim Burkhard, Kate Hardin, Shankari Srinivasan, and Michael Stoppard. I would also like to thank my present and past teammates in IHS Cambridge Energy Research Associates' Russian and Caspian Energy service; in addition to those already mentioned, they include Malcolm Brown, Steve Haggett, Kelly Knight, Konstantin Kovalenko, Timothy Krysiek, Sergej Mahnovski, Paulina Mirenkova, Laurent Ruseckas, Christine Telyan, Tatyana Ustyantseva, Sergey Vakulenko, and Vitaly Yermakov, as well as many other colleagues in IHS's other research services, especially Judson Jacobs, Peter Jackson, Chuck Movit, Suriya Rajan, and Leta Smith. I'm also very grateful to the superb staff at IHS's Moscow office, under the capable leadership of Irina Zamarina, for their kind help over the years in arranging meetings and interviews. Special mention goes to Igor Solovyov, the best driver in Moscow.

I am equally grateful to my colleagues and students in the Department of Government at Georgetown University, which has been a happy and productive home for many years. In addition to those already mentioned, I would like to express my deep appreciation to the succession of able colleagues who have served as department chairmen over the years, beginning with Bruce Douglass, who first welcomed me to the department three decades ago, followed by John Bailey, Bob Lieber, and George Shambaugh, who have shaped my teaching and thinking in so many ways.

I have benefited over three decades from the energy and talent of many students at Georgetown University, especially those in my graduate seminar in Russian politics. I am especially grateful to Artem Agoulnik, Jon Askonas, Ilya Breyman, Igor Danchenko, John Gledhill, Leonid Godunov, Anthony Martinez, Meghan McConaughey, Anton Strezhnev, Eric Swinn, and Maria Vassileva.

I would like to express my deep appreciation to my editors at Harvard University Press, Mike Aronson and his deputy Kathleen Drummy, as well as John Donohue and Julie Palmer-Hoffman at Westchester Publishing Services. Virginia Mason and Sean McNaughton did the excellent maps and graphics. Brendan McElroy, one of Georgetown's talented graduate students, compiled the index. Many thanks to all of them for tolerating cheerfully and patiently my endless revisions.

Many friends and teachers have given valuable help and counsel along the way. I am grateful to Eqbal Ahmad, Abe Becker, Jacob and Ruby Brunstein, Paul Cocks, Robert Comunale, Merle Fainsod, Walter and Anne Gustafson, Değer

Heriş, Ruth Jacobi, Edward Keenan, Terry Killen, David Kindermann, Francis Koenig, Walter and Will Lippincott, Arthur Maass, Serge Masson, Audrey McMahon, Bruce Mainous, Francis Nachtmann, and Ida Shimanouchi. Lastly, my thanks to Robert W. Campbell, who may be surprised to learn that he sparked my early interest in Russian oil in a lecture at the University of Illinois in 1964.

My family, Nil, Peri, Farah, and Kenan, have been the inspiration for this book as for all of life. I am forever grateful to them for their love and support.

Index